William Blake
JERUSALEM
SELECTED POEMS AND PROSE

"Ancient of Days," colored relief etching. By permission of the Pierpont Morgan Library.

William Blake
JERUSALEM,
SELECTED POEMS AND PROSE

EDITED WITH INTRODUCTION, NOTES,
AND COMMENTARY BY *Hazard Adams*

HOLT, RINEHART AND WINSTON, INC.

NEW YORK   CHICAGO   SAN FRANCISCO   ATLANTA
DALLAS   MONTREAL   TORONTO   LONDON   SYDNEY

Introduction

I

William Blake, one of the greatest geniuses England has produced, died at the age of seventy on August 12, 1827. Three obituaries appeared in the London press. In none of them was it so much as mentioned that Blake was a poet. His modest reputation was as an illustrator, a "designer," and "artist." The *Literary Gazette* remarked: "He has left *nothing* except some pictures, copperplates, and his principal work of a series of a hundred large designs from Dante." The *Gentleman's Magazine* referred briefly to *Songs of Experience, America,* and *Europe,* but did not indicate that these works were poems. During Blake's lifetime only two of his works were actually printed. One, the *Poetical Sketches,* was never sold, apparently because Blake disliked the condescending introduction written by the Reverend Matthews, who was obviously overacting the part of patron. The second, *A Descriptive Catalogue,* was printed for Blake's unsuccessful exhibition of paintings in 1809. Of the rest of Blake's poetic works that were published at all, most were illuminated books; that is, books in which Blake's own designs and illustrations were closely integrated with the text. The designs and text were engraved and run off from copper plates by Blake himself. Few copies of these remain, and they are highly prized. The plates are lost.

Blake and his wife Catherine lived a life of poverty, though not of desperate want. Apparently frugal, they managed carefully and efficiently on the very modest income Blake gained, mainly from executing commissions or occasionally selling one of his own works. On the surface, it was not an eventful life. At an early age, we are told, he saw visions—angels in a tree, God's face at the window. Not formally educated, he went to drawing school, then was apprenticed to a prominent engraver, who sent him to Westminster Abbey to make drawings. His great love of the Gothic and his peculiar sense of tradition were no doubt partially formed by these frequent visits.

Blake exhibited a work in the Royal Academy exhibition when he was twenty-three. At twenty-five he married a young woman who could neither read nor write, but who learned to do both and to assist him at his drawing and engraving and in the coloring of his books. They had no children.

Blake lived all of his life in London except for three years from 1800 to 1803, during which time he worked for commissions mainly from the poetaster William Hayley at Felpham in Sussex. It was there one day, in the summer of 1803, that Blake discovered a drunken soldier in his garden and asked him to leave. From that point on there is a disagreement as to what transpired. The soldier, Scofield by name, asserted in a formal complaint that Blake

> did utter the following seditious expressions, viz. that we (meaning the people of England) were like a Parcel of Children, that they would play with themselves till they got scalded and burnt; that the French knew our Strength very well, and if Bonaparte should come he would be master of Europe in an hour's time; that England might depend upon it . . . that he damned the King of England, his country, & his Subjects; that his Soldiers were all bound for Slaves, and all the Poor People in general . . .

Although it is very unlikely that Blake said all or any of this (Blake vehemently denied all of it), it is almost certain that he had *thought* some of it. What Blake, who was not quite five feet six inches tall, did do was to take Scofield by his two arms and propel him out of the garden and a good distance down the road toward the village. But Blake had damned the king in "sublime allegory" many years before and more than once. His prophetic poem *America* sides with the colonists, and in *Europe* "Albion's Angel," or King George III, is consumed in the fires of Blake's mythological rebel, Orc. It is just as well that those who presided over Blake's trial for sedition in January 1804 knew nothing of these works or of Blake's strongly republican sympathies. England was at war; the government was very jittery. People had been hanged for less, but Blake was acquitted to the cheers of the people in the courtroom.

At Felpham there was another crisis, probably more profound than the Scofield episode. Blake was forced to make a choice.

The Augustan style of William Hayley, his friendly though rather domineering patronage, and his urging Blake to execute miniature paintings for good commissions were arrayed against all Blake's training as an artist and the vision Blake had of his own purpose. This situation provides some of the "plot" of *Milton,* with Hayley as Satan, and, later on, a number of epigrams of which the following are examples:

ON H_____'S FRIENDSHIP

When H_____y finds out what you cannot do,
That is the very thing he'll set you to.

TO H

Thy Friendship has made my heart to ache;
So be my Enemy for Friendship's sake.

After the mental struggle with his "Satanic" friend Hayley, Blake returned to London to poverty but to his own freedom of invention. The decision was a brave one, made when he was forty-six with most of his great poetry already written. A more conventional and comfortable career had beckoned, but he had withstood the temptation.

These occurrences at Felpham were the major outward events of Blake's life. As an artist he held only one exhibition, in his brother's house in 1809. Robert Hunt attacked the pictures unmercifully, in a review in the *Examiner,* as the work of a lunatic. The exhibition was not a success, yet Blake continued his work and in later years gained the admiration of a number of younger artists.

Blake's life is a tribute to the power of the imagination, not just to overcome some great obstacle in its path, but simply to endure in single-minded devotion to its own activity. Blake managed, against the current of fashion, to maintain a clear vision of what he ought to be doing with his time. To keep a roof over his head, he was a journeyman engraver, an illustrator; but even on these jobs his work bore the mark of his unique point of view, as his interpretive illustrations to *Job,* Dante, Milton, and others amply demonstrate. From him, on his own, came lyrics, prophecies, illuminated books, water colors, engravings, and frescoes.

Although Wordsworth, Coleridge, and Lamb had read some of his lyrics, Blake seems not to have been on intimate terms with any prominent poets. He was born, for one thing, into a different class from that which produced the creators of English letters. Unlike most of the other great poets of his time, he did not have Oxford or Cambridge ties. His taste had been formed neither by the Augustans, whom he attacked, nor by the Romantics who were younger than he, but by the period of Ossian, Chatterton, Percy's *Reliques,* and those poets sometimes labeled "pre-Romantic." He was acquainted with a number of artists—John Flaxman, Henry Fuseli, and later John Linnell, George Richmond, Edward Calvert, and Samuel Palmer, all of whom greatly esteemed him. One of the most interesting and moving accounts of Blake is Palmer's letter written to Blake's biographer Alexander Gilchrist in 1855. An excerpt follows:

> In him you saw at once the Maker, the Inventor; one of the few in any age: a fitting companion for Dante. He was energy itself, and shed around him a kindling influence; an atmosphere of life, full of the ideal. To walk with him in the country was to perceive the soul of beauty through the forms of matter; and the high gloomy buildings between which, from his study window, a glimpse was caught of the Thames and the Surrey shore, assumed a kind grandeur from the man dwelling near them. Those may laugh at this who never knew such an one as Blake; but of him it is the simple truth.
>
> He was a man without a mask; his aim single, his path straightforwards, and his wants few; so he was free, noble, and happy.

As a painter Blake was never in style during his career. Indeed, he held out vigorously against the modern fashions and advocated a return to the methods of Raphael and Michelangelo. In this he influenced the later pre-Raphaelite movement and was revered by the Rossettis and Swinburne. He had some particularly scathing things to say about the painters of the Venetian school and the Dutch. Rembrandt and Rubens were his villains. In about 1808 he annotated his volume of Sir Joshua Reynolds' *Discourses on Art,* attacking the fashionable and gifted portrait painter, spokesman of the establishment, for countenancing "blots and blurs."

Blake vehemently defended the principle of "definite outline" against generalized vagueness:

> To My Eye Rubens's Colouring is most Contemptible. His Shadows are of a Filthy Brown somewhat of the Colour of Excrement; these are filled with tints & messes of yellow and red. His lights are all the Colours of the Rainbow, laid on Indiscriminately & broken one into another. Altogether his Colouring is Contrary to the Colouring of Real Art & Science.
> The Man who asserts that there is no Such Thing as Softness in Art, & that everything in Art is Definite & Determinate has not been told this by Practise, but by Inspiration & Vision. . . .

Blake particulary disliked oil painting, which "will not drink or absorb colour enough to stand the test of very little Time and of the Air; it grows yellow, and at length brown." The *Descriptive Catalogue* of his unsuccessful exhibition is an attempt to justify an art which would return to the principles of an earlier age, in which "all depends upon Form and outline." In this Blake was alone against the fashion, but a room in the Tate Gallery is now devoted to his paintings. Unfortunately many of his works, including the large fresco version of The Last Judgment, are lost, partly for want of a sympathetic audience in his own time.

II

Blake lived in à revolutionary age that brought about changes in many important phases of human life. The Reformation had destroyed the unity of the Christian Church; subsequent events saw a further division of Christians into a multiplicity of sects. Post-Renaissance thought, mainly the development of materialist science, created the Deist myth of God as the great designer, the machine-builder. One of Blake's best-known paintings, "The Ancient of Days," depicts a bearded patriarchal god of the sky spreading a pair of compasses over the earth. For Blake, this god, the idea that only the measurable is real, and the assumption that man and the universe are merely machines were all manifestations of error. Blake's religious views, vehemently anti-Deistic, were in the tradition of individualistic Christianity with not a little infusion of the rhetoric of evangelical dissent. He advocated a return to the Bible, not as a historical document but as an encyclopaedia of spiritual vision. Rather than looking to the sky for an alien and distant lawgiver, Blake would discover God in Man, in every man.

In a way this individualistic religion is a sort of ultimate *reductio* of the multiplication of sects, every man finally making his own religion. The danger in this, of course, is a sort of spiritual solipsism and, perhaps, social isolation. Blake attempted to express an ultimately communal vision in poetry, but without capitulation to any spiritual or social institution that hands down an abstract moral code. In *The Marriage of Heaven and Hell,* one of the Devil's proverbs is: "One law for the lion and the ox is oppression." In Blake's symbolism, devils are often very much worth listening to, for Blake thinks of them as creatures of imaginative energy, as opposed to the angels of abstract law.

The drive toward the release of the individual was evident in Blake's time in laissez-faire economic theory and practice and in the political revolutions of America and France. Although he became more and more suspicious of anarchic revolt after the French debacle, Blake supported both revolutions and wrote poems celebrating them. A story, perhaps apocryphal, says that Thomas Paine escaped England on Blake's warning. Most republicans of Paine's stripe found little difficulty in squaring their republicanism with a Deistic religious position. Blake did not find that they jibed so well.

All of these movements, whether ultimately consistent with each other or not, did emphasize individual emancipation from dying forms of belief and social behavior. But with emancipation came the man trapped in the cave, Blake's tragic figure, Urizen, isolated in a brutalizing mechanistic philosophy of nature and man, seeking frantically to impose abstract moral codes upon apparent chaos. The man in the cave is man driven to a rejection of his own humanity. Blake's art is by his own admission an effort to restore, or, better, to create a mythical golden age or visionary frame of mind in the individual man, so that he can again discover that other men are a part of him.

III

The issue Blake deals with can be put in epistemological terms. In *The Recluse,* Wordsworth wrote the following lines about the relation of mind to nature or the world around the mind:

How exquisitely the individual Mind
(And the progressive powers perhaps no less
Of the whole species) to the external World
Is fitted:—& how exquisitely, too,
Theme this but little heard among Men,
The external World is fitted to the Mind.

Blake's annotation to this reads: "You shall not bring me down to believe such fitting & fitted."

Philosophers and poets of the age were deeply concerned with this matter of the relation or disrelation between mind and nature, subject and object. One attempted resolution of this dualism was to assert that the mind *knows* nature by rational means but *feels* nature by poetic intuition. But in the face of the Lockean principle that the world is divided into primary measurable qualities of experience, which are objective and "real," and the secondary qualities of experience (taste, smell, texture, and so on), which are subjective and differ from individual to individual, the mind is apparently turned back upon itself and ends up as solipsistic and merely expressive of its own isolation.

The romantic poets sought to deal with this problem by raising questions about the objectivity of objectivity. Do not the tools of "objective" reason—analysis and generalization—distance, deaden, and dissect reality into parts, isolating the mind from its objects? Can the mind, in some intuitive act, put the world back together, synthesize rather than analyze? Synthesis and communion seem to be the aim of Wordsworth's *Prelude,* of Shelley's *Prometheus Unbound.* Blake's objection to Wordsworth's vision of nature as somehow "fitted" to the mind, aside from his dislike of its implied materialism and mechanism, is that two things fitted together are not really synthesized. The shoe surrounds the foot but never becomes part of the foot.

Blake supposes another situation: The world is as we make it, but we make it always in two fundamentally contrary ways. The mind posits nature as an "other," surrounding it; *but* it also posits itself as turning nature inside out, so to speak, and containing nature in its own imaginative acts and productions. In both cases, of course, it is the mind that is acting, but according to two competing myths. In both, nature is *made,* but in each it is made differently, and the two depend upon each other: "Without Contraries is no Progression." Neither view can triumph by negation or annihilation of the other. They are in a dialectical relationship. Blake's view is reminiscent of Heraclitus' remark that Homer was wrong in praying that strife disappear from the universe, for should that happen, all would fall into chaos. Blake, however, wants to raise strife to its proper mental level rather than allow it to operate destructively in its fallen form of war.

The two myths are represented in Blake's prophecies by two of his "giant forms" or Zoas (*Ezekiel* I, 5); Urizen (your reason, horizon) and Los (Sol, the sun, reversed). Urizen, who is roughly the power of analytic procedures that work toward generalizations about man and nature, invents in his mind the split between subject and object that enables him to generalize and objectify. The fall is brought about by Urizen's going on to insist that only the objective and general are real, that man is born into and surrounded by a material universe, which is reducible in its operations to general laws. Man objectified, being a part of this universe, is also subject to these laws and to the moral laws apparently derivable from them. Urizen's symbols in his fallen state are thus the cave of surrounding matter and the tablets of the law handed down to Moses on Mount Sinai. The Urizen of Blake's age is a Deist and a Newtonian. He winds up the universe and makes it run; anyone who rebels against his view is accused of sin.

In the story Blake tells, in the golden age, outside of time as we measure it or objectify it, Urizen possessed the sun. He was the true prince of light, but once convinced that he required no opposition, he found himself surrounded by dead matter. He lived in a cavern; he had fallen into the condition he imagined for the remainder of history.

In the same golden age Los, whose name was then Urthona, the giant of the earth, inhabited the place where the valuable metals of the mental life could be mined for ultimate refinement in the fire of the prince of light. Urthona's domain was the caverns and mountains, not of a material universe, but of the mind itself, the world of the artists of the imagination, the gnomes of fairy tales. But in the cataclysm of Urizen's fall into the unopposed idea that a surrounding material nature was the only reality, Urthona was cast into the Promethean role of saving fire for man. He became Los, or fallen Sol, and had to shape man's destiny on his blacksmith's anvil. He is obviously the imaginative foundation upon which reason must stand. An archetype of the artist, he is reminiscent of Hephaestus and Vulcan. Since Urizen has lost his true form, one of Los's jobs is to rebuild Urizen's spiritual body. This task continues through history; it is the eschatological principle in Blake's poetry.

In his desire to assume total power, Urizen has no use for Los's activity and does not recognize it as the contrary necessary to his own prolific existence. Instead he "negates" it. Los, on the other hand, not without numerous struggles with himself, recognizes that his task is not to destroy the tyrant but to restore his proper form, to rebuild his body. Thus Blake sees Los's activity finally as that of a sculptor.

The next step in understanding Blake is to think of this contrariety, this apparent struggle in the universe, as going on within man, not just in Blake but in all men. In Blake this Everyman is Albion, who is each of us, but also the whole world, for if we somehow make the world, then there is a sense in which the world is in us. No matter which of the two myths one accepts (and the point is to accept both at once, thus to live where both are fictions and yet are "equally true"), both myths are emanations of the mind. In that sense they are interior to man, even though one creates a poem of an outer material reality while the other creates a poem of an inner one. In Blake, it should be clear, there is no point in trying to locate anything by what the philosopher Whitehead called "simple location" in space and time. The world is not simply "given" to us. It is constantly being made by us. It is changing and growing as our imagination and reason debate its nature. Alone, Urizen's reason tends to harden into unchanging laws. Without reason as the "outward bound and circumference of energy" the imagination, as represented by Los, would fall into a dreamlike anarchy. Fallen Urizen, having negated the imagination, negates change; but he finds that he cannot annihilate it. Everything he creates becomes something different and horrible before his eyes. Los could say to him, as Blake does, in *The Marriage of Heaven and Hell,* to the angel: "All that we saw was owing to your metaphysics."

IV

Another way of discussing all of this is to invoke the two modes of time that inform Blake's poems. The first is the time most suitable to Urizen's view—measurable or spatialized time. When we speak of spaces of time, make chronological charts, or construct clock faces, we spatialize time. Soon we discover that this mode of imagining time puts us *in* time, just as Urizen assumes that we are *in* space. With a little reflection we recognize that linear chronology *constructs* a past that is forever gone; yet we manage to create the *fiction* of its presence in our accounts of it. It is present, of course, in the spatializing symbolic formulations we employ. The ancient Romans exist in books, not "back there" because there isn't any "back there" except in our creation of it.

For Los there are symbolizations which do not formulate a "back there" but insist within themselves on their presentness. Such a symbolization is the Bible, which for Blake is the supreme and archetypal work of art. Blake's point is that the Jesus present in the Bible is the real Jesus, not the historical Jesus who must always remain alienated from us "back there" in time. Jesus *comes* in the Bible; it is not that he *came.* By the same token we rehearse plots in novels in the present tense even though the convention of fiction is to employ the past tense, as in a chronicle. Blake's criticism of Chaucer's *Canterbury Tales* makes this point.

To spatialize and historicize is to surround oneself with time, which is the same sort of illusion as Urizen's cave. At this point the contrary had better be introduced: "The bright sculptures of Los's Halls." This is the potential presence for each individual of everything, regardless of location in time, in the "minute particulars" of art. Thus, as Blake says of Chaucer's pilgrims, they still exist "unaltered, and consequently they are the physiognomies or lineaments of universal human life." Blake's Los is the spirit of time, but of immeasurable time, time lived and time now, time that is made by imaginative work rather than time in which things occur:

Every Time less than a pulsation of the artery
Is equal in its period & value to Six Thousand Years;
For in this time the poet's work is done.

Urizen's time is spatial and external; Los's time is dynamic and inner. It is difficult to imagine human life progressing satisfactorily without the opposition of these two modes.

V

The idea of a giant man who fell into a nightmare world from an Edenic existence has the sanction of religious and literary traditions. Blake makes his archetypal giant Albion fourfold; there are two other Zoas besides Urthona (Los) and Urizen. They are the shadowy Tharmas, whose fall is described in *Night the First* of *Vala,* a figure representing primal power, instinct, and unity, and Luvah, who is passion and generation, and appears in the fallen world as thwarted desire in the figure of the revolutionary, fiery, Oedipal child Orc (an anagram of Cor, heart, a play on the Greek word for the sexual organs, and a suggestion of hell, Orcus). For a while in the early prophecies this Orc is Blake's hero, but soon Blake imagines him locked with Urizen in an endless opposition of oppression and revolt. Urizen seems to assume the role of Orc's father, and we realize that in some sense he was once an Orc himself. The true parents of Orc are Los and his female "emanation," Enitharmon; Urizen, in his negation of the imagination, cannot be prolific, only a foster-father. Orc and Urizen symbolize cyclical time without progression, tyranny, and anarchy by turn. Neither can break the cycle. Every Orc becomes Urizen. This is where Los must enter, true father of Orc and revolt, but worker with the materials at hand, shaper of tradition. Los is work itself; Orc is the quest for gratification. But gratification and happiness are abstractions and cannot be pursued. They are, if anything, a by-product of work, though even this formulation may provide them with too great a status.

Blake treats history, or measured time, as a dream. Having succumbed to the total domination of the Urizenic myth of an outer material reality, and having therefore negated the imaginative world contained by man, Albion falls *into* history, or sleep. The archetypal man must be redeemed by his own imagination's righting the balance between living *in* time and *making* time through work. Los must build the body of the world in imaginative form. This body is equivalent to the city of God in the Apocalypse.

Albion not only dreams the nightmare of history; his Zoas are at war "within his members." Another way of expressing this is in sexual terms. On one level of the symbolism Albion is fourfold; on another he is a synthesis through contrariety of male and female. In the fall, he becomes alienated from his female "emanation," who is called Jerusalem. In this separate "natural" state ("nature" is a state of alienation in Blake), the emanation is no longer *inside* Albion, or imaginatively conceived by him, but *outside* and separate. She is thus equivalent to nature itself—mother nature, whom Blake calls Vala (veil). She is the surrounding material world insisted upon by the Urizenic portion of Albion when that portion gains control at the expense of imagination. Separated from her in this way, Albion becomes a "spectre" of his true self, and we see the battle of the sexes played out before us. When this occurs each Zoa loses his emanation as well. One of the best expressions of this situation occurs in the unfinished manuscript poem "My Spectre around me. . . ." It is given extended treatment along with the cyclical opposition of Orc to Urizen in the cryptic poem, "The Mental Traveller."

Spectre and Emanation is one way of describing an aspect of the fallen condition, but there are other states as well. Blake sees all human life as existing potentially in four "states," and each of these has a presiding Zoa. The states are called Eden, Beulah, Generation, and Ulro. Eden, which is not the Biblical Eden of Genesis, but the city of Revelation, is properly the realm of Urizen, prince of light, and is associated with the sun and the head of the body of the archetypal world-man Albion. The breast or heart of Albion is ruled by Tharmas. His land is Beulah, the "married land" of Isaiah, the Eden of Genesis or lovers' paradise, the realm of child and protective mother, shepherd and flock, lover and beloved, the source of idyllic art. The loins and genitals belong to Luvah, the state Blake calls Generation. Here man plays subject to the world's object, and that world must be "planted and sown." It is a world upon which the seasonal cycle impresses itself, a world of birth, growth, decay, and death. It has an elegaic quality about it. Finally, beneath these three states, in the strong legs of Albion and in the caves and mountains of the earth, complete with working gnomes, there is Ulro, which is properly Urthona's world; here are mined the crude but valuable mental materials of dream and imagination, ready for the blacksmith's shaping art. In the unfallen world, these states represent prolific contrariety or mental war, imagination through generation, procreation, and unification, to apocalyptic ordering of the whole world of experience. In *Night the Ninth* of *Vala,* with Albion once again awakened from the nightmare of spatial and temporal enclosure, Blake offers the following lines as partial illustration of the proper relation of the Zoas, and states:

For Tharmas brought his flocks upon the hills, & in the Vales
Around the Eternal Man's bright tent, the little children play
Among the woolly flocks. The hammer of Urthona sounds
In the deep caves beneath; his limbs renewed, his Lions roar
Around the furnaces.

But when Albion falls as a result of the tyranny of Urizen, he falls into "death" or sleep and becomes, rather than a standing, upright man, an upside-down one. He begins to think only in Urizen's terms; the world is around him like a coffin. His head is in Ulro. His Zoas have fallen into the wrong states: Urizen in Ulro, Tharmas in Generation, Luvah in Beulah, and Urthona (now called Los) in Eden. In other words, if Urizen falls, there is nothing better than for the imagination to deal with light as best it can. Los becomes, therefore, Blake's hero, seeking to rebuild the City of Eden, now fallen, or Urizen's body, or nature into what Blake calls Golgonooza, the city of art. The name is composed of the beginning and ending of the word Golgotha, place of the skull, but with something workable buried within it—the primordial *ooze,* perhaps. And, of course, it is a new "Golgotha."

A MAP OF THE UNFALLEN MAN ALBION
(The Tree of Life)

RELATED SYMBOLS:

ZOA: Urizen; the head
AREA: Eden; the city

ZOA: Tharmas; the breast
AREA: Beulah; the garden

ZOA: Luvah; the loins
AREA: Generation; the soil

ZOA: Urthona (Los); the legs
AREA: Ulro; the caves

A MAP OF THE FALLEN MAN
(The Tree of the Knowledge of Good and Evil)

ZOA: Los (Urthona)
AREA: City of Golgonooza

ZOA: Luvah (Orc)
AREA: Beulah; the garden

ZOA: Tharmas
AREA: Generation; the soil

ZOA: Urizen
AREA: Ulro; the caves

Upside-down and upright Albion may be described by the diagram on opposite page[1] though some of the correspondences mentioned are not as fully developed by Blake as others, and there are occasional inconsistencies.

Blake's earliest treatment of human states was twofold rather than fourfold, encompassing Beulah and Generation as Innocence and Experience respectively. These two states form the basis for Blake's most famous lyrics, *Songs of Innocence and Experience,* which present situations typical of innocent childhood and of the emergence into experience, or the fall from Beulah. These *Songs,* often paired for ironic contrast, exploiting a variety of speaking voices and attitudes, are the first works of Blake to have gained critical acceptance. A remarkable body of lyric poems, they serve also as a fine introduction to the more difficult later prophecies. My own introduction properly closes with reference to them, where, with those earlier juvenilia *Poetical Sketches,* the reader's experience with Blake properly begins.

[1] Reproduced from my *William Blake: A Reading of the Shorter Poems,* Seattle, 1963, p. 39. By permission of the University of Washington Press.

A Note on the Text

This generous selection of Blake's work is the only one that offers a complete text of one of Blake's three longer prophecies. I have chosen to include *Jerusalem* over *The Four Zoas* or *Milton,* because *The Four Zoas* is unfinished and chaotic in parts, and *Milton* seems to me not quite the encyclopaedic effort of *Jerusalem.* Nevertheless, I have printed selections from *The Four Zoas,* including the whole of the apocalyptic ninth night, and many important and beautiful passages from *Milton,* which is, in my opinion, a very fine poem with great and passionate moments.

Blake published most of his own works in illuminated books from his own designs and engraved plates. Some works were never published and have been recovered from manuscript notebooks. Except for *Poetical Sketches* and *A Descriptive Catalogue,* none of the works was conventionally printed in his own lifetime. Blake's punctuation, capitalization, and spelling are eccentric. The two major texts of Blake take different attitudes toward the problems this presents. Sir Geoffrey Keynes's *The Complete Writings of William Blake* modernizes the punctuation but preserves Blake's spelling and his capitalization. David V. Erdman's *The Poetry and Prose of William Blake* seeks to print the works exactly as Blake wrote them. The result in the latter case is a scholar's text, but one that is very difficult to read. (For example, Blake hardly punctuates the poems from the Pickering Manuscript at all, and he sprinkles all of his poetry with periods where commas or semicolons would clearly be a wiser choice from our point of view.) In Keynes's edition, there are occasional inaccuracies of transcription and, in my opinion, some questionable decisions of punctuation.

I have chosen to punctuate Blake anew and to modernize, in most cases, the spelling. Anyone who makes this effort will soon discover places where there is simply no resolution of a thorny syntactical thicket. There are real problems of interpretation that are subject to intelligent disagreement. I offer a modernized version because I believe that Blake is difficult enough for the student even with the help of modern punctuation and spelling. I have kept the capitalization, adding a capital here and there where I have started a new sentence and for an occasional proper name. The ground for keeping the capitals is that Blake was using them for emphasis. I only wish that I could believe that this is always the case.

No doubt I have chosen a messy solution, but it is offered as a workable one. The other texts are available for more advanced scholarly work and should be consulted finally on any interpretive matter.

In all of this I have been very ably assisted by Mrs. Mary Gazlay, to whom I owe a great debt for the preparation of the text and many helpful suggestions.

Irvine, California   Hazard Adams
September 1969

Chronology of Blake's Life

1757   November 28. Blake was born at 28 Broad Street, London, the second of five children, to James and Catherine Blake. The father was a retail hosier.

1767   Educated at home, Blake was sent to Pars' drawing school, Strand.

1769   The earliest poems of *Poetical Sketches* are said to have been written in this year.

1771   Blake's apprenticeship to James Basire, a well-known engraver, began. The apprenticeship lasted seven years, during which period Blake was frequently sent to make drawings in Westminster Abbey.

1778   Blake commenced study in the Royal Academy Antique School.

1780   Blake exhibited his first work in the Royal Academy Exhibition. On the evening of June 6, Blake, walking in the evening, was caught up in a mob during the Lord George Gordon No-Popery riots.

1782   August 18. Blake was married to Catherine Boucher in Battersea Church. The Blakes lived at 23 Green Street, Leicester Fields. In this year Blake met the artists Flaxman and Fuseli.

1783   *Poetical Sketches* printed but never sold.

1784   Blake's father died. Blake began a print shop with Parker at 27 Broad Street.

1784   Four drawings were exhibited at the Royal Academy.

ca. 1784   *An Island in the Moon* was written.

1787   The business at 27 Broad Street was closed. Blake began, about this time, his new method of illuminated printing.

ca. 1788   *There is no Natural Religion* and *All Religions are One*.

1789   *Songs of Innocence* were issued. *Tiriel. The Book of Thel.*

1791   *The French Revolution* was printed but never published.

1792   Blake's mother died.

ca. 1790 -

1793   *The Marriage of Heaven and Hell.*

1793   Blake met Thomas Butts, long his patron. The Blakes moved to 13 Hercules Buildings, Lambeth. *For Children: The Gates of Paradise; America.*

1794   *Songs of Innocence and Experience; Visions of the Daughters of Albion; The [First] Book of Urizen; Europe.*

1795   *The Song of Los; The Book of Ahania; The Book of Los.*

1797   Nights 1 - 4 of Young's *Night Thoughts* with forty-three engravings by Blake.

1799   Blake exhibited a painting at Royal Academy.

1800   Under the urging of William Hayley, the Blakes moved to a cottage in Felpham, Sussex. Blake taught himself Greek, Latin, and Hebrew. Blake executed various drawings and engravings for Hayley and others.

1803   August 12. Blake evicted the drunken soldier Scofield from his garden and was formally accused by Scofield of uttering treasonous remarks against the king.

1803   September. The Blakes left Felpham to take lodging at 17 South Molton Street, London.

ca. 1803   The poems from the Pickering Manuscript were written.

1804   January 11. Blake stood trial at Chichester for high treason and was acquitted.

1795 -

1804   and perhaps later. Blake worked on the unfinished *Vala, or the Four Zoas.*

1804 -

1805   Blake did drawings for Blair's *The Grave.*

1802 -

1808   *Milton* was composed.

1804 -

1820   Blake wrote *Jerusalem.*

1808   Blake exhibited, for the last time, two drawings at the Royal Academy.

ca. 1808   Blake annotated Sir Joshua Reynolds' *Discourses.*

1809   From May to September, Blake held his only exhibition in his birthplace, then his brother James's house. It was violently attacked by Robert Hunt, visited by Charles Lamb and Robert Southey. For this exhibition *A Descriptive Catalogue* was written.

1810   *A Vision of the Last Judgment.*

ca. 1818   *The Everlasting Gospel.*

1818   Blake met the painter, John Linnell.

ca. 1820   *On Homer's Poetry; On Virgil; The Laocoön.*

1821   The Blakes moved to 3 Fountain Court, Strand.

1822   Linnell commissioned from Blake a series of Illustrations to Dante's *Divine Comedy.* Blake taught himself Italian.

1825   Fuseli died.

1826   Flaxman died.

1827   August 12. Blake died. He was buried in Bunhill Fields, the grave unmarked.

1831   October 18. Mrs. Blake died and was buried next to her husband's grave.

1863   Alexander Gilchrist's *Life of William Blake.*

Selected Bibliography

Biographies

The best biography remains that of Alexander Gilchrist, *The Life of William Blake* (1863, 1880). The later Everyman edition with introduction and notes by Ruthven Todd, is the most trustworthy. Subsequent biographies by Wright and Wilson are derivative of Gilchrist's without adding much new information. Recent work by G. E. Bentley, Jr., appearing in periodicals, will result in a book of studies on Blake's life.

Reference Books

A *Blake Bibliography* by G. E. Bentley, Jr., and Martin K. Nurmi (1964).

A *Blake Dictionary* by S. Foster Damon annotates Blake's symbols.

Texts

There are two fundamental texts:

The Writings of William Blake (1957), edited by Geoffrey Keynes, is a complete text modernized in respect to punctuation.

The Prose and Poetry of William Blake (1965), edited by David V. Erdman, with a commentary by Harold Bloom, attempts to preserve Blake's punctuation. Only a selection of the letters, however, is provided.

The Letters of William Blake were edited by Geoffrey Keynes in 1956. Revised edition, 1969.

Commentaries and Criticism

The earliest interpretative books on Blake, both with their own idiosyncrasies, are Swinburne's *William Blake: A Critical*

Study (1867), and the three-volume edition of Blake's works edited with commentary and notes by E. J. Ellis and W. B. Yeats (1893).

The modern interpretation of Blake really begins with S. Foster Damon's *William Blake: His Philosophy and Symbols* (1924, 1947). Among the most useful subsequent books are:

M. O. Percival, *William Blake's Circle of Destiny* (1938), mainly on the earlier prophecies.

Mark Schorer, *William Blake: The Politics of Vision* (1946).

Northrop Frye, *Fearful Symmetry* (1947), very important.

David V. Erdman, *Blake: Prophet Against Empire* (1954), on the political and social background and allegory.

Robert F. Gleckner, *The Piper and the Bard* (1959), on the early prophecies.

Peter F. Fisher, *The Valley of Vision* (1961), on the intellectual context of Blake's work, incomplete at Fisher's death.

Hazard Adams, *William Blake: A Reading of the Shorter Poems* (1963).

Harold Bloom, *Blake's Apocalypse* (1963), a very useful general introduction.

There are two particularly good collections of essays. *Blake* (Northrop Frye, editor), 1966, and *Discussions of William Blake* (John E. Grant, editor), 1961. The latter contains the best introductory essay on Blake ever written, Northrop Frye's "Blake's Treatment of the Archetype," originally published in *English Institute Essays,* 1950.

On Blake's Pictorial Art

There are numerous books which reproduce Blake's drawings and etchings. The Blake Trust has over the years published colored reproductions of Blake's prophetic books, including a remarkably fine *Jerusalem* (1952). There are also collections of Blake's paintings by Darrell Figgis (1925), his engravings by Laurence Binyon (1926), and his line drawings by Geoffrey

Keynes (1927 and 1956). See also G. E. Bentley, Jr.'s edition of *Vala; or The Four Zoas* (1963), which includes a facsimile, Albert S. Roe's *Blake's Illustrations to the Divine Comedy* (1953), and S. Foster Damon's, *Blake's Job: William Blake's Illustrations of the Book of Job* (1966).

Useful books on Blake's art are:

Anthony Blunt, *The Art of William Blake* (1959).
Jean H. Hagstrum, *William Blake: Poet and Painter* (1964).

Contents

A Selection of *Poems, Epigrams, and Fragments from the Rossetti Manuscript* (1793 - 1811), 52

PART FOUR: SELECTED MARGINALIA, 591

PART FIVE: SELECTED LETTERS, 633

NOTES AND COMMENTARIES, 685

Part One
SHORTER POEMS

Selections from *Poetical Sketches* (1783)

TO SPRING

O thou with dewy locks, who lookest down
Through the clear windows of the morning, turn
Thine angel eyes upon our western isle,
Which in full choir hails thy approach, O Spring!

The hills tell each other, and the list'ning   5
Valleys hear; all our longing eyes are turned
Up to thy bright pavilions; issue forth,
And let thy holy feet visit our clime.

Come o'er the eastern hills, and let our winds
Kiss thy perfumed garments; let us taste   10
Thy morn and evening breath; scatter thy pearls
Upon our lovesick land, that mourns for thee.

O deck her forth with thy fair fingers; pour
Thy soft kisses on her bosom; and put
Thy golden crown upon her languished head,   15
Whose modest tresses were bound up for thee!

TO SUMMER

O thou, who passest through our valleys in
Thy strength, curb thy fierce steeds, allay the heat
That flames from their large nostrils! Thou, O Summer,
Oft pitched'st here thy golden tent, and oft
Beneath our oaks hast slept, while we beheld   5
With joy thy ruddy limbs and flourishing hair.

Beneath our thickest shades we oft have heard
Thy voice, when noon upon his fervid car
Rode o'er the deep of heaven; beside our springs
Sit down, and in our mossy valleys, on   10
Some bank beside a river clear, throw thy
Silk draperies off and rush into the stream;
Our valleys love the Summer in his pride.

Our bards are famed who strike the silver wire;
Our youths are bolder than the southern swains;   15
Our maidens fairer in the sprightly dance;
We lack not songs, nor instruments of joy,
Nor echoes sweet, nor waters clear as heaven,
Nor laurel wreaths against the sultry heat.

TO AUTUMN

O Autumn, laden with fruit, and stained
With the blood of the grape, pass not, but sit
Beneath my shady roof; there thou may'st rest
And tune thy jolly voice to my fresh pipe,
And all the daughters of the year shall dance!   5
Sing now the lusty song of fruits and flowers:

"The narrow bud opens her beauties to
The sun, and love runs in her thrilling veins;
Blossoms hang round the brows of morning and
Flourish down the bright cheek of modest eve,   10
Till clust'ring Summer breaks forth into singing,
And feathered clouds strew flowers round her head.

"The spirits of the air live on the smells
Of fruit; and joy, with pinions light, roves round
The gardens, or sits singing in the trees."   15
Thus sang the jolly Autumn as he sat,
Then rose, girded himself, and o'er the bleak
Hills fled from our sight, but left his golden load.

TO WINTER

O Winter! bar thine adamantine doors;
The north is thine; there hast thou built thy dark
Deep-founded habitation. Shake not thy roofs,
Nor bend thy pillars with thine iron car.

He hears me not, but o'er the yawning deep   5
Rides heavy; his storms are unchained, sheathed
In ribbed steel; I dare not lift mine eyes,
For he hath reared his sceptre o'er the world.

Lo! now the direful monster, whose skin clings
To his strong bones, strides o'er the groaning rocks;   10
He withers all in silence, and his hand
Unclothes the earth and freezes up frail life.

He takes his seat upon the cliffs; the mariner
Cries in vain, Poor little wretch! that deal'st
With storms; till heaven smiles, and the monster   15
Is driven yelling to his caves beneath Mount Hecla.

TO THE EVENING STAR

Thou fair-haired angel of the evening,
Now, while the sun rests on the mountains, light
Thy bright torch of love; thy radiant crown
Put on, and smile upon our evening bed!
Smile on our loves; and, while thou drawest the   5
Blue curtains of the sky, scatter thy silver dew
On every flower that shuts its sweet eyes
In timely sleep. Let thy west wind sleep on
The lake; speak silence with thy glimmering eyes,
And wash the dusk with silver. Soon, full soon,   10
Dost thou withdraw; then the wolf rages wide,

And the lion glares through the dun forest;
The fleeces of our flocks are covered with
Thy sacred dew; protect them with thine influence.

TO MORNING

O holy virgin! clad in purest white,
Unlock heaven's golden gates, and issue forth;
Awake the dawn that sleeps in heaven; let light
Rise from the chambers of the east, and bring
The honeyed dew that cometh on waking day.   5
O radiant morning, salute the sun,
Roused like a huntsman to the chase, and, with
Thy buskined feet, appear upon our hills.

SONG

How sweet I roamed from field to field
    And tasted all the summer's pride,
Till I the prince of love beheld,
    Who in the sunny beams did glide!

He showed me lilies for my hair   5
    And blushing roses for my brow;
He led me through his gardens fair,
    Where all his golden pleasures grow.

With sweet May dews my wings were wet,
    And Phoebus fired my vocal rage;   10
He caught me in his silken net
    And shut me in his golden cage.

He loves to sit and hear me sing,
    Then, laughing, sports and plays with me,
Then stretches out my golden wing   15
    And mocks my loss of liberty.

SONG

My silks and fine array,
  My smiles and languished air,
By love are driven away;
  And mournful lean Despair
Brings me yew to deck my grave: 5
Such end true lovers have.

His face is fair as heaven,
  When springing buds unfold;
O why to him was't given,
  Whose heart is wintry cold?   10
His breast is love's all worshiped tomb,
Where all love's pilgrims come.

Bring me an axe and spade,
  Bring me a winding sheet;
When I my grave have made,   15
  Let winds and tempests beat:
Then down I'll lie, as cold as clay.
True love doth pass away!

SONG

Love and harmony combine
And around our souls intwine,
While thy branches mix with mine,
And our roots together join.

Joys upon our branches sit,   5
Chirping loud and singing sweet;
Like gentle streams beneath our feet
Innocence and virtue meet.

Thou the golden fruit dost bear;
I am clad in flowers fair.   10
Thy sweet boughs perfume the air,
And the turtle buildeth there.

There she sits and feeds her young;
Sweet I hear her mournful song.
And thy lovely leaves among,   15
There is love: I hear his tongue.

There his charming nest doth lay;
There he sleeps the night away;
There he sports along the day
And doth among our branches play.   20

SONG

I love the jocund dance,
  The softly breathing song,
Where innocent eyes do glance,
  And where lisps the maiden's tongue.

I love the laughing vale,   5
  I love the echoing hill,
Where mirth does never fail,
  And the jolly swain laughs his fill.

I love the pleasant cot,
  I love the innocent bower,   10
Where white and brown is our lot,
  Or fruit in the midday hour.

I love the oaken seat
  Beneath the oaken tree,
Where all the old villagers meet   15
  And laugh our sports to see.

I love our neighbours all,
  But, Kitty, I better love thee;

And love them I ever shall,
  But thou art all to me.   20

SONG

Memory, hither come,
  And tune your merry notes;
And, while upon the wind
  Your music floats,

I'll pore upon the stream,   5
  Where sighing lovers dream,
And fish for fancies as they pass
  Within the watery glass.

I'll drink of the clear stream
  And hear the linnet's song,   10
And there I'll lie and dream
  The day along,

And when night comes, I'll go
  To places fit for woe,
Walking along the darkened valley   15
  With silent Melancholy.

MAD SONG

The wild winds weep,
  And the night is a-cold;
Come hither, Sleep,
  And my griefs infold;
But lo! the morning peeps   5
  Over the eastern steeps,
And the rustling birds of dawn
The earth do scorn.

Lo! to the vault
  Of paved heaven,   10
With sorrow fraught
  My notes are driven;
They strike the ear of night,
  Make weep the eyes of day;
They make mad the roaring winds   15
  And with tempests play.

Like a fiend in a cloud
  With howling woe,
After night I do crowd
  And with night will go;   20
I turn my back to the east,
From whence comforts have increased;
For light doth seize my brain
With frantic pain.

SONG

Fresh from the dewy hill, the merry year
Smiles on my head and mounts his flaming car;
Round my young brows the laurel wreathes a shade,
And rising glories beam around my head.

My feet are wing'd, while o'er the dewy lawn,   5
I meet my maiden, risen like the morn.
Oh bless those holy feet, like angels' feet;
Oh bless those limbs, beaming with heavenly light,

Like as an angel glitt'ring in the sky
In times of innocence and holy joy.   10
The joyful shepherd stops his grateful song
To hear the music of an angel's tongue.

So when she speaks, the voice of Heaven I hear;
So when we walk, nothing impure comes near;
Each field seems Eden, and each calm retreat;   15
Each village seems the haunt of holy feet.

But that sweet village where my black-eyed maid,
Closes her eyes in sleep beneath night's shade,
Whene'er I enter, more than mortal fire
Burns in my soul and does my song inspire. 20

SONG

When early morn walks forth in sober grey,
Then to my black-eyed maid I haste away;
When evening sits beneath her dusky bower
And gently sighs away the silent hour,
The village bell alarms, away I go, 5
And the vale darkens at my pensive woe.

To that sweet village where my black-eyed maid
Doth drop a tear beneath the silent shade
I turn my eyes and, pensive as I go,
Curse my black stars and bless my pleasing woe. 10

Oft when the summer sleeps among the trees,
Whisp'ring faint murmurs to the scanty breeze,
I walk the village round; if at her side
A youth doth walk in stolen joy and pride,
I curse my stars in bitter grief and woe, 15
That made my love so high, and me so low.

O should she e'er prove false, his limbs I'd tear
And throw all pity on the burning air;
I'd curse bright fortune for my mixed lot,
And then I'd die in peace, and be forgot. 20

TO THE MUSES

Whether on Ida's shady brow
  Or in the chambers of the East,
The chambers of the sun, that now
  From ancient melody have ceased;

Whether in Heaven ye wander fair,   5
  Or the green corners of the earth,
Or the blue regions of the air,
  Where the melodious winds have birth;

Whether on crystal rocks ye rove,
  Beneath the bosom of the sea   10
Wand'ring in many a coral grove,
  Fair Nine, forsaking Poetry!

How have you left the ancient love
  That bards of old enjoyed in you!
The languid strings do scarcely move!   15
  The sound is forced, the notes are few!

GWIN, KING OF NORWAY

Come, Kings, and listen to my song:
  When Gwin, the son of Nore,
Over the nations of the North
  His cruel sceptre bore,

The Nobles of the land did feed   5
  Upon the hungry Poor;
They tear the poor man's lamb and drive
  The needy from their door!

"The land is desolate; our wives
  And children cry for bread;   10
Arise, and pull the tyrant down;
  Let Gwin be humbled."

Gordred the giant roused himself
  From sleeping in his cave;
He shook the hills, and in the clouds   15
  The troubled banners wave.

Beneath them rolled, like tempests black,
  The num'rous sons of blood;

Like lions' whelps, roaring abroad,
    Seeking their nightly food.   20

Down Bleron's hills they dreadful rush;
    Their cry ascends the clouds;
The trampling horse and clanging arms,
    Like rushing mighty floods,

Their wives and children, weeping loud,   25
    Follow in wild array,
Howling like ghosts, furious as wolves
    In the bleak wintry day.

"Pull down the tyrant to the dust;
    Let Gwin be humbled,"   30
They cry, "and let ten thousand lives
    Pay for the tyrant's head."

From tower to tower the watchmen cry,
    "O Gwin, the son of Nore,
Arouse thyself! The nations black,   35
    Like clouds, come rolling o'er!"

Gwin reared his shield, his palace shakes,
    His chiefs come rushing round;
Each, like an awful thunder cloud,
    With voice of solemn sound.   40

Like reared stones around a grave
    They stand around the King;
Then suddenly each seized his spear,
    And clashing steel does ring.

The husbandman does leave his plow   45
    To wade through fields of gore;
The merchant binds his brows in steel
    And leaves the trading shore.

The shepherd leaves his mellow pipe
    And sounds the trumpet shrill;   50
The workman throws his hammer down
    To heave the bloody bill.

Like the tall ghost of Barraton,
  Who sports in stormy sky,
Gwin leads his host as black as night,   55
  When pestilence does fly.

With horses and with chariots—
  And all his spearmen bold
March to the sound of mournful song,
  Like clouds around him rolled.   60

Gwin lifts his hand—the nations halt;
  "Prepare for war," he cries—
"Gordred appears!—His frowning brow
  Troubles our northern skies."

The armies stand like balances   65
  Held in th' Almighty's hand;—
"Gwin, thou hast filled thy measure up;
  Thou'rt swept from out the land."

And now the raging armies rushed
  Like warring mighty seas;   70
The Heavens are shook with roaring war;
  The dust ascends the skies!

Earth smokes with blood and groans and shakes,
  To drink her children's gore,
A sea of blood; nor can the eye   75
  See to the trembling shore!

And on the verge of this wild sea
  Famine and death doth cry;
The cries of women and of babes
  Over the field doth fly.   80

The King is seen raging afar
  With all his men of might,
Like blazing comets, scattering death
  Through the red fev'rous night.

Beneath his arm like sheep they die   85
  And groan upon the plain;

The battle faints, and bloody men
  Fight upon hills of slain.

Now death is sick, and riven men
  Labour and toil for life;
Steed rolls on steed, and shield on shield,   90
  Sunk in this sea of strife!

The god of war is drunk with blood;
  The earth doth faint and fail;
The stench of blood makes sick the heavens;   95
  Ghosts glut the throat of hell!

O, what have Kings to answer for,
  Before that awful throne,
When thousand deaths for vengeance cry,
  And ghosts accusing groan!   100

Like blazing comets in the sky,
  That shake the stars of light,
Which drop like fruit unto the earth,
  Through the fierce burning night—

Like these did Gwin and Gordred meet,   105
  And the first blow decides;
Down from the brow unto the breast
  Gordred his head divides!

Gwin fell; the Sons of Norway fled,
  All that remained alive;   110
The rest did fill the vale of death;
  For them the eagles strive.

The river Dorman rolled their blood
  Into the northern sea,
Who mourned his sons and overwhelmed   115
  The pleasant south country.

Figure 1. "Infant Joy" from *Songs of Innocence*

SONGS OF INNOCENCE
AND OF EXPERIENCE

Showing the two contrary states of the human soul

Songs of Innocence (1789)

INTRODUCTION

Piping down the valleys wild,
Piping songs of pleasant glee,
On a cloud I saw a child,
And he laughing said to me:

"Pipe a song about a Lamb."   5
So I piped with merry cheer.
"Piper, pipe that song again."
So I piped; he wept to hear.

"Drop thy pipe, thy happy pipe;
Sing thy songs of happy cheer."   10
So I sung the same again,
While he wept with joy to hear.

"Piper, sit thee down and write
In a book that all may read."
So he vanished from my sight,   15
And I plucked a hollow reed,

And I made a rural pen,
And I stained the water clear,
And I wrote my happy songs
Every child may joy to hear.   20

THE SHEPHERD

How sweet is the Shepherd's sweet lot!
From the morn to the evening he strays.
He shall follow his sheep all the day,
And his tongue shall be filled with praise.

For he hears the lamb's innocent call,   5
And he hears the ewe's tender reply;
He is watchful while they are in peace,
For they know when their Shepherd is nigh.

THE ECHOING GREEN

The Sun does arise
And make happy the skies.
The merry bells ring
To welcome the Spring.
The skylark and thrush,   5
The birds of the bush,
Sing louder around
To the bells' cheerful sound,
While our sports shall be seen
On the Echoing Green.   10

Old John with white hair
Does laugh away care,
Sitting under the oak,
Among the old folk.
They laugh at our play,   15
And soon they all say:
"Such, such were the joys,
When we all girls & boys,

In our youth time were seen
On the Echoing Green."   20

Till the little ones weary
No more can be merry,
The sun does descend,
And our sports have an end;
Round the laps of their mothers,   25
Many sisters and brothers,
Like birds in their nest,
Are ready for rest,
And sport no more seen
On the darkening Green.   30

THE LAMB

Little Lamb, who made thee?
Dost thou know who made thee,
Gave thee life & bid thee feed
By the stream & o'er the mead;
Gave thee clothing of delight,   5
Softest clothing woolly bright;
Gave thee such a tender voice,
Making all the vales rejoice?
Little Lamb, who made thee?
Dost thou know who made thee?   10

Little Lamb, I'll tell thee!
Little Lamb, I'll tell thee!
He is called by thy name,
For he calls himself a Lamb.
He is meek & he is mild;   15
He became a little child.
I a child & thou a lamb,
We are called by his name.
Little Lamb, God bless thee!
Little Lamb, God bless thee!   20

THE LITTLE BLACK BOY

My mother bore me in the southern wild,
And I am black, but O! my soul is white;
White as an angel is the English child,
But I am black, as if bereaved of light.

My mother taught me underneath a tree,   5
And sitting down before the heat of day,
She took me on her lap and kissed me
And pointing to the east began to say:

"Look on the rising sun: there God does live
And gives his light and gives his heat away;   10
And flowers and trees and beasts and men receive
Comfort in morning, joy in the noon day.

And we are put on earth a little space
That we may learn to bear the beams of love,
And these black bodies and this sunburnt face   15
Is but a cloud and like a shady grove.

For when our souls have learned the heat to bear,
The cloud will vanish; we shall hear his voice,
Saying: 'Come out from the grove, my love & care,
And round my golden tent like lambs rejoice.'   20

Thus did my mother say and kissed me,
And thus I say to little English boy:
When I from black and he from white cloud free,
And round the tent of God like lambs we joy,

I'll shade him from the heat till he can bear,   25
To lean in joy upon our father's knee.
And then I'll stand and stroke his silver hair,
And be like him, and he will then love me.

THE BLOSSOM

Merry, Merry Sparrow!
Under leaves so green
A happy Blossom
Sees you swift as arrow
Seek your cradle narrow   5
Near my Bosom.

Pretty, Pretty Robin!
Under leaves so green
A happy Blossom
Hears you sobbing, sobbing,   10
Pretty, Pretty Robin,
Near my Bosom.

THE CHIMNEY SWEEPER

When my mother died I was very young,
And my father sold me while yet my tongue
Could scarcely cry, "weep, weep, weep, weep."
So your chimneys I sweep, & in soot I sleep.

There's little Tom Dacre, who cried when his head,   5
That curled like a lamb's back, was shaved, so I said:
"Hush, Tom, never mind it, for when your head's bare,
You know that the soot cannot spoil your white hair."

And so he was quiet, & that very night,
As Tom was a-sleeping, he had such a sight,   10
That thousands of sweepers, Dick, Joe, Ned & Jack,
Were all of them locked up in coffins of black.

And by came an Angel who had a bright key,
And he opened the coffins & set them all free.
Then down a green plain, leaping, laughing, they run   15
And wash in a river and shine in the Sun.

Then naked & white, all their bags left behind,
They rise upon clouds and sport in the wind.
And the Angel told Tom, if he'd be a good boy,
He'd have God for his father & never want joy.   20

And so Tom awoke, and we rose in the dark
And got with our bags & our brushes to work.
Though the morning was cold, Tom was happy & warm.
So if all do their duty, they need not fear harm.

THE LITTLE BOY LOST

"Father, father, where are you going?
O do not walk so fast.
Speak, father, speak to your little boy,
Or else I shall be lost."

The night was dark; no father was there.   5
The child was wet with dew.
The mire was deep, & the child did weep,
And away the vapour flew.

THE LITTLE BOY FOUND

The little boy lost in the lonely fen,
Led by the wand'ring light,
Began to cry, but God ever nigh,
Appeared like his father in white.

He kissed the child & by the hand led
And to his mother brought,
Who in sorrow pale, through the lonely dale,
Her little boy weeping sought.

LAUGHING SONG

When the green woods laugh with the voice of joy,
And the dimpling stream runs laughing by;
When the air does laugh with our merry wit,
And the green hill laughs with the noise of it;

When the meadows laugh with lively green,   5
And the grasshopper laughs in the merry scene;
When Mary and Susan and Emily
With their sweet round mouths sing, "Ha, Ha, He";

When the painted birds laugh in the shade;
Where our table with cherries and nuts is spread,   10
Come live & be merry and join with me
To sing the sweet chorus of "Ha, Ha, He."

A CRADLE SONG

Sweet dreams, form a shade
O'er my lovely infant's head,
Sweet dreams of pleasant streams
By happy, silent, moony beams.

Sweet sleep, with soft down   5
Weave thy brows an infant crown.
Sweet sleep, Angel mild,
Hover o'er my happy child.

Sweet smiles, in the night
Hover over my delight.   10
Sweet smiles, Mother's smiles,
All the livelong night beguiles.

Sweet moans, dovelike sighs,
Chase not slumber from thy eyes.
Sweet moans, sweeter smiles,   15
All the dovelike moans beguiles.

Sleep, sleep, happy child.
All creation slept and smiled.
Sleep, sleep, happy sleep,
While o'er thee thy mother weep.   20

Sweet babe, in thy face
Holy image I can trace.
Sweet babe, once like thee,
Thy maker lay and wept for me,

Wept for me, for thee, for all,   25
When he was an infant small.
Thou his image ever see,
Heavenly face that smiles on thee,

Smiles on thee, on me, on all,
Who became an infant small.   30
Infant smiles are his own smiles;
Heaven & earth to peace beguiles.

THE DIVINE IMAGE

To Mercy, Pity, Peace and Love,
All pray in their distress,
And to these virtues of delight
Return their thankfulness.

For Mercy, Pity, Peace and Love   5
Is God our father dear;

And Mercy, Pity, Peace and Love
Is Man, his child and care.

For Mercy has a human heart,
Pity a human face,   10
And Love the human form divine,
And Peace the human dress.

Then every man of every clime
That prays in his distress
Prays to the human form divine,   15
Love, Mercy, Pity, Peace.

And all must love the human form
In heathen, Turk or Jew.
Where Mercy, Love & Pity dwell,
There God is dwelling too.   20

HOLY THURSDAY

'Twas on a Holy Thursday, their innocent faces clean,
The children walking two & two in red & blue & green.
Grey-headed beadles walked before with wands as white
        as snow,
Till into the high dome of Paul's they like Thames' waters
        flow.

O what a multitude they seemed, these flowers of London
        town!   5
Seated in companies they sit with radiance all their own.
The hum of multitudes was there, but multitudes of lambs,
Thousands of little boys & girls raising their innocent hands.

Now like a mighty wind they raise to heaven the voice
        of song,
Or like harmonious thunderings the seats of heaven among. 10
Beneath them sit the aged men, wise guardians of the poor;
Then cherish pity, lest you drive an angel from your door.

NIGHT

The sun descending in the west,
The evening star does shine.
The birds are silent in their nest,
And I must seek for mine.
The moon like a flower   5
In heaven's high bower
With silent delight
Sits and smiles on the night.

Farewell green fields and happy groves,
Where flocks have took delight;   10
Where lambs have nibbled, silent moves
The feet of angels bright;
Unseen they pour blessing
And joy without ceasing
On each bud and blossom   15
And each sleeping bosom.

They look in every thoughtless nest,
Where birds are covered warm;
They visit caves of every beast
To keep them all from harm;   20
If they see any weeping
That should have been sleeping,
They pour sleep on their head
And sit down by their bed.

When wolves and tigers howl for prey,   25
They pitying stand and weep,
Seeking to drive their thirst away
And keep them from the sheep.
But if they rush dreadful,
The angels, most heedful,   30

Receive each mild spirit,
New worlds to inherit.

And there the lion's ruddy eyes
Shall flow with tears of gold,
And pitying the tender cries   35
And walking round the fold,
Saying: "Wrath by his meekness
And, by his health, sickness
Is driven away
From our immortal day.   40

"And now beside thee, bleating lamb,
I can lie down and sleep,
Or think on him who bore thy name,
Graze after thee and weep.
For washed in life's river,   45
My bright name forever
Shall shine like the gold
As I guard o'er the fold."

SPRING

Sound the Flute!
Now it's mute.
Birds delight
Day and Night.
Nightingale   5
In the dale,
Lark in Sky,
Merrily,
Merrily, Merrily, to welcome in the Year.

Little Boy   10
Full of joy,
Little Girl

Sweet and small,
Cock does crow;
So do you.   15
Merry voice,
Infant noise,
Merrily, Merrily, to welcome in the Year.

Little Lamb,
Here I am   20
Come and lick
My white neck.
Let me pull
Your soft Wool.
Let me kiss   25
Your soft face.
Merrily, Merrily, we welcome in the Year.

NURSE'S SONG

When the voices of children are heard on the green
And laughing is heard on the hill,
My heart is at rest within my breast,
And every thing else is still.

"Then come home, my children; the sun is gone down,   5
And the dews of night arise.
Come, come, leave off play, and let us away
Till the morning appears in the skies."

"No, no, let us play, for it is yet day,
And we cannot go to sleep.   10
Besides, in the sky the little birds fly,
And the hills are all covered with sheep."

"Well, well, go & play till the light fades away,
And then go home to bed."
The little ones leaped & shouted & laughed,   15
And all the hills echoed.

INFANT JOY

"I have no name.
I am but two days old."
"What shall I call thee?"
"I happy am.
Joy is my name."   5
"Sweet joy befall thee!

"Pretty joy!
Sweet joy but two days old,
Sweet joy I call thee.
Thou dost smile.   10
I sing the while.
Sweet joy befall thee."

A DREAM

Once a dream did weave a shade
O'er my Angel-guarded bed
That an Emmet lost its way
Where on grass methought I lay.

Troubled, 'wildered and forlorn,   5
Dark benighted, travel-worn,
Over many a tangled spray,
All heartbroke I heard her say:

"O, my children! do they cry?
Do they hear their father sigh?   10
Now they look abroad to see,
Now return and weep for me."

Pitying, I dropped a tear,
But I saw a glow-worm near,

Who replied: "What wailing wight 15
Calls the watchman of the night?

"I am set to light the ground,
While the beetle goes his round;
Follow now the beetle's hum;
Little wanderer, hie thee home." 20

ON ANOTHER'S SORROW

Can I see another's woe
And not be in sorrow too?
Can I see another's grief
And not seek for kind relief?

Can I see a falling tear 5
And not feel my sorrow's share?
Can a father see his child
Weep, nor be with sorrow filled?

Can a mother sit and hear
An infant groan, an infant fear? 10
No, no, never can it be.
Never, never can it be.

And can he who smiles on all
Hear the wren with sorrows small,
Hear the small bird's grief & care, 15
Hear the woes that infants bear,

And not sit beside the nest,
Pouring pity in their breast,
And not sit the cradle near,
Weeping tear on infant's tear. 20

And not sit both night & day,
Wiping all our tears away?
O! no, never can it be.
Never, never can it be.

He doth give his joy to all.   25
He becomes an infant small.
He becomes a man of woe.
He doth feel the sorrow too.

Think not thou canst sigh a sigh,
And thy maker is not by.   30
Think not thou canst weep a tear,
And thy maker is not near.

O! he gives to us his joy
That our grief he may destroy;
Till our grief is fled & gone   35
He doth sit by us and moan.

Figure 2. "The Sick Rose" from *Songs of Experience*

INTRODUCTION

Hear the voice of the Bard!
Who Present, Past & Future sees,
Whose ears have heard
The Holy Word,
That walked among the ancient trees,   5

Calling the lapsed Soul
And weeping in the evening dew,
That might control
The starry pole
And fallen, fallen light renew!   10

O Earth, O Earth, return!
Arise from out the dewy grass;
Night is worn,
And the morn
Rises from the slumberous mass.   15

Turn away no more;
Why wilt thou turn away?
The starry floor,
The wat'ry shore,
Is given thee till the break of day.   20

EARTH'S ANSWER

Earth raised up her head
From the darkness dread & drear.
Her light fled,

Stony dread!
And her locks covered with grey despair: 5

"Prisoned on wat'ry shore,
Starry Jealousy does keep my den.
Cold and hoar,
Weeping o'er,
I hear the Father of the ancient men.   10

"Selfish father of men,
Cruel, jealous, selfish fear,
Can delight
Chained in night
The virgins of youth and morning bear?   15

"Does spring hide its joy
When buds and blossoms grow?
Does the sower
Sow by night,
Or the plowman in darkness plow?   20

"Break this heavy chain
That does freeze my bones around.
Selfish, vain,
Eternal bane,
That free Love with bondage bound."   25

THE CLOD AND THE PEBBLE

"Love seeketh not Itself to please,
Nor for itself hath any care,
But for another gives its ease,
And builds a Heaven in Hell's despair."

So sang a little Clod of Clay,   5
Trodden with the cattle's feet,
But a Pebble of the brook
Warbled out these metres meet:

"Love seeketh only Self to please,
To bind another to its delight,   10
Joys in another's loss of ease
And builds a Hell in Heaven's despite."

HOLY THURSDAY

Is this a holy thing to see
In a rich and fruitful land
Babes reduced to misery,
Fed with cold and usurous hand?

Is that trembling cry a song?   5
Can it be a song of joy?
And so many children poor;
It is a land of poverty!

And their sun does never shine.
And their fields are bleak & bare.   10
And their ways are filled with thorns.
It is eternal winter there.

For where'er the sun does shine,
And where'er the rain does fall,
Babe can never hunger there,   15
Nor poverty the mind appall.

THE LITTLE GIRL LOST

In futurity
I prophetic see
That the earth from sleep
(Grave the sentence deep)

Shall arise and seek   5
For her maker meek

And the desert wild
Become a garden mild.

In the southern clime,
Where the summer's prime   10
Never fades away,
Lovely Lyca lay.

Seven summers old
Lovely Lyca told;
She had wandered long   15
Hearing wild birds' song.

"Sweet sleep, come to me
Underneath this tree.
Do father, mother weep:
'Where can Lyca sleep?'   20

"Lost in desert wild
Is your little child.
How can Lyca sleep
If her mother weep?

"If her heart does ache,   25
Then let Lyca wake;
If my mother sleep,
Lyca shall not weep.

"Frowning, frowning night,
O'er this desert bright,   30
Let thy moon arise,
While I close my eyes."

Sleeping Lyca lay,
While the beasts of prey,
Come from caverns deep,   35
Viewed the maid asleep.

The kingly lion stood
And the virgin viewed,
Then he gamboled round
O'er the hallowed ground.   40

Leopards, tigers play
Round her as she lay,
While the lion old
Bowed his mane of gold

And her bosom lick, 45
And upon her neck,
From his eyes of flame
Ruby tears there came,

While the lioness
Loosed her slender dress, 50
And naked they conveyed
To caves the sleeping maid.

THE LITTLE GIRL FOUND

All the night in woe
Lyca's parents go.
Over valleys deep,
While the deserts weep.

Tired and woebegone, 5
Hoarse with making moan,
Arm in arm seven days,
They traced the desert ways.

Seven nights they sleep
Among shadows deep 10
And dream they see their child
Starved in desert wild.

Pale through pathless ways
The fancied image strays;
Famished, weeping, weak, 15
With hollow piteous shriek,

Rising from unrest,
The trembling woman pressed

With feet of weary woe;
She could no further go.   20

In his arms he bore
Her, armed with sorrow sore,
Till before their way
A couching lion lay.

Turning back was vain;   25
Soon his heavy mane
Bore them to the ground;
Then he stalked around,

Smelling to his prey.
But their fears allay   30
When he licks their hands
And silent by them stands.

They look upon his eyes,
Filled with deep surprise,
And wondering behold   35
A spirit armed in gold.

On his head a crown,
On his shoulders down
Flowed his golden hair.
Gone was all their care.   40

"Follow me," he said;
"Weep not for the maid;
In my palace deep,
Lyca lies asleep."

Then they followed   45
Where the vision led
And saw their sleeping child
Among tigers wild.

To this day they dwell
In a lonely dell,   50
Nor fear the wolvish howl,
Nor the lion's growl.

THE CHIMNEY SWEEPER

A little black thing among the snow,
Crying "weep, weep," in notes of woe!
"Where are thy father & mother, say?"
"They are both gone up to the church to pray.

"Because I was happy upon the heath   5
And smiled among the winter's snow,
They clothed me in the clothes of death
And taught me to sing the notes of woe.

"And because I am happy & dance & sing,
They think they have done me no injury   10
And are gone to praise God & his Priest & King,
Who make up a heaven of our misery.

NURSE'S SONG

When the voices of children are heard on the green
And whisp'rings are in the dale,
The days of my youth rise fresh in my mind,
My face turns green and pale.

Then come home my children, the sun is gone down,   5
And the dews of night arise.
Your spring & your day are wasted in play,
And your winter and night in disguise.

THE SICK ROSE

O Rose, thou art sick!
The invisible worm,

That flies in the night
In the howling storm,

Has found out thy bed   5
Of crimson joy,
And his dark, secret love
Does thy life destroy.

THE FLY

Little Fly,
Thy summer's play
My thoughtless hand
Has brushed away.

Am not I   5
A fly like thee?
Or art not thou
A man like me?

For I dance
And drink & sing,   10
Till some blind hand
Shall brush my wing.

If thought is life
And strength & breath,
And the want   15
Of thought is death,

Then am I
A happy fly,
If I live,
Or if I die.   20

THE ANGEL

I Dreamt a Dream! What can it mean?
And that I was a maiden Queen

Guarded by an Angel mild;
Wiltless woe was ne'er beguiled!

And I wept both night and day,   5
And he wiped my tears away,
And I wept both day and night
And hid from him my heart's delight.

So he took his wings and fled;
Then the morn blushed rosy red;   10
I dried my tears & armed my fears
With ten thousand shields and spears.

Soon my Angel came again;
I was armed, he came in vain;
For the time of youth was fled,   15
And grey hairs were on my head.

THE TIGER

Tiger, tiger, burning bright
In the forests of the night,
What immortal hand or eye
Could frame thy fearful symmetry?

In what distant deeps or skies   5
Burnt the fire of thine eyes?
On what wings dare he aspire?
What the hand dare seize the fire?

And what shoulder & what art,
Could twist the sinews of thy heart?   10
And when thy heart began to beat,
What dread hand, & what dread feet?

What the hammer? What the chain?
In what furnace was thy brain?
What the anvil? What dread grasp   15
Dare its deadly terrors clasp?

When the stars threw down their spears

And watered heaven with their tears,
Did he smile his work to see?
Did he who made the Lamb make thee?   20

Tiger, tiger, burning bright
In the forests of the night,
What immortal hand or eye
Dare frame thy fearful symmetry?

MY PRETTY ROSE TREE

A flower was offered to me,
Such a flower as May never bore;
But I said, "I've a Pretty Rose tree,"
And I passed the sweet flower o'er.

Then I went to my Pretty Rose tree   5
To tend her by day and by night;
But my Rose turned away with jealousy,
And her thorns were my only delight.

AH! SUNFLOWER

Ah, Sunflower! weary of time,
Who countest the steps of the Sun,
Seeking after that sweet golden clime
Where the traveller's journey is done,

Where the Youth pined away with desire   5
And the pale Virgin shrouded in snow
Arise from their graves and aspire,
Where my Sunflower wishes to go.

THE LILY

The modest Rose puts forth a thorn,
The humble Sheep a threat'ning horn;
While the Lily white shall in Love delight,
Nor a thorn nor a threat stain her beauty bright.

THE GARDEN OF LOVE

I went to the Garden of Love
And saw what I never had seen:
A Chapel was built in the midst,
Where I used to play on the green.

And the gates of this Chapel were shut,   5
And "Thou shalt not" writ over the door;
So I turned to the Garden of Love,
That so many sweet flowers bore,

And I saw it was filled with graves
And tombstones where flowers should be;   10
And Priests in black gowns were walking
    their rounds
And binding with briars my joys & desires.

THE LITTLE VAGABOND

Dear Mother, dear Mother, the Church is cold,
But the Alehouse is healthy & pleasant & warm;

Besides, I can tell where I am used well;
Such usage in heaven will never do well.

But if at the Church they would give us some Ale   5
And a pleasant fire our souls to regale,
We'd sing and we'd pray all the livelong day
Nor ever once wish from the Church to stray.

Then the Parson might preach & drink & sing,
And we'd be as happy as birds in the spring,   10
And modest dame Lurch, who is always at Church,
Would not have bandy children nor fasting nor birch.

And God, like a father rejoicing to see
His children as pleasant and happy as he,
Would have no more quarrel with the Devil
      or the barrel   15
But kiss him & give him both drink and apparel.

LONDON

I wander through each chartered street
Near where the chartered Thames does flow
And mark in every face I meet
Marks of weakness, marks of woe.

In every cry of every Man,   5
In every Infant's cry of fear,
In every voice, in every ban,
The mind-forged manacles I hear:

How the Chimney sweeper's cry
Every black'ning Church appalls,   10
And the hapless Soldier's sigh
Runs in blood down Palace walls.

But most through midnight streets I hear
How the youthful Harlot's curse
Blasts the newborn Infant's tear   15
And blights with plagues the Marriage hearse.

THE HUMAN ABSTRACT

Pity would be no more
If we did not make somebody Poor,
And Mercy no more could be
If all were as happy as we.

And mutual fear brings peace   5
Till the selfish loves increase.
Then Cruelty knits a snare
And spreads his baits with care.

He sits down with holy fears
And waters the ground with tears.   10
Then Humility takes its root
Underneath his foot.

Soon spreads the dismal shade
Of Mystery over his head;
And the Caterpillar and Fly   15
Feed on the Mystery.

And it bears the fruit of Deceit,
Ruddy and sweet to eat;
And the Raven his nest has made
In its thickest shade.   20

The Gods of the earth and sea
Sought through Nature to find this Tree,
But their search was all in vain:
There grows one in the Human Brain.

INFANT SORROW

My mother groaned! My father wept.
Into the dangerous world I leapt,
Helpless, naked, piping loud,
Like a fiend hid in a cloud.

Struggling in my father's hands,   5
Striving against my swaddling bands,
Bound and weary, I thought best
To sulk upon my mother's breast.

A POISON TREE

I was angry with my friend:
I told my wrath, my wrath did end.
I was angry with my foe:
I told it not, my wrath did grow.

And I watered it in fears,   5
Night & morning with my tears;
And I sunned it with smiles,
And with soft deceitful wiles.

And it grew both day and night
Till it bore an apple bright,   10
And my foe beheld it shine,
And he knew that it was mine,

And into my garden stole
When the night had veiled the pole;
In the morning glad I see   15
My foe outstretched beneath the tree.

A LITTLE BOY LOST

"Naught loves another as itself
Nor venerates another so,
Nor is it possible to Thought
A greater than itself to know;

"And Father, how can I love you,   5
Or any of my brothers more?
I love you like the little bird
That picks up crumbs around the door."

The Priest sat by and heard the child.
In trembling zeal he seized his hair;   10
He led him by his little coat,
And all admired the Priestly care.

And standing on the altar high,
"Lo, what a fiend is here!" said he,
"One who sets reason up for judge   15
Of our most holy Mystery."

The weeping child could not be heard.
The weeping parents wept in vain.
They stripped him to his little shirt
And bound him in an iron chain,   20

And burned him in a holy place,
Where many had been burned before.
The weeping parents wept in vain.
Are such things done on Albion's shore?

A LITTLE GIRL LOST

Children of the future Age,
Reading this indignant page,

Know that in a former time
Love! sweet Love! was thought a crime.

In the Age of Gold,   5
Free from winter's cold,
Youth and maiden bright
To the holy light
Naked in the sunny beams delight.

Once a youthful pair,   10
Filled with softest care,
Met in garden bright
Where the holy light
Had just removed the curtains of the night.

There in rising day   15
On the grass they play;
Parents were afar;
Strangers came not near,
And the maiden soon forgot her fear.

Tired with kisses sweet,   20
They agree to meet
When the silent sleep
Waves o'er heaven's deep
And the weary tired wanderers weep.

To her father white   25
Came the maiden bright,
But his loving look,
Like the holy book,
All her tender limbs with terror shook.

"Ona! pale and weak!   30
To thy father speak.
O, the trembling fear!
O, the dismal care!
That shakes the blossoms of my hoary hair."

TO TIRZAH

Whate'er is Born of Mortal Birth
Must be consumed with the Earth
To rise from Generation free;
Then what have I to do with thee?

The Sexes sprung from Shame & Pride   5
Blowed in the morn, in evening died;
But Mercy changed Death into Sleep;
The Sexes rose to work & weep.

Thou Mother of my Mortal part
With cruelty didst mould my Heart,   10
And with false self-deceiving tears
Didst bind my Nostrils, Eyes & Ears,

Didst close my Tongue in senseless clay
And me to Mortal Life betray.
The Death of Jesus set me free;   15
Then what have I to do with thee?

THE SCHOOL BOY

I love to rise in a summer morn
When the birds sing on every tree,
The distant huntsman winds his horn,
And the skylark sings with me.
O! what sweet company.   5

But to go to school in a summer morn
O! it drives all joy away;
Under a cruel eye outworn

The little ones spend the day
In sighing and dismay.   10

Ah! then at times I drooping sit
And spend many an anxious hour,
Nor in my book can I take delight
Nor sit in learning's bower,
Worn through with the dreary shower.   15

How can the bird that is born for joy
Sit in a cage and sing?
How can a child when fears annoy
But droop his tender wing
And forget his youthful spring?   20

O! father & mother, if buds are nipped
And blossoms blown away,
And if the tender plants are stripped
Of their joy in the springing day
By sorrow and care's dismay,   25

How shall the summer arise in joy
Or the summer fruits appear?
Or how shall we gather what griefs destroy
Or bless the mellowing year
When the blasts of winter appear?   30

THE VOICE OF THE ANCIENT BARD

Youth of delight, come hither
And see the opening morn,
Image of truth new born.
Doubt is fled & clouds of reason,
Dark disputes & artful teasing.   5
Folly is an endless maze;
Tangled roots perplex her ways.
How many have fallen there!
They stumble all night over bones of the dead

And feel they know not what but care 10
And wish to lead others when they should be led.

A DIVINE IMAGE
(etched circa 1794,
but not included in the Songs)

Cruelty has a Human Heart
And Jealousy a Human Face,
Terror the Human Form Divine
And Secrecy the Human Dress.

The Human Dress is forged Iron, 5
The Human Form a fiery Forge,
The Human Face a Furnace sealed,
The Human Heart its hungry Gorge.

A Selection of Poems, Epigrams and Fragments from the Rossetti Manuscript

(1793-1811)

Never pain to tell thy love
Love that never told can be,
For the gentle wind does move
Silently, invisibly.

I told my love, I told my love,   5
I told her all my heart.
Trembling cold, in ghastly fears,
Ah, she doth depart.

Soon as she was gone from me
A traveller came by.   10
Silently, invisibly,
O, was no deny.

I laid me down upon a bank
Where love lay sleeping.
I heard among the rushes dank
Weeping, Weeping.

Then I went to the heath & the wild, 5
To the thistles & thorns of the waste;
And they told me how they were beguiled,
Driven out & compelled to be chaste.

I saw a chapel all of gold,
That none did dare to enter in,
And many weeping stood without,
Weeping, mourning, worshipping.

I saw a serpent rise between   5
The white pillars of the door,
And he forced & forced & forced,
Down the golden hinges tore.

And along the pavement sweet,
Set with pearls & rubies bright,   10
All his slimy length he drew,
Till upon the altar white,

Vomiting his poison out
On the bread & on the wine,
So I turned into a sty   15
And laid me down among the swine.

I asked a thief to steal me a peach:
He turned up his eyes.
I asked a lithe lady to lie her down:
Holy & meek she cries.

As soon as I went   5
An angel came.
He winked at the thief
And smiled at the dame,

And without one word said
Had a peach from the tree   10
And 'twixt earnest and joke
Enjoyed the lady.

I heard an Angel singing
When the day was springing:
"Mercy, Pity, Peace
Is the world's release."

Thus he sung all day   5
Over the new mown hay,
Till the sun went down
And haycocks looked brown.

I heard a Devil curse
Over the heath & the furze: 10
"Mercy could be no more
If there was nobody poor,

And pity no more could be
If all were as happy as we."
At his curse the sun went down,   15
And the heavens gave a frown.

Down poured the heavy rain
Over the new reaped grain,
And Miseries' increase
Is Mercy, Pity, Peace.   20

A CRADLE SONG

Sleep, Sleep, beauty bright,
Dreaming o'er the joys of night.
Sleep, Sleep, in thy sleep
Little sorrows sit & weep.

Sweet Babe, in thy face   5
Soft desires I can trace,
Secret joys & secret smiles,
Little pretty infant wiles.

As thy softest limbs I feel
Smiles as of the morning steal   10
O'er thy cheek & o'er thy breast,
Where thy little heart does rest.

O, the cunning wiles that creep,
In thy little heart asleep.
When thy little heart does wake,   15
Then the dreadful lightnings break.

From thy cheek & from thy eye
O'er the youthful harvests nigh.

Infant wiles & infant smiles
Heaven & Earth of peace beguiles.   20

I feared the fury of my wind
Would blight all blossoms fair & true,
And my sun it shined & shined,
And my wind it never blew.

But a blossom fair or true   5
Was not found on any tree,
For all blossoms grew & grew
Fruitless, false, though fair to see.

Why should I care for the men of Thames
Or the cheating waves of chartered streams
Or shrink at the little blasts of fear
That the hireling blows into my ear?

Though born on the cheating banks of Thames,   5
Though his waters bathed my infant limbs,
The Ohio shall wash his stains from me;
I was born a slave, but I go to be free.

Silent, Silent Night,
Quench the holy light
Of thy torches bright,

For possessed of Day,
Thousand spirits stray   5
That sweet joys betray.

Why should joys be sweet,
Used with deceit,
Nor with sorrows meet?

But an honest joy   10
Does itself destroy
For a harlot coy.

O lapwing, thou fliest around the heath
Nor seest the net that is spread beneath.
Why dost thou not fly among the cornfields?
They cannot spread nets where a harvest yields.

Thou hast a lap full of seed,
And this is a fine country.
Why dost thou not cast thy seed
And live in it merrily?

Shall I cast it on the sand 5
And turn it into fruitful land?
For on no other ground
Can I sow my seed
Without tearing up
Some stinking weed. 10

IN A MYRTLE SHADE

"Why should I be bound to thee,
O my lovely myrtle tree?
Love, free love, cannot be bound
To any tree that grows on ground.

O, how sick & weary I 5
Underneath my myrtle lie,
Like to dung upon the ground
Underneath my myrtle bound."

Oft my myrtle sighed in vain
To behold my heavy chain. 10
Oft my father saw us sigh
And laughed at our simplicity.

So I smote him, & his gore
Stained the roots my myrtle bore,

But the time of youth is fled   15
And grey hairs are on my head.

TO NOBODADDY

Why art thou silent & invisible,
Father of Jealousy?
Why dost thou hide thyself in clouds
From every searching Eye?

Why darkness & obscurity   5
In all thy words & laws,
That none dare eat the fruit but from
The wily serpent's jaws?
Or is it because Secrecy
Gains females' loud applause?   10

Are not the joys of morning sweeter
Than the joys of night?
And are the vig'rous joys of youth
Ashamed of the light?

Let age & sickness silent rob   5
The vineyards in the night,
But those who burn with vig'rous youth
Pluck fruits before the light.

Love to faults is always blind,
Always is to joy inclined,
Lawless winged & unconfined,
And breaks all chains from every mind.

Deceit to secrecy confined,   5
Lawful, cautious & refined,

To every thing but interest blind,
And forges fetters for the mind.

SOFT SNOW

I walked abroad in a snowy day,
I asked the soft snow with me to play.
She played & she melted in all her prime,
And the winter called it a dreadful crime.

AN ANCIENT PROVERB

Remove away that black'ning church.
Remove away that marriage hearse.
Remove away that_____of blood.
You'll quite remove the ancient curse.

TO MY MYRTLE

To a lovely myrtle bound,
Blossoms show'ring all around:
O, how sick & weary I
Underneath my myrtle lie.
Why should I be bound to thee,
O, my lovely myrtle tree?

5

MERLIN'S PROPHECY

The harvest shall flourish in wintry weather
When two virginities meet together.

The King & the Priest must be tied in a tether
Before two virgins can meet together.

DAY

The Sun arises in the East,
Clothed in robes of blood & gold.
Swords & spears & wrath increased,
All around his bosom rolled,
Crowned with warlike fires & raging
    desires.   5

THE FAIRY

"Come hither, my sparrows,
My little arrows.
If a tear or a smile
Will a man beguile,
If an amorous delay   5
Clouds a sunshiny day,
If the step of a foot
Smites the heart to its root,

'Tis the marriage ring
Makes each fairy a king."   10

So a fairy sung.
From the leaves I sprung:
He leaped from the spray
To flee away;
But in my hat caught,   15
He soon shall be taught.
Let him laugh, let him cry,
He's my butterfly;
For I've pulled out the Sting
Of the marriage ring.   20

The sword sung on the barren heath,
The sickle in the fruitful field.
The sword he sung a song of death,
But could not make the sickle yield.

Abstinence sows sand all over
The ruddy limbs & flaming hair,
But Desire Gratified
Plants fruits of life & beauty there.

In a wife I would desire
What in whores is always found,
The lineaments of Gratified desire.

If you trap the moment before it's ripe,
The tears of repentance you'll certainly wipe;
But if once you let the ripe moment go,
You can never wipe off the tears of woe.

ETERNITY

He who binds to himself a joy
Does the winged life destroy,
But he who kisses the joy as it flies
Lives in eternity's sun rise.

What is it men in women do require?
The lineaments of Gratified Desire.
What is it women do in men require?
The lineaments of Gratified Desire.

LACEDEMONIAN INSTRUCTION

"Come hither, my boy; tell me what thou
    seest there."
"A fool tangled in a religious snare."

RICHES

The countless gold of a merry heart,
The rubies & pearls of a loving eye,
The indolent never can bring to the mart,
Nor the secret hoard up in his treasury.

AN ANSWER TO THE PARSON

"Why of the sheep do you not learn peace?"
"Because I don't want you to shear my fleece."

The look of love alarms
Because 'tis filled with fire,
But the look of soft deceit
Shall Win the lover's hire.

Soft deceit & Idleness:
These are Beauty's sweetest dress.

MOTTO TO THE SONGS OF

INNOCENCE & OF EXPERIENCE

The Good are attracted by Men's perceptions
And Think not for themselves,
Till Experience teaches them to catch
And to cage the Fairies & Elves.

And then the Knave begins to snarl,   5
And the Hypocrite to howl;
And all his good Friends show their private ends,
And the Eagle is known from the Owl.

Her whole Life is an Epigram: smack, smooth &
      neatly penned,

Platted quite neat to catch applause, with a
    a sliding noose at the end.

An old maid early, e'er I knew
Aught but the love that on me grew,
And now I'm covered o'er & o'er
And wish that I had been a Whore.

O I cannot, cannot find   5
The undaunted courage of a Virgin Mind;
For Early I in love was crossed
Before my flower of love was lost.

"Let the Brothels of Paris be opened
With many an alluring dance
To awake the Physicians through the city,"
Said the beautiful Queen of France.

Then old Nobodaddy aloft   5
Farted & belched & coughed
And said, "I love hanging & drawing & quartering
Every bit as well as war & slaughtering."

Then he swore a great & solemn Oath:
"To kill the people I am loth,   10
But if they rebel, they must go to hell.
They shall have a Priest & a passing bell."

The King awoke on his couch of gold
As soon as he heard these tidings told:
"Arise & come, both fife & drum,   15
And the Famine shall eat both crust & crumb."

The Queen of France just touched this Globe,
And the Pestilence darted from her robe;
But our good Queen quite grows to the ground,
And a great many suckers grow all around.   20·

Who will exchange his own fireside
For the stone of another's door?
Who will exchange his wheaten loaf
For the links of a dungeon floor?

Fayette beheld the King & Queen   25
In curses & iron bound,
But mute Fayette wept tear for tear
And guarded them around.
O who would smile on the wintry seas
& Pity the stormy roar?   30
Or who will exchange his newborn child
For the dog at the wintry door?

When Klopstock England defied,
Up rose terrible Blake in his pride,
For old Nobodaddy aloft
Farted & Belched & coughed,
Then swore a great oath that made heaven quake   5
And called aloud to English Blake.
Blake was giving his body ease
At Lambeth beneath the poplar trees.
From his seat then started he
And turned himself round three times three.   10
The Moon at that sight blushed scarlet red,
The stars threw down their cups & fled,
And all the devils that were in hell
Answered with a ninefold yell.
Klopstock felt the intripled turn,   15
And all his bowels began to churn;
And his bowels turned round three times three
And locked in his soul with a ninefold key,
That from his body it ne'er could be parted
Till to the last trumpet it was farted.   20
Then again old Nobodaddy swore
He ne'er had seen such a thing before,

Since Noah was shut in the ark,
Since Eve first chose her hellfire spark,
Since 'twas the fashion to go naked,   25
Since the old anything was created.
And so feeling, he begged him to turn again
And ease poor Klopstock's ninefold pain.
Thrice Blushing, he reddened round,
And the Spell turned & unwound.   30
It spun Back on the Stile,
Whereat Klopstock did smile.

If Blake could do this when he rose up from shite,
What might he not do if he sat down to write?

A fairy skipped upon my knee
Singing & dancing merrily;
I said, "Thou thing of patches, rings,
Pins, Necklaces & such like things,
Disguiser of the Female Form,   5
Thou paltry, gilded, poisonous worm!"
Weeping, he fell upon my thigh
And thus in tears did soft reply:
"Knowest thou not, O Fairies' Lord,
How much by us Contemned, Abhorred,   10
Whatever hides the Female form
That cannot bear the Mental storm?
Therefore in Pity still we give
Our lives to make the Female live,
And what would turn into disease   15
We turn to what will joy & please."

"My Spectre around me night & day
Like a Wild beast guards my way.
My Emanation far within
Weeps incessantly for my Sin.

"A Fathomless & boundless deep,   5
There we wander, there we weep;
On the hungry craving wind
My Spectre follows thee behind.

"He scents thy footsteps in the snow,
Wheresoever thou dost go,   10
Through the wintry hail & rain.
When wilt thou return again?

"Dost thou not in Pride & Scorn
Fill with tempests all my morn
And with jealousies & fears   15
Fill my pleasant nights with tears?

"Seven of my sweet loves thy knife
Has bereaved of their life.
Their marble tombs I built with tears
And with cold & shuddering fears.   20

"Seven more loves weep night & day
Round the tombs where my loves lay,
And seven more loves attend each night
Around my couch with torches bright,

"And seven more Loves in my bed   25
Crown with wine my mournful head,
Pitying & forgiving all
Thy transgressions great & small.

"When wilt thou return & view
My loves & them to life renew?   30
When wilt thou return & live?
When wilt thou pity as I forgive?"

"Never, Never, I return.
Still for Victory I burn.
Living thee alone I'll have,   35
And when dead I'll be thy Grave.

"Through the Heaven & Earth & Hell
Thou shalt never, never quell.

I will fly & thou pursue,
Night & Morn the flight renew."   40

"Till I turn from Female Love
And root up the Infernal Grove,
I shall never worthy be
To Step into Eternity,

"And to end thy cruel mocks   45
Annihilate thee on the rocks
And another form create
To be subservient to my Fate.

"Let us agree to give up Love
And root up the infernal grove.   50
Then shall we return & see
The worlds of happy Eternity,

& Throughout all Eternity
I forgive you, you forgive me.
As our Dear Redeemer said,   55
'This the Wine & this the Bread'."

[Additional Stanzas]

"O'er my Sins Thou sit & moan.
Hast thou no sins of thy own?
O'er my Sins thou sit & weep
And lull thy own Sins fast asleep.   60

"What transgressions I commit
Are for thy Transgressions fit.
They thy Harlots, thou their Slave,
And my Bed becomes their Grave.

"Poor pale pitiable form   65
That I follow in a Storm,
Iron tears & groans of lead
Bind around my aching head,

"And let us go to the_____downs
With many pleasing wiles,   70

The Woman that does not love your Frowns
Will never embrace your smiles."

———————

When a Man has Married a Wife,
    he finds out whether
Her knees & elbows are only
    glued together.

———————

ON THE VIRGINITY OF
THE VIRGIN MARY &
JOHANNA SOUTHCOTT

Whate'er is done to her she cannot know,
And if you'll ask her she will swear it so.
Whether 'tis good or evil, none's to blame,
No one can take the pride, no one the shame.

———————

Mock on, Mock on, Voltaire, Rousseau.
Mock on, Mock on, 'tis all in vain.
You throw the sand against the wind,
And the wind blows it back again.

And every sand becomes a Gem   5
Reflected in the beams divine.
Blown back, they blind the mocking Eye,
But still in Israel's paths they shine.

The Atoms of Democritus
And Newton's Particles of Light   10
Are sands upon the Red sea shore,
Where Israel's tents do shine so bright.

———————

MORNING

To find the Western path
Right through the Gates of Wrath
I urge my way.
Sweet Mercy leads me on.
With soft repentant moan   5
I see the break of day.

The war of swords & spears,
Melted by dewy tears,
Exhales on high.
The Sun is freed from fears   10
And with soft grateful tears
Ascends the sky.

———————

Terror in the house does roar,
But Pity stands before the door.

———————

Each Man is in his Spectre's power
Until the arrival of that hour
When his Humanity awake
And cast his own Spectre into the Lake.

———————

THE BIRDS

He: Where thou dwellest, in what Grove
     Tell me, Fair one, tell me, love;
     Where thou thy charming Nest dost build,
     O thou pride of every field.

She: Yonder stands a lonely tree.   5
      There I live & mourn for thee.
      Morning drinks my silent tear,
      And evening winds my sorrows bear.

 He: O thou Summer's harmony,
      I have lived & mourned for thee.   10
      Each day I mourn along the wood,
      And night hath heard my sorrows loud.

She: Dost thou truly long for me,
      And am I thus sweet to thee?
      Sorrow now is at an End,   15
      O my Lover & my Friend.

 He: Come, on wings of joy we'll fly
      To where my Bower hangs on high.
      Come & make thy calm retreat
      Among green leaves & blossoms sweet.   20

You don't believe—I won't attempt to make ye,
You are asleep—I won't attempt to wake ye.
Sleep on, Sleep on, while in your pleasant dreams
Of Reason you may drink of Life's clear streams.
Reason and Newton, they are quite two things,   5
For so the Swallow & the Sparrow sings.
Reason says "Miracle." Newton says "Doubt."
Aye, that's the way to make all Nature out.
Doubt, Doubt, & don't believe without experiment.
That is the very thing that Jesus meant   10
When he said, "Only Believe, Believe & try,
Try, Try, & never mind the Reason why."

Anger & Wrath my bosom rends:
I thought them the Errors of friends;
But all my limbs with warmth glow:
I find them the Errors of the foe.

The Sussex Men are Noted Fools,
And weak is their brain pan.
I wonder if H_____ the painter
Is not a Sussex Man.

"Madman," I have been called. "Fool," they
    call thee.
I wonder which they Envy, Thee or Me.

TO H

You think Fuseli is not a Great Painter. I'm Glad.
This is one of the best compliments he ever had.

TO F

I mock thee not, though I by thee am Mocked.
Thou call'st me Madman, but I call thee Blockhead.

Of H's birth this was the happy lot:
His Mother on his Father him begot.

He's a Blockhead who wants a proof of what
    he Can't Perceive,
And he's a Fool who tries to make such a Blockhead
    believe.

———————

He has observed the Golden Rule
Till he's become the Golden Fool.

———————

The Angel that presided o'er my birth
Said, "Little creature, formed of Joy & Mirth,
Go love without the help of any Thing on Earth."

———————

To forgive Enemies H———— does pretend,
Who never in his Life forgave a friend.

———————

ON H————Y'S FRIENDSHIP

When H———— finds out what you cannot do,
That is the very thing he'll set you to.
If you break not your Neck, 'tis not his fault;
But pecks of poison are not pecks of salt.
And when he could not act upon my wife,   5
Hired a Villain to bereave my Life.

———————

TO H

Thy Friendship oft has made my heart to ache.
Do be my Enemy for Friendship's sake.

———————

ANOTHER

Here lies John Trot, the Friend of all mankind.
He has not left one Enemy behind.

Friends were quite hard to find, old authors say,
But now they stand in everybody's way.

———————

My title as a Genius thus is proved:
Not Praised by Hayley nor by Flaxman loved.

———————

ON H_____ THE PICK THANK

I write the Rascal Thanks till he & I
With Thanks & Compliments are quite drawn dry.

———————

Great things are done when Men & Mountains meet.
This is not done by Jostling in the Street.

———————

Grown old in Love from Seven till Seven times Seven,
I oft have wished for Hell for Ease from Heaven.

———————

Why was Cupid a Boy,
And why a boy was he?
He should have been a Girl
For aught that I can see.

For he shoots with his bow,   5
And the Girl shoots with her Eye,
And they both are merry & glad
And laugh when we do cry.

And to make Cupid a Boy
Was the Cupid Girl's mocking plan,   10
For a boy can't interpret the thing
Till he is become a man.

And then he's so pierced with care
And wounded with arrowy smarts
That the whole business of his life   15
Is to pick out the heads of the darts.

'Twas the Greeks' love of war
Turned Love into a Boy
And Woman into a Statue of Stone,
And away fled every Joy.   20

———————

I asked my Dear Friend, Orator Prigg,
"What's the first part of Oratory?" He said,
      "A great wig."
"And what is the second?" Then dancing a jig
And bowing profoundly, he said, "A great wig."
"And what is the third?" Then he snored like
      a pig,   5
And, puffing his cheeks, he replied, "A Great wig."

So if a Great Painter with Questions you push,
"What's the first Part of Painting?" He'll say,
      "A Paint Brush."
"And what is the second?" With modest blush,
He'll smile like a Cherub & say, "A paint
      Brush."   10
"And what is the third?" He'll bow like a rush.
With a leer in his Eye, he'll reply, "A Paint
      Brush."
Perhaps this is all a Painter can want,
But look yonder, that house is the house of
      Rembrandt.

"O dear Mother outline, of knowledge most sage, 15
What's the First Part of Painting?" She said,
      "Patronage."
"And what is the second, to Please & Engage?"
She frowned like a Fury and said, "Patronage."

"And what is the Third?" She put off Old Age
And smiled like a Siren & said, "Patronage."   20

---

23 May, 1810, found the Word Golden.

TO GOD

If you have formed a Circle to go into,
Go into it yourself & see how you would do.

"Now Art has lost its mental Charms;
France shall subdue the World in Arms."
So spoke an Angel at my birth,
Then said, "Descend thou upon Earth.
Renew the Arts on Britain's Shore,   5
And France shall fall down & adore.
With works of Art their Armies meet,
And War shall sink beneath thy feet;
But if thy Nation Arts refuse,
And if they scorn the immortal Muse,   10
France shall the arts of Peace restore
And save thee from the Ungrateful shore."

Spirit who lov'st Britannia's Isle,
Round which the Fiends of Commerce smile. . . .

The Caverns of the Grave I've seen,
And these I showed to England's Queen,
But now the Caves of Hell I view.
Who shall I dare to show them to?

What mighty Soul in Beauty's form   5
Shall dauntless View the Infernal Storm?
Egremont's Countess can control
The flames of Hell that round me roll.
If she refuse I still go on
Till the Heavens & Earth are gone,   10
Still admired by Noble minds,
Followed by Envy on the winds.
Re-engraved Time after Time,
Ever in their youthful prime,
My Designs unchanged remain.   15
Time may rage but rage in vain,
For above Time's troubled Fountains
On the Great Atlantic Mountains
In my Golden House on high
There they Shine Eternally.   20

I rose up at the dawn of day.
"Get thee away, get thee away.
Pray'st thou for Riches, away, away.
This is the Throne of Mammon grey."

Said I, "This sure is very odd.   5
I took it to be the Throne of God,
For every Thing besides I have.
It is only for Riches that I can crave.

"I have Mental Joy & Mental Health
And Mental Friends & Mental wealth.   10
I've a Wife I love & that loves me.
I've all But Riches Bodily.

"I am in God's presence night & day,
And he never turns his face away.
The accuser of sins by my side does stand,   15
And he holds my money bag in his hand.

"For my worldly things God makes him pay,
And he'd pay for more if to him I would pray;

And so you may do the worst you can do.
Be assured, Mr. Devil, I won't pray to you.   20

"Then if for Riches I must not Pray,
God knows I little of Prayers need say.
So as a Church is known by its Steeple
If I pray it must be for other People.

"He says if I do not worship him for a God   25
I shall eat coarser food & go worse shod,
So as I don't value such things as these
You must do, Mr. Devil, just as God please."

Poems from the Pickering Manuscript
(circa 1803)

THE SMILE

There is a Smile of Love,
And there is a Smile of Deceit,
And there is a Smile of Smiles
In which these two Smiles meet.

And there is a Frown of Hate,   5
And there is a Frown of disdain,
And there is a Frown of Frowns
Which you strive to forget in vain;

For it sticks in the Heart's deep Core,
And it sticks in the deep Backbone,   10
And no Smile that ever was smiled,
But only one Smile alone,

That betwixt the Cradle & Grave,
It only once Smiled can be,
But when it once is Smiled;   15
There's an end to all Misery.

THE GOLDEN NET

Three Virgins at the break of day:
"Whither, young Man, whither away?
Alas for woe! alas for woe!"
They cry, & tears forever flow.
The one was Clothed in flames of fire,   5
The other Clothed in iron wire,
The other Clothed in tears & sighs,

Dazzling bright before my Eyes.
They bore a Net of Golden twine
To hang upon the Branches fine.   10
Pitying I wept to see the woe
That Love & Beauty undergo.
To be consumed in burning Fires
And in ungratified desires
And in tears clothed Night & day   15
Melted all my Soul away.
When they saw my Tears, a Smile
That did Heaven itself beguile
Bore the Golden Net aloft
As on downy Pinions soft   20
Over the Morning of my day.
Underneath the Net I stray,
Now entreating Burning Fire,
Now entreating Iron Wire,
Now entreating Tears & Sighs,   25
O, when will the morning rise?

THE MENTAL TRAVELLER

I travelled through a Land of Men,
A Land of Men & Women too,
And heard & saw such dreadful things
As cold Earth wanderers never knew.

For there the Babe is born in joy   5
That was begotten in dire woe,
Just as we Reap in joy the fruit
Which we in bitter tears did sow.

And if the Babe is born a Boy
He's given to a Woman Old,   10
Who nails him down upon a rock,
Catches his shrieks in cups of gold.

She binds iron thorns around his head,
She pierces both his hands & feet,
She cuts his heart out at his side   15
To make it feel both cold & heat.

Her fingers number every Nerve,
Just as a Miser counts his gold.
She lives upon his shrieks & cries,
And she grows young as he grows old,   20

Till he becomes a bleeding youth,
And she becomes a Virgin bright.
Then he rends up his Manacles
And binds her down for his delight.

He plants himself in all her Nerves,   25
Just as a Husbandman his mould,
And she becomes his dwelling place
And Garden fruitful seventyfold.

An aged Shadow, soon he fades,
Wand'ring round an Earthly Cot,   30
Full filled all with gems & gold
Which he by industry had got.

And these are the gems of the
    Human Soul,
The rubies & pearls of a lovesick eye,
The countless gold of the aching heart,   35
The martyr's groan & the lover's sigh.

They are his meat, they are his drink.
He feeds the Beggar & the Poor
And the wayfaring Traveller;
Forever open is his door.   40

His grief is their eternal joy.
They make the roofs & walls to ring,
Till from the fire on the hearth
A little Female Babe does spring.

And she is all of solid fire   45
And gems & gold, that none his hand
Dares stretch to touch her Baby form
Or wrap her in his swaddling band.

But She comes to the Man she loves,
If young or old or rich or poor.   50
They soon drive out the aged Host,
A Beggar at another's door.

He wanders weeping far away,
Until some other take him in,
Oft blind & age-bent, sore distressed,   55
Until he can a Maiden win.

And to allay his freezing Age
The Poor Man takes her in his arms;
The Cottage fades before his sight,
The Garden & its lovely Charms.   60

The Guests are scattered through the land,
For the Eye altering alters all;
The Senses roll themselves in fear,
And the flat Earth becomes a Ball.

The stars, Sun, Moon all shrink away,   65
A desert vast without a bound,
And nothing left to eat or drink,
And a dark desert all around.

The honey of her Infant lips,
The bread & wine of her sweet smile,   70
The wild game of her roving Eye
Does him to Infancy beguile.

For as he eats & drinks he grows
Younger & younger every day;
And on the desert wild they both   75
Wander in terror & dismay.

Like the wild Stag she flees away;
Her fear plants many a thicket wild,

While he pursues her night & day,
By various arts of Love beguiled,   80

By various arts of Love & Hate,
Till the wide desert planted o'er
With Labyrinths of wayward Love,
Where roams the Lion, Wolf & Boar,

Till he becomes a wayward Babe   85
And she a weeping Woman Old.
Then many a Lover wanders here;
The Sun & Stars are nearer rolled.

The trees bring forth sweet Ecstasy
To all who in the desert roam,   90
Till many a City there is Built
And many a pleasant Shepherd's home.

But when they find the frowning Babe,
Terror strikes through the region wide
They cry, "The Babe, the Babe is Born!"   95
And flee away on Every side.

For who dare touch the frowning form;
His arm is withered to its root.
Lions, Boars, Wolves, all howling flee,
And every Tree does shed its fruit.   100

And none can touch that frowning form,
Except it be a Woman Old.
She nails him down upon the Rock,
And all is done as I have told.

THE LAND OF DREAMS

"Awake, awake, my little Boy,
Thou wast thy Mother's only joy.
Why dost thou weep in thy gentle sleep?
Awake, thy Father does thee keep."

"O, what Land is the Land of Dreams?   5
What are its Mountains, & what are its Streams?
O Father, I saw my Mother there
Among the Lilies by waters fair.

"Among the Lambs, clothed in white,
She walked with her Thomas in sweet delight.   10
I wept for joy; like a dove I mourn.
O when shall I again return?"

"Dear Child, I also by pleasant Streams
Have wandered all Night in the Land of Dreams.
But though calm & warm the waters wide,   15
I could not get to the other side."

"Father, O Father, what do we here
In this Land of unbelief & fear?
The Land of Dreams is better far,
Above the light of the Morning Star."   20

MARY

Sweet Mary, the first time she ever was there,
Came into the Ballroom among the Fair.
The young Men & Maidens around her throng,
And these are the words upon every tongue:

"An Angel is here from the heavenly Climes,   5
Or again does return the Golden times.
Her eyes outshine every brilliant ray;
She opens her lips—'tis the Month of May."

Mary moves in soft beauty & conscious delight
To augment with sweet smiles all the joys
        of the Night,   10

Nor once blushes to own to the rest of the Fair
That sweet Love & Beauty are worthy our care.

In the Morning the Villagers rose with delight
And repeated with pleasure the joys of the night,
And Mary arose among Friends to be free, 15
But no Friend from henceforward thou, Mary,
    shalt see.

Some said she was proud, some called her a whore,
And some when she passed by shut to the door.
A damp cold came o'er her, her blushes all fled;
Her lilies & roses are blighted & shed. 20

"O, why was I born with a different Face?
Why was I not born like this Envious Race?
Why did Heaven adorn me with bountiful hand
And then set me down in an envious Land?

"To be weak as a Lamb & smooth as a dove 25
And not to raise Envy is called Christian Love,
But if you raise Envy your Merit's to blame
For planting such spite in the weak & the tame.

"I will humble my Beauty, I will not dress fine,
I will keep from the Ball, & my Eyes shall
    not shine; 30
And if any Girl's Lover forsakes her for me,
I'll refuse him my hand & from Envy be free."

She went out in Morning attired plain & neat.
"Proud Mary's gone Mad," said the Child in the Street,
She went out in Morning in plain neat attire 35
And came home in Evening bespattered with mire.

She trembled & wept, sitting on the Bed side.
She forgot it was Night, & she trembled & cried.
She forgot it was Night, she forgot it was Morn,
Her soft Memory imprinted with Faces of Scorn, 40

With Faces of Scorn & with Eyes of disdain
Like foul Fiends inhabiting Mary's mild Brain.
She remembers no Face like the Human Divine.
All Faces have Envy, sweet Mary, but thine,

And thine is a Face of sweet Love in Despair,   45
And thine is a Face of mild sorrow & care,
And thine is a Face of wild terror & fear
That shall never be quiet till laid on its bier.

THE CRYSTAL CABINET

The Maiden caught me in the Wild,
Where I was dancing merrily.
She put me into her Cabinet
And Locked me up with a golden Key.

This Cabinet is formed of Gold
And Pearl & Crystal, shining bright,   5
And within it opens into a World
And a little lovely Moony Night.

Another England there I saw,
Another London with its Tower,   10
Another Thames & other Hills
And another pleasant Surrey Bower.

Another Maiden like herself,
Translucent, lovely, shining clear,
Threefold each in the other closed—   15
O, what a pleasant trembling fear!

O, what a smile, a threefold Smile,
Filled me that like a flame I burned.
I bent to Kiss the lovely Maid
And found a Threefold Kiss returned.   20

I strove to seize the inmost Form
With ardor fierce & hands of flame,
But burst the Crystal Cabinet
And like a Weeping Babe became,

A weeping Babe upon the wild   25
And Weeping Woman pale reclined,

And in the outward air again
I filled with woes the passing Wind.

THE GREY MONK

"I die, I die!" the Mother said.
"My Children die for lack of Bread.
What more has the merciless Tyrant said?"
The Monk sat down on the Stony Bed.

The blood red ran from the Grey Monk's side.   5
His hands & feet were wounded wide,
His Body bent, his arms & knees
Like to the roots of ancient trees.

His eye was dry; no tear could flow.
A hollow groan first spoke his woe.   10
He trembled & shuddered upon the Bed.
At length with a feeble cry he said:

"When God commanded this hand to write
In the studious hours of deep midnight,
He told me the writing I wrote should prove   15
The Bane of all that on Earth I loved.

"My Brother starved between two Walls.
His Children's Cry my Soul appalls.
I mocked at the wrack & griding chain;
My bent body mocks their torturing pain.   20

"Thy Father drew his sword in the North.
With his thousands strong he marched forth.
Thy Brother has armed himself in Steel
To avenge the wrongs thy Children feel.

"But vain the Sword & vain the Bow.   25
They never can work War's overthrow.
The Hermit's Prayer & the Widow's tear
Alone can free the World from fear.

"For a Tear is an Intellectual Thing,
And a Sigh is the Sword of an Angel King,   30
And the bitter groan of the Martyr's woe
Is an Arrow from the Almighty's Bow.

"The hand of Vengeance found the Bed
To which the Purple Tyrant fled.
The iron hand crushed the Tyrant's head   35
And became a Tyrant in his stead."

AUGURIES OF INNOCENCE

To see a World in a Grain of Sand
And a Heaven in a Wild Flower,
Hold Infinity in the palm of your hand
And Eternity in an hour.
A Robin Redbreast in a Cage   5
Puts all Heaven in a Rage.
A dove house filled with doves & Pigeons
Shudders Hell through all its regions.
A dog starved at his Master's Gate
Predicts the ruin of the State.   10
A Horse misused upon the Road
Calls to Heaven for Human blood.
Each outcry of the hunted Hare
A fibre from the Brain does tear.
A Skylark wounded in the wing,   15
A Cherubim does cease to sing.
The Game Cock clipped & armed for fight
Does the Rising Sun affright.
Every Wolf's & Lion's howl
Raises from Hell a Human Soul.   20
The wild deer wand'ring here & there
Keeps the Human Soul from Care.
The Lamb misused breeds Public strife
And yet forgives the Butcher's Knife.
The Bat that flits at close of Eve

Has left the Brain that won't Believe.   25
The Owl that calls upon the Night
Speaks the Unbeliever's fright.
He who shall hurt the little Wren
Shall never be beloved by Men.   30
He who the Ox to wrath has moved
Shall never be by Woman loved.
The wanton Boy that kills the Fly
Shall feel the Spider's enmity.
He who torments the Chafer's sprite   35
Weaves a Bower in endless Night.
The Caterpillar on the Leaf
Repeats to thee thy Mother's grief.
Kill not the Moth nor Butterfly,
For the Last Judgment draweth nigh.   40
He who shall train the Horse to War
Shall never pass the Polar Bar.
The Beggar's Dog & Widow's Cat,
Feed them & thou wilt grow fat.
The Gnat that sings his Summer's song   45
Poison gets from Slander's tongue.
The poison of the Snake & Newt
Is the sweat of Envy's Foot.
The Poison of the Honey Bee
Is the Artist's Jealousy.   50
The Prince's Robes & Beggar's Rags
Are Toadstools on the Miser's Bags.
A truth that's told with bad intent
Beats all the Lies you can invent.
It is right it should be so: 55
Man was made for Joy & Woe,
And when this we rightly know
Through the World we safely go.
Joy & Woe are woven fine,
A Clothing for the Soul divine.   60
Under every grief & pine
Runs a joy with silken twine.
The Babe is more than swaddling Bands

Throughout all these Human Lands.
Tools were made, & Born were hands,   65
Every Farmer Understands.
Every Tear from Every Eye
Becomes a Babe in Eternity;
This is caught by Females bright
And returned to its own delight.   70
The Bleat, the Bark, Bellow & Roar
Are Waves that Beat on Heaven's Shore.
The Babe that weeps the Rod beneath
Writes Revenge in realms of death.
The Beggar's Rags fluttering in Air   75
Does to Rags the Heavens tear.
The Soldier armed with Sword & Gun
Palsied strikes the Summer's Sun.
The poor Man's Farthing is worth more
Than all the Gold on Afric's Shore.   80
One Mite wrung from the Lab'rer's hands
Shall buy & sell the Miser's Lands,
Or if protected from on high
Does that whole Nation sell & buy.
He who mocks the Infant's Faith   85
Shall be mocked in Age & Death.
He who shall teach the Child to Doubt
The rotting Grave shall ne'er get out.
He who respects the Infant's faith
Triumphs over Hell & Death.   90
The Child's Toys & the Old Man's Reasons
Are the Fruits of the Two seasons.
The Questioner who sits so sly
Shall never know how to Reply.
He who replies to words of Doubt   95
Doth put the Light of Knowledge out.
The Strongest Poison ever known
Came from Caesar's Laurel Crown.
Naught can deform the Human Race
Like to the Armour's iron brace.   100
When Gold & Gems adorn the Plow

To peaceful Arts shall Envy Bow.
A Riddle or the Cricket's Cry
Is to Doubt a fit Reply.
The Emmet's Inch & Eagle's Mile   105
Make Lame Philosophy to smile.
He who Doubts from what he sees
Will ne'er Believe, do what you Please.
If the Sun & Moon should doubt,
They'd immediately Go out.   110
To be in a Passion you Good may do,
But no Good if a Passion is in you.
The Whore & Gambler by the State
Licensed build that Nation's Fate.
The Harlot's cry from Street to Street   115
Shall weave Old England's winding Sheet.
The Winner's Shout, the Loser's Curse
Dance before dead England's Hearse.
Every Night & every Morn
Some to Misery are Born.   120
Every Morn & every Night
Some are Born to sweet delight.
Some are Born to sweet delight,
Some are Born to Endless Night.
We are led to Believe a Lie   125
When we see not Through the Eye,
Which was Born in a Night to perish in a Night
When the Soul Slept in Beams of Light.
God Appears & God is Light
To those poor Souls who dwell in Night,   130
But does a Human Form Display
To those who Dwell in Realms of day.

LONG JOHN BROWN &

LITTLE MARY BELL

Little Mary Bell had a Fairy in a Nut;
Long John Brown had the Devil in his Gut.

Long John Brown loved Little Mary Bell,
And the Fairy drew the Devil into the Nutshell.

Her Fairy skipped out, & her Fairy skipped in;   5
He laughed at the devil saying Love is a Sin.
The devil he raged, & the devil he was wroth;
And the devil entered into the Young Man's broth.

He was soon in the Gut of the loving Young Swain,
For John eat & drank to drive away Love's pain;   10
But all he could do he grew thinner & thinner,
Though he eat & drank as much as ten Men for
      his dinner.

Some said he had a Wolf in his stomach day & night;
Some said he had the devil, & they guessed right.
The fairy skipped about in his glory, Joy & Pride;   15
And he laughed at the devil till poor John Brown died.

Then the Fairy skipped out of the old Nutshell,
And woe & alack for Pretty Mary Bell;
For the Devil crept in when the Fairy skipped out,
And there goes Miss Bell with her fusty old Nut.   20

WILLIAM BOND

I wonder whether the Girls are mad,
And I wonder whether they mean to kill,
And I wonder if William Bond will die,
For assuredly he is very ill.

He went to Church in a May morning   5
Attended by Fairies, one, two & three,
But the Angels of Providence drove them away,
And he returned home in Misery.

He went not out to the Field nor Fold;
He went not out to the Village nor Town;   10
But he came home in a black, black cloud
And took to his Bed & there lay down.

And an Angel of Providence at his Feet,
And an Angel of Providence at his Head,
And in the midst a Black, Black Cloud,   15
And in the midst the Sick Man on his Bed.

And on his Right hand was Mary Green,
And on his Left hand was his Sister Jane,
And their tears fell through the black,
    black Cloud
To drive away the sick man's pain.   20

"O William, if thou dost another Love,
Dost another Love better than poor Mary,
Go & take that other to be thy Wife,
And Mary Green shall her Servant be."

"Yes, Mary, I do another Love,   25
Another I Love far better than thee,
And Another I will have for my Wife.
Then what have I to do with thee?

"For thou art Melancholy Pale,
And on thy Head is the cold Moon's shine;   30
But she is ruddy & bright as day,
And the sunbeams dazzle from her eyne."

Mary trembled, & Mary chilled,
And Mary fell down on the right-hand floor,
That William Bond & his Sister Jane   35
Scarce could recover Mary more.

When Mary woke & found her Laid
On the Right hand of her William dear,
On the Right hand of his loved Bed,
And saw her William Bond so near,   40

The Fairies that fled from William Bond
Danced around her Shining Head;
They danced over the Pillow white,
And the Angels of Providence left the Bed.

I thought Love lived in the hot sunshine,   45
But, O, he lives in the Moony light.

I thought to find Love in the heat of day,
But sweet Love is the Comforter of Night.

Seek Love in the Pity of others' Woe,
In the gentle relief of another's care,
In the darkness of night & the winter's snow,
In the naked & outcast, Seek Love there.

50

Dedication of Blake's Illustration
To Blair's Grave (1808)

TO THE QUEEN

The Door of Death is made of Gold
That Mortal Eyes cannot behold;
But when the Mortal Eyes are closed,
And cold and pale the Limbs reposed,
The Soul awakes and, wond'ring, sees   5
In her mild Hand the golden Key.
The Grave is Heaven's golden Gate,
And rich and poor around it wait.
O Shepherdess of England's Fold,
Behold this Gate of Pearl and Gold!   10

To dedicate to England's Queen
The Visions that my Soul has seen,
And, by Her kind permission, bring
What I have borne on solemn Wing
From the vast regions of the Grave,   15
Before Her Throne my Wings I wave,
Bowing before my Sov'reign's Feet,
"The Grave produced these Blossoms sweet
In mild repose from Earthly strife,
The Blossoms of Eternal Life!"   20

The Everlasting Gospel (circa 1818)

The passages of the poem are scattered through the Rossetti MS
and on a separate folded leaf of notepaper. The order of the parts of
the poem is conjectural.

1

[*folded leaf, p. 1*]

There is not one Moral Virtue that Jesus Inculcated but Plato
& Cicero did Inculcate before him. What then did Christ Inculcate? Forgiveness of Sins. This alone is the Gospel, & this is the
Life & Immortality brought to light by Jesus, Even the Covenant
of Jehovah, which is This: If you forgive one another your Trespasses, so shall Jehovah forgive you, That he himself may dwell
among you; but if you Avenge, you Murder the Divine Image,
& he cannot dwell among you. Because you Murder him, he arises
Again, & you deny that he is Arisen & are blind to Spirit.

2

[*folded leaf, p. 4*]

If Moral Virtue was Christianity,
Christ's Pretensions were all Vanity,
And Caiaphas & Pilate Men
Praiseworthy, & the Lion's Den
And not the Sheepfold Allegories   5
Of God & Heaven & their Glories.
The Moral Christian is the Cause
Of the Unbeliever & his Laws.
The Roman Virtues, Warlike Fame,
Take Jesus' & Jehovah's Name.   10

For what is Antichrist but those
Who against Sinners Heaven close
With Iron bars in Virtuous State,
And Rhadamanthus at the Gate?

3

[*folded leaf, p. 2*]

What can this Gospel of Jesus be?
What Life & Immortality,
What was it that he brought to Light
That Plato & Cicero did not write?
The Heathen Deities wrote them all,   5
These Moral Virtues, great & small.
What is the Accusation of Sin
But Moral Virtues' deadly Gin?
The Moral Virtues in their Pride
Did o'er the World triumphant ride   10
In Wars & Sacrifice for Sin,
And Souls to Hell ran trooping in.
The Accuser, Holy God of All
This Pharisaic Worldly Ball,
Amidst them in his Glory Beams   15
Upon the Rivers & the Streams.
Then Jesus rose & said to Me,
"Thy Sins are all forgiven thee."
Loud Pilate Howled, loud Caiaphas yelled,
When they the Gospel Light beheld.   20
It was when Jesus said to Me,
"Thy Sins are all forgiven thee."
The Christian trumpets loud proclaim
Through all the World in Jesus' name
Mutual forgiveness of each Vice,   25
And oped the Gates of Paradise.
The Moral Virtues in Great fear
Formed the Cross & Nails & Spear,

And the Accuser standing by
Cried out, "Crucify! Crucify!   30
Our Moral Virtues ne'er can be,
Nor Warlike pomp & Majesty;
For Moral Virtues all begin
In the Accusations of Sin,
And all the Heroic Virtues End   35
In destroying the Sinners' Friend.
Am I not Lucifer the Great,
And you my daughters in Great State,
The Fruit of my Mysterious Tree
Of Good & Evil & Misery   40
And Death & Hell, which now begin
On everyone who Forgives Sin?"

4

[*MS, p. 120*]

Was Jesus Born of a Virgin Pure
With narrow Soul & looks demure?
If he intended to take on Sin
The Mother should an Harlot been,
Just such a one as Magdalen   5
With seven devils in her Pen;
Or were Jew Virgins still more Curst
And more sucking devils nurst?
Or what was it which he took on
That he might bring Salvation?   10
A Body subject to be Tempted,
From neither pain nor grief Exempted?
Or such a body as might not feel
The passions that with Sinners deal?
Yes, but they say he never fell.   15
Ask Caiaphas; for he can tell:
"He mocked the Sabbath, & he mocked
The Sabbath's God, & he unlocked
The Evil spirits from their Shrines,
And turned Fishermen to Divines;   20

O'erturned the Tent of Secret Sins,
& its Golden cords & Pins—
'Tis the Bloody Shrine of War
Pinned around from Star to Star,
Halls of justice, hating Vice,   25
Where the devil Combs his lice.
He turned the devils into Swine
That he might tempt the Jews to dine;
Since which, a Pig has got a look
That for a Jew may be mistook.   30
'Obey your parents.' —What says he?
'Woman, what have I to do with thee?
No Earthly Parents I confess:
I am doing my Father's Business.'
He scorned Earth's Parents, scorned Earth's
        God,   35
And mocked the one & the other's Rod;
His Seventy Disciples sent
Against Religion & Government:
They by the Sword of Justice fell
And him their Cruel Murderer tell.   40
He left his Father's trade to roam
A wand'ring Vagrant without Home;
And thus he others' labour stole
That he might live above Control.
The Publicans & Harlots he   45
Selected for his Company,
And from the Adulteress turned away
God's righteous Law, that lost its Prey."

5

[*MS, p. 48*]

Did Jesus teach doubt, or did he
Give any lessons of Philosophy,
Charge Visionaries with deceiving,
Or call Men wise for not Believing?

6

[*MS, pp. 52-54*]

Was Jesus Humble, or did he
Give any Proofs of Humility,
Boast of high Things with Humble tone
And give with Charity a Stone?
When but a Child he ran away   5
And left his Parents in dismay,
When they had wandered three days long,
These were the words upon his tongue:
"No Earthly Parents I confess,
I am doing my Father's business."   10
When the rich learned Pharisee
Came to consult him secretly,
Upon his heart with Iron pen
He wrote, "Ye must be born again."
He was too proud to take a bribe.   15
He spoke with authority, not like a Scribe.
He says with most consummate Art,
"Follow me; I am meek & lowly of heart,"
As that is the only way to escape
The Miser's net & the Glutton's trap.   20
What can be done with such desperate Fools,
Who follow after the Heathen Schools?
I was standing by when Jesus died;
What I called Humility they called Pride.
He who loves his Enemies betrays his
    Friends.   25
This surely is not what Jesus intends,
But the sneaking Pride of Heroic Schools
And the Scribes' & Pharisees' Virtuous Rules;
For he acts with honest triumphant Pride,
And this is the cause that Jesus died.   30
He did not die with Christian Ease,
Asking pardon of his Enemies.
If he had, Caiaphas would forgive;
Sneaking submission can always live,

He had only to say that God was the devil   35
And the devil was God, like a Christian Civil,
Mild Christian regrets to the devil confess
For affronting him thrice in the Wilderness,
He had soon been bloody Caesar's Elf,
And at last he would have been Caesar's
    himself   40
Like Dr. Priestley & Bacon & Newton.
Poor Spiritual Knowledge is not worth a button,
For thus the Gospel Sir Isaac confutes:
God can only be known by his Attributes;
And as for the Indwelling of the Holy
    Ghost   45
Or of Christ & his Father, it's all a boast
And Pride & Vanity of the imagination
That disdains to follow this World's Fashion.
To teach doubt & Experiment
Certainly was not what Christ meant.   50
What was he doing all that time
From twelve years old to manly prime?
Was he then Idle or the Less
About his Father's business,
Or was his wisdom held in scorn   55
Before his wrath began to burn
In Miracles throughout the Land
That quite unnerved Caiaphas' hand
If he had been Antichrist, Creeping
    Jesus,
He'd have done anything to please us,   60
Gone sneaking into Synagogues
And not used the Elders & Priests like dogs,
But, Humble as a Lamb or Ass,
Obeyed himself to Caiaphas.
God wants not Man to Humble himself: 65
This is the trick of the ancient Elf.
This is the Race that Jesus ran:
Humble to God, Haughty to Man,
Cursing the Rulers before the People

Even to the temple's highest Steeple;   70
And when he Humbled himself to God,
Then descended the Cruel Rod.
"If thou humblest thyself, thou humblest me,
Thou also dwell'st in Eternity.
Thou art a Man, God is no more.   75
Thy own humanity learn to adore,
For that is my Spirit of Life.
Awake, arise to Spiritual Strife,
And thy Revenge abroad display
In terrors at the Last Judgment day.   80
God's Mercy & Long Suffering
Is but the Sinner to Judgment to bring.
Thou on the Cross for them shalt pray
And take Revenge at the Last Day."
Jesus replied & thunders hurled—   85
"I never will Pray for the World
Once I did so when I prayed in the
        Garden.
I wished to take with me a Bodily Pardon."
Can that which was of woman born
In the absence of the Morn
When the Soul fell into Sleep   90
And Archangels round it weep,
Shooting out against the Light
Fibres of a deadly night,
Reasoning upon its own dark Fiction   95
In doubt which is Self Contradiction?
Humility is only doubt
And does the Sun & Moon blot out,
Rooting over with thorns & stems
The buried Soul & all its Gems.   100
This Life's dim Windows of the Soul
Distorts the Heavens from Pole to Pole
And leads you to Believe a Lie
When you see with not through the Eye,
That was born in a night to perish in a night   105
When the Soul slept in the beams of Light.

7

[*MS, pp. 48-52*]

Was Jesus Chaste, or did he
Give any Lessons of Chastity?
The morning blushed fiery red;
Mary was found in Adulterous bed.
Earth groaned beneath, & Heaven above   5
Trembled at discovery of Love.
Jesus was sitting in Moses' Chair.
They brought the trembling Woman There.
Moses commands she be stoned to death.
What was the sound of Jesus' breath?   10
He laid His hand on Moses' Law.
The Ancient Heavens in Silent Awe,
Writ with Curses from Pole to Pole,
All away began to roll.
The Earth trembling & Naked lay   15
In secret bed of Mortal Clay,
On Sinai felt the hand Divine
Putting back the bloody shrine,
And she heard the breath of God
As she heard by Eden's flood: 20
"Good & Evil are no more!
Sinai's trumpets cease to roar!
Cease, finger of God, to write!
The Heavens are not clean in thy Sight.
Thou art Good, & thou Alone,   25
Nor may the sinner cast one stone.
To be Good only is to be
A God or else a Pharisee.
Thou, Angel of the Presence Divine,
That didst create this Body of Mine,   30
Wherefore has thou writ these Laws
And Created Hell's dark jaws?
My Presence I will take from thee.
A Cold Leper thou shalt be,

Though thou wast so pure & bright   35
That Heaven was Impure in thy Sight.
Though thy Oath turned Heaven Pale,
Though thy Covenant built Hell's Jail,
Though thou didst all to Chaos roll
With the Serpent for its soul,   40
Still the breath Divine does move,
And the breath Divine is Love.
Mary, Fear Not! Let me see
The Seven Devils that torment thee.
Hide not from my Sight thy Sin   45
That forgiveness thou may'st win.
Has no Man Condemned thee?"
"No Man, Lord!" "Then what is he
Who shall Accuse thee? Come Ye forth,
Fallen Fiends of Heavenly birth   50
That have forgot your Ancient love
And driven away my trembling Dove.
You shall bow before her feet;
You shall lick the dust for Meat,
And though you cannot Love, but Hate,   55
Shall be beggars at Love's Gate.
What was thy love? Let me see it.
Was it love or Dark Deceit?"
"Love too long from Me has fled.
'Twas dark deceit to Earn my bread.   60
'Twas Covet or 'twas Custom or
Some trifle not worth caring for
That they may call a shame & Sin,
Love's temple that God dwelleth in,
And hide in secret hidden Shrine   65
The Naked Human form divine,
And render that a Lawless thing
On which the Soul Expands its wing.
But this, O Lord, this was my Sin
When first I let these Devils in   70
In dark pretense to Chastity:
Blaspheming Love, blaspheming thee.
Then Rose Secret Adulteries,

And thence did Covet also rise.
My sin thou hast forgiven me.   75
Canst thou forgive my Blasphemy?
Canst thou return to this dark Hell
And in my burning bosom dwell,
And canst thou die that I may live,
And canst thou Pity & forgive?"   80
Then Rolled the shadowy Man away
From the Limbs of Jesus to make them his prey,
An Ever-devouring appetite
Glittering with festering Venoms bright,
Crying, "Crucify this cause of distress   85
Who don't keep the secrets of Holiness.
All Mental Powers by Diseases we bind,
But he heals the Deaf & the Dumb & the Blind.
Whom God has afflicted for Secret Ends,
He comforts & Heals & calls them Friends."   90
But when Jesus was Crucified,
Then was perfected his glittering pride.
In three Nights he devoured his prey,
And still he devours the Body of Clay,
For dust & Clay is the Serpent's meat,   95
Which never was made for Man to Eat.

8

[*MS, pp. 100 - 101*]

Was Jesus gentle, or did he
Give any marks of Gentility?
When twelve years old he ran away
And left his Parents in dismay,
When after three days' sorrow found,   5
Loud as Sinai's trumpet sound:
"No Earthly Parents I confess,
My Heavenly Father's business.
Ye understand not what I say
And, angry, force me to obey."   10

Obedience is a duty then,
And favour gains with God & Men.
John from the Wilderness loud cried,
Satan gloried in his Pride.
"Come," said Satan, "come away.   15
I'll soon see if you'll obey.
John for disobedience bled,
But you can turn the stones to bread.
God's high king & God's high Priest
Shall Plant their Glories in your breast.   20
If Caiaphas you will obey,
If Herod you with bloody Prey
Feed with the Sacrifice & be
Obedient, fall down, worship me."
Thunders & lightnings broke around,   25
And Jesus' voice in thunders sound:
"Thus I seize the Spiritual Prey.
Ye smiters with disease, make way.
I come Your King & God to seize.
Is God a Smiter with disease?"   30
The God of this World raged in vain.
He bound Old Satan in his Chain,
And bursting forth, his furious ire
Became a Chariot of fire.
Throughout the land he took his course   35
And traced diseases to their source.
He cursed the Scribe & Pharisee,
Trampling down Hypocrisy.
Where'er his Chariot took its way,
There Gates of Death let in the day,   40
Broke down from every Chain & Bar;
And Satan in his Spiritual War
Dragged at his Chariot wheels; loud howled
The God of this world; louder rolled
The Chariot Wheels, & louder still   45
His voice was heard from Zion's hill;
And in his hand the Scourge shone bright.
He scourged the Merchant Canaanite.

From out the Temple of his Mind
And in his Body tight does bind   50
Satan & all his Hellish Crew,
And thus with wrath he did subdue
The Serpent Bulk of Nature's dross,
Till he had nailed it to the Cross.
He took on Sin in the Virgin's Womb   55
And put it off on the Cross & Tomb,
To be Worshipped by the Church of Rome.

9

[*MS, p. 33*]

The Vision of Christ that thou dost see
Is my Vision's Greatest Enemy.
Thine has a great hook nose like thine;
Mine has a snub nose like to mine.
Thine is the friend of All Mankind;   5
Mine speaks in parables to the Blind.
Thine loves the same world that mine hates;
Thy Heaven doors are my Hell Gates.
Socrates taught what Melitus
Loathed as a Nation's bitterest Curse,   10
And Caiaphas was in his own Mind
A benefactor to Mankind.
Both read the Bible day & night,
But thou read'st black where I read white.

TO THE ACCUSER WHO IS THE GOD OF THIS WORLD (CIRCA 1818)

Truly, My Satan, thou art but a Dunce
And dost not know the Garment from the Man.
Every Harlot was a Virgin once,
Nor canst thou ever change Kate into Nan.

Though thou art Worshiped by the Names
    Divine   5
Of Jesus & Jehovah, thou art still
The Son of Morn in weary Night's decline,
The lost Traveller's Dream under the Hill.

Part Two
PROPHECIES

There is No Natural Religion (circa 1788)

[A]

The Argument: Man has no notion of moral fitness but from Education. Naturally he is only a natural organ subject to Sense.

I. Man cannot naturally Perceive, but through his natural or bodily organs.

II. Man by his reasoning power can only compare & judge of what he has already perceived.

III. From a perception of only 3 senses or 3 elements none could deduce a fourth or fifth.

IV. None could have other than natural or organic thoughts if he had none but organic perceptions.

V. Man's desires are limited by his perceptions. None can desire what he has not perceived.

VI. The desires & perceptions of man, untaught by anything but organs of sense, must be limited to objects of sense.

Conclusion: If it were not for the Poetic or Prophetic character the Philosophic & Experimental would soon be at the ratio of all things & stand still, unable to do other than repeat the same dull round over again.

There is No Natural Religion (circa 1788)

[B]

I. Man's perceptions are not bounded by organs of perception. He perceives more than sense (though ever so acute) can discover.

II. Reason, or the ratio of all we have already known, is not the same that it shall be when we know more.

[III. lacking]

IV. The bounded is loathed by its possessor. The same dull round even of a universe would soon become a mill with complicated wheels.

V. If the many become the same as the few when possessed, More! More! is the cry of a mistaken soul. Less than All cannot satisfy Man.

VI. If any could desire what he is incapable of possessing, despair must be his eternal lot.

VII. The desire of Man being Infinite, the possession is Infinite & himself Infinite.

Application: He who sees the Infinite in all things sees God. He who sees the Ratio only sees himself only.

Therefore God becomes as we are, that we may be as he is.

All Religions Are One (circa 1788)

THE VOICE OF ONE CRYING IN THE WILDERNESS

The Argument: As the true method of knowledge is experiment, the true faculty of knowing must be the faculty which experiences. This faculty I treat of.

Principle 1st. That the Poetic Genius is the true Man, and that the body or outward form of Man is derived from the Poetic Genius. Likewise that the forms of all things are derived from their Genius, which by the Ancients was called an Angel & Spirit & Demon.

Principle 2nd. As all men are alike in outward form, So (and with the same infinite variety) all are alike in the Poetic Genius.

Principle 3rd. No man can think, write or speak from his heart, but he must intend truth. Thus all sects of Philosophy are from the Poetic Genius, adapted to the weaknesses of every individual.

Principle 4th. As none by travelling over known lands can find out the unknown, So from already acquired knowledge Man could not acquire more. Therefore an universal Poetic Genius exists.

Principle 5th. The Religions of all Nations are derived from each Nation's different reception of the Poetic Genius, which is everywhere called the Spirit of Prophecy.

Principle 6th. The Jewish & Christian Testaments are An original derivation from the Poetic Genius. This is necessary from the confined nature of bodily sensation.

Principle 7th. As all men are alike (though infinitely various), So all Religions &, as all similars, have one source.

The true Man is the source, he being the Poetic Genius.

The Book of Thel (1789)

Plate i
THEL'S *MOTTO*

Does the Eagle know what is in the pit?
Or wilt thou go ask the Mole?
Can Wisdom be put in a silver rod?
Or Love in a golden bowl?

Plate 1

I

The daughters of Mne Seraphim led round their sunny
    flocks.
All but the youngest: she in paleness sought the
    secret air,
To fade away like morning beauty from her mortal day.
Down by the river of Adona her soft voice is heard,
And thus her gentle lamentation falls like morning
    dew: 5

"O life of this our spring, why fades the lotus of
    the water?
Why fade these children of the spring, born but to
    smile & fall?
Ah! Thel is like a wat'ry bow and like a parting
    cloud,
Like a reflection in a glass, like shadows in
    the water.
Like dreams of infants, like a smile upon an
    infant's face,   10
Like the dove's voice, like transient day, like
    music in the air.
Ah! gentle may I lay me down, and gentle rest
    my head,

And gentle sleep the sleep of death, and gentle
    hear the voice
Of him that walketh in the garden in the evening
    time."

The Lily of the valley breathing in the humble grass   15
Answered the lovely maid and said: "I am a
    wat'ry weed,
And I am very small and love to dwell in lowly vales,
So weak, the gilded butterfly scarce perches on my
    head.
Yet I am visited from heaven, and he that smiles
    on all
Walks in the valley and each morn over me spreads
    his hand,   20
Saying, 'Rejoice, thou humble grass, thou newborn
    lily flower,
Thou gentle maid of silent valleys and of modest
    brooks;
For thou shalt be clothed in light and fed with
    morning manna,
Till summer's heat melts thee beside the fountains
    and the springs
To flourish in eternal vales.' Then why should
    Thel complain?   25

Plate 2

Why should the mistress of the vales of Har
    utter a sigh?"

She ceased & smiled in tears, then sat down in
    her silver shrine.

Thel answered: "O thou little virgin of the
    peaceful valley,
Giving to those that cannot crave, the voiceless,
    the o'ertired,
Thy breath doth nourish the innocent lamb; he smells
    thy milky garments;   5

He crops thy flowers, while thou sittest smiling
    in his face,
Wiping his mild and meekin mouth from all
    contagious taints.
Thy wine doth purify the golden honey; thy perfume,
Which thou dost scatter on every little blade of
    grass that springs,
Revives the milked cow & tames the fire-breathing
    steed.   10
But Thel is like a faint cloud kindled at the
    rising sun;
I vanish from my pearly throne, and who shall find
    my place?"

"Queen of the vales," the Lily answered, "ask the
    tender cloud,
And it shall tell thee why it glitters in the
    morning sky
And why it scatters its bright beauty through the
    humid air.   15
Descend, O little cloud, & hover before the eyes
    of Thel."

The Cloud descended, and the Lily bowed her
    modest head
And went to mind her numerous charge among the
    verdant grass.

Plate 3

II

"O little Cloud," the virgin said, "I charge thee tell to
    me
Why thou complainest not when in one hour thou
    fade away.
Then we shall seek thee but not find; ah Thel is
    like to Thee.
I pass away; yet I complain, and no one hears
    my voice."

The Cloud then showed his golden head, & his
    bright form emerged,   5
Hovering and glittering on the air before the
    face of Thel.

"O virgin, know'st thou not our steeds drink of
    the golden springs
Where Luvah doth renew his horses? Look'st thou
    on my youth,
And fearest thou, because I vanish and am seen
    no more,
Nothing remains? O maid, I tell thee, when I
    pass away,   10
It is to tenfold life, to love, to peace; and
    raptures holy,
Unseen descending, weigh my light wings upon
    balmy flowers
And court the fair-eyed dew to take me to her
    shining tent;
The weeping virgin trembling kneels before the
    risen sun,
Till we arise linked in a golden band and never
    part,   15
But walk united, bearing food to all our tender
    flowers."
"Dost thou, O little Cloud? I fear that I am
    not like thee,
For I walk through the vales of Har and smell the
    sweetest flowers,
But I feed not the little flowers.
    I hear the warbling birds,
But I feed not the warbling birds; they fly and
    seek their food.   20
But Thel delights in these no more because I
    fade away,
And all shall say, 'Without a use this shining
    woman lived,
Or did she only live to be at death the food
    of worms?'"

The Cloud reclined upon his airy throne and
    answered thus:

"Then if thou art the food of, worms, O' virgin
    of the skies,   25
How great thy use, how great thy blessing! Every
    thing that lives
Lives not alone, nor for itself. Fear not, and
    I will call
The weak worm from its lowly bed, and thou shalt
    hear its voice.
Come forth, worm of the silent valley, to thy
    pensive queen."

The helpless worm arose and sat upon the Lily's
    leaf,   30
And the bright Cloud sailed on, to find his
    partner in the vale.

Plate 4

III

Then Thel astonished viewed the Worm upon its
    dewy bed.

"Art thou a Worm, image of weakness, art thou
    but a Worm?
I see thee like an infant wrapped in the Lily's leaf.
Ah, weep not, little voice; thou canst not speak,
    but thou canst weep.
Is this a Worm? I see thee lay helpless & naked,
    weeping,   5
And none to answer, none to cherish thee with
    mother's smiles."

The Clod of Clay heard the Worm's voice & raised her
    pitying head;
She bowed over the weeping infant, and her life
    exhaled

In milky fondness, then on Thel she fixed her
    humble eyes.

"O beauty of the vales of Har, we live not for
    ourselves;   10
Thou seest me the meanest thing, and so I am indeed;
My bosom of itself is cold and of itself is dark,

Plate 5

But he that loves the lowly pours his oil upon my head
And kisses me and binds his nuptial bands around my
    breast
And says: "Thou mother of my children, I have
    loved thee,
And I have given thee a crown that none can
    take away,   5
But how this is, sweet maid, I know not, and I
    cannot know;
I ponder, and I cannot ponder; yet I live and love."

The daughter of beauty wiped her pitying tears
    with her white veil
And said: "Alas! I knew not this, and therefore
    did I weep.
That God would love a Worm I knew, and punish the
    evil foot
That, wilful, bruised its helpless form; but that
    he cherished it   10
With milk and oil I never knew; and therefore
    did I weep,
And I complained in the mild air, because I
    fade away
And lay me down in thy cold bed and leave my
    shining lot."

"Queen of the vales," the matron Clay answered,
    "I heard thy sighs,
And all thy moans flew o'er my roof, but I have
    called them down.   15

Wilt thou, O Queen, enter my house? 'Tis given
    thee to enter
And to return; fear nothing. Enter with thy
    virgin feet."

Plate 6

IV

The eternal gates' terrific porter lifted the
    northern bar.
Thel entered in & saw the secrets of the land
    unknown;
She saw the couches of the dead & where the
    fibrous roots
Of every heart on earth infixes deep its restless
    twists:
A land of sorrows & of tears where never
    smile was seen.   5

She wandered in the land of clouds through valleys
    dark, list'ning
Dolours & lamentations. Waiting oft beside a dewy
    grave,
She stood in silence, list'ning to the voices of
    the ground,
Till to her own grave plot she came, & there she
    sat down
And heard this voice of sorrow breathed from the
    hollow pit: 10

"Why cannot the Ear be closed to its own
    destruction?
Or the glist'ning Eye to the poison of a smile?
Why are Eyelids stored with arrows ready drawn,
Where a thousand fighting men in ambush lie?
Or an Eye of gifts & graces, show'ring fruits
    & coined gold?   15
Why a Tongue impressed with honey from every wind?

Why an Ear, a whirlpool fierce to draw creations in?
Why a Nostril wide, inhaling terror, trembling
    & affright?
Why a tender curb upon the youthful burning boy?
Why a little curtain of flesh on the bed of our
    desire?   20

The Virgin started from her seat & with a shriek
Fled back unhindered till she came into the vales
    of Har.

Figure 3. "Ezekiel's Vision" Courtesy, Museum of Fine Arts, Boston

The Marriage of Heaven and Hell
(circa 1790-1793)

Plate 2

THE ARGUMENT

Rintrah roars & shakes his fires in the burdened air;
Hungry clouds swag on the deep.

Once meek, and in a perilous path,
The just man kept his course along
The vale of death.   5
Roses are planted where thorns grow,
And on the barren heath
Sing the honey bees.

Then the perilous path was planted,
And a river and a spring   10
On every cliff and tomb,
And on the bleached bones
Red clay brought forth,

Till the villain left the paths of ease
To walk in perilous paths and drive   15
The just man into barren climes.

Now the sneaking serpent walks
In mild humility,
And the just man rages in the wilds
Where lions roam.   20

Rintrah roars & shakes his fires in the burdened air;
Hungry clouds swag on the deep.

Plate 3

As a new heaven is begun, and it is now thirty-three years since its advent, the Eternal Hell revives. And lo! Swedenborg is the Angel sitting at the tomb; his writings are the linen clothes folded up. Now is the dominion of Edom & the return of Adam into Paradise; see Isaiah xxxiv & xxxv Chap.

Without Contraries is no progression. Attraction and Repulsion, Reason and Energy, Love and Hate are necessary to Human existence.

From these contraries spring what the religious call Good & Evil. Good is the passive that obeys Reason. Evil is the active springing from Energy.

Good is Heaven. Evil is Hell.

Plate 4

THE VOICE OF THE DEVIL

All Bibles or sacred codes have been the causes of the following Errors:

1. That Man has two real existing principles: Viz: a Body & a Soul.

2. That Energy, called Evil, is alone from the Body; & that Reason, called Good, is alone from the Soul.

3. That God will torment Man in Eternity for following his Energies. But the following Contraries to these are True:

1. Man has no Body distinct from his Soul, for that called Body is a portion of Soul discerned by the five Senses, the chief inlets of Soul in this age.

2. Energy is the only life and is from the Body, and Reason is the bound or outward circumference of Energy.

3. Energy is Eternal Delight.

Plates 5-6

Those who restrain desire do so because theirs is weak enough to be restrained, and the restrainer or reason usurps its place & governs the unwilling.

And being restrained, it by degrees becomes passive, till it is only the shadow of desire.

The history of this is written in Paradise Lost, & the Governor or Reason is called Messiah.

And the original Archangel, or possessor of the command of the heavenly host, is called the Devil or Satan, and his children are called Sin & Death.

But in the Book of Job, Milton's Messiah is called Satan.

For this history has been adopted by both parties.

It indeed appeared to Reason as if Desire was cast out, but the Devil's account is that the Messiah fell & formed a heaven of what he stole from the Abyss.

This is shown in the Gospel, where he prays to the Father to send the comforter, or Desire, that Reason may have Ideas to build on, the Jehovah of the Bible being no other than he who dwells in flaming fire.

Know that after Christ's death he became Jehovah.

But in Milton, the Father is Destiny, the Son a Ratio of the five senses, & the Holy-ghost Vacuum!

Note: The reason Milton wrote in fetters when he wrote of Angels & God and at liberty when of Devils & Hell is because he was a true Poet and of the Devil's party without knowing it.

Plates 6-7

A MEMORABLE FANCY

As I was walking among the fires of hell, delighted with the enjoyments of Genius, which to Angels look like torment and insanity, I collected some of their Proverbs, thinking that as the sayings used in a nation mark its character, so the Proverbs of Hell show the nature of Infernal wisdom better than any description of buildings or garments.

When I came home, on the abyss of the five senses, where a flat-sided steep frowns over the present world, I saw a mighty Devil folded in black clouds, hovering on the sides of the rock.

With corroding fires he wrote the following sentence, now perceived by the minds of men & read by them on earth:

How do you know but ev'ry Bird that cuts the airy way
Is an immense world of delight closed by your senses five?

Plate 7

PROVERBS OF HELL

In seed time learn, in harvest teach, in winter enjoy.
Drive your cart and your plow over the bones of the
    dead.
The road of excess leads to the palace of wisdom.
Prudence is a rich, ugly old maid courted by
    Incapacity.
He who desires but acts not breeds
    pestilence.
The cut worm forgives the plow.
Dip him in the river who loves water.
A fool sees not the same tree that a wise man sees.
He whose face gives no light shall never become a
    star.
Eternity is in love with the productions of time.
The busy bee has no time for sorrow.
The hours of folly are measured by the clock, but
    of wisdom no clock can measure.
All wholesome food is caught without a net or a trap.
Bring out number, weight & measure in a year of
    dearth.
No bird soars too high if he soars with his own wings.
A dead body revenges not injuries.
The most sublime act is to set another before you.
If the fool would persist in his folly he would
    become wise.
Folly is the cloak of knavery.
Shame is Pride's cloak.

Plate 8

Prisons are built with stones of Law, Brothels with
  bricks of Religion.
The pride of the peacock is the glory of God.
The lust of the goat is the bounty of God.
The wrath of the lion is the wisdom of God.
The nakedness of woman is the work of God.
Excess of sorrow laughs. Excess of joy weeps.
The roaring of lions, the howling of wolves, the
  raging of the stormy sea, and the destructive
  sword are portions of eternity too great for the
  eye of man.
The fox condemns the trap, not himself.
Joys impregnate. Sorrows bring forth.
Let man wear the fell of the lion, woman the fleece
  of the sheep.
The bird a nest, the spider a web, man friendship.
The selfish smiling fool & the sullen frowning
  fool shall be both thought wise that they may
  be a rod.
What is now proved was once only imagined.
The rat, the mouse, the fox, the rabbit watch the
  roots; the lion, the tiger, the horse, the
  elephant watch the fruits.
The cistern contains; the fountain overflows.
One thought fills immensity.
Always be ready to speak your mind, and a base man
  will avoid you.
Every thing possible to be believed is an image of truth.
The eagle never lost so much time as when he submitted
  to learn of the crow.

Plate 9

The fox provides for himself, but God provides for
  the lion.

Think in the morning, Act in the noon, Eat in the
    evening, Sleep in the night.
He who has suffered you to impose on him knows you.
As the plow follows words, so God rewards prayers.
The tigers of wrath are wiser than the horses of
    instruction.
Expect poison from the standing water.
You never know what is enough unless you know what
    is more than enough.
Listen to the fool's reproach! It is a kingly title!
The eyes of fire, the nostrils of air, the mouth
    of water, the beard of earth.
The weak in courage is strong in cunning.
The apple tree never asks the beech how he shall
    grow, nor the lion the horse how he shall take
    his prey.
The thankful receiver bears a plentiful harvest.
If others had not been foolish, we should be so.
The soul of sweet delight can never be defiled.
When thou seest an Eagle, thou seest a portion of
    Genius. Lift up thy head!
As the caterpillar chooses the fairest leaves to
    lay her eggs on, so the priest lays his curse
    on the fairest joys.
To create a little flower is the labour of ages.
Damn braces; Bless relaxes.
The best wine is the oldest, the best water the
    newest.
Prayers plow not! Praises reap not!
Joys laugh not! Sorrows weep not!

Plate 10

The head Sublime, the heart Pathos, the genitals
Beauty, the hands & feet Proportion.
As the air to a bird or the sea to a fish, so is contempt to
    the contemptible.

The crow wished everything was black, the owl that
    everything was white.
Exuberance is Beauty.
If the lion was advised by the fox, he would be
    cunning.
Improvement makes straight roads, but the crooked
    roads without Improvement are roads of Genius.
Sooner murder an infant in its cradle than nurse
    unacted desires.
Where man is not nature is barren.
Truth can never be told so as to be understood and
    not be believed.

Enough! or Too much.

Plate 11

The ancient Poets animated all sensible objects with Gods or Geniuses, calling them by the names and adorning them with the properties of woods, rivers, mountains, lakes, cities, nations, and whatever their enlarged & numerous senses could perceive.

And particularly they studied the genius of each city & country, placing it under its mental deity.

Till a system was formed, which some took advantage of, & enslaved the vulgar by attempting to realize or abstract the mental deities from their objects: thus began Priesthood.

Choosing forms of worship from poetic tales.

And at length they pronounced that the Gods had ordered such things.

Thus men forgot that All deities reside in the human breast.

Plates 12-13

A MEMORABLE FANCY

The Prophets Isaiah and Ezekiel dined with me, and I asked them how they dared so roundly to assert that God spake to them, and whether they did not think at the time that they would be misunderstood & so be the cause of imposition.

Isaiah answered: "I saw no God, nor heard any, in a finite organical perception; but my senses discovered the infinite in everything, and as I was then persuaded, & remain confirmed, that the voice of honest indignation is the voice of God, I cared not for consequences but wrote."

Then I asked: "Does a firm persuasion that a thing is so make it so?"

He replied: "All poets believe that it does, & in ages of imagination this firm persuasion removed mountains; but many are not capable of a firm persuasion of anything."

Then Ezekiel said: "The philosophy of the East taught the first principles of human perception. Some nations held one principle for the origin, & some another; we of Israel taught that the Poetic Genius (as you now call it) was the first principle and all the others merely derivative, which was the cause of our despising the Priests & Philosophers of other countries and prophesying that all Gods would at last be proved to originate in ours & to be the tributaries of the Poetic Genius. It was this that our great poet King David desired so fervently & invokes so pathetic'ly, saying by this he conquers enemies & governs kingdoms; and we so loved our God that we cursed in his name all the deities of surrounding nations and asserted that they had rebelled; from these opinions the vulgar came to think that all nations would at last be subject to the Jews.

"This," said he, "like all firm persuasions, is come to pass, for all nations believe the Jews' code and worship the Jews' god, and what greater subjection can be?"

I heard this with some wonder & must confess my own conviction. After dinner I asked Isaiah to favour the world with his lost works; he said none of equal value was lost. Ezekiel said the same of his.

I also asked Isaiah what made him go naked and barefoot three years. He answered: "The same that made our friend Diogenes the Grecian."

I then asked Ezekiel why he eat dung and lay so long on his right & left side. He answered: "The desire of raising other men into a perception of the infinite. This the North American tribes practice; & is he honest who resists his genius or conscience only for the sake of present ease or gratification?"

Plate 14

The ancient tradition that the world will be consumed in fire at the end of six thousand years is true, as I have heard from Hell.

For the cherub with his flaming sword is hereby commanded to leave his guard at the tree of life; and when he does, the whole creation will be consumed and appear infinite and holy, whereas it now appears finite & corrupt.

This will come to pass by an improvement of sensual enjoyment.

But first the notion that man has a body distinct from his soul is to be expunged; this I shall do by printing in the infernal method, by corrosives, which in Hell are salutary and medicinal, melting apparent surfaces away and displaying the infinite which was hid.

If the doors of perception were cleansed, every thing would appear to man as it is, infinite.

For man has closed himself up, till he sees all things through narrow chinks of his cavern.

Plate 15

A MEMORABLE FANCY

I was in a Printing house in Hell & saw the method in which knowledge is transmitted from generation to generation.

In the first chamber was a Dragon-Man, clearing away the rubbish from a cave's mouth; within, a number of Dragons were hollowing the cave.

In the second chamber was a Viper folding round the rock & the cave, and others adorning it with gold, silver and precious stones.

In the third chamber was an Eagle with wings and feathers of air; he caused the inside of the cave to be infinite; around were numbers of Eagle-like men, who built palaces in the immense cliffs.

In the fourth chamber were Lions of flaming fire, raging around & melting the metals into living fluids.

In the fifth chamber were Unnamed forms, which cast the metals into the expanse.

There they were received by Men, who occupied the sixth chamber, and took the forms of books & were arranged in libraries.

Plates 16 - 17

The Giants who formed this world into its sensual existence and now seem to live in it in chains are in truth the causes of its life & the sources of all activity, but the chains are the cunning of weak and tame minds, which have power to resist energy; according to the proverb, the weak in courage is strong in cunning.

Thus one portion of being is the Prolific, the other the Devouring; to the devourer it seems as if the producer was in his chains, but it is not so; he only takes portions of existence and fancies that the whole.

But the Prolific would cease to be Prolific unless the Devourer as a sea received the excess of his delights.

Some will say: "Is not God alone the Prolific?" I answer: "God only Acts & Is in existing beings or Men."

These two classes of men arc always upon earth, & they should be enemies; whoever tries to reconcile them seeks to destroy existence.

Religion is an endeavour to reconcile the two.

Note: Jesus Christ did not wish to unite but to separate them, as in the Parable of sheep and goats; & he says: "I came not to send Peace, but a Sword."

Messiah, or Satan, or Tempter, was formerly thought to be one of the Antediluvians, who are our Energies.

Plates 17 - 18 - 19 - 20

A MEMORABLE FANCY

An Angel came to me and said: "O pitiable foolish young man! O horrible! O dreadful state! Consider the hot burning dungeon thou art preparing for thyself to all eternity, to which thou art going in such career."

I said: "Perhaps you will be willing to show me my eternal lot, & we will contemplate together upon it and see whether your lot or mine is most desirable."

So he took me through a stable & through a church & down into the church vault, at the end of which was a mill; through the mill we went and came to a cave. Down the winding cavern we groped our tedious way, till a void boundless as a nether sky appeared beneath us & we held by the roots of trees and hung over this immensity; but I said, "If you please, we will commit ourselves to this void, and see whether providence is here also; if you will not, I will. But he answered: "Do not presume, O young man, but as we here remain, behold thy lot, which will soon appear when the darkness passes away."

So I remained with him, sitting in the twisted root of an oak. He was suspended in a fungus which hung with the head downward into the deep.

By degrees we beheld the infinite Abyss, fiery as the smoke of a burning city; beneath us at an immense distance was the sun, black but shining; round it were fiery tracks on which revolved vast spiders, crawling after their prey, which flew, or rather swum, in the infinite deep, in the most terrific shapes of animals sprung from corruption; & the air was full of them & seemed composed of them; these are Devils and are called Powers of the air. I now asked my companion which was my eternal lot. He said, "Between the black & white spiders."

But now, from between the black & white spiders a cloud and fire burst and rolled through the deep, black'ning all beneath, so that the nether deep grew black as a sea & rolled with a terrible noise; beneath us was nothing now to be seen but a black tempest, till looking east between the clouds & the waves, we saw a cataract of blood mixed with fire and not many stones' throw from us appeared and sunk again the scaly fold of a monstrous serpent. At last to the east, distant about three degrees, appeared a fiery crest above the waves. Slowly it reared like a ridge of golden rocks, till we discovered two globes of crimson fire, from which the sea fled away in clouds of smoke; and now we saw it was the head of Leviathan; his forehead was divided into streaks of green & purple like those on a tiger's forehead; soon we saw his mouth & red gills hang just above the raging foam, tinging the black deep with beams of blood, advancing toward us with all the fury of a spiritual existence.

My friend the Angel climbed up from his station into the mill; I remained alone, & then this appearance was no more, but I found myself sitting on a pleasant bank beside a river by moonlight hearing a harper who sung to the harp, & his theme was, "The man who never alters his opinion is like standing water & breeds reptiles of the mind."

But I arose and sought for the mill, & there I found my Angel, who, surprised, asked me how I escaped.

I answered: "All that we saw was owing to your metaphysics; for when you ran away, I found myself on a bank by moonlight hearing a harper. But now we have seen my eternal lot; shall I show you yours?" He laughed at my proposal; but I by force suddenly caught him in my arms & flew westerly through the night, till we were elevated above the earth's shadow; then I flung myself with him directly into the body of the sun; here I clothed myself in white &, taking in my hand Swedenborg's volumes, sunk from the glorious clime and passed all the planets, till we came to Saturn; here I stayed to rest & then leaped into the void between Saturn & the fixed stars.

"Here," said I, "is your lot, in this space, if space it may be called." Soon we saw the stable and the church, & I took him to the altar and opened the Bible, and lo! it was a deep pit, into which I descended driving the Angel before me; soon we saw seven houses of brick; one we entered; in it were a number of monkeys, baboons & all of that species, chained by the middle, grinning and snatching at one another, but withheld by the shortness of their chains. However, I saw that they sometimes grew numerous, and then the weak were caught by the strong and, with a grinning aspect, first coupled with & then devoured by plucking off first one limb and then another, till the body was left a helpless trunk. This after grinning and kissing it with seeming fondness they devoured too; and here & there I saw one savourily picking the flesh off of his own tail; as the stench terribly annoyed us both, we went into the mill, & I in my hand brought the skeleton of a body, which in the mill was Aristotle's Analytics.

So the Angel said: "Thy phantasy has imposed upon me, & thou oughtest to be ashamed."

I answered: "We impose on one another, & it is but lost time to converse with you whose works are only Analytics."

Plates 21-22

OPPOSITION IS TRUE FRIENDSHIP

I have always found that Angels have the vanity to speak of themselves as the only wise; this they do with a confident insolence sprouting from systematic reasoning.

Thus Swedenborg boasts that what he writes is new; though it is only the Contents or Index of already published books.

A man carried a monkey about for a show, & because he was a little wiser than the monkey, grew vain and conceived himself as much wiser than seven men. It is so with Swedenborg; he shows the folly of churches & exposes hypocrites, till he imagines that all are religious & himself the single one on earth that ever broke a net.

Now hear a plain fact: Swedenborg has not written one new truth. Now hear another: he has written all the old falsehoods.

And now hear the reason: He conversed with Angels, who are all religious, & conversed not with Devils, who all hate religion, for he was incapable through his conceited notions.

Thus Swedenborg's writings are a recapitulation of all superficial opinions and an analysis of the more sublime, but no further.

Have now another plain fact: Any man of mechanical talents may from the writings of Paracelsus or Jacob Behmen, produce ten thousand volumes of equal value with Swedenborg's, and from those of Dante or Shakespeare an infinite number.

But when he has done this, let him not say that he knows better than his master, for he only holds a candle in sunshine.

Plates 22-23-24

A MEMORABLE FANCY

Once I saw a Devil in a flame of fire who arose before an Angel that sat on a cloud, and the Devil uttered these words:

"The worship of God is: Honouring his gifts in other men, each according to his genius, and loving the greatest men best; those who envy or calumniate great men hate God, for there is no other God."

The Angel, hearing this, became almost blue; but mastering himself, he grew yellow & at last white, pink & smiling, and then replied:

"Thou Idolater, is not God One? & is not he visible in Jesus Christ? And has not Jesus Christ given his sanction to the law of ten commandments, and are not all other men fools, sinners & nothings?"

The Devil answered: "Bray a fool in a mortar with wheat; yet shall not his folly be beaten out of him; if Jesus Christ is the greatest man, you ought to love him in the greatest degree; now hear how he has given his sanction to the law of ten commandments: did he not mock at the sabbath and so mock the sabbath's God? Murder those who were murdered because of him? Turn away the law from the woman taken in adultery? Steal the labor of others to support him? Bear false witness when he omitted making a defense before Pilate? Covet when he prayed for his disciples and when he bid them shake off the dust of their feet against such as refused to lodge them? I tell you, no virtue can exist without breaking these ten commandments. Jesus was all virtue and acted from impulse, not from rules."

When he had so spoken, I beheld the Angel, who stretched out his arms embracing the flame of fire, & he was consumed and arose as Elijah.

Note: This Angel, who is now become a Devil, is my particular friend; we often read the Bible together in its infernal or diabolical sense, which the world shall have if they behave well.

I have also the Bible of Hell, which the world shall have whether they will or no.

One Law for the Lion & Ox is Oppression.

Plate 25

A SONG OF LIBERTY

1. The Eternal Female groaned! It was heard over all the Earth.
2. Albion's coast is sick, silent; the American meadows faint!

3. Shadows of Prophecy shiver along by the lakes and the rivers and mutter across the ocean. France, rend down thy dungeon!

4. Golden Spain, burst the barriers of old Rome.

5. Cast thy keys, O Rome, into the deep, down falling, even to eternity down falling,

6. And weep.

7. In her trembling hands she took the newborn terror howling.

8. On those infinite mountains of light, now barred out by the Atlantic sea, the newborn fire stood before the starry king!

9. Flagged with grey-browed snows and thunderous visages, the jealous wings waved over the deep.

10. The speary hand burned aloft; unbuckled was the shield; forth went the hand of jealousy among the flaming hair and hurled the newborn wonder through the starry night.

11. The fire, the fire is falling!

12. Look up! Look up! O citizen of London. Enlarge thy countenance; O Jew, leave counting gold! Return to thy oil and wine; O African! black African! (go, winged thought, widen his forehead.)

13. The fiery limbs, the flaming hair, shot like the sinking sun into the western sea.

14. Waked from his eternal sleep, the hoary element roaring fled away.

15. Down rushed, beating his wings in vain, the jealous king; his grey-browed councillors, thunderous warriors, curled veterans, among helms, and shields, and chariots, horses, elephants, banners, castles, slings and rocks,

16. Falling, rushing, ruining! Buried in the ruins, on Urthona's dens,

17. All night beneath the ruins; then, their sullen flames faded, emerge round the gloomy king.

18. With thunder and fire, leading his starry hosts through the waste wilderness, he promulgates his ten commands, glancing his beamy eyelids over the deep in dark dismay,

19. Where the son of fire in his eastern cloud, while the morning plumes her golden breast,

20. Spurning the clouds written with curses, stamps the stony

law to dust, loosing the eternal horses from the dens of night, crying:

"Empire is no more! And now the lion & wolf shall cease."

CHORUS

Let the Priests of the Raven of dawn no longer in deadly black with hoarse note curse the sons of joy. Nor his accepted brethren, whom, tyrant, he calls free, lay the bound or build the roof. Nor pale religious lechery call that virginity that wishes but acts not!
For every thing that lives is Holy.

Visions of the Daughters of Albion (1793)

The Eye sees more than the Heart knows.

Plate iii

THE ARGUMENT

I loved Theotormon,
And I was not ashamed.
I trembled in my virgin fears,
And I hid in Leutha's vale!

I plucked Leutha's flower,   5
And I rose up from the vale;
But the terrible thunders tore
My virgin mantle in twain.

Plate 1

VISIONS

Enslaved, the Daughters of Albion weep: a trembling
    lamentation
Upon their mountains; in their valleys, sighs
    toward America.

For the soft soul of America, Oothoon, wandered in
    woe
Along the vales of Leutha, seeking flowers to comfort
    her;
And thus she spoke to the bright Marigold of Leutha's
    vale: 5

"Art thou a flower? Art thou a nymph? I see thee now
    a flower,
Now a nymph! I dare not pluck thee from thy dewy
    bed!"

The Golden nymph replied: "Pluck thou my flower,
    Oothoon the mild.

Another flower shall spring, because the soul
   of sweet delight
Can never pass away." She ceased & closed her golden
   shrine.   10

Then Oothoon plucked the flower, saying, "I pluck
   thee from thy bed,
Sweet flower, and put thee here to glow between my
   breasts;
And thus I turn my face to where my whole soul seeks."

Over the waves she went in wing'd exulting swift
   delight,
And over Theotormon's reign took her impetuous course.   15

Bromion rent her with his thunders. On his stormy bed
Lay the faint maid, and soon her woes appalled his
   thunders hoarse.

Bromion spoke: "Behold this harlot here on Bromion's
   bed,
And let the jealous dolphins sport around the lovely
   maid:
Thy soft American plains are mine, and mine thy north
   & south;   20
Stamped with my signet are the swarthy children of the
   sun;
They are obedient, they resist not, they obey the
   scourge:
Their daughters worship terrors and obey the violent.

Plate 2

Now thou may'st marry Bromion's harlot, and protect
   the child
Of Bromion's rage that Oothoon shall put forth in
   nine moons' time."

Then storms rent Theotormon's limbs; he rolled his
   waves around

And folded his black jealous waters round the
    adulterate pair.
Bound back to back in Bromion's caves, terror &
    meekness dwell.   5

At entrance Theotormon sits, wearing the threshold
    hard
With secret tears; beneath him sound like waves on a
    desert shore
The voice of slaves beneath the sun and children
    bought with money,
That shiver in religious caves beneath the burning
    fires
Of lust, that belch incessant from the summits of the
    earth.   10

Oothoon weeps not; she cannot weep! Her tears are
    locked up;
But she can howl incessant, writhing her soft snowy
    limbs
And calling Theotormon's Eagles to prey upon her flesh:

"I call with holy voice! Kings of the sounding air,
Rend away this defiled bosom that I may reflect   15
The image of Theotormon on my pure transparent breast."

The Eagles at her call descend & rend their bleeding
    prey.
Theotormon severely smiles. Her soul reflects the smile,
As the clear spring, mudded with feet of beasts,
    grows pure & smiles.

The Daughters of Albion hear her woes & echo back her
    sighs.   20

"Why does my Theotormon sit weeping upon the threshold,
And Oothoon hovers by his side, persuading him in vain?
I cry, 'Arise, O Theotormon,' for the village dog
Barks at the breaking day, the nightingale has done
    lamenting,
The lark does rustle in the ripe corn, and the Eagle
    returns.

From nightly prey and lifts his golden beak to the pure
    east,
Shaking the dust from his immortal pinions to awake
The sun that sleeps too long. Arise, my Theotormon! I
    am pure,
Because the night is gone that closed me in its
    deadly black.
They told me that the night & day were all that I
    could see;   30
They told me that I had five senses to inclose me up.
And they inclosed my infinite brain into a narrow
    circle,
And sunk my heart into the Abyss, a red round globe
    hot burning,
Instead of morn arises a bright shadow, like an eye   35
In the eastern cloud; instead of night a sickly
    charnel house;
That Theotormon hears me not! To him the night and morn
Are both alike, a night of sighs, a morning of fresh
    tears;
Till all from life I was obliterated and erased.

Plate 3

And none but Bromion can hear my lamentations.

"With what sense is it that the chicken shuns the
    ravenous hawk?
With what sense does the tame pigeon measure out the
    expanse?
With what sense does the bee form cells? Have not
    the mouse & frog
Eyes and ears and sense of touch? Yet are their
    habitations   5
And their pursuits as different as their forms and as
    their joys?
Ask the wild ass why he refuses burdens, and the meek
    camel
Why he loves man. Is it because of eye, ear, mouth or
    skin

Or breathing nostrils? No, for these the wolf and tiger
    have.
Ask the blind worm the secrets of the grave, and why
    her spires   10
Love to curl round the bones of death; and ask the
    rav'nous snake
Where she gets poison, & the wing'd eagle why he loves
    the sun;
And then tell me the thoughts of man, that have been
    hid of old.

"Silent I hover all the night, and all day could be
    silent
If Theotormon once would turn his loved eyes upon me.   15
How can I be defiled when I reflect thy image pure?
Sweetest the fruit that the worm feeds on & the soul
    preyed on by woe,
The new washed lamb tinged with the village smoke,
    & the bright swan
By the red earth of our immortal river. I bathe my
    wings,
And I am white and pure to hover round Theotormon's
    breast."   20
Then Theotormon broke his silence, and he answered:
"Tell me what is the night or day to one o'erflowed
    with woe?
Tell me what is a thought, & of what substance is it
    made?
Tell me what is a joy, & in what gardens do joys grow?
And in what rivers swim the sorrows, and upon what
    mountains   25

Plate 4

Wave shadows of discontent, and in what houses dwell
    the wretched,
Drunken with woe forgotten, and shut up from cold
    despair?

"Tell me where dwell the thoughts forgotten till
    thou call them forth?
Tell me where dwell the joys of old, & where the
    ancient loves?
And when will they renew again, & the night of
    oblivion past,   5
That I might traverse times & spaces far remote and
    bring
Comforts into a present sorrow and a night of pain?
Where goest thou, O thought? To what remote land is
    thy flight?
If thou returnest to the present moment of affliction,
Wilt thou bring comforts on thy wings and dews and
    honey and balm   10
Or poison from the desert wilds, from the eyes of the
    envier?"

Then Bromion said, and shook the cavern with his
    lamentation:

"Thou knowest that the ancient trees seen by thine
    eyes have fruit,
But knowest thou that trees and fruits flourish upon
    the earth
To gratify senses unknown—trees, beasts and birds
    unknown: 15
Unknown, not unperceived, spread in the infinite
    microscope,
In places yet unvisited by the voyager, and in worlds
Over another kind of seas, and in atmospheres unknown?
Ah! Are there other wars, beside the wars of sword
    and fire?
And are there other sorrows beside the sorrows of
    poverty?   20
And are there other joys beside the joys of riches
    and ease?
And is there not one law for both the lion and the ox?
And is there not eternal fire, and eternal chains
To bind the phantoms of existence from eternal life?"

Then Oothoon waited silent all the day and all the
    night,   25

Plate 5

But when the morn arose, her lamentation renewed.
The Daughters of Albion hear her woes & echo back her
    sighs:

"O Urizen! Creator of men! mistaken Demon of heaven,
Thy joys are tears, thy labour vain, to form men to
    thine image.
How can one joy absorb another? Are not different joys   5
Holy, eternal, infinite? And each joy is a Love.

"Does not the great mouth laugh at a gift, & the
    narrow eyelids mock
At the labour that is above payment, and wilt thou
    take the ape
For thy counsellor, or the dog for a schoolmaster to
    thy children?
Does he who contemns poverty and he who turns with
    abhorrence   10
From usury feel the same passion, or are they moved
    alike?
How can the giver of gifts experience the delights of
    the merchant?
How the industrious citizen the pains of the husbandman?
How different far the fat fed hireling with hollow
    drum,
Who buys whole cornfields into wastes and sings upon
    the heath!   15
How different their eye and ear! How different the
    world to them!
With what sense does the parson claim the labour of
    the farmer?
What are his nets & gins & traps, & how does he
    surround him

With cold floods of abstraction and with forests of
    solitude,
To build him castles and high spires, where kings &
    priests may dwell,   20
Till she who burns with youth and knows no fixed lot
    is bound
In spells of law to one she loathes? And must she drag
    the chain
Of life in weary lust? Must chilling, murderous
    thoughts obscure
The clear heaven of her eternal spring, to bear the
    wintry rage
Of a harsh terror, driv'n to madness, bound to hold
    a rod   25
Over her shrinking shoulders all the day, & all the
    night
To turn the wheel of false desire and longings
    that wake her womb
To the abhorred birth of cherubs in the human form,
That live a pestilence & die a meteor & are no more;
Till the child dwell with one he hates and do the
    deed he loathes,   30
And the impure scourge force his seed into its unripe
    birth
E'er yet his eyelids can behold the arrows of the
    day?
"Does the whale worship at thy footsteps as the
    hungry dog?
Or does he scent the mountain prey because his nostrils
    wide
Draw in the ocean? Does his eye discern the flying
    cloud   35
As the raven's eye, or does he measure the expanse
    like the vulture?
Does the still spider view the cliffs where eagles
    hide their young,
Or does the fly rejoice because the harvest is brought
    in?

Does not the eagle scorn the earth & despise the
    treasures beneath?
But the mole knoweth what is there, & the worm shall
    tell it thee.   40
Does not the worm erect a pillar in the mouldering
    churchyard

Plate 6

And a palace of eternity in the jaws of the hungry
    grave?
Over his porch these words are written: 'Take thy
    bliss, O Man!
And sweet shall be thy taste, & sweet thy infant joys
    renew!'
"Infancy, fearless, lustful, happy, nestling for
    delight
In laps of pleasure; Innocence, honest, open, seeking   5
The vigorous joys of morning light, open to virgin
    bliss.
Who taught thee modesty, subtle modesty, child of
    night & sleep?
When thou awakest, wilt thou dissemble all thy
    secret joys,
Or wert thou not awake when all this mystery was
    disclosed?
Then com'st thou forth a modest virgin, knowing to
    dissemble   10
With nets found under thy night pillow, to catch
    virgin joy
And brand it with the name of whore & sell it in the
    night,
In silence, ev'n without a whisper, and in seeming sleep.
Religious dreams and holy vespers light thy smoky fires.
Once were thy fires lighted by the eyes of honest morn.   15
And does my Theotormon seek this hypocrite modesty,
This knowing, artful, secret, fearful, cautious,
    trembling hypocrite?

Then is Oothoon a whore indeed! And all the virgin joys
Of life are harlots, and Theotormon is a sick man's
    dream,
And Oothoon is the crafty slave of selfish holiness.   20
But Oothoon is not so, a virgin filled with virgin
    fancies
Open to joy and to delight wherever beauty appears.
If in the morning sun I find it, there my eyes are fixed

Plate 7

In happy copulation; if in evening mild, wearied with
    work,
Sit on a bank and draw the pleasures of this freeborn joy.
The moment of desire! The moment of desire! The virgin
That pines for man shall awaken her womb to enormous joys
In the secret shadows of her chamber; the youth shut
    up from   5
The lustful joy shall forget to generate & create an
    amorous image
In the shadows of his curtains and in the folds of his
    silent pillow.
Are not these the places of religion, the rewards of
    continence,
The self-enjoyings of self-denial? Why dost thou seek
    religion?
Is it because acts are not lovely that thou seekest
    solitude,   10
Where the horrible darkness is impressed with
    reflections of desire?

Father of Jealousy, be thou accursed from the earth!
Why hast thou taught my Theotormon this accursed thing?
Till beauty fades from off my shoulders, darkened and
    cast out,
A solitary shadow wailing on the margin of non-Entity.   15

"I cry, Love! Love! Love! happy happy Love! free as
    the mountain wind!

Can that be Love that drinks another as a sponge
    drinks water,
That clouds with jealousy his nights, with weepings
    all the day,
To spin a web of age around him, grey and hoary, dark,
Till his eyes sicken at the fruit that hangs before
    his sight?   20
Such is self-love that envies all, a creeping skeleton
With lamplike eyes watching around the frozen marriage
    bed.

"But silken nets and traps of adamant will Oothoon
    spread,
And catch for thee girls of mild silver, or of furious
    gold.
I'll lie beside thee on a bank & view their wanton play   25
In lovely copulation, bliss on bliss, with Theotormon.
Red as the rosy morning, lustful as the firstborn beam,
Oothoon shall view his dear delight, nor e'er with
    jealous cloud
Come in the heaven of generous love, nor selfish
    blightings bring.

"Does the sun walk in glorious raiment on the secret
    floor   30

Plate 8

Where the cold miser spreads his gold? Or does the
    bright cloud drop
On his stone threshold? Does his eye behold the beam
    that brings
Expansion to the eye of pity, or will he bind himself
Beside the ox to thy hard furrow? Does not that mild
    beam blot
The bat, the owl, the glowing tiger, and the king of
    night?   5
The sea fowl takes the wintry blast for a cov'ring to
    her limbs,

And the wild snake, the pestilence to adorn him with
 gems & gold.
And trees & birds & beasts & men behold their eternal
 joy.
Arise, you little glancing wings, and sing your infant
 joy!
Arise and drink your bliss, for everything that lives
 is holy!"   10

Thus every morning wails Oothoon, but Theotormon sits
Upon the margined ocean conversing with shadows dire.

The Daughters of Albion hear her woes, & echo back
 her sighs.

Europe: A Prophecy (1794)

Plate iii

"Five windows light the caverned Man; through one
  he breathes the air;
Through one hears music of the spheres; through one
  the eternal vine
Flourishes, that he may receive the grapes; through
  one can look
And see small portions of the eternal world that ever
  groweth;
Through one himself pass out what time he please, but
  he will not,   5
For stolen joys are sweet, & bread eaten in secret
  pleasant."

So sang a Fairy, mocking as he sat on a streaked Tulip,
Thinking none saw him. When he ceased, I started from
  the trees
And caught him in my hat as boys knock down a
  butterfly.
"How know you this," said I, "small Sir? Where did
  you learn this song?"   10
Seeing himself in my possession, thus he answered me:

"My master, I am yours. Command me, for I must obey."
"Then tell me, what is the material world, and is it
  dead?"
He, laughing, answered: "I will write a book on
  leaves of flowers,
If you will feed me on love-thoughts & give me now and
  then   15
A cup of sparkling poetic fancies; so when I am tipsy,
I'll sing to you to this soft lute and show you all alive

The world, where every particle of dust breathes forth
    its joy."
I took him home in my warm bosom: as we went along
Wild flowers I gathered, & he showed me each eternal
    flower.   20
He laughed aloud to see them whimper because they were
    plucked.
They hovered round me like a cloud of incense. When I
    came
Into my parlour and sat down and took my pen to write,
My Fairy sat upon the table and dictated EUROPE.

Plate 1

PRELUDIUM

The nameless shadowy female rose from out the breast
    of Orc,
Her snaky hair brandishing in the winds of Enitharmon;
And thus her voice arose:

"O mother Enitharmon, wilt thou bring forth other sons
To cause my name to vanish, that my place may not be
    found?   5
For I am faint with travel
Like the dark cloud disburdened in the day of
    dismal thunder.

"My roots are brandished in the heavens; my fruits
    in earth beneath
Surge, foam and labour into life, first born and first
    consumed,
Consumed and consuming!   10
Then why should'st thou, accursed mother, bring me
    into life?

"I wrap my turban of thick clouds around my lab'ring
    head
And fold the sheety waters as a mantle round my limbs.

Yet the red sun and moon
And all the overflowing stars rain down prolific pains.   15

Plate 2

"Unwilling, I look up to heaven, unwilling count the
          stars
Sitting in fathomless abyss of my immortal shrine;
I seize their burning power
And bring forth howling terrors, all-devouring fiery
          kings,

"Devouring & devoured, roaming on dark and desolate
          mountains   20
In forests of eternal death, shrieking in hollow trees.
Ah mother Enitharmon!
Stamp not with solid form this vig'rous progeny of fires.

"I bring forth from my teeming bosom myriads of
          flames,
And thou dost stamp them with a signet; then they
          roam abroad   25
And leave me void as death.
Ah! I am drowned in shady woe and visionary joy.

"And who shall bind the infinite with an eternal band
To compass it with swaddling bands? And who shall
          cherish it
With milk and honey?   30
I see it smile, & I roll inward, & my voice is past."

                    She ceased & rolled her shady clouds
                    Into the secret place.

Plate 3

A PROPHECY

                    The deep of winter came,
                    What time the secret child

Descended through the orient gates of the eternal day:
War ceased, & all the troops like shadows fled to their
    abodes.
Then Enitharmon saw her sons & daughters rise around.   5
Like pearly clouds they meet together in the crystal
    house;
And Los, possessor of the moon, joyed in the peaceful
    night,
Thus speaking while his num'rous sons shook their
    bright fiery wings:

"Again the night is come
That strong Urthona takes his rest,   10
And Urizen, unloosed from chains,
Glows like a meteor in the distant north.
Stretch forth your hands and strike the elemental
    strings!
Awake the thunders of the deep!

Plate 4

"The shrill winds wake,
Till all the sons of Urizen look out and envy Los.
Seize all the spirits of life and bind
Their warbling joys to our loud strings.
Bind all the nourishing sweets of earth   5
To give us bliss, that we may drink the sparkling wine
    of Los;
And let us laugh at war,
Despising toil and care,
Because the days and nights of joy in lucky hours renew.

"Arise, O Orc, from thy deep den!   10
Firstborn of Enitharmon, rise!
And we will crown thy head with garlands of the ruddy
    vine,
For now thou are bound,
And I may see thee in the hour of bliss, my eldest
    born."

The horrent Demon rose, surrounded with red stars of
    fire,   15
Whirling about in furious circles round the immortal
    fiend.

Then Enitharmon down descended into his red light,
And thus her voice rose to her children; the distant
    heavens reply:

Plate 6

"Now comes the night of Enitharmon's joy!
Who shall I call? Who shall I send,
That Woman, lovely Woman, may have dominion?
Arise, O Rintrah, thee I call! & Palamabron, thee!
Go! Tell the Human race that Woman's love is Sin,   5
That an Eternal life awaits the worms of sixty winters
In an allegorical abode where existence hath never come.
Forbid all Joy, & from her childhood shall the little
    female
Spread nets in every secret path.

"My weary eyelids draw towards the evening; my bliss
    is yet but new.   10

Plate 8

Arise, O Rintrah, eldest born, second to none but Orc!
O lion Rintrah, raise thy fury from thy forests black!
Bring Palamabron, horned priest, skipping upon the
    mountains,
And silent Elynittria, the silver-bowed queen.
Rintrah, where hast thou hid thy bride?   5
Weeps she in desert shades?
Alas, my Rintrah, bring the lovely jealous Ocalythron.

"Arise, my son! Bring all thy brethren, O thou king
    of fire!
Prince of the sun, I see thee with thy innumerable race,
Thick as the summer stars;   10

But each, ramping, his golden mane shakes,
And thine eyes rejoice because of strength, O Rintrah,
    furious king."

Plate 9

Enitharmon slept,
Eighteen hundred years; Man was a Dream!
The night of Nature and their harps unstrung!
She slept in middle of her nightly song,
Eighteen hundred years, a female dream!   5

Shadows of men in fleeting bands upon the winds
Divide the heavens of Europe,
Till Albion's Angel, smitten with his own plagues,
    fled with his bands.
The cloud bears hard on Albion's shore,
Filled with immortal demons of futurity.   10
In council gather the smitten Angels of
    Albion.
The cloud bears hard upon the council house, down
    rushing
On the heads of Albion's Angels.

One hour they lay buried beneath the ruins of that hall,
But as stars rise from the salt lake, they arise in pain,   15
In troubled mists o'erclouded by the terrors of
    struggling times.

Plate 10

In thoughts perturbed, they rose from the bright ruins,
    silent following
The fiery King, who sought his ancient temple,
    serpent-formed,
That stretches out its shady length along the
    Island white.
Round him rolled his clouds of war; silent the Angel
    went,   5
Along the infinite shores of Thames to golden Verulam.

There stand the venerable porches that, high-towering,
    rear
Their oak-surrounded pillars, formed of massy stones,
    uncut
With tool, stones precious, such eternal in the
    heavens,
Of colours twelve, few known on earth, give light in
    the opaque,
Placed in the order of the stars, when the five senses
    whelmed   10
In deluge o'er the earthborn man; then turned the
    fluxile eyes
Into two stationary orbs, concentrating all things.
The ever-varying spiral ascents to the heavens of
    heavens
Were bended downward; and the nostrils' golden gates
    shut,
Turned outward, barred and petrified against the
    infinite.   15

Thought changed the infinite to a serpent, that which
    pitieth
To a devouring flame; and man fled from its face and hid
In forests of night; then all the eternal forests were
    divided
Into earths, rolling circles of space, that like an ocean
    rushed
And overwhelmed all except this finite wall of
    flesh.   20
Then was the serpent temple formed, image of infinite
Shut up in finite revolutions, and man became an Angel,
Heaven a mighty circle turning, God a tyrant crowned.

Now arrived the ancient Guardian at the southern porch
That planted thick with trees of blackest leaf, & in a
    vale   25
Obscure, enclosed the Stone of Night; oblique it stood,
    o'erhung
With purple flowers and berries red, image of that sweet
    South,

Once open to the heavens and elevated on the human neck,
Now overgrown with hair and covered with a stony
    roof;
Downward 'tis sunk beneath th'attractive North, that
    round the feet   30
A raging whirlpool draws the dizzy enquirer to his grave.

Plate 11

        Albion's Angel rose upon the Stone of Night.
        He saw Urizen on the Atlantic;
        And his brazen Book,
         That Kings & Priests had copied on Earth,
         Expanded from North to South.   5

Plate 12

And the clouds & fires pale rolled round in the
    night of Enitharmon,
Round Albion's cliffs & London's walls; still
    Enitharmon slept!
Rolling volumes of grey mist involve Churches,
    Palaces, Towers;
For Urizen unclasped his Book, feeding his soul
    with pity.
The youth of England, hid in gloom, curse the pained
    heavens; compelled   5
Into the deadly night to see the form of Albion's Angel.
Their parents brought them forth, & aged ignorance preaches,
    canting,
On a vast rock, perceived by those senses that are
    closed from thought.
Bleak, dark, abrupt, it stands & overshadows London city.
They saw his bony feet on the rock, the flesh consumed
    in flames.   10
They saw the Serpent temple lifted above, shadowing the
    Island white;
They heard the voice of Albion's Angel howling in flames
    of Orc,
Seeking the trump of the last doom.

Above the rest the howl was heard from Westminster louder
    & louder;
The Guardian of the secret codes forsook his ancient
    mansion,   15
Driven out by the flames of Orc; his furred robes & false
    locks
Adhered and grew one with his flesh, and nerves & veins
    shot through them
With dismal torment sick, hanging upon the wind;
    he fled
Groveling along Great George Street through the Park gate;
    all the soldiers
Fled from his sight; he dragged his torments to the
    wilderness.   20

Thus was the howl through Europe!
For Orc rejoiced to hear the howling shadows,
But Palamabron shot his lightnings, trenching down his
    wide back,
And Rintrah hung with all his legions in the nether deep.

Enitharmon laughed in her sleep to see (O woman's
    triumph)   25
Every house a den, every man bound; the shadows are
    filled
With spectres, and the windows wove over with curses
    of iron;
Over the doors "Thou shalt not" & over the chimneys
    "Fear" is written.
With bands of iron round their necks fastened into the
    walls
The citizens, in leaden gyves the inhabitants of
    suburbs   30
Walk heavy; soft and bent are the bones of villagers.

Between the clouds of Urizen the flames of Orc roll
    heavy
Around the limbs of Albion's Guardian, his flesh
    consuming.
Howlings & hissings, shrieks & groans, & voices of despair

Arise around him in the cloudy   35
Heavens of Albion. Furious,

Plate 13

The red-limbed Angel seized in horror and torment
The Trump of the last doom; but he could not blow the
    iron tube!
Thrice he assayed presumptuous to awake the dead to
    Judgment.
A mighty Spirit leaped from the land of Albion,
Named Newton; he seized the Trump & blowed the
    enormous blast!   5

Yellow as leaves of Autumn, the myriads of Angelic
    hosts
Fell through the wintry skies, seeking their graves,
Rattling their hollow bones in howling and lamentation.

Then Enitharmon woke, nor knew that she had slept,
And eighteen hundred years were fled   10
As if they had not been.
She called her sons & daughters
To the sports of night
Within her crystal house;
And thus her song proceeds: 15

"Arise Ethinthus! Though the earthworm call,
Let him call in vain,
Till the night of holy shadows
And human solitude is past!

Plate 14

"Ethinthus, queen of waters, how thou shinest in the sky!
My daughter, how do I rejoice! For thy children flock
    around
Like the gay fishes on the wave when the cold moon
    drinks the dew.
Ethinthus! Thou art sweet as comforts to my fainting soul,

For now thy waters warble round the feet of
    Enitharmon.   5

"Manathu-Vorcyon! I behold thee flaming in my halls,
Light of thy mother's soul! I see thy lovely eagles
    round;
Thy golden wings are my delight, & thy flames of soft
    delusion.

"Where is my luring bird of Eden, Leutha, silent love?
Leutha, the many-coloured bow delights upon thy wings!   10
Soft soul of flowers, Leutha!
Sweet smiling pestilence! I see thy blushing light!
Thy daughters, many changing,
Revolve like sweet perfumes ascending, O Leutha, silken
    queen!

"Where is the youthful Antamon, prince of the pearly
    dew?
O Antamon, why wilt thou leave thy mother Enitharmon?   15
Alone I see thee, crystal form,
Floating upon the bosomed air
With lineaments of gratified desire.
My Antamon, the seven churches of Leutha seek thy
    love.   20

"I hear the soft Oothoon in Enitharmon's tents:
Why wilt thou give up woman's secrecy, my melancholy
    child?
Between two moments bliss is ripe.
O Theotormon, robbed of joy, I see thy salt tears flow
Down the steps of my crystal house.   25

"Sotha & Thiralatha, secret dwellers of dreamful caves,
Arise and please the horrent fiend with your melodious
    songs.
Still all your thunders, golden-hoofed, & bind your horses
    black.
Orc! smile upon my children!
Smile, son of my afflictions.   30
Arise, O Orc, and give our mountains joy of thy red
    light."

She ceased, for All were forth at sport beneath the
    solemn moon,
Waking the stars of Urizen with their immortal songs,
That nature felt through all her pores the enormous
    revelry,
Till morning oped the eastern gate.   35
Then everyone fled to his station, & Enitharmon wept.

But terrible Orc, when he beheld the morning in the east,

Plate 15

Shot from the heights of Enitharmon;
And in the vineyards of red France appeared the light of
    his fury.

The sun glowed fiery red!
The furious terrors flew around
On golden chariots raging, with red wheels dropping
    with blood!   5
The Lions lash their wrathful tails!
The Tigers couch upon the prey & suck the ruddy tide,
And Enitharmon groans & cries in anguish and dismay.

Then Los arose. His head he reared in snaky thunders
    clad,
And with a cry that shook all nature to the utmost pole,   10
Called all his sons to the strife of blood.

Chap: IV: -ment
1: Los smitten with astonish-
Frightend at the hurtling bones

2: And at the surging sulphure-
-ous
Perturbed Immortal mad raging

3: In whirlwinds & pitch & nitre
Round the furious limbs of Los

4: And Los formed nets & gins
And threw the nets round about

5. He watch'd in shuddring fear
The dark changes & bound every
change
With rivets of iron & brass:

6. And these were the changes
of Urizen

Figure 4. "Page 10, The Book of Urizen." By permission of Library of Congress.

The [First] Book of Urizen   (1794)

Plate 2

PRELUDIUM TO THE [FIRST] BOOK OF URIZEN

Of the primeval Priest's assumed power,
When Eternals spurned back his religion
And gave him a place in the north,
Obscure, shadowy, void, solitary.

Eternals, I hear your call gladly.   5
Dictate swift winged words, & fear not
To unfold your dark visions of torment.

Plate 3

Chapter I

1.   Lo, a shadow of horror is risen
In Eternity! Unknown, unprolific,
Self-closed, all-repelling. What Demon
Hath formed this abominable void,
This soul-shudd'ring vacuum? Some said,   5
"It is Urizen," But unknown, abstracted,
Brooding secret, the dark power hid.

2.   Times on times he divided, & measured
Space by space in his ninefold darkness,
Unseen, unknown! Changes appeared   10
In his desolate mountains, rifted furious
By the black winds of perturbation.

3.   For he strove in battles dire,
In unseen conflictions with shapes

Bred from his forsaken wilderness   15
Of beast, bird, fish, serpent & element,
Combustion, blast, vapour and cloud.

4. Dark revolving in silent activity,
    Unseen in tormenting passions,
    An activity unknown and horrible,   20
    A self-contemplating shadow,
    In enormous labours occupied.

5. But Eternals beheld his vast forests.
    Age on ages he lay, closed, unknown,
    Brooding shut in the deep; all avoid   25
    The petrific, abominable chaos.

6. His cold horror silent, dark Urizen
    Prepared: his ten thousands of thunders,
    Ranged in gloomed array, stretch out across
    The dread world, & the rolling of wheels   30
    As of swelling seas sound in his clouds,
    In his hills of stored snows, in his mountains
    Of hail & ice; voices of terror
    Are heard like thunders of autumn
    When the cloud blazes over the harvests.   35

Chapter II

1. Earth was not, nor globes of attraction.
    The will of the Immortal expanded
    Or contracted his all flexible senses.
    Death was not, but eternal life sprung.

2. The sound of a trumpet the heavens   40
    Awoke, & vast clouds of blood rolled
    Round the dim rocks of Urizen, so named
    That solitary one in Immensity.

3. Shrill the trumpet, & myriads of Eternity

Plate 4

        Muster around the bleak deserts,
        Now filled with clouds, darkness & waters,

That rolled perplexed, lab'ring, & uttered
Words articulate, bursting in thunders
That rolled on the tops of his mountains.   5

4. "From the depths of dark solitude, From
     The eternal abode in my holiness,
     Hidden, set apart, in my stern counsels,
     Reserved for the days of futurity,
     I have sought for a joy without pain,   10
     For a solid without fluctuation.
     Why will you die, O Eternals?
     Why live in unquenchable burnings?

5. "First I fought with the fire, consumed
     Inwàrds, into a deep world within,   15
     A void immense, wild, dark & deep,
     Where nothing was, Nature's wide womb.
     And self-balanced, stretched o'er the void,
     I alone, even I, the winds merciless
     Bound; but condensing in torrents   20
     They fall & fall; strong, I repelled
     The vast waves, & arose on the waters
     A wide world of solid obstruction.

6. "Here alone I in books formed of metals
     Have written the secrets of wisdom,   25
     The secrets of dark contemplation,
     By fightings and conflicts dire
     With terrible monsters, Sin-bred,
     Which the bosoms of all inhabit,
     Seven deadly Sins of the soul.   30

7. "Lo! I unfold my darkness and on
     This rock place with strong hand the Book
     Of eternal brass, written in my solitude:

8. "Laws of peace, of love, of unity,
     Of pity, compassion, forgiveness.   35
     Let each choose one habitation,
     His ancient infinite mansion,
     One command, one joy, one desire,

One curse, one weight, one measure,
One King, one God, one Law."   40

Chapter III

1. The voice ended; they saw his pale visage
    Emerge from the darkness, his hand
    On the rock of eternity unclasping
    The Book of brass. Rage seized the strong,

2. Rage, fury, intense indignation   45
    In cataracts of fire, blood & gall,
    In whirlwinds of sulphurous smoke
    And enormous forms of energy.
    All the seven deadly sins of the soul

Plate 5

    In living creations appeared
    In the flames of eternal fury.

3. Sund'ring, dark'ning, thund'ring!
    Rent away with a terrible crash,
    Eternity rolled wide apart,   5
    Wide asunder rolling,
    Mountainous all around,
    Departing, departing, departing,
    Leaving ruinous fragments of life
    Hanging, frowning cliffs, &, all between,   10
    An ocean of voidness unfathomable.

4. The roaring fires ran o'er the heavens
    In whirlwinds & cataracts of blood
    And o'er the dark deserts of Urizen.
    Fires pour through the void on all sides   15
    On Urizen's self-begotten armies.

5. But no light from the fires: all was darkness
    In the flames of Eternal fury.

6. In Fierce anguish & quenchless flames
    To the deserts and rocks He ran raging   20
    To hide, but He could not. Combining,
    He dug mountains & hills in vast strength;
    He piled them in incessant labour,
    In howlings & pangs & fierce madness,
    Long periods in burning fires labouring,   25
    Till hoary and age-broke and aged,
    In despair and the shadows of death.

7. And a roof, vast, petrific around,
    On all sides He framed, like a womb,
    Where thousands of rivers in veins   30
    Of blood pour down the mountains to cool
    The eternal fires, beating, without
    From Eternals; & like a black globe
    Viewed by sons of Eternity, standing
    On the shore of the infinite ocean,   35
    Like a human heart struggling & beating,
    The vast world of Urizen appeared.

8. And Los, round the dark globe of Urizen,
    Kept watch for Eternals, to confine
    The obscure separation alone;   40
    For Eternity stood wide apart,

Plate 6

    As the stars are apart from the earth.

9. Los wept, howling around the dark Demon
    And cursing his lot; for in anguish
    Urizen was rent from his side;
    And a fathomless void for his feet,   5
    And intense fires for his dwelling.

10. But Urizen laid in a stony sleep
    Unorganized, rent from Eternity.

11. The Eternals said: "What is this? Death.
    Urizen is a clod of clay."   10

Plate 7

12. Los howled in a dismal stupor,
     Groaning! gnashing! groaning!
     Till the wrenching apart was healed.

13. But the wrenching of Urizen healed not.
     Cold, featureless, flesh or clay,   5
     Rifted with direful changes,
     He lay in a dreamless night.

14. Till Los roused his fires, affrighted
     At the formless unmeasurable death.

Plate 8

Chapter IV [a]

1. Los, smitten with astonishment,
    Frightened at the hurtling bones

2. And at the surging, sulphureous,
    Perturbed Immortal, mad, raging,

3. In whirlwinds & pitch & nitre   5
    Round the furious limbs of Los.

4. And Los formed nets & gins
    And threw the nets round about.

5. He watched in shudd'ring fear
    The dark changes & bound every change   10
    With rivets of iron & brass.

6. And these were the changes of Urizen:

Plate 10

Chapter IV [b]

1. Ages on ages rolled over him!
    In stony sleep ages rolled over him!

Like a dark waste stretching changeable
By earthquakes riven, belching sullen fires,
On ages rolled ages in ghastly   5
Sick torment; around him in whirlwinds
Of darkness the eternal Prophet howled,
Beating still on his rivets of iron,
Pouring solder of iron, dividing
The horrible night into watches.   10

2. And Urizen (so his eternal name)
    His prolific delight obscured more & more
    In dark secrecy hiding in surging
    Sulphureous fluid his phantasies.
    The Eternal Prophet heaved the dark bellows   15
    And turned restless the tongs and the hammer
    Incessant beat, forging chains new & new
    Numb'ring with links, hours, days & years.

3. The eternal mind, bounded, began to roll
    Eddies of wrath ceaseless round & round.   20
    And the sulphureous foam, surging thick,
    Settled, a lake, bright & shining clear,
    White as the snow on the mountains cold.

4. Forgetfulness, dumbness, necessity,
    In chains of the mind locked up,   25
    Like fetters of ice shrinking together
    Disorganized, rent from Eternity,
    Los beat on his fetters of iron
    And heated his furnaces & poured
    Iron solder and solder of brass.   30

5. Restless turned the immortal, enchained,
    Heaving dolorous, anguished, unbearable;
    Till a roof, shaggy, wild, enclosed
    In an orb his fountain of thought.

6. In a horrible dreamful slumber   35
    Like the linked infernal chain,
    A vast Spine writhed in torment

Upon the winds, shooting pained
Ribs like a bending cavern;
And bones of solidness froze   40
Over all his nerves of joy.
And a first Age passed over,
And a state of dismal woe.

Plate 11

7. From the caverns of his jointed Spine,
    Down sunk with fright a red
    Round globe, hot, burning deep,
    Deep down into the Abyss,
    Panting, Conglobing, Trembling,   5
    Shooting out ten thousand branches
    Around his solid bones.
    And a second Age passed over,
    And a state of dismal woe.

8. In harrowing fear rolling round,   10
    His nervous brain shot branches
    Round the branches of his heart.
    On high into two little orbs
    And fixed in two little caves,
    Hiding carefully from the wind,   15
    His Eyes beheld the deep.
    And a third Age passed over,
    And a state of dismal woe.

9. The pangs of hope began,
    In heavy pain striving, struggling.   20
    Two Ears in close volutions
    From beneath his orbs of vision
    Shot spiring out and petrified
    As they grew. And a fourth Age passed
    And a state of dismal woe.   25

10. In ghastly torment sick,
    Hanging upon the wind,

Plate 13

Two Nostrils bent down to the deep.
And a fifth Age passed over,
And a state of dismal woe.

11. In ghastly torment sick,
     Within his ribs bloated round,   5
     A craving Hungry Cavern,
     Thence arose his channeled Throat,
     And like a red flame a Tongue
     Of thirst & of hunger appeared.
     And a sixth Age passed over,   10
     And a state of dismal woe.

12. Enraged & stifled with torment,
     He threw his right Arm to the North,
     His left Arm to the South,
     Shooting out in anguish deep,   15
     And his Feet stamped the nether Abyss
     In trembling & howling and dismay.
     And a seventh Age passed over,
     And a state of dismal woe.

Chapter V

1. In terrors Los shrunk from his task;   20
    His great hammer fell from his hand.
    His fires beheld and, sickening,
    Hid their strong limbs in smoke.
    For with noises, ruinous, loud,
    With hurtlings & clashings & groans,   25
    The Immortal endured his chains,
    Though bound in a deadly sleep.

2. All the myriads of Eternity,
    All the wisdom & joy of life
    Roll like a sea around him,   30

Except what his little orbs
Of sight by degrees unfold.

3. And now his eternal life
Like a dream was obliterated.

4. Shudd'ring, the Eternal Prophet smote   35
With a stroke from his north to south region.
The bellows & hammer are silent now.
A nerveless silence his prophetic voice
Seized, a cold solitude & dark void.
The Eternal Prophet & Urizen closed.   40

5. Ages on ages rolled over them,
Cut off from life & light, frozen
Into horrible forms of deformity.
Los suffered his fires to decay.
Then he looked back with anxious desire,   45
But the space, undivided by existence,
Struck horror into his soul.

6. Los wept, obscured with mourning;
His bosom earthquaked with sighs.
He saw Urizen, deadly black,   50
In his chains bound, & Pity began,

7. In anguish, dividing & dividing,
For pity divides the soul
In pangs, eternity on eternity.
Life in cataracts poured down his cliffs.   55
The void shrunk the lymph into Nerves
Wand'ring wide on the bosom of night
And left a round globe of blood
Trembling upon the Void.

Plate 15

Thus the Eternal Prophet was divided
Before the death-image of Urizen;
For in changeable clouds and darkness,

In a winterly night beneath,
The Abyss of Los stretched immense;   5
And, now seen, now obscured to the eyes
Of Eternals, the visions remote
Of the dark separation appeared.
As glasses discover Worlds
In the endless Abyss of space,   10
So the expanding eyes of Immortals
Beheld the dark visions of Los
And the globe of life blood trembling.

Plate 18

8. The globe of life blood trembled,
    Branching out into roots,
    Fibrous, writhing upon the winds,
    Fibres of blood, milk and tears,
    In pangs, eternity on eternity.   5
    At length in tears & cries embodied,
    A female form, trembling and pale,
    Waves before his deathy face.

9. All Eternity shuddered at sight
    Of the first female now separate,   10
    Pale as a cloud of snow
    Waving before the face of Los.

10. Wonder, awe, fear, astonishment
    Petrify the eternal myriads
    At the first female form now separate.   15

Plate 19

They called her Pity and fled:

11. "Spread a Tent with strong curtains around them.
    Let cords & stakes bind in the Void
    That Eternals may no more behold them."

12. They began to weave curtains of darkness.   5
    They erected large pillars round the Void
    With golden hooks fastened in the pillars.
    With infinite labour the Eternals
    A woof wove and called it Science.

Chapter VI

1. But Los saw the Female & pitied.   10
   He embraced her; she wept, she refused;
   In perverse and cruel delight
   She fled from his arms, yet he followed.

2. Eternity shuddered when they saw
   Man begetting his likeness   15
   On his own divided image.

3. A time passed over; the Eternals
   Began to erect the tent,
   When Enitharmon, sick,
   Felt a Worm within her womb.   20

4. Yet helpless, it lay like a Worm
   In the trembling womb,
   To be moulded into existence.

5. All day the worm lay on her bosom;
   All night within her womb   25
   The worm lay, till it grew to a serpent
   With dolorous hissings & poisons
   Round Enitharmon's lions folding.

6. Coiled within Enitharmon's womb,
   The serpent grew, casting its scales;   30
   With sharp pangs the hissings began
   To change to a grating cry.
   Many sorrows and dismal throes,
   Many forms of fish, bird & beast
   Brought forth an Infant form   35
   Where was a worm before.

7. The Eternals, their tent finished,
    Alarmed with these gloomy visions
    When Enitharmon, groaning,
    Produced a man Child to the light.   40

8. A shriek ran through Eternity,
    And a paralytic stroke,
    At the birth of the Human shadow.

9. Delving earth in his resistless way,
    Howling, the Child with fierce flames   45
    Issued from Enitharmon.

10. The Eternals closed the tent.
    They beat down the stakes, the cords

Plate 20

    Stretched for a work of eternity.
    No more Los beheld Eternity.

11. In his hands he seized the infant.
    He bathed him in springs of sorrow.
    He gave him to Enitharmon.   5

Chapter VII

1. They named the child Orc; he grew,
    Fed with milk of Enitharmon.

2. Los awoke her; O sorrow & pain!
    A tight'ning girdle grew
    Around his bosom. In sobbings   10
    He burst the girdle in twain,
    But still another girdle
    Oppressed his bosom. In sobbings
    Again he burst it. Again
    Another girdle succeeds.   15
    The girdle was formed by day,
    By night was burst in twain,

3.   These falling down on the rock
     Into an iron Chain,
     In each other link by link locked.   20

4.   They took Orc to the top of a mountain.
     O how Enitharmon wept!
     They chained his young limbs to the rock
     With the Chain of Jealousy
     Beneath Urizen's deathful shadow.   25

5.   The dead heard the voice of the child
     And began to awake from sleep.
     All things heard the voice of the child
     And began to awake to life.

6.   And Urizen, craving with hunger,   30
     Stung with the odours of Nature,
     Explored his dens around.

7.   He formed a line & a plummet
     To divide the Abyss beneath;
     He formed a dividing rule;   35

8.   He formed scales to weigh;
     He formed massy weights;
     He formed a brazen quadrant;
     He formed golden compasses
     And began to explore the Abyss,   40
     And he planted a garden of fruits.

9.   But Los encircled Enitharmon
     With fires of Prophecy
     From the sight of Urizen & Orc.

10. And she bore an enormous race.   45

Chapter VIII

1.   Urizen explored his dens,
     Mountain, moor & wilderness,
     With a globe of fire lighting his journey,

A fearful journey, annoyed
By cruel enormities, forms   50

Plate 23

Of life on his forsaken mountains.

2.   And his world teemed vast enormities,
Fright'ning, faithless, fawning
Portions of life, similitudes
Of a foot, or a hand, or a head,   5
Or a heart, or an eye; they swam mischievous,
Dread terrors, delighting in blood.

3.   Most Urizen sickened to see
His eternal creations appear,
Sons & daughters of sorrow on mountains,   10
Weeping, wailing. First Thiriel appeared,
Astonished at his own existence,
Like a man from a cloud born; & Utha,
From the waters emerging, laments!
Grodna rent the deep earth, howling   15
Amazed! His heavens immense cracks
Like the ground parched with heat. Then Fuzon
Flamed out, first begotten, last born;
All his eternal sons in like manner,
His daughters from green herbs & cattle,   20
From monsters & worms of the pit.

4.   He, in darkness closed, viewed all his race,
And his soul sickened! He cursed
Both sons & daughters, for he saw
That no flesh nor spirit could keep   25
His iron laws one moment.

5.   For he saw that life lived upon death:

Plate 25

The Ox in the slaughterhouse moans,
The Dog at the wintry door;

And he wept, & he called it Pity,
And his tears flowed down on the winds.

6. Cold he wandered on high, over their cities   5
    In weeping & pain & woe;
    And wherever he wandered in sorrows
    Upon the aged heavens,
    A cold shadow followed behind him
    Like a spider's web, moist, cold & dim,   10
    Drawing out from his sorrowing soul
    The dungeon-like heaven, dividing
    Wherever the footsteps of Urizen
    Walked over the cities in sorrow;

7. Till a Web, dark & cold, throughout all   15
    The tormented element stretched
    From the sorrows of Urizen's soul,
    And the Web is a Female in embryo.
    None could break the Web, no wings of fire,

8. So twisted the cords & so knotted   20
    The meshes, twisted like to the human brain.

9. And all called it The Net of Religion.

Chapter IX

1. Then the Inhabitants of those Cities
    Felt their Nerves change into Marrow,
    And hardening Bones began   25
    In swift diseases and torments,
    In throbbings & shootings & grindings
    Through all the coasts, till, weakened,
    The Senses inward rushed, shrinking
    Beneath the dark net of infection,   30

2. Till the shrunken eyes, clouded over,
    Discerned not the woven hypocrisy;
    But the streaky slime in their heavens,
    Brought together by narrowing perceptions,

Appeared transparent air; for their eyes   35
Grew small like the eyes of a man,
And in reptile forms shrinking together
Of seven feet stature they remained.

3. Six days they shrunk up from existence,
    And on the seventh day they rested,   40
    And they blessed the seventh day in sick hope
    And forgot their eternal life,

4. And their thirty cities divided
    In form of a human heart.
    No more could they rise at will   45
    In the infinite void, but bound down
    To earth by their narrowing perceptions,

Plate 28

They lived a period of years,
Then left a noisome body
To the jaws of devouring darkness.

5. And their children wept & built
    Tombs in the desolate places   5
    And formed laws of prudence and called them
    The eternal laws of God.

6. And the thirty cities remained
    Surrounded by salt floods, now called
    Africa: its name was then Egypt.   10

7. The remaining sons of Urizen
    Beheld their brethren shrink together
    Beneath the Net of Urizen.
    Persuasion was in vain,
    For the ears of the inhabitants   15
    Were withered & deafened & cold;
    And their eyes could not discern
    Their brethren of other cities.

8. So Fuzon called all together,
    The remaining children of Urizen,   20
    And they left the pendulous earth.
    They called it Egypt & left it.

9. And the salt ocean rolled englobed.

The Book of Ahania (1795)

Plate 2

Chapter I

1. Fuzon, on a chariot iron-wing'd,
   On spiked flames rose; his hot visage
   Flamed furious! Sparkles his hair & beard
   Shot down his wide bosom and shoulders.
   On clouds of smoke rages his chariot,   5
   And his right hand burns red in its cloud,
   Moulding into a vast globe his wrath
   As the thunder-stone is moulded,
   Son of Urizen's silent burnings.

2. "Shall we worship this Demon of smoke,"   10
   Said Fuzon, "this abstract non-Entity,
   This cloudy God seated on waters,
   Now seen, now obscured, King of sorrow?"

3. So he spoke in a fiery flame,
   On Urizen frowning indignant,   15
   The Globe of wrath shaking on high.
   Roaring with fury, he threw
   The howling Globe; burning, it flew,
   Length'ning into a hungry beam. Swiftly

4. Opposed to the exulting flamed beam,   20
   The broad Disk of Urizen upheaved
   Across the Void many a mile.

5. It was forged in mills where the winter
   Beats incessant; ten winters the disk
   Unremitting endured the cold hammer.   25

6. But the strong arm that sent it, remembered
   The sounding beam; laughing, it tore through

That beaten mass, keeping its direction,
The cold loins of Urizen dividing.

7. Dire shrieked his invisible Lust.   30
    Deep groaned Urizen! Stretching his awful hand,
    Ahania (so name his parted soul)
    He seized on his mountains of Jealousy.
    He groaned anguished & called her Sin,
    Kissing her and weeping over her,   35
    Then hid her in darkness, in silence,
    Jealous, though she was invisible.

8. She fell down, a faint shadow wand'ring
    In chaos and circling dark Urizen,
    As the moon anguished circles the earth;   40
    Hopeless! abhorred! a death-shadow,
    Unseen, unbodied, unknown,
    The mother of Pestilence.

9. But the fiery beam of Fuzon
    Was a pillar of fire to Egypt,   45
    Five hundred years wand'ring on earth,
    Till Los seized it and beat in a mass
    With the body of the sun.

Plate 3

Chapter II

1. But the forehead of Urizen gathering
    And his eyes pale with anguish, his lips
    Blue & changing, in tears and bitter
    Contrition he prepared his Bow,

2. Formed of Ribs, that in his dark solitude,   5
    When obscured in his forests, fell monsters
    Arose. For his dire Contemplations
    Rushed down like floods from his mountains
    In torrents of mud settling thick,

    With Eggs of unnatural production;   10
    Forthwith hatching, some howled on his hills,
    Some in vales, some aloft flew in air.

3. Of these, an enormous dread Serpent,
    Scaled and poisonous horned,
    Approached Urizen even to his knees,   15
    As he sat on his dark rooted Oak.

4. With his horns he pushed furious.
    Great the conflict & great the jealousy
    In cold poisons, but Urizen smote him.

5. First he poisoned the rocks with his blood,   20
    Then polished his ribs, and his sinews
    Dried, laid them apart till winter;
    Then a Bow black prepared; on this Bow
    A poisoned rock placed in silence.
    He uttered these words to the Bow: 25

6. "O Bow of the clouds of secrecy!
    O nerve of that lust-formed monster!
    Send this rock swift, invisible, through
    The Black clouds on the bosom of Fuzon."

7. So saying, In torment of his wounds,   30
    He bent the enormous ribs slowly,
    A circle of darkness, then fixed
    The sinew in its rest, then the Rock,
    Poisonous source, placed with art, lifting difficult
    Its weighty bulk; silent the rock lay,   35

8. While Fuzon, his tigers unloosing,
    Thought Urizen slain by his wrath.
    "I am God," said he, "eldest of things!"

9. Sudden sings the rock; swift & invisible
    On Fuzon flew, entered his bosom;   40
    His beautiful visage, his tresses,
    That gave light to the mornings of heaven,

Were smitten with darkness, deformed
And outstretched on the edge of the forest.

10.   But the rock fell upon the Earth,   45
       Mount Sinai, in Arabia.

Chapter III

1.   The Globe shook; and Urizen, seated
      On black clouds, his sore wound anointed.
      The ointment flowed down on the void,
      Mixed with blood; here the snake gets her poison.   50

2.   With difficulty & great pain Urizen
      Lifted on high the dead corse;
      On his shoulders he bore it to where
      A Tree hung over the Immensity.

3.   For when Urizen shrunk away   55
      From Eternals, he sat on a rock
      Barren, a rock which himself
      From redounding fancies had petrified.
      Many tears fell on the rock,
      Many sparks of vegetation;   60
      Soon shot the pained root
      Of Mystery under his heel:
      It grew a thick tree; he wrote
      In silence his book of iron;
      Till the horrid plant, bending its boughs,   65
      Grew to roots when it felt the earth,
      And again sprung to many a tree.

4.   Amazed started Urizen when
      He beheld himself compassed round
      And high roofed over with trees.   70
      He arose, but the stems stood so thick
      He with difficulty and great pain
      Brought his Books, all but the Book

Plate 4

    Of iron, from the dismal shade.

5. The Tree still grows over the Void,
     Enrooting itself all around,
     An endless labyrinth of woe!

6. The corse of his first begotten   5
     On the accursed Tree of Mystery,
     On the topmost stem of this Tree
     Urizen nailed Fuzon's corse.

Chapter IV

1. Forth flew the arrows of pestilence
     Round the pale living Corse on the tree.   10

2. For in Urizen's slumbers of abstraction
     In the infinite ages of Eternity,
     When his Nerves of Joy melted & flowed,
     A white Lake on the dark blue air
     In perturbed pain and dismal torment   15
     Now stretching out, now swift conglobing,

3. Effluvia vapored above
     In noxious clouds—these hovered thick
     Over the disorganized Immortal,
     Till petrific pain scurfed o'er the Lakes   20
     As the bones of man, solid & dark.

4. The clouds of disease hovered wide
     Around the Immortal in torment,
     Perching around the hurtling bones,
     Disease on disease, shape on shape,   25
     Winged, screaming in blood & torment.

5. The Eternal Prophet beat on his anvils.
     Enraged in the desolate darkness,

He forged nets of iron around,   30
And Los threw them around the bones.

6.   The shapes, screaming, fluttered vain,
     Some combined into muscles & glands,
     Some organs for craving & lust.
     Most remained on the tormented void,
     Urizen's army of horrors.   35

7.   Round the pale living Corse on the Tree
     Forty years flew the arrows of pestilence.

8.   Wailing and terror and woe
     Ran through all his dismal world.
     Forty years all his sons & daughters   40
     Felt their skulls harden; then Asia
     Arose in the pendulous deep.

9.   They reptilize upon the Earth.

10. Fuzon groaned on the Tree.

Chapter V

1.   The lamenting voice of Ahania   45
     Weeping upon the void.
     And round the Tree of Fuzon,
     Distant in solitary night,
     Her voice was heard, but no form
     Had she; but her tears from clouds   50
     Eternal fell round the Tree.

2.   And the voice cried: "Ah, Urizen! Love!
     Flower of morning! I weep on the verge
     Of non-Entity; how wide the Abyss
     Between Ahania and thee!   55

3.   "I lie on the verge of the deep.
     I see thy dark clouds ascend;
     I see thy black forests and floods,
     A horrible waste to my eyes!

4. "Weeping I walk over rocks,   60
    Over dens & through valleys of death.
    Why didst thou despise Ahania,
    To cast me from thy bright presence
    Into the World of Loneness?

5. "I cannot touch his hand,   65
    Nor weep on his knees, nor hear
    His voice & bow, nor see his eyes
    And joy, nor hear his footsteps, and
    My heart leap at the lovely sound!
    I cannot kiss the place   70
    Whereon his bright feet have trod,

Plate 5

    But I wander on the rocks
    With hard necessity.

6. "Where is my golden palace?
    Where my ivory bed?
    Where the joy of my morning hour?   5
    Where the sons of eternity, singing

7. "To awake bright Urizen, my king,
    To arise to the mountain sport,
    To the bliss of eternal valleys,

8. "To awake my king in the morn,   10
    To embrace Ahania's joy,
    On the breadth of his open bosom,
    From my soft cloud of dew to fall
    In showers of life on his harvests?

9. "When he gave my happy soul   15
    To the sons of eternal joy,
    When he took the daughters of life
    Into my chambers of love,

10. "When I found babes of bliss on my beds
    And bosoms of milk in my chambers   20

Filled with eternal seed,
O, eternal births sung round Ahania
In interchange sweet of their joys.

11. "Swelled with ripeness & fat with fatness,
     Bursting on winds, my odours,   25
     My ripe figs and rich pomegranates
     In infant joy at thy feet,
     O Urizen, sported and sang.

12. "Then thou, with thy lap full of seed,
     With thy hand full of generous fire,   30
     Walked forth from the clouds of morning
     On the virgins of springing joy,
     On the human soul, to cast
     The seed of eternal science.

13. "The sweat poured down thy temples;   35
     To Ahania returned in evening,
     The moisture awoke to birth
     My mother's-joys, sleeping in bliss.

14. "But now alone over rocks, mountains,
     Cast out from thy lovely bosom,   40
     Cruel jealousy! selfish fear!
     Self-destroying, how can delight
     Renew in these chains of darkness,
     Where bones of beasts are strown
     On the bleak and snowy mountains,   45
     Where bones from the birth are buried
     Before they see the light?"

Selections from *Vala; or the Four Zoas*
(1795-?)

Page 3

The Song of the Aged Mother, which shook the heavens
  with wrath,
Hearing the march of long-resounding, strong, heroic Verse
Marshalled in order for the day of Intellectual Battle:
The heavens quake; the earth was moved & shuddered, &
  the mountains
With all their woods; the streams & valleys wailed in dismal
  fear.   5

Four Mighty Ones are in every Man.
  a Perfect Unity   John XVII c. 21 & 22 & 23 v
Cannot Exist but from the Universal
  Brotherhood of Eden,   John I c. 14 v
The Universal Man, To Whom be
  Glory Evermore, Amen.   Καὶ ἐσχήνωσέν ἡμῖν

What are the Natures of those Living Creatures
  the Heavenly Father only
Knoweth. No Individual Knoweth nor Can know in all
  Eternity.   10

Los was the fourth immortal starry one, & in the Earth
Of a bright Universe Empery attended day & night,
Days & nights of revolving joy. Urthona was his name

Page 4

In Eden; in the Auricular Nerves of Human life
Which is the Earth of Eden, he his Emanations propagated
Fairies of Albion, afterwards Gods of the Heathen.
    Daughter of Beulah, Sing
His fall into Division & his Resurrection to Unity,
His fall into the Generation of Decay and Death, & his   5
Regeneration by the Resurrection from the dead.

Begin with Tharmas, Parent power, dark'ning in the
    West:

"Lost! Lost! Lost! are my Emanations! Enion, O
    Enion,
We are become a Victim to the Living. We hide in secret.
I have hidden Jerusalem in Silent Contrition, O Pity
    Me.   10
I will build thee a Labyrinth also, O pity me. O
    Enion,
Why hast thou taken sweet Jerusalem from my inmost Soul?
Let her Lay secret in the Soft recess of darkness &
    silence.
It is not Love I bear to Enitharmon. It is Pity.
She hath taken refuge in my bosom, & I cannot cast
    her out.   15

"The Men have received their death wounds, & their
    Emanations are fled
To me for refuge, & I cannot turn them out for Pity's
    sake."

Enion said: "Thy fear has made me tremble; thy
    terrors have surrounded me.
All Love is lost. Terror succeeds, & Hatred instead
    of Love,
And stern demands of Right & Duty instead of Liberty.   20
Once thou wast to Me the loveliest son of heaven. But
    now,
Why art thou Terrible? And yet I love thee in thy
    terror till
I am almost Extinct & soon shall be a Shadow in
    Oblivion,
Unless some way can be found that I may look upon
    thee & live.
Hide me some Shadowy semblance, secret whisp'ring
    in my Ear   25
In secret of soft wings, in mazes of delusive beauty.
I have looked into the secret soul of him I loved
And in the Dark recesses found Sin & cannot return."

Trembling & pale sat Tharmas, weeping in his clouds:

"Why wilt thou Examine every little fibre of my soul,   30
Spreading them out before the Sun like Stalks of flax
    to dry?
The infant joy is beautiful, but its anatomy
Horrible, Ghast & Deadly. Naught shalt thou find in it
But Death, Despair & Everlasting brooding Melancholy.
Thou wilt go mad with horror if thou dost Examine thus   35
Every moment of my secret hours. Yea, I know
That I have sinned & that my Emanations are become
    harlots.
I am already distracted at their deeds & if I look
Upon them more, Despair will bring self-murder on my
    soul.
O Enion, thou art thyself a root growing in hell,   40
Though thus heavenly beautiful to draw me to
    destruction.

Sometimes I think thou art a flower expanding.
Sometimes I think thou art fruit breaking from its bud
In dreadful dolor & pain & I am like an atom,
A Nothing left in darkness; yet I am an identity.   45
I wish & feel & weep & groan. Ah, terrible! terrible!"

Page 5

In Eden Females sleep the winter in soft silken
    veils
Woven by their own hands to hide them in the
    darksome grave,
But Males immortal live renewed by female deaths.
    In soft
Delight they die, & they revive in spring with music
    & songs.
Enion said: "Farewell, I die. I hide from thy
    searching eyes."   5

So saying, From her bosom, weaving soft in Sinewy
    threads
A tabernacle for Jerusalem, she sat among the Rocks,

Singing her lamentation. Tharmas groaned among his
    Clouds
Weeping; then bending from his Clouds, he stooped his
    innocent head,
And, stretching out his holy hand in the vast Deep
    sublime,   10
Turned round the circle of Destiny with tears & bitter
    sighs
And said: "Return, O Wanderer, when the Day of
    Clouds is o'er."

So saying, he sunk down into the sea, a pale white corse.
In torment he sunk down & flowed among her filmy Woof,
His Spectre issuing from his feet in flames of fire.   15
In gnawing pain drawn out by her loved fingers, every
    nerve
She counted, every vein & lacteal, threading them
    among
Her woof of terror. Terrified & drinking tears of woe,
Shudd'ring, she wove nine days & nights, Sleepless;
    her food was tears.
Wond'ring she saw her woof begin to animate, & not   20
As Garments woven subservient to her hands, but having
    a will
Of its own, perverse & wayward. Enion loved & wept.
Nine days she laboured at her work & nine dark sleepless
    nights,
But on the tenth trembling morn, the Circle of
    Destiny complete,
Round rolled the Sea, Englobing in a wat'ry Globe,
    self-balanced.   25
A Frowning Continent appeared Where Enion in the Desert,
Terrified in her own Creation, viewing her woven shadow,
Sat in a dread intoxication of Repentance & Contrition.

There is from Great Eternity a mild & pleasant rest
Named Beulah, a Soft Moony Universe, feminine, lovely,   30
Pure, mild & Gentle, given in Mercy to those who sleep,
Eternally Created by the Lamb of God around,
On all sides, within & without the Universal Man.

The Daughters of Beulah follow sleepers in all their
    Dreams,
Creating Spaces lest they fall into Eternal Death.   35
The Circle of Destiny complete, they gave to it a
    Space
And named the Space Ulro & brooded over it in care
    & love.
They said: "The Spectre is in every man insane & most
Deformed. Through the three heavens descending in fury
    & fire
We meet it with our Songs & loving blandishments & give   40
To it a form of vegetation. But this Spectre of
    Tharmas
Is Eternal Death. What shall we do? O God, pity & help."
So spoke they & closed the Gate of the Tongue in
    trembling fear.

Page 6

She drew the Spectre forth from Tharmas in
    her shining loom
Of Vegetation, weeping in wayward infancy & sullen
    youth.
List'ning to her soft lamentations, soon his tongue
    began
To Lisp out words, & soon, in masculine strength
    augmenting, he
Reared up, a form of gold, & stood upon the glittering
    rock,   5
A shadowy human form, winged; & in his depths
The dazzlings as of gems shone clear, rapturous, in
    fury
Glorying in his own eyes.

From Night the Second

Urizen rose from the bright Feast like a star
    through the evening sky,

Exulting at the voice that called him from the Feast
    of envy.   10
First he beheld the body of Man, pale, cold; the horrors
    of death
Beneath his feet shot through him as he stood in the
    Human Brain,
And all its golden porches grew pale with his
    sickening light,
No more Exulting, for he saw Eternal Death beneath.
Pale, he beheld futurity; pale, he beheld the
    Abyss,   15
Where Enion, blind & age-bent, wept in direful hunger
    craving,
All rav'ning like the hungry worm, & like the silent
    grave.

Page 24

Mighty was the draught of Voidness to draw
    Existence in.

Terrific, Urizen strode above; in fear & pale dismay
He saw the indefinite space beneath, & his soul
    shrunk with horror,
His feet upon the verge of Non-Existence; his voice
    went forth.

Luvah & Vala, trembling & shrinking, beheld the great
    Work master   5
And heard his Word: "Divide, ye bands, influence by
    influence.
Build we a Bower for heaven's darling in the grisly deep.
Build we the Mundane Shell around the Rock of Albion."

The Bands of Heaven flew through the air singing &
    shouting to Urizen.
Some fixed the anvil, some the loom erected, some the
    plow   10
And harrow formed & framed the harness of silver &
    ivory,

The golden compasses, the quadrant & the rule & balance.
They erected the furnaces; they formed the anvils of gold
    beaten in mills
Where winter beats incessant, fixing them firm on
    their base.
The bellows began to blow, & the Lions of Urizen
    stood round the anvil,   15

Page 25

And the leopards, covered with skins of
    beasts, tended the roaring fires,
Sublime, distinct their lineaments divine of human
    beauty.
The tigers of wrath called the horses of instruction
    from their mangers.
They unloosed them & put on the harness of gold &
    silver & ivory.
In human forms distinct they stood round Urizen,
    prince of Light,   5
Petrifying all the Human Imagination into rock & sand.
Groans ran along Tyburn's brook and along the River
    of Oxford
Among the Druid Temples. Albion groaned on Tyburn's
    brook;
Albion gave his loud death groan. The Atlantic
    Mountains trembled.
Aloft the Moon fled with a cry, the Sun with streams
    of blood.   10
From Albion's Loins fled all Peoples and Nations of
    the Earth,
Fled with the noise of Slaughter, & the stars of heaven
    Fled.
Jerusalem came down in a dire ruin over all the Earth.
She fell cold from Lambeth's Vales in groans & Dewy
    death,
The dew of anxious souls, the death-sweat of the dying   15
In every pillared hall & arched roof of Albion's skies.

The brother & the brother bathe in blood upon the
    Severn,
The Maiden weeping by. The father & the mother with
The Maiden's father & her mother fainting over the body,
And the Young Man, the Murderer, fleeing over the
    mountains.   20

Page 34

Night passed, & Enitharmon, e'er the dawn,
    returned in bliss.   55
She sang O'er Los, reviving him to Life. His groans
    were terrible,
But thus she sang: "I seize the sphery harp; I
    strike the strings.

"At the first Sound the Golden sun arises from the Deep
And shakes his awful hair.
The Echo wakes the moon to unbind her silver locks.   60
The golden sun bears on my song,
And nine bright spheres of harmony rise round the
    fiery King.

"The joy of woman is the Death of her most best beloved,
Who dies for Love of her
In torments of fierce jealousy & pangs of adoration.   65
The Lover's night bears on my song,
And the nine Spheres rejoice beneath my powerful
    control.

"They sing unceasing to the notes of my immortal hand.
The solemn, silent moon
Reverberates the living harmony upon my limbs.   70
The birds & beasts rejoice & play,
And everyone seeks for his mate to prove his inmost
    joy.

"Furious & terrible they sport & rend the nether deeps.
The deep lifts up his rugged head

And, lost in infinite humming wings, vanishes with a
    cry.   75
The fading cry is ever dying.
The living voice is ever living in its inmost joy.

"Arise, you little glancing wings, & sing your infant
    joy.
Arise & drink your bliss.
For everything that lives is holy; for the source
    of life   80
Descends to be a weeping babe.
For the Earthworm renews the moisture of the sandy
    plain.

"Now my left hand I stretch to earth beneath
And strike the terrible string.
I wake sweet joy in dens of sorrow, & I plant a smile   85
In forests of affliction
And wake the bubbling springs of life in regions of dark
    death.

"O, I am weary. Lay thine hand upon me or I faint.
I faint beneath these beams of thine,
For thou hast touched my five senses, & they
    answered thee.
Now I am nothing, & I sink   90
And on the bed of silence sleep till thou awakest
    me."

Thus sang the Lovely one in Rapturous, delusive trance.
Los heard. Reviving, he seized her in his arms.
    Delusive hopes
Kindling, She led him into Shadows & thence fled
    outstretched   95
Upon the immense like a bright rainbow, weeping &
    smiling & fading.

Thus lived Los, driving Enion far into the deathful
    infinite
That he may also draw Ahania's spirit into her Vortex.

Ah, happy blindness! Enion sees not the terrors of the
    uncertain.
And thus wails from the dark deep; the golden heavens
    tremble.   100

Page 35

"I am made to sow the thistle for wheat,
    the nettle for a nourishing dainty.
I have planted a false oath in the earth; it has
    brought forth a poison tree.
I have chosen the serpent for a counsellor & the dog
For a schoolmaster to my children.
I have blotted out from light & living the dove &
    nightingale,   5
And I have caused the earthworm to beg from door to
    door.
I have taught the thief a secret path into the house
    of the just.
I have taught pale artifice to spread his nets upon
    the morning.
My heavens are brass, my earth is iron, my moon a clod
    of clay,
My sun a pestilence burning at noon & a vapour of
    death in night.   10

"What is the price of Experience? Do men buy it for
    a song?
Or wisdom for a dance in the street? No, it is bought
    with the price
Of all that a man hath—his house, his wife, his
    children.
Wisdom is sold in the desolate market where none come
    to buy,
And in the withered field where the farmer plows for
    bread in vain.   15

"It is an easy thing to triumph in the summer's sun
And in the vintage & to sing on the wagon loaded with
    corn.

It is an easy thing to talk of patience to the
    afflicted,
To speak the laws of prudence to the houseless
    wanderer,

Page 36

"To listen to the hungry raven's cry in wintry season
When the red blood is filled with wine & with the
    marrow of lambs.

It is an easy thing to laugh at wrathful elements,
To hear the dog howl at the wintry door, the ox in
    the slaughterhouse moan,
To see a god on every wind & a blessing on every blast,   5
To hear sounds of love in the thunderstorm that
    destroys our enemies' house,
To rejoice in the blight that covers his field & the
    sickness that cuts off his children,
While our olive & vine sing & laugh round our door,
    & our children bring fruits & flowers.

"Then the groan & the dolor are quite forgotten, & the
    slave grinding at the mill,
And the captive in chains, & the poor in the prison,
    & the soldier in the field   10
When the shattered bone hath laid him groaning among
    the happier dead.

"It is an easy thing to rejoice in the tents of
    prosperity.
Thus could I sing & thus rejoice, but it is not so
    with me."

From Night the Fifth

From Page 59

Enitharmon nursed her fiery child in the dark
    deeps,   25

Sitting in darkness. Over her Los mourned in anguish
    fierce,
Covered with gloom. The fiery boy grew, fed by the
    milk
Of Enitharmon. Los around her builded pillars of iron

Page 60

And brass & silver & gold, fourfold in dark
    prophetic fear;
For now he feared Eternal Death & uttermost
    Extinction.
He builded Golgonooza on the Lake of Udan Adan,
Upon the Limit of Translucence; then he builded Luban,
Tharmas laid the Foundations, & Los finished it in
    howling woe. 5

But when fourteen summers & winters had revolved over
Their solemn habitation, Los beheld the ruddy boy
Embracing his bright mother & beheld malignant fires
In his young eyes, discerning plain that Orc plotted
    his death.
Grief rose upon his ruddy brows; a tightening girdle
    grew 10
Around his bosom like a bloody cord. In secret sobs
He burst it, but next morn another girdle succeeds
Around his bosom. Every day he viewed the fiery youth
With silent fear, & his immortal cheeks grew deadly
    pale,
Till many a morn & many a night passed over in dire
    woe, 15
Forming a girdle in the day & bursting it at night.
The girdle was formed by day, by night was burst in
    twain,
Falling down on the rock, an iron chain link by link
    locked.

Enitharmon beheld the bloody chain of nights & days
Depending from the bosom of Los & how with griding pain 20

He went each morning to his labours with the spectre dark,
Called it the chain of Jealousy. Now Los began to speak
His woes aloud to Enitharmon, since he could not hide
His uncouth plague. He seized the boy in his immortal hands,
While Enitharmon followed him weeping in dismal woe   25
Up to the iron mountain's top, & there the Jealous chain
Fell from his bosom on the mountain. The Spectre dark
Held the fierce boy; Los nailed him down, binding around
        his limbs
The accursed chain. O how bright Enitharmon howled & cried
Over her son. Obdurate, Los bound down her loved Joy.   30

From Page 62

But when returned to Golgonooza, Los & Enitharmon
Felt all the sorrow Parents feel; They wept toward one
        another,
And Los repented that he had chained Orc upon the
        mountain,
And Enitharmon's tears prevailed. Parental love returned,
Though terrible his dread of that infernal chain. They rose
At midnight, hasting to their much beloved care.
Nine days they traveled through the Gloom of Entuthon-   15
        Benithon.
Los taking Enitharmon by the hand led her along
The dismal vales & up to the iron mountain's top where Orc
Howled in the furious wind. He thought to give to Enitharmon
Her son in tenfold joy & to compensate for her tears,
Even if his own death resulted, so much pity him pained,   20

But when they came to the dark rock & to the spectrous
        cave,
Lo, the young limbs had strucken root into the rock, & strong
Fibres had from the Chain of Jealousy inwove themselves
In a swift vegetation round the rock & round the Cave
And over the immortal limbs of the terrible fiery boy.   25
In vain they strove now to unchain, In vain with bitter
        tears

To melt the chain of Jealousy. Not Enitharmon's death
Nor the Consummation of Los could ever melt the chain,
Nor unroot the infernal fibres from their rocky bed,
Nor all Urthona's strength, nor all the power of Luvah's Bulls,   30
Though they each morning drag the unwilling Sun out of the
    deep,
Could uproot the infernal chain; for it had taken root

Page 63

Into the iron rock & grew a chain beneath the
    Earth,
Even to the Center, wrapping round the Center; & the
    limbs
Of Orc, entering with fibres, became one with him, a
    living Chain
Sustained by the Demon's life. Despair & Terror & Woe
    & Rage
Inwrap the Parents in cold clouds as they bend howling
    over   5
The terrible boy, till, fainting by his side, the
    Parents fell.

———————

From Night the Sixth

Page 67

So Urizen arose &, leaning on his Spear,
    explored his dens.
He threw his flight through the dark air to where
    a river flowed,
And, taking off his silver helmet, filled it & drank;
But when, unsatiated his thirst, he assayed to gather
    more,
Lo, three terrific women at the verge of the bright
    flood   5

Who would not suffer him to approach, but drove him
    back with storms.

Urizen knew them not & thus addressed the spirits of
    darkness:

"Who art thou, Eldest Woman, sitting in thy clouds?
What is that name written on thy forehead? What art
    thou?
And wherefore dost thou pour this water forth in sighs
    & care?"   10

She answered not, but filled her urn & poured it
    forth abroad:

"Answerest thou not?" said Urizen. "Then thou
    may'st answer me,
Thou terrible woman, clad in blue, whose strong
    attractive power
Draws all into a fountain. At the rock of thy
    attraction
With frowning brow thou sittest, mistress of these
    mighty waters."   15

She answered not, but stretched her arms & threw her
    limbs abroad.

"Or wilt thou answer, youngest Woman, clad in shining
    green?
With labour & care thou dost divide the current into
    four.
Queen of these dreadful rivers, speak & let me hear
    thy voice."

Page 68

They reared up a wall of rocks, and Urizen
    raised his spear.
They gave a scream; they knew their father; Urizen
    knew his daughters.

They shrunk into their channels, dry the rocky strand
    beneath his feet,
Hiding themselves in rocky forms from the
    Eyes of Urizen.

———————

From Page 70

For Urizen beheld the terrors of the Abyss,
    wand'ring among   5
The ruined spirits, once his children & the children
    of Luvah.
Scared at the sound of their own sigh, that seems to
    shake the immense,
They wander Moping, in their heart a Sun, a Dreary
    moon,
A Universe of fiery constellations in their brain,
An Earth of wintry woe beneath their feet, & round
    their loins   10
Waters or winds or clouds or brooding lightnings &
    pestilential plagues.
Beyond the bounds of their own self their senses cannot
    penetrate.
As the tree knows not what is outside of its leaves
    & bark
And yet it drinks the summer joy & fears the winter
    sorrow,
So in the regions of the grave none knows his dark
    compeer,   15
Though he partakes of his dire woes & mutual returns
    the pang,
The throb, the dolor, the convulsion, in soul-sickening
    woes.

The horrid shapes & sights of torment in burning
    dungeons & in
Fetters of red-hot iron, some with crowns of serpents
    & some

With monsters girding round their bosoms, Some lying
    on beds of sulphur   20
On racks & wheels; he beheld women marching o'er
    burning wastes
Of Sand in bands of hundreds & of fifties & of
    thousands, strucken with
Lightnings, which blazed after them upon their
    shoulders in their march
In successive volleys with loud thunders; swift flew
    the King of Light
Over the burning deserts. Then the deserts passed,
    involved in clouds   25
Of smoke, with myriads moping in the stifling
    vapours. Swift
Flew the King though flagged his powers, lab'ring
    till over rocks
And Mountains, faint, weary, he wandered where
    multitudes were shut
Up in the solid mountains & in rocks which heaved with
    their torments.
Then came he among fiery cities & castles built
    of burning steel.   30
Then he beheld the forms of tigers & of Lions,
    dishumanized men.
Many in serpents & in worms, stretched out, enormous
    length,
Over the sullen mould & slimy tracks, obstruct his way,
Drawn out from deep to deep, woven by ribbed
And scaled monsters or armed in iron shell or shell
    of brass   35
Or gold, a glittering torment, shining & hissing in
    eternal pain,
Some columns of fire or of water, sometimes stretched
    out in height,
Sometimes in length, sometimes englobing, wandering
    in vain seeking for ease.
His voice to them was but an inarticulate thunder, for
    their Ears

Were heavy & dull & their eyes & nostrils closed up.   40
Oft he stood by a howling victim, Questioning in words
Soothing or Furious; no one answered; every one,
    wrapped up
In his own sorrow, howled regardless of his words;
    nor voice
Of sweet response could he obtain, though oft assayed
    with tears.
He knew they were his Children, ruined in his ruined
    world.   45

Page 71

Oft would he stand & question a fierce scorpion
    glowing with gold.
In vain terror heard not. Then a lion he would
    Seize
By the fierce mane, staying his howling course; in vain
    the voice
Of Urizen, in vain the Eloquent tongue. A Rock, a
    Cloud, a Mountain
Were now not Vocal as in Climes of happy Eternity,   5
Where the lamb replies to the infant voice & the lion
    to the man of years,
Giving them sweet instructions, Where the Cloud, the
    River & the Field
Talk with the husbandman & shepherd. But these attacked
    him sore,
Seizing upon his feet & rending the Sinews, that in
    Caves
He hid to recure his obstructed powers with rest &
    oblivion.   10

Page 70

Here he had time enough to repent of his
    rashly threatened curse.

He saw them cursed beyond his Curse; his soul melted
    with fear.

Page 71

He could not take their fetters off, for they
    grew from the soul.
Nor could he quench the fires, for they flamed out
    from the heart.
Nor could he calm the Elements, because himself was
    Subject.
So he threw his flight in terror & pain & in
    repentant tears.

From Page 72

Oft would he sit in a dark rift & regulate
    his books,
Or sleep such sleep as spirits eternal, wearied in his
    dark
Tearful & sorrowful state, then rise, look out & ponder
His dismal voyage, eyeing the next sphere though far
    remote,
Then darting into the Abyss of night his venturous limbs   10
Through lightnings, thunders, earthquakes & concussions,
    fires & floods,
Stemming his downward fall, labouring up against
    futurity,
Creating many a Vortex, fixing many a Science in the
    deep,
And thence throwing his venturous limbs into the Vast
    unknown,
Swift, Swift from Chaos to chaos, from void to void,
    a road immense.
    15
For when he came to where a Vortex ceased to operate,
Nor down nor up remained; then if he turned & looked
    back

From whence he came, 'twas upward all; & if he turned
    and viewed
The unpassed void, upward was still his mighty
    wand'ring,
The midst between, an Equilibrium grey of air serene   20
Where he might live in peace & where his life might
    meet repose.
But Urizen said: "Can I not leave this world of Cumbrous
    wheels,
Circle o'er Circle, nor on high attain a void
Where, self-sustaining, I may view all things beneath
    my feet,
Or sinking through these Elemental wonders, swift to
    fall,   25
I thought perhaps to find an End, a world beneath of
    voidness,
Whence I might travel round the outside of this Dark
    confusion?
When I bend downward, bending my head downward into the
    deep,
'Tis upward all which way soever I my course begin;
But when A Vortex formed on high by labour & sorrow
    & care   30
And weariness begins on all my limbs, then sleep
    revives
My wearied spirits waking, then 'tis downward all
    which way
Soever I my spirits turn; no end I find of all.
O, what a world is here, unlike those climes of bliss
Where my sons gathered round my knees. O, thou poor
    ruined world!   35
Thou horrible ruin! Once, like me, thou wast all
    glorious.
And now, like me, partaking desolate thy master's lot,
Art thou, O ruin, the once glorious heaven? Are these
    thy rocks
Where joy sang in the trees, & pleasure sported on the
    rivers,

Page 73

And laughter sat beneath the Oaks, & innocence
    sported round
Upon the green plains, & sweet friendship met in palaces,
And books & instruments of song & pictures of delight?
Where are they, whelmed beneath these ruins in horrible
    destruction?
And if Eternal falling, I repose on the dark bosom   5
Of winds & waters or thence fall into a Void where air
Is not, down falling through immensity ever & ever,
I lose my powers, weakened every revolution, till a
    death
Shuts up my powers, then a seed in the vast womb
    of darkness,
I dwell in dim oblivion. Brooding over me, the Enormous
    worlds   10
Reorganize me, shooting forth in bones & flesh & blood.
I am regenerated to fall or rise at will or to remain
A labourer of ages, a dire discontent, a living woe,
Wand'ring in vain. Here will I fix my foot & here
    rebuild;
Here Mountains of Brass promise much riches in their
    dreadful bosoms."   15

So he began to dig, form of gold, silver & iron
And brass vast instruments to measure out the immense
    & fix
The whole into another world better suited to obey
His will, where none should dare oppose his will,
    himself being King
Of All, & all futurity be bound in his vast chain.   20

And the Sciences were fixed, & the Vortexes began to
    operate
On all the sons of men, & every human soul, terrified
At the turning wheels of heaven, shrunk away inward,
    with'ring away.

———

From Night the Seventh (A)

From Page 77

But Urizen silent descended to the Caves of
    Orc & saw   5
A Caverned Universe of flaming fire. The horses of
    Urizen,
Here bound to fiery mangers, furious dash their golden
    hooves,
Striking fierce sparkles from their brazen fetters.
    Fierce his lions
Howl in the burning dens; his tigers roam in the
    redounding smoke,
In forests of affliction; the adamantine scales of
    justice   10
Consuming in the raging lamps of mercy, poured in rivers.
The holy oil rages through all the caverned rocks.
    Fierce flames
Dance on the rivers & the rocks, howling & drunk
    with fury.
The plow of ages & the golden harrow wade through
    fields
Of gory blood; the immortal seed is nourished for the
    slaughter.   15
The bulls of Luvah, breathing fire, bellow on burning
    pastures
Round howling Orc, whose awful limbs cast forth red
    smoke & fire,
That Urizen approached not near, but took his seat on
    a rock
And ranged his books around him, brooding Envious
    over Orc.

Howling & rending his dark caves, the awful Demon lay;   20
Pulse after pulse beat on his fetters; pulse after
    pulse his spirit

Darted & darted higher & higher to the shrine of
    Enitharmon;
As when the thunder folds himself in thickest clouds,
The wat'ry nations couch & hide in the profoundest deeps,
Then bursting from his troubled head with terrible
    visages & flaming hair,   25
His swift-wing'd daughters sweep across the vast black
    ocean.
Los felt the Envy in his limbs like to a blighted tree.

Page 78

For Urizen, fixed in Envy, sat brooding &
    covered with snow.
His book of iron on his knees, he traced the dreadful
    letters
While his snows fell & his storms beat to cool the
    flames of Orc
Age after Age, till underneath his heel a deadly root
Struck through the rock, the root of Mystery
    accursed, shooting up   5
Branches into the heaven of Los. They, pipe-formed,
    bending down,
Take root again wherever they touch again, branching
    forth
In intricate labyrinths, o'erspreading many a grizzly
    deep.
Amazed started Urizen when he found himself compassed
    round
And high roofed over with trees. He arose, but the
    stems   10
Stood so thick he with difficulty & great pain
    brought
His books out of the dismal shade, all but the book
    of iron.
Again he took his seat & ranged his Books around
On a rock of iron frowning over the foaming fires of
    Orc.

And Urizen hung over Orc & viewed his terrible wrath,   15
Sitting upon an iron Crag; at length his words broke
    forth:
"Image of dread, whence art thou? Whence is this most
    woeful place?
Whence these fierce fires, but from thyself? No other
    living thing
In all this Chasm I behold. No other living thing.
Dare thy most terrible wrath abide? Bound here to waste
    in pain   20
Thy vital substance in these fires that issue new &
    new
Around thee, sometimes like a flood & sometimes like
    a rock
Of living pangs, thy horrible bed glowing with
    ceaseless fires
Beneath thee & around. Above a Shower of fire now beats,
Moulded to globes & arrowy wedges, rending thy bleeding
    limbs;   25
And now a whirling pillar of burning sands to
    overwhelm thee
Steeping thy wounds in salts infernal & in bitter
    anguish;
And now a rock moves on the surface of this lake of
    fire
To bear thee down beneath the waves in stifling
    despair.
Pity for thee moved me to break my dark & long repose   30
And to reveal myself before thee in a form of wisdom.
Yet thou dost laugh at all these tortures & this
    horrible place.
Yet throw thy limbs these fires abroad that back
    return upon thee,
While thou reposest, throwing rage on rage, feeding
    thyself
With visions of sweet bliss far other than this
    burning clime.   35

Sure thou art bathed in rivers of delight on verdant
    fields,
Walking in joy in bright Expanses, sleeping on bright
    clouds
With visions of delight so lovely that they urge thy
    rage
Tenfold with fierce desire to rend thy chain & howl in
    fury
And dim oblivion of all woe & desperate repose.   40
Or is thy joy founded on torment which others bear for
    thee?"

Orc answered: "Curse thy hoary brows. What dost thou
    in this deep?
Thy Pity I contemn. Scatter thy snows elsewhere.

Page 79

I rage in the deep, for Lo, my feet & hands
    are nailed to the burning rock,
Yet my fierce fires are better than thy snows.
    Shudd'ring thou sittest.
Thou are not chained. Why should'st thou sit, cold
    grovelling demon of woe,
In tortures of dire coldness? Now a Lake of waters deep
Sweeps over thee, freezing to solid. Still thou
    sit'st closed up   5
In that transparent rock as if in joy of thy bright
    prison,
Till overburdened with its own weight, drawn out
    through immensity
With a crash breaking across, the horrible mass comes
    down
Thund'ring, & hail & frozen iron hailed from the Element
Rends thy white hair. Yet thou dost, fixed, obdurate,
    brooding, sit   10
Writing thy books. Anon a cloud filled with a waste
    of snows

Covers thee, still obdurate, still resolved & writing
    still.
Though rocks roll o'er thee, though floods pour, though
    winds black as the Sea
Cut thee in gashes, though the blood pours down around
    thy ankles
Freezing thy feet to the hard rock, still thy pen
    obdurate   15
Traces the wonders of Futurity in horrible fear of the
    future.
I rage furious in the deep, for, lo, my feet & hands
    are nailed
To the hard rock, or thou shouldst feel my enmity &
    hate
In all the diseases of man falling upon thy grey,
    accursed front."

Urizen answered: "Read my books, explore my
    Constellations,   20
Inquire of my Sons, & they shall teach thee how to War.
Inquire of my Daughters, who accursed in the dark depths
Knead bread of Sorrow by my stern command, for I am God
Of all this dreadful ruin. Rise, O daughters, at my
    Stern command."

Rending the Rocks, Eleth & Uveth rose, & Ona rose,   25
Terrific with their iron vessels, driving them across
In the dim air. They took the book of iron & placed
    above
On clouds of death & sang their songs, Kneading the
    bread of Orc.
Orc listened to the song, compelled, hung'ring on the
    cold wind
That swagged heavy with the accursed dough. The hoar
    frost raged   30
Through Ona's sieve. The torrent rain poured from the
    iron pail
Of Eleth, & the icy hands of Uveth kneaded the bread.
The heavens bow with terror underneath their iron hands,

Singing at their dire work the words of Urizen's book
    of iron,
While the enormous scrolls rolled dreadful in the
    heavens above.   35
And still the burden of their song in tears was poured
    forth:
"The bread is Kneaded. Let us rest, O cruel father
    of children."

But Urizen remitted not their labours upon his rock.

Page 80

And Urizen Read in his book of brass in sounding tones:

"Listen, O Daughters, to my voice. Listen to the Words
    of Wisdom.
So shall ye govern over all. Let Moral Duty tune your
    tongue,
But be your hearts harder than the nether millstone,
To bring the shadow of Enitharmon beneath our wondrous
    tree,   5
That Los may Evaporate like smoke & be no more.
Draw down Enitharmon to the Spectre of Urthona,
And let him have dominion over Los, the terrible shade.
Compel the poor to live upon a Crust of bread by soft
    mild arts.
Smile when they frown, frown when they smile, & when
    a man looks pale   10
With labour & abstinence, say he looks healthy & happy,
And when his children sicken, let them die. There are
    enough
Born, even too many, & our Earth will be overrun
Without these arts. If you would make the poor live
    with temper,
With pomp give every crust of bread you give; with
    gracious cunning   15
Magnify small gifts; reduce the man to want a gift,
    & then give with pomp.

Say he smiles if you hear him sigh. If pale, say he is
    ruddy.
Preach temperance. Say he is overgorged & drowns his wit
In strong drink, though you know that bread & water
    are all
He can afford. Flatter his wife, pity his children,
    till we can   20
Reduce all to our will, as spaniels are taught with art.
Lo, how the heart & brain are formed in the breeding
    womb
Of Enitharmon, how it buds with life & forms the bones,
The little heart, the liver & the red blood in its
    labyrinths.
By gratified desire, by strong devouring appetite,
    she fills   25
Los with ambitious fury that his race shall all devour."
Then Orc cried: "Curse thy Cold hypocrisy.
    Already round thy Tree
In scales that shine with gold & rubies thou beginnest
    to weaken
My divided Spirit. Like a worm I rise in peace, unbound
From wrath. Now When I rage, my fetters bind me more.   30
O torment! O torment! A Worm compelled. Am I a worm?
Is it in strong deceit that man is born? In strong deceit
Thou dost restrain my fury, that the worm may fold
    the tree.
Avaunt, Cold hypocrite. I am chained or thou couldst
    not use me thus.
The Man shall rage bound with this Chain, the worm in
    silence creep.   35
Thou wilt not cease from rage, Grey Demon. Silence
    all thy storms;
Give me example of thy mildness, King of furious
    hailstorms.
Art thou the cold attractive power that holds me in
    this chain?
I well remember how I stole thy light & it became fire

Consuming. Thou Know'st me now, O Urizen, Prince of
    Light,   40
And I know thee. Is this the triumph, this the Godlike
    State
That lies beyond the bounds of Science in the Grey
    obscure?"

Terrified, Urizen heard Orc, now certain that he was
    Luvah;
And Orc began to Organize a Serpent body,
Despising Urizen's light & turning it into flaming
    fire,   45
Receiving as a poisoned Cup Receives the heavenly wine
And turning affection into fury & thought into
    abstraction,
A Self-consuming dark devourer rising into the heavens.

Urizen, envious, brooding, sat & saw the secret terror
Flame high in pride & laugh to scorn the source of
    his deceit,   50
Nor knew the source of his own, but thought himself
    the Sole author

Page 81

Of all his wandering Experiments in the horrible
    Abyss.
He knew that weakness stretches out in breadth &
    length; he knew
That wisdom reaches high & deep; & therefore he made
    Orc,
In Serpent form compelled, stretch out & up the
    mysterious tree.
He suffered him to Climb, that he might draw all
    human forms   5
Into submission to his will, nor knew the dread result.

―――――――

From Night the Eighth
Page 101

When Urizen saw the Lamb of God clothed in
    Luvah's robes,
Perplexed & terrified he Stood, though well he knew
    that Orc
Was Luvah, But he now beheld a new Luvah, or Orc,
Who assumed Luvah's form & stood before him opposite.
But he saw Orc a Serpent form augmenting times on times   5
In the fierce battle, & he saw the Lamb of God & the
    World of Los
Surrounded by his dark machines, for Orc augmented
    swift
In fury, a Serpent wondrous among the Constellations
    of Urizen.
A crest of fire rose on his forehead, red as the
    carbuncle,
Beneath down to his eyelids scales of pearl, then gold
    & silver   10
Immingled with the ruby overspread his Visage. Down
His furious neck, writhing contortive in dire budding
    pains,
The scaly armour shot out. Stubborn down his back &
    bosom
The Emerald, Onyx, Sapphire, jasper, beryl, amethyst
Strove in terrific emulation which should gain a place   15
Upon the mighty Fiend, the fruit of the mysterious tree
Kneaded in Uveth's kneading trough. Still Orc
    devoured the food
In raging hunger. Still the pestilential food in gems
    & gold
Exuded round his awful limbs, Stretching to serpent
    length
His human bulk, While the dark shadowy female,
    brooding over,   20

Measured his food morning & evening in cups & baskets
    of iron.

With tears of sorrow incessant she laboured the food
    of Orc,
Compelled by the iron-hearted sisters, Daughters of
    Urizen,
Gath'ring the fruit of that mysterious tree. Circling
    its root,
She spread herself through all the branches in the power
    of Orc.   25

Thus Urizen in self-deceit his warlike preparations
    fabricated,
And when all things were finished, sudden waved among
    the Stars,
His hurtling hand gave the dire signal: thunderous
    Clarions blow,
And all the hollow deep rebellowed with the wonderous
    war.
But Urizen his mighty rage let loose in the mid deep.   30
Sparkles of Dire affliction issued round his frozen
    limbs.
Horrible hooks & nets he formed, twisting the cords
    of iron
And brass, & molten metals cast in hollow globes, &
    bored
Tubes in petrific steel, & rammed combustibles, &
    wheels
And chains & pulleys, fabricated all round the heavens
    of Los,   35
Communing with the Serpent of Orc in dark dissimulation,
And with the Synagogue of Satan in dark Sanhedrim,
To undermine the World of Los & tear bright Enitharmon
To the four winds, hopeless of future. All futurity
Seems teeming with Endless destruction never to be
    expelled.   40
Desperate remorse swallows the present in a
    quenchless rage.

Terrified & astonished, Urizen beheld the battle take
    a form
Which he intended not, a Shadowy hermaphrodite,
    black & opaque.
The Soldiers named it Satan, but he was yet unformed
    & vast,
Hermaphroditic it at length became, hiding the Male   45
Within as in a Tabernacle, Abominable, Deadly.

The battle howls; the terrors fired rage in the work
    of death.
Enormous Works Los Contemplated, inspired by the
    holy Spirit.
Los builds the Walls of Golgonooza against the stirring
    battle,
That only through the Gates of Death they can enter
    to Enitharmon.   50
Raging they take the human visage & the human form,
Feeling the hand of Los in Golgonooza & the force
Attractive of his hammers beating & the Silver looms
Of Enitharmon singing lulling cadences on the wind.
They humanize in the fierce battle, where in direful
    pain   55
Troop by troop the bestial droves rend one another,
    sounding loud
The instruments of sound; & troop by troop, in human
    forms, they urge

Page 102

The dire confusion till the battle faints;
    those that remain
Return in pangs & horrible convulsions to their
    bestial state;
For the monsters of the Elements, Lions or Tigers or
    Wolves,
Sound loud the howling music Inspired by Los &
    Enitharmon, Sounding loud. Terrific men

They seem to one another, laughing terrible among the
    banners,   5
And when the revolution of their day of battles over,
Relapsing in dire torment, they return to forms of woe,
To moping visages, returning inanimate though furious,
No more erect though strong, drawn out in length, they
    ravin
For senseless gratification; & their visages thrust
    forth   10
Flatten above & beneath & stretch out into bestial
    length.
Weakened, they stretch beyond their power in dire droves
    till war begins
Or Secret religion in their temples before secret
    shrines.

And Urizen gave life & sense by his immortal power
To all his Engines of deceit, that linked chains might
    run   15
Through ranks of war spontaneous, & that hooks & boring
    screws
Might act according to their forms by innate cruelty.
He formed also harsh instruments of sound,
To grate the soul into destruction or to inflame with
    fury
The spirits of life, to pervert all the faculties
    of sense   20
Into their own destruction, if perhaps he might avert
His own despair even at the cost of everything that
    breathes.

From Page 104

The war roared round Jerusalem's Gates. It
    took a hideous form
Seen in the aggregate: a Vast Hermaphroditic form   20
Heaved like an Earthquake lab'ring with convulsive
    groans

Intolerable. At length an awful wonder burst
From the Hermaphroditic bosom. Satan he was named,
Sons of Perdition terrible, his form dishumanized,
    monstrous,
A male without a female counterpart, a howling fiend,   25
Forlorn of Eden & repugnant to the forms of life,
Yet hiding the shadowy female Vala as in an ark &
    Curtains,
Abhorred, accursed, ever dying an Eternal death,
Being multitudes of tyrant Men in union blasphemous
Against the divine image, Congregated Assemblies of
    wicked men.   30

Los said to Enitharmon: "Pitying, I saw."
Pitying, the Lamb of God Descended through Jerusalem's
    gates
To put off Mystery time after time, & as a Man
Is born on Earth, so was he born of Fair Jerusalem
In mystery's woven mantle & in the Robes of Luvah.   35

He stood in fair Jerusalem to awake up into Eden
The fallen Man, but first to Give his vegetated body
To be cut off & separated, that the Spiritual body
    may be Revealed.

Page 105

The Lamb of God stood before Satan opposite
In Entuthon Benithon, in the shadows of torments & woe,
Upon the heights of Amalek. Taking refuge in his arms,
The Victims fled from punishment, for all his words
    were peace.

Urizen called together the Synagogue of Satan in dire
    Sanhedrim   5
To Judge the Lamb of God to Death as a murderer &
    robber.
As it is written, he was numbered among the transgressors.

Cold, dark, opaque, the Assembly met twelvefold in
    Amalek.
Twelve rocky unshaped forms, terrific forms of torture
    & woe,
Such seemed the Synagogue to distant view, amidst
    them beamed   10
A False Feminine Counterpart of Lovely Delusive
    Beauty,
Dividing & Uniting at will in the Cruelties of
    Holiness,
Vala drawn down into a Vegetated body, now triumphant.
The Synagogue of Satan Clothed her with Scarlet robes
    & Gems
And on her forehead was her name written in blood:
    "Mystery."   15
When viewed remote She is One; when viewed near she
    divides
To multitude, as it is in Eden, so permitted because
It was the best possible in the State called Satan
    to Save
From Death Eternal & to put off Satan Eternally.
The Synagogue Created her from Fruit of Urizen's tree   20
By devilish arts abominable, unlawful, unutterable,
Perpetually vegetating in detestable births
Of Female forms, beautiful through poisons hidden
    in secret,
Which give a tincture to false beauty. There was
    hidden within
The bosom of Satan The false Female as in an ark & veil,   25
Which Christ must rend & her reveal. Her Daughters
    are Called
Tirzah. She is named Rahab. Their various divisions
    are called
The Daughters of Amalek, Canaan & Moab, binding on the
    Stones
Their victims & with knives tormenting them, singing
    with tears
Over their victims.   30

―――――――

Page 106

Thus was the Lamb of God condemned to Death.
They nailed him upon the tree of Mystery, weeping over
    him
And then mocking & then worshipping, calling
    him Lord & King.
Sometimes as twelve daughters lovely & sometimes as
    five
They stood in beaming beauty, & sometimes as one, even
    Rahab,   5
Who is Mystery, Babylon the Great, the Mother of Harlots.

Jerusalem saw the Body dead upon the Cross. She fled
    away
Saying, "Is this Eternal Death? Where shall I hide
    from Death?
Pity me, Los; pity me, Urizen, & let us build
A Sepulcher & worship Death in fear while yet we
    live.   10
Death! God of All, from whom we rise, to whom we all
    return.
And Let all Nations of the Earth worship at the
    Sepulcher
With Gifts & Spices, with lamps rich embossed, jewels
    & gold."

―――――――

From Page 115

Rahab burning with pride & revenge departed
    from Los.
Los dropped a tear at her departure, but he wiped it
    away in hope.

She went to Urizen in pride. The Prince of Light beheld
Revealed before the face of heaven his secret holiness.

Page 106

Darkness & sorrow covered all flesh. Eternity
    was darkened.

Urizen sitting in his web of deceitful Religion
Felt the female death, a dull & numbing stupor such
    as ne'er
Before assaulted the bright human form. He felt his
    pores   20
Drink in the deadly dull delusion. Horrors of Eternal
    death
Shot through him. Urizen sat stonied upon his rock.
Forgetful of his own Laws, pitying, he began to Embrace
The Shadowy Female. Since life cannot be quenched, Life
    exuded.
His eyes shot outwards. Then, his breathing nostrils
    drawn forth,   25
Scales covered over a cold forehead, & a neck
    outstretched
Into the deep to seize the shadow; scales his neck &
    bosom
Covered & scales his hands & feet upon his belly falling
Outstretched through the immense, his mouth wide opening,
    tongueless,
His teeth a triple row. He strove to seize the shadow
    in vain,   30
And his immense tail lashed the Abyss. His human form
    a Stone,
A form of Senseless Stone, remained in terrors on the
    rock,
Abominable to the eyes of mortals who explore his books.
His wisdom still remained, & all his memory stored with
    woe.

And still his stony form remained in the Abyss
    immense,   35
Like the pale visage in its sheet of lead that cannot
    follow.
Incessant stern disdain his scaly form gnaws inwardly,
With deep repentance for the loss of that fair form of
    Man.
With Envy he saw Los, with Envy Tharmas & the Spectre,
With Envy, & in vain he swam around his stony form.   40

No longer now Erect, the King of Light, outstretched
    in fury,
Lashes his tail in the wild deep. His Eyelids, like the
    Sun
Arising in his pride, enlighten all the Grisly deeps;
His scales transparent give forth light like windows
    of the morning.
His neck flames with wrath & majesty; he lashes the
    Abyss,   45
Beating the Deserts & the rocks. The deserts feel his
    power.
They shake their slumbers off. They wave in awful fear,
Calling the Lion & the Tiger, the horse & the wild Stag,

Page 107

The Elephant, the wolf, the Bear, the Lamia, the
    Satyr.
His Eyelids give their light around; his folding tail
    aspires
Among the stars. The Earth & all the Abysses feel his
    fury.

———————

Page 111

Rahab triumphs over all. She took Jerusalem
Captive, A Willing Captive, by delusive arts impelled

To worship Urizen's Dragon form, to offer her own
    Children
Upon the bloody Altar. John Saw these things Revealed
    in Heaven
On Patmos Isle & heard the Souls cry out to be
    delivered.   5
He saw the Harlot of the Kings of Earth & saw her Cup
Of fornication, food of Orc & Satan, pressed from the
    fruit of Mystery.
But when she saw the form of Ahania weeping on the
    Void
And heard Enion's voice sound from the caverns of the
    Grave,
No more spirit remained in her. She secretly left the
    Synagogue of Satan.   10
She communed with Orc in secret. She hid him with the
    flax
That Enitharmon had numbered away from the Heavens.
She gathered it together to consume her Harlot Robes.
In bitterest Contrition, sometimes Self-condemning,
    repentant,
And Sometimes kissing her Robes & Jewels & weeping over
    them,   15
Sometimes returning to the Synagogue of Satan in Pride,
And Sometimes weeping before Orc in humility &
    trembling,
The Synagogue of Satan, therefore uniting against
    Mystery,
Satan divided against Satan, resolved in open Sanhedrim
To burn Mystery with fire & form another from her
    ashes;   20
For God put it into their heart to fulfill all his will.

The Ashes of Mystery began to animate. They called it
    Deism
And Natural religion as of old. So now anew began
Babylon again in Infancy, Called Natural Religion.

Night the Ninth

Being The Last Judgment

Page 117

And Los & Enitharmon builded Jerusalem, weeping
Over the Sepulcher & over the Crucified body,
Which to their Phantom Eyes appeared still in the
　　　Sepulcher.
But Jesus stood beside them in the Spirit, Separating
Their Spirit from their body. Terrified at
　　　Non-Existence,　　　　　　　　　　　　　　　　5
For such they deemed the death of the body. Los, his
　　　vegetable hands
Outstretched, his right hand branching out in fibrous
　　　Strength,
Seized the Sun. His left hand like dark roots covered
　　　the Moon
And tore them down, cracking the heavens across from
　　　immense to immense.
Then fell the fires of Eternity with loud & shrill　　　10
Sound of Loud Trumpet thundering along from heaven to
　　　heaven,
A mighty sound articulate: "Awake, ye dead, & come
To Judgment from the four winds! Awake & Come away!"
Folding like scrolls of the Enormous volume of Heaven
　　　& Earth,
With thunderous noise & dreadful shakings rocking to &
　　　fro,　　　　　　　　　　　　　　　　　　　　15
The heavens are shaken & the Earth removed from its
　　　place,
The foundations of the Eternal hills discovered.
The thrones of Kings are shaken; they have lost their
　　　robes & crowns.
The poor smite their oppressors; they awake up to the
　　　harvest.

The naked warriors rush together down to the seashore,   20
Trembling before the multitudes of slaves now set at
    liberty.
They are become like wintry flocks, like forests stripped
    of leaves.
The oppressed pursue like the wind; there is no room
    for escape.
The Spectre of Enitharmon, let loose on the troubled
    deep,
Wailed shrill in the confusion, & the Spectre of
    Urthona   25

Page 118

Received her in the dark'ning South. Their bodies lost,
    they stood
Trembling & weak, a faint embrace, a fierce desire, as
    when
Two shadows mingle on a wall. They wail, & shadowy tears
Fell down, & shadowy forms of joy mixed with despair &
    grief,
Their bodies buried in the ruins of the Universe,   5
Mingled with the confusion. Who shall call them from
    the Grave?

Rahab & Tirzah wail aloud in the wild flames; they give
    up themselves to Consummation.
The books of Urizen unroll with dreadful noise; the
    folding Serpent
Of Orc began to Consume in fierce raving fire; his
    fierce flames
Issued on all sides, gath'ring strength in animating
    volumes,   10
Roaming abroad on all the winds, raging intense,
    reddening
Into resistless pillars of fire, rolling round & round,
    gathering

Strength from the Earths consumed & heavens & all hidden
 abysses,
Wherever the Eagle has Explored, or Lion or Tiger trod,
Or where the Comets of the night or stars of asterial
 day   15
Have shot their arrows or long-beamed spears in wrath
 & fury.

And all the while the trumpet sounds. From the clotted
 gore & from the hollow den
Start forth the trembling millions into flames of mental
 fire,
Bathing their limbs in the bright visions of Eternity.

Then like the doves from pillars of Smoke the trembling
 families   20
Of women & children throughout every nation under heaven
Cling round the men in bands of twenties & of fifties,
 pale
As snow that falls around a leafless tree upon the green.
Their oppressors are fallen; they have Stricken them;
 they awake to life.
Yet pale the just man stands erect & looking up to
 heaven.   25
Trembling & strucken by the Universal stroke, the trees
 unroot;
The rocks groan horrible & run about. The mountains &
Their rivers cry with a dismal cry. The cattle gather
 together.
Lowing they kneel before the heavens. The wild beasts
 of the forests
Tremble. The Lion, shuddering, asks the Leopard:
 "Feelest thou   30
The dread I feel, unknown before? My voice refuses to
 roar,
And in weak moans I speak to thee. This night,
Before the morning's dawn, the Eagle called the Vulture;
The Raven called the hawk. I heard them from my forests
 black,

Saying, 'Let us go up far, for soon I smell upon the
  wind   35
A terror coming from the South.' The Eagle & Hawk fled
  away
At dawn; & E'er the sun arose, the raven & Vulture
  followed.
Let us flee also to the North." They fled. The Sons of
  Men
Saw them depart in dismal droves. The trumpet sounded
  loud,
And all the Sons of Eternity Descended into Beulah.   40

Page 119

In the fierce flames the limbs of Mystery lay
  consuming with howling
And deep despair. Rattling go up the flames around the
  Synagogue
Of Satan. Loud the Serpent Orc raged through his
  twenty-Seven
Folds. The tree of Mystery went up in folding flames.
Blood issued out in mighty volumes, pouring in whirlpools
  fierce   5
From out the floodgates of the Sky. The Gates are burst;
  down pour
The torrents black upon the Earth; the blood pours down
  incessant.
Kings in their palaces lie drowned. Shepherds, their
  flocks, their tents
Roll down the mountains in black torrents. Cities,
  Villages,
High spires & Castles drowned in the black deluge. Shoal
  on Shoal   10
Float the dead carcasses of Men & Beasts, driven to &
  fro on waves
Of foaming blood beneath the black incessant Sky, till
  all
Mystery's tyrants are cut off & not one left on Earth.

And when all Tyranny was cut off from the face of Earth
Around the Dragon form of Urizen & round his stony
    form,   15
The flames rolling intense through the wide Universe
Began to Enter the Holy City. Ent'ring, the dismal clouds
In furrowed lightnings break their way, the wild flames
    lightening up
The Bloody Deluge; living flames, winged with intellect
And Reason round the Earth. They march in order, flame
    by flame.   20
From the clotted gore & from the hollow den
Start forth the trembling millions into flames of mental
    fire,
Bathing their Limbs in the bright visions of Eternity.

Beyond this Universal Confusion, beyond the remotest
    Pole,
Where their vortexes begin to operate, there stands   25
A Horrible rock far in the South. It was forsaken when
Urizen gave the horses of Light into the hands of Luvah.
On this rock lay the faded head of the Eternal Man
Enwrapped round with weeds of death, pale cold in sorrow
    & woe.
He lifts the blue lamps of his Eyes & cries with
    heavenly voice.   30
Bowing his head over the consuming Universe, he cried:
"O weakness & O weariness! O war within my members!
My sons, exiled from my breast, pass to & fro before me.
My birds are silent on my hills; flocks die beneath my
    branches.
My tents are fallen, my trumpets & the sweet sound of
    my harp   35
Is silent on my clouded hills, that belch forth storms
    & fires.
My milk of cows & honey of bees & fruit of golden harvest
Are gathered in the scorching heat & in the driving rain.
My robe is turned to confusion & my bright gold to
    stones.

Where once I sat, I weary walk in misery & pain;   40
For from within my withered breast, grown narrow with
    my woes,
The Corn is turned to thistles & the apples into poison,
The birds of song to murderous crows, My joys to bitter
    groans,

Page 120

The voices of children in my tents to cries of
    helpless infants,
And all exiled from the face of light & shine of morning.
In this dark world, a narrow house, I wander up & down.
I hear Mystery howling in these flames of Consummation.
When shall the Man of future times become as in days
    of old.   5
O weary life, why sit I here & give up all my powers
To indolence, to the night of death, when indolence &
    mourning
Sit hov'ring over my dark threshold? Though I arise,
    look out
And scorn the war within my members, yet my heart is
    weak
And my head faint. Yet will I look again unto the
    morning.   10
Whence is this sound of rage of Men drinking each other's
    blood,
Drunk with the smoking gore, & red, but not with
    nourishing wine?"

The Eternal Man sat on the Rocks & cried with awful
    voice:

"O Prince of Light, where art thou? I behold thee not
    as once
In those Eternal fields in clouds of morning, stepping
    forth   15
With harps & songs, where bright Ahania sang before thy
    face,

And all thy sons & daughters gathered round my ample
     table.
See you not all this wracking, furious confusion?
Come forth from slumbers of thy cold abstraction. Come
     forth.
Arise to Eternal births. Shake off thy cold repose.   20
Schoolmaster of souls, great opposer of change, arise,
That the Eternal worlds may see thy face in peace & joy,
That, thou dread form of Certainty, may'st sit in town
     & village
While little children play around thy feet in gentle awe,
Fearing thy frown, loving thy smile, O Urizen, Prince
     of light."   25

He called; the deep buried his voice, & answer none
     returned.

Then wrath burst round; the Eternal Man was wrath. Again
     he cried:

"Arise, O stony form of death, O dragon of the Deeps.
Lie down before my feet, O Dragon. Let Urizen arise.
O how couldst thou deform those beautiful proportions   30
Of life & person? For as the Person, so is his life
     proportioned,
Let Luvah rage in the dark deep, even to Consummation;
For if thou feedest not his rage, it will subside in
     peace;
But if thou darest, obstinate, refuse my stern behest,
Thy crown & scepter I will seize & regulate all my
     members   35
In stern severity & cast thee out into the indefinite,
Where nothing lives, there to wander; & if thou
     return'st weary,
Weeping at the threshold of Existence, I will steel
     my heart
Against thee to Eternity & never receive thee more.
Thy self-destroying beast-formed Science shall be thy
     eternal lot.   40

My anger against thee is greater than against this
    Luvah,
For war is energy Enslaved; but thy religion,
The first author of this war & the distracting of
    honest minds
Into confused perturbation & strife & honour & pride,
Is a deceit so detestable that I will cast thee out   45
If thou repentest not, & leave thee as a rotten branch
    to be burned
With Mystery the Harlot & with Satan for Ever & Ever.
Error can never be redeemed in all Eternity;
But Sin, Even Rahab, is redeemed in blood & fury &
    jealousy—
That line of blood that stretched across the windows
    of the morning—   50
Redeemed from Error's power. Wake, thou dragon of the
    deeps!"

Page 121

Urizen wept in the dark deep, anxious his Scaly
    form
To reassume the human, & he wept in the dark deep,

Saying, "O that I had never drank the wine nor eat
    the bread
Of dark mortality, nor cast my view into futurity, nor
    turned
My back, dark'ning the present clouding with a cloud   5
And building arches high & cities, turrets & towers &
    domes,
Whose smoke destroyed the pleasant garden, & whose
    running Kennels
Choked the bright rivers, burd'ning with my Ships the
    angry deep;
Through Chaos seeking for delight, & in spaces remote
Seeking the Eternal, which is always present to the
    wise;   10

Seeking for pleasure which unsought falls round the
    infant's path
And on the fleeces of mild flocks, who neither care nor
    labour.
But I, the labourer of ages, whose unwearied hands
Are thus deformed with hardness, with the sword & with
    the spear
And with the Chisel & the mallet, I whose labours
    vast   15
Order the nations, separating family by family,
Alone enjoy not. I alone, in misery supreme,
Ungratified give all my joy unto this Luvah & Vala.
Then Go, O dark futurity. I will cast thee forth from
    these
Heavens of my brain, nor will I look upon futurity
    more.   20
I cast futurity away & turn my back upon that void
Which I have made; for, lo, futurity is in this moment.
Let Orc consume, let Tharmas rage, let dark Urthona give
All strength to Los & Enitharmon, & let Los self-cursed
Rend down this fabric as a wall ruined & family extinct.   25
Rage, Orc! Rage, Tharmas! Urizen no longer curbs your
    rage."

So Urizen spoke. He shook his snows from off his
    Shoulders & arose
As on a Pyramid of mist, his white robes scattering
The fleecy white; renewed, he shook his aged mantles off
Into the fires. Then glorious bright, Exulting in his
    joy   30
He sounding rose into the heavens in naked majesty,
In radiant Youth; when Lo, like garlands in the Eastern
    sky
When vocal May comes dancing from the East, Ahania came
Exulting in her flight, as when a bubble rises up
Onto the surface of a lake. Ahania rose in joy,   35
Excess of Joy is worse than grief; her heart beat high,
    her blood

Burst its bright Vessels. She fell down dead at the feet
    of Urizen
Outstretched, a Smiling corse. They buried her in a
    silent cave.
Urizen dropped a tear; the Eternal Man Darkened with
    sorrow.

The three daughters of Urizen guard Ahania's Death
    couch,   40
Rising from the confusion in tears & howlings & despair,
Calling upon their father's Name upon their Rivers dark.

And the Eternal Man Said: "Hear my words, O Prince of
    Light;

Page 122

Behold Jerusalem, in whose bosom the Lamb of God
Is seen, though slain before her Gates. He, self-renewed,
    remains
Eternal, & I through him awake from death's dark vale.
The times revolve. The time is coming when all these
    delights
Shall be renewed, & all these Elements that now
    consume   5
Shall reflourish. Then bright Ahania shall awake from
    death,
A glorious Vision to thine Eyes, a Self-renewing Vision,
The spring, the summer to be thine. Then sleep the
    wintry days
In silken garments spun by her own hands against her
    funeral.
The winter thou shalt plow & lay thy stores into thy
    barns   10
Expecting to receive Ahania in the spring with joy.
Immortal thou, Regenerate She, & all the lovely Sex
From her shall learn obedience & prepare for a wintry
    grave,

That spring may see them rise in tenfold joy & sweet
    delight.
Thus shall the male & female live the life of Eternity,   15
Because the Lamb of God Creates himself a bride & wife,
That we his Children evermore may live in Jerusalem,
Which now descendeth out of heaven, a City yet a Woman,
Mother of myriads redeemed & born in her spiritual
    palaces,
By a New Spiritual birth Regenerated from Death."   20

Urizen said: "I have Erred, & my Error remains with me.
What Chain encompasses? In what Lock is the river of
    light confined
That issues forth in the morning by measure & the
    evening by carefulness?
Where shall we take our stand to view the infinite &
    unbounded?
Or where are human feet? For Lo, our eyes are in the
    heavens."   25

He ceased, for riven link from link, the bursting
    Universe explodes.
All things reversed flew from their centers; rattling
    bones
To bones Join; shaking convulsed, the shivering clay
    breathes.
Each speck of dust to the Earth's center nestles round
    & round
In pangs of an Eternal Birth; in torment & awe & fear   30
All spirits deceased, let loose from reptile prisons,
    come in shoals:
Wild furies from the tiger's brain & from the lion's
    Eyes;
And from the ox & ass come moping terrors, from the
    Eagle
And raven; numerous as the leaves of autumn, every
    species
Flock to the trumpet mutt'ring over the sides of the
    grave & crying   35

In the fierce wind round heaving rocks & mountains
    filled with groans.
On rifted rocks suspended in the air by inward fires,
Many a woeful company & many on clouds & waters,
Fathers & friends, Mothers & Infants, Kings & Warriors,
Priests & chained Captives met together in a horrible
    fear;   40
And every one of the dead appears as he had lived before.

Page 123

And all the marks remain of the slave's scourge
    & tyrant's Crown,
And of the Priest's o'ergorged Abdomen, & of the
    merchant's thin
Sinewy deception, & of the warrior's outbraving &
    thoughtlessness
In lineaments too extended & in bones too straight &
    long.

They show their wounds; they accuse; they seize the
    oppressor; howlings began   5
On the golden palace, Songs & joy on the desert. The
    Cold babe
Stands in the furious air; he cries; the children of
    six thousand years
Who died in infancy rage furious; a mighty multitude
    rage furious,
Naked & pale standing on the expecting air to be
    delivered,
Rend limb from limb the Warrior & the tyrant, reuniting
    in pain.   10
The furious wind still rends around; they flee in
    sluggish effort.
They beg, they entreat in vain now; they Listened not
    to entreaty.
They view the flames red rolling on through the wide
    universe,

From the dark jaws of death beneath & desolate shores
    remote,
These covering Vaults of heaven & these trembling globes
    of Earth.   15
One Planet calls to another, & one star enquires of
    another:
"What flames are these coming from the South? What
    noise? What dreadful rout
As of a battle in the heavens? Hark, heard you not the
    trumpet
As of fierce battle?" While they spoke, the flames
    come on, intense, roaring.

They see him whom they have pierced; they wail because
    of him.   20
They magnify themselves no more against Jerusalem, Nor
Against her little ones; the innocent, accused before
    the Judges,
Shines with immortal Glory; trembling, the Judge springs
    from his throne,
Hiding his face in the dust beneath the prisoner's
    feet, & saying,
"Brother of Jesus, what have I done? Entreat thy lord
    for me;   25
Perhaps I may be forgiven." While he speaks, the flames
    roll on,
And after the flames appears the Cloud of the Son of
    Man,
Descending from Jerusalem with power and great Glory.
All nations look up to the Cloud & behold him who was
    Crucified.
The Prisoner answers: "You scourged my father to death
    before my face   30
While I stood bound with cords & heavy chains. Your
    hypocrisy
Shall now avail you naught." So speaking, he dashed
    him with his foot.

The Cloud is Blood dazzling upon the heavens, & in the
    cloud,

Above, upon its volumes, is beheld a throne & a
    pavement
Of precious stones surrounded by twenty-four venerable
    patriarchs,   35
And these again surrounded by four Wonders of the
    Almighty,
Incomprehensible, pervading all, amidst & round about,
Fourfold each in the other reflected. They are named
    Life's (in Eternity)
Four Starry Universes, going forward from Eternity to
    Eternity.
And the Fallen Man, who was arisen upon the Rock of
    Ages,   40

Page 124

Beheld the Vision of God; & he arose up from the
    Rock,
And Urizen arose up with him, walking through the flames
To meet the Lord, coming to Judgment; but the flames
    repelled them.
Still to the Rock in vain they strove to Enter the
    Consummation
Together, for the Redeemed Man could not enter the
    Consummation.   5

Then seized the Sons of Urizen the Plow. They polished
    it
From rust of ages; all its ornaments of Gold & silver &
    ivory
Reshone across the field immense where all the nations
Darkened like Mould in the divided fallows, where the
    weed
Triumphs in its own destruction; they took down the
    harness   10
From the blue walls of heaven, starry, jingling,
    ornamented
With beautiful art, the study of angels, the workmanship
    of Demons

When Heaven & Hell in Emulation strove in sports of
    Glory.

The noise of rural work resounded through the heaven
    of heavens.
The horses neigh from the battle, the wild bulls from
    the sultry waste,   15
The tigers from the forests, & the lions from the sandy
    deserts.
They Sing; they seize the instruments of harmony; they
    throw away
The spear, the bow, the gun, the mortar; they level
    the fortifications;
They beat the iron engines of destruction into wedges;
They give them to Urthona's Sons. Ringing, the hammers
    sound   20
In dens of death, to forge the spade, the mattock & the
    ax,
The heavy roller, to break the clods, to pass over the
    nations.

The Sons of Urizen Shout. Their father rose. The Eternal
    horses
Harnessed, They called to Urizen; the heavens moved at
    their call.
The limbs of Urizen shone with ardor. He laid his hand
    on the Plow,   25
Through dismal darkness drave the Plow of ages over
    Cities
And all their Villages, over Mountains & all their
    Valleys,
Over the graves & caverns of the dead, Over the Planets
And over the void Spaces, over Sun & moon & star &
    constellation.

Then Urizen commanded, & they brought the Seed of
    Men.   30
The trembling souls of All the Dead stood before Urizen,
Weak wailing in the troubled air, East, west & north
    & south.

Page 125

He turned the horses loose & laid his Plow in
    the northern corner
Of the wide Universal field, then Stepped forth into
    the immense.

Then he began to sow the seed; he girded round his loins
With a bright girdle, & his skirt filled with immortal
    souls.
Howling & Wailing fly the souls from Urizen's strong
    hand,   5

For from the hand of Urizen the myriads fall like stars
Into their own appointed places, driven back by the winds.
The naked warriors rush together down to the sea shores.
They are become like wintry flocks, like forests stripped
    of leaves.
The Kings & Princes of the Earth cry with a feeble cry,   10
Driven on the unproducing sands & on the hardened rocks.
And all the while the flames of Orc follow the vent'rous
    feet
Of Urizen, & all the while the Trump of Tharmas sounds.
Weeping & wailing fly the souls from Urizen's strong
    hand.
The daughters of Urizen stand with Cups & measures of
    foaming wine   15
Immense upon the heavens with bread & delicate repasts.
Then follows the golden harrow in the midst of Mental
    fires.
To ravishing melody of flutes & harps & softest voice
The seed is harrowed in, while flames heat the black
    mould & cause
The human harvest to begin. Towards the south first
    sprang   20
The myriads, & in silent fear they look out from their
    graves.

Then Urizen sits down to rest, & all his wearied Sons
Take their repose on beds; they drink, they sing, they
    view the flames
Of Orc. In joy they view the human harvest springing up.
A time they give to sweet repose till all the harvest is
    ripe.   25

And Lo, like the harvest Moon, Ahania cast off her death
    clothes.
She folded them up in care, in silence; & her bright'ning
    limbs
Bathed in the clear spring of the rock, then from her
    darksome cave
Issued in majesty divine. Urizen rose up from his couch
On wings of tenfold joy, clapping his hands, his feet,
    his radiant wings   30
In the immense, as when the Sun dances upon the mountains
A shout of jubilee in lovely notes responds from daughter
    to daughter,
From son to Son, as if the Stars, beaming innumerable
Through night, should sing, soft warbling, filling Earth
    & heaven;
And bright Ahania took her seat by Urizen in songs &
    joy.   35

The Eternal Man also sat down upon the Couches of Beulah,
Sorrowful that he could not put off his new risen body
In mental flames. The flames refused, they drove him
    back to Beulah.
His body was redeemed to be permanent through the Mercy
    Divine.

Page 126

And now fierce Orc had quite consumed himself
    in Mental flames,
Expending all his energy against the fuel of fire.
The Regenerate Man stooped his head over the Universe &
    in

His holy hands received the flaming Demon and Demoness
    of Smoke
And gave them to Urizen's hands. The immortal frowned,
    Saying,   5

"Luvah & Vala, henceforth you are Servants. Obey & live.
You shall forget your former state. Return & Love in
    peace
Into your place, the place of seed, not in the brain or
    heart.
If Gods combine against Man, Setting their Dominion above
The Human form Divine, Thrown down from their high
    Station   10
In the Eternal heavens of Human Imagination, buried
    beneath
In dark oblivion with incessant pangs ages on ages,
In Enmity & war first weakened, then in stern repentance,
They must renew their brightness & their disorganized
    functions
Again reorganize, till they resume the image of the
    human,   15
Cooperating in the bliss of Man, obeying his Will,
Servants to the infinite & Eternal of the Human form."

Luvah & Vala descended and entered the Gates of Dark
    Urthona
And walked from the hands of Urizen in the shadows of
    Vala's Garden,
Where the impressions of Despair & Hope forever vegetate   20
In flowers, in fruits, in fishes, birds & beasts & clouds
    & waters,
The land of doubts & shadows, sweet delusions, unformed
    hopes.
They saw no more the terrible confusion of the wracking
    universe.
They heard not, saw not, felt not all the terrible
    confusion;
For in their orbed senses within closed up they wandered
    at will.   25

And those upon the Couches viewed them in the dreams
    of Beulah
As they reposed from the terrible wide universal harvest.
Invisible Luvah in bright clouds hovered over Vala's
    head,
And thus their ancient golden age renewed, for Luvah
    spoke
With voice mild from his golden Cloud upon the breath
    of morning: 30

"Come forth, O Vala, from the grass & from the silent
    Dew.
Rise from the dews of death, for the Eternal Man is
    Risen."

She rises among flowers & looks toward the Eastern
    clearness,
She walks, yea, runs; her feet are wing'd on the tops
    of the bending grass.
Her garments rejoice in the vocal wind, & her hair
    glistens with dew.   35

She answered thus: "Whose voice is this in the voice
    of the nourishing air,
In the spirit of the morning, awaking the Soul from
    its grassy bed?

Page 127

Where dost thou dwell? For it is thee I seek,
    & but for thee
I must have slept Eternally, nor have felt the dew
    of thy morning.
Look how the opening dawn advances with vocal harmony.
Look how the beams foreshow the rising of some
    glorious power.
The sun is thine; he goeth forth in his majestic
    brightness.   5
O thou creating voice that callest, & who shall answer
    thee?

"Where dost thou flee, O fair one? Where dost thou
    seek thy happy place?"

"To yonder brightness, there I haste, for sure I
    came from thence,
Or I must have slept eternally, nor have felt the dew
    of morning."

"Eternally thou must have slept, nor have felt the
    morning dew,   10
But for yon nourishing sun; 'tis that by which thou
    art arisen.
The birds adore the sun; the beasts rise up & play
    in his beams;
And every flower & every leaf rejoices in his light.
Then, O thou fair one, sit thee down; for thou art as
    the grass.
Thou risest in the dew of morning & at night art
    folded up."   15

"Alas, am I but as a flower? Then will I sit me down,
Then will I weep; then I'll complain & sigh for
    immortality
And chide my maker, thee, O Sun, that raisedst me to
    fall."

So saying, she sat down & wept beneath the apple trees.

"O be thou blotted out, thou Sun, that raisedst me
    to trouble,   20
That gavest me a heart to crave & raisedst me, thy
    phantom,
To feel thy heat & see thy light & wander here alone,
Hopeless, if I am like the grass & so shall pass away."

"Rise, sluggish Soul, why sit'st thou here? Why dost
    thou sit & weep?
Yon Sun shall wax old & decay, but thou shalt ever
    flourish.   25
The fruit shall ripen & fall down & the flowers
    consume away,

But thou shalt still survive. Arise, O dry thy
    dewy tears."

"Hah! Shall I still survive? Whence came that sweet
    & comforting voice?
And whence that voice of sorrow? O sun, thou art
    nothing now to me.
Go on thy course rejoicing, & let us both rejoice
    together.   30
I walk among his flocks & hear the bleating of his lambs.
O that I could behold his face & follow his pure feet.
I walk by the footsteps of his flocks. Come hither,
    tender flocks.
Can you converse with a pure Soul that seeketh for
    her maker?
You answer not; then am I set your mistress in this
    garden.   35
I'll watch you & attend your footsteps. You are not
    like the birds

Page 128

That sing & fly in the bright air, but you do
    lick my feet
And let me touch your woolly backs. Follow me as I
    sing,
For in my bosom a new song arises to my Lord:

"Rise up, O Sun, most glorious minister & light of
    day.
Flow on, ye gentle airs, & bear the voice of my
    rejoicing.   5
Wave freshly, clear waters, flowing around the tender
    grass;
And thou, sweet-smelling ground, put forth thy life
    in fruits & flowers.
Follow me, O my flocks, & hear me sing my rapturous
    Song.
I will cause my voice to be heard on the clouds that
    glitter in the sun.

I will call, & who shall answer me? I will sing. Who
    shall reply?   10
For from my pleasant hills behold the living, living
    springs
Running among my green pastures, delighting ámong my
    trees.
I am not here alone; my flocks, you are my brethren;
And you birds that sing & adorn the sky, you are my
    sisters.
I sing, & you reply to my Song. I rejoice, & you are
    glad.   15
Follow me, O my flocks; we will now descend into the
    valley.
O how delicious are the grapes flourishing in the Sun,
How clear the spring of the rock running among the
    golden sand,
How cool the breezes of the valley & the arms of the
    branching trees.
Cover us from the Sun; come & let us sit in the Shade.   20
My Luvah here hath placed me in a Sweet & pleasant
    Land
And given me fruits & pleasant waters & warm hills &
    cool valleys.
Here will I build myself a house, & here I'll call on
    his name,
Here I'll return when I am weary & take my pleasant
    rest."

So spoke the Sinless Soul & laid her head on the
    downy fleece   25
Of a curled Ram, who stretched himself in sleep beside
    his mistress,
And soft sleep fell upon her eyelids in the silent
    noon of day.

Then Luvah passed by & saw the sinless Soul
And said: "Let a pleasant house arise to be the
    dwelling place
Of this immortal Spirit, growing in lower
    Paradise."   30

He spoke, & pillars were builded & walls as white as
  ivory.
The grass she slept upon was paved with pavement as
  of pearl.
Beneath her rose a downy bed, & a ceiling covered all.

Vala awoke. "When in the pleasant gates of sleep I
  entered,
I saw my Luvah like a spirit stand in the bright air.   35
Round him stood spirits like me, who reared me a bright
  house;
And here I see thee, house; remain in my most
  pleasant world.

Page 129

My Luvah smiled; I kneeled down; he laid his
  hand on my head;
And when he laid his hand upon me, from the gates of
  sleep I came
Into this bodily house to tend my flocks in my
  pleasant garden."

So saying, she arose & walked round her beautiful
  house,
And then from her white door she looked to see her
  bleating lambs,   5
But her flocks were gone up from beneath the trees
  into the hills.

"I see the hand that leadeth me doth also lead my
  flocks."
She went up to her flocks & turned oft to see her
  shining house.
She stopped to drink of the clear spring & eat the
  grapes & apples.
She bore the fruits in her lap, she gathered flowers
  for her bosom.   10
She called to her flocks, saying, "Follow me, O my
  flocks."

They followed her to the silent valley beneath the
  spreading trees,
And on the river's margin she ungirded her golden
  girdle.
She stood in the river & viewed herself within the wat'ry
  glass,
And her bright hair was wet with the waters. She rose
  up from the river,   15
And as she rose her Eyes were opened to the world of
  waters.
She saw Tharmas sitting upon the rocks beside the wavy
  sea.
He stroked the water from his beard & mourned faint
  through the summer vales.

And Vala stood on the rocks of Tharmas & heard his
  mournful voice:

"O Enion, my weary head is in the bed of death,   20
For weeds of death have wrapped around my limbs in the
  hoary deeps.
I sit in the place of shells & mourn, & thou art closed
  in clouds.
When will the time of Clouds be past, & the dismal
  night of Tharmas?
Arise, O Enion. Arise & smile upon my head
As thou dost smile upon the barren mountains and they
  rejoice.   25
When wilt thou smile on Tharmas, O thou bringer of
  golden day?
Arise, O Enion, arise; for Lo, I have calmed my seas."

So saying, his faint head he laid upon the Oozy rock,
And darkness covered all the deep; the light of Enion
  faded
Like a faint flame quivering upon the surface of the
  darkness.   30

Then Vala lifted up her hands to heaven to call on
  Enion.

She called, but none could answer her, & the Echo of
her voice returned:

"Where is the voice of God, that called me from the
silent dew?
Where is the Lord of Vala? Dost thou hide in clefts
of the rock?
Why shouldst thou hide thyself from Vala, from the
soul that wanders desolate?"   35
She ceased, & light beamed round her like the glory
of the morning.

Page 130

And She arose out of the river & girded her
golden girdle.

And now her feet step on the grassy bosom of the ground
Among her flocks, & she turned her eyes toward her
pleasant house
And saw in the doorway beneath the trees two little
children playing.
She drew near to her house, & her flocks followed her
footsteps.   5
The Children clung around her knees; she embraced them
& wept over them:

"Thou, little Boy, art Tharmas, & thou, bright Girl,
Enion.
How are ye thus renewed & brought into the Gardens of
Vala?"

She embraced them in tears, till the sun descended the
western hills,
And then she entered her bright house, leading her
mighty children.   10
And when night came, the flocks laid round the house
beneath the trees.
She laid the Children on the beds which she saw
prepared in the house,

Then last herself laid down & closed her Eyelids in
    soft slumbers.

And in the morning, when the Sun arose in the crystal
    sky,
Vala awoke & called the children from their gentle
    slumbers: 15

"Awake, O Enion, awake & let thine innocent Eyes
Enlighten all the Crystal house of Vala. Awake, awake!
Awake, Tharmas! Awake, awake, thou child of dewy tears!
Open the orbs of thy blue eyes & smile upon my gardens."

The Children woke & smiled on Vala. She kneeled by the
    golden couch;   20
She pressed them to her bosom, & her pearly tears
    dropped down.
"O my sweet Children! Enion, let Tharmas kiss thy
    Cheek.
Why dost thou turn thyself away from his sweet wat'ry
    eyes?
Tharmas, henceforth in Vala's bosom thou shalt find
    sweet peace.
O bless the lovely eyes of Tharmas & the Eyes of Enion."   25

They rose; they went out wand'ring, sometimes together,
    sometimes alone.
Why weepest thou, Tharmas, Child of tears, in the
    bright house of joy?
Doth Enion avoid the sight of thy blue heavenly Eyes?
And dost thou wander with my lambs & wet their
    innocent faces
With thy bright tears because the steps of Enion are
    in the gardens?   30
Arise, sweet boy, & let us follow the path of Enion."

So saying they went down into the garden among the
    fruits,
And Enion sang among the flowers that grew among the
    trees;
And Vala said: "Go, Tharmas. Weep not, Go to Enion."

Page 131

He said: "O Vala, I am sick, & all this garden
    of Pleasure
Swims like a dream before my eyes; but the sweet-smelling
    fruit
Revives me to new deaths. I fade even like a water lily
In the sun's heat, till in the night on the couch of Enion
I drink new life & feel the breath of sleeping Enion.   5
But in the morning she arises to avoid my Eyes.
Then my loins fade, & in the house I sit me down &
    weep."

"Cheer up thy Countenance, bright boy, & go to Enion.
Tell her that Vala waits her in the shadows of her
    garden."

He went with timid steps & Enion, like the ruddy morn   10
When infant spring appears in swelling buds & opening
    flowers
Behind her Veil, withdraws; so Enion turned her modest
    head.

But Tharmas spoke: "Vala seeks thee, sweet Enion, in
    the shades.
Follow the steps of Tharmas, O thou brightness of the
    gardens."
He took her hand reluctant; she followed in infant
    doubts.   15

Thus in Eternal Childhood, straying among Vala's flocks,
In infant sorrow & joy alternate, Enion & Tharmas played
Round Vala in the Gardens of Vala & by her river's
    margin.
They are the shadows of Tharmas & of Enion in Vala's
    world.

And the sleepers who rested from their harvest work
    beheld these visions.   20

Thus were the sleepers entertained upon the Couches
    of Beulah.

When Luvah & Vala were closed up in their world of
    shadowy forms,
Darkness was all beneath the heavens; only a little
    light
Such as glows out from sleeping spirits appeared in
    the deeps beneath.
As when the wind sweeps over a Cornfield, the noise
    of souls   25
Through all the immense, borne down by Clouds swagging
    in autumnal heat,
Muttering along from heaven to heaven, hoarse roll the
    human forms
Beneath thick clouds, dreadful lightnings burst, &
    thunders roll;
Down pour the torrent Floods of heaven on all the
    human harvest.
Then Urizen, sitting at his repose on beds in the
    bright South,   30
Cried: "Times are Ended!" He Exulted; he arose in
    joy; he exulted.
He poured his light, & all his Sons & daughters poured
    their light
To exhale the spirits of Luvah & Vala through the
    atmosphere.
And Luvah & Vala saw the Light. Their spirits were
    Exhaled
In all their ancient innocence. The floods depart, the
    clouds   35
Dissipate or sink into the Seas of Tharmas. Luvah sat
Above on the bright heavens in peace. The Spirits of
    Men beneath
Cried out to be delivered, & the Spirit of Luvah wept
Over the human harvest & over Vala, the sweet wanderer.
In pain the human harvest waved in horrible groans
    of woe.   40

Page 132

The Universal Groan went up; the Eternal Man
    was Darkened.

Then Urizen arose & took his Sickle in his
    hand.
There is a brazen sickle & a scythe of iron hid
Deep in the South, guarded by a few solitary stars.
This sickle Urizen took; the scythe his sons embraced   5
And went forth & began to reap, & all his joyful sons
Reaped the wide Universe & bound in Sheaves a wondrous
    harvest.
They took them into the wide barns with loud rejoicings
    & triumph
Of flute & harp & drum & trumpet, horn & clarion.

The feast was spread in the bright South, & the
    Regenerate Man   10
Sat at the feast rejoicing, & the wine of Eternity
Was served round by the flames of Luvah all Day & all
    the Night;
And when Morning began to dawn upon the distant hills,
A whirlwind rose up in the Center, & in the Whirlwind
    a shriek,
And in the Shriek a rattling of bones, & in the rattling
    of bones   15
A dolorous groan, & from the dolorous groan in tears
Rose Enion like a gentle light; & Enion spoke, saying,

"O Dreams of Death, the human form dissolving,
    'companied
By beasts & worms & creeping things & darkness &
    despair,
The clouds fall off from my wet brow, the dust from
    my cold limbs   20
Into the Sea of Tharmas. Soon renewed, a Golden Moth,
I shall cast off my death clothes & Embrace Tharmas
    again.

For Lo, the winter melted away upon the distant hills,
And all the black mould sings." She speaks to her
    infant race; her milk
Descends down on the sand. The thirsty sand drinks
    & rejoices,   25
Wondering to behold the Emmet, the Grasshopper, the
    jointed worm.
The roots shoot thick through the solid rocks,
    bursting their way.
They cry out in joys of existence. The broad stems
Rear on the mountains, stem after stem. The scaly newt
    creeps
From the stone, & the armed fly springs from the rocky
    crevice.   30
The spider, the bat burst from the hardened slime
    crying
To one another, "What are we, & whence is our joy &
    delight?
Lo, the little moss begins to spring, & the tender weed
Creeps round our secret nest." Flocks brighten the
    Mountains;
Herds throng up the Valley; wild beasts fill the
    forests.   35

Joy thrilled through all the Furious form of Tharmas,
    humanizing.
Mild he Embraced her whom he sought; he raised her
    through the heavens,
Sounding his trumpet to awake the dead; on high he
    soared
Over the ruined worlds, the smoking tomb of the
    Eternal Prophet.

Page 133

The Eternal Man arose; He welcomed them to the
    Feast.
The feast was spread in the bright South, & the Eternal
    Man

Sat at the feast rejoicing, & the wine of Eternity
Was served round by the flames of Luvah all day & all
    the night.

And Many Eternal Men sat at the golden feast to see   5
The female form now separate. They shuddered at the
    horrible thing,
Not born for the sport and amusement of Man, but born
    to drink up all his powers.
They wept to see their shadows; they said to one
    another: "This is Sin.
This is the Generative world." They remembered the
    Days of old.

And One of the Eternals spoke. All was silent at the
    feast: 10

"Man is a Worm; wearied with joy, he seeks the caves
    of sleep
Among the Flowers of Beulah in his Selfish cold repose,
Forsaking Brotherhood & Universal love in selfish clay,
Folding the pure wings of his mind, seeking the places
    dark,
Abstracted from the roots of Science; then enclosed
    around   15
In walls of Gold, we cast him like a Seed into the Earth
Till times & spaces have passed over him; duly every
    morn
We visit him, covering with a Veil the immortal seed.
With windows from the inclement sky we cover him &
    with walls
And hearths protect the Selfish terror, till divided
    all   20
In families, we see our shadows born; & thence we
    know   Ephesi-
That Man subsists by Brotherhood & Universal Love.   ans iii c.
We fall on one another's necks; more closely we   10 v
    embrace.
Not for ourselves, but for the Eternal family we live.

Man liveth not by Self alone, but in his brother's face   25
Each shall behold the Eternal Father, & love & joy
    abound."

So spoke the Eternal at the Feast. They embraced the
    Newborn Man,
Calling him Brother, image of the Eternal Father. They
    sat down
At the immortal tables, sounding loud their instruments
    of joy.
Calling the Morning into Beulah, the Eternal Man
    rejoiced.   30

When Morning dawned, The Eternals rose to labour at
    the Vintage.
Beneath they saw their sons & daughters, wondering
    inconceivable
At the dark myriads in Shadows in the worlds beneath.

The morning dawned, Urizen rose, & in his hand the
    Flail
Sounds on the Floor, heard terrible by all beneath
    the heavens.   35
Dismal, loud redounding, the nether floor shakes with
    the sound;

Page 134

And all Nations were threshed out, & the stars
    threshed from their husks.

Then Tharmas took the Winnowing fan; the winnowing
    wind furious
Above, veered round by the violent whirlwind, driven
    west & south,
Tossed the Nations like Chaff into the seas of Tharmas:

"O Mystery," Fierce Tharmas cries, "Behold, thy end
    is come.   5
Art thou she that made the nations drunk with the cup
    of Religion?

Go down, ye Kings & Councillors & Giant Warriors,
Go down into the depths, go down & hide yourselves
    beneath,
Go down with horse & Chariots & Trumpets of hoarse war.

"Lo, how the Pomp of Mystery goes down into the Caves.   10
Her great men howl & throw the dust & rend their hoary
    hair;
Her delicate women & children shriek upon the bitter
    wind,
Spoiled of their beauty, their hair rent & their
    skin shriveled up.
Lo, darkness covers the long pomp of banners on the wind,
And black horses & armed men & miserable bound captives.   15
Where shall the graves receive them all, & where
    shall be their place?
And who shall mourn for Mystery, who never loosed her
    Captives?

"Let the slave grinding at the mill run out into the
    field.
Let him look up into the heavens & laugh in the bright
    air.
Let the inchained soul, shut up in darkness &
    in sighing,   20
Whose face has never seen a smile in thirty
    weary years,
Rise & look out. His chains are loose; his dungeon
    doors are open.
And let his wife & children return from the
    oppressor's scourge.

"They look behind at every step & believe it is a dream.
Are these the Slaves that groaned along the streets
    of Mystery?   25
Where are your bonds & taskmasters? Are these the
    prisoners?
Where are your chains? Where are your tears? Why do
    you look around?

If you are thirsty, there is the river; go bathe your
    parched limbs.
The good of all the Land is before you, for Mystery is
    no more."

Then All the Slaves from every Earth in the wide
    Universe   30
Sing a New Song, drowning confusion in its happy notes,
While the flail of Urizen sounded loud & the winnowing
    wind of Tharmas
So loud, so clear in the wide heavens; & the song that
    they sung was this,
Composed by an African Black from the little Earth
    of Sotha:

"Aha, Aha, how came I here so soon in my sweet native
    land?   35
How came I here? Methinks I am as I was in my youth,

Page 135

When in my father's house I sat & heard his
    cheering voice.
Methinks I see his flocks & herds & feel my limbs
    renewed.
And Lo, my Brethren in their tents & their little
    ones around them."

The song arose to the Golden feast; the Eternal Man
    rejoiced.
Then the Eternal Man said: "Luvah, the Vintage is
    ripe; arise.   5
The sons of Urizen shall gather the vintage with
    sharp hooks,
And all thy sons, O Luvah, bear away the families
    of Earth.
I hear the flail of Urizen; his barns are full. No
    room
Remains, & in the Vineyards stand the abounding
    sheaves beneath

The falling Grapes that odorous burst upon the winds.
  Arise! 10
My flocks & herds trample the Corn; my cattle browse
  upon
The ripe Clusters. The shepherds shout for Luvah,
  prince of Love.
Let the Bulls of Luvah tread the Corn & draw the
  loaded wagon
Into the Barn while children glean the Ears around
  the door.
Then shall they lift their innocent hands & stroke
  his furious nose, 15
And he shall lick the little girl's white neck & on
  her head
Scatter the perfume of his breath, while from his
  mountains high
The lion of terror shall come down &, bending his
  bright mane,
And couching at their side, shall eat from the curled
  boy's white lap
His golden food, and in the evening sleep before the
  Door." 20

"Attempting to be more than Man We become less,"
  said Luvah
As he arose from the Bright feast, drunk with the
  wine of ages.
His crown of thorns fell from his head; he hung his
  living Lyre
Behind the seat of the Eternal Man & took his way,
Sounding the Song of Los, descending to the Vineyards
  bright. 25
His sons, arising from the feast with golden baskets,
  follow,
A fiery train, as when the Sun sings in the ripe
  vineyards.
Then Luvah stood before the winepress. All his fiery
  sons

Brought up the loaded Wagons with shoutings. Ramping
    tigers play
In the jingling traces; furious lions sound the song
    of joy   30
To the golden wheels circling upon the pavement of
    heaven, & all
The Villages of Luvah ring; the golden tiles of the
    villages
Reply to violins & tabors, to the pipe, flute, lyre
    & cymbal,
Then fell the Legions of Mystery in madd'ning
    confusion,
Down, Down through the immense with outcry, fury &
    despair   35
Into the winepresses of Luvah; howling fell the Clusters
Of human families through the deep. The winepresses
    were filled.
The blood of life flowed plentiful. Odors of life
    arose
All round the heavenly arches, & the Odors rose
    singing this song:

Page 136

"O terrible Winepresses of Luvah! O caverns
    of the Grave!
How lovely the delights of those risen again from
    death.
O trembling joy, excess of joy is like Excess of grief."

So sang the Human Odors round the Winepresses of Luvah.

But in the Winepresses is wailing, terror & despair.   5
Forsaken of their Elements, they vanish & are no more,
No more but a desire of Being, a distracted ravening
    desire,
Desiring like the hungry worm & like the gaping grave.
They plunge into the Elements; the Elements cast them
    forth

Or else consume their shadowy semblance; Yet they,
    obstinate   10
Though pained to distraction, Cry: "O let us Exist,
    for
This dreadful Non-Existence is worse than pains of
    Eternal Birth.
Eternal Death who can Endure? Let us consume in fires,
In waters stifling or in air corroding or in earth shut
    up.
The Pangs of Eternal birth are better than the Pangs
    of Eternal Death."   15

How red the sons & daughters of Luvah! How they tread
    the Grapes!
Laughing & shouting, drunk with odors, many fall
    o'erwearied.
Drowned in the wine is many a youth & maiden. Those
    around
Lay them on skins of tigers or the spotted Leopard or
    wild Ass,
Till they revive, or bury them in cool Grots, making
    lamentation.   20

But in the Winepresses the Human Grapes Sing not, nor
    dance.
They howl & writhe in shoals of torment, in fierce
    flames consuming,
In chains of iron & in dungeons circled with ceaseless
    fires,
In pits & dens & shades of death, in shapes of torment
    & woe,
The Plates, the Screws, and Racks & Saws & cords & fires
    & floods,   25
The cruel joy of Luvah's daughters, lacerating with
    knives
And whips their Victims, & the deadly sports of Luvah's
    sons.

Timbrels & Violins sport round the Winepresses. The
    little Seed,

The Sportive root, the Earthworm, the small beetle,
    the wise Emmet
Dance round the Winepresses of Luvah. The Centipede
    is there,   30
The ground Spider with many Eyes, the Mole clothed in
    Velvet,
The Earwig armed, the tender maggot, emblem of
    Immortality,
The Slow Slug, the grasshopper, that sings & laughs
    & drinks.
The winter comes, he folds his slender bones without
    a murmur.
There is the Nettle, that stings with soft down, &
    there   35
The indignant Thistle, whose bitterness is bred in
    his milk
And who lives on the contempt of his neighbour. There
    all the idle weeds
That creep about the obscure places show their various
    limbs,
Naked in all their beauty, dancing round the Winepresses.
They Dance around the Dying, & they Drink the howl &
    groan.   40

Page 137

They catch the Shrieks in cups of gold; they
    hand them to one another.
These are the sports of love, & these the sweet delights
    of amorous play,
Tears of the grape, the death sweat of the Cluster, the
    last sigh
Of the mild youth who listens to the luring songs of
    Luvah.
The Eternal Man darkened with Sorrow, & a wintry
    mantle   5
Covered the ills. He said: "O Tharmas, rise, & O
    Urthona!

Then Tharmas & Urthona rose from the Golden feast,
    satiated
With Mirth & Joy. Urthona, limping from his fall, on
    Tharmas leaned,
In his right hand his hammer. Tharmas held his
    Shepherd's crook,
Beset with gold. Gold were the ornaments formed by sons
    of Urizen.   10

Then Enion & Ahania & Vala & the wife of Dark Urthona
Rose from the feast in joy, ascending to their Golden
    Looms.
There the wing'd shuttle Sang; the spindle & the
    distaff & the Reel
Rang sweet the praise of industry. Through all the
    golden rooms
Heaven rang with winged Exultation. All beneath
    howled loud.   15
With tenfold rout & desolation roared the Chasms
    beneath,
Where the wide woof flowed down & where the Nations
    are gathered together.

Tharmas went down to the Winepresses & beheld the sons
    & daughters
Of Luvah quite exhausted with the Labour & quite filled
With new wine, that they began to torment one another
    and to tread   20
The weak. Luvah & Vala slept on the floor o'erwearied.

Urthona called his Sons around him. Tharmas called his
    sons
Num'rous. They took the wine; they separated the Lees,
And Luvah was put for dung on the ground by the Sons of
    Tharmas & Urthona.
They formed heavens of sweetest woods, of gold & silver
    & ivory,   25
Of glass and precious stones. They loaded all the wagons
    of heaven

And took away the wine of ages with solemn songs & joy.

Luvah & Vala woke, & all the sons & daughters of Luvah
Awoke. They wept to one another, & they reascended
To the Eternal Man. In woe he cast them wailing into   30
The world of shadows through the air till winter is over
    & gone.

But the Human Wine stood wondering in all their
    delightful Expanses.
The Elements subside; the heavens roll'd on with vocal
    harmony.

Then Los, who is Urthona, rose in all his regenerate
    power.
The Sea that rolled & foamed with darkness & the shadows
    of death   35
Vomited out & gave up all; the floods lift up their hands
Singing & shouting to the Man. They bow their hoary heads
And, murmuring in their channels, flow & circle round
  his feet.

Page 138

Then Dark Urthona took the Corn out of the Stores
    of Urizen.
He ground it in his rumbling Mills. Terrible the distress
Of all the Nations of Earth ground in the Mills of Urthona.
In his hand Tharmas takes the Storms; he turns the
    whirlwind Loose
Upon the wheels; the stormy seas howl at his dread
    command   5
And, Eddying fierce, rejoice in the fierce agitation
    of the wheels
Of Dark Urthona. Thunders, Earthquakes, Fires, Water,
    floods
Rejoice to one another. Loud their voices shake the
    Abyss,
Their dread forms tending the dire mills. The grey hoar
    frost was there,

And his pale wife, the aged Snow; they watch over the
   fires;   10
And build the Ovens of Urthona. Nature in darkness
   groans,
And Men are bound to sullen contemplations in the night.
Restless they turn on beds of sorrow. In their inmost
   brain,
Feeling the crushing Wheels, they rise; they write the
   bitter words
Of Stern Philosophy & knead the bread of knowledge
   with tears & groans.   15

Such are the works of Dark Urthona. Tharmas sifted the
   corn.
Urthona made the Bread of Ages, & he placed it
In golden & in silver baskets in heavens of precious
   stone
And then took his repose in Winter in the night of Time.

The Sun has left his blackness & has found a fresher
   morning,   20
And the mild moon rejoices in the clear & cloudless
   night,
And Man walks forth from midst of the fires; the evil
   is all consumed.
His eyes behold the Angelic spheres, arising night &
   day,
The stars consumed like a lamp blown out, & in their
   stead, behold
The Expanding Eyes of Man behold the depths of wondrous
   worlds.   25
One Earth, one sea beneath, nor Erring Globes wander,
   but Stars
Of fire rise up nightly from the Ocean, & one Sun
Each morning like a Newborn Man issues with songs & Joy,
Calling the Plowman to his Labour & the Shepherd to his
   rest.
He walks upon the Eternal Mountains, raising his
   heavenly voice,   30

Conversing with the Animal forms of wisdom night & day,
That, risen from the Sea of fire, renewed, walk o'er
    the Earth.

For Tharmas brought his flocks upon the hills & in the
    Vales.
Around the Eternal Man's bright tent the little
    Children play
Among the woolly flocks. The hammer of Urthona sounds   35
In the deep caves beneath, his limbs renewed; his Lions
    roar
Around the Furnaces & in Evening sport upon the plains.
They raise their faces from the Earth, conversing with
    the Man:

"How is it we have walked through fires & yet are not
    consumed?
How is it that all things are changed, even as in
    ancient times?"   40

Page 139

The Sun arises from his dewy bed, & the fresh
    airs
Play in his smiling beams, giving the seeds of life to
    grow;
And the fresh Earth beams forth ten thousand thousand
    springs of life.
Urthona is arisen in his strength, no longer now
Divided from Enitharmon, no longer the Spectre Los.   5
Where is the Spectre of Prophecy? Where the delusive
    Phantom?
Departed; & Urthona rises from the ruinous walls
In all his ancient strength to form the golden armour
    of science
For intellectual War. The war of swords departed now,
The dark Religions are departed, & sweet Science reigns.   10

End of The Dream

Figure 5. "Behemoth and Leviathan" No. 15, from *The Book of Job.*
By permission of the Pierpont Morgan Library.

Selections from *Milton* (1802-1808)

To Justify the Ways of God to Men

Plate 1

Preface

The Stolen and Perverted Writings of Homer & Ovid, of Plato & Cicero, which all Men ought to contemn, are set up by artifice against the Sublime of the Bible; but when the New Age is at leisure to Pronounce, all will be set right, & those Grand Works of the more ancient & consciously & professedly Inspired Men will hold their proper rank, & the Daughters of Memory shall become the Daughters of Inspiration. Shakespeare & Milton were both curbed by the general malady & infection from the silly Greek & Latin slaves of the Sword.

Rouse up, O Young Men of the New Age! Set your foreheads against the ignorant Hirelings! For we have Hirelings in the Camp, the Court & the University, who would, if they could, forever depress Mental & prolong Corporeal War. Painters, on you I call! Sculptors! Architects! Suffer not the fashionable Fools to depress your powers by the prices they pretend to give for contemptible works or the expensive advertising boasts that they make of such works; believe Christ & his Apostles that there is a Class of Men whose whole delight is in Destroying. We do not want either Greek or Roman Models if we are but just & true to our own Imaginations, those Worlds of Eternity in which we shall live forever, in Jesus our Lord.

> And did those feet in ancient time
> Walk upon England's mountains green ?
> And was the holy Lamb of God
> On England's pleasant pastures seen?
>
> And did the Countenance Divine   5
> Shine forth upon our clouded hills?
> And was Jerusalem builded here
> Among these dark Satanic Mills?

> Bring me my Bow of burning gold,
> Bring me my Arrows of desire,   10
> Bring me my Spear! O clouds unfold!
> Bring me my Chariot of fire!
>
> I will not cease from Mental Fight,
> Nor shall my Sword sleep in my hand,
> Till we have built Jerusalem   15
> In England's green & pleasant land.

*Would to God that all the Lord's people were
    Prophets.*

Numbers XI. ch 29 v.

From Plate 2

From Book the First

Daughters of Beulah! Muses who inspire the Poet's Song,
Record the journey of immortal Milton through your
    Realms
Of terror & mild moony lustre, in soft sexual
    delusions
Of varied beauty, to delight the wanderer and repose
His burning thirst & freezing hunger! Come into my
    hand   5
By your mild power, descending down the Nerves of my
    right arm
From out the Portals of my Brain, where by your
    ministry
The Eternal Great Humanity Divine planted his Paradise
And in it caused the Spectres of the Dead to take
    sweet forms
In likeness of himself. Tell also of the False Tongue,
    vegetated   10
Beneath your land of shadows, of its sacrifices and
Its offerings, even till Jesus, the image of the
    Invisible God,

Became its prey, a curse, an offering and an
    atonement
For Death Eternal in the heavens of Albion & before
    the Gates
Of Jerusalem, his Emanation, in the heavens beneath
    Beulah.   15

Say first! What moved Milton, who walked about in
    Eternity
One hundred years, pond'ring the intricate mazes of
    Providence
(Unhappy though in heaven, he obeyed, he murmured
    not, he was silent,
Viewing his Sixfold Emanation scattered through the
    deep
In torment!) To go into the deep her to redeem &
    himself perish?   20

From Plate 14

Then Milton rose up from the heavens of Albion
    ardorous!   10
The whole Assembly wept prophetic, seeing in
    Milton's face
And in his lineaments divine the shades of Death &
    Ulro,
He took off the robe of the promise & ungirded
    himself from the oath of God.

And Milton said: "I go to Eternal Death! The
    Nations still
Follow after the detestable Gods of Priam in
    pomp   15
Of warlike selfhood, contradicting and blaspheming.
When will the Resurrection come to deliver the
    sleeping body

From corruptibility? O when, Lord Jesus, wilt thou
    come?
Tarry no longer, for my soul lies at the gates of
    death.
I will arise and look forth for the morning of the
    grave.   20
I will go down to the sepulcher to see if morning
    breaks!
I will go down to self-annihilation and eternal
    death,
Lest the Last Judgment come & find me unannihilate
And I be seized & given into the hands of my own
    Selfhood.
The Lamb of God is seen through mists & shadows,
    hov'ring   25
Over the sepulchers in clouds of Jehovah & winds
    of Elohim,
A disk of blood, distant; & heavens & earths roll
    dark between.
What do I here before the Judgment without my
    Emanation,
With the daughters of memory & not with the daughters
    of inspiration?
I in my Selfhood am that Satan; I am that Evil
    One!   30
He is my Spectre! In my obedience to loose him from
    my Hells,
To claim the Hells, my Furnaces, I go to Eternal
    Death."

And Milton said: "I go to Eternal Death!" Eternity
    shuddered,
For he took the outside course, among the graves of
    the dead,
A mournful shade. Eternity shuddered at the image of
    eternal death.   35

Then on the verge of Beulah he beheld his own Shadow,
A mournful form, double, hermaphroditic, male & female

In one wonderful body; and he entered into it
In direful pain; for the dread shadow, twenty-seven-fold,
Reached to the depths of direst Hell, & thence to
    Albion's land,   40
Which is this earth of vegetation on which now I
    write.

The Seven Angels of the Presence wept over Milton's
    Shadow!

Plate 15

As when a man dreams, he reflects not that his
    body sleeps,
Else he would wake, so seemed he entering his
    Shadow; but
With him, the Spirits of the Seven Angels of the
    Presence
Entering, they gave him still perceptions of his
    Sleeping Body,
Which now arose and walked with them in Eden as
    an Eighth   5
Image Divine, though darkened, and though walking
    as one walks
In sleep; and the Seven comforted and supported him.

Like as a Polypus that vegetates beneath the deep,
They saw his Shadow vegetated underneath the Couch
Of death; for when he entered into his Shadow,
    Himself,   10
His real and immortal Self, was as appeared to
    those
Who dwell in immortality, as One sleeping on a couch
Of gold; and those in immortality gave forth their
    Emanations,
Like Females of sweet beauty, to guard round him &
    to feed
His lips with food of Eden in his cold and dim
    repose!   15

But to himself he seemed a wanderer lost in dreary
    night.

Onwards his Shadow kept its course among the Spectres,
    called
Satan; but swift as lightning passing them;
    startled, the shades
Of Hell beheld him in a trail of light as of a comet
That travels into Chaos; so Milton went guarded
    within.   20

The nature of infinity is this: That every thing
    has its
Own Vortex, and when once a traveller through
    Eternity
Has passed that Vortex, he perceives it roll
    backward behind
His path into a globe itself infolding like a
    sun,
Or like a moon, or like a universe of starry
    majesty,   25
While he keeps onwards in his wondrous journey
    on the earth,
Or like a human form, a friend with whom he lived
    benevolent.
As the eye of man views both the East & West,
    encompassing
Its vortex, and the North & South, with all their
    starry host,
Also the rising sun & setting moon, he views
    surrounding   30
His cornfields and his valleys of five hundred
    acres square.
Thus is the earth one infinite plane, and not as
    apparent
To the weak traveller confined beneath the moony
    shade.
Thus is the heaven a vortex passed already, and the
    earth

A vortex not yet passed by the traveller through
    Eternity.   35

First Milton saw Albion upon the Rock of
    Ages,
Deadly pale, outstretched and snowy cold, storm-covered,
A Giant form of perfect beauty outstretched on the
    rock
In solemn death. The Sea of Time & Space thundered
    aloud
Against the rock, which was inwrapped with the weeds of
    death   40
Hovering over the cold bosom, in its vortex, Milton
    bent down
To the bosom of death; what was underneath soon
    seemed above.
A cloudy heaven mingled with stormy seas in loudest
    ruin;
But as a wintry globe descends precipitant, through
    Beulah bursting
With thunders loud, and terrible, so Milton's
    shadow fell,   45
Precipitant, loud thund'ring into the Sea of Time
    & Space.

Then first I saw him in the Zenith as a falling
    star,
Descending perpendicular, swift as the swallow
    or swift,
And on my left foot falling on the tarsus, entered
    there;
But from my left foot a black cloud redounding
    spread over Europe.   50

Then Milton knew that the Three Heavens of Beulah
    were beheld
By him on earth in his bright pilgrimage of sixty
    years

From Plate 17

In those three females whom his Wives & those three
    whom his Daughters
Had represented and contained, that they might be
    resumed
By giving up of Selfhood; & they distant viewed his
    journey
In their eternal spheres, now Human, though their
    Bodies remain closed
In the dark Ulro till the Judgment. Also Milton knew
    they and   5
Himself was Human, though now wandering through
    Death's Vale
In conflict with those Female forms, which in blood
    & jealousy
Surrounded him, dividing & uniting without end or
    number.

He saw the Cruelties of Ulro, and he wrote them down
In iron tablets, and his Wives' & Daughters' names were
    these: 10
Rahab and Tirzah, & Milcah & Malah & Noah & Hoglah.
They sat ranged round him as the rocks of Horeb
    round the land
Of Canaan; and they wrote in thunder smoke and fire
His dictate; and his body was the Rock Sinai, that
    body
Which was on earth born to corruption; & the six
    Females   15
Are Hor & Peor & Bashan & Abarim & Lebanon & Hermon,
Seven rocky masses terrible in the Deserts of Midian.

But Milton's Human Shadow continued journeying above
The rocky masses of The Mundane Shell in the Lands
Of Edom & Aram & Moab & Midian & Amalek.   20

The Mundane Shell is a vast Concave Earth, an
    immense

Hardened shadow of all things upon our Vegetated
    Earth,
Enlarged into dimension & deformed into indefinite
    space,
In Twenty-seven Heavens and all their Hells, with
    Chaos
And Ancient Night & Purgatory. It is a cavernous
    Earth   25
Of labyrinthine intricacy, twenty-seven folds of
    opaqueness,
And finishes where the lark mounts; here Milton
    journeyed
In that Region called Midian, among the Rocks of
    Horeb.
For travellers from Eternity pass outward to
    Satan's seat,
But travellers to Eternity pass inward to
    Golgonooza.   30

From Plate 18

Urizen emerged from his Rocky Form & from his Snows,

Plate 19

And he also darkened his brows, freezing dark rocks
    between
The footsteps and infixing deep the feet in marble beds,
That Milton laboured with his journey, & his feet bled
    sore
Upon the clay, now changed to marble; also Urizen rose
And met him on the shores of Arnon; & by the streams
    of the brooks   5

Silent they met, and silent strove among the streams
    of Arnon
Even to Mahanaim, when with cold hand Urizen
    stooped down

And took up water from the river Jordan, pouring on
To Milton's brain the icy fluid from his broad cold
    palm.
But Milton took of the red clay of Succoth, moulding
    it with care   10
Between his palms and filling up the furrows of many
    years,
Beginning at the feet of Urizen, and on the bones
Creating new flesh on the Demon cold, and building
    him.
As with new clay a Human form in the Valley of Beth
    Peor.

Four Universes round the Mundane Egg remain Chaotic: 15
One to the North, named Urthona; One to the South,
    named Urizen;
One to the East, named Luvah; One to the West,
    named Tharmas.
They are the Four Zoas that stood around the Throne
    Divine!
But when Luvah assumed the World of Urizen to the
    South
And Albion was slain upon his mountains & in his tent,   20
All fell towards the Center in dire ruin, sinking down.
And in the South remains a burning fire, in the East
    a void.
In the West, a world of raging waters; in the North,
    a solid,
Unfathomable, without end. But in the midst of these
Is built eternally the Universe of Los and
    Enitharmon,   25
Towards which Milton went, but Urizen opposed his
    path.

———

From Plate 20
                Silent, Milton stood before
The darkened Urizen, as the sculptor silent stands
    before

His forming image; he walks round it, patient,
    labouring.
Thus Milton stood forming bright Urizen, while his
    Mortal part   10
Sat frozen in the rock of Horeb, and his
    Redeemed portion
Thus formed the Clay of Urizen; but within that
    portion
His real Human walked above in power and majesty,
Though darkened; and the Seven Angels of the
    Presence attended him.

Now Albion's sleeping Humanity began to turn upon his
    Couch   25
Feeling the electric flame of Milton's awful precipitate
    descent.
Seest thou the little winged fly, smaller than a grain
    of sand?
It has a heart like thee, a brain open to heaven &
    hell,
Withinside wondrous & expansive; its gates are not
    closed;
I hope thine are not. Hence it clothes itself in
    rich array   30
Hence thou art clothed with human beauty, O thou
    mortal man.
Seek not thy heavenly father then beyond the skies;
There Chaos dwells & ancient Night & Og & Anak old;
For every human heart has gates of brass & bars of
    adamant,
Which few dare unbar, because dread Og & Anak guard
    the gates   35
Terrific! And each mortal brain is walled and moated
    round
Within, and Og & Anak watch here; here is the Seat
    of Satan in its Webs; for in brain and heart and loins
Gates open behind Satan's Seat to the City of
    Golgonooza,

Which is the spiritual fourfold London, in the loins
 of Albion.   40

Thus Milton fell through Albion's heart, travelling
 outside of Humanity
Beyond the Stars in Chaos, in Caverns of the
 Mundane Shell.

———————

From Plate 21

But Milton entering my Foot, I saw in the nether
Regions of the Imagination; also all men on Earth,   5
And all in Heaven, saw in the nether regions of the
 Imagination,
In Ulro beneath Beulah, the vast breach of Milton's
 descent.
But I knew not that it was Milton, for man cannot
 know
What passes in his members till periods of Space & Time
Reveal the secrets of Eternity; for more extensive   10
Than any other earthly things are Man's earthly
 lineaments.

And all this Vegetable World appeared on my left
 Foot
As a bright sandal formed immortal of precious
 stones & gold;
I stooped down & bound it on to walk forward
 through Eternity.

———————

From Plate 22

While Los heard indistinct in fear, what time I
 bound my sandals
On to walk forward through Eternity, Los descended
 to me;   5
And Los behind me stood, a terrible flaming Sun just
 close

Behind my back; I turned round in terror, and, behold,
Los stood in that fierce glowing fire; & he also
    stooped down
And bound my sandals on in Udan-Adan; trembling, I
    stood
Exceedingly with fear & terror, standing in the Vale   10
Of Lambeth; but he kissed me and wished me health.
And I became One Man with him, arising in my
    strength.
'Twas too late now to recede: Los had entered into
    my soul;
His terrors now possessed me whole! I arose in fury
    & strength.

"I am that Shadowy Prophet who Six Thousand Years
    ago   15
Fell from my station in the Eternal bosom. Six
    Thousand Years
Are finished. I return! Both Time & Space obey my
    will.
I in Six Thousand Years walk up and down, for
    not one Moment
Of Time is lost, nor one Event of Space unpermanent.
But all remain, every fabric of Six Thousand Years   20
Remains permanent, though on the Earth, where Satan
Fell and was cut off, all things vanish & are seen
    no more.
They vanish not from me & mine; we guard them first
    & last.
The generations of men run on in the tide of Time
But leave their destined lineaments permanent forever
    & ever."   25

So spoke Los as we went along to his supreme abode.

From Plate 24

Los is by mortals named Time. Enitharmon is named
    Space.

But they depict him bald & aged who is in eternal
  youth
All powerful, and his locks flourish like the brows
  of morning.   70
He is the Spirit of Prophecy, the ever-apparent Elias.
Time is the mercy of Eternity; without Time's
  swiftness,
Which is the swiftest of all things, all were eternal
  torment.
All the Gods of the Kingdoms of Earth labour in Los's
  Halls.
Every one is a fallen Son of the Spirit of
  Prophecy.   75
He is the Fourth Zoa, that stood around the Throne
  Divine.

From Plate 25

And Los stood & cried to the Labourers of the Vintage
  in voice of awe:

"Fellow Labourers! The Great Vintage & Harvest is
  now upon Earth.
The whole extent of the Globe is explored: Every
  scattered Atom
Of Human Intellect now is flocking to the sound of
  the Trumpet;
All the Wisdom which was hidden in caves & dens from
  ancient   20
Time is now sought out from Animal & Vegetable &
  Mineral.
The Awakener is come, outstretched over Europe! The
  Vision of God is fulfilled.
The Ancient Man upon the Rock of Albion Awakes;
He listens to the sounds of War astonished & ashamed;
He sees his Children mock at Faith and deny Providence.   25
Therefore you must bind the Sheaves not by Nations
  or Families.

You shall bind them in Three Classes; according
    to their Classes
So shall you bind them, Separating What has been
    Mixed
Since Men began to be Wove into Nations by Rahab &
    Tirzah,
Since Albion's Death & Satan's Cutting-off from our
    awful Fields,   30
When under pretense to benevolence the Elect Subdued
    All
From the Foundation of the World. The Elect is one
    Class: You
Shall bind them separate; they cannot Believe in
    Eternal Life
Except by Miracle & a New Birth. The other two
    Classes,
The Reprobate, who never cease to Believe, and the
    Redeemed,   35
Who live in doubts & fears, perpetually tormented
    by the Elect—
These you shall bind in a twin-bundle for the
    Consummation.
But the Elect must be saved from fires of Eternal
    Death
To be formed into the Churches of Beulah, that
    they destroy not the Earth.
. . . ."

Plate 28

Some Sons of Los surround the Passions with porches
    of iron & silver
Creating form & beauty around the dark regions of
    sorrow,
Giving to airy nothing a name and a habitation
Delightful, with bounds to the Infinite putting
    off the Indefinite

Into most holy forms of Thought; such is the power
    of inspiration.   5
They labour incessant with many tears &
    afflictions,
Creating the beautiful House for the piteous
    sufferer.

Others Cabinets richly fabricate of gold & ivory
For Doubts & fears unformed & wretched & melancholy.
The little weeping Spectre stands on the threshold of
    Death   10
Eternal, and sometime two Spectres; like lamps
    quivering
And often malignant, they combat, heart-breaking,
    sorrowful & piteous.
Antamon takes them into his beautiful flexible hands
As the Sower takes the seed, or as the Artist his clay
Or fine wax, to mould artful a model for golden
    ornaments.   15
The soft hands of Antamon draw the indelible line,
Form immortal with golden pen, such as the Spectre,
    admiring,
Puts on the sweet form; then smiles Antamon bright
    through his windows.
The Daughters of beauty look up from their Loom &
    prepare
The integument soft for its clothing with joy &
    delight.   20

But others of the Sons of Los build Moments & Minutes
    & Hours
And Days & Months & Years & Ages & Periods, wondrous
    buildings;   45
And every Moment has a Couch of gold for soft repose
(A Moment equals a pulsation of the artery),
And between every two Moments stands a Daughter of
    Beulah

To feed the Sleepers on their Couches with maternal
    care.

And every Minute has an azure Tent with silken Veils.   50
And every Hour has a bright golden Gate carved with
    skill.
And every Day & Night has Walls of brass & Gates of
    adamant,
Shining like precious stones & ornamented with
    appropriate signs.
And every Month, a silver-paved Terrace builded high.
And every Year, invulnerable Barriers with high
    Towers.   55
And every Age is Moated deep with Bridges of silver
    & gold.
And every Seven Ages is Incircled with a Flaming Fire.
Now Seven Ages is amounting to Two Hundred Years.
Each has its Guard, each Moment, Minute, Hour, Day,
    Month & Year.
All are the work of Fairy hands of the Four Elements.   60
The Guard are Angels of Providence on duty evermore.
Every Time less than a pulsation of the artery
Is equal in its period & value to Six Thousand Years,

From Plate 29

For in this Period the Poet's Work is Done, and all
    the Great
Events of Time start forth & are conceived in such
    a Period,
Within a Moment, a Pulsation of the Artery.

The Sky is an immortal Tent built by the Sons of Los,
And every Space that a Man views around his
    dwelling-place,   5
Standing on his own roof, or in his garden on a mount
Of twenty-five cubits in height, such space is his
    Universe;
And on its verge the Sun rises & sets, the Clouds bow

To meet the flat Earth & the Sea in such an ordered
    Space.
The Starry heavens reach no further, but here bend
    and set   10
On all sides, & the two Poles turn on their valves
    of gold;
And if he move his dwelling-place, his heavens also
    move
Where'er he goes, & all his neighbourhood bewail his
    loss.
Such are the Spaces called Earth, & such its dimension.
As to that false appearance which appears to the
    reasoner   15
As of a Globe rolling through Voidness, it is a delusion
    of Ulro.
The Microscope knows not of this, nor the Telescope.
    They alter
The ratio of the Spectator's Organs but leave Objects
    untouched,
For every Space larger than a red Globule of Man's
    blood
Is visionary and is created by the Hammer of Los.   20
And every Space smaller than a Globule of Man's blood
    opens
Into Eternity, of which this vegetable Earth is but
    a shadow.

From Book the Second

From Plate 30

There is a place where Contrarieties are equally True.
This place is called Beulah. It is a pleasant lovely
    Shadow
Where no dispute can come, Because of those who Sleep.
Into this place the Sons & Daughters of Ololon
    descended

With solemn mourning into Beulah's moony shades &
   hills,   5
Weeping for Milton; mute wonder held the Daughters
   of Beulah
Enraptured with affection sweet and mild benevolence.

Beulah is evermore Created around Eternity, appearing
To the Inhabitants of Eden around them on all sides.
But Beulah to its Inhabitants appears within each district   10
As the beloved infant in his mother's bosom, round
   incircled
With arms of love & pity & sweet compassion. But to
The Sons of Eden the moony habitations of Beulah
Are from Great Eternity a mild & pleasant Rest.

From Plate 31

Into this pleasant Shadow all the weak & weary
Like Women & Children were taken away as on wings
Of dovelike softness, & shadowy habitations prepared
   for them.
But every Man returned & went, still going forward
   through
The Bosom of the Father in Eternity on Eternity.   5
Neither did any lack or fall into Error without
A Shadow to repose in all the Days of happy Eternity.

Into this pleasant Shadow, Beulah, all Ololon
   descended;
And when the Daughters of Beulah heard the lamentation
All Beulah wept, for they saw the Lord coming in the
   Clouds.   10
And the Shadows of Beulah terminate in rocky Albion.

Thou hearest the Nightingale begin the Song of Spring;
The Lark, sitting upon his earthy bed just as the morn

Appears, listens silent; then, springing from the
    waving Cornfield, loud   30
He leads the Choir of Day! trill, trill, trill, trill,
Mounting upon the wings of light into the Great Expanse,
Reechoing against the lovely blue & shining heavenly
    Shell.
His little throat labours with inspiration; every
    feather
On throat & breast & wings vibrates with the effluence
    Divine.   35
All Nature listens silent to him, & the awful Sun
Stands still upon the Mountain, looking on this little
    Bird
With eyes of soft humility & wonder, love & awe.
Then loud from their green covert all the Birds begin
    their Song.
The Thrush, the Linnet & the Goldfinch, Robin & the
    Wren   40
Awake the Sun from his sweet reverie upon the Mountain.
The Nightingale again assays his song & through the
    day
And through the night warbles luxuriant, every Bird of
    Song
Attending his loud harmony with admiration & love.
This is a Vision of the lamentation of Beulah over
    Ololon!   45

Thou perceivest the Flowers put forth their precious
    Odours!
And none can tell how from so small a center comes
    such sweets,
Forgetting that within that Center Eternity expands
Its ever 'during doors, that Og & Anak fiercely guard.
First e'er the morning breaks joy opens in the
    flowery bosoms,   50
Joy even to tears, which the Sun rising dries; first
    the Wild Thyme
And Meadow-sweet, downy & soft, waving among the reeds,

Light springing on the air, lead the sweet Dance; they
  wake
The Honeysuckle sleeping on the Oak; the flaunting
  beauty
Revels along upon the wind; the White-thorn lovely
  May   55
Opens her many lovely eyes; listening the Rose still
  sleeps.
None dare to wake her. Soon she bursts her
  crimson-curtained bed
And comes forth in the majesty of beauty; every
  Flower—
The Pink, the Jessamine, the Wall-flower, the
  Carnation,
The Jonquil, the mild Lily—opes her heavens! Every
  Tree   60
And Flower & Herb soon fill the air with an innumerable
  Dance,
Yet all in order sweet & lovely; Men are sick with Love!
Such is a Vision of the lamentation of Beulah
  over Ololon.

From Plate 32

And Milton oft sat up on the Couch of Death & oft
  conversed
In vision & dream beatific with the Seven Angels of
  the Presence:
"I have turned my back upon these Heavens builded on
  cruelty.
My Spectre, still wandering through them, follows my
  Emanation.
He hunts her footsteps through the snow & the wintry
  hail & rain.   5
The idiot Reasoner laughs at the Man of
  Imagination
And from laughter proceeds to murder by undervaluing
  calumny."

From Plate 35

There is a Moment in each Day that Satan cannot find,
Nor can his Watch-Fiends find it, but the Industrious
    find
This Moment & it multiply, & when it once is found
It renovates every Moment of the Day, if rightly
    placed.   45
In this Moment Ololon descended to Los & Enitharmon,
Unseen beyond the Mundane Shell, Southward in Milton's
    track.

Just in this Moment when the morning odours rise
    abroad,
And first from the Wild Thyme, stands a Fountain in a
    rock
Of crystal flowing into two Streams; one flows through
    Golgonooza   50
And through Beulah to Eden beneath Los's western Wall.
The other flows through the Aerial Void & all the
    Churches,
Meeting again in Golgonooza beyond Satan's Seat.

The Wild Thyme is Los's Messenger to Eden, a mighty
    Demon
Terrible, deadly & poisonous his presence in Ulro
    dark.   55
Therefore he appears only a small Root creeping in
    grass,
Covering over the Rock of Odours his bright purple
    mantle,
Beside the Fount above the Lark's nest in Golgonooza.
Luvah slept here in death, & here is Luvah's empty Tomb.
Ololon sat beside this Fountain on the Rock of Odours.   60

Just at the place to where the Lark mounts is a
    Crystal Gate,
It is the entrance of the First Heaven, named Luther;
    for

The Lark is Los's Messenger through the Twenty-seven
    Churches,
That the Seven Eyes of God, who walk even to Satan's Seat
Through all the Twenty-seven Heavens, may not slumber
    nor sleep.   65
But the Lark's Nest is at the Gate of Los, at the
    eastern
Gate of wide Golgonooza, & the Lark is Los's Messenger.

Plate 36

When on the highest lift of his light pinions he
    arrives
At that bright Gate, another Lark meets him, & back to
    back
They touch their pinions, tip tip, and each descend
To their respective Earths & there all night consult
    with Angels
Of Providence & with the Eyes of God all night in
    slumbers   5
Inspired, & at the dawn of day send out another Lark
Into another Heaven to carry news upon his wings.
Thus are the Messengers dispatched till they reach
    the Earth again
In the East Gate of Golgonooza, & the Twenty-eighth
    bright
Lark met the Female Ololon descending into my Garden.   10
Thus it appears to Mortal eyes & those of the Ulro
    Heavens,
But not thus to Immortals; the Lark is a mighty Angel.

For Ololon stepped into the Polypus within the Mundane
    Shell.
They could not step into Vegetable Worlds without becoming
The enemies of Humanity, except in a Female Form;   15
And as One Female, Ololon and all its mighty Hosts
Appeared, a Virgin of twelve years; nor time nor space
    was
To the perception of the Virgin Ololon; but as the

Flash of lightning, but more quick, the Virgin in my
 Garden
Before my Cottage stood, for the Satanic Space is
 delusion.   20

For when Los joined with me he took me in his fiery
 whirlwind,
My Vegetated portion was hurried from Lambeth's shades;
He set me down in Felpham's Vale & prepared a beautiful
Cottage for me, that in three years I might write
 all these Visions,
To display Nature's cruel holiness, the deceits of
 Natural Religion.   25
Walking in my Cottage Garden, sudden I beheld
The Virgin Ololon & addressed her as a Daughter of
 Beulah:

"Virgin of Providence, fear not to enter into my
 Cottage.
What is thy message to thy friend? What am I now to do?
Is it again to plunge into deeper affliction? Behold
 me   30
Ready to obey, but pity thou my Shadow of Delight.
Enter my Cottage, comfort her, for she is sick with
 fatigue."

From Plate 37

The Virgin answered: "Knowest thou of Milton who
 descended
Driven from Eternity? Him I seek, terrified at my Act
In Great Eternity, which thou knowest! I come him to seek."

From Plate 38

And Milton, collecting all his fibres into
 impregnable strength,   5
Descended down a Paved work of all kinds of precious
 stones

Out from the eastern sky, descending down into my
    Cottage
Garden; clothed in black, severe & silent he descended.
The Spectre of Satan stood upon the roaring
    sea & beheld
Milton within his sleeping Humanity! Trembling &
    shudd'ring   10
He stood upon the waves, a Twenty-seven-fold mighty
    Demon,
Gorgeous & beautiful; loud roll his thunders against
    Milton.
Loud Satan thundered, loud & dark upon mild Felpham
    shore.
Not daring to touch one fibre, he howled round upon the
    Sea

I also stood in Satan's bosom & beheld its desolations: 15
A ruined Man, a ruined building of God not made with
    hands,
Its plains of burning sand, its mountains of marble
    terrible,
Its pits & declivities flowing with molten ore &
    fountains.
Of pitch & nitre, its ruined palaces & cities & mighty
    works
Its furnaces of affliction, in which his Angels &
    Emanations   20
Labour with blackened visages among its stupendous ruins,
Arches & pyramids & porches, colonnades & domes,
In which dwells Mystery Babylon; here is her secret
    place.
From hence she comes forth on the Churches in delight.
Here is her Cup filled with its poisons, in these horrid
    vales,   25
And here her scarlet Veil woven in pestilence & war.
Here is Jerusalem bound in chains, in the Dens of Babylon.
In the Eastern porch of Satan's Universe Milton stood
    & said:

"Satan! my Spectre! I know my power thee to annihilate
And be a greater in thy place & be thy Tabernacle,   30
A covering for thee to do thy will, till one greater
        comes
And smites me as I smote thee, & becomes my covering.
Such are the Laws of thy false Heavens, but Laws of
        Eternity
Are not such; know thou I come to Self-Annihilation.
Such are the Laws of Eternity that each shall
        mutually   35
Annihilate himself for other's good, as I for thee.
Thy purpose & the purpose of thy Priests & of thy
        Churches
Is to impress on men the fear of death, to teach
Trembling & fear, terror, constriction, abject
        selfishness.
Mine is to teach Men to despise death & to go on   40
In fearless majesty annihilating Self, laughing to
        scorn
Thy Laws & terrors, shaking down thy Synagogues as
        webs.
I come to discover before Heaven & Hell the
        Self-righteousness
In all its Hypocritic turpitude, opening to every eye
These wonders of Satan's holiness, showing to the
        Earth   45
The Idol Virtues of the Natural Heart, & Satan's Seat
Explore in all its Selfish Natural Virtue, & put off
In Self-annihilation all that is not of God alone,
To put off Self & all I have, ever & ever, Amen."

Satan heard! coming in a cloud, with trumpets &
        flaming fire,   50
Saying, "I am God the judge of all, the living & the
        dead.
Fall therefore down & worship me. Submit they supreme
Dictate to my eternal Will, & to my dictate bow.
I hold the Balances of Right & Just, & mine the Sword.

Seven Angels bear my Name, & in those Seven I appear,   55
But I alone am God, & I alone in Heaven and Earth
Of all that live dare utter this; others tremble & bow,

From Plate 39

Till All Things become One Great Satan, in Holiness
Opposed to Mercy, and the Divine Delusion, Jesus, be
    no more."

Suddenly around Milton on my Path the Starry Seven
Burned terrible! My Path became a solid fire, as bright
As the clear Sun, & Milton silent came down on my Path.   5
And there went forth from the Starry limbs of the Seven
    Forms
Human, with Trumpets innumerable, sounding articulate
As the Seven spake; and they stood in a mighty Column
    of Fire
Surrounding Felpham's Vale, reaching to the Mundane
    Shell, Saying,

"Awake, Albion, awake! Reclaim thy Reasoning Spectre.
    Subdue   10
Him to the Divine Mercy; Cast him down into the Lake
Of Los, that ever burneth with fire, ever & ever, Amen!
Let the Four Zoas awake from Slumbers of Six Thousand
    Years."

From Plate 40

But turning toward Ololon in terrible majesty, Milton
Replied: "Obey thou the Words of the Inspired Man.
All that can be annihilated must be annihilated,   30
That the Children of Jerusalem may be saved from slavery.
There is a Negation, & there is a Contrary.
The Negation must be destroyed to redeem the Contraries.
The Negation is the Spectre, the Reasoning Power in Man.
This is a false Body, an Incrustation over my Immortal   35

Spirit, a Selfhood, which must be put off & annihilated
    alway.
To cleanse the Face of my Spirit by Self-examination,

From Plate 41

To bathe in the Waters of Life, to wash off the Not
    Human,
I come in Self-annihilation & the grandeur of Inspiration,
To cast off Rational Demonstration by Faith in the
    Saviour,
To cast off the rotten rags of Memory by Inspiration,
To cast off Bacon, Locke & Newton from Albion's
    covering,   5
To take off his filthy garments & clothe him with
    Imagination,
To cast aside from Poetry all that is not Inspiration,
That it no longer shall dare to mock with the aspersion
    of Madness
Cast on the Inspired, by the tame high finisher of
    paltry Blots
Indefinite, or paltry Rhymes, or paltry Harmonies,   10
Who creeps into State Government like a caterpillar to
    destroy,
To cast off the idiot Questioner who is always questioning
But never capable of answering, who sits with a sly grin
Silent plotting when to question, like a thief in a cave,
Who publishes doubt & calls it knowledge, whose Science
    is Despair,   15
Whose pretense to knowledge is Envy, whose whole
    Science is
To destroy the wisdom of ages to gratify ravenous Envy,
That rages round him like a Wolf day & night without
    rest.
He smiles with condescension; he talks of Benevolence &
    Virtue,
And those who act with Benevolence & Virtue, they murder
    time on time.   20

These are the destroyers of Jerusalem; these are the
    murderers
Of Jesus, who deny the Faith & mock at Eternal Life,
Who pretend to Poetry that they may destroy Imagination,
By imitation of Nature's Images drawn from Remembrance.
These are the Sexual Garments, the Abomination of
    Desolation,   25
Hiding the Human Lineaments as with an Ark & Curtains,
Which Jesus rent & now shall wholly purge away with
    Fire
Till Generation is swallowed up in Regeneration."

From Plate 42

And I beheld the Twenty-four Cities of Albion
Arise upon their Thrones to Judge the Nations of the
    Earth,
And the Immortal Four in whom the Twenty-four appear
    Fourfold
Arose around Albion's body. Jesus wept & walked forth
From Felpham's Vale clothed in Clouds of blood, to
    enter into   20
Albion's Bosom, the bosom of death, & the Four
    surrounded him
In the Column of Fire in Felpham's Vale; then to their
    mouths the Four
Applied their Four Trumpets & them sounded to the
    Four winds.

Terror struck in the Vale. I stood at that immortal
    sound.
My bones trembled. I fell outstretched upon the path   25
A moment, & my Soul returned into its mortal state,
To Resurrection & Judgment in the Vegetable Body,
And my sweet Shadow of Delight stood trembling by my
    side.

Immediately the Lark mounted with a loud
    trill from Felpham's Vale,

And the Wild Thyme from Wimbledon's green & impurpled
    Hills
                                   30
And Los & Enitharmon rose over the Hills of Surrey.
Their clouds roll over London with a south wind;
    soft Oothoon
Pants in the Vales of Lambeth, weeping o'er her Human
    Harvest.
Los listens to the Cry of the Poor Man. His Cloud
Over London in volume terrific low bended in anger.   35

Rintrah & Palamabron view the Human Harvest beneath.
Their Winepresses & Barns stand open; the Ovens are
    prepared,
The Wagons ready; terrific Lions & Tigers sport & play.
All Animals upon the Earth are prepared in all their
    strength

Plate 43

To go forth to the Great Harvest & Vintage of the
    Nations.

———————

Figure 6. *Jerusalem,* page 70. By permission of The British Museum.

Jerusalem: *The Emanation of The Giant Albion (1804-1820)*

Plate 1

FRONTISPIECE

ABOVE THE ARCHWAY:

There is a Void, outside of Existence, which if
    entered into
Englobes itself & becomes a Womb; such was Albion's
    Couch,
A pleasant Shadow of Repose called Albion's lovely
    Land.

His Sublime & Pathos become Two Rocks fixed in the
    Earth.
His Reason, his Spectrous Power, covers them above.
Jerusalem, his Emanation, is a Stone laying beneath.
O behold the Vision of Albion.

ON THE RIGHT SIDE OF ARCHWAY:

"Half Friendship is the bitterest Enmity," said Los
As he entered the Door of Death for Albion's sake
    Inspired.
The long sufferings of God are not forever; there is
    a Judgment.

ON THE LEFT SIDE IN REVERSED WRITING:

Every Thing has its Vermin, O Spectre of the Sleeping
    Dead!

Plate 3

SHEEP   GOATS

TO THE PUBLIC

After my three years' slumber on the banks of the Ocean, I
again display my Giant forms to the Public. My former Giants

& Fairies having received the highest reward possible, the love
and friendship of those with whom to be connected is to be
blessed, I cannot doubt that this more consolidated & extended
Work will be as kindly received.

The Enthusiasm of the following Poem, the Author hopes. . . .
I also hope the Reader will be with me, wholly One in Jesus our
Lord, who is the God of Fire and Lord of Love to whom the Ancients looked and saw his day afar off with trembling and amazement.

The Spirit of Jesus is continual forgiveness of Sin: he who waits
to be righteous before he enters into the Saviour's kingdom, the
Divine Body, will never enter there. I am perhaps the most sinful of men; I pretend not to holiness; yet I pretend to love, to
see, to converse with daily, as man with man, & the more to have
an interest in the Friend of Sinners. Therefore, Dear Reader,
forgive what you do not approve, & love me for this energetic
exertion of my talent.

> Reader! lover of books! lover of heaven,
> And of that God from whom all books are given,
> Who in mysterious Sinai's awful cave
> To Man the wondrous art of writing gave,
> Again he speaks in thunder and in fire!
> Thunder of Thought & flames of fierce desire.
> Even from the depths of Hell his voice I hear
> Within the unfathomed caverns of my Ear.
> Therefore I print, nor vain my types shall be:
> Heaven, Earth & Hell henceforth shall live in
>   harmony.

> Of the Measure in which
> the following Poem is written:

We who dwell on Earth can do nothing of ourselves; everything is conducted by Spirits, no less than Digestion or Sleep.

When this Verse was first dictated to me I considered a Monotonous Cadence like that used by Milton & Shakespeare & all
writers of English Blank Verse, derived from the modern bondage
of Rhyming, to be a necessary and indispensable part of Verse.
But I soon found that in the mouth of a true Orator such mo-

notony was not only awkward, but as much a bondage as rhyme itself. I therefore have produced a variety in every line, both of cadences & number of syllables. Every word and every letter is studied and put into its fit place: the terrific numbers are reserved for the terrific parts, the mild & gentle for the mild & gentle parts, and the prosaic for inferior parts: all are necessary to each other. Poetry Fettered, Fetters the Human Race! Nations are Destroyed, or Flourish in proportion as their Poetry, Painting and Music are Destroyed or Flourish! The Primeval State of Man was Wisdom, Art and Science.

Plate 4

JERUSALEM

Chapter I

Of the Sleep of Ulro! and of the passage through
Eternal Death! and of the awaking to Eternal Life.

This theme calls me in sleep night after night, & ev'ry
    morn
Awakes me at sunrise; then I see the Saviour over me
Spreading his beams of love & dictating the words of
    this mild song: 5

"Awake! awake! O sleeper of the land of shadows, wake!
    expand!
I am in you and you in me, mutual in love divine:
Fibres of love from man to man through Albion's pleasant
    land.
In all the dark Atlantic vale down from the hills of
    Surrey
A black water accumulates; return, Albion! return!   10
Thy brethren call thee, and thy fathers, and thy sons;
Thy nurses and thy mothers, thy sisters and thy
    daughters
Weep at thy soul's disease, and the Divine Vision is
    darkened;

Thy Emanation, that was wont to play before thy face,
Beaming forth with her daughters into the Divine
    bosom—   15
Where hast thou hidden thy Emanation, lovely Jerusalem,
From the vision and fruition of the Holy one?
I am not a God afar off, I am a brother and friend;
Within your bosoms I reside, and you reside in me.
Lo! we are One, forgiving all Evil, Not seeking
    recompense!   20
Ye are my members, O ye sleepers of Beulah, land of
    shades!"

But the perturbed Man away turns down the valleys dark:
"Phantom of the overheated brain! shadow of immortality!
Seeking to keep my soul a victim to thy Love, which binds
Man, the enemy of man, into deceitful friendships.   25
Jerusalem is not! Her daughters are indefinite.
By demonstration man alone can live, and not by faith.
My mountains are my own, and I will keep them to
    myself:
The Malvern and the Cheviot, the Wolds, Plinlimmon &
    Snowdon
Are mine: here will I build my Laws of Moral Virtue.   30
Humanity shall be no more, but war & princedom &
    victory."

So spoke Albion in jealous fears, hiding his Emanation
Upon the Thames and Medway, rivers of Beulah, dissembling
His jealousy before the throne divine, darkening, cold!

Plate 5

The banks of the Thames are clouded! The ancient porches
    of Albion are
Darkened! They are drawn through unbounded space,
    scattered upon
The Void in incoherent despair! Cambridge & Oxford &
    London
Are driven among the starry Wheels, rent away and dissipated

In Chasms & Abysses of sorrow, enlarged without
    dimension, terrible.   5
Albion's mountains run with blood; the cries of war
    & of tumult
Resound into the unbounded night; every Human
    perfection
Of mountain & river & city are small & withered &
    darkened.
Cam is a little stream! Ely is almost swallowed up!
Lincoln & Norwich stand trembling on the brink of
    Udan-Adan!   10
Wales and Scotland shrink themselves to the West and to
    the North!
Mourning for fear of the warriors in the Vale of
    Entuthon-Benython,
Jerusalem is scattered abroad like a cloud of smoke
    through non-Entity;
Moab & Ammon & Amalek & Canaan & Egypt & Aram
Receive her little ones for sacrifices and the delights
    of cruelty.   15
Trembling I sit day and night; my friends are
    astonished at me,
Yet they forgive my wanderings. I rest not from my
    great task!
To open the Eternal Worlds, to open the immortal Eyes
Of man inwards into the Worlds of Thought: into Eternity,
Ever-expanding in the Bosom of God, the Human
    Imagination.   20
O Saviour, pour upon me thy Spirit of meekness & love;
Annihilate the Selfhood in me; be thou all my life!
Guide thou my hand, which trembles exceedingly upon
    the rock of ages,
While I write of the building of Golgonooza & of the
    terrors of Entuthon,
Of Hand & Hyle & Coban, of Guantok, Peachey, Brereton,
    Slade & Hutton,   25
Of the terrible sons & daughters of Albion, and their
    Generations.

Scofield, Kox, Kotope and Bowen revolve most
    mightily upon
The Furnace of Los before the eastern gate, bending
    their fury.
They war to destroy the Furnaces, to desolate Golgonooza,
And to devour the Sleeping Humanity of Albion in rage
    & hunger.   30
They revolve into the Furnaces Southward & are driven
    forth Northward,
Divided into Male and Female forms time after time.
From these Twelve all the Families of England spread
    abroad.

The Male is a Furnace of beryl; the Female is a golden
    Loom;
I behold them, and their rushing fires overwhelm my
    Soul,   35
In London's darkness; and my tears fall day and night
Upon the Emanations of Albion's Sons, the Daughters of
    Albion,
Names anciently remembered, but now contemned as
    fictions;
Although in every bosom they control our Vegetative
    powers.

These are united into Tirzah and her Sisters on
    Mount Gilead,   40
Cambel & Gwendolen & Conwenna & Cordella & Ignoge.
And these united into Rahab in the Covering Cherub on
    Euphrates:
Gwiniverra & Gwinefred & Gonorill & Sabrina beautiful,
Estrild, Mehetabel & Ragan, lovely Daughters of Albion:
They are the beautiful Emanations of the Twelve Sons of
    Albion.   45

The Starry Wheels revolved heavily over the Furnaces,
Drawing Jerusalem in anguish of maternal love
Eastward, a pillar of a cloud, with Vala upon the
    mountains,

Howling in pain, redounding from the arms of Beulah's
    Daughters
Out from the Furnaces of Los above the head of
    Los,   50
A pillar of smoke writhing afar into non-Entity,
    redounding
Till the cloud reaches afar outstretched among the
    Starry Wheels,
Which revolve heavily in the mighty Void above the
    Furnaces.

O, what avail the loves & tears of Beulah's lovely
    Daughters?
They hold the Immortal Form in the gentle bands &
    tender tears,   55
But all within is opened into the deeps of Entuthon-Benython,
A dark and unknown night, indefinite, unmeasurable, without
    end,
Abstract Philosophy warring in enmity against Imagination
(Which is the Divine Body of the Lord Jesus, blessed
    forever).
And there Jerusalem wanders with Vala upon the
    mountains,   60
Attracted by the revolutions of those Wheels, the
    Cloud of smoke
Immense; and Jerusalem & Vala, weeping in the Cloud,
Wander away into the Chaotic Void, lamenting with her
    Shadow
Among the Daughters of Albion, among the Starry
    Wheels;
Lamenting for her children, for the sons & daughters
    of Albion.   65

Los heard her lamentations in the deeps afar! His tears
    fall
Incessant before the Furnaces, and his Emanation
    divided in pain
Eastward toward the Starry Wheels. But Westward, a
    black Horror,

Plate 6

His spectre, driven by the Starry Wheels of Albion's
    sons, black and
Opaque, divided from his back; he labours and he mourns!

For as his Emanation divided, his Spectre also
    divided
In terror of those starry wheels; and the Spectre stood
    over Los
Howling in pain, a black'ning Shadow, black'ning, dark
    & opaque,   5
Cursing the terrible Los, bitterly cursing him for his
    friendship
To Albion, suggesting murderous thoughts against
    Albion.

Los raged and stamped the earth in his might & terrible
    wrath!
He stood and stamped the earth! Then he threw down
    his hammer in rage &
In fury; then he sat down and wept, terrified! Then
    arose   10
And chanted his song, labouring with the tongs and
    hammer;
But still the Spectre divided, and still his pain
    increased!

In pain the Spectre divided, in pain of hunger and
    thirst,
To devour Los's Human Perfection; but when he saw
    that Los

Plate 7

Was living, panting like a frighted wolf, and howling,
He stood over the Immortal in the solitude and
    darkness

Upon the dark'ning Thames, across the whole Island
    westward,
A horrible Shadow of Death among the Furnaces beneath
The pillar of folding smoke; and he sought by other
    means   5
To lure Los: by tears, by arguments of science & by
    terrors,
Terrors in every Nerve, by spasms & extended pains;
While Los answered unterrified to the opaque blackening
    Fiend.

And thus the Spectre spoke: "Wilt thou still go
    on to destruction
Till thy life is all taken away by this deceitful
    Friendship?   10
He drinks thee up like water! Like wine he pours thee
Into his tuns; thy Daughters are trodden in his vintage.
He makes thy Sons the trampling of his bulls; they
    are plowed
And harrowed for his profit; lo! thy stolen Emanation
Is his garden of pleasure! All the Spectres of his Sons
    mock thee.   15
Look how they scorn thy once-admired palaces,
    now in ruins
Because of Albion! Because of deceit and friendship!
    For Lo!
Hand has peopled Babel & Nineveh; Hyle, Ashur & Aram;
Coban's son is Nimrod; his son Cush is adjoined to Aram
By the Daughter of Babel in a woven mantle of pestilence
    & war.   20
They put forth their spectrous cloudy sails, which drive
    their immense
Constellations over the deadly deeps of indefinite
    Udan-Adan.
Kox is the Father of Shem & Ham & Japheth; he is the
    Noah
Of the Flood of Udan-Adan. Hutton is the Father of
    the Seven

From Enoch to Adam; Scofield is Adam who was New-   25
Created in Edom. I saw it indignant, & thou art not
    moved!
This has divided thee in sunder, and wilt thou still
    forgive?
O! thou seest not what I see, what is done in the
    Furnaces.
Listen, I will tell thee what is done in moments to
    thee unknown:
Luvah was cast into the Furnaces of affliction and
    sealed,   30
And Vala fed in cruel delight the Furnaces with fire.
Stern Urizen beheld, urged by necessity to keep
The evil day afar, and if perchance with iron power
He might avert his own despair; in woe & fear he saw
Vala incircle round the Furnaces where Luvah
    was closed.   35
With joy she heard his howlings, & forgot he was her
    Luvah,
With whom she lived in bliss in times of innocence &
    youth!
Vala comes from the Furnace in a cloud, but wretched
    Luvah
Is howling in the Furnaces, in flames among Albion's
    Spectres,
To prepare the Spectre of Albion to reign over thee,
    O Los,   40
Forming the Spectres of Albion according to his rage,
To prepare the Spectre sons of Adam, who is Scofield,
    the Ninth
Of Albion's sons & the father of all his brethren in
    the Shadowy
Generation. Cambel & Gwendolen wove webs of war & of
Religion to involve all Albion's sons, and when they
    had   45
Involved Eight, their webs rolled outwards into
    darkness,

And Scofield the Ninth remained on the outside of the
    Eight,
And Kox, Kotope, & Bowen, One in him, a Fourfold
    Wonder,
Involved the Eight. Such are the Generations of the
    Giant Albion,
To separate a Law of Sin, to punish thee in thy
    members."   50

Los answered: "Although I know not this, I know far
    worse than this:
I know that Albion hath divided me, and that thou, O
    my Spectre,
Hast just cause to be irritated; but look steadfastly
    upon me;
Comfort thyself in my strength; the time will arrive
When all Albion's injuries shall cease, and when we
    shall   55
Embrace him, tenfold bright, rising from his tomb in
    immortality.
They have divided themselves by Wrath; they must be
    united by
Pity. Let us therefore take example & warning, O my
    Spectre.
O that I could abstain from wrath! O that the Lamb
Of God would look upon me and pity me in my fury.   60
In anguish of regeneration, in terrors of
    self-annihilation,
Pity must join together those whom wrath has torn in
    sunder,
And the Religion of Generation, which was meant for
    the destruction
Of Jerusalem, become her covering till the time of
    the End.
O holy Generation, Image of regeneration!   65
O point of mutual forgiveness between Enemies!
Birthplace of the Lamb of God incomprehensible!

The Dead despise & scorn thee & cast thee out as
    accursed,
Seeing the Lamb of God in thy gardens & thy palaces,
Where they desire to place the Abomination of
    Desolation.   70
Hand sits before his furnace; scorn of others & furious
    pride
Freeze round him to bars of steel & to iron rocks
    beneath
His feet; indignant self-righteousness like whirlwinds
    of the North

Plate 8

Rose up against me, thundering from the Brook of
    Albion's River,
From Ranelagh & Strumbolo, from Cromwell's gardens &
    Chelsea,
The place of wounded Soldiers; but when he saw my Mace
Whirled round from heaven to earth, trembling he sat;
    his cold
Poisons rose up, & his sweet deceits covered them all
    over   5
With a tender cloud. As thou art now, such was he, O
    Spectre.
I know thy deceit & thy revenges, and unless thou desist
I will certainly create an eternal Hell for thee.
    Listen!
Be attentive! Be obedient! Lo, the Furnaces are ready to
    receive thee.
I will break thee into shivers & melt thee in the
    furnaces of death;   10
I will cast thee into forms of abhorrence & torment if
    thou
Desist not from thine own will & obey not my stern
    command!
I am closed up from my children; my Emanation is
    dividing,

And thou my Spectre art divided against me. But mark,
I will compel thee to assist me in my terrible labours:
      To beat   15
These hypocritic Selfhoods on the Anvils of bitter Death.
I am inspired: I act not for myself; for Albion's sake
I now am what I am, a horror and an astonishment,
Shudd'ring the heavens to look upon me. Behold
      what cruelties
Are practiced in Babel & Shinar & have approached to
      Zion's Hill."   20

While Los spoke, the terrible Spectre fell
      shudd'ring before him,
Watching his time with glowing eyes to leap upon
      his prey.
Los opened the Furnaces in fear. The Spectre saw to
      Babel & Shinar
Across all Europe & Asia. He saw the tortures of the
      Victims.
He saw now from the outside what he before saw & felt
      from within.   25
He saw that Los was the sole, uncontrolled Lord of
      the Furnaces.
Groaning, he kneeled before Los's iron-shod feet
      on London Stone,
Hung'ring & thirsting for Los's life, yet pretending
      obedience.
While Los pursued his speech in threat'nings loud &
      fierce:

"Thou art my Pride & Self-righteousness; I have
      found thee out.   30
Thou art revealed before me in all thy magnitude &
      power.
The Uncircumcised pretenses to Chastity must be cut
      in sunder!
Thy holy wrath & deep deceit cannot avail against me,
Nor shalt thou ever assume the triple form of Albion's
      Spectre,

For I am one of the living; dare not to mock my inspired
      fury.   35
If thou wast cast forth from my life, if I was dead
      upon the mountains,
Thou mightest be pitied & loved; but now I am living.
      Unless
Thou abstain ravening I will create an eternal Hell
      for thee.
Take thou this Hammer & in patience heave the thundering
      Bellows.
Take thou these Tongs; strike thou alternate with me;
      labour obedient.   40
Hand & Hyle & Coban, Scofield, Kox & Kotope labour
      mightily.
In the Wars of Babel & Shinar, all their Emanations were
Condensed. Hand has absorbed all his Brethren in his
      might.
All the infant Loves & Graces were lost, for the mighty
      Hand

Plate 9

Condensed his Emanations into hard, opaque substances
And his infant thoughts & desires into cold, dark
      cliffs of death.
His hammer of gold he seized, and his anvil of adamant.
He seized the bars of condensed thoughts to forge them
Into the sword of war, into the bow and arrow,   5
Into the thundering cannon and into the murdering
      gun.
I saw the limbs, formed for exercise, contemned, &
      the beauty of
Eternity looked upon as deformity, & loveliness as a
      dry tree.
I saw disease forming a Body of Death around the Lamb
Of God to destroy Jerusalem & to devour the body of
      Albion,   10
By war and stratagem to win the labour of the husbandman.
Awkwardness armed in steel, folly in a helmet of gold,

Weakness with horns & talons, ignorance with a
    rav'ning beak,
Every Emanative joy forbidden as a Crime,
And the Emanations buried alive in the earth with pomp
    of religion,   15
Inspiration denied, Genius forbidden by laws of punishment
I saw, terrified. I took the sighs & tears & bitter
    groans;
I lifted them into my Furnaces to form the spiritual
    sword
That lays open the hidden heart; I drew forth the pang
Of sorrow red-hot; I worked it on my resolute
    anvil;   20
I heated it in the flames of Hand & Hyle & Coban
Nine times; Gwendolen & Cambel & Gwiniverra
Are melted into the gold, the silver, the liquid ruby,
The chrysolite, the topaz, the jacinth & every precious
    stone.
Loud roar my Furnaces and loud my hammer is heard.   25
I labour day and night. I behold the soft
    affections
Condense beneath my hammer into forms of cruelty,
But still I labour in hope, though still my tears
    flow down.
That he who will not defend Truth may be compelled
    to defend
A Lie, that he may be snared and caught and snared and
    taken,   30
That Enthusiasm and Life may not cease, arise,
    Spectre, arise!"

Thus they contended among the Furnaces with groans
    & tears;
Groaning, the Spectre heaved the bellows, obeying
    Los's frowns,
Till the Spaces of Erin were perfected in the furnaces
Of affliction and Los drew them forth, compelling
    the harsh Spectre   35

Plate 10

Into the Furnaces & into the valleys of the Anvils
    of Death
And into the mountains of the Anvils & of the heavy
    Hammers,
Till he should bring the Sons & Daughters of
    Jerusalem to be
The Sons & Daughters of Los, that he might protect
    them from
Albion's dread Spectres; storming, loud, thunderous
    & mighty,   5
The Bellows & the Hammers move, compelled by
    Los's hand.

And this is the manner of the Sons of Albion in
    their strength:
They take the Two Contraries, which are called Qualities,
    with which
Every Substance is clothed; they name them Good
    & Evil.
From them they make an Abstract, which is a Negation   10
Not only of the Substance from which it is derived,
A murderer of its own Body, but also a murderer
Of every Divine Member; it is the Reasoning Power,
An Abstract objecting power that Negatives everything.
This is the Spectre of Man, the Holy Reasoning Power,   15.
And in its Holiness is closed the Abomination of
    Desolation.

Therefore Los stands in London building Golgonooza,
Compelling his Spectre to labours mighty; trembling in
    fear,
The Spectre weeps, but Los, unmoved by tears or threats,
    remains.

"I must Create a System or be enslaved by another
    Man's.   20

I will not Reason & Compare; my business is to Create."

So Los, in fury & strength, in indignation & burning
    wrath.
Shudd'ring, the Spectre howls. His howlings terrify
    the night.
He stamps around the Anvil, beating blows of stern
    despair.
He curses Heaven & Earth, Day & Night & Sun & Moon;   25
He curses Forest, Spring & River, Desert & sandy Waste,
Cities & Nations, Families & Peoples, Tongues & Laws,
Driven to desperation by Los's terrors & threat'ning
    fears.

Los cries, "Obey my voice & never deviate from my will,
And I will be merciful to thee; be thou invisible to
    all
                                                                   30
To whom I make thee invisible, but chief to my own
    Children,
O Spectre of Urthona. Reason not against their dear
    approach,
Nor them obstruct with thy temptations of doubt &
    despair.
O Shame, O strong & mighty Shame, I break thy brazen
    fetters.
If thou refuse, thy present torments will seem southern
    breezes
                                                                   35
To what thou shalt endure if thou obey not my great
    will."

The Spectre answered, "Art thou not ashamed of
    those thy Sins
That thou callest thy Children? Lo, the Law of God
    commands
That they be offered upon his Altar. O cruelty &
    torment,
For thine are also mine! I have kept silent hitherto   40
Concerning my chief delight, but thou hast broken
    silence.

Now I will speak my mind! Where is my lovely Enitharmon,
O thou my enemy? Where is my Great Sin? 'She is also
    thine,'
I said; now is my grief at worst, incapable of being
Surpassed; but every moment it accumulates more &
    more.   45
It continues accumulating to eternity! The joys of
    God advance,
For he is Righteous; he is not a Being of Pity &
    Compassion;
He cannot feel Distress; he feeds on Sacrifice &
    Offering,
Delighting in cries & tears & clothed in holiness
    & solitude;
But my griefs advance also, forever & ever without
    end.   50
O that I could cease to be! Despair! I am Despair,
Created to be the great example of horror & agony;
    also my
Prayer is vain. I called for compassion; compassion
    mocked;
Mercy & pity threw the gravestone over me & with
    lead
And iron bound it over me forever. Life lives on my   55
Consuming, & the Almighty hath made me his Contrary,
To be all evil, all reversed & forever dead, knowing
And seeing life, yet living not. How can I then behold
And not tremble? How can I be beheld & not abhorred?"

So spoke the Spectre shudd'ring, & dark tears ran down
    his shadowy face,   60
Which Los wiped off, but comfort none could give, or
    beam of hope.
Yet ceased he not from labouring at the roaring of
    his Forge
With iron & brass, Building Golgonooza in great
    contendings,
Till his Sons & Daughters came forth from the
    Furnaces

At the sublime Labours; for Los compelled
   the invisible Spectre   65

Plate 11

To labours mighty, with vast strength, with his
   mighty chains,
In pulsations of time & extensions of space, like Urns
   of Beulah,
With great labour upon his anvils; & in his ladles the
   Ore
He lifted, pouring it into the clay ground prepared
   with art,
Striving with Systems to deliver Individuals from
   those Systems,   5
That whenever any Spectre began to devour the Dead,
He might feel the pain as if a man gnawed his own
   tender nerves.
Then Erin came forth from the Furnaces, & all the
   Daughters of Beulah
Came from the Furnaces by Los's mighty power for
   Jerusalem's
Sake, walking up and down among the Spaces of Erin;   10
And the Sons and Daughters of Los came forth in
   perfection lovely!
And the Spaces of Erin reached from the starry height
   to the starry depth.

Los wept with exceeding joy, & all wept with joy
   together!
They feared they never more should see their Father,
   who
Was built in from Eternity in the Cliffs of Albion.   15

But when the joy of meeting was exhausted in loving
   embrace,
Again they lament: "O what shall we do for lovely
   Jerusalem
To protect the Emanations of Albion's mighty ones from
   cruelty?

Sabrina & Ignoge begin to sharpen their beamy spears
Of light and love; their little children stand with
    arrows of gold.   20
Ragan is wholly cruel; Scofield is bound in iron
    armour!
He is like a mandrake in the earth before Reuben's
    gate.
He shoots beneath Jerusalem's walls to undermine her
    foundations!
Vala is but thy Shadow, O thou loveliest among women!
A shadow animated by thy tears, O mournful Jerusalem!   25

Plate 12

Why wilt thou give to her a Body whose life is but a
    Shade?
Her joy and love, a shade, a shade of sweet repose;
But animated and vegetated, she is a devouring worm.
What shall we do for thee, O lovely mild Jerusalem?"

And Los said, "I behold the finger of God in terrors!   5
Albion is dead! His Emanation is divided from him!
But I am living, yet I feel my Emanation also dividing.
Such thing was never known! O pity me, thou
    all-piteous one!
What shall I do, or how exist, divided from Enitharmon?
Yet why despair? I saw the finger of God go forth   10
Upon my Furnaces from within the Wheels of Albion's
    Sons,
Fixing their Systems permanent by mathematic power,
Giving a body to Falsehood that it may be cast off
    forever,
With Demonstrative Science piercing Apollyon with
    his own bow!
God is within & without! He is even in the depths of
    Hell!"   15

Such were the lamentations of the Labourers in the
    Furnaces!

And they appeared within & without incircling on both
    sides
The Starry Wheels of Albion's Sons with Spaces for
    Jerusalem,
And for Vala, the shadow of Jerusalem, the
    ever-mourning shade,
On both sides, within & without, beaming gloriously!   20

Terrified at the sublime Wonder, Los stood before
    his Furnaces.
And they stood around, terrified with admiration at
    Erin's Spaces,
For the Spaces reached from the starry height to the
    starry depth;
And they builded Golgonooza: terrible eternal labour!

What are those golden builders doing? Where was the
    burying-place   25
Of soft Ethinthus? Near Tyburn's fatal Tree? Is that
Mild Zion's hill's most ancient promontory near
    mournful
Ever-weeping Paddington? Is that Calvary and Golgotha
Becoming a building of pity and compassion? Lo!
The stones are pity, and the bricks well-wrought
    affections   30
Enameled with love & kindness, & the tiles engraven
    gold,
Labour of merciful hands; the beams & rafters
    are forgiveness;
The mortar & cement of the work, tears of honesty;
    the nails
And the screws & iron braces are well-wrought
    blandishments
And well-contrived words, firm-fixing, never forgotten,   35
Always comforting the remembrance; the floors, humility;
The ceilings, devotion; the hearths, thanksgiving.
Prepare the furniture, O Lambeth, in thy pitying
    looms,

The curtains, woven tears & sighs, wrought into lovely
    forms
For comfort. There the secret furniture of Jerusalem's
    chamber   40
Is wrought. Lambeth! the Bride, the Lamb's Wife,
    loveth thee.
Thou art one with her & knowest not of self in thy
    supreme joy.
Go on, builders, in hope, though Jerusalem
    wanders far away
Without the gate of Los, among the dark Satanic
    wheels.

Fourfold the Sons of Los in their divisions, and
    fourfold   45
The great City of Golgonooza: fourfold toward the
    North,
And toward the South fourfold, & fourfold toward the
    East & West,
Each within other toward the four points: that toward
Eden, and that toward the World of Generation,
And that toward Beulah, and that toward Ulro.   50
Ulro is the space of the terrible starry wheels of
    Albion's sons,
But that toward Eden is walled up till time of
    renovation,
Yet it is perfect in its building, ornaments & perfection.

And the Four Points are thus beheld in Great Eternity:
West, the Circumference; South, the Zenith; North,   55
The Nadir; East, the Center, unapproachable forever.
These are the four Faces towards the Four Worlds
    of Humanity
In every Man. Ezekiel saw them by Chebar's flood.
And the Eyes are the South, and the Nostrils are the
    East,
And the Tongue is the West, and the Ear is the
    North.   60

And the North Gate of Golgonooza toward Generation
Has four sculptured Bulls terrible before the
    Gate of iron,
And iron the Bulls; and that which looks toward Ulro,
Clay baked & enameled; eternal glowing as four furnaces,
Turning upon the Wheels of Albion's sons with enormous
    power;   65
And that toward Beulah four, gold, silver, brass
    & iron;

Plate 13

And that toward Eden four, formed of gold, silver,
    brass & iron.

The South, a golden Gate, has four Lions terrible,
    living;
That toward Generation four, of iron carved wondrous;
That toward Ulro four, clay-baked, laborious workmanship;
That toward Eden four, immortal gold, silver, brass
    & iron.   5

The Western Gate, fourfold, is closed, having four
    Cherubim
Its guards, living, the work of elemental hands,
    laborious task,
Like Men, hermaphroditic, each winged with eight
    wings:
That towards Generation, iron; that toward Beulah,
    stone;
That toward Ulro, clay; that toward Eden, metals;   10
But all closed up till the last day, when the graves
    shall yield their dead.

The Eastern Gate fourfold, terrible & deadly its
    ornaments,
Taking their forms from the Wheels of Albion's sons
    as cogs

Are formed in a wheel, to fit the cogs of the adverse
    wheel.

That toward Eden, eternal ice, frozen in seven
    folds   15
Of forms of death; and that toward Beulah, stone:
The seven diseases of the earth are carved
    terrible;
And that toward Ulro, forms of war: seven enormities;
And that toward Generation, seven generative forms.

And every part of the City is fourfold; & every
    inhabitant, fourfold.   20
And every pot & vessel & garment & utensil of the
    houses,
And every house, fourfold; but the third Gate in
    every one
Is closed as with a threefold curtain of ivory
    & fine linen & ermine.
And Luban stands in middle of the City. A moat of fire
Surrounds Luban, Los's Palace, & the golden Looms of
    Cathedron.   25

And sixty-four thousand Genii guard the Eastern Gate,
And sixty-four thousand Gnomes guard the Northern Gate,
And sixty-four thousand Nymphs guard the Western Gate,
And sixty-four thousand Fairies guard the Southern Gate.

Around Golgonooza lies the land of death eternal, a
    Land   30
Of pain and misery and despair and ever-brooding
    melancholy
In all the Twenty-seven Heavens, numbered from Adam to
    Luther,
From the blue Mundane Shell, reaching to the Vegetative
    Earth.

The Vegetative Universe opens like a flower from the
    Earth's center,

In which is Eternity. It expands in Stars to the Mundane
    Shell,   35
And there it meets Eternity again, both within and
    without,
And the abstract Voids between the Stars are the
    Satanic Wheels.

There is the Cave, the Rock, the Tree, the Lake
    of Udan-Adan,
The Forest, and the Marsh, and the Pits of bitumen
    deadly,
The Rocks of solid fire, the Ice valleys, the Plains   40
Of burning sand, the rivers, cataract & Lakes of Fire,
The Islands of the fiery Lakes, the Trees of Malice,
    Revenge
And black Anxiety, and the Cities of the Salamandrine
    men
(But whatever is visible to the Generated Man
Is a Creation of mercy & love from the Satanic
    Void).   45
The land of darkness flamed, but no light & no repose;
The land of snows, of trembling & of iron hail
    incessant;
The land of earthquakes and the land of woven
    labyrinths;
The land of snares & traps & wheels & pitfalls & dire
    mills;
The Voids, the Solids & the land of clouds & regions of
    waters   50
With their inhabitants in the Twenty-seven Heavens
    beneath Beulah:
Self-righteousnesses conglomerating against the Divine
    Vision,
A Concave Earth, wondrous, Chasmal, Abyssal,
    Incoherent,
Forming the Mundane Shell above, beneath, on all sides
    surrounding

Golgonooza. Los walks round the walls night and day.   55

He views the City of Golgonooza & its smaller Cities,
The Looms & Mills & Prisons & Workhouses of Og &
        Anak,
The Amalekite, the Canaanite, the Moabite, the Egyptian,
And all that has existed in the space of six thousand
        years,
Permanent & not lost, not lost nor vanished, & every
        little act,   60
Word, work & wish that has existed, all remaining still
In those Churches, ever-consuming & ever-building by
        the Spectres
Of all the inhabitants of Earth wailing to be Created,
Shadowy to those who dwell not in them,
        mere possibilities;
But to those who enter into them they seem the only
        substances,   65
For every thing exists, & not one sigh nor smile nor
        tear,

Plate 14

One hair nor particle of dust, not one can pass
        away.

He views the Cherub at the Tree of Life, also the
        Serpent
Orc, the firstborn, coiled in the south, the Dragon
        Urizen,
Tharmas, the Vegetated Tongue, even the Devouring
        Tongue:
A threefold region, a false brain, a false heart   5
And false bowels, altogether composing the False
        Tongue,
Beneath Beulah as a wat'ry flame revolving every way
And as dark roots and stems, a Forest of affliction, growing
In seas of sorrow. Los also views the Four Females,

Ahania and Enion and Vala and Enitharmon lovely;   10
And from them all the lovely beaming Daughters of Albion.
Ahania & Enion & Vala are three evanescent shades.
Enitharmon is a vegetated mortal Wife of Los,
His Emanation, yet his Wife, till the sleep of Death is past.

Such are the Buildings of Los, & such are the Woofs of
    Enitharmon.   15

And Los beheld his Sons, and he beheld his Daughters,
Every one a translucent Wonder, a Universe within,
Increasing inwards into length and breadth and height,
Starry & glorious, and they every one in their bright loins
Have a beautiful golden gate which opens into the
    vegetative world;   20
And every one a gate of rubies & all sorts of precious stones
In their translucent hearts, which opens into the vegetative
    world;
And every one a gate of iron dreadful and wonderful
In their translucent heads, which opens into the vegetative
    world;
And every one has the three regions, Childhood,
    Manhood & Age;   25
But the gate of the tongue, the western gate in
    them, is closed,
Having a wall builded against it; and thereby the gates
Eastward & Southward & Northward are incircled with
    flaming fires.
And the North is Breadth, the South is Height & Depth,
The East is Inwards, & the West is Outwards every way.   30

And Los beheld the mild Emanation Jerusalem, eastward
    bending
Her revolutions toward the Starry Wheels in maternal
    anguish
Like a pale cloud arising from the arms of Beulah's
    Daughters
In Entuthon-Benython's deep Vales beneath Golgonooza.

Plate 15

And Hand and Hyle rooted into Jerusalem by a fibre
Of strong revenge, & Scofield Vegetated by Reuben's
  Gate
In every Nation of the Earth, till the Twelve Sons of
  Albion
Enrooted into every Nation, a mighty Polypus growing
From Albion over the whole Earth: such is my awful
  Vision.   5

I see the Fourfold Man, The Humanity, in deadly sleep
And its fallen Emanation, The Spectre & its cruel
  Shadow.
I see the Past, Present & Future existing all at once
Before me; O Divine Spirit, sustain me on thy wings,
That I may awake Albion from his long & cold repose.   10
For Bacon & Newton sheathed in dismal steel; their
  terrors hang
Like iron scourges over Albion. Reasonings like vast
  Serpents
Infold around my limbs, bruising my minute articulations.

I turn my eyes to the Schools & Universities of
  Europe
And there behold the Loom of Locke, whose Woof rages
  dire,   15
Washed by the Waterwheels of Newton. Black the cloth
In heavy wreaths folds over every Nation; cruel Works
Of many Wheels I view, wheel without wheel, with cogs
  tyrannic
Moving by compulsion each other, not as those in Eden,
  which,
Wheel within Wheel, in freedom revolve in harmony &
  peace.   20
I see in deadly fear in London Los raging round his
  Anvil

Of death, forming an Ax of gold; the Four Sons of Los
Stand round him cutting the Fibres from Albion's hills,
That Albion's Sons may roll apart over the Nations,
While Reuben enroots his brethren in the narrow Canaanite   25
From the Limit Noah to the Limit Abram, in whose Loins
Reuben in his Twelvefold majesty & beauty shall take
 refuge
As Abraham flees from Chaldea, shaking his gory locks.
But first Albion must sleep, divided from the Nations.
I see Albion sitting upon his Rock in the first
 Winter,   30
And thence I see the Chaos of Satan & the World of
 Adam
When the Divine Hand went forth on Albion in the mid
 Winter
And at the place of Death when Albion sat in Eternal
 Death
Among the Furnaces of Los in the Valley of the Son of
 Hinnom.

Plate 16

Hampstead, Highgate, Finchley, Hendon, Muswell hill
 rage loud
Before Bromion's iron Tongs & glowing Poker, reddening
 fierce.
Hertfordshire glows with fierce Vegetation! In the
 Forests
The Oak frowns terrible; the Beech & Ash & Elm enroot
Among the Spiritual fires; loud the Cornfields thunder
 along,   5
The Soldier's fife, the Harlot's shriek, the Virgin's
 dismal groan,
The Parent's fear, the Brother's jealousy, the Sister's
 curse
Beneath the Storms of Theotormon; & the thund'ring
 Bellows

Heaves in the hand of Palamabron, who in
    London's darkness
Before the Anvil watches the bellowing flames.
    Thundering,   10
The Hammer loud rages in Rintrah's strong grasp,
    swinging loud
Round from heaven to earth, down falling with heavy
    blow
Dead on the Anvil, where the red-hot wedge groans in
    pain.
He quenches it in the black trough of his Forge; London's
    River
Feeds the dread Forge, trembling & shuddering along the
    Valleys.   15

Humber & Trent roll dreadful before the Seventh
    Furnace,
And Tweed & Tyne, anxious, give up their Souls for
    Albion's sake.
Lincolnshire, Derbyshire, Nottinghamshire, Leicestershire,
From Oxfordshire to Norfolk on the Lake of Udan-Adan,
Labour within the Furnaces, walking among the Fires   20
With Ladles huge & iron Pokers over the Island white.

Scotland pours out his Sons to labour at the Furnaces.
Wales gives his Daughters to the Looms; England nursing
    Mothers
Gives to the Children of Albion & to the Children of
    Jerusalem.
From the blue Mundane Shell even to the Earth of
    Vegetation   25
Throughout the whole Creation, which groans to be
    delivered,
Albion groans in the deep slumbers of Death upon his
    Rock.

Here Los fixed down the Fifty-two Counties of England
    & Wales,

The Thirty-six of Scotland & the Thirty-four of Ireland
With mighty power, when they fled out at Jerusalem's
    Gates   30
Away from the Conflict of Luvah & Urizen, fixing the
    Gates
In the Twelve Counties of Wales, & thence Gates looking
    every way
To the Four Points conduct to England & Scotland
    & Ireland
And thence to all the Kingdoms & Nations & Families
    of the Earth.
The Gate of Reuben in Carmarthenshire, the Gate of
    Simeon in   35
Cardiganshire, & the Gate of Levi in Montgomeryshire;
The Gate of Judah, Merionethshire, the Gate of Dan,
    Flintshire;
The Gate of Naphtali, Radnorshire; the Gate of
    Gad, Pembrokeshire;
The Gate of Asher, Carnarvonshire; the Gate of Issachar,
    Brecknockshire;
The Gate of Zebulun in Anglesea & Sodor (so is Wales
    divided)   40
The Gate of Joseph, Denbighshire; the Gate of Benjamin,
    Glamorganshire;
For the protection of the Twelve Emanations of Albion's
    Sons.

And the Forty Counties of England are thus divided:
    in the Gates
Of Reuben: Norfolk, Suffolk, Essex; Simeon:
    Lincoln, York, Lancashire;
Levi: Middlesex, Kent, Surrey; Judah: Somerset,
    Glou'ster, Wiltshire.   45
Dan: Cornwall, Devon, Dorset; Naphtali: Warwick,
    Leicester, Worcester;
Gad: Oxford, Bucks, Harford; Asher: Sussex, Hampshire,
    Berkshire;

Issachar: Northampton, Rutland, Nott'gham; Zebulun:
   Bedford, Hunt'g'n, Camb.;
Joseph: Stafford, Shrops., Heref.; Benjamin: Derby,
   Cheshire, Monmouth;
And Cumberland, Northumberland, Westmoreland &
   Durham are   50
Divided in the Gates of Reuben, Judah, Dan & Joseph.

And the Thirty-six Counties of Scotland, divided in
   the Gates
Of Reuben: Kincard, Hadd'n't'n, Forfar; Simeon: Ayr,
   Argyll, Banff;
Levi: Edinburgh, Roxbro, Ross; Judah: Aberdeen, Berwick,
   Dumfries;
Dan: Bute, Caithness, Clackmannan; Naphtali: Nairn,
   Inverness, Linlithgow,   55
Gad: Peebles, Perth, Renfrew; Asher: Sutherland,
   Stirling, Wigtown;
Issachar: Selkirk, Dumbarton, Glasgow; Zebulun: Orkney,
   Shetland, Skye;
Joseph: Elgin, Lanark., Kinross; Benjamin: Cromarty,
   Moray, Kirkcudbright;
Governing all by the sweet delights of secret
   amorous glances
In Enitharmon's Halls, builded by Los & his mighty
   Children.   60

All things acted on Earth are seen in the bright
   Sculptures of
Los's Halls, & every Age renews its powers from these
   Works
With every pathetic story possible to happen from Hate or
Wayward Love, & every sorrow & distress is carved here;
Every Affinity of Parents, Marriages & Friendships are
   here   65
In all their various combinations, wrought with
   wondrous Art;
All that can happen to Man in his pilgrimage of seventy
   years.

Such is the Divine Written Law of Horeb & Sinai,
And such the Holy Gospel of Mount Olivet & Calvary.

Plate 17

His Spectre divides, & Los in fury compels it to
    divide,
To labour in the fire, in the water, in the earth, in
    the air,
To follow the Daughters of Albion as the hound follows
    the scent
Of the wild inhabitant of the forest, to drive them from
    his own,
To make a way for the Children of Los to come from the
    Furnaces.   5
But Los himself against Albion's Sons his fury bends, for
    he
Dare not approach the Daughters openly lest he be
    consumed
In the fires of their beauty & perfection & be Vegetated
    beneath
Their Looms in a Generation of death & resurrection to
    forgetfulness.
They woo Los continually to subdue his strength;
    he continually   10
Shows them his Spectre, sending him abroad over the four
    points of heaven
In the fierce desires of beauty & in the tortures of
    repulse! He is
The Spectre of the Living pursuing the Emanations of
    the Dead.
Shudd'ring they flee; they hide in the Druid Temples
    in cold chastity,
Subdued by the Spectre of the Living & terrified by
    undisguised desire.   15

For Los said: "Though my Spectre is divided, as I
    am a Living Man

I must compel him to obey me wholly, that Enitharmon
    may not
Be lost, & lest he should devour Enitharmon. Ah me!
Piteous image of my soft desires & loves, O Enitharmon!
I will compel my Spectre to obey, I will restore to thee
    thy Children.   20
No one bruises or starves himself to make himself fit for
    labour!

"Tormented with sweet desire for these beauties of
    Albion,
They would never love my power if they did not seek to
    destroy
Enitharmon. Vala would never have sought & loved Albion
If she had not sought to destroy Jerusalem; such is that
    false   25
And Generating Love, a pretense of love to destroy love,
Cruel hypocrisy unlike the lovely delusions of Beulah,
And cruel forms unlike the merciful forms of
    Beulah's Night.

"They know not why they love nor wherefore they sicken
    & die,
Calling that Holy Love which is Envy, Revenge & Cruelty,   30
Which separated the stars from the mountains, the
    mountains from Man
And left man a little grovelling Root outside of
    Himself.
Negations are not Contraries: Contraries mutually Exist,
But Negations Exist Not; Exceptions & Objections &
    Unbeliefs
Exist not; nor shall they ever be Organized forever
    & ever.   35
If thou separate from me, thou are a Negation, a mere
Reasoning & Derogation from me, an Objecting & cruel
    Spite
And Malice & Envy; but my Emanation, Alas! will become
My Contrary. O thou Negation, I will continually compel
Thee to be invisible to any but whom I please, & when   40

And where & how I please, and never, never, shalt
 thou be Organized
But as a distorted & reversed Reflection in
 the Darkness
And in the non-Entity; nor shall that which is above
Ever descend into thee; but thou shalt be a non-Entity
 forever;
And if any enter into thee, thou shalt be an
 Unquenchable Fire,   45
And he shall be a never-dying Worm, mutually tormented
 by
Those that thou tormentest, a Hell & Despair forever
 & ever."

So Los in secret with himself communed, & Enitharmon
 heard
In her darkness & was comforted; yet still she divided away
In gnawing pain from Los's bosom in the deadly Night;   50
First as a red Globe of blood trembling beneath his
 bosom
Suspended over her he hung; he infolded her in his
 garments
Of wool; he hid her from the Spectre in shame &
 confusion of
Face: in terrors & pains of Hell & Eternal Death the
Trembling Globe shot forth Self-living, & Los howled over
 it,   55
Feeding it with his groans & tears day & night without
 ceasing;
And the Spectrous Darkness from his back divided in
 temptations
And in grinding agonies, in threats, stiflings & direful
 strugglings.

"Go thou to Scofield; ask him if he is Bath or if he is
 Canterbury.
Tell him to be no more dubious; demand explicit words.   60
Tell him I will dash him into shivers where & at what
 time

I please; tell Hand & Scofield they are my ministers
    of evil
To those I hate, for I can hate also as well as they!"

Plate 18

From every one of the Four Regions of Human Majesty
There is an Outside spread Without & an Outside spread
    Within,
Beyond the Outline of Identity both ways, which meet
    in One:
An orbed Void of doubt, despair, hunger & thirst &
    sorrow.
Here the Twelve Sons of Albion joined in dark Assembly,   5
Jealous of Jerusalem's children, ashamed of her little
    ones
(For Vala produced the Bodies; Jerusalem gave the Souls),
Became as Three Immense Wheels turning upon one
    another
Into non-Entity, and their thunders hoarse appall the
    Dead,
To murder their own Souls, to build a Kingdom among the
    Dead.   10

"Cast, Cast ye Jerusalem forth! The Shadow of delusions!
The Harlot daughter! Mother of pity and dishonourable
    forgiveness!
Our Father Albion's sin and shame! But father now no
    more!
Nor sons! Nor hateful peace & love, nor soft complacencies
With transgressors meeting in brotherhood around the
    table,   15
Or in the porch or garden. No more the sinful delights
Of age and youth, and boy and girl, and animal and herb,
And river and mountain, and city & village, and house
    & family,
Beneath the Oak & Palm, beneath the Vine and Fig tree,
In self-denial!—But War and deadly contention, Between   20
Father and Son, and light and love! All bold asperities

Of Haters met in deadly strife, rending the house &
    garden,
The unforgiving porches, the tables of enmity, and
    beds
And chambers of trembling & suspicion, hatreds of age
    & youth,
And boy & girl, & animal & herb, & river & mountain,   25
And city & village, and house & family, That the Perfect
May live in glory, redeemed by Sacrifice of the Lamb
And of his children before sinful Jerusalem, To build
Babylon the City of Vala, the Goddess Virgin-Mother.
She is our Mother! Nature! Jerusalem is our
    Harlot-Sister   30
Returned with Children of pollution to defile our House
With Sin and Shame. Cast! Cast her into the Potter's
    field.
Her little ones She must slay upon our Altars, and her
    aged
Parents must be carried into captivity to redeem her
    Soul,
To be for a Shame & a Curse, and to be our Slaves
    forever."   35

So cry Hand & Hyle, the eldest of the fathers of
    Albion's
Little ones, to destroy the Divine Saviour, the Friend
    of Sinners,
Building Castles in desolated places, and strong
    Fortifications.
Soon Hand mightily devoured & absorbed Albion's Twelve
    Sons.
Out from his bosom a mighty Polypus, vegetating in
    darkness;   40
And Hyle & Coban were his two chosen ones for
    Emissaries
In War; forth from his bosom they went and returned,
Like Wheels from a great Wheel reflected in the Deep.
Hoarse turned the Starry Wheels, rending a way in
    Albion's Loins

Beyond the Night of Beulah. In a dark & unknown
    Night   45
Outstretched his Giant beauty on the ground in
    pain & tears.

Plate 19

His Children exiled from his breast pass to and fro
    before him.
His birds are silent on his hills; flocks die beneath
    his branches:
His tents are fallen; his trumpets and the sweet sound
    of his harp
Are silent on his clouded hills, that belch forth
    storms & fire.
His milk of Cows & honey of Bees & fruit of golden
    harvest   5
Is gathered in the scorching heat & in the driving rain.
Where once he sat he weary walks in misery and pain,
His Giant beauty and perfection fallen into dust;
Till from within his withered breast, grown narrow
    with his woes,
The corn is turned to thistles & the apples into
    poison,   10
The birds of song to murderous crows, his joys to
    bitter groans!
The voices of children in his tents to cries of
    helpless infants!
And self-exiled from the face of light & shine of
    morning,
In the dark world, a narrow house, he wanders up and
    down,
Seeking for rest and finding none; and hidden far
    within,   15
His Eon weeping in the cold and desolated Earth.

All his Affections now appear withoutside: all his Sons,
Hand, Hyle & Coban, Guantok, Peachey, Brereton, Slade
    & Hutton,

Scofield, Kox, Kotope & Bowen; his Twelve Sons, Satanic
    Mill.
Who are the Spectres of the Twenty-four, each
    Double-formed,   20
Revolve upon his mountains, groaning pain beneath
The dark incessant sky, seeking for rest and finding
    none,
Raging against their Human natures, ravening to
    gormandize
The Human majesty and beauty of the Twenty-four,
Condensing them into solid rocks with cruelty and
    abhorrence,   25
Suspicion & revenge; & the seven diseases of the Soul
Settled around Albion and around Luvah in his secret
    cloud.
Willing, the Friends endured for Albion's sake and for
Jerusalem, his Emanation, shut within his bosom,
Which hardened against them more and more as he
    builded onwards   30
On the Gulf of Death in self-righteousness, that
    rolled
Before his awful feet in pride of virtue for victory;
And Los was roofed in from Eternity in Albion's Cliffs,
Which stand upon the ends of Beulah; and withoutside
    all
Appeared a rocky form against the Divine Humanity.   35

Albion's Circumference was closed; his Center began
    darkening
Into the Night of Beulah, and the Moon of Beulah rose
Clouded with storms; Los, his strong Guard, walked
    round beneath the Moon,
And Albion fled inward among the currents of his rivers.

He found Jerusalem upon the River of his City soft
    reposed   40
In the arms of Vala, assimilating in one with Vala
The Lily of Havilah; and they sang soft through
    Lambeth's vales
In a sweet moony night & silence that they had created

With a blue sky spread over with wings and a mild moon,
Dividing & uniting into many female forms, Jerusalem   45
Trembling, then in one commingling in eternal tears,
Sighing to melt his Giant beauty, on the moony river.

Plate 20

But when they saw Albion fallen upon mild Lambeth's
    vale,
Astonished! Terrified! they hovered over his Giant
    limbs.
Then thus Jerusalem spoke, while Vala wove the veil
    of tears,
Weeping in pleadings of Love, in the web of despair:

"Wherefore hast thou shut me into the winter of
    human life   5
And closed up the sweet regions of youth and virgin
    innocence,
Where we live, forgetting error, not pondering on
    evil,
Among my lambs & brooks of water, among my warbling
    birds,
Where we delight in innocence before the face of the
    Lamb,
Going in and out before him in his love and sweet
    affection?"   10

Vala replied, weeping & trembling, hiding in her veil:

"When winter rends the hungry family and the snow falls
Upon the ways of men, hiding the paths of man and beast,
Then mourns the wanderer; then he repents his wanderings
    & eyes
The distant forest; then the slave groans in the dungeon
    of stone,   15
The captive in the mill of the stranger, sold for
    scanty hire.
They view their former life; they number moments over
    and over,

Stringing them on their remembrance as on a thread of
    sorrow.
Thou art my sister and my daughter! Thy shame is mine
    also!
Ask me not of my griefs! Thou knowest all my griefs."   20

Jerusalem answered with soft tears over the valleys:

"O Vala, what is Sin that thou shudderest and weepest
At sight of thy once-loved Jerusalem? What is Sin but
    a little
Error & fault that is soon forgiven? But mercy is not
    a Sin
Nor pity nor love nor kind forgiveness. O! if I have
    Sinned   25
Forgive & pity me! O! unfold thy Veil in mercy & love!
Slay not my little ones, beloved Virgin daughter of
    Babylon;
Slay not my infant loves & graces, beautiful daughter
    of Moab.
I cannot put off the human form; I strive but strive
    in vain.
When Albion rent thy beautiful net of gold and silver
    twine,   30
Thou hadst woven it with art; thou hadst caught
    me in the bands
Of love; thou refusedst to let me go. Albion beheld
    thy beauty,
Beautiful through our Love's comeliness, beautiful
    through pity.
The Veil shone with thy brightness in the eyes of
    Albion,
Because it enclosed pity & love; because we loved
    one another!   35
Albion loved thee! he rent thy Veil! He embraced thee!
    He loved thee!
Astonished at his beauty & perfection, thou forgavest
    his furious love.
I redounded from Albion's bosom in my virgin
    loveliness.

The Lamb of God received me in his arms; he smiled
    upon us;
He made me his Bride & Wife; he gave thee to Albion.   40
Then was a time of love. O why is it passed away?"

Then Albion broke silence and with groans replied:

Plate 21

"O Vala! O Jerusalem! do you delight in my groans?
You, O lovely forms, you have prepared my death
    cup;
The disease of Shame covers me from head to feet; I
    have no hope.
Every boil upon my body is a separate & deadly Sin.
Doubt first assailed me; then Shame took possession of
    me.   5
Shame divides Families; Shame hath divided Albion in
    sunder.
First fled my Sons, & then my Daughters, then my Wild
    Animations,
My Cattle next, last even the Dog of my Gate. The
    Forests fled,
The Cornfields, & the breathing Gardens outside
    separated;
The Sea, the Stars, the Sun, the Moon, driven forth
    by my disease.   10
All is Eternal Death unless you can weave a chaste
Body over an unchaste Mind! Vala! O that thou wert pure!
That the deep wound of Sin might be closed up with the
    Needle
And with the Loom to cover Gwendolen & Ragan with costly
    Robes
Of Natural Virtue, for their Spiritual forms without
    a Veil   15
Wither in Luvah's Sepulcher. I thrust him from my
    presence,
And all my Children followed his loud howlings into
    the Deep.
Jerusalem! dissembler Jerusalem! I look into thy bosom;

I discover thy secret places. Cordella! I behold
Thee whom I thought pure as the heavens in innocence
    & fear,   20
Thy Tabernacle taken down, thy secret Cherubim
    disclosed.
Art thou broken? Ah me, Sabrina, running by my side,
In childhood what wert thou? Unutterable anguish!
    Conwenna,
Thy cradled infancy is most piteous. O hide, O hide!
Their secret gardens were made paths to the
    traveller.   25
I knew not of their secret loves with those I hated
    most,
Nor that their every thought was Sin & secret appetite.
Hyle sees in fear; he howls in fury over them. Hand
    sees
In jealous fear; in stern accusation with cruel
    stripes
He drives them through the Streets of Babylon before
    my face,   30
Because they taught Luvah to rise into my clouded
    heavens.
Battersea and Chelsea mourn for Cambel &
    Gwendolen!
Hackney and Holloway sicken for Estrild & Ignoge!
Because the Peak, Malvern, & Cheviot Reason in
    Cruelty,
Penmaenmawr & Dhinas-bran Demonstrate in Unbelief.   35
Manchester & Liverpool are in tortures of Doubt
    & Despair.
Malden & Colchester Demonstrate. I hear my Children's
    voices;
I see their piteous faces gleam out upon the cruel
    winds
From Lincoln & Norwich, from Edinburgh & Monmouth;
I see them distant from my bosom scourged along the
    roads,   40
Then lost in clouds; I hear their tender voices!
    Clouds divide.

I see them die beneath the whips of the Captains;
    they are taken
In solemn pomp into Chaldea across the breadths
    of Europe.
Six months they lie embalmed in silent death,
    worshipped,
Carried in Arks of Oak, before the armies in the
    spring.   45
Bursting their Arks, they rise again to life; they
    play before
The Armies. I hear their loud cymbals & their deadly
    cries.
Are the Dead cruel? Are those who are infolded in
    moral Law
Revengeful? O that Death & Annihilation were the
    same!"

Then Vala answered, spreading her scarlet Veil over
    Albion: 50

Plate 22

  "Albion, thy fear has made me tremble; thy terrors
    have surrounded me.
Thy Sons have nailed me on the Gates, piercing my
    hands & feet,
Till Scofield's Nimrod, the mighty Huntsman Jehovah,
    came
With Cush his Son & took me down. He in a golden Ark
Bears me before his Armies, though my shadow hovers
    here.   5
The flesh of multitudes fed & nourished me in my
    childhood.
My morn & evening food were prepared in Battles of
    Men.
Great is the cry of the Hounds of Nimrod along the
    Valley
Of Vision; they scent the odor of War in the Valley
    of Vision.

All Love is lost! Terror succeeds, & Hatred instead
   of Love,   10
And stern demands of Right & Duty instead of Liberty.
Once thou wast to me the loveliest Son of heaven, but
   now
Where shall I hide from thy dread countenance &
   searching eyes?
I have looked into the secret Soul of him I loved
And in the dark recesses found Sin & can never return."   15

Albion again uttered his voice beneath the silent
   Moon:

"I brought Love into light of day to pride in chaste
   beauty.
I brought Love into light & fancied Innocence is
   no more."

Then spoke Jerusalem, "O Albion! my Father Albion,
Why wilt thou number every little fibre of my Soul,   20
Spreading them out before the Sun like stalks of flax
   to dry?

The Infant Joy is beautiful, but its anatomy
Horrible, ghast & deadly! Naught shalt thou find in it
But dark despair & everlasting brooding melancholy!"

Then Albion turned his face toward Jerusalem & spoke: 25

"Hide thou, Jerusalem, in impalpable voidness, not
   to be
Touched by the hand nor seen with the eye. O Jerusalem,
Would thou wert not & that thy place might never be
   found;
But come, O Vala, with knife & cup; drain my blood
To the last drop! Then hide me in thy Scarlet
   Tabernacle,   30
For I see Luvah, whom I slew. I behold him in my
   Spectre
As I behold Jerusalem in thee, O Vala, dark and
   cold."

Jerusalem then stretched her hand toward the Moon
    & spoke:
"Why should Punishment Weave the Veil with Iron
    Wheels of War,
When Forgiveness might it Weave with Wings of
    Cherubim?"   35

Loud groaned Albion from mountain to mountain &
    replied:

Plate 23

"Jerusalem! Jerusalem! deluding shadow of Albion!
Daughter of my phantasy! unlawful pleasure! Albion's
    curse!
I came here with intention to annihilate thee! But
My soul is melted away, inwoven within the Veil.
Hast thou again knitted the Veil of Vala, which
    I, for thee   5
Pitying, rent in ancient times? I see it whole and
    more
Perfect, and shining with beauty!" "But thou! O
    wretched Father!"

Jerusalem replied, like a voice heard from a sepulcher:
"Father, once piteous! Is Pity a Sin? Embalmed in
    Vala's bosom
In an Eternal Death for Albion's sake, our best
    beloved.   10
Thou art my Father & my Brother. Why hast thou
    hidden me
Remote from the divine Vision, my Lord and Saviour?"

Trembling stood Albion at her words in jealous
    dark despair.
He felt that Love and Pity are the same, a soft
    repose,
Inward complacency of Soul, a Self-annihilation!   15

"I have erred! I am ashamed! and will never
    return more.

I have taught my children sacrifices of cruelty.
  What shall I answer?
I will hide it from Eternals! I will give myself
  for my Children!
Which way soever I turn, I behold Humanity and
  Pity!"

He recoiled; he rushed outwards; he bore the Veil
  whole away.   20
His fires redound from his Dragon Altars in Errors
  returning.
He drew the Veil of Moral Virtue, woven for Cruel
  Laws,
And cast it into the Atlantic Deep to catch the
  Souls of the Dead.
He stood between the Palm tree & the Oak of
  weeping,
Which stand upon the edge of Beulah; and there
  Albion sunk   25
Down in sick pallid languor. These were his last
  words, relapsing
Hoarse from his rocks, from caverns of Derbyshire
  & Wales
And Scotland, uttered from the Circumference into
  Eternity:

"Blasphemous Sons of Feminine delusion! God
  in the dreary Void
Dwells from Eternity, wide separated from the Human
  Soul;   30
But thou, deluding Image by whom imbued the Veil I
  rent,
Lo, here is Vala's Veil, whole for a Law, a
  Terror & a Curse!
And therefore God takes vengeance on me: from my
  clay-cold bosom
My children wander, trembling victims of his Moral
  Justice.
His snows fall on me and cover me, while in the Veil
  I fold   35

My dying limbs. Therefore, O Manhood, if thou art
    aught
But a mere Phantasy, hear dying Albion's Curse!
May God, who dwells in this dark Ulro & voidness,
    vengeance take
And draw thee down into this Abyss of sorrow and
    torture
Like me thy Victim. O that Death & Annihilation
    were the same!   40

Plate 24

What have I said? What have I done? O all-powerful
    Human Words!
You recoil back upon me in the blood of the Lamb
    slain in his Children.
Two bleeding Contraries, equally true, are his
    Witnesses against me.
We reared mighty Stones; we danced naked around
    them,
Thinking to bring Love into light of day to Jerusalem's
    shame,   5
Displaying our Giant limbs to all the winds of heaven!
    Sudden
Shame seized us; we could not look on one another for
    abhorrence; the Blue
Of our immortal Veins & all their Hosts fled from our Limbs
And wandered distant is a dismal Night, clouded & dark.
The Sun fled from the Briton's forehead, the Moon
    from his mighty loins;   10
Scandinavia fled with all his mountains, filled
    with groans.

O what is Life & what is Man? O what is Death?
    Wherefore
Are you, my Children, natives in the Grave to
    where I go,
Or are you born to feed the hungry ravenings of
    Destruction

To be the sport of Accident, to waste in Wrath &
    Love, a weary   15
Life, in brooding cares & anxious labours, that
    prove but chaff?
O Jerusalem, Jerusalem, I have forsaken thy Courts,
Thy Pillars of ivory & gold, thy Curtains of silk
    & fine
Linen, thy Pavements of precious stones, thy Walls
    of pearl
And gold, thy Gates of Thanksgiving, thy Windows
    of Praise,   20
Thy Clouds of Blessing, thy Cherubims of Tender
    mercy,
Stretching their Wings sublime over the Little ones
    of Albion.
O Human Imagination, O Divine Body, I have
    Crucified,
I have turned my back upon thee into the Wastes
    of Moral Law.
There Babylon is builded in the Waste, founded in
    Human desolation.   25
O Babylon, thy Watchman stands over thee in the
    night.
Thy severe Judge all the day long proves thee,
    O Babylon,
With provings of destruction, with giving thee thy
    heart's desire.
But Albion is cast forth to the Potter, his Children
    to the Builders
To build Babylon, because they have forsaken
    Jerusalem.   30
The Walls of Babylon are Souls of Men, her Gates
    the Groans
Of Nations; her Towers are the Miseries of once
    happy Families.
Her Streets are paved with Destruction, her Houses
    built with Death,
Her Palaces with Hell & the Grave, her Synagogues
    with Torments

Of ever-hardening Despair, squared & polished with
    cruel skill.   35
Yet thou wast lovely as the summer cloud upon my
    hills
When Jerusalem was thy heart's desire in times of
    youth & love.
Thy Sons came to Jerusalem with gifts; she sent them
    away
With blessings on their hands & on their feet,
    blessings of gold,
And pearl & diamond; thy Daughters sang in her
    Courts;   40
They came up to Jerusalem; they walked
    before Albion.
In the Exchanges of London every Nation walked,
And London walked in every Nation, mutual in love
    & harmony.
Albion covered the whole Earth; England encompassed
    the Nations,
Mutual each within other's bosom in Visions of
    Regeneration.   45
Jerusalem covered the Atlantic Mountains & the
    Erythrean,
From bright Japan & China to Hesperia, France &
    England.
Mount Zion lifted his head in every Nation under
    heaven
And the Mount of Olives was beheld over the whole
    Earth.
The footsteps of the Lamb of God were there, but now
    no more,   50
No more shall I behold him; he is closed in Luvah's
    Sepulcher.
Yet why these smitings of Luvah, the gentlest
    mildest Zoa?
If God was Merciful this could not be. O Lamb of
    God,
Thou art a delusion and Jerusalem is my Sin! O my
    Children,

I have educated you in the crucifying cruelties of
    Demonstration,   55
Till you have assumed the Providence of God & slain
    your Father.
Dost thou appear before me, who liest dead in
    Luvah's Sepulcher?
Dost thou forgive me, thou who wast Dead and art
    Alive?
Look not so merciful upon me, O thou Slain Lamb of
    God.
I die! I die in thy arms though Hope is banished
    from me."   60

Thundering, the Veil rushes from his hand, Vegetating
    Knot by
Knot, Day by Day, Night by Night; loud roll the
    indignant Atlantic
Waves & the Erythrean, turning up the bottoms of
    the Deeps;

Plate 25

And there was heard a great lamenting in Beulah;
    all the Regions
Of Beulah were moved as the tender bowels are moved,
    & they said:

"Why did you take Vengeance, O ye Sons of the
    mighty Albion,
Planting these Oaken Groves, Erecting these Dragon
    Temples?
Injury the Lord heals, but Vengeance cannot be
    healed.   5
As the Sons of Albion have done to Luvah, so they
    have in him
Done to the Divine Lord & Saviour, who suffers
    with those that suffer;
For not one sparrow can suffer & the whole Universe
    not suffer also

In all its Regions, & its Father & Saviour not
    pity and weep.
But Vengeance is the destroyer of Grace & Repentance
    in the bosom   10
Of the Injurer, in which the Divine Lamb is cruelly
    slain.
Descend, O Lamb of God, & take away the imputation
    of Sin
By the Creation of States & the deliverance of
    Individuals.Evermore. Amen."

Thus wept they in Beulah over the Four Regions of
    Albion,
But many doubted & despaired & imputed Sin &
    Righteousness   15
To Individuals & not to States, and these Slept
    in Ulro.

Plate 26

> *SUCH VISIONS HAVE APPEARED TO ME*
> *AS I MY ORDERED RACE HAVE RUN.*
> *JERUSALEM IS NAMED LIBERTY*
> *AMONG THE SONS OF ALBION.*

Plate 27

TO THE JEWS

   Jerusalem the Emanation of the Giant Albion! Can it be? Is
it a Truth that the Learned have explored? Was Britain the Primitive Seat of the Patriarchal Religion? If it is true, my title page
is also True, that Jerusalem was & is the Emanation of the Giant
Albion. It is True and cannot be controverted. Ye are united,
O ye Inhabitants of Earth in One Religion, The Religion of Jesus,
the most Ancient, the Eternal & the Everlasting Gospel—The
Wicked will turn it to Wickedness, the Righteous to Righteousness. Amen! Huzza! Selah!
   "All things Begin & End in Albion's Ancient Druid Rocky
Shore."

Your Ancestors derived their origin from Abraham, Heber, Shem, and Noah, who were Druids, as the Druid Temples (which are the Patriarchal Pillars & Oak Groves) over the whole Earth witness to this day.

You have a tradition that Man anciently contained in his mighty limbs all things in Heaven & Earth. This you received from the Druids. "But now the Starry Heavens are fled from the mighty limbs of Albion."

Albion was the Parent of the Druids & in his Chaotic State of Sleep Satan & Adam & the whole World was Created by the Elohim.

The fields from Islington to Marybone,
To Primrose Hill and Saint John's Wood,
   Were builded over with pillars of gold,
And there Jerusalem's pillars stood.

Her Little ones ran on the fields,   5
The Lamb of God among them seen,
   And fair Jerusalem his Bride
Among the little meadows green.

Pancras & Kentish-town repose
Among her golden pillars high,   10
   Among her golden arches, which
Shine upon the starry sky.

The Jew's-harp-house & the Green Man,
The Ponds where Boys to bathe delight,
   The fields of Cows by Willan's farm   15
Shine in Jerusalem's pleasant sight.

She walks upon our meadows green;
The Lamb of God walks by her side,
   And every English Child is seen,
Children of Jesus & his Bride,   20

   Forgiving trespasses and sins,
Lest Babylon with cruel Og,
   With Moral & Self-righteous Law
Should Crucify in Satan's Synagogue!

What are those golden Builders doing   25
Near mournful, ever-weeping Paddington,
  Standing above that mighty Ruin
Where Satan the first victory won,

  Where Albion slept beneath the Fatal Tree,
And the Druids' golden Knife   30
  Rioted in human gore
In Offerings of Human Life?

  They groaned aloud on London Stone;
They groaned aloud on Tyburn's Brook;
  Albion gave his deadly groan,   35
And all the Atlantic Mountains shook.

  Albion's Spectre from his Loins
Tore forth in all the pomp of War!
  Satan his name; in flames of fire
He stretched his Druid Pillars far.   40

  Jerusalem fell from Lambeth's Vale
Down through Poplar & Old Bow,
  Through Maldon & across the Sea
In War & howling death & woe.

  The Rhine was red with human blood;   45
The Danube rolled a purple tide.
  On the Euphrates Satan stood,
And over Asia stretched his pride.

  He withered up sweet Zion's Hill
From every Nation of the Earth.   50
  He withered up Jerusalem's Gates
And in a dark Land gave her birth.

  He withered up the Human Form
By laws of sacrifice for sin,
  Till it became a Mortal Worm,   55
But O! translucent all within.

  The Divine Vision still was seen,
Still was the Human Form Divine

Weeping in weak & mortal clay.
O Jesus, still the Form was thine.   60

And thine the Human Face & thine
The Human Hands & Feet & Breath,
    Entering through the Gates of Birth
And passing through the Gates of Death,

    And O thou Lamb of God, whom I   65
Slew in my dark self-righteous pride,
    Art thou returned to Albion's Land?
And is Jerusalem thy Bride?

    Come to my arms & nevermore
Depart, but dwell forever here;   70
    Create my Spirit to thy Love;
Subdue my Spectre to thy Fear.

    Spectre of Albion! warlike Fiend!
In clouds of blood & ruin rolled,
    I here reclaim thee as my own,   75
My Selfhood! Satan! armed in gold.

    Is this thy soft Family-Love
Thy cruel Patriarchal pride,
    Planting thy Family alone.
Destroying all the World beside?   80

    A man's worst enemies are those
Of his own house & family,
    And he who makes his law a curse
By his own law shall surely die.

    In my Exchanges every Land   85
Shall walk, & mine in every Land
    Mutual shall build Jerusalem,
Both heart in heart & hand in hand.

If Humility is Christianity, you, O Jews, are the true Christians.
If your tradition that Man contained in his Limbs all Animals
is True & they were separated from him by cruel Sacrifices; and
when compulsory cruel Sacrifices had brought Humanity into

a Feminine Tabernacle, in the loins of Abraham & David, the Lamb of God, the Saviour became apparent on Earth as the Prophets had foretold. The Return of Israel is a Return to Mental Sacrifice & War. Take up the Cross, O Israel, & follow Jesus.

Plate 28

JERUSALEM

Chapter 2

Every ornament of perfection and every labour
    of love
In all the Garden of Eden & in all the golden mountains
Was become an envied horror and a remembrance of
    jealousy,
And every Act a Crime, and Albion the punisher
    & judge.

And Albion spoke from his secret seat and said: 5

"All these ornaments are crimes; they are made by
    the labours
Of loves, of unnatural consanguinities and friendships,
Horrid to think of when inquired deeply into; and all
These hills & valleys are accursed witnesses of Sin.
I therefore condense them into solid rocks,
    steadfast,   10
A foundation and certainty and demonstrative truth,
That Man be separate from Man; & here I plant my seat."

Cold snows drifted around him; ice covered his
    loins around.
He sat by Tyburn's brook, and underneath his heel
    shot up
A deadly Tree; he named it Moral Virtue and the Law   15
Of God, who dwells in Chaos hidden from the human sight.
The Tree spread over him its cold shadows (Albion
    groaned).
They bent down; they felt the earth and again enrooting
Shot into many a Tree, an endless labyrinth of woe!

From willing sacrifice of Self to sacrifice of (miscalled)
     Enemies   20
For Atonement, Albion began to erect twelve Altars
Of rough unhewn rocks before the Potter's
     Furnace.
He named them Justice and Truth. And Albion's Sons
Must have become the first Victims, being the first
     transgressors,
But they fled to the mountains to seek ransom, building
     A Strong   25
Fortification against the Divine Humanity and Mercy,
In Shame & Jealousy to annihilate Jerusalem!

Plate 29 [*33*]

Turning his back to the Divine Vision, his
     Spectrous
Chaos before his face appeared, an Unformed Memory.

Then spoke the Spectrous Chaos to Albion, darkening cold
From the back & loins, where dwell the Spectrous Dead:

"I am your Rational Power, O Albion; & that Human
     Form   5
You call Divine is but a Worm seventy inches long
That creeps forth in a night & is dried in the
     morning sun
In fortuitous concourse of memories accumulated & lost.
It plows the Earth in its own conceit; it overwhelms
     the Hills
Beneath its winding labyrinths, till a stone of the
     brook   10
Stops it in midst of its pride among its hills & rivers.
Battersea & Chelsea mourn; London & Canterbury tremble.
Their place shall not be found as the wind passes over.
The ancient Cities of the Earth remove as a traveller.
And shall Albion's Cities remain when I pass over
     them   15
With my deluge of forgotten remembrances over the tablet?"

So spoke the Spectre to Albion. He is the Great Selfhood,
Satan, Worshiped as God by the Mighty Ones of the Earth,
Having a white Dot called a Center, from
    which branches out
A Circle in continual gyrations. This became a
    Heart,   20
From which sprang numerous branches, varying their
    motions,
Producing many Heads, three or seven or ten, & hands
    & feet
Innumerable at will of the unfortunate contemplator,
Who becomes his food. Such is the way of the Devouring
    Power.

And this is the cause of the appearance in the
    frowning Chaos.   25
Albion's Emanation, which he had hidden in Jealousy,
Appeared now in the frowning Chaos, prolific upon the
    Chaos,
Reflecting back to Albion in Sexual Reasoning Hermaphroditic.

Albion spoke: "Who art thou that appearest in gloomy pomp
Involving the Divine Vision in colours of autumn
    ripeness?   30
I never saw thee till this time, nor beheld life abstracted,
Nor darkness immingled with light on my furrowed field.
Whence camest thou? Who art thou, O loveliest? The
    Divine Vision
Is as nothing before thee. Faded is all life and joy."

Vala replied in clouds of tears, Albion's garment
    embracing: 35

"I was a City & a Temple built by Albion's Children.
I was a Garden planted with beauty. I allured on hill
    & valley
The River of Life to flow against my walls & among my trees.
Vala was Albion's Bride & Wife in great Eternity,
The loveliest of the daughters of Eternity when in
    daybreak   40
I emanated from Luvah over the Towers of Jerusalem

And in her Courts among her little Children,
    offering up
The Sacrifice of fanatic love! Why loved I Jerusalem?
Why was I one with her, embracing in the
    Vision of Jesus?
Wherefore did I, loving, create love, which never yet   45
Immingled God & Man, when thou & I, hid the Divine Vision
In cloud of secret gloom which, behold, involve me
    round about?
Know me now, Albion; look upon me, I alone am Beauty.
The Imaginative Human Form is but a breathing of Vala.
I breathe him forth into the Heaven from my secret
    Cave,   50
Born of the Woman to obey the Woman, O Albion the mighty,
For the Divine appearance is Brotherhood, but I am Love

Plate 30 [34]

Elevate into the Region of Brotherhood with my
    red fires."

"Art thou Vala," replied Albion, "image of my repose?
O how I tremble! How my members pour down milky fear!
A dewy garment covers me all over; all manhood is gone!
At thy word & at thy look death enrobes me about   5
From head to feet, a garment of death & eternal fear.
Is not that Sun thy husband & that Moon thy glimmering
    Veil?
Are not the Stars of heaven thy Children? Art thou not
    Babylon?
Art thou Nature, Mother of all? Is Jerusalem thy Daughter?
Why have thou elevate inward, O dweller of outward
    chambers,   10
From grot & cave beneath the Moon, dim region of death
Where I laid my Plow in the hot noon, where my hot
    team fed,
Where implements of War are forged, the Plow to go over
    the Nations,

In pain girding me round like a rib of iron in heaven?
    O Vala,
In Eternity they neither marry nor are
    given in marriage.   15
Albion, the high Cliff of the Atlantic is become a
    barren Land."

Los stood at his Anvil; he heard the contentions of Vala;
He heaved his thund'ring Bellows upon the valleys of
    Middlesex;
He opened his Furnaces before Vala. Then Albion frowned
    in anger
On his Rock, ere yet the Starry Heavens were fled
    away   20
From his awful Members; and thus Los cried aloud
To the Sons of Albion & to Hand, the eldest Son of Albion:

"I hear the screech of Childbirth, loud pealing, &
    the groans
Of Death, in Albion's clouds, dreadful, uttered over all
    the Earth.
What may Man be? Who can tell? But what may Woman
    be   25
To have power over Man from Cradle to corruptible Grave?
There is a Throne in every Man; it is the Throne of God
This Woman has claimed as her own, & Man is no more!
Albion is the Tabernacle of Vala & her Temple
And not the Tabernacle & Temple of the Most High.   30
O Albion, why wilt thou Create a Female Will
To hide the most evident God in a hidden covert, even
In the shadows of a Woman & a secluded Holy Place,
That we may pry after him as after a stolen treasure
Hidden among the Dead & mured up from the paths of
    life?   35
Hand, art thou not Reuben enrooting thyself into Bashan,
Till thou remainest a vaporous Shadow in a Void?
    O Merlin,
Unknown among the Dead, where never before
    Existence came.

Is this the Female Will, O ye lovely Daughters of
    Albion: To
Converse concerning Weight & Distance in the Wilds of
    Newton & Locke?"   40

So Los spoke, standing on Mam-Tor, looking over Europe
    & Asia.
The Graves thunder beneath his feet from Ireland to Japan.

Reuben slept in Bashan like one dead in the valley,
Cut off from Albion's mountains & from all the Earth's
    summits,
Between Succoth & Zaretan beside the Stone of Bohan.   45
While the Daughters of Albion divided Luvah into three
    Bodies,
Los bended his Nostrils down to the Earth, then sent
    him over
Jordan to the Land of the Hittite. Every one that saw him
Fled! They fled at his horrible Form; they hid in caves
And dens; they looked on one another & became what they
    beheld.   50

Reuben returned to Bashan; in despair he slept on the Stone.
Then Gwendolen divided into Rahab & Tirzah in Twelve
    Portions.
Los rolled his Eyes into two narrow circles, then sent him
Over Jordan; all terrified fled; they became what they beheld.

"If Perceptive Organs vary, Objects of Perception seem
    to vary.
If the Perceptive Organs close, their Objects seem to   55
    close also.
Consider this, O mortal Man, O worm of sixty winters,"
    said Los;
"Consider Sexual Organization, & hide thee in the dust."

Plate 31 [*35*]

Then the Divine hand found the Two Limits,
    Satan and Adam,

In Albion's bosom; for in every Human bosom those
    Limits stand.
And the Divine voice came from the Furnaces
    as multitudes without
Number, the voices of the innumerable multitudes of
    Eternity.
And the appearance of a Man was seen in the Furnaces,   5
Saving those who have sinned from the punishment of the Law
(In pity of the punisher, whose state is eternal death)
And keeping them from Sin by the mild counsels of his love.

"Albion goes to Eternal Death; In Me all Eternity
Must pass through condemnation and awake beyond the
    Grave!   10
No individual can keep these Laws, for they are death
To every energy of man, and forbid the springs of life.
Albion hath entered the State Satan! Be permanent, O State!
And be thou forever accursed, that Albion may arise again;
And be thou created into a State! I go forth to
    Create   15
States, to deliver Individuals evermore! Amen."

So spoke the voice from the Furnaces, descending into
    non-Entity.

Plate 32 [*36*]

Reuben returned to his place; in vain he sought
    beautiful Tirzah,
For his Eyelids were narrowed, & his Nostrils scented
    the ground.
And Sixty Winters Los raged in the Divisions of Reuben,
Building the Moon of Ulro, plank by plank & rib by rib.
Reuben slept in the Cave of Adam, and Los folded his Tongue   5
Between Lips of mire & clay, then sent him forth over Jordan.
In the love of Tirzah. He said, "Doubt is my food day
    & night."
All that beheld him fled howling and gnawed
    their tongues

For pain; they became what they beheld. In reasonings
     Reuben returned
To Heshbon. Disconsolate he walked through Moab, & he
     stood   10
Before the Furnaces of Los in a horrible dreamful slumber,
On Mount Gilead looking toward Gilgal; and Los bended
His Ear in a spiral circle outward, then sent him over Jordan.

The Seven Nations fled before him; they became what they
     beheld.
Hand, Hyle & Coban fled; they became what they
     beheld.   15
Guantok & Peachey hid in Damascus beneath Mount Lebanon,
Brereton & Slade in Egypt. Hutton & Scofield & Kox
Fled over Chaldea in terror, in pains in every nerve.
Kotope & Bowen became what they beheld, fleeing over the
     Earth;
And the Twelve Female Emanations fled with them,
     agonizing.   20

Jerusalem trembled seeing her Children driven by Los's
     Hammer
In the visions of the dreams of Beulah on the edge of
     non-Entity.
Hand stood between Reuben & Merlin, as the Reasoning
     Spectre
Stands between the Vegetative Man & his Immortal
     Imagination.
And the Four Zoas, clouded, rage East & West & North
     & South.   25
They change their situations in the Universal Man.
Albion groans; he sees the Elements divide before his face.
And England, who is Britannia, divided into Jerusalem
     & Vala;
And Urizen assumes the East. Luvah assumes the South
In his dark Spectre, ravening from his open Sepulcher.   30

And the Four Zoas, who are the Four Eternal Senses of Man,
Became Four Elements, separating from the Limbs of Albion.

These are their names in the Vegetative Generation,
And Accident & Chance were found hidden in Length, Breadth
    & Height,
And they divided into Four ravening deathlike Forms,   35
Fairies & Genii & Nymphs & Gnomes of the Elements.
These are States Permanently Fixed by the Divine Power.
The Atlantic Continent sunk round Albion's cliffy shore,
And the Sea poured in amain upon the Giants of
    Albion
As Los bended the Senses of Reuben. Reuben is
    Merlin   40
Exploring the Three States of Ulro: Creation, Redemption
    & Judgment.

And many of the Eternal Ones laughed after their manner:

"Have you known the Judgment that is arisen among the
Zoas of Albion? Where a Man dare hardly to embrace
His own Wife, for the terrors of Chastity that they
    call   45
By the name of Morality? Their Daughters govern all
In hidden deceit! They are Vegetable, only fit for
    burning.
Art & Science cannot exist but by Naked Beauty displayed."
Then those in Great Eternity, who contemplate on Death,
Said thus: "What seems to Be Is To those to whom   50
It seems to Be, & is productive of the most dreadful
Consequences to those to whom it seems to Be, even of
Torments, Despair, Eternal Death; but the Divine Mercy
Steps beyond and Redeems Man in the Body of Jesus, Amen.
And Length, Breadth, Height again Obey the Divine Vision.
    Hallelujah."   55

Plate 33 [*37*]

And One stood forth from the Divine family & said:

"I feel my Spectre rising upon me! Albion! arouse thyself!
Why dost thou thunder with frozen Spectrous wrath
    against us?

The Spectre is in Giant Man insane and most deformed.
Thou wilt certainly provoke my Spectre against thine
    in fury!   5
He has a Sepulcher hewn out of a Rock ready for thee
And a Death of Eight thousand years, forged by thyself,
    upon
The point of his Spear, if thou persistest to forbid
    with Laws
Our Emanations and to attack our secret supreme delights."

So Los spoke. But when he saw blue death in Albion's
    feet,   10
Again he joined the Divine Body, following merciful,
While Albion fled more indignant, revengeful, covering

Plate 34 [*38*]

His face and bosom with petrific hardness,
    and his hands
And feet, lest any should enter his bosom & embrace
His hidden heart; his Emanation wept & trembled
    within him,
Uttering not his jealousy, but hiding it as with
Iron and steel, dark and opaque, with clouds & tempests
    brooding.   5
His strong limbs shuddered upon his mountains high and dark.

Turning from Universal Love petrific as he went,
His cold against the warmth of Eden raged with loud
Thunders of deadly war (the fever of the human soul),
Fires and clouds of rolling smoke! But mild, the Saviour
    followed him,   10

Displaying the Eternal Vision, the Divine
    Similitude,
In loves and tears of brothers, sisters, sons, fathers,
    and friends,
Which if Man ceases to behold, he ceases to exist,

Saying, "Albion! Our wars are wars of life & wounds
    of love

With intellectual spears & long winged arrows of
    thought.   15
Mutual in one another's love and wrath all-renewing,
We live as One Man; for contracting our infinite senses
We behold multitude, or expanding we behold as one,
As One Man all the Universal Family; and that One Man
We call Jesus the Christ; and he in us, and we in him,   20
Live in perfect harmony in Eden, the land of life,
Giving, receiving, and forgiving each other's trespasses.
He is the Good shepherd; he is the Lord and master;
He is the Shepherd of Albion; he is all in all,
In Eden, in the garden of God and in heavenly
    Jerusalem.   25
If we have offended, forgive us; take not vengeance
    against us."

Thus speaking, the Divine Family follow Albion.
I see them in the Vision of God upon my pleasant
    valleys.

I behold London, a Human awful wonder of God!
He says: "Return, Albion, return! I give myself for
    thee;   30
My Streets are my Ideas of Imagination.
Awake, Albion, awake! and let us awake up together.
My Houses are Thoughts; my Inhabitants, Affections,
The children of my thoughts, walking within my blood
    vessels,
Shut from my nervous form, which sleeps upon
    the verge of Beulah   35
In dreams of darkness, while my vegetating blood in
    veiny pipes,
Rolls dreadful through the Furnaces of Los and the Mills
    of Satan.
For Albion's sake, and for Jerusalem, thy Emanation,
I give myself, and these my brethren give themselves
    for Albion."

So spoke London, immortal Guardian! I heard in Lambeth's
    shades;   40

In Felpham I heard and saw the Visions of Albion.
I write in South Molton Street what I both see and hear
In regions of Humanity, in London's opening streets.

I see thee, awful Parent Land, in light; behold, I see!
Verulam! Canterbury! venerable parent of men,   45
Generous, immortal Guardian, golden clad! For Cities
Are Men, fathers of multitudes, and Rivers & Mountains
Are also Men; every thing is Human, mighty! sublime!
In every bosom a Universe expands, as wings
Let down at will around, and called the Universal Tent.   50
York, crowned with loving kindness; Edinburgh, clothed
With fortitude as with a garment of immortal texture
Woven in looms of Eden, in spiritual deaths of mighty men
Who give themselves in Golgotha, Victims to Justice, where
There is in Albion a Gate of Precious stones and gold   55
Seen only by Emanations, by vegetations viewless,
Bending across the road of Oxford Street; it from Hyde
    Park
To Tyburn's deathful shades admits the wandering souls
Of multitudes who die from Earth. This Gate cannot be
    found

Plate 35 [39]

By Satan's Watch-fiends. Though they search, numbering
    every grain
Of sand on Earth every night, they never find this Gate.
It is the Gate of Los. Withoutside is the Mill, intricate,
    dreadful
And filled with cruel tortures; but no mortal man can
    find the Mill
Of Satan in his mortal pilgrimage of seventy years.   5
For Human beauty knows it not, nor can Mercy find it! But
In the Fourth region of Humanity, Urthona, named
Mortality, begins to roll the billows of Eternal Death
Before the Gate of Los. Urthona here is named Los.
And here begins the System of Moral Virtue, named
    Rahab.   10

Albion fled through the Gate of Los, and he stood in
    the Gate.

Los was the friend of Albion who most loved him. In
    Cambridgeshire,
His eternal station, he is the twenty-eighth & is fourfold.
Seeing Albion had turned his back against the Divine Vision,
Los said to Albion, "Whither fleest thou?" Albion
    replied: 15

"I die! I go to Eternal Death! The shades of death
Hover within me & beneath; and spreading themselves outside
Like rocky clouds, build me a gloomy monument of woe.
Will none accompany me in my death or be a Ransom for
    me
In that dark Valley? I have girded round my cloak, and
    on my feet   20
Bound these black shoes of death, & on my
    hands, death's iron gloves.
God hath forsaken me, & my friends are become a burden,
A weariness to me, & the human footstep is a terror to me."

Los answered, troubled; and his soul was rent in twain:
"Must the Wise die for an Atonement? Does Mercy endure
    Atonement?   25
No! It is Moral Severity & destroys Mercy in its Victim."
So speaking, not yet infected with the Error & Illusion,

Plate 36 [40]

Los shuddered at beholding Albion, for his disease
Arose upon him, pale and ghastly; and he called around
The Friends of Albion. Trembling at the sight of Eternal
    Death,
The four appeared with their Emanations in fiery
Chariots. Black their fires roll, beholding Albion's
    House of Eternity.   5
Damp couch the flames beneath and silent, sick, stand
    shuddering
Before the Porch of sixteen pillars. Weeping, every one

Descended and fell down upon their knees round Albion's knees,
Swearing the Oath of God with awful voice of thunders round
Upon the hills & valleys, and the cloudy Oath rolled far
    and wide.   10

"Albion is sick!" said every Valley, every mournful
    Hill
And every River. "Our brother Albion is sick to death.
He hath leagued himself with robbers! He
    hath studied the arts
Of unbelief! Envy hovers over him! His Friends
    are his abhorrence!
Those who give their lives for him are despised!   15
Those who devour his soul are taken into his bosom!
To destroy his Emanation is their intention.
Arise! awake, O Friends of the Giant Albion.
They have persuaded him of horrible falsehoods!
They have sown errors over all his fruitful fields!"   20

The Twenty-four heard! They came trembling on wat'ry
    chariots
Borne by the Living Creatures of the third procession
Of Human Majesty; the Living Creatures wept aloud as they
Went along Albion's roads, till they arrived at Albion's House.

O! how the torments of Eternal Death waited on Man,   25
And the loud-rending bars of the Creation ready to burst,
That the wide world might fly from its hinges, & the
    immortal mansion
Of Man forever be possessed by monsters of the deeps;
And Man himself become a Fiend, wrapped in an endless curse,
Consuming and consumed forever in flames of Moral
    Justice.   30

For had the Body of Albion fallen down, and from its
    dreadful ruins
Let loose the enormous Spectre on the darkness of the deep,
At enmity with the Merciful & filled with devouring fire,
A netherworld must have received the foul enormous spirit,
Under pretense of Moral Virtue, filled with
    Revenge and Law,   35

There to eternity chained down, and issuing in red flames
And curses, with his mighty arms brandished against the
 heavens,
Breathing cruelty, blood & vengeance, gnashing his teeth
 with pain,
Torn with black storms & ceaseless torrents of his own
 consuming fire,
Within his breast his mighty Sons chained down & filled
 with cursings,   40
And his dark Eon, that once fair crystal form divinely
 clear,
Within his ribs producing serpents whose souls are
 flames of fire.
But, glory to the Merciful One, for he is of tender mercies!
And the Divine Family wept over him as One Man.

And these the Twenty-four in whom the Divine Family   45
Appeared; and they were One in Him, A Human Vision,
Human Divine, Jesus the Saviour, blessed forever and ever.

Selsey, true friend, who afterwards submitted to be
 devoured
By the waves of Despair, whose Emanation rose above
The flood, and was named Chichester, lovely, mild &
 gentle! Lo!   50
Her lambs bleat to the sea fowl's cry, lamenting still
 for Albion.
Submitting to be called the son of Los, the terrible vision,
Winchester stood devoting himself for Albion, his tents
Outspread with abundant riches, and his Emanations
Submitting to be called Enitharmon's daughters and be
 born   55
In vegetable mould, created by the Hammer and Loom
In Bowlahoola & Allamanda, where the Dead wail night
 & day.

(I call them by their English names: English, the rough
 basement.
Los built the stubborn structure of the Language, acting
 against

Albion's melancholy, who must else have been a Dumb
    despair.)   60
Gloucester and Exeter and Salisbury and Bristol: and
    benevolent Bath,

Plate 37 [*41*]

Bath who is Legions; he is the Seventh, the
    physician and
The poisoner, the best and worst in Heaven and Hell,
Whose Spectre first assimilated with Luvah in Albion's
    mountains.
A triple octave he took, to reduce Jerusalem to twelve,
To cast Jerusalem forth upon the wilds to Poplar &
    Bow,   5
To Maldon & Canterbury in the delights of cruelty.
The Shuttles of death sing in the sky to Islington &
    Pancras,
Round Marybone to Tyburn's River, weaving black melancholy
    as a net,
And despair as meshes closely wove over the West of London,
Where mild Jerusalem sought to repose in death & be no
    more.   10
She fled to Lambeth's mild Vale and hid herself beneath
The Surrey Hills where Rephaim terminates. Her Sons are
    seized
For victims of sacrifice, but Jerusalem cannot be found,
    Hid
By the Daughters of Beulah, gently snatched away and hid
    in Beulah.

There is a Grain of Sand in Lambeth that
    Satan cannot find,   15
Nor can his Watch-Fiends find it; 'tis translucent & has
    many Angles;
But he who finds it will find Oothoon's palace, for within,
Opening into Beulah, every angle is a lovely heaven;
But should the Watch-Fiends find it, they would call it Sin

And lay its Heavens & their inhabitants in blood of
    punishment.   20
Here Jerusalem & Vala were hid in soft slumberous repose,
Hid from the terrible East, shut up in the South & West.

The Twenty-eight trembled in Death's dark caves in cold
    despair.
They kneeled around the Couch of Death in
    deep humiliation
And tortures of self-condemnation while their Spectres
    raged within.   25
The Four Zoas in terrible combustion clouded rage,
Drinking the shuddering fears & loves of Albion's
    Families,
Destroying by selfish affections the things that they
    most admire,
Drinking & eating, & pitying & weeping, as at a tragic scene
The soul drinks murder & revenge & applauds its own
    holiness.   30

They saw Albion endeavouring to destroy their Emanations.
[In reverse printing in the illustration:
              Each Man is in
                  his Spectre's power
              Until the arrival
                  of that hour
              When his Humanity
                  awake
              And cast his Spectre
                  into the Lake.]

Plate 38 [*43*]

They saw their Wheels rising up poisonous
    against Albion:
Urizen, cold & scientific, Luvah, pitying & weeping,
Tharmas, indolent & sullen, Urthona, doubting &
    despairing,
Victims to one another & dreadfully plotting against
    each other

To prevent Albion walking about in the Four
     Complexions.   5

They saw America closed out by the Oaks of the western
     shore
And Tharmas dashed on the Rocks of the Altars of Victims
     in Mexico.
"If we are wrathful, Albion will destroy Jerusalem with
     rooty Groves.
If we are merciful, ourselves must suffer destruction on
     his Oaks.
Why should we enter into our Spectres to behold our own
     corruptions?   10
O God of Albion, descend! Deliver Jerusalem from the
     Oaken Groves!"

Then Los grew furious, raging: "Why stand we here
     trembling around,
Calling on God for help; and not ourselves, in whom God
     dwells,
Stretching a hand to save the falling Man?
     Are we not Four
Beholding Albion upon the Precipice, ready to fall into
     non-Entity,   15
Seeing these Heavens & Hells conglobing in the Void,
     Heavens over Hells
Brooding in holy hypocritic lust, drinking the cries of pain
From howling victims of Law, building Heavens
     Twenty-seven-fold,
Swelled & bloated General Forms, repugnant to the Divine
Humanity, who is the Only General and Universal
     Form   20
To which all Lineaments tend & seek with love & sympathy?
All broad & general principles belong to benevolence,
Who protects minute particulars, every one in their
     own identity.
But here the affectionate touch of the tongue is closed
     in by deadly teeth,
And the soft smile of friendship & the open dawn of
     benevolence   25

Become a net & a trap, & every energy rendered cruel,
Till the existence of friendship & benevolence is denied.
The wine of the Spirit & the vineyards of the Holy One
Here turn into poisonous stupor & deadly intoxication,
That they may be condemned by Law & the Lamb of God
    be slain.   30
And the two Sources of Life in Eternity, Hunting and War,
Are become the Sources of dark & bitter Death & of
    corroding Hell.
The open heart is shut up in integuments of frozen silence,
That the spear that lights it forth may shatter the
    ribs & bosom,
A pretense of Art to destroy Art, a pretense of
    Liberty   35
To destroy Liberty, a pretense of Religion
    to destroy Religion.
Joshua and Caleb fight; they contend in the valleys of
    Peor,
In the terrible Family Contentions of those who love
    each other.
The Armies of Balaam weep—no women come to the field.
Dead corses lay before them, & not as in Wars of
    old.   40
For the Soldier who fights for Truth calls his enemy
    his brother.
They fight & contend for life, & not for eternal death!
But here the Soldier strikes, & a dead corse falls at
    his feet.
Nor Daughter nor Sister nor Mother come forth to embosom
    the Slain!
But Death, Eternal Death, remains in the Valleys of
    Peor.   45
The English are scattered over the face of the Nations.
    Are these
Jerusalem's children? Hark! Hear the Giants of Albion
    cry at night:
"We smell the blood of the English! We delight in their
    blood on our Altars!
The living & the dead shall be ground in our rumbling Mills

For bread of the Sons of Albion, of the Giants Hand &
    Scofield.   50
Scofield & Kox are let loose upon my Saxons! They
    accumulate
A World in which Man is by his Nature the Enemy of Man,
In pride of Selfhood unwieldy, stretching out into
    non-Entity,
Generalizing Art & Science till Art & Science is lost.
Bristol & Bath, listen to my words, & ye Seventeen,
    give ear!   55
It is easy to acknowledge a man to be great & good while we
Derogate from him in the trifles & small articles of
    that goodness.
Those alone are his friends who admire his
    minutest powers.
Instead of Albion's lovely mountains & the curtains of
    Jerusalem,
I see a Cave, a Rock, a Tree, deadly and poisonous,
    unimaginative;   60
Instead of the Mutual Forgivenesses, the Minute
    Particulars, I see
Pits of bitumen ever burning, artificial Riches of the
    Canaanite
Like Lakes of liquid lead; instead of heavenly Chapels
    built
By our dear Lord, I see Worlds crusted with snows & ice;
I see a Wicker Idol woven round Jerusalem's children.
    I see   65
The Canaanite, the Amalekite, the Moabite, the Egyptian,
By Demonstrations the cruel Sons of Quality & Negation.
Driven on the Void in incoherent despair into
    non-Entity,
I see America closed apart & Jerusalem driven in terror
Away from Albion's mountains, far away from London's
    spires.   70
I will not endure this thing! I alone withstand to death
This outrage! Ah me! How sick & pale you all stand round me!
Ah me! pitiable ones! Do you also go to death's vale?
All you my Friends & Brothers, all you my beloved Companions,

Have you also caught the infection of Sin & stern
    Repentance?   75
I see Disease arise upon you! Yet speak to me and give
Me some comfort! Why do you all stand silent? I alone
Remain in permanent strength. Or is all this goodness
    & pity only
That you may take the greater vengeance in your Sepulcher?"

So Los spoke. Pale they stood around the House of
    Death   80
In the midst of temptations & despair, among the
    rooted Oaks,
Among reared Rocks of Albion's Sons; at length they rose

Plate 39 [44]

With one accord in love sublime, & as
    on Cherub's wings
They Albion surround with kindest violence to bear him back
Against his will through Los's Gate to Eden, Fourfold, Loud
Their Wings waving over the bottomless Immense, to bear
Their awful charge back to his native home; but Albion,
    dark,   5
Repugnant, rolled his Wheels backward into non-Entity.
Loud roll the Starry Wheels of Albion into the World of Death
And all the Gate of Los, clouded with clouds redounding
    from
Albion's dread Wheels, stretching out spaces immense
    between,
That every little particle of light & air became
    Opaque,   10
Black & immense, a Rock of difficulty & a Cliff
Of black despair that the immortal Wings laboured
    against,
Cliff after cliff, & over Valleys of despair & death.
The narrow Sea between Albion & the Atlantic Continent:
Its waves of pearl became a boundless Ocean,
    bottomless,   15

Of grey obscurity, filled with clouds & rocks &
    whirling waters
And Albion's Sons, ascending & descending in the horrid
    Void.

But as the Will must not be bended but in the day of Divine
Power, silent, calm & motionless in the mid-air sublime,
The Family Divine hover around the darkened Albion.   20

Such is the nature of the Ulro, that whatever enters
Becomes Sexual & is Created and Vegetated and Born.
From Hyde Park spread their vegetating roots beneath
    Albion
In dreadful pain the Spectrous Uncircumcised Vegetation,
Forming a Sexual Machine, an Aged Virgin
    Form,   25
In Erin's Land toward the North, joint after joint
    & burning
In love & jealousy immingled & calling it Religion;
And feeling the damps of death, they with one accord
    delegated Los,
Conjuring him by the Highest that he should Watch over
    them
Till Jesus shall appear; & they gave their power to
    Los,   30
Naming him the Spirit of Prophecy, calling him Elijah.

Strucken with Albion's disease, they become what they
    behold;
They assimilate with Albion in pity & compassion;
Their Emanations return not; their Spectres rage in the
    Deep.
The Slumbers of Death came over them around the Couch
    of Death   35
Among the Furnaces of Los, among the Oaks of Albion.

Man is adjoined to Man by his Emanative portion,
Who is Jerusalem in every individual Man, and her
Shadow is Vala, builded by the Reasoning power in
    Man.

O search & see; turn your eyes inward; open, O thou World   40
Of Love & Harmony in Man; expand thy ever lovely Gates.

They wept into the deeps a little space. At length was heard
The voice of Bath, faint as the voice of the Dead in the
   House of Death.

Plate 40 [45]

Bath, healing City! whose wisdom in midst of Poetic
Fervor mild spoke through the Western Porch in soft gentle
   tears:

"O Albion, mildest Son of Eden! Closed is thy
   Western Gate.
Brothers of Eternity! This Man, whose great example
We all admired & loved, whose all-benevolent countenance,
   seen   5
In Eden, in lovely Jerusalem, drew even from envy
The tear and the confession of honesty, open & undisguised
From mistrust and suspicion, The Man is himself become
A piteous example of oblivion, To teach the Sons
Of Eden that however great and glorious, however
   loving   10
And merciful the Individuality, however high
Our palaces and cities, and however fruitful are
   our fields,
In Selfhood we are nothing, but fade away in morning's
   breath.
Our mildness is nothing; the greatest mildness we can use
Is incapable and nothing. None but the Lamb of God can
   heal   15
This dread disease, none but Jesus. O Lord, descend and
   save!
Albion's Western Gate is closed; his death is coming apace!
Jesus alone can save him; for alas, we none can know
How soon his lot may be our own. When Africa in sleep
Rose in the night of Beulah and bound down the Sun &
   Moon,   20
His friends cut his strong chains & overwhelmed his dark

Machines in fury & destruction, and the Man, reviving,
    repented.
He wept before his wrathful brethren, thankful & considerate
For their well-timed wrath. But Albion's sleep is not
Like Africa's, and his machines are woven with his
    life.   25
Nothing but mercy can save him, nothing but mercy
    interposing,
Lest he should slay Jerusalem in his fearful jealousy.
O God, descend! Gather our brethren; deliver Jerusalem.
But that we may omit no office of the friendly spirit,
Oxford, take thou these leaves of the Tree of
    Life; with eloquence   30
That thy immortal tongue inspires, present them to Albion.
Perhaps he may receive them, offered from thy loved hands."

So spoke, unheard by Albion, the merciful Son of Heaven
To those whose Western Gates were open, as they stood
    weeping
Around Albion; but Albion heard him not; obdurate,
    hard,   35
He frowned on all his Friends, counting them enemies in
    his sorrow.

And the Seventeen conjoining with Bath, the Seventh,
In whom the other Ten shone manifest, a Divine Vision,
Assimilated and embraced Eternal Death for Albion's sake.

And these the names of the Eighteen combining with those
    Ten: 40

Plate 41 [46]

Bath, mild Physician of Eternity, mysterious
    power
Whose springs are unsearchable & knowledge infinite.
Hereford, ancient Guardian of Wales, whose hands
Builded the mountain palaces of Eden, stupendous works!
Lincoln, Durham & Carlisle, Counsellors of Los.   5
And Ely, Scribe of Los, whose pen no other hand

Dare touch! Oxford, immortal Bard! With eloquence
Divine he wept over Albion, speaking the words of God
In mild persuasion, bringing leaves of the Tree of Life:

"Thou art in Error, Albion, the Land of Ulro.   10
One Error not removed will destroy a human Soul.
Repose in Beulah's night, till the Error is
      removed.
Reason not on both sides; Repose upon our bosoms
Till the Plow of Jehovah, and the Harrow of Shaddai
Have passed over the Dead, to awake the Dead to
      Judgment."   15
But Albion turned away, refusing comfort.

Oxford trembled while he spoke, then fainted in the arms
Of Norwich, Peterborough, Rochester, Chester awful,
      Worcester,
Lichfield, Saint David's, Llandaff, Asaph, Bangor, Sodor,
Bowing their heads, devoted; and the Furnaces of Los   20
Began to rage; thundering loud, the storms began to roar
Upon the Furnaces, and loud the Furnaces re-bellow beneath.

And these the Four in whom the twenty-four appeared
      fourfold:
Verulam, London, York, Edinburgh, mourning one towards
      another.
Alas! The time will come, when a man's worst enemies   25
Shall be those of his own house and family, in a Religion
Of Generation, to destroy by Sin and Atonement happy
      Jerusalem,
The Bride and Wife of the Lamb. O God, thou art Not an
      Avenger!

Plate 42

Thus Albion sat, studious of others in his
      pale disease,
Brooding on evil; but when Los opened the Furnaces
      before him,
He saw that the accursed things were his own affections

And his own beloveds: then he turned sick! His soul died
    within him.
Also Los, sick & terrified, beheld the Furnaces of
    Death   5
And must have died, but the Divine Saviour descended
Among the infant loves & affections, and
    the Divine Vision wept
Like evening dew on every herb upon the breathing ground.

Albion spoke in his dismal dreams: "O thou deceitful
    friend,
Worshipping mercy & beholding thy friend in such
    affliction.   10
Los! thou now discoverest thy turpitude to the heavens.
I demand righteousness & justice. O thou ingratitude!
Give me my Emanations back, food for my dying soul.
My daughters are harlots; my sons are accursed before me.
Enitharmon is my daughter, accursed with a father's
    curse.   15
O! I have utterly been wasted. I have given my daughters
    to devils."

So spoke Albion in gloomy majesty, and deepest night
Of Ulro rolled round his skirts from Dover to Cornwall.
Los answered: "Righteousness & justice I give thee
    in return
For thy righteousness, but I add mercy also and
    bind   20
Thee from destroying these little ones; am I to be only
Merciful to thee and cruel to all that thou hatest?
Thou wast the Image of God surrounded by the Four Zoas.
Three thou hast slain. I am the Fourth; thou canst not
    destroy me.
Thou art in Error; trouble me not with thy
    righteousness.   25
I have innocence to defend and ignorance to instruct;
I have no time for seeming, and little arts of compliment
In morality and virtue, in self-glorying and pride.
There is a limit of Opaqueness and a limit of Contraction
In every Individual Man, and the limit of Opaqueness   30

Is named Satan, and the limit of Contraction
    is named Adam.
But when Man sleeps in Beulah, the Saviour in mercy takes
Contraction's Limit, and of the Limit he forms Woman,
    That
Himself may in process of time be born, Man to redeem.
But there is no Limit of Expansion; there is no Limit of
    Translucence   35
In the bosom of Man forever from eternity to eternity.
Therefore I break thy bonds of righteousness; I crush
    thy messengers,
That they may not crush me and mine; do thou be righteous,
And I will return it; otherwise I defy thy worst revenge.
Consider me as thine enemy; on me turn all thy fury,   40
But destroy not these little ones, nor mock the Lord's
    anointed;
Destroy not by Moral Virtue the little ones whom he hath
    chosen,
The little ones whom he hath chosen in preference to thee.
He hath cast thee off forever; the little ones he hath
    anointed!
Thy Selfhood is forever accursed from the Divine
    presence."   45

So Los spoke, then turned his face & wept for Albion.

Albion replied: "Go, Hand & Hyle, seize the abhorred friend,
As you Have seized the Twenty-four rebellious ingratitudes,
To atone for you, for spiritual death. Man lives by
    deaths of Men.
Bring him to justice before heaven here upon London
    Stone,   50
Between Blackheath & Hounslow, between Norwood &
    Finchley.
All that they have is mine; from my free generous gift
They now hold all they have: ingratitude to me.
To me their benefactor calls aloud for vengeance deep."

Los stood before his Furnaces, awaiting the
    fury of the Dead;   55

And the Divine hand was upon him, strengthening him
  mightily.

The Spectres of the Dead cry out from the deeps beneath
Upon the hills of Albion; Oxford groans in his iron
  furnace,
Winchester in his den & cavern; they lament against
Albion; they curse their human kindness & affection;   60
They rage like wild beasts in the forests of affliction.
In the dreams of Ulro they repent of their human
  kindness.

"Come up, build Babylon; Rahab is ours & all her
  multitudes
With her in pomp and glory of victory. Depart,
Ye twenty-four, into the deeps; let us depart to
  glory."   65

Their Human majestic forms sit up upon their Couches
Of death; they curb their Spectres as with iron curbs;
They inquire after Jerusalem in the regions of the dead
With the voices of dead men, low, scarcely articulate;
And with tears cold on their cheeks they weary
  repose.   70

"O when shall the morning of the grave appear, and when
Shall our salvation come? We sleep upon our watch.
We cannot awake! And our Spectres rage in the forests.
O God of Albion, where art thou? Pity the watchers!"

Thus mourn they. Loud the Furnaces of Los thunder
  upon   75
The clouds of Europe & Asia, among the Serpent Temples.

And Los drew his Seven Furnaces around Albion's Altars,
And as Albion built his frozen Altars, Los built the
  Mundane Shell,
In the Four Regions of Humanity, East &
  West & North & South,
Till Norwood & Finchley & Blackheath & Hounslow covered
  the whole Earth.   80
This is the Net & Veil of Vala among the Souls of the Dead.

Plate 43 [*29*]

Then the Divine Vision like a silent Sun
    appeared above
Albion's dark rocks, setting behind the Gardens of
    Kensington
On Tyburn's River, in clouds of blood, where was mild
    Zion Hill's
Most ancient promontory; and in the Sun, a Human Form
    appeared,
And thus the Voice Divine went forth upon the rocks of
    Albion: 5

"I elected Albion for my glory; I gave to him the Nations
Of the whole Earth. He was the Angel of my Presence,
    and all
The Sons of God were Albion's Sons, and Jerusalem was
    my joy.
The Reactor hath hid himself through envy. I behold him.
But you cannot behold him till he be revealed in his
    System.   10
Albion's Reactor must have a Place prepared; Albion
    must Sleep
The Sleep of Death, till the Man of Sin & Repentance
    be revealed.
Hidden in Albion's Forests he lurks; he admits of no Reply
From Albion, but hath founded his Reaction into a Law
Of Action, for Obedience to destroy the Contraries
    of Man.   15
He hath compelled Albion to become a Punisher & hath
    possessed
Himself of Albion's Forests & Wilds, and Jerusalem is
    taken;
The City of the Woods in the Forest of Ephratah is taken.
London is a stone of her ruins; Oxford is the dust of
    her walls!
Sussex & Kent are her scattered garments, Ireland her
    holy place;   20

And the murdered bodies of her little ones are Scotland
    and Wales.
The Cities of the Nations are the smoke of
    her consummation.
The Nations are her dust, ground by the chariot wheels
Of her lordly conquerors, her palaces levelled with
    the dust.
I come that I may find a way for my banished ones to
    return.   25
Fear not, O little Flock, I come. Albion shall rise again."

So saying, the mild Sun enclosed the Human Family.

Forthwith from Albion's darkening locks came two
    Immortal forms
Saying: "We alone are escaped. O merciful Lord and
    Saviour,
We flee from the interiors of Albion's hills and
    mountains!   30
From his Valleys Eastward, from Amalek, Canaan & Moab,
Beneath his vast ranges of hills surrounding Jerusalem.

"Albion walked on the steps of fire before his Halls,
And Vala walked with him in dreams of soft deluding slumber.
He looked up & saw the Prince of Light with splendor
    faded.   35
Then Albion ascended mourning into the porches of his
    Palace.
Above him rose a Shadow from his wearied intellect,
Of living gold, pure, perfect, holy; in white linen
    pure he hovered,
A sweet entrancing self-delusion, a watery vision of
    Albion,
Soft-exulting in existence, all the Man absorbing!   40

"Albion fell upon his face prostrate before the wat'ry
    Shadow,
Saying, 'O Lord, whence is this change? Thou knowest
    I am nothing!'
And Vala trembled & covered her face, & her locks were
    spread on the pavement.

"We heard, astonished at the Vision, & our hearts
    trembled within us;
We heard the voice of slumberous Albion,
    and thus he spake,   45
Idolatrous, to his own Shadow words of eternity, uttering:

"'O I am nothing when I enter into judgment with thee!
If thou withdraw thy breath, I die & vanish into Hades.
If thou dost lay thine hand upon me, behold I am silent.
If thou withhold thine hand, I perish like a fallen
    leaf.   50
O I am nothing and to nothing must return again.
If thou withdraw thy breath, Behold I am oblivion.'

"He ceased; the shadowy voice was silent, but the cloud
    hovered over their heads
In golden wreaths, the sorrow of Man; & the balmy drops
    fell down.
And Lo! that son of Man, that Shadowy Spirit of mild
    Albion,   55
Luvah, descended from the cloud; in terror Albion rose;
Indignant rose the awful Man & turned his back on Vala.

"We heard the voice of Albion starting from his sleep:

"'Whence is this voice crying, "Enion!" that soundeth
    in my ears?
O cruel pity! O dark deceit! Can Love seek for
    dominion?'   60

"And Luvah strove to gain dominion over Albion.
They strove together above the Body where Vala was
    enclosed
And the dark Body of Albion left prostrate upon the
    crystal pavement,
Covered with boils from head to foot, the terrible
    smitings of Luvah.

"Then frowned the fallen Man and put forth Luvah from
    his presence,   65
Saying: 'Go and Die the Death of Man for Vala, the
    sweet wanderer.

I will turn the volutions of your ears outward and bend
    your nostrils
Downward, and your fluxile eyes englobed roll round
    in fear.
Your with'ring lips and tongue shrink up into a narrow
    circle,
Till into narrow forms you creep; go take your fiery
    way   70
And learn what 'tis to absorb the Man, you Spirits
    of Pity & Love.'

"They heard the voice and fled swift as the winter's
    setting sun.
And now the human blood foamed high; the Spirits Luvah
    & Vala
Went down the Human Heart, where Paradise & its joys
    abounded,
In jealous fears & fury & rage, & flames roll round their
    fervid feet;   75
And the vast form of Nature like a serpent played before
    them.
And as they fled in folding fires & thunders of the deep,
Vala shrunk in like the dark sea that leaves its slimy
    banks.
And from her bosom Luvah fell far as the East and West.
And the vast form of Nature like a serpent rolled
    between,   80
Whether of Jerusalem's or Vala's ruins congenerated, we
    know not.
All is confusion, all is tumult, & we alone are escaped."

So spoke the fugitives; they joined the Divine Family,
    trembling;

Plate 44 [*30*]

And the Two that escaped were the Emanation of
    Los & his
Spectre; for wherever the Emanation goes, the Spectre

Attends her as her Guard, & Los's Emanation is named
Enitharmon, & his Spectre is named Urthona;
   they knew
Not where to flee; they had been on a visit to Albion's
   Children,   5
And they strove to weave a Shadow of the Emanation
To hide themselves, weeping & lamenting for the Vegetation
Of Albion's Children, fleeing through Albion's vales in
   streams of gore.
Being not irritated by insult bearing insulting benevolences,
They perceived that corporeal friends are spiritual
   enemies.   10
They saw the Sexual Religion in its embryon Uncircumcision,
And the Divine hand was upon them, bearing them through
   darkness
Back safe to their Humanity as doves to their windows.
Therefore the Sons of Eden praise Urthona's Spectre in Songs,
Because he kept the Divine Vision in time of trouble.   15

They wept & trembled, & Los put forth his hand & took
   them in,
Into his Bosom, from which Albion shrunk in dismal pain,
Rending the fibres of Brotherhood & in Feminine Allegories
Enclosing Los; but the Divine Vision appeared with Los,
Following Albion into his Central Void among his
   Oaks.   20

And Los prayed and said: "O Divine Saviour, arise
Upon the Mountains of Albion as in ancient time. Behold!
The Cities of Albion seek thy face; London groans in pain
From Hill to Hill; & the Thames laments along the Valleys.
The little Villages of Middlesex & Surrey hunger
   & thirst.   25
The Twenty-eight Cities of Albion stretch their hands
   to thee,
Because of the Oppressors of Albion in every City & Village.
They mock at the Labourer's limbs; they mock
   at his starved Children.
They buy his Daughters that they may have power to sell
   his Sons.

They compel the Poor to live upon a crust of bread by
    soft mild arts.   30
They reduce the Man to want, then give with pomp &
    ceremony.
The praise of Jehovah is chanted from lips of hunger
    & thirst.

"Humanity knows not of Sex; wherefore are Sexes
    in Beulah?
In Beulah the Female lets down her beautiful Tabernacle,
Which the Male enters magnificent between her
    Cherubim   35
And becomes One with her, mingling, condensing in
    Self-love
The Rocky Law of Condemnation & double Generation &
    Death.
Albion hath entered the Loins, the place of the Last
    Judgment;
And Luvah hath drawn the Curtains around Albion in Vala's
    bosom.
The Dead awake to Generation! Arise, O Lord, & rend the
    Veil!"   40

So Los in lamentations followed Albion. Albion covered

Plate 45 [*31*]

His western heaven with rocky clouds of death
    & despair.

Fearing that Albion should turn his back against the
    Divine Vision,
Los took his globe of fire to search the interiors of
    Albion's
Bosom, in all the terrors of friendship, entering the
    caves
Of despair & death, to search the tempters out, walking
    among   5
Albion's rocks & precipices, caves of solitude & dark
    despair,

And saw every Minute Particular of Albion
    degraded & murdered,
But saw not by whom; they were hidden within in the
    minute particulars
Of which they had possessed themselves; and there they
    take up
The articulations of a man's soul, and laughing throw
    it down   10
Into the frame, then knock it out upon the plank; & souls
    are baked
In bricks to build the pyramids of Heber & Terah. But Los
Searched in vain; closed from the minutia he walked, difficult.
He came down from Highgate through Hackney & Holloway
    towards London,
Till he came to old Stratford, & thence to Stepney & the
    Isle   15
Of Leutha's Dogs, thence through the narrows of the River's
    side,
And saw every minute particular, the jewels of Albion,
    running down
The kennels of the streets & lanes as if they were abhorred.
Every Universal Form was become barren mountains of Moral
Virtue, and every Minute Particular hardened into grains
    of sand,   20
And all the tendernesses of the soul cast forth
    as filth & mire
Among the winding places of deep contemplation intricate,
To where the Tower of London frowned dreadful over
    Jerusalem,
A building of Luvah builded in Jerusalem's eastern gate to be
His secluded Court, thence to Bethlehem where was
    builded   25
Dens of despair in the house of bread. Inquiring in vain
Of stones and rocks, he took his way, for human
    form was none;
And thus he spoke, looking on Albion's City with many tears:

"What shall I do? What could I do? If I could find these
    Criminals,

I could not dare to take vengeance; for all things are so
    constructed   30
And builded by the Divine hand that the sinner shall always
    escape,
And he who takes vengeance alone is the criminal of
    Providence.
If I should dare to lay my finger on a grain of sand
In way of vengeance, I punish the already punished. O
    whom
Should I pity if I pity not the sinner who is gone
    astray?   35
O Albion, if thou takest vengeance, if thou revengest
    thy wrongs,
Thou art forever lost! What can I do to hinder the Sons
Of Albion from taking vengeance? Or how shall I them
    persuade?"

So spoke Los, travelling through darkness & horrid solitude;
And he beheld Jerusalem in Westminster & Marybone,   40
Among the ruins of the Temple, and Vala, who is her Shadow,
Jerusalem's Shadow bent northward over the Island
    white.
At length he sat on London stone & heard Jerusalem's voice:

"Albion, I cannot be thy Wife. Thine own Minute Particulars
Belong to God alone, and all thy little ones are holy.   45
They are of Faith & not of Demonstration. Wherefore
    is Vala
Clothed in black mourning upon my river's currents?
    Vala awake!
I hear thy shuttles sing in the sky, and round my limbs
I feel the iron threads of love & jealousy & despair."

Vala replied: "Albion is mine! Luvah gave me to
    Albion   50
And now receives reproach & hate. Was it not said of old,

"'Set your Son before a man, & he shall take
    you & your sons
For slaves; but set your Daughter before a man & She
Shall make him & his sons & daughters your slaves for ever'?

And is this Faith? Behold the strife of Albion &
    Luvah   55
Is great in the East; their spears of blood rage in the
    eastern heaven.
Urizen is the champion of Albion; they will slay my Luvah.
And thou, O harlot daughter, daughter of despair,
    art all
This cause of these shakings of my towers on Euphrates.
Here is the House of Albion, & here is thy secluded
    place,   60
And here we have found thy sins, & hence we turn
    thee forth,
For all to avoid thee, to be astonished at thee for
    thy sins,
Because thou art the impurity & the harlot, & thy
    children,
Children of whoredoms, born for Sacrifice, for the meat
    & drink
Offering, to sustain the glorious combat & the battle
    & war,   65
That Man may be purified by the death of thy delusions."

So saying, she her dark threads cast over the trembling
    River
And over the valleys from the hills of Hertfordshire to
    the hills
Of Surrey, across Middlesex & across Albion's House
Of Eternity! Pale stood Albion at his eastern gate,   70

Plate 46 [32]

Leaning against the pillars, & his disease rose
    from his skirts.
Upon the Precipice he stood, ready to fall into
    non-Entity.

Los was all astonishment & terror; he trembled sitting
    on the Stone
Of London; but the interiors of Albion's
    fibres & nerves were hidden

From Los; astonished he beheld only the petrified
    surfaces   5
And saw his Furnaces in ruins, for Los is the Demon of
    the Furnaces.
He saw also the Four Points of Albion reversed inwards;
He seized his Hammer & Tongs, his iron Poker & his
    Bellows,
Upon the valleys of Middlesex, Shouting loud for aid Divine.

In stern defiance came from Albion's bosom Hand, Hyle,
    Coban,   10
Guantok, Peachey, Brereton, Slade, Hutton, Scofield, Kox,
    Kotope,
Bowen, Albion's Sons; they bore him a golden couch into
    the porch,
And on the Couch reposed his limbs, trembling from
    the bloody field,
Rearing their Druid Patriarchal rocky Temples around
    his limbs.
(All things begin & end in Albion's Ancient Druid Rocky
    Shore.)   15

Plate 47

From Camberwell to Highgate, where the mighty
    Thames shudders along,
Where Los's Furnaces stand, where Jerusalem & Vala howl,
Luvah tore forth from Albion's Loins, in fibrous veins,
    in rivers
Of blood over Europe, a Vegetating Root in grinding pain,
Animating the Dragon Temples, soon to become that Holy
    Fiend   5
The Wicker Man of Scandinavia, in which, cruelly consumed,
The Captives reared to heaven howl in flames
    among the stars.
Loud the cries of War on the Rhine & Danube, with
    Albion's Sons.
Away from Beulah's hills & vales break forth the Souls
    of the Dead,

With cymbal, trumpet, clarion & the scythed chariots of
    Britain.   10

And the Veil of Vala is composed of the Spectres of the Dead.

Hark! The mingling cries of Luvah with the Sons of Albion.
Hark! & Record the terrible wonder! that the Punisher
Mingles with his Victim's Spectre, enslaved and
    tormented
To him whom he has murdered, bound in vengeance
    & enmity.   15
Shudder not, but Write, & the hand of God will assist you!
Therefore I write Albion's last words: "Hope is banished
    from me."

Plate 48

These were his last words, and the merciful
    Saviour in his arms
Received him, in the arms of tender mercy, and reposed
The pale limbs of his Eternal Individuality
Upon the Rock of Ages. Then, surrounded with a Cloud,
In silence, the Divine Lord builded with immortal
    labour   5
Of gold & jewels a sublime Ornament, a Couch of repose
With Sixteen pillars canopied with emblems & written
    verse,
Spiritual Verse, ordered & measured, from whence time
    shall reveal
The Five books of the Decalogue, the books of Joshua
    & Judges,
Samuel, a double book, & Kings, a double book, the Psalms
    & Prophets,   10
The Fourfold Gospel, and the Revelations
    everlasting.
Eternity groaned & was troubled at the image of Eternal
    Death!

Beneath the bottoms of the Graves, which is Earth's
    central joint,

There is a place where Contrarieties are equally true:
(To protect from the Giant blows in the sports of
        intellect,   15
Thunder in the midst of kindness, & love that kills its
        beloved,
Because Death is for a period, and they renew tenfold.)
From this sweet Place Maternal Love awoke Jerusalem.
With pangs she forsook Beulah's pleasant lovely
        shadowy Universe,
Where no dispute can come, created for those who
        Sleep.   20

Weeping was in all Beulah, and all the Daughters of Beulah
Wept for their Sister, the Daughter of Albion, Jerusalem,
When out of Beulah the Emanation of the Sleeper descended
With solemn mourning out of Beulah's moony shades and hills,
Within the Human Heart, whose Gates closed with solemn
        sound.   25

And this the manner of the terrible Separation:
The Emanations of the grievously afflicted Friends of Albion
Concenter in one Female form, an Aged pensive Woman.
Astonished! lovely! Embracing the sublime shade the
        Daughters of Beulah
Beheld her with wonder! With awful hands she took   30
A Moment of Time, drawing it out with many tears &
        afflictions
And many sorrows, oblique across the Atlantic Vale,
Which is the Vale of Rephaim dreadful, from East to West,
Where the Human Harvest waves abundant in the beams
        of Eden
Into a Rainbow of jewels and gold, a mild Reflection from   35
Albion's dread Tomb, Eight thousand and five hundred years
In its extension. Every two hundred years has a door to
        Eden.
She also took an Atom of Space, with dire pain opening
        it a Center
Into Beulah; trembling the Daughters of Beulah dried
Her tears. She ardent embraced her sorrows, occupied
        in labours   40

Of sublime mercy in Rephaim's Vale. Perusing Albion's Tomb
She sat; she walked among the ornaments, solemn mourning.
The Daughters attended her shudderings, wiping the death sweat.
Los also saw her in his seventh Furnace; he also,
    terrified,
Saw the finger of God go forth upon his seventh
    Furnace,   45
Away from the Starry Wheels to prepare Jerusalem a place,
When with a dreadful groan the Emanation mild of Albion
Burst from his bosom in the Tomb like a pale, snowy cloud,
Female and lovely, struggling to put off the Human form,
Writhing in pain. The Daughters of Beulah in kind arms
    received   50
Jerusalem, weeping over her among the Spaces of Erin,
In the Ends of Beulah, where the Dead wail night & day.

And thus Erin spoke to the Daughters of Beulah in
    soft tears:

"Albion, the Vortex of the Dead! Albion the Generous!
Albion, the mildest son of Heaven! The Place of Holy
    Sacrifice,   55
Where Friends Die for each other, will become the Place,
Of Murder & unforgiving, Never-awaking Sacrifice of Enemies.
The Children must be sacrificed (a horror never known
Till now in Beulah), unless a Refuge can be found
To hide them from the wrath of Albion's Law, that
    freezes sore   60
Upon his Sons & Daughters, self-exiled from his bosom.
Draw ye Jerusalem away from Albion's Mountains
To give a Place for Redemption; let Sihon and Og
Remove Eastward to Bashan and Gilead, and leave

Plate 49

The secret coverts of Albion & the hidden places
    of America.
Jerusalem, Jerusalem! why wilt thou turn away?
Come ye, O Daughters of Beulah, lament for Og & Sihon
Upon the Lakes of Ireland from Rathlin to Baltimore.

Stand ye upon the Dargle from Wicklow to Drogheda.   5
Come & mourn over Albion, the White Cliff of the Atlantic,
The Mountain of Giants; all the Giants of Albion are become
Weak, withered, darkened, & Jerusalem is cast forth from
     Albion.
They deny that they ever knew Jerusalem or ever dwelt in
     Shiloh.
The Gigantic roots & twigs of the vegetating Sons of
     Albion,   10
Filled with the little ones, are consumed in the Fires
     of their Altars.
The vegetating Cities are burned & consumed from the Earth,
And the Bodies in which all Animals & Vegetations, the
     Earth & Heaven
Were contained in the All-Glorious Imagination are
     withered & darkened.
The golden Gate of Havilah and all the Garden of God   15
Was caught up with the Sun in one day of fury and war.
The Lungs, the Heart, the Liver shrunk away
     far distant from Man
And left a little slimy substance floating upon the tides.
In one night the Atlantic Continent was caught up with
     the Moon
And became an Opaque Globe far distant, clad with moony
     beams.   20
The Visions of Eternity, by reason of narrowed perceptions,
Are become weak Visions of Time & Space, fixed into
     furrows of death,
Till deep dissimulation is the only defense an honest
     man has left.
O Polypus of Death, O Spectre over Europe and Asia,
Withering the Human Form by Laws of Sacrifice for
     Sin,   25
By Laws of Chastity & Abhorrence, I am withered up,
Striving to Create a Heaven in which all shall be pure
     & holy
In their Own Selfhoods, in Natural Selfish Chastity to
     banish Pity
And dear Mutual Forgiveness, & to become One Great Satan

Enslaved to the most powerful Selfhood, to murder the
    Divine Humanity,   30
In whose sight all are as the dust, & who chargeth
    his Angels with folly!
Ah! weak & wide astray! Ah, shut in narrow doleful form,
Creeping in reptile flesh upon the bosom of the ground!
The Eye of Man, a little narrow orb, closed up & dark,
Scarcely beholding the Great Light, conversing with
    the ground.   35
The Ear, a little shell, in small volutions shutting out
True Harmonies, & comprehending great, as very small.
The Nostrils, bent down to the earth & closed with
    senseless flesh,
That odours cannot them expand, nor joy on
    them exult.
The Tongue a little moisture fills, a little food it
    cloys,   40
A little sound it utters, & its cries are faintly heard.
Therefore they are removed; therefore they have taken root
In Egypt & Philistea, in Moab & Edom & Aram;
In the Erythrean Sea their Uncircumcision in Heart & Loins
Be lost forever & ever. Then they shall arise from
    Self   45
By Self-Annihilation into Jerusalem's Courts & into Shiloh,
Shiloh the Masculine Emanation among the Flowers of
    Beulah.
Lo, Shiloh dwells over France, as Jerusalem dwells over
    Albion.
Build & prepare a Wall & Curtain for America's shore!
Rush on! Rush on! Rush on! ye vegetating Sons of
    Albion.   50
The Sun shall go before you in Day; the Moon shall go
Before you in Night. Come on! Come on! Come on! The Lord
Jehovah is before, behind, above, beneath, around.
He has builded the arches of Albion's Tomb, binding the
    Stars
In merciful Order, bending the Laws of Cruelty to
    Peace.   55

He hath placed Og & Anak, the Giants of Albion, for
    their Guards,
Building the Body of Moses in the Valley of Peor, the Body
Of Divine Analogy; and Og & Sihon in the tears of Balaam,
The Son of Beor, have given their power to Joshua & Caleb.
Remove from Albion; far remove these terrible
    surfaces.   60
They are beginning to form Heavens & Hells in immense
Circles, the Hells for food to the Heavens, food of torment,
Food of despair; they drink the condemned Soul & rejoice
In cruel holiness, in their Heavens of Chastity &
    Uncircumcision.
Yet they are blameless, & Iniquity must be imputed
    only   65
To the State they are entered into, that
    they may be delivered.
Satan is the State of Death & not a Human existence;
But Luvah is named Satan because he has entered that State,
A World where Man is by Nature the enemy of Man,
Because the Evil is Created into a State, that
    Men   70
May be delivered time after time evermore. Amen.
Learn therefore, O Sisters, to distinguish the Eternal
    Human,
That walks about among the stones of fire in bliss & woe
Alternate, from those States or Worlds in which the
    Spirit travels.
This is the only means to Forgiveness of Enemies.   75
Therefore remove from Albion these terrible Surfaces
And let wild seas & rocks close up Jerusalem away from

Plate 50

The Atlantic Mountains, where Giants dwelt in
    Intellect,
Now given to stony Druids, and Allegoric Generation,
To the Twelve Gods of Asia, the Spectres of those who Sleep,
Swayed by a Providence opposed to the Divine Lord Jesus,

A murderous Providence! A Creation groans, living
    on Death,   5
Where Fish & Bird & Beast & Man & Tree & Metal & Stone
Live by Devouring, going into Eternal Death continually.
Albion is now possessed by the War of Blood! The Sacrifice
Of envy Albion is become, and his Emanation cast out.
Come, Lord Jesus, Lamb of God, descend; for if, O
    Lord,   10
If thou hadst been here, our brother Albion had not died.
Arise, sisters! Go ye & meet the Lord, while I remain.
Behold the foggy mornings of the Dead on Albion's cliffs!
Ye know that if the Emanation remains in them
She will become an Eternal Death, an Avenger of
    Sin,   15
A Self-righteousness, the proud Virgin-Harlot,
    Mother of War!
And we also & all Beulah consume beneath Albion's curse."

So Erin spoke to the Daughters of Beulah. Shuddering
With their wings, they sat in the Furnace, in a night
Of stars; for all the Sons of Albion appeared distant
    stars,   20
Ascending and descending into Albion's sea of death.
And Erin's lovely Bow enclosed the Wheels of Albion's Sons.

Expanding on wing, the Daughters of Beulah replied in
    sweet response:

"Come, O thou Lamb of God, and take away the remembrance
    of Sin.
To Sin & to hide the Sin in sweet deceit is
    lovely!   25
To Sin in the open face of day is cruel & pitiless! But
To record the Sin for a reproach, to let the Sun go down
In a remembrance of the Sin is a Woe & a Horror,
A brooder of an Evil Day, and a Sun rising in blood.
Come then, O Lamb of God, and take away the remembrance
    of Sin."   30

Plate 52

Rahab is an Eternal State.	To the Deists.	The Spiritual States of the Soul are all Eternal. Distinguish between the Man & his present State.

He never can be a Friend to the Human Race who is the Preacher of Natural Morality or Natural Religion; he is a flatterer who means to betray, to perpetuate Tyrant Pride & the Laws of that Babylon which he foresees shall shortly be destroyed, with the Spiritual and not the Natural Sword. He is in the State named Rahab, which State must be put off before he can be the Friend of Man.

You, O Deists, profess yourselves the Enemies of Christianity, and you are so; you are also the Enemies of the Human Race & of Universal Nature. Man is born a Spectre or Satan & is altogether an Evil & requires a New Selfhood continually & must continually be changed into his direct Contrary. But your Greek Philosophy (which is a remnant of Druidism) teaches that Man is Righteous in his Vegetated Spectre: An Opinion of fatal & accursed consequence to Man, as the Ancients saw plainly by Revelation to the entire abrogation of Experimental Theory; and many believed what they saw, and Prophesied of Jesus.

Man must & will have Some Religion; if he has not the Religion of Jesus, he will have the Religion of Satan, & will erect the Synagogue of Satan, calling the Prince of this World, God; and destroying all who do not worship Satan under the Name of God. Will anyone say: "Where are those who worship Satan under the Name of God?" Where are they? Listen! Every Religion that Preaches Vengeance for Sin is the Religion of the Enemy & Avenger, and not of the Forgiver of Sin, and their God is Satan, Named by the Divine Name. Your Religion, O Deists, Deism, is the Worship of the God of this World by the means of what you call Natural Religion and Natural Philosophy, and of Natural Morality or Self-Righteousness, the Selfish Virtues of the Natural Heart.

This was the Religion of the Pharisees who murdered Jesus. Deism
is the same & ends in the same.

Voltaire, Rousseau, Gibbon, Hume charge the Spiritually Religious with Hypocrisy! But how a Monk, or a Methodist either,
can be a Hypocrite I cannot conceive. We are Men of like passions with others & pretend not be be holier than others; therefore, when a Religious Man falls into Sin, he ought not to be called
a Hypocrite; this title is more properly to be given to a Player
who falls into Sin, whose profession is Virtue & Morality & the
making Men Self-Righteous. Foote in calling Whitefield Hypocrite was himself one; for Whitefield pretended not to be holier
than others but confessed his Sins before all the World. Voltaire!
Rousseau! You cannot escape my charge that you are Pharisees
& Hypocrites, for you are constantly talking of the Virtues of
the Human Heart, and particularly of your own, that you may
accuse others & especially the Religious, whose errors you, by
this display of pretended Virtue, chiefly design to expose. Rousseau thought Men Good by Nature; he found them Evil & found
no friend. Friendship cannot exist without Forgiveness of Sins
continually. The Book written by Rousseau called his Confes-
sions is an apology & cloak for his sin & not a confession.

But you also charge the poor Monks & Religious with being
the causes of War, while you acquit & flatter the Alexanders &
Caesars, the Louises & Fredericks, who alone are its causes &
its actors. But the Religion of Jesus, Forgiveness of Sin, can never
be the cause of a War nor of a single Martyrdom.

Those who Martyr others or who cause War are Deists, but
never can be Forgivers of Sin. The Glory of Christianity is To
Conquer by Forgiveness. All the Destruction, therefore, in Christian Europe has arisen from Deism, which is Natural Religion.

I saw a Monk of Charlemagne
Arise before my sight;
I talked with the Grey Monk as we stood
In beams of infernal light.

Gibbon arose with a lash of steel   5
And Voltaire with a wracking wheel.

The Schools, in clouds of learning rolled,
Arose with War in iron & gold.

"Thou lazy Monk," they sound afar,
"In vain condemning glorious War,   10
   And in your Cell you shall ever dwell.
Rise, War, & bind him in his Cell."

The blood red ran from the Grey Monk's side,
His hands & feet were wounded wide,
   His body bent, his arms & knees   15
Like to the roots of ancient trees.

When Satan first the black bow bent
And the Moral Law from the Gospel rent,
   He forged the Law into a Sword
And spilled the blood of mercy's Lord.   20

Titus! Constantine! Charlemagne!
O Voltaire! Rousseau! Gibbon! Vain
   Your Grecian Mocks & Roman Sword
Against this image of his Lord!

For a Tear is an Intellectual thing,   25
And a Sigh is the Sword of an Angel King,
   And the bitter groan of a Martyr's woe
Is an Arrow from the Almighty's Bow!

Plate 53

JERUSALEM

Chapter 3

But Los, who is the Vehicular Form of strong
    Urthona,
Wept vehemently over Albion where Thames' currents
    spring
From the rivers of Beulah; pleasant river! soft, mild,
    parent stream.

And the roots of Albion's Tree entered the Soul of Los
As he sat before his Furnaces clothed in sackcloth
    of hair,   5
In gnawing pain dividing him from his Emanation,
Enclosing all the children of Los time after time,

Their Giant forms condensing into Nations & Peoples
    & Tongues.
Translucent the Furnaces, of Beryl & Emerald immortal,
And Sevenfold each within other, incomprehensible   10
To the Vegetated Mortal Eye's perverted & single vision.
The Bellows are the Animal Lungs, the Hammers the
    Animal Heart,
The Furnaces the Stomach for Digestion; terrible their
    fury
Like seven burning heavens ranged from South to North.

Here on the banks of the Thames, Los builded Golgonooza,   15
Outside of the Gates of the Human Heart, beneath Beulah
In the midst of the rocks of the Altars of Albion. In
    fears
He builded it, in rage & in fury. It is the Spiritual
    Fourfold
London, continually building & continually decaying
    desolate!
In eternal labours, loud the Furnaces & loud the Anvils   20
Of Death thunder incessant around the flaming Couches of
The Twenty-four Friends of Albion and round the awful
    Four
For the protection of the Twelve Emanations of Albion's
    Sons,
The Mystic Union of the Emanation in the Lord. Because
Man divided from his Emanation is a dark Spectre,   25
His Emanation is an ever-weeping melancholy Shadow,
But she is made receptive of Generation through mercy
In the Potter's Furnace, among the Funeral Urns of
    Beulah,
From Surrey hills, through Italy and Greece, to Hinnom's
    vale.

Plate 54

In Great Eternity, every particular Form gives
     forth or Emanates
Its own peculiar Light, & the Form is the Divine Vision,
And the Light is his Garment. This is Jerusalem in
     every Man,
A Tent & Tabernacle of Mutual Forgiveness, Male &
     Female Clothings.
And Jerusalem is called Liberty among the
     Children of Albion.   5

But Albion fell down, a Rocky fragment from Eternity
     hurled
By his own Spectre, who is the Reasoning Power in
     every Man,
Into his own Chaos which is the Memory between Man &
     Man.

The silent broodings of deadly revenge springing from the
All-powerful parental affection fills Albion from head
     to foot,   10
Seeing his Sons assimilate with Luvah, bound in the bonds
Of spiritual Hate, from which springs Sexual Love as
     iron chains,
He tosses like a cloud outstretched among Jerusalem's
     Ruins,
Which overspread all the Earth; he groans among his
     ruined porches.

[In the illustration:

Reason
Pity   Wrath
This   World
Desire
                ]

But the Spectre like a hoar frost & a Mildew rose over
     Albion,   15

Saying, "I am God, O Sons of Men! I am your Rational
    Power!
Am I not Bacon & Newton & Locke, who teach Humility to
    Man,
Who teach Doubt & Experiment, & my two Wings, Voltaire,
    Rousseau?
Where is that Friend of Sinners, that Rebel against my
    Laws,
Who teaches Belief to the Nations & an unknown Eternal
    Life?   20
Come hither into the Desert & turn these stones to
    bread.
Vain, foolish Man, wilt thou believe without Experiment
And build a World of Phantasy upon my Great Abyss,
A World of Shapes in craving lust & devouring appetite?"

So spoke the hard, cold, constrictive Spectre; he is
    named Arthur,   25
Constricting into Druid Rocks round Canaan, Agag &
    Aram & Pharaoh.

Then Albion drew England into his bosom in groans &
    tears,
But she stretched out her starry Night in Spaces against
    him, like
A long Serpent, in the Abyss of the Spectre, which
    augmented
The Night with Dragon wings covered with stars, & in
    the Wings   30
Jerusalem & Vala appeared, & above, between the Wings
    magnificent
The Divine Vision dimly appeared in clouds of blood,
    weeping.

Plate 55

When those who disregard all Mortal Things saw a
    Mighty One
Among the Flowers of Beulah still retain his awful
    strength,

They wondered, checking their wild flames; & Many
    gathering
Together into an Assembly, they said: "Let us go down
And see these changes!" Others said: "If you do so,
    prepare   5
For being driven from our fields; what have we to do with
    the Dead?
To be their inferiors or superiors we equally abhor;
Superior none we know; inferior none; all equal share
Divine Benevolence & joy, for the Eternal Man
Walketh among us, calling us his Brothers & his Friends,   10
Forbidding us that Veil which Satan puts between Eve &
    Adam
By which the Princes of the Dead enslave their Votaries,
Teaching them to form the Serpent of precious stones &
    gold,
To seize the Sons of Jerusalem & plant them in One Man's
    Loins,
To make One Family of Contraries, that Joseph may be sold   15
Into Egypt for Negation, a Veil the Saviour born &
    dying rends."

But others said: "Let us to him who only Is & who
Walketh among us give decision. Bring forth all your
    fires!"

So Saying, an eternal deed was done: in fiery flames
The Universal Concave raged such thunderous sounds as
    never   20
Were sounded from a mortal cloud, nor on Mount Sinai
    old,
Nor in Havilah, where the Cherub rolled his redounding
    flame.

Loud! loud! the Mountains lifted up their voices, loud
    the Forests;
Rivers thundered against their banks; loud Winds
    furious fought;
Cities & Nations contended in fires & clouds & tempests.   25
The Seas raised up their voices & lifted their hands on
    high;

The Stars in their courses fought. The Sun! Moon!
    Heaven, Earth,
Contending for Albion & for Jerusalem, his Emanation,
And for Shiloh, the Emanation of France, & for lovely
    Vala.

Then far the greatest number were about to make a
    Separation,   30
And they Elected Seven, called the Seven Eyes of God:
Lucifer, Molech, Elohim, Shaddai, Pahad, Jehovah, Jesus.
They named the Eighth. He came not, he hid in Albion's
    Forests.
But first they said (& their Words stood in Chariots,
    in array,
Curbing their Tigers with golden bits & bridles of
    silver & ivory):   35

"Let the Human Organs be kept in their perfect Integrity,
At will Contracting into Worms or Expanding into Gods;
And then behold! What are these Ulro Visions of Chastity?
Then as the moss upon the tree, or dust upon the plow,
Or as the sweat upon the labouring shoulder, or as the
    chaff   40
Of the wheat floor, or as the dregs of the sweet
    winepress:
Such are these Ulro Visions, for though we sit down
    within
The plowed furrow, list'ning to the weeping clods till
    we
Contract or Expand Space at will, or if we raise
    ourselves
Upon the chariots of the morning, Contracting or
    Expanding Time,   45
Everyone knows we are One Family: One Man blessed
    forever."

Silence remained & everyone resumed his Human Majesty.
And many conversed on these things as they laboured at
    the furrow,

Saying: "It is better to prevent misery than to
    release from misery;
It is better to prevent error than to forgive the
    criminal.   50
Labour well the Minute Particulars, attend to the Little
    ones,
And those who are in misery cannot remain so long
If we do but our duty: labour well the teeming Earth."

They Plowed in tears, the trumpets sounded before the
    golden Plow,
And the voices of the Living Creatures were heard in
    the clouds of heaven,   55
Crying, "Compel the Reasoner to Demonstrate with
    unhewn Demonstrations.
Let the Indefinite be explored, and let every Man be
    Judged
By his own Works. Let all Indefinites be thrown into
    Demonstrations,
To be pounded to dust & melted in the Furnaces of
    Affliction.
He who would do good to another must do it in Minute
    Particulars;   60
General Good is the plea of the scoundrel, hypocrite &
    flatterer;
For Art & Science cannot exist but in minutely
    organized Particulars
And not in generalizing Demonstrations of the Rational
    Power.
The Infinite alone resides in Definite & Determinate
    Identity.
Establishment of Truth depends on destruction of
    Falsehood continually,   65
On Circumcision, not on Virginity, O Reasoners of
    Albion."
So cried they at the Plow. Albion's Rock frowned above,
And the Great Voice of Eternity rolled above, terrible
    in clouds,

Saying, "Who will go forth for us, & Who shall we send
    before our face?"

Plate 56

Then Los heaved his thund'ring Bellows on the
    Valley of Middlesex,
And thus he chanted his Song; the Daughters of Albion
    reply:

"What may Man be? Who can Tell? But what may Woman be
To have power over Man from Cradle to corruptible Grave?
He who is an Infant and whose Cradle is a Manger   5
Knoweth the Infant sorrow, whence it came, and where
    it goeth,
And who weave it a Cradle of the grass that withereth
    away.
This World is all a Cradle for the erred wandering
    Phantom,
Rocked by Year, Month, Day & Hour; and every
    two Moments
Between, dwells a Daughter of Beulah, to feed the Human
    Vegetable.   10
Entune, Daughters of Albion, your hymning Chorus mildly,
Cord of affection thrilling ecstatic on the iron Reel
To the golden Loom of Love,to the moth-laboured Woof,
A Garment and Cradle weaving for the infantine
    Terror,
For fear, at entering the gate into our World of cruel   15
Lamentation, it flee back & hide in non-Entity's dark
    wild,
Where dwells the Spectre of Albion, destroyer of Definite
    Form.
The Sun shall be a Scythed Chariot of Britain, the Moon
    a Ship
In the British Ocean, Created by Los's Hammer,
    measured out
Into Days & Nights & Years & Months, to travel with
    my feet   20

Over these desolate rocks of Albion. O daughters of
    despair!
Rock the Cradle, and in mild melodies tell me where
    found
What you have enwoven with so much tears & care, so
    much
Tender artifice, to laugh, to weep, to learn, to know;
Remember, recollect, what dark befell in wintry days."   25

"O it was lost forever, and we found it not; it came
And wept at our wintry Door. Look! look! behold!
    Gwendolen
Is become a Clod of Clay! Merlin is a Worm of the Valley."

Then Los uttered with Hammer & Anvil: "Chant! revoice!
I mind not your laugh, and your frown I not fear, and   30
You must my dictate obey from your gold-beamed Looms;
    trill
Gentle to Albion's Watchman on Albion's mountains;
    reecho
And rock the Cradle while! Ah, me! Of that Eternal Man
And of the cradled Infancy in his bowels of compassion
Who fell beneath his instruments of husbandry & became   35
Subservient to the clods of the furrow, the cattle and
    even
The emmet and Earthworms are his superiors & his lords."

Then the response came warbling from trilling Looms in
    Albion:

"We Women tremble at the light, therefore hiding
    fearful
The Divine Vision with Curtain & Veil & fleshly
    Tabernacle."   40

Los uttered, swift as the rattling thunder upon the
    mountains:
"Look back into the Church Paul! Look! Three Women
    around
The Cross! O Albion, why didst thou a Female Will Create?"

Plate 57

And the voices of Bath & Canterbury & York &
    Edinburgh Cry
Over the Plow of Nations in the strong hand of Albion,
    thundering along
Among the Fires of the Druid & the deep black rethundering
    Waters
Of the Atlantic, which poured in, impetuous, loud, loud,
    louder & louder.
And the Great Voice of the Atlantic howled over the
    Druid Altars,   5
Weeping over his Children in Stonehenge, in Maldon &
    Colchester,
Round the Rocky Peak of Derbyshire, London Stone &
    Rosamond's Bower:

"What is a Wife & what is a Harlot? What is a Church?
    & What
Is a Theatre? Are they Two & not One? Can they Exist
    Separate?
Are not Religion & Politics the Same Thing? Brotherhood
    is Religion.   10
O Demonstrations of Reason Dividing Families in Cruelty
    & Pride!"

But Albion fled from the Divine Vision, with the Plow
    of Nations enflaming;
The Living Creatures maddened; and Albion fell into
    the Furrow; and
The Plow went over him; & the Living was Plowed in among
    the Dead.
But his Spectre rose over the starry Plow. Albion
    fled beneath the Plow   15
Till he came to the Rock of Ages, & he took his Seat
    upon the Rock.

Wonder seized all in Eternity to behold the Divine
    Vision open

The Center into an Expanse, & the Center rolled out into
    an Expanse.

Plate 58

In beauty the Daughters of Albion divide & unite
    at will.
Naked & drunk with blood, Gwendolen dancing to the timbrel
Of War, reeling up the Street of London: she divides
    in twain
Among the Inhabitants of Albion. The People fall around.
The Daughters of Albion divide & unite in jealousy &
    cruelty.   5
The Inhabitants of Albion at the Harvest & the Vintage
Feel their Brain cut round beneath the temples,
    shrieking,
Bonifying into a Skull, the Marrow exuding in dismal
    pain.
They flee over the rocks bonifying. Horses, Oxen feel
    the knife.
And while the Sons of Albion by severe War & Judgment
    bonify,   10
The Hermaphroditic Condensations are divided by the
    Knife.
The obdurate Forms are cut asunder by Jealousy & Pity.

Rational Philosophy and Mathematic Demonstration
Is divided in the intoxications of pleasure & affection.
Two Contraries War against each other in fury & blood,   15
And Los fixes them on his Anvil, incessant his blows;
He fixes them with strong blows, placing the stones &
    timbers
To Create a World of Generation from the World of Death,
Dividing the Masculine & Feminine, for the commingling
Of Albion's & Luvah's Spectres was Hermaphroditic.   20

Urizen wrathful strode above, directing the awful Building
As a Mighty Temple, delivering Form out of confusion.

Jordan sprang beneath its threshold, bubbling from
    beneath
Its pillars; Euphrates ran under its arches; white sails
And silver oars reflect on its pillars, & sound on its
    echoing   25
Pavements, where walk the Sons of Jerusalem who remain
    Ungenerate.
But the revolving Sun and Moon pass through its porticos,
Day & night; in sublime majesty & silence they revolve
And shine glorious within! Hand & Coban arched over the
    Sun
In the hot noon, as he traveled through his journey;
    Hyle & Scofield   30
Arched over the Moon at midnight, & Los Fixed them there
With his thunderous Hammer; terrified the Spectres rage
    & flee!
Canaan is his portico; Jordan is a fountain in his porch,
A fountain of milk & wine to relieve the traveller;
Egypt is the eight steps within. Ethiopia supports his
    pillars;   35
Libya & the Lands unknown are the ascent without;
Within is Asia & Greece, ornamented with exquisite art;
Persia & Media are his halls; his inmost hall is Great
    Tartary.
China & India & Siberia are his temples for entertainment,
Poland & Russia & Sweden his soft retired chambers.   40
France & Spain & Italy & Denmark & Holland & Germany
Are the temples among his pillars. Britain is Los's
    Forge;
America North & South are his baths of living waters.

Such is the Ancient World of Urizen in the Satanic Void,
Created from the Valley of Middlesex by London's River   45
From Stonehenge and from London Stone, from Cornwall to
    Caithness.
The Four Zoas rush around on all sides in dire ruin.
Furious in pride of Selfhood, the terrible Spectres of
    Albion

Rear their dark Rocks among the Stars of God, stupendous
Works! A World of Generation continually Creating out
    of   50
The Hermaphroditic, Satanic World of rocky destiny,

Plate 59

And formed into Four precious stones for entrance
    from Beulah.

For the Veil of Vala, which Albion cast into the Atlantic
    Deep
To catch the Souls of the Dead, began to Vegetate &
    Petrify
Around the Earth of Albion among the Roots of his Tree.
This Los formed into the Gates & mighty Wall between
    the Oak   5
Of Weeping & the Palm of Suffering beneath Albion's
    Tomb.
Thus in process of time it became the beautiful Mundane
    Shell,
The Habitation of the Spectres of the Dead & the Place
Of Redemption & of awaking again into Eternity.

For Four Universes round the Mundane Egg remain Chaotic: 10
One to the North, Urthona; One to the South, Urizen;
One to the East, Luvah; One to the West, Tharmas;
They are the Four Zoas that stood around the Throne
    Divine.
Verulam, London, York & Edinburgh, their English names;
But when Luvah assumed the World of Urizen Southward   15
And Albion was slain upon his Mountains & in his Tent,
All fell towards the Center, sinking downwards in dire
    ruin.
In the South remains a burning Fire; in the East, a
    Void;
In the West, a World of raging Waters; in the North,
    solid Darkness,

Unfathomable without end; but in the midst of these   20
Is Built eternally the sublime Universe of Los
    & Enitharmon.

And in the North Gate, in the West of the North toward
    Beulah,
Cathedron's Looms are builded, and Los's Furnaces
    in the South.
A wondrous golden Building immense with ornaments sublime
Is bright Cathedron's golden Hall, its Courts, Towers
    & Pinnacles.   25

And one Daughter of Los sat at the fiery Reel, & another
Sat at the shining Loom with her Sisters attending round.
Terrible their distress, & their sorrow cannot be uttered.
And another Daughter of Los sat at the Spinning Wheel.
Endless their labour, with bitter food, void of sleep.   30
Though hungry, they labour; they rouse themselves anxious,
Hour after hour labouring at the whirling Wheel,
Many Wheels, & as many lovely Daughters sit weeping.

Yet the intoxicating delight that they take in their work
Obliterates every other evil; none pities their tears,   35
Yet they regard not pity, & they expect no one to pity,
For they labour for life & love, regardless of anyone
But the poor Spectres that they work for, always,
    incessantly.

They are mocked by everyone that passes by. They regard
    not.
They labour, & when their Wheels are broken by scorn
    & malice   40
They mend them, sorrowing with many tears & afflictions.

Other Daughters Weave on the Cushion & Pillow Network
    fine,
That Rahab & Tirzah may exist & live & breathe & love.
Ah, that it could be as the Daughters of Beulah wish!

Other Daughters of Los, labouring at Looms less fine,   45
Create the Silkworm & the Spider & the Caterpillar

To assist in their most grievous work of pity &
    compassion.
And others Create the woolly Lamb & the downy Fowl
To assist in the work; the Lamb bleats; the Seafowl cries.
Men understand not the distress & the labour & sorrow   50
That in the Interior Worlds is carried on in fear &
    trembling,
Weaving the shudd'ring fears & loves of Albion's
    Families.
Thunderous rage the Spindles of iron, & the iron Distaff
Maddens in the fury of their hands, weaving in
    bitter tears
The Veil of Goat's hair & Purple & Scarlet & fine-twined
    Linen.   55

Plate 60

The clouds of Albion's Druid Temples rage in the
    eastern heaven,
While Los sat terrified, beholding Albion's Spectre, who
    is Luvah,
Spreading in bloody veins in torments over Europe &
    Asia,
Not yet formed but a wretched torment, unformed & abyssal
In flaming fire; within the Furnaces the Divine Vision
    appeared   5
On Albion's hills, often walking from the Furnaces in
    clouds
And flames among the Druid Temples & the Starry Wheels,
Gathered Jerusalem's Children in his arms & bore them
    like
A Shepherd in the night of Albion, which overspread all
    the Earth.

"I gave thee liberty and life, O lovely Jerusalem,   10
And thou hast bound me down upon the Stems of Vegetation.
I gave thee Sheepwalks upon the Spanish Mountains,
    Jerusalem.

I gave thee Prima's City and the Isles of Grecia lovely!
I gave thee Hand & Scofield & the Counties of Albion;
They spread forth like a lovely root into the Garden of
    God;   15
They were as Adam before me; united into One Man,
They stood in innocence, & their skyey tent reached
    over Asia
To Nimrod's Tower, to Ham & Canaan walking with Mizraim
Upon the Egyptian Nile, with solemn songs to Grecia
And sweet Hesperia, even to Great Chaldea & Tesshina,   20
Following thee as a Shepherd by the Four Rivers of Eden.
Why wilt thou rend thyself apart, Jerusalem,
And build this Babylon & sacrifice in secret Groves,
Among the Gods of Asia, among the fountains of pitch
    & nitre?

"Therefore thy Mountains are become barren, Jerusalem!   25
Thy Valleys, Plains of burning sand; thy Rivers, waters
    of death.
Thy Villages die of the Famine, and thy Cities
Beg bread from house to house. Lovely Jerusalem,
Why wilt thou deface thy beauty & the beauty of thy
    little ones
To please thy Idols in the pretended chastities of
    Uncircumcision?   30
Thy Sons are lovelier than Egypt or Assyria; wherefore
Dost thou blacken their beauty by a Secluded place of
    rest
And a peculiar Tabernacle, to cut the integuments of
    beauty
Into veils of tears and sorrows, O lovely Jerusalem?
They have persuaded thee to this; therefore their end
    shall come,   35
And I will lead thee through the Wilderness in shadow
    of my cloud,
And in my love I will lead thee, lovely Shadow of
    Sleeping Albion."

This is the Song of the Lamb, sung by Slaves in
    evening time.

But Jerusalem faintly saw him, closed in the Dungeons
    of Babylon.
Her Form was held by Beulah's Daughters; but all within
    unseen,   40
She sat at the Mills, her hair unbound, her feet naked,
Cut with the flints; her tears run down; her reason
    grows like
The Wheel of Hand, incessant turning day & night without
    rest.
Insane she raves upon the winds, hoarse, inarticulate;
All night Vala hears. She triumphs in pride of holiness   45
To see Jerusalem deface her lineaments with bitter blows
Of despair, while the Satanic Holiness triumphed
    in Vala
In a Religion of Chastity & Uncircumcised Selfishness
Both of the Head & Heart & Loins, closed up in Moral
    Pride.

But the Divine Lamb stood beside Jerusalem. Oft she saw   50
The lineaments Divine & oft the Voice heard, & oft she
    said:

"O Lord & Saviour, have the Gods of the Heathen pierced
    thee?
Or hast thou been pierced in the House of thy Friends?
Art thou alive & livest thou forevermore? Or art thou
Not but a delusive shadow, a thought that liveth not.   55
Babel mocks, saying there is no God nor Son of God,
That thou, O Human Imagination, O Divine Body, art all
A delusion. But I know thee, O Lord, when thou arisest
    upon
My weary eyes, even in this dungeon & this iron mill.
The Stars of Albion cruel rise; thou bindest to sweet
    influences,   60
For thou also sufferest with me, although I behold thee not;

And although I sin & blaspheme thy holy name, thou
    pitiest me;
Because thou knowest I am deluded by the turning mills.
And by these visions of pity & love because of Albion's
    death."

Thus spake Jerusalem, & thus the Divine Voice replied: 65

"Mild Shade of Man, pitiest thou these Visions of
    terror & woe!
Give forth thy pity & love. Fear not! Lo, I am with thee
    always.
Only believe in me that I have power to raise from death
Thy Brother who Sleepeth in Albion; fear not, trembling
    Shade.

Plate 61

Behold, in the Visions of Elohim Jehovah. Behold
    Joseph & Mary,
And be comforted, O Jerusalem, in the Visions of Jehovah
    Elohim."

She looked & saw Joseph the Carpenter in Nazareth &
    Mary,
His espoused Wife. And Mary said: "If thou put me away
    from thee
Dost thou not murder me?" Joseph spoke in anger & fury:
    "Should I   5
Marry a Harlot & an Adulteress?" Mary answered: "Art
    thou more pure
Than thy Maker, who forgiveth Sins & calls again Her
    that is Lost,
Though She hates? He calls her again in love. I love
    my dear Joseph,
But he driveth me away from his presence, yet I hear the
    voice of God
In the voice of my Husband. Though he is angry for a
    moment, he will not   10

Utterly cast me away. If I were pure, never could I
    taste the sweets
Of the Forgiveness of Sins! If I were holy, I never
    could behold the tears
Of love, of him who loves me in the midst of his anger
    in furnace of fire."

"Ah, my Mary," said Joseph, weeping over & embracing
    her closely in
His arms, "Doth he forgive Jerusalem & not exact Purity
    from her who is   15
Polluted? I heard his voice in my sleep & his Angel in
    my dream
Saying, 'Doth Jehovah Forgive a Debt only on condition
    that it shall
Be Paid? Doth he Forgive Pollution only on conditions
    of Purity?
That Debt is not Forgiven! That Pollution is not Forgiven.
Such is the Forgiveness of the Gods, the Moral Virtues
    of the   20
Heathen, whose tender Mercies are Cruelty. But Jehovah's
    Salvation
Is without Money & without Price, in the Continual
    Forgiveness of Sins,
In the Perpetual Mutual Sacrifice in Great Eternity!
    For behold!
There is none that liveth & Sinneth not! And this is the
    Covenant
Of Jehovah: If you Forgive one another, so shall Jehovah
    Forgive You,   25
That He Himself may Dwell among You. Fear not then to
    take
To Thee Mary thy Wife, for she is with Child by the Holy
    Ghost.'"

Then Mary burst forth into a Song! She flowed like a
    River of
Many Streams in the arms of Joseph & gave forth her tears
    of joy

Like many waters, and Emanating into gardens &
    palaces upon   30
Euphrates & to forests & floods & animals wild & tame
    from
Gihon to Hiddekel, & to cornfields & villages &
    inhabitants
Upon Pison & Arnon & Jordan. And I heard the voice among
The Reapers Saying, "Am I Jerusalem the lost Adulteress,
    or am I
Babylon come up to Jerusalem?" And another voice
    answered, Saying,   35

"Does the voice of my Lord call me again? Am I pure
    through his Mercy
And Pity? Am I become lovely as a Virgin in his sight,
    who am
Indeed a Harlot drunken with the Sacrifice of Idols?
    Does he
Call her pure as he did in the days of her Infancy when
    She
Was cast out to the loathing of her person? The
    Chaldean took   40
Me from my Cradle. The Amalekite stole me away upon
    his Camels
Before I had ever beheld with love the Face of Jehovah,
    or known
That there was a God of Mercy. O Mercy, O Divine
    Humanity!
O Forgiveness & Pity & Compassion! If I were Pure I
    should never
Have known Thee; If I were Unpolluted I should never
    have   45
Glorified thy Holiness, or rejoiced in thy great
    Salvation."

Mary leaned her side against Jerusalem; Jerusalem
    received
The Infant into her hands in the Visions of Jehovah.
    Times passed on.

Jerusalem fainted over the Cross & Sepulcher. She
    heard the voice:
"Wilt thou make Rome thy Patriarch Druid & the Kings
    of Europe his   50
Horsemen? Man in the Resurrection changes his Sexual
    Garments at will.
Every Harlot was once a Virgin, every Criminal an
    Infant Love!

Plate 62

Repose on me till the morning of the Grave. I
    am thy life."

Jerusalem replied: "I am an outcast: Albion is dead;
I am left to the trampling foot & the spurning heel!
A Harlot I am called. I am sold from street to street!
I am defaced with blows & with the dirt of the Prison!   5
And wilt thou become my Husband, O my Lord & Saviour?
Shall Vala bring thee forth? Shall the Chaste be
    ashamed also?
I see the Maternal Line, I behold the Seed of the Woman!
Caina & Adah & Zillah & Naamah, Wife of Noah,
Shuah's daughter & Tamar & Rahab the Canaanites,   10
Ruth the Moabite & Bathsheba of the daughters of Heth,
Naamah the Ammonite, Zibeah the Philistine, & Mary:
These are the Daughters of Vala, Mother of the Body of
    death.
But I, thy Magdalen, behold thy Spiritual Risen Body.
Shall Albion arise? I know he shall arise at the Last
    Day!   15
I know that in my flesh I shall see God, but
    Emanations
Are weak. They know not whence they are, nor whither
    tend."

Jesus replied: "I am the Resurrection & the Life.
I Die & pass the limits of possibility as it appears
To individual perception. Luvah must be Created,   20

And Vala; for I cannot leave them in the gnawing Grave
But will prepare a way for my banished ones to return.
Come now with me into the villages; walk through all
    the cities.
Though thou art taken to prison & judgment, starved in
    the streets,
I will command the cloud to give thee food & the hard
    rock   25
To flow with milk & wine, though thou seest me not a
    season,
Even a long season & a hard journey & a howling
    wilderness,
Though Vala's cloud hide thee & Luvah's fires follow thee,
Only believe & trust in me. Lo, I am always with thee!"

So spoke the Lamb of God while Luvah's Cloud, reddening
    above,   30
Burst forth in streams of blood upon the heavens, &
    dark night
Involved Jerusalem, & the Wheels of Albion's Sons turned
    hoarse
Over the Mountains, & the fires blazed on Druid Altars,
And the Sun set in Tyburn's Brook, where Victims howl
    & cry.

But Los beheld the Divine Vision among the flames of the
    Furnaces.   35
Therefore he lived & breathed in hope, but his tears
    fell incessant
Because his Children were closed from his apart &
    Enitharmon
Dividing in fierce pain; also the Vision of God was
    closed in clouds
Of Albion's Spectres, that Los in despair oft sat &
    often pondered
On Death Eternal in fierce shudders, upon the mountains
    of Albion   40
Walking & in the vales in howlings fierce; then to his
    Anvils
Turning, anew began his labours, though in terrible pains!

Plate 63

Jehovah stood among the Druids in the Valley of Annandale
When the Four Zoas of Albion, the Four Living Creatures,
    the Cherubim
Of Albion, tremble before the Spectre, in the starry
    Harness of the Plow
Of Nations. And their Names are Urizen & Luvah &
    Tharmas & Urthona.

Luvah slew Tharmas; the Angel of the Tongue, & Albion
    brought him   5
To Justice in his own City of Paris, denying the
    Resurrection.
Then Vala, the Wife of Albion, who is the Daughter of
    Luvah,
Took vengeance Twelvefold among the Chaotic Rocks of the
    Druids,
Where the Human Victims howl to the Moon, & Thor
    & Friga
Dance the dance of death, contending with Jehovah among
    the Cherubim.   10
The Chariot Wheels filled with Eyes rage along the
    howling Valley
In the Dividing of Reuben & Benjamin, bleeding from
    Chester's River.

The Giants & the Witches & the Ghosts of Albion dance
    with
Thor & Friga, & the Fairies lead the Moon along the
    Valley of Cherubim,
Bleeding in torrents from Mountain to Mountain, a lovely
    Victim;   15
And Jehovah stood in the Gates of the Victim, & he
    appeared
A weeping Infant in the Gates of Birth in the midst of
    Heaven.

The Cities & Villages of Albion became Rock & Sand
    Unhumanized,
The Druid Sons of Albion, & the Heavens a Void around
    unfathomable,
No Human Form but Sexual, & a little weeping Infant pale
    reflected 20
Multitudinous in the Looking Glass of Enitharmon, on all
    sides
Around, in the clouds of the Female, on Albion's Cliffs
    of the Dead.

Such the appearance in Cheviot, in the Divisions of Reuben,
When the Cherubim hid their heads under their wings in
    deep slumbers,
When the Druids demanded Chastity from Woman & all
    was lost. 25

"How can the Female be Chaste, O thou stupid Druid,"
    Cried Los,
"Without the Forgiveness of Sins in the merciful clouds
    of Jehovah
And without the Baptism of Repentance to wash away
    Calumnies and
The Accusations of Sin, that each may be Pure in their
    Neighbours' sight?
O when shall Jehovah give us Victims from his Flocks &
    Herds 30
Instead of Human Victims by the Daughters of Albion &
    Canaan?"

Then laughed Gwendolen, & her laughter shook the Nations
    & Families of
The Dead beneath Beulah from Tyburn to Golgotha, and
    from
Ireland to Japan. Furious, her Lions & Tigers & Wolves
    sport before
Los on the Thames & Medway. London & Canterbury
    groan in pain. 35

Los knew not yet what was done; he thought it was all in
    Vision,

In Visions of the Dreams of Beulah among the Daughters
    of Albion.
Therefore the Murder was put apart in the Looking Glass
    of Enitharmon.

He saw in Vala's hand the Druid Knife of Revenge & the
    Poison Cup
Of Jealousy and thought it a Poetic Vision of the
    Atmospheres,   40
Till Canaan rolled apart from Albion across the Rhine,
    along the Danube,

And all the Land of Canaan suspended over the Valley of
    Cheviot
From Bashan to Tyre & from Troy to Gaza of the Amalekite,
And Reuben fled with his head downwards among the
    Caverns

Plate 64

Of the Mundane Shell, which froze on all sides
    round Canaan on
The vast Expanse, where the Daughters of Albion Weave
    the Web
Of Ages & Generations, folding & unfolding it, like a
    Veil of Cherubim.
And sometimes it touches the Earth's summits & sometimes
    spreads
Abroad into the Indefinite Spectre, who is the Rational
    Power.   5

Then All the Daughters of Albion became One before Los,
    even Vala!
And she put forth her hand upon the Looms in dreadful
    howlings
Till she vegetated into a hungry Stomach & a devouring
    Tongue.
Her Hand is a Court of Justice, her Feet two Armies in
    Battle,

Storms & Pestilence in her Locks, & in her Loins
    Earthquake   10
And Fire & the Ruin of Cities & Nations & Families &
    Tongues.

She cries: "The Human is but a Worm, & thou, O Male,
    Thou art
Thyself Female, a Male, a breeder of Seed, a Son &
    Husband, & Lo,
The Human Divine is Woman's Shadow, a Vapor in the
    summer's heat.
Go assume Papal dignity, thou Spectre, thou Male Harlot!
    Arthur,   15
Divide into the Kings of Europe in times remote, O
    Woman-born
And Woman-nourished & Woman-educated & Woman-
    scorned!"

"Wherefore art thou living," said Los, "& Man cannot
    live in thy presence?
Art thou Vala, the Wife of Albion, O thou lovely Daughter
    of Luvah?
All Quarrels arise from Reasoning: the secret Murder
    and   20
The violent Manslaughter, these are the Spectre's double
    Cave,
The Sexual Death living on accusation of Sin & Judgment,
To freeze Love & Innocence into the gold & silver of the
    Merchant.
Without Forgiveness of Sin Love is Itself Eternal Death."

Then the Spectre drew Vala into his bosom, magnificent,
    terrific,   25
Glittering with precious stones & gold, with Garments of
    blood & fire.
He wept in deadly wrath of the Spectre, in
    self-contradicting agony,
Crimson with Wrath & green with Jealousy, dazzling with
    Love

And Jealousy immingled; & the purple of the violet
    darkened deep
Over the Plow of Nations, thundering in the hand of
    Albion's Spectre.   30

A dark Hermaphrodite, they stood frowning upon London's
    River,
And the Distaff & Spindle in the hands of Vala with
    the Flax of
Human Miseries turned fierce with the Lives of Men
    along the Valley
As Reuben fled before the Daughters of Albion, Taxing
    the Nations.

Derby Peak yawned a horrid Chasm at the Cries of
    Gwendolen & at   35
The stamping feet of Ragan upon the flaming Treadles of
    her Loom,
That drop with crimson gore with the Loves of Albion
    & Canaan,
Opening along the Valley of Rephaim, weaving over the
    Caves of Machpelah,

Plate 65

To decide Two Worlds with a great decision, a
    World of Mercy and
A World of Justice, the World of Mercy for Salvation,
To cast Luvah into the Wrath and Albion into the Pity,
In the Two Contraries of Humanity & in the Four Regions.

For in the depths of Albion's bosom in the eastern
    heaven,   5
They sound the clarions strong! They chain the howling
    Captives!
They cast the lots into the helmet; they give the oath
    of blood in Lambeth;
They vote the death of Luvah; & they nailed him to
    Albion's Tree in Bath;

They stained him with poisonous blue, they inwove him
  in cruel roots
To die a death of Six thousand years bound round with
  vegetation.   10
The sun was black, & the moon rolled a useless globe
  through Britain!

Then left the Sons of Urizen the plow & harrow, the
  loom,
The hammer & the chisel, & the rule & compasses; from
  London fleeing,
They forged the sword on Cheviot, the chariot of war
  & the battle-ax,
The trumpet fitted to mortal battle, & the flute of summer
  in Annandale;   15
And all the Arts of Life they changed into the Arts of
  Death in Albion.
The hourglass contemned because its simple workmanship
Was, like the workmanship of the plowman, & the
  waterwheel,
That raises water into cisterns, broken & burned with
  fire
Because its workmanship was like the workmanship of the
  shepherd.   20
And in their stead, intricate wheels invented, wheel
  without wheel,
To perplex youth in their outgoings, & to bind to labours
  in Albion
Of day & night the myriads of eternity that they may
  grind
And polish brass & iron hour after hour, laborious task,
Kept ignorant of its use, that they might spend the days
  of wisdom   25
In sorrowful drudgery, to obtain a scanty pittance of
  bread,
In ignorance to view a small portion & think that All,
And call it Demonstration, blind to all the simple rules
  of life.

"Now, now the battle rages round thy tender limbs, O
    Vala.
Now smile among thy bitter tears, now put on all thy
    beauty.   30
Is not the wound of the sword sweet? & the broken bone
    delightful?
Wilt thou now smile among the scythes when the wounded
    groan in the field?
We were carried away in thousands from London, & in tens
Of thousands from Westminster & Marybone in ships closed
    up,
Chained hand & foot, compelled to fight under the iron
    whips   35
Of our captains, fearing our officers more than the
    enemy.
Lift up thy blue eyes, Vala, & put on thy sapphire shoes.
O melancholy Magdalen, behold the morning over Maldon
    break.
Gird on thy flaming zone, descend into the sepulcher of
    Canterbury.
Scatter the blood from thy golden brow, the tears from
    thy silver locks;   40
Shake off the waters from thy wings & the dust from thy
    white garments!
Remember all thy feigned terrors on the secret couch of
    Lambeth's Vale,
When the sun rose in glowing morn, with arms of mighty
    hosts
Marching to battle, who was wont to rise with Urizen's
    harps,
Girt as a sower with his seed, to scatter life abroad
    over Albion.   45
Arise, O Vala! Bring the bow of Urizen; bring the swift
    arrows of light.
How raged the golden horses of Urizen, compelled to the
    chariot of love,
Compelled to leave the plow to the ox, to snuff up the
    winds of desolation,

To trample the cornfields in boastful neighings; this is
    no gentle harp,
This is no warbling brook, nor shadow of a myrtle tree,   50
But blood and wounds and dismal cries, and shadows of
    the oak,
And hearts laid open to the light by the broad grisly
    sword,
And bowels hid in hammered steel ripped quivering on the
    ground.
Call forth thy smiles of soft deceit; call forth thy
    cloudy tears.
We hear thy sighs in trumpets shrill when morn shall blood
    renew."   55

So sang the Spectre Sons of Albion round Luvah's Stone
    of Trial,
Mocking and deriding at the writhings of their Victim
    on Salisbury,
Drinking his Emanation in intoxicating bliss, rejoicing
    in Giant dance;
For a Spectre has no Emanation but what he imbibes from
    deceiving
A Victim! Then he becomes her Priest & she his Tabernacle   60
And his Oak Grove, till the Victim rend the woven Veil
In the end of his sleep when Jesus calls him from his
    grave.

Howling, the Victims on the Druid Altars yield their
    souls
To the stern Warriors; lovely sport the Daughters round
    their Victims,
Drinking their lives in sweet intoxication. Hence arose
    from Bath   65
Soft deluding odours, in spiral volutions intricately
    winding
Over Albion's mountains, a feminine, indefinite, cruel
    delusion.
Astonished, terrified & in pain & torment, Sudden they
    behold

Their own Parent, the Emanation of their murdered Enemy,
Become their Emanation and their Temple and Tabernacle.   70
They knew not this Vala was their beloved Mother Vala,
    Albion's Wife.

Terrified at the sight of the Victim, at his distorted
    sinews,
The tremblings of Vala vibrate through the limbs of
    Albion's Sons,
While they rejoice over Luvah in mockery & bitter scorn.
Sudden they become like what they behold in howlings &
    deadly pain.   75
Spasms smite their features, sinews & limbs; pale they
    look on one another.
They turn, contorted; their iron necks bend unwilling
    towards
Luvah; their lips tremble; their muscular fibres are
    cramped & smitten.
They become like what they behold! Yet immense in
    strength & power,

Plate 66

In awful pomp & gold, in all the precious unhewn
    stones of Eden,
They build a stupendous Building on the Plain of Salisbury
    with chains
Of rocks round London Stone, of Reasonings, of unhewn
    Demonstrations
In labyrinthine arches (Mighty Urizen the Architect)
    through which
The Heavens might revolve & Eternity be bound in their
    chain.   5
Labour unparalleled! a wondrous rocky World of cruel
    destiny,
Rocks piled on rocks reaching the stars, stretching from
    pole to pole.
The Building is Natural Religion & its Altars Natural
    Morality,

A building of eternal death; whose proportions are
    eternal despair.
Here Vala stood turning the iron Spindle of destruction   10
From heaven to earth, howling! invisible! but not
    invisible
Her Two Covering Cherubs, afterwards named Voltaire &
    Rousseau,
Two frowning Rocks on each side of the Cove & Stone of
    Torture,
Frozen Sons of the feminine Tabernacle of Bacon, Newton
    & Locke.
For Luvah is France, the Victim of the Spectres of
    Albion.   15

Los beheld in terror; he poured his loud storms on the
    Furnaces.
The Daughters of Albion, clothed in garments of
    needlework,
Strip them off from their shoulders and bosoms; they lay
    aside
Their garments; they sit naked upon the Stone of trial.
The Knife of flint passes over the howling Victim; his
    blood   20
Gushes & stains the fair side of the fair Daughters of
    Albion.
They put aside his curls; they divide his seven locks
    upon
His forehead; they bind his forehead with thorns of iron;
They put into his hand a reed; they mock, Saying: "Behold
The King of Canaan, whose are seven hundred chariots of
    iron!"   25
They take off his vesture whole with their Knives of
    flint;

But they cut asunder his inner garments, searching with
Their cruel fingers for his heart, & there they enter in
    pomp,
In many tears, & there they erect a temple & an altar.
They pour cold water on his brain in front, to cause   30
Lids to grow over his eyes in veils of tears, and caverns

To freeze over his nostrils, while they feed his tongue
    from cups
And dishes of painted clay. Glowing with beauty & cruelty;
They obscure the sun & the moon; no eye can look upon
    them.

Ah! alas! at the sight of the Victim, & at sight of those
    who are smitten,   35
All who see become what they behold. Their eyes are
    covered
With veils of tears and their nostrils & tongues shrunk
    up,
Their ear bent outwards. As their Victim, so are they in
    the pangs
Of unconquerable fear amidst delights of revenge
    Earth-shaking!
And as their eye & ear shrunk, the heavens shrunk away.   40
The Divine Vision became First a burning flame, then a
    column
Of fire, then an awful fiery wheel surrounding earth &
    heaven,
And then a globe of blood wandering distant in an unknown
    night.
Afar into the unknown night the mountains fled away:
Six months of mortality, a summer, & six months of
    mortality, a winter.   45
The Human form began to be altered by the Daughters of
    Albion,
And the perceptions to be dissipated into the Indefinite,
    Becoming
A mighty Polypus named Albion's Tree; they tie the Veins
And Nerves into two knots, & the Seed into a double knot;
They look forth: the Sun is shrunk, the Heavens are
    shrunk   50
Away into the far remote, and the Trees & Mountains
    withered
Into indefinite cloudy shadows in darkness & separation.
By Invisible Hatreds adjoined, they seem remote and
    separate
From each other and yet are a Mighty Polypus in the Deep!

As the Mistletoe grows on the Oak, so Albion's Tree on
    Eternity, Lo!   55
He who will not commingle in Love must be adjoined by
    Hate.

They look forth from Stonehenge! From the Cove round
    London Stone
They look on one another; the mountain calls out to
    the mountain;
Plinlimmon shrunk away; Snowdon trembled; the mountains
Of Wales & Scotland beheld the descending War, the routed
    flying.   60
Red run the streams of Albion: Thames is drunk with blood,
As Gwendolen cast the shuttle of war, as Cambel returned
    the beam.
The Humber & the Severn are drunk with the blood of the
    slain.
London feels his brain cut round; Edinburgh's heart is
    circumscribed!
York & Lincoln hide among the flocks because of the
    griding Knife.   65
Worcester & Hereford, Oxford & Cambridge reel & stagger,
Overwearied with howling; Wales & Scotland alone sustain
    the fight!
The inhabitants are sick to death; they labour to divide
    into Days
And Nights the uncertain Periods, and into Weeks &
    Months. In vain
They send the Dove & Raven & in vain the Serpent over the
    mountains   70
And in vain the Eagle & Lion over the fourfold wilderness.
They return not, but generate in rocky places desolate.
They return not, but build a habitation separate from
    Man.
The Sun forgets his course like a drunken man; he
    hesitates
Upon the Cheselden hills, thinking to sleep on the
    Severn   75
In vain; he is hurried afar into an unknown Night.

He bleeds in torrents of blood as he rolls through heaven
    above.
He chokes up the paths of the sky; the Moon is leprous
    as snow,
Trembling & descending down, seeking to rest upon high
    Mona,
Scattering her leprous snows in flakes of disease over
    Albion.   80
The Stars flee remote, the heaven is iron, the earth is
    sulphur,
And all the mountains & hills shrink up like a withering
    gourd,
As the Senses of Men shrink together under the Knife of
    flint
In the hands of Albion's Daughters, among the Druid
    Temples,

Plate 67

By those who drink their blood & the blood of
    their Covenant.

And the Twelve Daughters of Albion united in Rahab &
    Tirzah,
A Double Female; and they drew out from the Rocky Stones
Fibres of Life to Weave, for every Female is a Golden
    Loom.
The Rocks are opaque hardnesses covering all Vegetated
    things,   5
And as they Wove & Cut from the Looms in various
    divisions
Stretching over Europe & Asia from Ireland to Japan,
They divided into many lovely Daughters to be
    counterparts
To those they Wove, for when they Wove a Male, they
    divided
Into a Female to the Woven Male. In opaque hardness   10
They cut the Fibres from the Rocks; groaning in pain
    they Weave,

Calling the Rocks Atomic Origins of Existence, denying
    Eternity
By the Atheistical Epicurean Philosophy of Albion's Tree.
Such are the Feminine & Masculine when separated from
    Man.
They call the Rocks Parents of Men & adore the frowning
    Chaos,   15
Dancing around in howling pain, clothed in the bloody
    Veil,
Hiding Albion's Sons within the Veil, closing Jerusalem's
Sons without, to feed with their Souls the Spectres of
    Albion,
Ashamed to give Love openly to the piteous & merciful
    Man,
Counting him an imbecile mockery; but the Warrior   20
They adore & his revenge cherish with the blood of the
    Innocent.
They drink up Dan & Gad, to feed with milk Scofield &
    Kotope.
They strip off Joseph's Coat & dip it in the blood of
    battle.

Tirzah sits weeping to hear the shrieks of the dying;
    her Knife
Of flint is in her hand; she passes it over the howling
    Victim.   25
The Daughters Weave their Work in loud cries over the Rock
Of Horeb, still eyeing Albion's Cliffs, eagerly seizing
    & twisting
The threads of Vala & Jerusalem running from mountain
    to mountain
Over the whole Earth; loud the Warriors rage in Beth Peor
Beneath the iron whips of their Captains & consecrated
    banners.   30
Loud the Sun & Moon rage in the conflict; loud the Stars
Shout in the night of battle, & their spears grow to
    their hands
With blood, weaving the deaths of the Mighty into a
    Tabernacle

For Rahab & Tirzah, till the Great Polypus of Generation
    covered the Earth.

In Verulam the Polypus's Head, winding around his bulk   35
Through Rochester, and Chichester, & Exeter, & Salisbury,
To Bristol, & his Heart beat strong on Salisbury Plain,
Shooting out Fibres round the Earth, through Gaul & Italy
And Greece, & along the Sea of Rephaim into Judea
To Sodom & Gomorrha, thence to India, China & Japan.   40

The Twelve Daughters in Rahab & Tirzah have circumscribed
    the Brain
Beneath & pierced it through the midst with a golden pin.
Blood hath stained her fair side beneath her bosom.

"O thou poor Human Form!" said she. "O thou poor child
    of woe!
Why wilt thou wander away from Tirzah? Why me compel to
    bind thee?   45
If thou dost go away from me I shall consume upon these
    Rocks.
These fibres of thine eyes, that used to beam in distant
    heavens
Away from me, I have bound down with a hot iron.
These nostrils, that expanded with delight in morning
    skies,
I have bent downward with lead melted in my roaring
    furnaces   50
Of affliction, of love, of sweet despair, of torment
    unendurable.
My soul is seven furnaces; incessant roars the bellows
Upon my terribly flaming heart; the molten metal runs
In channels through my fiery limbs. O love! O pity! O
    fear!
O pain! O the pangs, the bitter pangs of love forsaken!   55
Ephraim was a wilderness of joy where all my wild beasts
    ran.
The River Kanah wandered by my sweet Manasseh's side
To see the boy spring into heavens, sounding from my
    sight!

Go, Noah, fetch the girdle of strong brass, heat it
    red-hot,
Press it around the loins of this ever-expanding cruelty.   60
Shriek not so, my only love! I refuse thy joys; I drink
Thy shrieks because Hand & Hyle are cruel & obdurate to
    me.

Plate 68

O Scofield, why art thou cruel? Lo, Joseph is
    thine, to make
You One, to weave you both in the same mantle of skin.
Bind him down, Sisters, bind him down on Ebal, Mount of
    cursing,
Malah come forth from Lebanon, & Hoglah from Mount Sinai.
Come circumscribe this tongue of sweets & with a screw
    of iron   5
Fasten this ear into the rock! Milcah, the task is thine.
Weep not so, Sisters! Weep not so! Our life depends on
    this,
Or mercy & truth are fled away from Shechem & Mount
    Gilead,
Unless my beloved is bound upon the Stems of Vegetation."

And thus the Warriors cry, in the hot day of Victory,
    in Songs: 10

"Look, the beautiful Daughter of Albion sits naked upon
    the Stone,
Her panting Victim beside her; her heart is drunk with
    blood,
Though her brain is not drunk with wine; she goes forth
    from Albion
In pride of beauty, in cruelty of holiness, in the
    brightness
Of her tabernacle & her ark & secret place. The beautiful
    Daughter   15
Of Albion delights the eyes of the Kings. Their hearts
    & the

Hearts of their Warriors glow hot before Thor & Friga.
  O Molech!
O Chemosh! O Bacchus! O Venus! O Double God of
  Generation!
The Heavens are cut like a mantle around the Cliffs of
  Albion
Across Europe, across Africa; in howlings & deadly War   20
A sheet & veil & curtain of blood is let down from Heaven
Across the hills of Ephraim & down Mount Olivet to
The Valley of the Jebusite. Molech rejoices in heaven;
He sees the Twelve Daughters naked upon the Twelve
  Stones,
Themselves condensing to rocks & into the Ribs of a Man.   25
Lo, they shoot forth in tender Nerves across Europe &
  Asia.
Lo, they rest upon the Tribes, where their panting Victims
  lie.
Molech rushes into the Kings, in love to the beautiful
  Daughters,
But they frown & delight in cruelty, refusing all other
  joy:
'Bring your Offerings, your first-begotten, pampered with
  milk & blood,   30
Your firstborn of seven years old, be they Males or
  Females,
To the beautiful Daughters of Albion!' They sport before
  the Kings
Clothed in the skin of the Victim! Blood, human blood,
  is the life
And delightful food of the Warrior; the well-fed Warrior's
  flesh
Of him who is slain in War fills the Valleys of Ephraim
  with   35
Breeding Women walking in pride & bringing forth under
  green trees
With pleasure, without pain, for their food is blood of
  the Captive.
Molech rejoices through the Land from Havilah to Shur;
  he rejoices

In moral law & its severe penalties; loud Shaddai &
    Jehovah
Thunder above when they see the Twelve panting Victims   40
Of the Twelve Stones of Power & the beautiful Daughters
    of Albion.
If you dare rend their Veil with your Spear, you are
    healed of Love!
From the Hills of Camberwell & Wimbledon, from the
    Valleys
Of Walton & Esher, from Stonehenge & from Maldon's Cove,
Jerusalem's Pillars fall in the rendings of fierce War.   45
Over France & Germany upon the Rhine & Danube
Reuben & Benjamin flee; they hide in the Valley of
    Rephaim.
Why trembles the Warrior's limbs when he beholds thy
    beauty
Spotted with Victim's blood? By the fires of thy secret
    tabernacle
And thy ark & holy place, at thy frowns, at thy dire
    revenge,   50
Smitten as Uzzah of old, his armour is softened, his
    spear
And sword faint in his hand, from Albion across Great
    Tartary.
O beautiful Daughter of Albion, cruelty is thy delight.
O Virgin of terrible eyes, who dwellest by Valleys of
    springs
Beneath the Mountains of Lebanon, in the City of Rehob
    in Hamath,   55
Taught to touch the harp, to dance in the Circle of
    Warriors
Before the Kings of Canaan, to cut the flesh from the
    Victim,
To roast the flesh in fire, to examine the Infant's limbs
In cruelties of holiness, to refuse the joys of love, to
    bring
The Spies from Egypt, to raise jealousy in the bosoms of
    the Twelve   60

Kings of Canaan, then to let the Spies depart to Meribah
    Kadesh,
To the place of the Amalekite, I am drunk with unsatiated
    love.
I must rush again to War, for the Virgin has frowned &
    refused.
Sometimes I curse & sometimes bless thy fascinating
    beauty.
Once Man was occupied in intellectual pleasures &
    energies,   65
But now my soul is harrowed with grief & fear & love &
    desire,
And now I hate & now I love, & Intellect is no more.
There is no time for anything but the torments of love
    & desire.
The Feminine & Masculine Shadows, soft, mild &
    ever-varying
In beauty, are Shadows now no more, but Rocks in Horeb."   70

Plate 69

Then all the Males combined into One Male, & every
    one
Became a ravening, eating Cancer growing in the Female,
A Polypus of Roots of Reasoning Doubt, Despair & Death,
Going forth & returning from Albion's Rocks to Canaan,
Devouring Jerusalem from every Nation of the Earth.   5

Envying stood the enormous Form at variance with Itself
In all its Members, in eternal torment of love & jealousy,
Driven forth by Los time after time from Albion's cliffy
    shore,
Drawing the free loves of Jerusalem into infernal bondage,
That they might be born in contentions of Chastity & in   10
Deadly Hate between Leah & Rachel, Daughters of Deceit
    & Fraud
Bearing the Images of various Species of Contention
And Jealousy & Abhorrence & Revenge & deadly Murder,

Till they refuse liberty to the Male, & not like Beulah,
Where every Female delights to give her maiden to her
    husband.   15
The Female searches sea & land for gratifications to the
Male Genius, who in return clothes her in gems & gold
And feeds her with the food of Eden. Hence all her beauty
    beams.
She Creates at her will a little moony night & silence
With Spaces of sweet gardens & a tent of elegant beauty   20
Closed in by a sandy desert & a night of stars shining
And a little tender moon & hovering angels on the wing.
And the Male gives a Time & Revolution to her Space
Till the time of love is passed in ever-varying delights.
For All Things Exist in the Human Imagination,   25
And thence in Beulah they are stolen by secret amorous
    theft,
Till they have had Punishment enough to make them commit
    Crimes.
Hence rose the Tabernacle in the Wilderness & all its
    Offerings,
From Male & Female Loves in Beulah & their Jealousies,
But no one can consummate Female bliss in Los's World
    without   30
Becoming a Generated Mortal, a Vegetating Death.

And now the Spectres of the Dead awake in Beulah; all
The Jealousies become Murderous, uniting together in
    Rahab
A Religion of Chastity, forming a Commerce to sell Loves,
With Moral Law, an Equal Balance, not going down with
    decision.   35
Therefore the Male, severe & cruel, filled with stern
    Revenge,
Mutual Hate returns & mutual Deceit & mutual Fear.

Hence the Infernal Veil grows in the disobedient Female,
Which Jesus rends & the whole Druid Law removes away
From the Inner Sanctuary, a False Holiness hid within
    the Center,   40

For the Sanctuary of Eden is in the Camp, in the Outline,
In the Circumference; & every Minute Particular is Holy.
Embraces are Comminglings from the Head even to the Feet,
And not a pompous High Priest entering by a Secret Place.

Jerusalem pined in her inmost soul over Wandering Reuben   45
As she slept in Beulah's Night, hid by the Daughters of
    Beulah.

Plate 70

And this the form of mighty Hand sitting on
    Albion's cliffs
Before the face of Albion, a mighty threat'ning Form:

His bosom wide & shoulders huge, overspreading wondrous,
Bear Three strong sinewy Necks & Three awful & terrible
    Heads,
Three Brains in contradictory council brooding
    incessantly,   5
Neither daring to put in act its councils, fearing each
    other,
Therefore rejecting Ideas as nothing & holding all Wisdom
To consist in the agreements & disagreements of Ideas,
Plotting to devour Albion's Body of Humanity & Love.

Such Form the aggregate of the Twelve Sons of Albion
    took, & such   10
Their appearance when combined; but often by birth pangs
    & loud groans
They divide to Twelve; the key-bones & the chest dividing
    in pain
Disclose a hideous orifice; thence issuing, the Giant
    brood
Arise as the smoke of the furnace, shaking the rocks
    from sea to sea;
And there they combine into Three Forms, named Bacon &
    Newton & Locke,   15

In the Oak Groves of Albion which overspread all the
    Earth.

Imputing Sin & Righteousness to Individuals, Rahab
Sat deep within him hid, his Feminine Power unrevealed,
Brooding Abstract Philosophy to destroy Imagination, the
    Divine
Humanity, A Threefold Wonder, feminine, most beautiful,
    Threefold   20
Each within other. On her white marble & even Neck, her
    Heart
Inorbed and bonified, with locks of shadowing modesty,
    shining
Over her beautiful Female features, soft-flourishing in
    beauty,
Beams mild, all love and all perfection, that when the
    lips
Receive a kiss from Gods or Men, a threefold kiss returns   25
From the pressed loveliness; so her whole immortal form
    three-fold
Threefold embrace returns, consuming lives of Gods & Men,
In fires of beauty melting them as gold & silver in the
    furnace.
Her Brain enlabyrinths the whole heaven of her bosom &
    loins
To put in act what her Heart wills. O who can withstand
    her power?   30
Her name is Vala in Eternity; in Time her name is Rahab.

The Starry Heavens all were fled from the mighty limbs
    of Albion,

Plate 71

And above Albion's Land was seen the Heavenly Canaan
As the Substance is to the Shadow, and above Albion's
    Twelve Sons
Were seen Jerusalem's Sons, and all the Twelve Tribes
    spreading

Over Albion. As the Soul is to the Body, so Jerusalem's
    Sons
Are to the Sons of Albion, and Jerusalem is Albion's
    Emanation.   5

What is Above is Within, for everything in Eternity is
    translucent;
The Circumference is Within; Without is formed the
    Selfish Center,
And the Circumference still expands, going forward to
    Eternity,
And the Center has Eternal States; these States we now
    explore:

And these the Names of Albion's Twelve Sons & of his
    Twelve Daughters   10
With their Districts: Hand dwelt in Selsey & had Sussex
    & Surrey
And Kent & Middlesex, all their Rivers & their Hills of
    flocks & herds,
Their Villages, Towns, Cities, Sea Ports, Temples,
    sublime Cathedrals;
All were his Friends, & their Sons & Daughters intermarry
    in Beulah,
For all are Men in Eternity. Rivers, Mountains, Cities,
    Villages,   15
All are Human, & when you enter into their Bosoms you
    walk
In Heavens & Earths, as in your own Bosom you bear your
    Heaven
And Earth & all you behold; though it appears Without
    it is Within,
In your Imagination, of which this World of Mortality
    is but a Shadow.

Hyle dwelt in Winchester, comprehending Hants., Dorset,
    Devon, Cornwall,   20
Their Villages, Cities, Sea Ports, their Cornfields &
    Gardens spacious,

Palaces, Rivers & Mountains; and between Hand & Hyle
    arose
Gwendolen & Cambel, who is Boadicea; they go abroad &
    return
Like lovely beams of light from the mingled affections
    of the Brothers.
The Inhabitants of the whole Earth rejoice in their
    beautiful light.   25

Coban dwelt in Bath. Somerset, Wiltshire, Gloucestershire
Obeyed his awful voice. Ignoge is his lovely Emanation;
She adjoined with Guantok's Children; soon lovely
    Cordella arose.
Guantok forgave & joyed over South Wales & all its
    Mountains.

Peachey had North Wales, Shropshire, Cheshire & the Isle
    of Man.   30
His Emanation is Mehetabel, terrible & lovely upon the
    Mountains.

Brereton had Yorkshire, Durham, Westmoreland, & his
    Emanation
Is Ragan; she adjoined to Slade, & produced Gonorill far
    beaming.

Slade had Lincoln, Stafford, Derby, Nottingham, & his
    lovely
Emanation, Gonorill, rejoices over hills & rocks & woods
    & rivers.   35

Hutton had Warwick, Northampton, Bedford, Buckingham,
Leicester & Berkshire, & his Emanation is Gwinefred
    beautiful.

Scofield had Ely, Rutland, Cambridge, Huntingdon,
    Norfolk,
Suffolk, Hartford & Essex, & his Emanation is Gwiniverra.
Beautiful, she beams towards the East, all kinds of
    precious stones   40
And pearl, with instruments of music in holy Jerusalem.

Kox had Oxford, Warwick, Wilts.; his Emanation is
　　Estrild;
Joined with Cordella, she shines southward over the
　　Atlantic.

Kotope had Hereford, Stafford, Worcester, & his Emanation
Is Sabrina; joined with Mehetabel, she shines west over
　　America.　　　　　　　　　　　　　　　　　　　　45

Bowen had all Scotland, the Isles, Northumberland &
　　Cumberland.
His Emanation is Conwenna; she shines a triple form
Over the north with pearly beams gorgeous & terrible.
Jerusalem & Vala rejoice in Bowen & Conwenna.

But the Four Sons of Jerusalem that never were Generated　　50
Are Rintrah and Palamabron and Theotormon and Bromion.
　　They
Dwell over the Four Provinces of Ireland in heavenly
　　light,
The Four Universities of Scotland, & in Oxford &
　　Cambridge & Winchester.

But now Albion is darkened & Jerusalem lies in ruins
Above the Mountains of Albion, above the head of Los.　　55

And Los shouted with ceaseless shoutings, & his tears
　　poured down
His immortal cheeks, rearing his hands to heaven for
　　aid Divine!
But he spoke not to Albion, fearing lest Albion should
　　turn his Back
Against the Divine Vision & fall over the Precipice of
　　Eternal Death.
But he receded before Albion & before Vala weaving the
　　Veil　　　　　　　　　　　　　　　　　　　　　　60
With the iron shuttle of War among the rooted Oaks of
　　Albion,
Weeping & shouting to the Lord day & night; and his
　　Children
Wept round him as a flock silent Seven Days of Eternity.

Plate 72

And the Thirty-two Counties of the Four Provinces
    of Ireland
Are thus divided: the Four Counties are in the Four
    Camps,
Munster South in Reuben's Gate, Connaught West in
    Joseph's Gate,
Ulster North in Dan's Gate, Leinster East in Judah's
    Gate.

For Albion in Eternity has Sixteen Gates among his
    Pillars,   5
But the Four towards the West were Walled up, & the
    Twelve
That front the Four other Points were turned Four Square
By Los for Jerusalem's sake & called the Gates of
    Jerusalem,
Because Twelve Sons of Jerusalem fled successive through
    the Gates.
But the Four Sons of Jerusalem who fled not but remained   10
Are Rintrah & Palamabron & Theotormon & Bromion,
The Four that remain with Los to guard the Western Wall;
And these Four remain to guard the Four Walls of
    Jerusalem,
Whose foundations remain in the Thirty-two Counties of
    Ireland
And in Twelve Counties of Wales & in the Forty Counties   15
Of England & in the Thirty-six Counties of Scotland.

And the names of the Thirty-two Counties of Ireland are
    these:
Under Judah & Issachar & Zebulun are Lowth, Longford,
Eastmeath, Westmeath, Dublin, Kildare, King's County,
Queen's County, Wicklow, Catherlogh, Wexford, Kilkenny.   20
And those under Reuben & Simeon & Levi are these:
Waterford, Tipperary, Cork, Limerick, Kerry, Clare.
And those under Ephraim, Manasseh & Benjamin are these:

Galway, Roscommon, Mayo, Sligo, Leitrim.
And those under Dan, Asher & Naphtali are these: 25
Donegal, Antrim, Tyrone, Fermanagh, Armagh,
    Londonderry,
Down, Monaghan, Cavan. These are the Land of Erin.

All these Center in London & in Golgonooza, from whence
They are Created continually East & West & North &
    South,
And from them are Created all the Nations of the Earth,   30
Europe & Asia & Africa & America, in fury Fourfold!

[in the illustration:
            Continually Building, Continually Decaying
                because of Love & Jealousy.]

And Thirty-two the Nations to dwell in Jerusalem's Gates.
O Come ye Nations, Come ye People, Come up to Jerusalem.
Return, Jerusalem, & dwell together as of old. Return,
Return! O Albion, let Jerusalem overspread all Nations   35
As in the times of old. O Albion awake! Reuben wanders.
The Nations wait for Jerusalem. They look up for the
    Bride.

France, Spain, Italy, Germany, Poland, Russia, Sweden,
    Turkey,
Arabia, Palestine, Persia, Hindustan, China, Tartary,
    Siberia,
Egypt, Libya, Ethiopia, Guinea, Kaffraria, Negroland,
    Morocco,   40
Congo, Zaara, Canada, Greenland, Carolina, Mexico,
Peru, Patagonia, Amazonia, Brazil: Thirty-two Nations,
And under these Thirty-two Classes of Islands in the
    Ocean
All the Nations, Peoples & Tongues throughout all the
    Earth.

And the Four Gates of Los surround the Universe Within
    and   45
Without; & whatever is visible in the Vegetable Earth,
    the same

Is visible in the Mundane Shell, reversed in mountain
    & vale.
And a Son of Eden was set over each Daughter of Beulah
    to guard
In Albion's Tomb the wondrous Creation, & the Fourfold
    Gate
Towards Beulah is to the South. Fénelon, Guyon, Teresa,   50
Whitefield & Hervey guard that Gate with all the gentle
    Souls
Who guide the great Winepress of Love. Four precious
    Stones that Gate.

[in reversed writing, in the illustration: Women the
    comforters of Men become the Tormenters & Punishers.]

Plate 73

Such are Cathedron's golden Halls in the City of
    Golgonooza.

And Los's Furnaces howl loud, living, self-moving,
    lamenting
With fury & despair, & they stretch from South to North
Through all the Four Points. Lo! the Labourers at the
    Furnaces,
Rintrah & Palamabron, Theotormon & Bromion, loud
    lab'ring   5
With the innumerable multitudes of Golgonooza, round
    the Anvils
Of Death. But how they came forth from the Furnaces &
    how long,
Vast & severe the anguish e'er they knew their Father
    were
Long to tell, & of the iron rollers, golden axle-trees
    & yokes
Of brass, iron chains & braces & the gold, silver &
    brass,   10
Mingled or separate, for swords, arrows, cannons, mortars,

The terrible ball, the wedge, the loud sounding hammer
    of destruction,
The sounding flail to thresh, the winnow to winnow
    kingdoms,
The waterwheel & mill of many innumerable wheels
    resistless
Over the Fourfold Monarchy from Earth to the Mundane
    Shell,   15

Perusing Albion's Tomb in the starry characters of Og
    & Anak,
To Create the lion & wolf, the bear, the tiger & ounce,
To Create the woolly lamb & downy fowl & scaly serpent,
The summer & winter, day & night, the sun & moon
    & stars,
The tree, the plant, the flower, the rock, the stone,
    the metal,   20
Of Vegetative Nature by their hard, restricting
    condensations.

Where Luvah's World of Opaqueness grew to a period, It
Became a Limit, a Rocky hardness without form & void,
Accumulating without end: here Los, who is of the Elohim,
Opens the Furnaces of affliction in the Emanation,   25
Fixing the Sexual into an ever-prolific Generation,
Naming the Limit of Opaqueness Satan & the Limit of
    Contraction
Adam, who is Peleg & Joktan, & Esau & Jacob, & Saul &
    David.

Voltaire insinuates that these Limits are the cruel
    work of God,
Mocking the Remover of Limits & the Resurrection of the
    Dead,   30
Setting up Kings in wrath, in holiness of Natural
    Religion,
Which Los with his mighty Hammer demolishes time on
    time
In miracles & wonders in the Fourfold Desert of Albion,

Permanently Creating, to be in Time Revealed &
    Demolished,
Satan, Cain, Tubal, Nimrod, Pharaoh, Priam, Bladud,
    Belin,   35
Arthur, Alfred, the Norman Conqueror, Richard, John,
And all the Kings & Nobles of the Earth & all their
    Glories.
These are Created by Rahab & Tirzah in Ulro, but around
These, to preserve them from Eternal Death, Los Creates
Adam, Noah, Abraham, Moses, Samuel, David, Ezekiel   40
Dissipating the rocky forms of Death by his thunderous
    Hammer.
As the Pilgrim passes while the Country permanent
    remains,
So Men pass on, but States remain permanent forever.

The Spectres of the Dead howl round the porches of Los
In the terrible Family feuds of Albion's cities &
    villages,   45
To devour the Body of Albion, hung'ring & thirsting &
    rav'ning.
The Sons of Los clothe them & feed, & provide houses &
    gardens.
And every Human Vegetated Form in its inward recesses
Is a house of pleasantness & a garden of delight Built
    by the
Sons & Daughters of Los in Bowlahoola & in Cathedron.   50

From London to York & Edinburgh the Furnaces rage terrible.
Primrose Hill is the mouth of the Furnace & the Iron Door.

Plate 74

The Four Zoas clouded rage; Urizen stood by Albion
With Rintrah and Palamabron and Theotormon and Bromion.
These Four are Verulam & London & York & Edinburgh.
And the Four Zoas are Urizen & Luvah & Tharmas & Urthona
In opposition deadly, and their Wheels in poisonous   5
And deadly stupor turned against each other loud & fierce,
Entering into the Reasoning Power; forsaking Imagination,

They became Spectres; & their Human Bodies were reposed
In Beulah by the Daughters of Beulah with tears &
    lamentations.

The Spectre is the Reasoning Power in Man; & when
    separated   10
From Imagination and closing itself as in steel, in a
    Ratio
Of the Things of Memory, It thence frames Laws &
    Moralities
To destroy Imagination, the Divine Body, by Martyrdoms
    & Wars.

Teach me, O Holy Spirit, the Testimony of Jesus! Let me
Comprehend wonderous things out of the Divine Law.   15
I behold Babylon in the opening Streets of London; I
    behold
Jerusalem in ruins wandering about from house to house.
This I behold; the shudderings of death attend my steps.
I walk up and down in Six Thousand Years; their Events
    are present before me:
To tell how Los in grief & anger, whirling round his
    Hammer on high   20
Drave the Sons & Daughters of Albion from their ancient
    mountains.
They became the Twelve Gods of Asia Opposing the Divine
    Vision.

The Sons of Albion are Twelve, the Sons of Jerusalem
    Sixteen.
I tell how Albion's Sons by Harmonies of Concords &
    Discords
Opposed to Melody, and by Lights & Shades opposed to
    Outline,   25
And by Abstraction opposed to the Visions of
    Imagination,
By cruel Laws divided Sixteen into Twelve Divisions;
How Hyle roofed Los in Albion's Cliffs, by the
    Affections rent
Asunder & opposed to Thought, to draw Jerusalem's Sons

Into the Vortex of his Wheels; therefore Hyle is called
    Gog,   30
Age after age drawing them away towards Babylon,
Babylon, the Rational Morality deluding to death the
    little ones
In strong temptations of stolen beauty. I tell how
    Reuben slept
On London Stone & the Daughters of Albion ran around
    admiring
His awful beauty; with Moral Virtue the fair deceiver,
    offspring   35
Of Good & Evil, they divided him in love upon the Thames
    & sent
Him over Europe in streams of gore out of Cathedron's
    Looms;
How Los drave them from Albion & they became Daughters
    of Canaan.
Hence Albion was called the Canaanite & all his Giant
    Sons.
Hence is my Theme. O Lord my Saviour, open thou the
    Gates   40
And I will lead forth thy Words, telling how the
    Daughters
Cut the Fibres of Reuben, how he rolled apart & took
    Root
In Bashan; terror-struck, Albion's Sons look toward
    Bashan.
They have divided Simeon; he also rolled apart in blood
Over the Nations till he took Root beneath the shining
    Looms   45
Of Albion's Daughters in Philistea by the side of Amalek.
They have divided Levi; he hath shot out into
    Forty-eight Roots
Over the Land of Canaan. They have divided Judah;
He hath took Root in Hebron, in the Land of Hand & Hyle.
Dan, Naphtali, Gad, Asher, Issachar, Zebulun roll apart   50
From all the Nations of the Earth to dissipate
    into non-Entity.

I see a Feminine Form arise from the Four terrible
    Zoas,
Beautiful but terrible, struggling to take a form of
    beauty,
Rooted in Shechem; this is Dinah, the youthful form
    of Erin.
The Wound I see in South Molton Street & Stratford
    place,   55
Whence Joseph & Benjamin rolled apart away from the
    Nations.
In vain they rolled apart; they are fixed into the
    Land of Cabul.

Plate 75

And Rahab, Babylon the Great, hath destroyed
    Jerusalem.

Bath stood upon the Severn with Merlin & Bladud &
    Arthur,
The Cup of Rahab in his hand. Her Poisons Twenty-seven-fold

And all her Twenty-seven Heavens, now hid & now revealed,
Appear in strong, delusive light of Time & Space,
    drawn out   5
In shadowy pomp, by the Eternal Prophet created evermore.

For Los in Six Thousand Years walks up & down continually,
That not one Moment of Time be lost; & every revolution
Of Space he makes permanent in Bowlahoola & Cathedron.

And these the names of the Twenty-seven Heavens & their
    Churches: 10
Adam, Seth, Enos, Cainan, Mahalaleel, Jared, Enoch,
Methuselah, Lamech—these are the Giants mighty,
    Hermaphroditic.
Noah, Shem, Arphaxad, Cainan the Second, Salah, Heber,
Peleg, Reu, Serug, Nahor, Terah—these are the Female
    Males,
A Male within a Female hid as in an Ark & Curtains.   15

Abraham, Moses, Solomon, Paul, Constantine, Charlemagne,
Luther—these Seven are the Male Females, the Dragon
    Forms
The Female hid within a Male; thus Rahab is revealed
Mystery, Babylon the Great, the Abomination of Desolation,
Religion hid in War, a Dragon red, & hidden Harlot.   20
But Jesus, breaking through the Central Zones of Death
    & Hell,
Opens Eternity in Time & Space, triumphant in Mercy.

Thus are the Heavens formed by Los within the Mundane
    Shell,
And where Luther ends Adam begins again in Eternal
    Circle,
To awake the Prisoners of Death, to bring Albion again   25
With Luvah into light eternal, in his eternal day.

But now the Starry Heavens are fled from the mighty
    limbs of Albion.

Plate 77

TO THE CHRISTIANS

    Devils are   I give you the end of a golden string,
False Religions   Only wind it into a ball,
     "Saul, Saul,   It will lead you in at Heaven's gate
Why persecutest thou me?"   Built in Jerusalem's wall.

We are told to abstain from fleshly desires that we may lose no
time from the Work of the Lord. Every moment lost is a moment
that cannot be redeemed. Every pleasure that intermingles with
the duty of our station is a folly unredeemable & is planted like
the seed of a wildflower among our wheat. All the tortures of
repentance are tortures of self-reproach on account of our leaving the Divine Harvest to the Enemy, the struggles of intangle-
ment with incoherent roots. I know of no other Christianity and
of no other Gospel than the liberty both of body & mind to exer-

cise the Divine Arts of Imagination; Imagination, the real & eternal World of which this Vegetable Universe is but a faint shadow & in which we shall live in our Eternal or Imaginative Bodies when these Vegetable Mortal Bodies are no more. The Apostles knew of no other Gospel. What were all their spiritual gifts? What is the Divine Spirit? Is the Holy Ghost any other than an Intellectual Fountain? What is the Harvest of the Gospel & its Labours? What is that Talent which it is a curse to hide? What are the Treasures of Heaven which we are to lay up for ourselves? Are they any other than Mental Studies & Performances? What are all the Gifts of the Gospel, are they not all Mental Gifts? Is God a Spirit who must be worshipped in Spirit & in Truth, and are not the Gifts of the Spirit Everything to Man? O ye Religious, discountenance every one among you who shall pretend to despise Art & Science! I call upon you in the Name of Jesus! What is the Life of Man but Art & Science? Is it Meat & Drink? Is not the Body more than Raiment? What is Mortality but the things relating to the Body, which Dies? What is Immortality but the things relating to the Spirit, which Lives Eternally! What is the Joy of Heaven but Improvement in the things of the Spirit? What are the Pains of Hell but Ignorance, Bodily Lust, Idleness & devastation of the things of the Spirit? Answer this to yourselves, & expel from among you those who pretend to despise the labours of Art & Science, which alone are the labours of the Gospel. Is not this plain & manifest to the thought? Can you think at all & not pronounce heartily That to Labour in Knowledge is to Build up Jerusalem, and to Despise Knowledge is to Despise Jerusalem & her Builders. And remember: He who despises & mocks a Mental Gift in another, calling it pride & selfishness & sin, mocks Jesus, the giver of every Mental Gift, which always appear to the ignorance-loving Hypocrite as Sins; but that which is a Sin in the sight of cruel Man is not so in the sight of our kind God. Let every Christian, as much as in him lies, engage himself openly & publicly before all the World in some Mental pursuit for the Building up of Jerusalem.

I stood among my valleys of the south
And saw a flame of fire, even as a Wheel

Of fire surrounding all the heavens: it went
From west to east against the current of
Creation and devoured all things in its loud   5
Fury & thundering course round heaven & earth.
By it the Sun was rolled into an orb;
By it the Moon faded into a globe
Travelling through the night; for from its dire
And restless fury, Man himself shrunk up   10
Into a little root a fathom long.
And I asked a Watcher & a Holy One
Its Name. He answered: "It is the Wheel of Religion."
I wept & said: "Is this the law of Jesus,
This terrible devouring sword turning every way?"   15
He answered: "Jesus died because he strove
Against the current of this Wheel; its Name
Is Caiaphas, the dark Preacher of Death,
Of sin, of sorrow, & of punishment,
Opposing Nature! It is Natural Religion,   20
But Jesus is the bright Preacher of Life,
Creating Nature from this fiery Law
By self-denial & forgiveness of Sin.
Go therefore, cast out devils in Christ's name,
Heal thou the sick of spiritual disease,   25
Pity the evil, for thou art not sent
To smite with terror & with punishments
Those that are sick, like to the Pharisees
Crucifying & encompassing sea & land
For proselytes to tyranny & wrath.   30
But to the Publicans & Harlots go!
Teach them True Happiness, but let no curse
Go forth out of thy mouth to blight their peace;
For Hell is opened to Heaven; thine eyes beheld
The dungeons burst & the Prisoners set free."   35

England! awake! awake! awake!
    Jerusalem thy Sister calls!
Why wilt thou sleep the sleep of death
    And close her from thy ancient walls?

Thy hills & valleys felt her feet   5
    Gently upon their bosoms move;
Thy gates beheld sweet Zion's ways;
    Then was a time of joy and love.

And now the time returns again:
    Our souls exult & London's towers   10
Receive the Lamb of God to dwell
    In England's green & pleasant bowers.

Plate 78

JERUSALEM

Chapter 4

The Spectres of Albion's Twelve Sons revolve
    mightily
Over the Tomb & over the Body, rav'ning to devour
The Sleeping Humanity. Los with his mace of iron
Walks round; loud his threats, loud his blows fall
On the rocky Spectres, as the Potter breaks the potsherds,   5
Dashing in pieces Self-righteousness, driving them
    from Albion's
Cliffs, dividing them into Male & Female forms in
    his Furnaces
And on his Anvils; lest they destroy the Feminine
    Affections,
They are broken. Loud howl the Spectres in his iron
    Furnace.

While Los laments at his dire labours, viewing Jerusalem,   10
Sitting before his Furnaces clothed in sackcloth of
    hair,
Albion's Twelve Sons surround the Forty-two Gates of
    Erin
In terrible armour, raging against the Lamb & against
    Jerusalem,

Surrounding them with armies, to destroy the Lamb of
    God.
They took their Mother Vala, and they crowned her with
    gold;   15
They named her Rahab & gave her power over the Earth,
The Concave Earth round Golgonooza in Entuthon-
    Benython,
Even to the stars exalting her Throne, to build beyond
    the Throne
Of God and the Lamb, to destroy the Lamb & usurp the
    Throne of God,
Drawing their Ulro Voidness round the Fourfold Humanity.   20

Naked Jerusalem lay before the Gates upon Mount Zion,
The Hill of Giants, all her foundations levelled with
    the dust,

Her Twelve Gates thrown down, her children carried into
    captivity,
Herself in chains; this from within was seen in a dismal
    night
Outside, unknown before in Beulah; & the twelve gates
    were filled   25
With blood from Japan eastward to the Giants' causeway,
    west
In Erin's Continent; and Jerusalem wept upon Euphrates'
    banks,
Disorganized; an evanescent shade, scarce seen or heard
    among
Her children's Druid Temples, dropping with blood,
    wandered weeping!
And thus her voice went forth in the darkness of
    Philistea: 30

"My brother & my father are no more! God hath forsaken
    me.
The arrows of the Almighty pour upon me & my children.
I have sinned and am an outcast from the Divine
    Presence!

Plate 79

My tents are fallen! My pillars are in ruins!
   My children dashed
Upon Egypt's iron floors & the marble pavements of
   Assyria;
I melt my soul in reasonings among the towers of
   Heshbon;
Mount Zion is become a cruel rock, & no more dew
Nor rain, no more the spring of the rock appears,
   but cold,   5
Hard & obdurate are the furrows of the mountain of wine
   & oil;
The mountain of blessing is itself a curse & an
   astonishment;
The hills of Judea are fallen with me into the deepest
   hell
Away from the Nations of the Earth, & from the Cities
   of the Nations;
I walk to Ephraim. I seek for Shiloh. I walk like a lost
   sheep   10
Among precipices of despair; in Goshen I seek for light
In vain; and in Gilead for a physician and a comforter.
Goshen hath followed Philistea; Gilead hath joined with
   Og!
They are become narrow places in a little and dark land.
How distant far from Albion! His hills & his valleys no
   more   15
Receive the feet of Jerusalem; they have cast me quite
   away;
And Albion is himself shrunk to a narrow rock in the
   midst of the sea!
The plains of Sussex & Surrey, their hills of flocks
   & herds
No more seek to Jerusalem nor to the sound of my Holy
   ones.

The Fifty-two Counties of England are hardened against
    me   20
As if I was not their Mother; they despise me & cast
    me out.
London covered the whole Earth. England encompassed the
    Nations,
And all the Nations of the Earth were seen in the
    Cities of Albion.
My pillars reached from sea to sea. London beheld me
    come
From my east & from my west; he blessed me and gave   25
His children to my breasts, his sons & daughters to
    my knees.
His aged parents sought me out in every city & village;
They discerned my countenance with joy, they showed me
    to their sons
Saying, 'Lo, Jerusalem is here! She sitteth in our secret
    chambers.
Levi and Judah & Issachar, Ephraim, Manasseh, Gad and
    Dan   30
Are seen in our hills & valleys; they keep our flocks
    & herds;
They watch them in the night; and the Lamb of God appears
    among us.'
The river Severn stayed his course at my command;
Thames poured his waters into my basins and baths;
Medway mingled with Kishon; Thames received the
    heavenly Jordan.   35
Albion gave me to the whole Earth to walk up & down,
    to pour
Joy upon every mountain, to teach songs to the shepherd
    & plowman.
I taught the ships of the Sea to sing the songs of Zion.
Italy saw me in sublime astonishment; France was wholly
    mine
As my garden & as my secret bath; Spain was my heavenly
    couch: 40
I slept in his golden hills; the Lamb of God met me
    there.

There we walked as in our secret chamber among our
    little ones.
They looked upon our loves with joy; they beheld our
    secret joys
With holy raptures of adoration, rapt sublime in the
    Visions of God.
Germany, Poland & the North wooed my footsteps; they
    found   45
My gates in all their mountains & my curtains in all
    their vales.
The furniture of their houses was the furniture of my
    chamber.
Turkey & Grecia saw my instruments of music; they arose;
They seized the harp, the flute, the mellow horn of
    Jerusalem's joy.
They sounded thanksgivings in my courts; Egypt & Libya
    heard.   50
The swarthy sons of Ethiopia stood round the Lamb of
    God,
Inquiring for Jerusalem; he led them up my steps to my
    altar.
And thou America! I once beheld thee but now behold no
    more
Thy golden mountains where my Cherubim & Seraphim
    rejoiced
Together among my little ones. But now my Altars run
    with blood!   55
My fires are corrupt! My incense is a cloudy pestilence
Of seven diseases! Once a continual cloud of salvation
    rose
From all my myriads; once the Fourfold World rejoiced
    among
The pillars of Jerusalem between my winged Cherubim;
But now I am closed out from them in the narrow passages   60
Of the valleys of destruction, into a dark land of pitch
    & bitumen,
From Albion's Tomb afar and from the fourfold wonders
    of God
Shrunk to a narrow doleful form in the dark land of Cabul.

There is Reuben & Gad & Joseph & Judah & Levi, closed
    up
In narrow vales. I walk & count the bones of my beloveds   65
Along the Valley of Destruction, among these Druid
    Temples,
Which overspread all the Earth in patriarchal pomp
    & cruel pride.
Tell me, O Vala, thy purposes; tell me wherefore thy
    shuttles
Drop with the gore of the slain, why Euphrates is red with
    blood,
Wherefore in dreadful majesty & beauty outside appears   70
Thy Masculine from thy Feminine, hardening against the
    heavens
To devour the Human? Why dost thou weep upon the wind
    among
These cruel Druid Temples? O Vala! Humanity is far
    above
Sexual organization & the Visions of the Night of Beulah,
Where Sexes wander in dreams of bliss among the
      Emanations,   75
Where the Masculine & Feminine are nursed into Youth
    & Maiden
By the tears & smiles of Beulah's Daughters till the
    time of Sleep is past.
Wherefore then do you realize these nets of beauty &
    delusion
In open day to draw the souls of the Dead into the light
Till Albion is shut out from every Nation under Heaven?   80

Plate 80

Encompassed by the frozen Net and by the rooted
    Tree,
I walk weeping in pangs of a Mother's torment for her
    Children:
I walk in affliction. I am a worm, and no living soul,
A worm going to eternal torment, raised up in a night
To an eternal night of pain, lost! lost! lost! forever!"   5

Beside her Vala howled upon the winds in pride of beauty,
Lamenting among the timbrels of the Warriors, among the
    Captives
In cruel holiness, and her lamenting songs were from
    Arnon
And Jordan to Euphrates. Jerusalem followed trembling,
Her children in captivity, listening to Vala's
    lamentation   10
In the thick cloud & darkness, & the voice went forth
    from
The cloud: "O rent in sunder from Jerusalem the Harlot
    daughter
In an eternal condemnation in fierce burning flames
Of torment unendurable! And if once a Delusion be found,
Woman must perish, & the Heavens of Heavens remain no
    more.   15

"My Father gave to me command to murder Albion
In unreviving Death; my Love, my Luvah, ordered me in
    night
To murder Albion, the King of Men. He fought in battles
    fierce;
He conquered Luvah, my beloved; he took me and my Father.
He slew them. I revived them to life in my warm bosom.   20
He saw them issue from my bosom; dark in Jealousy
He burned before me: Luvah framed the Knife, & Luvah
    gave
The Knife into his daughter's hand; such thing was never
    known
Before in Albion's land, that one should die a death
    never to be revived!
For in our battles we the Slain men view with pity and
    love;   25
We soon revive them in the secret of our tabernacles.
But I, Vala, Luvah's daughter, keep his body embalmed in
    moral laws
With spices of sweet odours of lovely jealous stupefaction
Within my bosom, lest he arise to life & slay my Luvah.
Pity me then, O Lamb of God! O Jesus pity me!   30

Come into Luvah's Tents, and seek not to revive the Dead!"

So sang she, and the Spindle turned furious as she sang.
The Children of Jerusalem, the Souls of those who sleep,
Were caught into the flax of her Distaff, & in her Cloud
To weave Jerusalem a body according to her will,   35
A Dragon form on Zion Hill's most ancient promontory.

The Spindle turned in blood & fire; loud sound the
     trumpets
Of war; the cymbals play loud before the Captains
With Cambel & Gwendolen in dance and solemn song.
The Cloud of Rahab vibrating with the Daughters of
     Albion   40
Los saw terrified; melted with pity & divided in wrath,
He sent them over the narrow seas in pity and love
Among the Four Forests of Albion, which overspread all
     the Earth.
They go forth & return swift as a flash of lightning
Among the tribes of warriors, among the Stones of power!   45
Against Jerusalem they rage through all the Nations of
     Europe,
Through Italy & Grecia, to Lebanon & Persia & India.

The Serpent Temples through the Earth, from the wide
     Plain of Salisbury,
Resound with cries of Victims, shouts & songs & dying
     groans
And flames of dusky fire, to Amalek, Canaan and Moab.   50
And Rahab, like a dismal and indefinite hovering Cloud,
Refused to take a definite form. She hovered over all
     the Earth
Calling the definite sin, defacing every definite form,
Invisible or Visible, stretched out in length or spread
     in breadth
Over the Temples, drinking groans of victims; weeping
     in pity   55
And joying in the pity, howling over Jerusalem's walls.

Hand slept on Skiddaw's top, drawn by the love of
     beautiful

Cambel, his bright, beaming Counterpart, divided from
    him,
And her delusive light beamed fierce above the Mountain,
Soft, invisible, drinking his sighs in sweet
    intoxication,   60
Drawing out fibre by fibre, returning to Albion's Tree
At night and in the morning to Skiddaw; she sent him over
Mountainous Wales into the Loom of Cathedron fibre by
    fibre.
He ran in tender nerves across Europe to Jerusalem's
    Shade
To weave Jerusalem a Body repugnant to the Lamb.   65

Hyle on East Moor in rocky Derbyshire raved to the Moon
For Gwendolen; she took up in bitter tears his anguished
    heart,
That, apparent to all in Eternity, glows like the Sun
    in the breast;
She hid it in his ribs & back; she hid his tongue with
    teeth.
In terrible convulsions, pitying & gratified,
    drunk with pity,   70
Glowing with loveliness before him, becoming apparent
According to his changes, she rolled his kidneys round
Into two irregular forms, and looking on Albion's dread
    Tree,
She wove two vessels of seed, beautiful as Skiddaw's
    snow.

Giving them bends of self-interest & selfish natural
    virtue,   75
She hid them in his loins; raving he ran among the rocks,
Compelled into a shape of Moral Virtue against the Lamb,
The invisible lovely one giving him a form according to
His Law, a form against the Lamb of God, opposed to Mercy
And playing in the thunderous Loom in sweet intoxication,   80
Filling cups of silver & crystal with shrieks & cries,
    with groans
And dolorous sobs, the wine of lovers in the Winepress
    of Luvah.

"O sister Cambel," said Gwendolen, as their long
    beaming light
Mingled above the Mountain, "what shall we do to keep
These awful forms in our soft bands, distracted with
    trembling?   85

Plate 81

I have mocked those who refused cruelty, & I
    have admired
The cruel Warrior. I have refused to give love to Merlin
    the piteous.
He brings to me the Images of his Love, & I reject in
    chastity
And turn them out into the streets for Harlots, to be
    food
To the stern Warrior. I am become perfect in beauty
    over my Warrior,   5
For Men are caught by Love; Woman is caught by Pride,
That Love may only be obtained in the passages of Death.
Let us look, let us examine: is the Cruel become an
    Infant,
Or is he still a cruel Warrior? Look, Sisters, look!
    O piteous!
I have destroyed Wand'ring Reuben, who strove to bind
    my Will.   10
I have stripped off Joseph's beautiful integument for my
    Beloved,
The Cruel one of Albion, to clothe him in gems of my
    Zone.
I have named him Jehovah of Hosts. Humanity is become
A weeping Infant in ruined lovely Jerusalem's folding
    Cloud.

[In the illustration in reversed writing:
In Heaven the only Art of Living
Is Forgetting and Forgiving
Especially to the Female.

But if you on Earth Forgive
You shall not find where to Live.]

In Heaven Love begets Love, but Fear is the Parent of
    Earthly Love,   15
And he who will not bend to Love must be subdued by
    Fear.

Plate 82

I have heard Jerusalem's groans; from Vala's
    cries & lamentations
I gather our eternal fate, Outcasts from life and love.
Unless we find a way to bind these awful Forms to our
Embrace, we shall perish annihilate, discovered our
    Delusions.
Look! I have wrought without delusion. Look! I have
    wept   5
And given soft milk mingled together with the spirits
    of flocks
Of lambs and doves, mingled together in cups and
    dishes
Of painted clay; the mighty Hyle is become a weeping
    infant.
Soon shall the Spectres of the Dead follow my weaving
    threads."

The Twelve Daughters of Albion attentive listen in
    secret shades,   10
On Cambridge and Oxford beaming soft, uniting with
    Rahab's cloud,
While Gwendolen spoke to Cambel, turning soft the
    spinning reel,
Or throwing the winged shuttle, or drawing the cords with
    softest songs.
The golden cords of the Looms animate beneath their
    touches soft,
Along the Island white, among the Druid Temples, while
    Gwendolen   15

Spoke to the Daughters of Albion, standing on Skiddaw's
    top.

So saying, she took a Falsehood & hid it in her left
    hand,
To entice her Sisters away to Babylon on Euphrates.
And thus she closed her left hand and uttered her
    Falsehood;
Forgetting that Falsehood is prophetic, she hid her
    hand behind her,   20
Upon her back behind her loins, & thus uttered her
    Deceit:

"I heard Enitharmon say to Los: 'Let the Daughters of
    Albion
Be scattered abroad and let the name of Albion be
    forgotten.
Divide them into three; name them Amalek, Cannan
    & Moab.
Let Albion remain a desolation without an inhabitant,   25
And let the Looms of Enitharmon & the Furnaces of Los
Create Jerusalem & Babylon & Egypt & Moab & Amalek,
And Helle & Hesperia & Hindustan & China & Japan.
But hide America, for a Curse, an Altar of Victims &
    a Holy Place.'
See, Sisters, Canaan is pleasant, Egypt is as the Garden
    of Eden,   30
Babylon is our chief desire, Moab our bath in summer;
Let us lead the stems of this Tree, let us plant it
    before Jerusalem
To judge the Friend of Sinners to death without the Veil,
To cut her off from America, to close up her secret Ark,
And the fury of Man exhaust in War! Woman permanent
    remain.   35
See how the fires of our loins point eastward to Babylon.
Look! Hyle is become an infant Love! look! behold! see
    him lie
Upon my bosom. Look! here is the lovely wayward form
That gave me sweet delight by his torments beneath my
    Veil;

By the fruit of Albion's Tree, I have fed him with
    sweet milk.   40
By contentions of the mighty for Sacrifice of Captives,
Humanity, the Great Delusion, is changed to War &
    Sacrifice.
I have nailed his hands on Beth Rabbim & his feet on
    Heshbon's Wall;
O that I could live in his sight. O that I could bind
    him to my arm."

So saying, She drew aside her Veil from Mam-Tor to
    Dovedale,   45
Discovering her own perfect beauty to the Daughters of
    Albion
And Hyle a winding Worm beneath, [erasure]
    [erasure] & not a weeping Infant.
Trembling & pitying she screamed & fled upon the wind.
Hyle was a winding Worm and herself perfect in
    beauty.   50
The deserts tremble at his wrath; they shrink themselves
    in fear.

Cambel trembled with jealousy; she trembled! She envied!
The envy ran through Cathedron's Looms into the Heart
Of mild Jerusalem, to destroy the Lamb of God. Jerusalem
Languished upon Mount Olivet, East of mild Zion's Hill.   55

Los saw the envious blight above his Seventh Furnace
On London's Tower on the Thames; he drew Cambel
    in wrath
Into his thundering Bellows, heaving it for a loud blast,
And with the blast of his Furnace upon fishy Billingsgate,
Beneath Albion's fatal Tree, before the Gate of Los,   60
Showed her the fibres of her beloved to ameliorate
The envy; loud she laboured in the Furnace of fire
To form the mighty form of Hand according to her will,
In the Furnaces of Los & in the Winepress, treading
    day & night.

Naked among the human clusters, bringing wine of
    anguish   65

To feed the afflicted in the Furnaces, she minded not
The raging flames, though she returned [erasure]
    [erasure] instead of beauty,
Deformity; she gave her beauty to another, bearing
    abroad
Her struggling torment in her iron arms, and like a
    chain   70
Binding his wrists & ankles with the iron arms of love.

Gwendolen saw the Infant in her sister's arms; she
    howled
Over the forests with bitter tears, and over the winding
    Worm,
Repentant; and she also in the eddying wind of Los's
    Bellows
Began her dolorous task of love in the Winepress of
    Luvah,   75
To form the Worm into a form of love by tears & pain.
The Sisters saw! Trembling ran through their Looms,
    softening mild
Towards London; then they saw the Furnaces opened, & in
    tears
Began to give their souls away in the Furnaces of
    affliction.

Los saw & was comforted at his Furnaces, uttering thus
    his voice: 80

"I know I am Urthona, keeper of the Gates of Heaven,
And that I can at will expatiate in the Gardens of bliss;
But pangs of love draw me down to my loins, which are
Become a fountain of veiny pipes. O Albion! my brother!

Plate 83

Corruptibility appears upon thy limbs, and
    nevermore
Can I arise and leave thy side, but labour here incessant
Till thy awaking; yet, alas, I shall forget Eternity.

Against the Patriarchal pomp and cruelty, labouring
    incessant,
I shall become an Infant horror. Enion! Tharmas! friends   5
Absorb me not in such dire grief. O Albion, my
    brother!
Jerusalem hungers in the desert; affection to her children!
The scorned and contemned youthful girl, where shall
    she fly?
Sussex shuts up her Villages. Hants., Devon & Wilts.,
Surrounded with masses of stone in ordered forms,
    determine then   10
A form for Vala and a form for Luvah, here on the Thames,
Where the Victim nightly howls beneath the Druid's knife,
A Form of Vegetation; nail them down on the stems of
    Mystery.
O when shall the Saxon return with the English, his
    redeemed brother?
O when shall the Lamb of God descend among the
    Reprobate?   15
I woo to Amalek to protect my fugitives. Amalek trembles.
I call to Canaan & Moab in my night watches; they mourn;
They listen not to my cry; they rejoice among their
    warriors.
Woden and Thor and Friga wholly consume my Saxons
On their enormous Altars built in the terrible north   20
From Ireland's rocks to Scandinavia, Persia and Tartary:
From the Atlantic Sea to the universal Erythrean.
Found ye London, enormous City? Weeps thy River?
Upon his parent bosom lay thy little ones, O Land
Forsaken. Surrey and Sussex are Enitharmon's Chamber,   25
Where I will build her a Couch of repose & my pillars
Shall surround her in beautiful labyrinths. Oothoon?
Where hides my child? In Oxford hidest thou with Antamon?
In graceful hidings of error, in merciful deceit
Lest Hand the terrible destroy his Affection, thou
    hidest her.   30
In chaste appearances for sweet deceits of love &
    modesty

Immingled, interwoven, glistening to the sickening
    sight,
Let Cambel and her Sisters sit within the Mundane
    Shell,
Forming the fluctuating Globe according to their will.
According as they weave the little embryon nerves &
    veins,   35
The Eye, the little Nostrils, & the delicate Tongue
    & Ears,
Of labyrinthine intricacy, so shall they fold the World,
That whatever is seen upon the Mundane Shell, the same
Be seen upon the Fluctuating Earth, woven by the Sisters.
And sometimes the Earth shall roll in the Abyss &
    sometimes   40
Stand in the Center & sometimes stretch flat in the
    Expanse,
According to the will of the lovely Daughters of Albion.
Sometimes it shall assimilate with mighty Golgonooza,
Touching its summits, & sometimes, divided, roll apart.
As a beautiful Veil, so these Females shall fold & unfold   45
According to their will the outside surface of the Earth,
An outside shadowy Surface superadded to the real Surface,
Which is unchangeable forever & ever, Amen; so be it!
Separate Albion's Sons gently from their Emanations,
Weaving bowers of delight on the current of infant
    Thames,   50
Where the old Parent still retains his youth, as I alas
Retain my youth eight thousand and five hundred years,
The labourer of ages in the Valleys of Despair!
The land is marked for desolation, & unless we plant
The seeds of Cities & of Villages in the Human bosom   55
Albion must be a rock of blood; mark ye the points
Where Cities shall remain & where Villages; for the rest,
It must lie in confusion till Albion's time of awaking.
Place the Tribes of Llewellyn in America for a hiding
    place
Till sweet Jerusalem emanates again into Eternity.   60
The night falls thick; I go upon my watch; be attentive;

The Sons of Albion go forth; I follow from my Furnaces,
That they return no more, that a place be prepared on
    Euphrates.
Listen to your Watchman's voice; sleep not before the
    Furnaces.
Eternal Death stands at the door. O God, pity our
    labours."   65

So Los spoke to the Daughters of Beulah while his
    Emanation
Like a faint rainbow waved before him in the awful
    gloom
Of London City on the Thames from Surrey Hills to
    Highgate.
Swift turn the silver spindles, & the golden weights
    play soft
And lulling harmonies beneath the Looms, from Caithness
    in the North   70
To Lizard Point & Dover in the South; his Emanation
Joyed in the many weaving threads in bright Cathedron's
    Dome,
Weaving the Web of life for Jerusalem; the Web of life,
Down flowing into Entuthon's Vales, glistens with soft
    affections.

While Los arose upon his Watch, and down from Golgonooza   75
Putting on his golden sandals to walk from mountain to
    mountain,
He takes his way, girding himself with gold & in his
    hand
Holding his iron mace, The Spectre remains attentive.
Alternate they watch in night; alternate labour in day,
Before the Furnaces labouring, while Los all night
    watches   80
The stars rising & setting, & the meteors & terrors of
    night.
With him went down the Dogs of Leutha; at his feet
They lap the water of the trembling Thames, then follow
    swift,

And thus he heard the voice of Albion's daughters on
    Euphrates:

"Our Father Albion's land, O it was a lovely land!
    & the Daughters of Beulah   85
Walked up and down in its green mountains, but Hand is
    fled
Away, & mighty Hyle, & after them Jerusalem is gone.
    Awake

Plate 84

Highgate's heights & Hampstead's; to Poplar, Hackney
    & Bow,
To Islington & Paddington & the Brook of Albion's River
We builded Jerusalem as a City & a Temple; from Lambeth
We began our Foundations, lovely Lambeth! O lovely Hills
Of Camberwell, we shall behold you no more in glory &
    pride,   5
For Jerusalem lies in ruins, & the Furnaces of Los are
    builded there.
You are now shrunk up to a narrow Rock in the midst
    of the Sea.
But here we build Babylon on Euphrates, compelled to
    build
And to inhabit, our Little ones to clothe in armour of
    the gold
Of Jerusalem's Cherubims & to forge them swords of her
    Altars.   10
I see London, blind & age-bent, begging through the
    Streets
Of Babylon, led by a child; his tears run down his beard.
The voice of Wandering Reuben echoes from street to street
In all the Cities of the Nations: Paris, Madrid,
    Amsterdam.

The Corner of Broad Street weeps; Poland Street languishes.   15
To Great Queen Street & Lincoln's Inn, all is distress
    & woe.

The night falls thick. Hand comes from Albion in his
    strength.
He combines into a Mighty one, the Double Molech &
    Chemosh,
Marching through Egypt in his fury; the East is pale at
    his course.
The Nations of India, the Wild Tartar that never knew
    Man,   20
Starts from his lofty places & casts down his tents
    & flees away;
But we woo him all the night in songs. O Los, come forth.
    O Los,
Divide us from these terrors, & give us power them to
    subdue.
Arise upon thy Watches; let us see thy Globe of fire
On Albion's Rocks, & let thy voice be heard upon
    Euphrates."   25

Thus sang the Daughters in lamentation, uniting into
    One
With Rahab as she turned the iron Spindle of destruction.

Terrified at the Sons of Albion, they took the Falsehood
    which
Gwendolen hid in her left hand. It grew & grew till it

Plate 85

Became a Space & an Allegory around the Winding
    Worm.
They named it Canaan & built for it a tender Moon.
Los smiled with joy, thinking on Enitharmon, & he
    brought
Reuben from his twelvefold wand'rings & led him into it,
Planting the Seeds of the Twelve Tribes & Moses & David   5
And gave a Time & Revolution to the Space Six Thousand
    Years.
He called it Divine Analogy, for in Beulah the Feminine
Emanations Create Space, the Masculine Create Time, &
    plant

The Seeds of beauty in the Space. List'ning to their
    lamentation,
Los walks upon his ancient Mountains in the deadly
    darkness   10
Among his Furnaces, directing his laborious Myriads,
    watchful,
Looking to the East; & his voice is heard over the whole
    Earth
As he watches the Furnaces by night & directs the
    labourers.

And thus Los replies upon his Watch; the Valleys listen
    silent;
The Stars stand still to hear; Jerusalem & Vala cease
    to mourn;   15
His voice is heard from Albion; the Alps & Appenines
Listen; Hermon & Lebanon bow their crowned heads;
Babel & Shinar look toward the Western Gate; they sit
    down
Silent at his voice; they view the red Globe of fire in
    Los's hand
As he walks from Furnace to Furnace directing the
    Labourers.   20
And this is the Song of Los, the Song that he sings on
    his Watch:

"O lovely mild Jerusalem! O Shiloh of Mount Ephraim!
I see thy Gates of precious stones, thy Walls of gold
    & silver.
Thou art the soft, reflected Image of the Sleeping Man
Who, stretched on Albion's rocks, reposes amidst his
    Twenty-eight   25
Cities, where Beulah lovely terminates, in the hills &
    valleys of Albion,
Cities not yet embodied in Time and Space; plant ye
The Seeds, O Sisters, in the bosom of Time & Space's womb,
To spring up for Jerusalem. Lovely Shadow of Sleeping
    Albion,
Why wilt thou rend thyself apart & build an Earthly
    Kingdom   30

To reign in pride & to oppress & to mix the Cup of
    Delusion,
O thou that dwellest with Babylon? Come forth, O lovely
    one.

Plate 86

I see thy Form, O lovely mild Jerusalem, Winged
    with Six Wings
In the opacious Bosom of the Sleeper, lovely, Threefold,
In Head & Heart & Reins, three Universes of love & beauty.
Thy forehead bright, Holiness to the Lord, with Gates of
    pearl
Reflects Eternity beneath thy azure wings of feathery
    down,   5
Ribbed delicate & clothed with feathered gold & azure
    & purple
From thy white shoulders shadowing, purity in holiness!
Thence feathered with soft crimson of the ruby, bright
    as fire,
Spreading into the azure Wings, which like a canopy
Bends over thy immortal Head, in which Eternity dwells.   10
Albion, beloved Land, I see thy mountains & thy hills
And valleys & thy pleasant Cities, Holiness to the Lord.
I see the Spectres of thy Dead, O Emanation of Albion.

"Thy Bosom, white, translucent, covered with immortal gems,
A sublime ornament not obscuring the outlines of beauty,   15
Terrible to behold for thy extreme beauty & perfection.
Twelvefold here all the Tribes of Israel I behold
Upon the Holy Land; I see the River of Life & Tree of
    Life;
I see the New Jerusalem descending out of Heaven
Between thy Wings of gold & silver, feathered immortal,   20
Clear as the rainbow, as the cloud of the Sun's tabernacle.

"Thy Reins, covered with Wings translucent, sometimes
    covering
And sometimes spread abroad, reveal the flames of
    holiness,

Which like a robe covers & like a Veil of Seraphim
In flaming fire unceasing burns from Eternity to Eternity.   25
Twelvefold I there behold Israel in her Tents.
A Pillar of a Cloud by day, a Pillar of fire by night
Guides them; there I behold Moab & Ammon & Amalek.
There, Bells of silver round thy knees, living articulate
Comforting sounds of love & Harmony, & on thy feet   30
Sandals of gold & pearl, & Egypt & Assyria before me,
The Isles of Javan, Philistea, Tyre and Lebanon."

Thus Los sings upon his Watch, walking from Furnace
    to Furnace.
He seizes his Hammer every hour, flames surround him as
He beats; seas roll beneath his feet; tempests muster   35
Around his head. The thick Hailstones stand ready to
    obey
His voice in the black cloud; his Sons labour in thunders
At his Furnaces; his Daughters at their Looms sing woes.
His Emanation separates in milky fibres, agonizing
Among the golden Looms of Cathedron, sending fibres of
    love   40
From Golgonooza with sweet visions for Jerusalem,
    wanderer.

Nor can any consummate bliss without being Generated
On Earth, of those whose Emanations weave the loves
Of Beulah for Jerusalem & Shiloh, in immortal
    Golgonooza,
Concentering in the majestic form of Erin in eternal
    tears,   45
Viewing the Winding Worm on the Deserts of Great Tartary,
Viewing Los in his shudderings, pouring balm on his
    sorrows.
So dread is Los's fury that none dare him to approach
Without becoming his Children in the Furnaces of
    affliction.

And Enitharmon like a faint rainbow waved before him,   50
Filling with Fibres from his loins, which reddened
    with desire

Into a Globe of blood beneath his bosom, trembling in
    darkness
Of Albion's clouds. He fed it with his tears & bitter
    groans,
Hiding his Spectre in invisibility from the timorous
    Shade
Till it became a separated cloud of beauty, grace &
    love   55
Among the darkness of his Furnaces, dividing asunder till
She, separated, stood before him, a lovely Female weeping,
Even Enitharmon separated outside; & his Loins closed
And healed after the separation; his pains he soon forgot,
Lured by her beauty outside of himself in shadowy grief.   60
Two Wills they had, Two Intellects, & not as in times
    of old.

Silent they wandered hand in hand like two Infants
    wand'ring
From Enion in the deserts, terrified at each other's
    beauty,
Envying each other, yet desiring, in all-devouring Love,

Plate 87

Repelling weeping Enion, blind & age-bent, into the
    fourfold
Deserts. Los first broke silence & began to utter his
    love:

"O lovely Enitharmon, I behold thy graceful forms,
Moving beside me till, intoxicated with the woven
    labyrinth
Of beauty & perfection, my wild fibres shoot in veins   5
Of blood through all my nervous limbs. Soon overgrown
    in roots,

"I shall be closed from thy sight. Seize therefore in
    thy hand
The small fibres as they shoot around me, draw out in
    pity

And let them run on the winds of thy bosom: I will fix
    them
With pulsations. We will divide them into Sons &
    Daughters   10
To live in thy Bosom's translucence as in an eternal
    morning."

Enitharmon answered: "No! I will seize thy Fibres &
    weave
Them, not as thou wilt, but as I will; for I will Create
A round Womb beneath my bosom, lest I also be overwoven
With Love; be thou assured I never will be thy slave.   15
Let Man's delight be Love, but Woman's delight be Pride.
In Eden our loves were the same; here they are opposite.
I have Loves of my own. I will weave them in Albion's
    Spectre.
Cast thou in Jerusalem's shadows thy Loves, silk of
    liquid,
Rubies, Jacinths, Chrysolites, issuing from thy
    Furnaces. While   20
Jerusalem divides thy care, while thou carest for
    Jerusalem,
Know that I never will be thine; also thou hidest Vala.
From her these fibres shoot to shut me in a Grave.
You are Albion's Victim; he has set his Daughter in
    your path."

Plate 88

Los answered, sighing like the Bellows of his
    Furnaces:

"I care not! The swing of my Hammer shall measure the
    starry round.
When in Eternity Man converses with Man they enter
Into each other's Bosom (which are Universes of delight)
In mutual interchange, and first their Emanations meet   5
Surrounded by their Children. If they embrace &
    commingle

The Human Fourfold Forms mingle also in thunders of
    Intellect;
But if the Emanations mingle not, with storms & agitations
Of earthquakes & consuming fires they roll apart in fear,
For Man cannot unite with Man but by their Emanations,   10
Which stand both Male & Female at the Gates of each
    Humanity.
How then can I ever again be united as Man with Man
While thou my Emanation refusest my Fibres of
    dominion?
When Souls mingle & join through all the Fibres of
    Brotherhood
Can there be any secret joy on Earth greater than this?"   15

Enitharmon answered: "This is Woman's World, nor need
    she any
Spectre to defend her from Man. I will Create secret
    places
And the masculine names of the places, Merlin
    & Arthur.
A triple Female Tabernacle for Moral Law I weave,
That he who loves Jesus may loathe, terrified, Female
    love,   20
Till God himself become a Male subservient to the
    Female."

She spoke in scorn & jealousy, alternate torments; and
So speaking she sat down on Sussex shore singing lulling
Cadences & playing in sweet intoxication among the
    glistening
Fibres of Los, sending them over the Ocean eastward into   25
The realms of dark death. O perverse to thyself,
    contrarious
To thy own purposes; for when she began to weave,
Shooting out in sweet pleasure, her bosom in milky Love
Flowed into the aching fibres of Los, yet contending
    against him
In pride, sending his Fibres over to her objects of
    jealousy   30

In the little lovely Allegoric Night of Albion's
    Daughters,
Which stretched abroad, expanding east & west & north
    & south
Through all the World of Erin & of Los & all their
    Children.

A sullen smile broke from the Spectre in mockery &
    scorn,
Knowing himself the author of their divisions &
    shrinkings, gratified   35
At their contentions; he wiped his tears; he washed
    his visage.

"The Man who respects Woman shall be despised by Woman,
And deadly cunning & mean abjectness only shall enjoy
    them;
For I will make their places of joy & love excrementitious,
Continually building, continually destroying in Family
    feuds,   40
While you are under the dominion of a jealous Female,
Unpermanent forever because of love & jealousy.
You shall want all the Minute Particulars of Life."

Thus joyed the Spectre in the dusky fires of Los's
    Forge, eyeing
Enitharmon, who at her shining Looms sings lulling
    cadences,   45
While Los stood at his Anvil in wrath, the victim of
    their love
And hate, dividing the Space of Love with brazen
    Compasses
In Golgonooza & in Udan-Adan & in Entuthon of Urizen.

The blow of his Hammer is Justice, the swing of his
    Hammer Mercy.
The force of Los's Hammer is eternal Forgiveness; but   50
His rage or his mildness were vain; she scattered his
    love on the wind
Eastward into her own Center, creating the Female Womb

In mild Jerusalem around the Lamb of God. Loud howl
The Furnaces of Los! Loud roll the Wheels of Enitharmon.
The Four Zoas in all their faded majesty burst out in
    fury   55
And fire. Jerusalem took the Cup which foamed in Vala's
    hand
Like the red Sun upon the mountains in the bloody day
Upon the Hermaphroditic Winepresses of Love & Wrath.

Plate 89

Though divided by the Cross & Nails & Thorns
    & Spear
In cruelties of Rahab & Tirzah, permanent endure
A terrible indefinite Hermaphroditic form,
A Winepress of Love & Wrath, double, Hermaphroditic,
Twelvefold in Allegoric pomp, in selfish holiness,   5
The Pharisaion, the Grammateis, the Presbyterion,
The Archiereus, the Iereus, the Saddusaion, double
Each withoutside of the other, covering eastern heaven.

Thus was the Covering Cherub revealed, majestic image
Of Selfhood, Body put off, the Antichrist accursed,   10
Covered with precious stones, a Human Dragon terrible
And bright, stretched over Europe & Asia gorgeous.
In three nights he devoured the rejected corse of death.

His Head dark, deadly, in its Brain encloses a reflection
Of Eden all perverted: Egypt on the Gihon, many-tongued   15
And many-mouthed: Ethiopia, Libya, the Sea of Rephaim,
Minute Particulars in slavery I behold among the brick
    kilns
Disorganized; & there is Pharaoh in his iron Court
And the Dragon of the River & the Furnaces of iron.
Outwoven from Thames & Tweed & Severn, awful streams,   20
Twelve ridges of Stone frown over all the Earth in
    tyrant pride,
Frown over each River, stupendous Works of Albion's
    Druid Sons,

And Albion's Forests of Oaks covered the Earth from Pole
    to Pole.

His Bosom wide reflects Moab & Ammon, on the River
Pison, since called Arnon; there is Heshbon beautiful,   25
The Rocks of Rabbath on the Arnon & the Fish-pools of
    Heshbon,
Whose currents flow into the Dead Sea by Sodom &
    Gomorrha.
Above his Head high-arching wings, black, filled with
    Eyes,
Spring upon iron sinews from the Scapulae & Os Humeri.
There Israel in bondage to his Generalizing Gods,   30
Molech & Chemosh; & in his left breast is Philistea
In Druid Temples over the whole Earth with Victims'
    Sacrifice,
From Gaza to Damascus, Tyre & Sidon & the Gods
Of Javan, through the Isles of Grecia & all Europe's
    Kings,
Where Hiddekel pursues his course among the rocks.   35

Two Wings spring from his ribs of brass, starry, black as
    night,
But translucent their blackness as the dazzling of gems.

His Loins enclose Babylon on Euphrates beautiful
And Rome in sweet Hesperia. There Israel, scattered
    abroad
In martyrdoms & slavery, I behold. Ah vision of sorrow,   40
Enclosed by eyeless Wings, glowing with fire as the iron
Heated in the Smith's forge, but cold the wind of their
    dread fury.

But in the midst of a devouring stomach, Jerusalem
Hidden within the Covering Cherub as in a Tabernacle
Of threefold workmanship, in allegoric delusion & woe.   45
There the Seven Kings of Canaan & Five Baalim of
    Philistea,
Sihon & Og, the Anakim & Emim, Nephilim & Gibborim,
From Babylon to Rome; & the Wings spread from Japan,

Where the Red Sea terminates the World of Generation &
    Death,
To Ireland's farthest rocks, where Giants builded their
    Causeway,   50
Into the Sea of Rephaim, but the Sea o'erwhelmed them
    all.

A Double Female now appeared within the Tabernacle,
Religion hid in War, a Dragon red & hidden Harlot,
Each within other, but without a Warlike Mighty one
Of dreadful power, sitting upon Horeb, pondering dire   55
And mighty preparations, mustering multitudes innumerable
Of warlike sons among the sands of Midian & Aram.
For multitudes of those who sleep in Alla descend,
Lured by his warlike symphonies of tab'ret, pipe & harp,
Burst the bottoms of the Graves & Funeral Arks of Beulah.   60
Wandering in that unknown Night beyond the silent Grave,
They become One with the Antichrist & are absorbed in
    him.

Plate 90

The Feminine separates from the Masculine, &
    both from Man,
Ceasing to be His Emanations, Life to Themselves
    assuming.
And while they circumscribe his Brain, & while they
    circumscribe
His Heart, & while they circumscribe his
    Loins, a Veil & Net
Of Veins of red Blood grows around them like a scarlet
    robe,   5
Covering them from the sight of Man like the woven Veil
    of Sleep
Such as the Flowers of Beulah weave to be their Funeral
    Mantles,
But dark, opaque, tender to touch, & painful & agonizing
To the embrace of love, & to the mingling of soft fibres

Of tender affection, that no more the Masculine mingles　　　10
With the Feminine, but the Sublime is shut out from
　　　the Pathos
In howling torment, to build stone walls of separation,
　　　compelling
The Pathos to weave curtains of hiding secrecy from
　　　the torment.

Bowen & Conwenna stood on Skiddaw, cutting the Fibres
Of Benjamin from Chester's River; loud the River, loud
　　　the Mersey　　　15
And the Ribble thunder into the Irish sea, as the Twelve
　　　Sons
Of Albion drank & imbibed the Life & eternal Form of
　　　Luvah.
Cheshire & Lancashire & Westmoreland groan in anguish
As they cut the fibres from the Rivers; he sears them
　　　with hot
Iron of his Forge & fixes them into Bones of chalk &
　　　Rock.　　　20
Conwenna sat above; with solemn cadences she drew
Fibres of life out from the Bones into her golden Loom.
Hand had his Furnace on Highgate's heights, & it reached
To Brockley Hills across the Thames; he with double
　　　Boadicea
In cruel pride cut Reuben apart from the Hills of Surrey,　　　25
Commingling with Luvah & with the Sepulcher of Luvah;
For the Male is a Furnace of beryl, the Female is a
　　　golden Loom.

Los cries: "No Individual ought to appropriate to Himself
Or to his Emanation any of the Universal Characteristics
Of David or of Eve, of the Woman or of the Lord,　　　30
Of Reuben or of Benjamin, of Joseph or Judah or Levi.
Those who dare appropriate to themselves Universal
　　　Attributes
Are the Blasphemous Selfhoods & must be broken asunder.
A Vegetated Christ & a Virgin Eve are the Hermaphroditic
Blasphemy; by his Maternal Birth he is that Evil One,　　　35

And his Maternal Humanity must be put off Eternally
Lest the Sexual Generation swallow up Regeneration.
Come, Lord Jesus, take on thee the Satanic Body of
    Holiness."

So Los cried in the Valleys of Middlesex in the Spirit
    of Prophecy,
While in Selfhood Hand & Hyle & Bowen & Scofield
    appropriate   40
The Divine Names, seeking to Vegetate the Divine Vision
In a corporeal & ever-dying Vegetation & Corruption.
Mingling with Luvah in One, they become One Great
    Satan.

Loud scream the Daughters of Albion beneath the Tongs
    & Hammer.
Dolorous are their lamentations in the burning Forge.   45
They drink Reuben & Benjamin as the iron drinks the fire;
They are red-hot with cruelty, raving along the Banks
    of Thames
And on Tyburn's Brook among the howling Victims in
    loveliness,
While Hand & Hyle condense the Little ones & erect them
    into
A mighty Temple even to the stars; but they Vegetate   50
Beneath Los's Hammer, that Life may not be blotted out.

For Los said: "When the Individual appropriates
    Universality
He divides into Male & Female, & when the Male &
    Female
Appropriate Individuality, they become an Eternal Death,
Hermaphroditic worshippers of a God of cruelty & law!   55
Your Slaves & Captives you compel to worship a God of
    Mercy.
These are the Demonstrations of Los, & the blows of my
    mighty Hammer."

So Los spoke. And the Giants of Albion, terrified &
    ashamed

With Los's thunderous Words, began to build trembling,
    rocking Stones,
For his Words roll in thunders & lightnings among
    the Temples,   60
Terrified, rocking to & fro upon the earth, & sometimes
Resting in a Circle in Maldon or in Strathness or Dura,
Plotting to devour Albion & Los, the friend of Albion,
Denying in private, mocking God & Eternal Life, & in
    Public
Collusion, calling themselves Deists, Worshipping the
    Maternal   65
Humanity, calling it Nature and Natural Religion.

But still the thunder of Los peals loud, & thus the
    thunders cry:

"These beautiful Witchcrafts of Albion are gratified by
    Cruelty.

Plate 91

It is easier to forgive an Enemy than to forgive
    a Friend.
The man who permits you to injure him deserves your
    vengeance;
He also will receive it; go, Spectre! Obey my most
    secret desire,
Which thou knowest without my speaking: Go to these
    Fiends of Righteousness,
Tell them to obey their Humanities & not pretend Holiness   5
When they are murderers; as far as my Hammer & Anvil
    permit,
Go, tell them that the Worship of God is honouring his
    gifts
In other men & loving the greatest men best, each
    according
To his Genius, which is the Holy Ghost in Man;
    there is no other

God than that God who is the intellectual fountain of
    Humanity;   10
He who envies or calumniates, which is murder & cruelty,
Murders the Holy one. Go tell them this & overthrow
    their cup,
Their bread, their altar-table, their incense & their oath.
Their marriage & their baptism, their burial & consecration.
I have tried to make friends by corporeal gifts but have
    only   15
Made enemies. I never made friends but by spiritual
    gifts,
By severe contentions of friendship & the burning fire
    of thought.
He who would see the Divinity must see him in his
    Children,
One first, in friendship & love, then a Divine Family,
    & in the midst
Jesus will appear; so he who wishes to see a Vision, a
    perfect Whole,   20
Must see it in its Minute Particulars, Organized, & not
    as thou,
O Fiend of Righteousness, pretendest; thine is a
    Disorganized
And snowy cloud, brooder of tempests & destructive War.
You smile with pomp & rigor; you talk of benevolence
    & virtue;
I act with benevolence & Virtue & get murdered time
    after time.   25
You accumulate Particulars, & murder by analyzing,
    that you
May take the aggregate; & you call the aggregate Moral
    Law;
And you call that Swelled & bloated Form a Minute
    Particular.
But General Forms have their vitality in Particulars,
    & every
Particular is a Man, a Divine Member of the Divine
    Jesus."   30

So Los cried at his Anvil in the horrible darkness,
    weeping.

The Spectre builded stupendous Works, taking the Starry
    Heavens
Like to a curtain & folding them according to his will,
Repeating the Smaragdine Table of Hermes to draw
    Los down
Into the Indefinite, refusing to believe without
    demonstration.   35
Los reads the Stars of Albion, the Spectre reads the
    Voids
Between the Stars among the arches of Albion's Tomb
    sublime,
Rolling the Sea in rocky paths, forming Leviathan
And Behemoth, the War by Sea enormous & the War
By Land astounding, erecting pillars in the deepest
    Hell,   40
To reach the heavenly arches; Los beheld undaunted;
    furious,
His heaved Hammer; he swung it round & at one blow,
In unpitying ruin driving down the pyramids of pride,
Smiting the Spectre on his Anvil & the integuments of
    his Eye
And Ear unbinding in dire pain, with many blows,   45
Of strict severity self-subduing & with many tears
    labouring.

Then he sent forth the Spectre; all his pyramids were
    grains
Of sand & his pillars dust on the fly's wing; & his starry
Heavens a moth of gold & silver mocking his anxious
    grasp.
Thus Los altered his Spectre, & every Ratio of his
    Reason   50
He altered time after time, with dire pain & many tears,
Till he had completely divided him into a separate
    space.

Terrified Los sat to behold, trembling & weeping &
   howling:
"I care not whether a Man is Good or Evil; all that I
   care
Is whether he is a Wise Man or a Fool. Go, put off
   Holiness   55
And put on Intellect, or my thund'rous Hammer shall
   drive thee
To wrath which thou condemnest, till thou obey my voice."

So Los terrified cries, trembling & weeping & howling:
   "Beholding,

Plate 92

What do I see? The Briton, Saxon, Roman, Norman
   amalgamating
In my Furnaces into One Nation, the English, & taking
   refuge
In the Loins of Albion. The Canaanite united with the
   fugitive
Hebrew, whom she divided into Twelve & sold into Egypt,
Then scattered the Egyptian & Hebrew to the four Winds!   5
This sinful Nation Created in our Furnaces & Looms is
   Albion."

So Los spoke. Enitharmon answered in great terror in
   Lambeth's Vale:

"The Poet's Song draws to its period, & Enitharmon is
   no more;
For if he be that Albion, I can never weave him in my
   Looms.
But when he touches the first fibrous thread, like
   filmy dew   10
My Looms will be nor more & I, annihilate, vanish forever.
Then thou wilt Create another Female according to thy
   Will."

Los answered swift as the shuttle of gold: "Sexes must
    vanish & cease
To be, when Albion arises from his dread repose, O lovely
    Enitharmon,
When all their Crimes, their Punishments, their
    Accusations of Sin,   15
All their Jealousies, Revenges, Murders, hidings of
    Cruelty in Deceit
Appear only in the Outward Spheres of Visionary Space
    and Time,
In the shadows of Possibility by Mutual Forgiveness
    forevermore,
And in the Vision & in the Prophecy, that we may Foresee
    & Avoid
The terrors of Creation & Redemption & Judgment,
    Beholding them   20
Displayed in the Emanative Visions of Canaan, in Jerusalem
    & in Shiloh
And in the Shadows of Remembrance, & in the Chaos of
    the Spectre,
Amalek, Edom, Egypt, Moab, Ammon, Ashur, Philistea,
    around Jerusalem,
Where the Druids reared their Rocky Circles to make
    permanent Remembrance
Of Sin, & the Tree of Good & Evil sprang from the Rocky
    Circle & Snake   25
Of the Druid, along the Valley of Rephaim, from
    Camberwell to Golgotha,
And framed the Mundane Shell Cavernous in Length, Breadth
    & Height."

Plate 93

[In the illustration:

    Anytus, Melitus & Lycon thought Socrates a Very
        Pernicious
    Man. So Caiaphas thought Jesus.]

Enitharmon heard. She raised her head like the mild
    Moon:

"O Rintrah! O Palamabron! What are your dire & awful
    purposes?
Enitharmon's name is nothing before you; you forget all
    my Love.
The Mother's love of obedience is forgotten, & you seek
    a Love
Of the pride of dominion that will Divorce Ocalythron
    & Elynittria   5
Upon East Moor in Derbyshire & along the Valleys of
    Cheviot.
Could you Love me, Rintrah, if you Pride not in my Love,
As Reuben found Mandrakes in the field & gave them to
    his Mother?
Pride meets with Pride upon the Mountains in the stormy
    day,
In that terrible Day of Rintrah's Plow & of Satan's
    driving the Team.   10
Ah! then I heard my little ones weeping along the Valley.
Ah! then I saw my beloved ones fleeing from my Tent.
Merlin was like thee, Rintrah, among the Giants of
    Albion;
Judah was like Palamabron. O Simeon! O Levi! ye fled
    away.
How can I hear my little ones weeping along the
    Valley.   15
Or how upon the distant Hills see my beloved's Tents?"

Then Los again took up his speech as Enitharmon ceased.

"Fear not, my Sons, this Waking Death. He is become
    One with me.
Behold him here! We shall not Die! We shall be united in
    Jesus.
Will you suffer this Satan, this Body of Doubt that
    Seems but Is Not   20
To occupy the very threshold of Eternal Life? If Bacon,
    Newton, Locke

Deny a Conscience in Man & the Communion of Saints &
    Angels,
Contemning the Divine Vision & Fruition, Worshiping
    the Deus
Of the Heathen, The God of This World, & the Goddess
    Nature,
Mystery, Babylon the Great, the Druid Dragon &
    hidden Harlot,   25
Is it not that Signal of the Morning which was told
    us in the Beginning?"

Thus they converse upon Mam-Tor. The Graves thunder
    under their feet.

Plate 94

Albion cold lays on his Rock; storms & snows
    beat round him
Beneath the Furnaces & the starry Wheels & the Immortal
    Tomb.
Howling winds cover him; roaring seas dash furious
    against him.
In the deep darkness broad lightnings glare; long thunders
    roll.

The weeds of Death inwrap his hands & feet, blown
    incessant   5
And washed incessant by the forever restless sea-waves
    foaming abroad
Upon the white Rock. England, a Female Shadow, as
    deadly damps
Of the Mines of Cornwall & Derbyshire, lays upon his
    bosom heavy,
Moved by the wind in volumes of thick cloud, returning,
    folding round
His loins & bosom, unremovable by swelling storms
    & loud rending   10
Of enraged thunders. Around them the Starry Wheels of
    their Giant Sons

Revolve, & over them the Furnaces of Los, & the Immortal
    Tomb around,
Erin sitting in the Tomb, to watch them unceasing night
    and day;
And the Body of Albion was closed apart from all
    Nations.

Over them the famished Eagle screams on bony Wings, and
    around   15
Them howls the Wolf of famine; deep heaves the Ocean
    black, thundering
Around the wormy Garments of Albion, then pausing in
    deathlike silence.

Time was Finished! The Breath Divine Breathed over Albion
Beneath the Furnaces & starry Wheels and in the Immortal
    Tomb,
And England, who is Britannia, awoke from Death on
    Albion's bosom.   20
She awoke pale & cold; she fainted seven times on the
    Body of Albion.

"O piteous Sleep, O piteous Dream! O God, O God, awake!
    I have slain
In Dreams of Chastity & Moral Law. I have Murdered
    Albion! Ah!
In Stonehenge & on London Stone & in the Oak Groves of
    Maldon
I have Slain him in my Sleep with the Knife of the
    Druid, O England!   25
O all ye Nations of the Earth, behold ye the Jealous
    Wife.
The Eagle & the Wolf & Monkey & Owl & the King & Priest
    were there."

Plate 95

Her voice pierced Albion's clay-cold ear. He
    moved upon the Rock.

The Breath Divine went forth upon the morning hills;
    Albion moved
Upon the Rock; he opened his eyelids in pain; in pain
    he moved
His stony members; he saw England. Ah! shall the Dead
    live again?

The Breath Divine went forth over the morning hills.
    Albion rose   5
In anger, the wrath of God breaking bright, flaming on
    all sides around
His awful limbs; into the Heavens he walked, clothed
    in flames,
Loud thund'ring, with broad flashes of flaming lightning
    & pillars
Of fire, speaking the Words of Eternity in Human Forms,
    in direful
Revolutions of Action & Passion, through the Four Elements
    on all sides   10
Surrounding his awful Members. Thou seest the Sun in
    heavy clouds
Struggling to rise above the Mountains. In his burning
    hand
He takes his Bow, then chooses out his arrows of flaming
    gold.
Murmuring, the Bowstring breathes with ardor! Clouds
    roll round the
Horns of the wide Bow; loud sounding winds sport on the
    mountain brows,   15
Compelling Urizen to his Furrow, & Tharmas to his
    Sheepfold,
And Luvah to his Loom. Urthona he beheld, mighty
    labouring at
His Anvil in the Great Spectre Los, unwearied labouring
    & weeping.
Therefore the Sons of Eden praise Urthona's Spectre in
    songs,
Because he kept the Divine Vision in time of trouble.   20

As the Sun & Moon lead forward the Visions of Heaven &
 Earth,
England, who is Britannia, entered Albion's bosom
 rejoicing,
Rejoicing in his indignation, adoring his wrathful rebuke.
She who adores not your frowns will only loathe your
 smiles.

Plate 96

As the Sun & Moon lead forward the Visions of
 Heaven & Earth,
England, who is Britannia, entered Albion's bosom
 rejoicing.

Then Jesus appeared, standing by Albion as the Good
 Shepherd
By the lost Sheep that he hath found, & Albion knew that
 it
Was the Lord, the Universal Humanity, & Albion saw his
 Form,   5
A Man, & they conversed as Man with Man, in Ages of
 Eternity,
And the Divine Appearance was the likeness & similitude
 of Los.

Albion said: "O Lord, what can I do? My Selfhood cruel
Marches against thee deceitful from Sinai & from Edom
Into the Wilderness of Judah to meet thee in his pride. 10
I behold the Visions of my deadly Sleep of Six Thousand
 Years
Dazzling around thy skirts like a Serpent of precious
 stones & gold.
I know it is my Self, O my Divine Creator & Redeemer."

Jesus replied: "Fear not, Albion, unless I die thou
 canst not live,
But if I die I shall arise again, & thou with me.   15
This is Friendship & Brotherhood; without it Man is Not."

So Jesus spoke. The Covering Cherub, coming on in
    darkness,
Overshadowed them, & Jesus said: "Thus do Men in Eternity
One for another to put off by forgiveness every sin."

Albion replied: "Cannot Man exist without Mysterious   20
Offering of Self for Another? Is this Friendship &
    Brotherhood?
I see thee in the likeness & similitude of Los my
    Friend."

Jesus said: "Wouldest thou love one who never died
For thee, or ever die for one who had not died for thee?
And if God dieth not for Man & giveth not himself   25
Eternally for Man, Man could not exist; for Man is Love
As God is Love; every kindness to another is a little
    Death
In the Divine Image, nor can Man exist but by Brotherhood."

So saying, the Cloud, overshadowing, divided them asunder.
Albion stood in terror, not for himself but for his
    Friend   30
Divine, & Self was lost in the contemplation of faith
And wonder at the Divine Mercy & at Los's sublime honour.

"Do I sleep amidst danger to Friends? O my Cities &
    Counties,
Do you sleep? Rouse up, rouse up. Eternal Death is abroad."

So Albion spoke & threw himself into the Furnaces of
    affliction.   35
All was a Vision, all a Dream: the Furnaces became
Fountains of Living Waters flowing from the Humanity
    Divine,
And all the Cities of Albion rose from their Slumbers,
    And All
The Sons & Daughters of Albion on soft clouds Waking
    from Sleep.
Soon all around remote the Heavens burnt with flaming
    fires,   40

And Urizen & Luvah & Tharmas & Urthona arose into
Albion's Bosom. Then Albion stood before Jesus in the
   Clouds
Of Heaven, Fourfold among the Visions of God in Eternity.

Plate 97

"Awake! Awake, Jerusalem! O lovely Emanation of
   Albion,
Awake and overspread all Nations as in Ancient Time;
For Lo, the Night of Death is past, and the Eternal Day
Appears upon our Hills. Awake, Jerusalem, and come away."

So spake the Vision of Albion, & in him so spake in my
   hearing   5
The Universal Father. Then Albion stretched his hand
   into Infinitude
And took his Bow. Fourfold the Vision, for bright beaming
   Urizen
Laid his hand on the South & took a breathing Bow of
   carved Gold;
Luvah his hand stretched to the East & bore a Silver Bow,
   bright shining;
Tharmas Westward a Bow of Brass, pure flaming, richly
   wrought;   10
Urthona Northward in thick storms a Bow of Iron, terrible
   thundering.

And the Bow is a Male & Female, & the Quiver of the Arrows
   of Love
Are the Children of this Bow, a Bow of Mercy & Loving
   kindness, laying
Open the hidden Heart in Wars of mutual Benevolence,
   Wars of Love.
And the Hand of Man grasps firm between the Male & Female
   Loves,   15
And he Clothed himself in Bow & Arrows in awful state
   Fourfold

In the midst of his Twenty-eight Cities, each with his
   Bow breathing.

Plate 98

Then each an Arrow flaming from his Quiver fitted
   carefully.
They drew fourfold the unreprovable String, bending
   through the wide Heavens
The horned Bow Fourfold; loud sounding flew the flaming
   Arrow fourfold.

Murmuring, the Bow-string breathes with ardor. Clouds
   roll round the horns
Of the wide Bow; loud sounding Winds sport on the
   Mountain's brows.   5
The Druid Spectre was Annihilate, loud-thund'ring,
   rejoicing terrific, vanishing,
Fourfold Annihilation; & at the clangor of the Arrows of
   Intellect
The innumerable Chariots of the Almighty appeared in
   Heaven,
And Bacon & Newton & Locke, & Milton & Shakespeare &
   Chaucer,
A Sun of blood-red wrath surrounding heaven on all sides
   around,   10
Glorious incomprehensible by Mortal Man, & each Chariot
   was Sexual Threefold.

And every Man stood Fourfold; each Four Faces had, One
   to the West,
One toward the East, One to the South, One to the North,
   the Horses Fourfold,
And the dim Chaos brightened beneath, above, around;
   Eyed as the Peacock,
According to the Human Nerves of Sensation, the Four
   Rivers of the Water of Life.   15

South stood the Nerves of the Eye; East in Rivers of
   bliss the Nerves of the

Expansive Nostrils; West flowed the Parent Sense, the
    Tongue; North stood
The labyrinthine Ear, Circumscribing & Circumcising the
    Excrementitious
Husk & Covering, into Vacuum evaporating, revealing the
    lineaments of Man,
Driving outward the Body of Death in an Eternal Death &
    Resurrection,   20
Awaking it to Life among the Flowers of Beulah, rejoicing
    in Unity,
In the Four Senses, in the Outline, the Circumference
    & Form, forever
In Forgiveness of Sins, which is Self-Annihilation. It
    is the Covenant of Jehovah.

The Four Living Creatures, Chariots of Humanity, Divine,
    Incomprehensible,
In beautiful Paradises expand. These are the Four Rivers
    of Paradise   25
And the Four Faces of Humanity, fronting the Four
    Cardinal Points
Of Heaven, going forward, forward irresistible from
    Eternity to Eternity.

And they conversed together in Visionary forms dramatic,
    which bright
Redounded from their Tongues in thunderous majesty, in
    Visions,
In new Expanses, creating exemplars of Memory and of
    Intellect,   30
Creating Space, Creating Time, according to the wonders
    Divine
Of Human Imagination, throughout all the Three Regions
    immense
Of Childhood, Manhood & Old Age; & the all-tremendous
    unfathomable Non Ens
Of Death was seen in regenerations terrific or
    complacent, varying
According to the subject of discourse, & every Word
    & Every Character   35

Was Human according to the Expansion or Contraction, the
    Translucence or
Opaqueness of Nervous fibres; such was the variation
    of Time & Space,
Which vary according as the Organs of Perception vary;
    & they walked
To & fro in Eternity as One Man, reflecting each in each
    & clearly seen
And seeing, according to fitness & order. And I heard
    Jehovah speak   40
Terrific from his Holy Place & saw the Words of the
    Mutual Covenant Divine
On Chariots of gold & jewels, with Living Creatures,
    starry & flaming,
With every Colour, Lion, Tiger, Horse, Elephant, Eagle
    Dove, Fly, Worm
And the all-wondrous Serpent clothed in gems & rich
    array, Humanize
In the Forgiveness of Sins according to the Covenant
    of Jehovah. They Cry: 45

"Where is the Covenant of Priam, the Moral Virtues of
    the Heathen?
Where is the Tree of Good & Evil that rooted beneath
    the cruel heel
Of Albion's Spectre, the Patriarch Druid? Where are all
    his Human Sacrifices
For Sin in War & in the Druid Temples of the Accuser of
    Sin, beneath
The Oak Groves of Albion that covered the whole Earth
    beneath his Spectre?   50
Where are the Kingdoms of the World & all their glory
    that grew on Desolation,
The Fruit of Albion's Poverty Tree, when the Triple-Headed
    Gog-Magog Giant
Of Albion Taxed the Nations into Desolation & then gave
    the Spectrous Oath?"

Such is the Cry from all the Earth, from the Living
    Creatures of the Earth

And from the great City of Golgonooza in the Shadowy
    Generation,   55
And from the Thirty-two Nations of the Earth among the
    Living Creatures.

Plate 99

All Human Forms identified, even Tree, Metal,
    Earth & Stone; all
Human Forms identified, living, going forth & returning
    wearied
Into the Planetary lives of Years, Months, Days & Hours,
    reposing

And then Awaking into his Bosom in the Life of
    Immortality.
And I heard the Name of their Emanations: they are
    named Jerusalem.   5

Part Three
SELECTED PROSE

An Island in the Moon (circa 1784)

CHAPTER 1

In the Moon is a certain Island near by a mighty continent, which small island seems to have some affinity to England, &, what is more extraordinary, the people are so much alike & their language so much the same that you would think you was among your friends. In this Island dwells three Philosophers—Suction the Epicurean, Quid the Cynic, & Sipsop the Pythagorean. I call them by the names of these sects, though the sects are not ever mentioned there, as being quite out of date. However, the things still remain, and the vanities are the same. The three Philosophers sat together thinking of nothing. In comes Etruscan Column the Antiquarian, & after an abundance of Inquiries to no purpose sat himself down & described something that nobody listened to. So they were employed when Mrs. Gimblet came in. The corners of her mouth seemed, I don't know how, but very odd, as if she hoped you had not an ill opinion of her. To be sure we are all poor creatures. Well, she seated & seemed to listen with great attention while the Antiquarian seemed to be talking of virtuous cats, but it was not so. She was thinking of the shape of her eyes & mouth, & he was thinking of his eternal fame. The three Philosophers at this time were each endeavouring to conceal his laughter, not at them but at his own imaginations. This was the situation of this improving company when, in a great hurry, Inflammable Gas the Wind-finder entered. They seemed to rise & salute each other.

Etruscan Column & Inflammable Gas fixed their eyes on each other; their tongues went in question & answer, but their thoughts were otherwise employed.

"I don't like his eyes," said Etruscan Column.

"He's a foolish puppy," said Inflammable Gas, smiling on him.

The three Philosophers—the Cynic smiling, the Epicurean seeming studying the flame of the candle & the Pythagorean playing with the cat—listened with open mouths to the edifying discourses.

"Sir," said the Antiquarian, "I have seen these works, & I do affirm that they are no such thing. They seem to me to be the most wretched, paltry, flimsy Stuff that ever—"

"What d'ye say? What d'ye say?" said Inflammable Gas, "why, why I wish I could see you write so."

"Sir," said the Antiquarian, "according to my opinion the author is an errant blockhead."

"Your reason, your reason," said Inflammable Gas, "why, why, I think it very abominable to call a man a blockhead that you know nothing of."

"Reason, Sir?" said the Antiquarian. "I'll give you an example for your reason: As I was walking along the street I saw a vast number of swallows on the rails of an old Gothic square. They seemed to be going on their passage, as Pliny says. As I was looking up, a little *outré* fellow, pulling me by the sleeve, cries, 'Pray, Sir, who do all they belong to?' I turned myself about with great contempt. Said I, 'Go along, you fool.' 'Fool,' said he, 'who do you call fool? I only asked you a civil question.' I had a great mind to have thrashed the fellow, only he was bigger than I." Here Etruscan Column left off.

Inflammable Gas, recollecting himself: "Indeed, I do not think the man was a fool, for he seems to me to have been desirous of inquiring into the works of nature."

"Ha, Ha, Ha," said the Pythagorean.

It was reechoed by Inflammable Gas to overthrow the argument. Etruscan Column, then starting up & clenching both his fists, was prepared to give a formal answer to the company. But Obtuse Angle, entering the room, having made a gentle bow, proceeded to empty his pockets of a vast number of papers, turned about & sat down, wiped his face with his pocket handkerchief &, shutting his eyes, began to scratch his head.

"Well, gentlemen," said he. "What is the cause of strife?"

The Cynic answered, "They are only quarreling about Voltaire."

"Yes," said the Epicurean, "& having a bit of fun with him."

"And," said the Pythagorean, "endeavouring to incorporate their souls with their bodies."

Obtuse Angle, giving a grin, said, "Voltaire understood nothing of the Mathematics, and a man must be a fool i'faith not to understand the Mathematics."

Inflammable Gas, turning round hastily in his chair, said, "Mathematics? He found out a number of Queries in Philosophy."

Obtuse Angle, shutting his eyes & saying that he always understood better when he shut his eyes, said, "In the first place, it is of no use for a man to make Queries, but to solve them, for a man may be a fool & make Queries, but a man must have good sound sense to solve them. A query & an answer are as different as a straight line & a crooked one. Secondly, I, I, I."

"Aye, Secondly, Voltaire's a fool," says the Epicurean.

"Pooh," says the Mathematician, scratching his head with double violence, "it is not worth Quarreling about."

The Antiquarian here got up &, hemming twice to show the strength of his Lungs, said, "But my good Sir, Voltaire was immersed in matter & seems to have understood very little but what he saw before his eyes, like the Animal upon the Pythagorean's lap always playing with its own tail."

"Ha, Ha, Ha," said Inflammable Gas, "he was the Glory of France. I have got a bottle of air that would spread a Plague."

Here the Antiquarian shrugged up his shoulders & was silent, while Inflammable Gas talked for half an hour.

When Steelyard, the lawgiver, coming in stalking, with an act of parliament in his hand, said that it was a shameful thing that acts of parliament should be in a free state; it had so engrossed his mind that he did not salute the company.

Mrs. Gimblet drew her mouth downwards.

CHAPTER 2

Tilly Lally, the Siptippidist, Aradobo, the Dean of Morocco, Miss Gittipin, Mrs. Nannicantipot, Mrs. Sigtagatist, Gibble Gabble, the wife of Inflammable Gas, & Little Scopprell entered the room.

(If I have not presented you with every character in the piece, call me ass.)

CHAPTER 3

In the Moon, as Phebus stood over his oriental Gardening, "O ay, come, I'll sing you a song," said the Cynic.

"The trumpeter shit in his hat," said the Epicurean.

"& clapped it on his head," said the Pythagorean.

"I'll begin again," said the Cynic:

> "Little Phebus came strutting in
> With his fat belly & his round chin.
> What is it you would please to have?
> Ho, Ho,
> I won't let it go at only so-&-so."

Mrs. Gimblet looked as if they meant her. Tilly Lally laughed like a Cherry clapper.

Aradobo asked, "Who was Phebus, Sir?"

Obtuse Angle answered quickly, "He was the God of Physic, Painting, Perspective, Geometry, Geography, Astronomy, Cookery, Chemistry, Mechanics, Tactics, Pathology, Phraseology, Theology, Mythology, Astrology, Osteology, Somatology—in short, every art & science adorned him as beads round his neck."

Here Aradobo looked Astonished & asked if he understood Engraving.

Obtuse Angle Answered, indeed he did.

"Well," said the other, "he was as great as Chatterton."

Tilly Lally turned round to Obtuse Angle & asked who it was that was as great as Chatterton.

"Hay, how should I know?" Answered Obtuse Angle. "Who was It, Aradobo?"

"Why, sir," said he, "the Gentleman that the song was about."

"Ah," said Tilly Lally, "I did not hear it. What was it, Obtuse Angle?"

"Pooh," said he. "Nonsense."

"Mhm," said Tilly Lally.

"It was Phebus," said the Epicurean.

"Ah, that was the Gentleman," said Aradobo.

"Pray, Sir," said Tilly Lally, "who was Phebus?"

Obtuse Angle answered, "The heathens in the old ages used to have Gods that they worshiped, & they used to sacrifice to them. You have read about that in the Bible."

"Ah," said Aradobo, "I thought I had read of Phebus in the Bible."

"Aradobo, you should always think before you speak," said Obtuse Angle.

"Ha, Ha, Ha, he means Pharaoh," said Tilly Lally.

"I am ashamed of you making use of the names in the Bible," said Mrs. Sigtagatist.

"I'll tell you what, Mrs. Sinagain; I don't think there's any harm in it," said Tilly Lally.

"No," said Inflammable Gas. "I have got a camera obscura at home. What was it you was talking about?"

"Law," said Tilly Lally. "What has that to do with Pharaoh?"

"Pho! Nonsense! Hang Pharaoh & all his host," said the Pythagorean. "Sing away, Quid."

Then the Cynic sung:

> "Honour & Genius is all I ask,
> And I ask the Gods no more
>   No more, No more, ⎱ the three Philosophers
>   No more, No more," ⎰ bear Chorus

Here Aradobo sucked his under lip.

CHAPTER 4

"Hang names!" said the Pythagorean. "What's Pharaoh better than Phebus, or Phebus than Pharaoh?"

"Hang them both," said the Cynic.

"Don't be profane," said Mrs. Sigtagatist.

"Why," said Mrs. Nannicantipot, "I don't think it's profane to say, 'hang Pharaoh.'"

"Ah," said Mrs. Sinagain, "I'm sure you ought to hold your tongue, for you never say anything about the scriptures, & you hinder your husband from going to church."

"Ha, Ha," said Inflammable Gas. "What? Don't you like to go to church?"

"No," said Mrs. Nannicantipot, "I think a person may be as good at home."

"If I had not a place of profit that forces me to go to church," said Inflammable Gas, "I'd see the parsons all hanged, a parcel of lying."

"O," said Mrs. Sigtagatist, "if it was not for churches & chapels, I should not have lived so long. There was I, up in a Morning at four o'clock when I was a Girl. I would run like the dickens till I was all in a heat. I would stand till I was ready to sink into the earth. Ah, Mr. Huffcap would kick the bottom of the Pulpit out with Passion, would tear off the sleeve of his Gown & set his wig on fire & throw it at the people. He'd cry & stamp & kick & sweat and all for the good of their souls."

"I'm sure he must be a wicked villain," said Mrs. Nannicantipot, "a passionate wretch. If I was a man, I'd wait at the bottom of the pulpit stairs & knock him down & run away."

"You would, you Ignorant jade! I wish I could see you hit any of the ministers. You deserve to have your ears boxed, you do."

"I'm sure this is not religion," answers the other.

Then Mr. Inflammable Gas ran & shoved his head into the fire & set his hair all in a flame & ran about the room. No, No, he did not. I was only making a fool of you.

CHAPTER 5

Obtuse Angle, Scopprell, Aradobo & Tilly Lally are all met in Obtuse Angle's study:

"Pray," said Aradobo, "is Chatterton a Mathematician?"

"No," said Obtuse Angle. "How can you be so foolish as to think he was?"

"Oh, I did not think he was; I only asked," said Aradobo.

"How could you think he was not, & ask if he was?" said Obtuse Angle.

"Oh no, Sir, I did think he was before you told me, but afterwards I thought he was not."

Obtuse Angle said, "In the first place you thought he was, & then afterwards when I said he was not, you thought he was not. Why, I know that."

"Oh no, sir, I thought that he was not, but I asked to know whether he was."

"How can that be?" said Obtuse Angle. "How could you ask & think that he was not?"

"Why," said he. "It came into my head that he was not."

"Why then," said Obtuse Angle, "you said that he was."

"Did I say so? Law, I did not think I said that."

"Did not he?" said Obtuse Angle.

"Yes," said Scopprell.

"But I meant," said Aradobo, "I, I, I can't think. Law, Sir, I wish you'd tell me how it is."

Then Obtuse Angle put his chin in his hand & said, "Whenever you think, you must always think for yourself."

"How, Sir," said Aradobo. "Whenever I think I must think myself? I think I do. In the first place—," said he with a grin.

"Poo, Poo," said Obtuse Angle, "don't be a fool."

Then Tilly Lally took up a Quadrant & asked, "Is not this a sun dial?"

"Yes," said Scopprell, "but it's broke."

At this moment the three Philosophers entered, and low'ring darkness hovered o'er the assembly.

"Come," said the Epicurean, "let's have some rum & water & hang the mathematics. Come, Aradobo, say something."

Then Aradobo began: "In the first place I think, I think in the first place that Chatterton was clever at Fissic Follogy, Pistinology, Aridology, Arography, Transmography, Phizography, Hogamy, Hatomy & hall that, but in the first place he eat wery little, wickly, that is, he slept very little which he brought into a consumsion, & what was that that he took? Fissic or somethink, & so died."

So all the people in the book entered into the room, & they could not talk any more to the present purpose.

CHAPTER 6

They all went home & left the Philosophers, then Suction Asked if Pindar was not a better Poet than Giotto was a Painter.

"Plutarch has not the life of Giotto," said Sipsop.

"No," said Quid. "To be sure he was an Italian."

"Well," said Suction, "that is not any proof."

"Plutarch was a nasty, ignorant puppy," said Quid. "I hate your sneaking rascals. There's Aradobo in ten or twelve years will be a far superior genius."

"Ah," said the Pythagorean, "Aradobo will make a very clever fellow."

"Why," said Quid, "I think that any natural fool would make a clever fellow if he was properly brought up."

"Ah, hang your reasoning," said the Epicurean. "I hate reasoning. I do everything by my feelings."

"Ah," said Sipsop, "I only wish Jack Tearguts had had the cutting of Plutarch. He understands anatomy better than any of the Ancients. He'll plunge his knife up to the hilt in a single drive and thrust his fist in, and all in the space of a Quarter of an hour. He does not mind their crying, though they cry ever so. He'll Swear at them & keep them down with his fist & tell them that he'll scrape their bones if they don't lay still & be quiet. What the devil should the people in the hospital that have it done for nothing make such a piece of work for?"

"Hang that," said Suction. "Let us have a Song."

Then the Cynic sang:

1

"When old corruption first begun,
Adorned in yellow vest,
He committed on flesh a whoredom,
O, what a wicked beast!

2

"From them a callow babe did spring,   5
And old corruption smiled
To think his race should never end,
For now he had a child.

3

"He call'd him Surgery & fed
The babe with his own milk,   10
For flesh & he could ne'er agree;
She would not let him suck.

4

"And this he always kept in mind
And formed a crooked knife
And ran about with bloody hands   15
To seek his mother's life.

5

"And as he ran to seek his mother,
He met with a dead woman.
He fell in love & married her,
A deed which is not common.   20

6

"She soon grew pregnant & brought forth
Scurvy & spotted fever.
The father grinned & skipped about
And said, 'I'm made forever.

7

" 'For now I have procured
        these imps,   25

I'll try experiments.'
With that he tied poor scurvy down
& stopped up all its vents.

8

"And when the child began to swell
He shouted out aloud,   30
'I've found the dropsy out & soon
Shall do the world more good.'

9

"He took up fever by the neck
And cut out all its spots,
And through the holes which he had made   35
He first discovered guts."

"Ah," said Sipsop, "you think we are rascals, & we think you
are rascals. I do as I choose. What is it to anybody what I do?
I am always unhappy too when I think of Surgery— I don't know;
I do it because I like it. My father does what he likes, & so do
I. I think somehow I'll leave it off. There was a woman having
her cancer cut, & she shrieked so that I was quite sick."

CHAPTER 7

"Good night," said Sipsop.
"Good night," said the other two.
Then Quid & Suction were left alone.
Then said Quid, "I think that Homer is bombast, & Shakespeare
is too wild, & Milton has no feelings. They might be easily out-
done. Chatterton never writ those poems. A parcel of fools going
to Bristol! If I was to go, I'd find it out in a minute, but I've found
it out already."
"If I don't knock them all up next year in the Exhibition, I'll
be hanged," said Suction. "Hang Philosophy. I would not give

a farthing for it. Do all by your feelings, and never think at all about it. I'm hanged if I don't get up tomorrow morning by four o'clock & work Sir Joshua."

"Before ten years are at an end," said Quid, "how I will work these poor milksop devils, an ignorant pack of wretches!"

So they went to bed.

CHAPTER 8

Steelyard the Lawgiver, sitting at his table taking extracts from Hervey's Meditations among the tombs & Young's Night thoughts: "He is not able to hurt me," said he, "more than making me Constable or taking away the parish business. Hah!

'My crop of corn is but a field of tares.'

Says Jerome. Happiness is not for us poor crawling reptiles of the earth. Talk of happiness & happiness. It's no such thing. Every person has a something.

Hear then the pride & knowledge of a Sailor,
His sprit sail, fore sail, main sail & his mizen,
A poor frail man, god wot, I know none frailer,
I know no greater sinner than John Taylor.

'If I had only myself to care for, I'd soon make Double Elephant look foolish, & Filigree Work I hope shall live to see.

'The wreck of matter & the crush of worlds,'

as Younge says."

Obtuse Angle entered the Room. "What news, Mr. Steelyard?"

"I am Reading Theron & Aspasio," said he.

Obtuse Angle took up the books one by one. "I don't find it here," said he.

"Oh no," said the other. "It was the meditations."

Obtuse Angle took up the book & read till the other was quite tired out.

Then Scopprell & Miss Gittipin coming in, Scopprell took up a book & read the following passage:

"An Easy of Huming Understanding, by John Lookye Gent."

"John Locke," said Obtuse Angle.

"O, ay, Lock," said Scopprell.

"Now here," said Miss Gittipin, "I never saw such company in my life. You are always talking of your books. I like to be where we talk. You had better take a walk, that we may have some pleasure. I am sure I never see any pleasure. There's Double Elephant's Girls; they have their own way; & there's Miss Filigree Work. She goes out in her coaches, & her footman & her maids, & Stormonts & Balloon hats, & a pair of Gloves every day, & the sorrows of Werter, & Robinsons, & the Queen of France's Puss colour; & my Cousin Gibble Gabble says that I am like nobody else. I might as well be in a nunnery. There they go in Post Chaises & Stages to Vauxhall & Ranelagh. And I hardly know what a coach is, except when I go to Mr. Jacko's. He knows what riding is, & his wife is the most agreeable woman. You hardly know she has a tongue in her head. And he is the funniest fellow, & I do believe he'll go in partnership with his master, & they have black servants lodge at their house. I never saw such a place in my life. He says he has Six & twenty rooms in his house, and I believe it, & he is not such a liar as Quid thinks he is."

"Poo, Poo, hold your tongue," said the Lawgiver.

This quite provoked Miss Gittipin to interrupt her in her favourite topic, & she proceeded to use every Provoking speech that ever she could, & he bore it more like a Saint than a Lawgiver, and with great Solemnity he addressed the company in these words:

"They call women the weakest vessel, but I think they are the strongest. A girl has always more tongue than a boy. I have seen a little brat no higher than a nettle, & she had as much tongue as a city clerk, but a boy would be such a fool, not have anything to say, and if anybody asked him a question, he would put his head into a hole & hide it. I am sure I take but little pleasure. You have as much pleasure as I have. There I stand & bear every fool's insult. If I had only myself to care for, I'd wring off their noses."

To this Scopprell answered, "I think the Ladies' discourses, Mr. Steelyard, are some of them more improving than any book. That is the way I have got some of my knowledge."

"Then," said Miss Gittipin, "Mr. Scopprell, do you know the song of Phebe and Jellicoe?"

"No, Miss," said Scopprell.

Then she repeated these verses, while Steelyard walked about the room:

"Phebe, dressed like beauty's Queen,
Jellicoe in faint peagreen,
Sitting all beneath a grot
Where the little lambkins trot.

"Maidens dancing, loves a-sporting,   5
All the country folks a-courting,
Susan, Johnny, Bet & Joe
Lightly tripping on a row.

"Happy people, who can be
In happiness compared with ye?   10
The Pilgrim with his crook & hat
Sees your happiness complete."

"A charming Song, indeed, miss," said Scopprell. Here they received a summons for a merrymaking at the Philosopher's house.

CHAPTER 9

"I say this evening we'll all get drunk. I say, dash, an Anthem, an Anthem!" said Suction.

"Lo, the Bat with Leathern wing,
Winking & blinking,
Winking & blinking,
Winking & blinking,
Like Doctor Johnson."   5

Quid: "'Oho,' said Doctor Johnson
To Scipio Africanus,
'If you don't own me a Philosopher
I'll kick your Roman Anus.'"

Suction: "'Aha,' To Doctor Johnson   10
Said Scipio Africanus,

'Lift up my Roman Petticoat
And kiss my Roman Anus.'"

"And the Cellar goes down with a Step." (Grand Chorus)

"Ho, Ho, Ho, Ho, Ho, Ho, Ho, Hooooo, my poooooor siiides!
I, I should die if I was to live here," said Scopprell. "Ho, Ho, Ho,
Ho, Ho!"

1st Vo.   "Want Matches?"
2nd Vo.   "Yes, Yes, Yes."
1st Vo.   "Want Matches?"
2nd Vo.   "No."

1st Vo.   "Want Matches?"
2nd Vo.   "Yes, Yes, Yes."
1st Vo.   "Want Matches?"
2nd Vo.   "No."

Here was Great confusion & disorder. Aradobo said that the
boys in the street sing something very pretty & funny about Matches. Then Mrs. Nannicantipot sung:

"I cry my matches as far as Guild hall.
God bless the duke & his aldermen all."

Then sung Scopprell:

"I ask the Gods no more,
        no more, no more."

Then, said Suction, "Come, Mr. Lawgiver, your song." And
the Lawgiver sung:

"As I walked forth one May morning
To see the fields so pleasant & so gay,
O there did I spy a young maiden sweet,
Among the Violets that smell so sweet,
        Smell so sweet,
        Smell so sweet,
Among the Violets that smell so sweet."

"Hang your Violets; here's your Rum & water."
"O, ay," said Tilly Lally. "Joe Bradley & I was going along one
day in the Sugar house. Joe Bradley saw—for he had but one eye—

saw a treacle Jar. So he goes of his blind side & dips his hand up to the shoulder in treacle. 'Here, lick, lick, lick,' said he. Ha, Ha, Ha, Ha, Ha! For he had but one eye. Ha, Ha, Ha, Ho!"

Then sung Scopprell:

> "And I ask the Gods no more,
>   no more, no more,
>   no more, more."

"Miss Gittipin," said he, "you sing like a harpsichord. Let your bounty descend to our fair ears and favour us with a fine song."

Then she sung:

> "This frog he would a-wooing ride,
>   Kitty alone, Kitty alone.
> This frog he would a-wooing ride,
> Kitty alone & I.
> Sing cock I cary, Kitty alone,
> Kitty alone, Kitty alone,
> Cock I cary, Kitty alone,
> Kitty alone & I."

"Charming, truly elegant," said Scopprell.

"And I ask the gods no more."

"Hang your Serious Songs," said Sipsop, & he sung as follows:

> "Fa ra so bo ro
>   Fa ra bo ra
> Sa ba ra ra ba rare roro
> Sa ra ra ra bo ro ro ro
> Radara
> Sarapodo no flo ro."

"Hang Italian songs; let's have English," said Quid. "English Genius forever! Here I go:

> "Hail, Matrimony, made of Love,
> To thy wide gates how great a drove
> On purpose to be yoked do come,

Widows & maids & Youths also,
That lightly trip on beauty's toe,   5
Or sit on beauty's bum.

"Hail, fingerfooted, lovely Creatures,
The females of our human Natures,
Formed to suckle all Mankind.
'Tis you that come in time of need,   10
Without you we should never Breed
Or any Comfort find.

"For if a Damsel's blind or lame,
Or Nature's hand has crooked her frame,
Or if she's deaf or is wall-eyed,   15
Yet if her heart is well inclined,
Some tender lover she shall find
That panteth for a Bride.

"The universal Poultice this,
To cure whatever is amiss   20
In damsel or in Widow gay.
It makes them smile, it makes them skip;
Like Birds just cured of the pip
They chirp & hop away.

"Then come, ye Maidens; come, ye Swains,   25
Come & be eased of all your pains
In Matrimony's Golden cage."

"Go & be hanged!" said Scopprell. "How can you have the
face to make game of Matrimony?"
Then Quid called upon Obtuse Angle for a Song, & he, wiping his face & looking on the corner of the ceiling, Sang:

"To be or not to be
Of great capacity
Like Sir Isaac Newton,
Or Locke, or Doctor South,
Or Sherlock upon death?   5
I'd rather be Sutton.

"For he did build a house
For aged men & youth
With walls of brick & stone.
He furnished it within   10
With whatever he could win,
And all his own.

"He drew out of the Stocks
His money in a box
And sent his servant   15
To Green the Bricklayer,
And to the Carpenter,
He was so fervent.

"The chimneys were three score,
The windows many more;   20
And for convenience
He sinks & gutters made,
And all the way he paved
To hinder pestilence.

"Was not this a good man,   25
Whose life was but a span
Whose name was Sutton,
As Locke, or Doctor South,
Or Sherlock upon Death,
Or Sir Isaac Newton?"   30

The Lawgiver was very attentive & begged to have it sung over
again & again, till the company were tired & insisted on the Lawgiver singing a song himself, which he readily complied with.

"This city & this country has brought forth many
    mayors
To sit in state & give forth laws out of their old
    oak chairs.
With face as brown as any nut with drinking of strong ale.
Good English hospitality, O then it did not fail!

"With scarlet gowns & broad gold lace would make
    a yeoman sweat,   5

With stockings rolled above their knees & shoes as
    black as jet,
With eating beef & drinking beer, O they were stout
    & hale!
Good English hospitality, O then it did not fail!

"Thus sitting at the table wide, the Mayor & Aldermen
Were fit to give law to the city; each eat as much as
    ten.   10
The hungry poor entered the hall to eat good beef & ale.
Good English hospitality, O then it did not fail!"

Here they gave a shout, & the company broke up.

CHAPTER 10

Thus these happy Islanders spent their time, but felicity does
not last long, for being met at the house of Inflammable Gas the
Wind-finder, the following affairs happened:

"Come, Flammable," said Gibble Gabble, "& let's enjoy ourselves. Bring the Puppets."

"Hay, Hay," said he, "you sho, why ya ya, how can you be so
foolish? Ha, Ha, Ha! She calls the experiments puppets!"

Then he went upstairs & loaded the maid with glasses & brass
tubes & magic pictures.

"Here, ladies & gentlemen," said he, "I'll show you a louse or
a flea or a butterfly or a cock chafer, the blade bone of a tittle
back. No, No! Here's a bottle of wind that I took up in the bog
house. O dear, O dear, the water's got into the sliders! Look here,
Gibble Gabble! Lend me your handkerchief, Tilly Lally."

Tilly Lally took out his handkerchief, which smeared the glass
worse than ever.

Then he screwed it on; then he took the sliders; & then he set
up the glasses for the Ladies to view the pictures. Thus he was
employed & quite out of breath.

While Tilly Lally & Scopprell were pumping at the air pump,
"Smack," went the glass.

"Hang," said Tilly Lally.

Inflammable Gas turned short round & threw down the table & Glasses & Pictures, & broke the bottles of wind & let out the Pestilence. He saw the Pestilence fly out of the bottle & cried out while he ran out of the room, "Come out, come out; we are putrefied; we are corrupted; our lungs are destroyed with the Flogiston. This will spread a plague all through the Island."

He was downstairs the very first. On the back of him came all the others in a heap.

So they need not bidding go.

CHAPTER 11

Another merry meeting at the house of Steelyard the Law-giver.

After Supper, Steelyard & Obtuse Angle had pumped Inflammable Gas quite dry. They played at forfeits & tried every method to get good humour.

Said Miss Gittipin: "Pray, Mr. Obtuse Angle, sing us a song. Then he sung:

> "Upon a Holy Thursday, their innocent faces clean,
> The children walking two & two in grey & blue & green,
> Grey-headed beadles walked before with wands as white
>   as snow,
> Till into the high dome of Paul's they like Thames'
>   waters flow.
>
> "O, what a multitude they seemed, these flowers of
>   London town,   5
> Seated in companies they sit with radiance all their own.
> The hum of multitudes were there, but multitudes of
>   lambs,
> Thousands of little girls & boys raising their innocent
>   hands.
>
> "Then like a mighty wind they raise to heaven the
>   voice of song,
> Or like harmonious thunderings the seats of heaven
>   among.   10

> Beneath them sit the rev'rend men, the guardians of
>   the poor.
> Then cherish pity lest you drive an angel from your
>   door."

After this, they all sat silent for a quarter of an hour and Mrs. Nannicantipot said, "It puts me in Mind of my mother's song:

> "When the tongues of children are
>   heard on the green,
> And laughing is heard on the hill,
> My heart is at rest within my breast,
> And everything else is still.
>
> "Then come home, my children, the sun is gone down,   5
> And the dews of night arise.
> Come, Come, leave off play, & let us away
> Till the morning appears in the skies.
>
> "No, No, let us play, for it is yet day,
> And we cannot go to sleep.   10
> Besides in the Sky the little birds fly,
> And the meadows are covered with Sheep.
>
> "Well, Well, go & play till the light fades away,
> And then go home to bed.
> The little ones leaped & shouted & laughed,   15
> And all the hills echoed."

Then sung Quid:

> "O father, father, where are you going?
> O do not walk so fast!
> O speak, father, speak to your little boy,
> Or else I shall be lost!
>
> "The night it was dark, & no father was there,   5
> And the child was wet with dew.
> The mire was deep, & the child did weep,
> And away the vapour flew."

Here nobody could sing any longer, till Tilly Lally plucked up a spirit, & he sung:

"O, I say you, Joe,
Throw us the ball.
I've a good mind to go
And leave you all.
I never saw saw such a bowler,   5
To bowl the ball in a tansey
And to clean it with my handkercher
Without saying a word.

"That Bill's a foolish fellow;
He has given me a black eye.   10
He does not know how to handle a bat
Any more than a dog or a cat.
He has knocked down the wicket
And broke the stumps
And runs without shoes to save his pumps."   15

Here a laugh began, and Miss Gittipin sung:

"Leave, O leave me to my sorrows
Here, I'll sit & fade away.
Till I'm nothing but a spirit,
And I lose this form of clay.

"Then if chance along this forest   5
Any walk in pathless ways,
Through the gloom he'll see my shadow,
Hear my voice upon the Breeze."

The Lawgiver all the while sat delighted to see them in such
a serious humour.

"Mr. Scopprell," said he, "you must be acquainted with a great
many songs."

"O, dear sir, Ho, Ho, Ho, I am no singer. I must beg of one of
these tenderhearted ladies to sing for me."

They all declined, & he was forced to sing himself:

"There's Doctor Clash
And Signior Falalasole;
O they sweep in the cash
Into their purse hole
Fa me la sol, La me fa Sol.   5

"Great A, little A,
Bouncing B,
Play away, Play away,
You're out of the key.
Fa me la sol, La me fa sol.   10

"Musicians should have
A pair of very good ears
And Long fingers & thumbs,
And not like clumsy bears.
Fa me la sol, La me fa sol.   15

"Gentlemen, Gentlemen,
Rap, Rap, Rap,
Fiddle, Fiddle, Fiddle,
Clap, Clap, Clap.
Fa me la sol, La me fa sol."   20

"Hm," said the Lawgiver, "funny enough. "Let's have Handel's waterpiece."

Sipsop sung:

"A crowned king,
On a white horse sitting
With his trumpets sounding
And Banners flying
Through the clouds of smoke he makes his way.   5

And the shout of his thousands fills his heart with rejoicing
    & victory.
And the shout of his thousands fills his heart with rejoicing
    & victory.
Victory! Victory! 'Twas William, the prince of Orange."
      [Here a leaf or more is missing.]
thus Illuminating the Manuscript."

"Ay," said she, "that would be excellent."

"Then," said he, "I would have all the writing Engraved instead of Printed, & at every other leaf a high finished print all in three Volumes folio, & sell them a hundred pounds apiece. They would print off two thousand."

"Then," said she, "whoever will not have them will be ignorant fools & will not deserve to live."

"Don't you think I have something of the Goat's face?" says he.

"Very like a Goat's face," she answered.

"I think your face," said he, "is like that noble beast, the Tiger."

"Oh, I was at Mrs. Sicknakens, & I was speaking of my abilities, but their nasty hearts, poor devils, are eat up with envy. They envy me my abilities & all the Women envy your abilities, my dear."

"They hate people who are of higher abilities than their nasty filthy selves. But do you outface them, & then Strangers will see you have an opinion."

"Now I think we should do as much good as we can when we are at Mr. Femality's. Do you snap, & take me up, and I will fall into such a passion I'll hollo, and stamp & frighten all the People there & show them what truth is."

At this Instant Obtuse Angle came in.

"Oh, I am glad you are come," said Quid.

A Descriptive Catalogue of Pictures

Poetical and Historical Inventions

Painted by William Blake, in Water Colours, Being the Ancient Method of Fresco Painting Restored; and Drawings, For Public Inspection, and for Sale by Private Contract.

(1809)

CONDITIONS OF SALE

I. One third of the price to be paid at the time of Purchase and remainder on Delivery.

II. The Pictures and Drawings to remain in the Exhibition till its close, which will be the 29th of September 1809; and the Picture of the Canterbury Pilgrims, which is to be engraved, will be Sold only on condition of its remaining in the Artist's hands twelve months, when it will be delivered to the Buyer.

PREFACE

The eye that can prefer the Colouring of Titian and Rubens to that of Michael Angelo and Rafael ought to be modest and to doubt its own powers. Connoisseurs talk as if Rafael and Michael Angelo had never seen the colouring of Titian or Correggio. They ought to know that Correggio was born two years before Michael Angelo, and Titian but four years after. Both Rafael and Michael Angelo knew the Venetian, and contemned and rejected all he did with the utmost disdain as that which is fabricated for the purpose to destroy art.

Mr. B. appeals to the Public from the judgment of those narrow blinking eyes that have too long governed art in a dark corner. The eyes of stupid cunning never will be pleased with the work any more than with the look of self-devoting genius. The quarrel of the Florentine with the Venetian is not because he does not understand Drawing, but because he does not understand Colouring. How should he, he who does not know how to draw a hand or a foot, know how to colour it?

538

Colouring does not depend on where the Colours are put, but on where the lights and darks are put, and all depends on Form or Outline, On where that is put. Where that is wrong, the Colouring never can be right; and it is always wrong in Titian and Correggio, Rubens and Rembrandt. Till we get rid of Titian and Correggio, Rubens and Rembrandt, We never shall equal Rafael and Albert Dürer, Michael Angelo and Julio Romano.

NUMBER I

The spiritual form of Nelson guiding Leviathan, in whose wreathings are infolded the Nations of the Earth.

Clearness and precision have been the chief objects in painting these Pictures. Clear colours, unmudded by oil, and firm and determinate lineaments, unbroken by shadows, which ought to display and not to hide form, as is the practice of the latter Schools of Italy and Flanders.

NUMBER II, ITS COMPANION

The spiritual form of Pitt, guiding Behemoth; he is that Angel who, pleased to perform the Almighty's orders, rides on the whirlwind, directing the storms of war. He is ordering the Reaper to reap the Vine of the Earth and the Plowman to plow up the Cities and Towers.

This Picture also is a proof of the power of colours unsullied with oil or with any cloggy vehicle. Oil has falsely been supposed to give strength to colours, but a little consideration must show the fallacy of this opinion. Oil will not drink or absorb colour enough to stand the test of very little time and of the air. It deadens every colour it is mixed with, at its first mixture, and in a little time becomes a yellow mask over all that it touches. Let the works of modern Artists since Rubens' time witness the villainy of someone at that time, who first brought oil Painting into general opinion and practice, since which we have never had a Picture painted that could show itself by the side of an earlier production. Whether Rubens or Vandyke, or both, were guilty of this villainy is to be inquired in another work on Painting, and who first forged the silly story and known falsehood about John of Bruges inventing oil colours; in the meantime let it be observed that before Vandyke's time, and in his time, all the genuine Pictures are on Plaster or Whiting grounds, and none since.

The two Pictures of Nelson and Pitt are compositions of a mythological cast, similar to those Apotheoses of Persian, Hindu, and Egyptian Antiquity, which are still preserved on rude monuments, being copies from some stupendous originals now lost or perhaps buried till some happier age. The Artist, having been taken in vision into the ancient republics, monarchies, and patriarchates of Asia, has seen those wonderful originals called in the Sacred Scriptures the Cherubim, which were sculptured and painted on walls of Temples, Towers, Cities, Palaces, and erected in the highly cultivated states of Egypt, Moab, Edom, Aram, among the Rivers of Paradise, being originals from which the Greeks and Hetrurians copied Hercules, Farnese, Venus of Medicis, Apollo Belvedere, and all the grand works of ancient art. They were executed in a very superior style to those justly admired copies, being with their accompaniments terrific and grand in the highest degree. The Artist has endeavoured to emulate the grandeur of those seen in his vision and to apply it to modern Heroes, on a smaller scale.

No man can believe that either Homer's Mythology, or Ovid's were the production of Greece, or of Latium; neither will anyone believe that the Greek statues, as they are called, were the invention of Greek Artists; perhaps the Torso is the only original work remaining; all the rest are evidently copies, though fine ones, from greater works of the Asiatic Patriarchs. The Greek Muses are daughters of Mnemosyne, or Memory, and not of Inspiration or Imagination, therefore not authors of such sublime conceptions. Those wonderful originals seen in my visions were some of them one hundred feet in height; some were painted as pictures, and some carved as *basso relievos,* and some as groups of statues, all containing mythological and recondite meaning, where more is meant than meets the eye. The Artist wishes it was now the fashion to make such monuments, and then he should not doubt of having a national commission to execute these two Pictures on a scale that is suitable to the grandeur of the nation, who is the parent of his heroes, in high finished fresco, where the colours would be as pure and as permanent as precious stones, though the figures were one hundred feet in height.

All Frescoes are as high finished as miniatures or enamels, and they are known to be unchangeable; but oil, being a body itself, will drink or absorb very little colour, and, changing yellow, and at length brown, destroys every colour it is mixed with, especially every delicate colour. It turns every permanent white to a yellow and brown putty, and has compelled the use of that destroyer of colour, white lead, which, when its protecting oil is evaporated, will become lead again. This is an awful thing to say to oil Painters; they may call it madness, but it is true. All the genuine old little Pictures, called Cabinet Pictures, are in fresco and not in oil. Oil was not used except by blundering ignorance till after Vandyke's time, but the art of fresco painting being lost, oil became a fetter to genius and a dungeon to art. But one convincing proof among many others that these assertions are true is that real gold and silver cannot be used with oil, as they are in all the old pictures and in Mr. B.'s frescoes.

NUMBER III

Sir Jeffery Chaucer and the nine and twenty Pilgrims on their journey to Canterbury.

The time chosen is early morning, before sunrise, when the jolly company are just quitting the Tabarde Inn. The Knight and Squire with the Squire's Yeoman lead the Procession; next follow the youthful Abbess, her nun and three priests; her greyhounds attend her.

> "Of small hounds had she that she fed
> With roast flesh, milk and wastel bread."

Next follow the Friar and Monk; then the Tapiser, the Pardoner, and the Summoner and Manciple. After these "Our Host," who occupies the center of the cavalcade, directs them to the Knight as the person who would be likely to commence their task of each telling a tale in their order. After the Host follow the Shipman, the Haberdasher, the Dyer, the Franklin, the Physician, the Plowman, the Lawyer, the poor Parson, the Merchant, the Wife of Bath, the Miller, the Cook, the Oxford Scholar, Chaucer himself; and the Reeve comes as Chaucer has described:

> "And ever he rode hinderest of the rout."

These last are issuing from the gateway of the Inn; the Cook and the Wife of Bath are both taking their morning's draught of comfort. Spectators stand at the gateway of the Inn and are composed of an old Man, a Woman and Children.

The Landscape is an eastward view of the country, from the Tabarde Inn, in Southwark, as it may be supposed to have appeared in Chaucer's time, interspersed with cottages and villages; the first beams of the Sun are seen above the horizon; some buildings and spires indicate the situation of the great City; the Inn is a Gothic building, which Thynne in his Glossary says was the lodging of the Abbot of Hyde, by Winchester. On the Inn is inscribed its title, and a proper advantage is taken of this circumstance to describe the subject of the Picture. The words written over the gateway of the Inn are as follow: "The Tabarde Inn, by Henry Baillie, the lodgynge-house for Pilgrims, who journey to Saint Thomas's Shrine at Canterbury."

The characters of Chaucer's Pilgrims are the characters which compose all ages and nations: as one age falls, another rises different to mortal sight, but to immortals only the same; for we see the same characters repeated again and again, in animals, vegetables, minerals, and in men; nothing new occurs in identical existence; Accident ever varies; Substance can never suffer change nor decay.

Of Chaucer's characters, as described in his Canterbury Tales, some of the names or titles are altered by time, but the characters themselves forever remain unaltered, and consequently they are the physiognomies or lineaments of universal human life, beyond which Nature never steps. Names alter; things never alter. I have known multitudes of those who would have been monks in the age of monkery, who in this deistical age are deists. As Newton numbered the stars, and as Linneus numbered the plants, so Chaucer numbered the classes of men.

The Painter has consequently varied the heads and forms of his personages into all Nature's varieties; the Horses he has also varied to accord to their Riders, the Costume is correct according to authentic monuments.

The Knight and Squire with the Squire's Yeoman lead the procession, as Chaucer has also placed them first in his prologue. The Knight is a true Hero, a good, great and wise man; his whole-length portrait on horseback, as written by Chaucer, cannot be surpassed. He has spent his life in the field; has ever been a conqueror, and is that species of character which in every age stands as the guardian of man against the oppressor. His son is like him with the germ of perhaps greater perfection still, as he blends literature and the arts with his warlike studies. Their dress and their horses are of the first rate, without ostentation, and with all the true grandeur that unaffected simplicity when in high rank always displays. The Squire's Yeoman is also a great character, a man perfectly knowing in his profession:

> "And in his hand he bare a mighty bow."

Chaucer describes here a mighty man; one who in war is the worthy attendant on noble heroes.

The Prioress follows these with her female chaplain.

> "Another Nonne also with her had she,
> That was her Chaplaine and Priests three."

This Lady is described also as of the first rank, rich and honoured. She has certain peculiarities and little delicate affectations, not unbecoming in her, being accompanied with what is truly grand and really polite; her person and face Chaucer has described with minuteness; it is very elegant and was the beauty of our ancestors till after Elizabeth's time, when voluptuousness and folly began to be accounted beautiful.

Her companion and her three priests were no doubt all perfectly delineated in those parts of Chaucer's work which are now lost; we ought to suppose them suitable attendants on rank and fashion.

The Monk follows these with the Friar. The Painter has also grouped with these the Pardoner and the Summoner and the Manciple, and has here also introduced one of the rich citizens of London. Characters likely to ride in company, all being above the common rank in life, or attendants on those who were so.

For the Monk is described by Chaucer as a man of the first rank in society, noble, rich and expensively attended: he is a leader of the age, with certain humourous accompaniments in his character that do not degrade, but render him an object of dignified mirth, but also with other accompaniments not so respectable.

The Friar is a character also of a mixed kind.

> "A friar there was, a wanton and a merry."

But in his office he is said to be a "full solemn man," eloquent, amorous, witty and satirical; young, handsome and rich, he is a complete rogue; with constitutional gaiety enough to make him a master of all the pleasures of the world.

> "His neck was white as the flour de lis,
> Thereto strong he was as a champioun."

It is necessary here to speak of Chaucer's own character, that I may set certain mistaken critics right in their conception of the humour and fun that occurs on the journey. Chaucer is himself the great poetical observer of men, who in every age is born to record and eternize its acts. This he does as a master, as a father and superior, who looks down on their little follies from the Emperor to the Miller, sometimes with severity, oftener with joke and sport.

Accordingly Chaucer has made his Monk a great tragedian, one who studied poetical art; So much so, that the generous Knight is, in the compassionate dictates of his soul, compelled to cry out:

> "Ho quoth the Knyght, good Sir, no more of this,
> That ye have said, is right yenough I wis;

> And mokell more, for little heaviness,
> Is right enough for much folk as I guesse.
> I say for me, it is a great disease,
> Whereas men have been in wealth and ease;
> To heare of their sudden fall alas,
> And the contrary is joy and solas."

The Monk's definition of tragedy in the proem to his tale is worth repeating:

> "Tragedie is to tell a certain story,
> As old books us maken memory;
> Of hem that stood in great prosperity.
> And be fallen out of high degree,
> Into miserie and ended wretchedly."

Though a man of luxury, pride and pleasure, he is a master of art and learning, though affecting to despise it. Those who can think that the proud Huntsman and noble Housekeeper, Chaucer's Monk, is intended for a buffoon or burlesque character know little of Chaucer.

For the Host, who follows this group and holds the center of the cavalcade, is a first-rate character, and his jokes are no trifles; they are always, though uttered with audacity, and equally free with the Lord and the Peasant, they are always substantially and weightily expressive of knowledge and experience; Henry Baillie, the keeper of the greatest Inn of the greatest City; for such was the Tabarde Inn in Southwark, near London; our Host was also a leader of the age.

By way of illustration, I instance Shakespeare's Witches in *Macbeth*. Those who dress them for the stage consider them as wretched old women, and not as Shakespeare intended, the Goddesses of Destiny; this shows how Chaucer has been misunderstood in his sublime work. Shakespeare's Fairies also are the rulers of the vegetable world, and so are Chaucer's; let them be so considered, and then the poet will be understood, and not else.

But I have omitted to speak of a very prominent character, the Pardoner, the Age's Knave, who always commands and domineers over the high and low vulgar. This man is sent in every age for a rod and scourge, and for a blight, for a trial of men, to divide the classes of men; he is in the most holy sanctuary, and he is suffered by Providence for wise ends and has also his great use and his grand leading destiny.

His companion, the Summoner, is also a Devil of the first magnitude, grand, terrific, rich and honoured in the rank of which he holds the destiny. The uses to society are perhaps equal of the Devil and of the Angel; their sublimity who can dispute?

> "In daunger had he at his own gise,
> The young girls of his diocese,
> And he knew well their counsel, &c."

The principal figure in the next group is the Good Parson, an Apostle, a real Messenger of Heaven, sent in every age for its light and its warmth. This man is beloved and venerated by all and neglected by all: He serves all and is served by none; he is, according to Christ's definition, the greatest of his age. Yet he is a Poor Parson of a town. Read Chaucer's description of the Good Parson and bow the head and the knee to him who in every age sends us such a burning and a shining light. Search, O ye rich and powerful, for these men and obey their counsel; then shall the golden age return. But alas, you will not easily distinguish him from the Friar or the Pardoner; they also are "full solemn men," and their counsel you will continue to follow.

I have placed by his side the Sergeant at Law, who appears delighted to ride in his company, and, between him and his brother, the Plowman, as I wish men of Law would always ride with them and take their counsel, especially in all difficult points. Chaucer's Lawyer is a character of great venerableness, a Judge, and a real master of the jurisprudence of his age.

The Doctor of Physic is in this group, and the Franklin, the voluptuous country gentleman, contrasted with the Physician, and on his other hand, with two Citizens of London. Chaucer's characters live age after age. Every age is a Canterbury Pilgrimage; we all pass on, each sustaining one or other of these characters; nor can a child be born who is not one of these characters of Chaucer. The Doctor of Physic is described as the first of his profession: perfect, learned, completely Master and Doctor in his art. Thus the reader will observe that Chaucer makes every one of his characters perfect in his kind, every one is an Antique Statue, the image of a class, and not of an imperfect individual.

This group also would furnish substantial matter, on which volumes might be written. The Franklin is one who keeps open table, who is the genius of eating and drinking, the Bacchus; as the Doctor of Physic is the Esculapius, the Host is the Silenus, the Squire is the Apollo, the Miller is the Hercules, &c. Chaucer's characters are a description of the eternal Principles that exist in all ages. The Franklin is voluptuousness itself most nobly portrayed:

> "It snewed in his house of meat and drink."

The Plowman is simplicity itself, with wisdom and strength for its stamina. Chaucer has divided the ancient character of Hercules between his Miller and his Plowman. Benevolence is the Plowman's great characteristic; he is thin with excessive labour, and not with old age, as some have supposed.

> "He would thresh and thereto dike and delve
> For Christe's sake, for every poore wight,
> Withouten hire, if it lay in his might."

Visions of these eternal principles or characters of human life appear to poets in all ages; the Grecian gods were the ancient Cherubim of Phoenicia; but the Greeks and, since them, the Moderns, have neglected to subdue the gods of Priam. These Gods are visions of the eternal attributes, or divine names, which, when erected into gods, become destructive to humanity. They ought to be the servants, and not the masters of man, or of society. They ought to be made to sacrifice to Man, and not man compelled to sacrifice to them; for when separated from man or humanity, who is Jesus the Saviour, the vine of eternity, they are thieves and rebels, they are destroyers.

The Plowman of Chaucer is Hercules in his supreme eternal state, divested of his spectrous shadow, which is the Miller, a terrible fellow, such as exists in all times and places for the trial of men, to astonish every neighbourhood with brutal strength and courage, to get rich and powerful to curb the pride of Man.

The Reeve and the Manciple are two characters of the most consummate worldly wisdom. The Shipman, or Sailor, is a similar genius of Ulyssean art, but with the highest courage superadded.

The Citizens and their Cook are each leaders of a class. Chaucer has been somehow made to number four citizens, which would make his whole company, himself included, thirty-one. But he says there was but nine and twenty in his company.

> "Full nine and twenty in a company."

The Webbe, or Weaver, and the Tapiser, or Tapestry Weaver, appear to me to be the same person; but this is only an opinion, for full nine and twenty may signify one more or less. But I dare say that Chaucer wrote "A Webbe Dyer," that is, a Cloth Dyer.

> "A Webbe Dyer and a Tapiser."

The Merchant cannot be one of the Three Citizens, as his dress is different, and his character is more marked, whereas Chaucer says of his rich citizens:

> "All were yclothed in o liverie."

The characters of Women Chaucer has divided into two classes, the Lady Prioress and the Wife of Bath. Are not these leaders of the ages of men? The lady prioress, in some ages, predominates; and in some the wife of Bath, in whose character Chaucer has been equally minute and exact, because she is also a scourge and a blight. I shall say no more of her, nor expose what Chaucer has left hidden; let the young reader study what he has said of her; it is useful as a scarecrow. There are of such characters born too many for the peace of the world.

I come at length to the Clerk of Oxenford. This character varies from that of Chaucer, as the contemplative philosopher varies from the poetical genius. There are always these two classes of learned sages, the poetical and the philosophical. The painter has put them side by side, as if the youthful clerk had put himself under the tuition of the mature poet. Let the Philosopher always be the servant and scholar of inspiration and all will be happy.

Such are the characters that compose this Picture, which was painted in self-defense against the insolent and envious imputation of unfitness for finished and scientific art; and this imputation most artfully and industriously endeavoured to be propagated among the public by ignorant hirelings. The painter courts comparison with his competitors, who, having received fourteen hundred guineas and more from the profits of his designs, in that well-known work, Designs for Blair's Grave, have left him to shift for himself, while others, more obedient to an employer's opinions and directions, are employed, at a great expense, to produce works, in succession to his, by which they acquired public patronage. This has hitherto been his lot—to get patronage for others and then to be left and neglected, and his work, which gained that patronage, cried down as eccentricity and madness, as unfinished and neglected by the artist's violent temper; he is sure the works now exhibited will give the lie to such aspersions.

Those who say that men are led by interest are knaves. A knavish character will often say, of what interest is it to me to do so-and-so? I answer, of none at all, but the contrary, as you well know. It is of malice and envy that you have done this; hence I am aware of you, because I know that you act not from interest but from malice, even to your own destruction. It is therefore become a duty which Mr. B. owes to the Public, who have always recognized him, and patronized him, however hidden by artifices, that he should not suffer such things to be done or be hindered from the public Exhibition of his finished productions by any calumnies in future.

The character and expression in this picture could never have been produced with Rubens' light and shadow, or with Rembrandt's, or anything Venetian or Flemish. The Venetian and Flemish practice is broken lines, broken masses, and broken colours. Mr. B.'s practice is unbroken lines, unbroken masses, and unbroken colours. Their art is to lose form, his art is to find form, and to keep it. His arts are opposite to theirs in all things.

As there is a class of men, whose whole delight is the destruction of men, so there is a class of artists, whose whole art and science is fabricated for the purpose of destroying art. Who these are is soon known: "by their works ye shall know them." All who endeavour to raise up a style against Rafael, Mich. Angelo, and the Antique, those who separate Painting from Drawing who look if a picture is well-Drawn and, if it is, immediately cry out that it cannot be well-Coloured—those are the men.

But to show the stupidity of this class of men, nothing need be done but to examine my rival's prospectus.

The two first characters in Chaucer, the Knight and the Squire, he has put among his rabble; and indeed his prospectus calls the Squire the fop of Chaucer's age. Now hear Chaucer:

> "Of his Stature, he was of even length,
> And wonderly deliver, and of great strength;
> And he had be sometime in Chivauchy,
> In Flanders, in Artois, and in Picardy,
> And borne him well as of so litele space."

Was this a fop?

> "Well could he sit a horse, and faire ride,
> He could songs make, and eke well indite
> Just, and eke dance, pourtray, and well write.

Was this a fop?

> "Curteis he was, and meek, and serviceable;
> And kerft before his fader at the table."

Was this a fop?

It is the same with all his characters; he has done all by chance, or perhaps his fortune, money, money. According to his prospectus he has Three Monks; these he cannot find in Chaucer, who has only One Monk, and that no vulgar character, as he has endeavoured to make him. When men cannot read they should not pretend to paint. To be sure, Chaucer is a little difficult to him who has only blundered over novels and catchpenny trifles of booksellers. Yet a little pains ought to be taken even by the ignorant and weak. He has put The Reeve, a vulgar fellow, between his Knight and Squire, as if he was resolved to go contrary in every thing to Chaucer, who says of the Reeve:

"And ever he rode hinderest of the rout."

In this manner he has jumbled his dumb dollies together and is praised by his equals for it, for both himself and his friend are equally masters of Chaucer's language. They both think that the Wife of Bath is a young, beautiful, blooming damsel; and H_____ says, that she is the Fair Wife of Bath, and that the Spring appears in her Cheeks. Now hear what Chaucer has made her say of herself, who is no modest one:

> "But Lord when it remembereth me
> Upon my youth and on my jollity,
> It tickleth me about the heart root.
> Unto this day it doth my heart boot,
> That I have had my world as in my time;   5
> But age, alas, that all will envenime,
> Hath me bireft, my beauty and my pith
> Let go; farewell: the devil go therewith,
> The flower is gone, there is no more to tell.
> The bran, as best, I can, I now mote sell;   10
> And yet, to be right merry, will I fond,
> Now forth to tell of my fourth husband."

She has had four husbands, a fit subject for this painter; yet the painter ought to be very much offended with his friend H_____, who has called his "a common scene" "and very ordinary forms"; which is the truest part of all, for it is so, and very wretchedly so indeed. What merit can there be in a picture of which such words are spoken with truth?

But the prospectus says that the Painter has represented Chaucer himself as a knave, who thrusts himself among honest people to make game of and laugh at them; though I must do justice to the painter and say that he has made him look more like a fool than a knave. But it appears, in all the writings of Chaucer, and particularly in his *Canterbury Tales,* that he was very devout and paid respect to true enthusiastic superstition. He has laughed at his knaves and fools as I do now. But he has respected his True Pilgrims, who are a majority of his company and are not thrown together in the random manner that Mr. S_____ has done. Chaucer has nowhere called the Plowman old, worn out with age and labour, as the prospectus has represented him and says that the picture has done so too. He is worn down with labour, but not with age. How spots of brown and yellow, smeared about at random, can be either young or old, I cannot see. It may be an old man; it may be a young one; it may be anything that a prospectus pleases. But I know that where there are no lineaments there can be no character. And what connoisseurs call touch, I know by experience must be the destruction of all character and expression, as it is of every lineament.

The scene of Mr. S——'s Picture is by Dulwich Hills, which was not the way to Canterbury; but perhaps the painter thought he would give them a ride round about, because they were a burlesque set of scarecrows, not worth any man's respect or care.

But the painter's thoughts being always upon gold, he has introduced a character that Chaucer has not; namely, a Goldsmith; for so the prospectus tells us. Why he has introduced a Goldsmith, and what is the wit of it, the prospectus does not explain. But it takes care to mention the reserve and modesty of the Painter; this makes a good epigram enough.

> "The fox, the owl, the spider, and the mole,
> By sweet reserve and modesty get fat."

But the prospectus tells us that the painter has introduced a Sea Captain; Chaucer has a Shipman, a Sailor, a Trading Master of a Vessel, called by courtesy Captain, as every master of a boat is; but this does not make him a Sea Captain. Chaucer has purposely omitted such a personage, as it only exists in certain periods; it is the soldier by sea. He who would be a Soldier in inland nations is a sea captain in commercial nations.

All is misconceived, and its misexecution is equal to its misconception. I have no objection to Rubens and Rembrandt being employed, or even to their living in a palace; but it shall not be at the expense of Rafael and Michael Angelo living in a cottage, and in contempt and derision. I have been scorned long enough by these fellows, who owe to me all that they have; it shall be so no longer.

> I found them blind, I taught them how to see;
> And, now, they know me not, nor yet themselves.

NUMBER IV

The Bard, from Gray

> On a rock, whose haughty brow
> Frown'd o'er old Conway's foaming flood,
> Robed in the sable garb of woe,
> With haggard eyes the Poet stood,
> Loose his beard, and hoary hair
> Stream'd like a meteor to the troubled air.
>
> Weave the warp, and weave the woof,
> The winding sheet of Edward's race.

Weaving the winding sheet of Edward's race by means of sounds of spiritual music and its accompanying expressions of articulate speech is a bold and daring and most masterly conception that the public have embraced and approved with avidity. Poetry consists in these conceptions; and shall Painting be confined to the sordid drudgery of facsimile representations of merely mortal and perishing substances, and not be as poetry and music are, elevated into its own proper sphere of invention and visionary conception? No, it shall not be so! Painting, as well as poetry and music, exists and exults in immortal thoughts. If Mr. B.'s Canterbury Pilgrims had been done by any other power than that of the poetic visionary, it would have been as dull as his adversary's.

The Spirits of the murdered bards assist in weaving the deadly woof.

> With me in dreadful harmony they join,
> And weave, with bloody hands, the tissue of thy line.

The connoisseurs and artists who have made objections to Mr. B.'s mode of representing spirits with real bodies would do well to consider that the Venus, the Minerva, the Jupiter, the Apollo, which they admire in Greek statues, are all of them representations of spiritual existences of Gods immortal to the mortal perishing organ of sight; and yet they are embodied and organized in solid marble. Mr. B. requires the same latitude and all is well. The Prophets describe what they saw in Vision as real and existing men whom they saw with their imaginative and immortal organs; the Apostles the same; the clearer the organ the more distinct the object. A Spirit and a Vision are not, as the modern philosophy supposes, a cloudy vapour or a nothing; they are organized and minutely articulated beyond all that the mortal and perishing nature can produce. He who does not imagine in stronger and better lineaments, and in stronger and better light than his perishing mortal eye can see, does not imagine at all. The painter of this work asserts that all his imaginations appear to him infinitely more perfect and more minutely organized than any thing seen by his mortal eye. Spirits are organized men. Moderns wish to draw figures without lines, and with great and heavy shadows; are not shadows more unmeaning than lines, and more heavy? O who can doubt this?

King Edward and his Queen Elenor are prostrated, with their horses, at the foot of a rock on which the Bard stands, prostrated by the terrors of his harp on the margin of the river Conway, whose waves bear up a corse of a slaughtered bard at the foot of the rock. The armies of Edward are seen winding among the mountains.

"He wound with toil-some march his long array."

Mortimer and Gloucester lie spellbound behind their king. The execution of this picture is also in Water Colours, or Fresco.

NUMBER V

The Ancient Britons

In the last Battle of King Arthur only Three Britons escaped. These were the Strongest Man, the Beautifullest Man and the Ugliest Man; these three marched through the field unsubdued, as Gods, and the Sun of Britain set, but shall arise again with tenfold splendor when Arthur shall awake from sleep and resume his dominion over earth and ocean.

The three general classes of men, who are represented by the most Beautiful, the most Strong and the most Ugly, could not be represented by any historical facts but those of our own country, the Ancient Britons, without violating costume. The Britons (say historians) were naked civilized men, learned, studious, abstruse in thought and contemplation; naked, simple, plain in their acts and manners; wiser than after-ages. They were overwhelmed by brutal arms, all but a small remnant; Strength, Beauty and Ugliness escaped the wreck and remain forever unsubdued, age after age.

The British Antiquities are now in the Artist's hands, all his visionary contemplations relating to his own country and its ancient glory, when it was, as it again shall be, the source of learning and inspiration. Arthur was a name for the constellation Arcturus, or Bootes, the Keeper of the North Pole. And all the fables of Arthur and his round table; of the warlike naked Britons; of Merlin; of Arthur's conquest of the whole world; of his death, or sleep, and promise to return again; of the Druid monuments, or temples; of the pavement of Watling street; of London Stone; of the caverns in Cornwall, Wales, Derbyshire, and Scotland; of the Giants of Ireland and Britain; of the elemental beings, called by us by the general name of Fairies; and of these three who escaped, namely, Beauty, Strength and Ugliness, Mr. B. has in his hands poems of the highest antiquity. Adam was a Druid, and Noah; also Abraham was called to succeed the Druidical age, which began to turn allegoric and mental signification into corporeal command, whereby human sacrifice would have depopulated the earth. All these things are written in Eden. The artist is an inhabitant of that happy country; and if every thing goes on as it has begun, the world of vegetation and generation may expect to be opened again to Heaven, through Eden, as it was in the beginning.

The Strong man represents the human sublime. The Beautiful man represents the human pathetic, which was in the wars of Eden divided into male and female. The Ugly man represents the human reason. They were originally one man, who was four-fold; he was self-divided, and his real humanity slain on the stems of generation, and the form of the fourth was like the Son of God. How he became divided is a subject of great sublimity and pathos. The Artist has written it under inspiration and will, if God please, publish it; it is voluminous and contains the ancient history of Britain and the world of Satan and of Adam.

In the meantime he has painted his Picture, which supposes that in the reign of that British Prince, who lived in the fifth century, there were remains of those naked Heroes in the Welsh Mountains; they are there now; Gray saw them in the person of his bard on Snowdon; there they dwell in naked simplicity; happy is he who can see and converse with them above the shadows of generation and death. The giant Albion was Patriarch of the Atlantic; he is the Atlas of the Greeks, one of those the Greeks called Titans. The stories of Arthur are the acts of Albion applied to a Prince of the fifth century, who conquered Europe and held the Empire of the world in the dark age, which the Romans never again recovered. In this Picture, believing with Milton the ancient British History, Mr. B. has done as all the ancients did, and as all the moderns, who are worthy of fame, given the historical fact in its poetical vigour; so as it always happens, and not in that dull way that some Historians pretend, who, being weakly organized themselves, cannot see either miracle or prodigy; all is to them a dull round of probabilities and possibilities; but the history of all times and places is nothing else but improbabilities and impossibilities, what we should say was impossible if we did not see it always before our eyes.

The antiquities of every Nation under Heaven is no less sacred than that of the Jews. They are the same thing, as Jacob Bryant and all antiquaries have proved. How other antiquities came to be neglected and disbelieved, while those of the Jews are collected and arranged, is an inquiry worthy of both the Antiquarian and the Divine. All had originally one language and one religion; this was the religion of Jesus, the everlasting Gospel. Antiquity preaches the Gospel of Jesus. The reasoning historian, turner and twister of causes and consequences, such as Hume, Gibbon and Voltaire, cannot with all their artifice turn or twist one fact or disarrange self-evident action and reality. Reasons and opinions concerning acts are not history. Acts themselves alone are history, and these are neither the exclusive property of Hume, Gibbon, nor Voltaire, Echard, Rapin, Plutarch, nor Herodotus. Tell me the Acts, O historian, and leave me to reason upon them as I please; away with your reasoning and your rubbish. All that is not action is not worth reading. Tell me the What; I do not want you to tell me the Why and the How; I can find that out myself as well as you can, and I will not be fooled by you into opinions that you please to impose, to disbelieve what you think improbable or impossible. His opinions, who does not see spiritual agency, is not worth any man's reading; he who rejects a fact because it is improbable must reject all History and retain doubts only.

It has been said to the Artist, take the Apollo for the model of your beautiful Man and the Hercules for your strong Man, and the Dancing Fawn for your Ugly Man. Now he comes to his trial. He knows that what he does is not inferior to the grandest Antiques. Superior they cannot be, for human power cannot go beyond either what he does, or what they have done; it is the gift of God; it is inspiration and vision. He has resolved to emulate those precious remains of antiquity; he has done so, and the result you behold; his ideas of strength and beauty have not been greatly different. Poetry as it exists now on earth, in the various remains of ancient authors, Music as it exists in old tunes or melodies, Painting and Sculpture as it exists in the remains of Antiquity and in the works of more modern genius is Inspiration and cannot be surpassed; it is perfect and eternal. Milton, Shakespeare, Michael Angelo, Rafael, the finest specimens of Ancient Sculpture and Painting, and Architecture, Gothic, Grecian, Hindu and Egyptian, are the extent of the human mind. The human mind cannot go beyond the gift of God, the Holy Ghost. To suppose that Art can go beyond the finest specimens of Art that are now in the world is not knowing what Art is; it is being blind to the gifts of the spirit.

It will be necessary for the Painter to say something concerning his ideas of Beauty, Strength and Ugliness.

The Beauty that is annexed and appended to folly is a lamentable accident and error of the mortal and perishing life; it does but seldom happen; but with this unnatural mixture the sublime

Artist can have nothing to do; it is fit for the burlesque. The Beauty proper for sublime art is lineaments, or forms and features that are capable of being the receptacles of intellect; accordingly the Painter has given in his beautiful man his own idea of intellectual Beauty. The face and limbs that deviates or alters least, from infancy to old age, is the face and limbs of greatest Beauty and perfection.

The Ugly likewise, when accompanied and annexed to imbecility and disease, is a subject for burlesque and not for historical grandeur; the Artist has imagined his Ugly man one approaching to the beast in features and form, his forehead small, without frontals; his jaws large; his nose high on the ridge, and narrow; his chest and the stamina of his make, comparatively little, and his joints and his extremities large; his eyes with scarce any whites, narrow and cunning, and every thing tending toward what is truly Ugly; the incapability of intellect.

The Artist has considered his strong Man as a receptacle of Wisdom, a sublime energizer; his features and limbs do not spindle out into length without strength, nor are they too large and unwieldy for his brain and bosom. Strength consists in accumulation of power to the principal seat, and from thence a regular gradation and subordination; strength is compactness, not extent nor bulk.

The strong Man acts from conscious superiority and marches on in fearless dependence on the divine decrees, raging with the inspirations of a prophetic mind. The Beautiful Man acts from duty and anxious solicitude for the fates of those for whom he combats. The Ugly Man acts from love of carnage and delight in the savage barbarities of war, rushing with sportive precipitation into the very teeth of the affrighted enemy.

The Roman Soldiers rolled together in a heap before them: "Like the rolling thing before the whirlwind"; each show a different character, and a different expression of fear, or revenge, or envy, or blank horror, or amazement, or devout wonder and unresisting awe.

The dead and the dying, Britons naked, mingled with armed Romans, strew the field beneath. Among these, the last of the Bards who were capable of attending warlike deeds is seen falling, outstretched among the dead and the dying, singing to his harp in the pains of death.

Distant among the mountains are Druid Temples, similar to Stone Henge. The Sun sets behind the mountains, bloody with the day of battle.

The flush of health in flesh, exposed to the open air, nourished by the spirits of forests and floods, in that ancient happy period, which history has recorded, cannot be like the sickly daubs of Titian or Rubens. Where will the copier of nature, as it now is, find a civilized man, who has been accustomed to go naked? Imagination only can furnish us with colouring appropriate, such as is found in the Frescoes of Rafael and Michael Angelo; the disposition of forms always directs colouring in works of true art. As to a modern Man, stripped from his load of clothing, he is like a dead corpse. Hence Rubens, Titian, Correggio, and all of that class, are like leather and chalk; their men are like leather, and their women like chalk, for the disposition of their forms will not admit of grand colouring; in Mr. B.'s Britons the blood is seen to circulate in their limbs; he defies competition in colouring.

NUMBER VI

A Spirit vaulting from a cloud to turn and wind a fiery Pegasus— Shakespeare. The Horse of Intellect is leaping from the cliffs of Memory and Reasoning; it is a barren Rock; it is also called the Barren Waste of Locke and Newton.

This Picture was done many years ago and was one of the first Mr. B. ever did in Fresco; fortunately, or rather providentially, he left it unblotted and unblurred, although molested continually by blotting and blurring demons; but he was also compelled to leave it unfinished for reasons that will be shown in the following:

NUMBER VII

The Goats, an experiment Picture

The subject is taken from the Missionary Voyage and varied from the literal fact for the sake of picturesque scenery. The savage girls had dressed themselves with vine leaves, and some goats on board the missionary ship stripped them off presently. This Picture was painted at intervals, for experiment with the colours, and is laboured to a superabundant blackness; it has however that about it which may be worthy the attention of the Artist and Connoisseur for reasons that follow.

NUMBER VIII

The spiritual Preceptor, an experiment Picture

This subject is taken from the visions of Emanuel Swedenborg, Universal Theology, No. 623. The Learned, who strive to ascend into Heaven by means of learning, appear to Children like dead horses when repelled by the celestial spheres. The works of this visionary are well worthy of the attention of Painters and Poets; they are foundations for grand things; the reason they have not been more attended to is because corporeal demons have gained a predominance; who the leaders of these are will be shown below. Unworthy Men who gain fame among Men continue to govern mankind after death, and in their spiritual bodies oppose the spirits of those who worthily are famous; and as Swedenborg observes, by entering into disease and excrement, drunkenness and concupiscence, they possess themselves of the bodies of mortal men, and shut the doors of mind and of thought by placing Learning above Inspiration. O Artist! you may disbelieve all this, but it shall be at your own peril.

NUMBER IX

Satan calling up his Legions, from Milton's Paradise Lost; *a composition for a more perfect Picture, afterward executed for a Lady of high rank. An experiment Picture.*

This Picture was likewise painted at intervals, for experiment on colours, without any oily vehicle; it may be worthy attention, not only on account of its composition, but of the great labour which has been bestowed on it, that is, three or four times as much as would have finished a more perfect Picture; the labour has destroyed the lineaments; it was with difficulty brought back again to a certain effect, which it had at first, when all the lineaments were perfect.

These Pictures, among numerous others painted for experiment, were the result of temptations and perturbations, labouring to destroy Imaginative power by means of that infernal machine called Chiaro Oscuro, in the hands of Venetian and Flemish Demons, whose enmity to the Painter himself and to all Artists who study in the Florentine and Roman Schools may be removed by an exhibition and exposure of their vile tricks. They cause that every thing in art shall become a Machine. They cause that the execution shall be all blocked up with brown shadows. They put the original Artist in fear and doubt of his own original conception. The spirit of Titian was particularly active in raising doubts concerning the possibility of executing without a model; and when once he had raised the doubt, it became easy for him to snatch away the vision time after time; for when the Artist took his pencil to execute his ideas, his power of imagination weakened so much and darkened, that memory of nature and of Pictures of the various Schools possessed his mind instead of appropriate execution resulting from the inventions, like walking in another man's style, or speaking or looking in another man's style and manner, unappropriate and repugnant to your own individual character, tormenting the true Artist till he leaves the Florentine and adopts the Venetian practice or does as Mr. B. has done, has the courage to suffer poverty and disgrace till he ultimately conquers.

Rubens is a most outrageous demon and by infusing the remembrances of his Pictures and style of execution hinders all power of individual thought, so that the man who is possessed by this demon loses all admiration of any other Artist but Rubens and those who were his imitators and journeymen; he causes to the Florentine and Roman Artist fear to execute; and though the original conception was all fire and animation, he loads it with hellish brownness and blocks up all its gates of light, except one, and that one he closes with iron bars, till the victim is obliged to give up the Florentine and Roman practice and adopt the Venetian and Flemish.

Correggio is a soft and effeminate and consequently a most cruel demon, whose whole delight is to cause endless labour to whoever suffers him to enter his mind. The story that is told in all Lives of the Painters about Correggio being poor and but badly paid for his Pictures is altogether false; he was a petty Prince in Italy and employed numerous Journeymen in manufacturing (as Rubens and Titian did) the Pictures that go under his name. The manual labour in these Pictures of Correggio is immense and was paid for originally at the immense prices that those who keep manufactories of art always charge to their employers, while they themselves pay their journeymen little enough. But though Correggio was not poor, he will make any true artist so, who permits him to enter his mind, and take possession of his affections; he infuses a love of soft and even tints without boundaries and of endless reflected lights that confuse one another and hinder all correct drawing from appearing to be correct; for if one of Rafael or Michael Angelo's figures was to be traced, and Correggio's reflections and refractions to be added to it, there would soon be an end of proportion and strength, and it would be weak and pappy and lumbering and thickheaded, like his own works; but then it would have softness and evenness, by a twelvemonth's labour, where a month would with judgment have finished it better and higher; and the poor wretch who executed it would be the Correggio that the life writers have written of: a drudge and a miserable man, compelled to softness by poverty. I say again, O Artist, you may disbelieve all this, but it shall be at your own peril.

Note: These experiment Pictures have been bruised and knocked about without mercy, to try all experiments.

NUMBER X

The Bramins—A Drawing

The subject is, Mr. Wilkin translating the Geeta, an ideal design, suggested by the first publication of that part of the Hindu Scriptures translated by Mr. Wilkin. I understand that my Costume is incorrect, but in this I plead the authority of the ancients, who often deviated from the Habits to preserve the Manners, as in the instance of Laocoön, who, though a priest, is represented naked.

NUMBER XI

The body of Abel found by Adam and Eve; Cain, who was about to bury it, fleeing from the face of his Parents.—A Drawing.

NUMBER XII

The Soldiers casting lots for Christ's Garment.—A Drawing.

NUMBER XIII

Jacob's Ladder.—A Drawing.

NUMBER XIV

The Angels hovering over the Body of Jesus in the Sepulcher.—
A Drawing.

The above four drawings the Artist wishes were in Fresco, on
an enlarged scale to ornament the altars of churches and to make
England like Italy, respected by respectable men of other countries on account of Art. It is not the want of genius that can here-
after be laid to our charge; the Artist who has done these Pictures
and Drawings will take care of that; let those who govern the
Nation take care of the other. The times require that everyone
should speak out boldly; England expects that every man should
do his duty, in Arts as well as in Arms, or in the Senate.

NUMBER XV

Ruth.—A Drawing.

This Design is taken from that most pathetic passage in the
Book of Ruth, where Naomi having taken leave of her daugh-
ters-in-law, with intent to return to her own country, Ruth cannot leave her, but says, "Whither thou goest I will go; and where
thou lodgest I will lodge; thy people shall be my people, and thy
God my God; where thou diest I will die, and there will I be buried; God do so to me and more also, if aught but death part thee
and me."

The distinction that is made in modern times between a Painting and a Drawing proceeds from ignorance of art. The merit
of a Picture is the same as the merit of a Drawing. The dauber
daubs his Drawings; he who draws his Drawings draws his Pictures. There is no difference between Rafael's Cartoons and his
Frescoes, or Pictures, except that the Frescoes, or Pictures, are

more finished. When Mr. B. formerly painted in oil colours his Pictures were shown to certain painters and connoisseurs, who said that they were very admirable Drawings on canvas, but not Pictures; but they said the same of Rafael's Pictures. Mr. B. thought this the greatest of compliments, though it was meant otherwise. If losing and obliterating the outline constitutes a Picture, Mr. B. will never be so foolish as to do one. Such art of losing the outlines is the art of Venice and Flanders; it loses all character, and leaves what some people call expression; but this is a false notion of expression; expression cannot exist without character as its stamina; and neither character nor expression can exist without firm and determinate outline. Fresco Painting is susceptible of higher finishing than Drawing on paper, or than any other method of Painting. But he must have a strange organization of sight who does not prefer a Drawing on Paper to a Daubing in Oil by the same master, supposing both to be done with equal care.

The great and golden rule of art, as well as of life, is this: That the more distinct, sharp and wiry the bounding line, the more perfect the work of art; and the less keen and sharp, the greater is the evidence of weak imitation, plagiarism and bungling. Great inventors in all ages knew this; Protogenes and Apelles knew each other by this line. Rafael and Michael Angelo, and Albert Dürer, are known by this and this alone. The want of this determinate and bounding form evidences the want of idea in the artist's mind, and the pretense of the plagiary in all its branches. How do we distinguish the oak from the beech, the horse from the ox but by the bounding outline? How do we distinguish one face or countenance from another but by the bounding line and its infinite inflections and movements? What is it that builds a house and plants a garden, but the definite and determinate? What is it that distinguishes honesty from knavery but the hard and wiry line of rectitude and certainty in the actions and intentions? Leave out this line and you leave out life itself; all is chaos again, and the line of the almighty must be drawn out upon it before man or beast can exist. Talk no more then of Correggio, or Rembrandt, or any other of those plagiaries of Venice or Flanders.

They were but the lame imitators of lines drawn by their predecessors, and their works prove themselves contemptible disarranged imitations and blundering misapplied copies.

NUMBER XVI

The Penance of Jane Shore in St. Paul's Church. — A Drawing.

This Drawing was done above Thirty Years ago and proves to the Author, and he thinks will prove to any discerning eye, that the productions of our youth and of our maturer age are equal in all essential points. If a man is master of his profession, he cannot be ignorant that he is so; and if he is not employed by those who pretend to encourage art, he will employ himself and laugh in secret at the pretenses of the ignorant, while he has every night dropped into his shoe, as soon as he puts it off, and puts out the candle, and gets into bed, a reward for the labours of the day such as the world cannot give, and patience and time await to give him all that the world can give.

Selections from *A Public Address*

(FROM THE ROSSETTI MANUSCRIPT, C. 1810)

The manner in which my Character has been blasted these thirty years, both as an artist & a Man, may be seen particularly in a Sunday Paper called the *Examiner,* Published in Beaufort Buildings. (We all know that Editors of Newspapers trouble their heads very little about art & science & that they are always paid for what they put in upon these ungracious Subjects), & the manner in which I have routed out the nest of villains will be seen in a Poem concerning my Three years' Herculean Labours at Felpham, which I will soon Publish. Secret Calumny & open Professions of Friendship are common enough all the world over, but have never been so good an occasion of Poetic Imagery. When a Base Man means to be your Enemy he always begins with being your Friend. Flaxman cannot deny that one of the very first Monuments he did I gratuitously designed for him. At the same time he was blasting my character as an Artist to Macklin my Employer, as Macklin told me at the time. How much of his Homer & Dante he will allow to be mine I do not know, as he went far enough off to Publish them, even to Italy; But the Public will know, & Posterity will know.

While the Works of Pope & Dryden are looked upon as the Same Art with those of Milton & Shakespeare, while the works of Strange & Woollet are looked upon as the same Art with those of Rafael & Albert Dürer, there can be no Art in a Nation but such as is Subservient to the interest of the Monopolizing Trader. Englishmen, rouse yourselves from the fatal Slumber into which Booksellers & Trading Dealers have thrown you, Under the artfully propagated pretense that a Translation or a Copy of any kind can be as honourable to a Nation as An Original, Belying the English Character in that well-known Saying, "Englishmen

Improve what others Invent." This Even Hogarth's Works Prove
a detestable Falsehood. No Man Can Improve An Original Invention, nor can an Original Invention Exist without Execution
Organized & minutely delineated & Articulated Either by God
or Man. I do not mean smoothed up & Niggled, Poco-Penned
and all the beauties picked out & blurred & blotted, but Drawn
with a firm and decided hand at once like Fuseli & Michael Angelo, Shakespeare & Milton.

I have heard many People say: Give me the Ideas, It is no matter what Words you put them into; & others say, Give me the
Design, it is no matter for the Execution. These People know
Enough of Artifice but Nothing of Art. Ideas cannot be Given
but in their minutely Appropriate Words, nor Can a Design be
made without its minutely Appropriate Execution. The unorgan-
ized Blots & Blurs of Rubens & Titian are not Art, nor can their
Method ever express Ideas or Imaginations any more than Pope's
Metaphysical Jargon of Rhyming. Unappropriate Execution is
the Most nauseous of all affectation & foppery. He who copies
does not Execute; he only Imitates what is already Executed.
Execution is only the result of Invention.

The wretched State of the Arts in this Country & in Europe,
originating in the wretched State of Political Science, which is
the Science of Sciences, Demands a firm & determinate conduct
on the part of Artists to Resist the Contemptible Counter Arts
established by such contemptible Politicians as Louis XIV & originally set on foot by Venetian Picture traders, Music traders &
Rhyme traders, to the destruction of all true art as it is this Day.
To recover Art has been the business of my life — to the Florentine
Original & if possible to go beyond that Original. This I thought
the only pursuit worthy of a Man. To Imitate I abhor. I obstinately
adhere to the true Style of Art, such as Michael Angelo, Rafael,
Jul. Rom., Alb. Dürer left it. I demand therefore of the Amateurs
of art the Encouragement which is my due. If they continue to
refuse, theirs is the loss, not mine, & theirs is the Contempt of

Posterity. I have Enough in the Approbation of fellow labourers. This is my glory & exceeding great reward. I go on, & nothing can hinder my course:

> And in Melodious Accents I
> Will sit me down & Cry, I, I.

An Example of these Contrary Arts is given us in the Characters of Milton & Dryden as they are written in a Poem signed with the name of Nat Lee, which perhaps he never wrote & perhaps he wrote in a paroxysm of insanity, In which it is said that Milton's Poem is a rough Unfinished Piece & Dryden has finished it. Now let Dryden's *Fall* & Milton's *Paradise* be read, & I will assert that everybody of Understanding must cry out Shame on such Niggling & Poco-Pen as Dryden has degraded Milton with. But at the same time I will allow that Stupidity will Prefer Dryden because it is in Rhyme & Monotonous Sing Song, Sing Song from beginning to end. Such are Bartollozzi, Woollet & Strange.

A Vision of the Last Judgment

(FROM THE ROSSETTI MANUSCRIPT, 1810)

For the Year 1810
Additions to Blake's Catalogue of Pictures &c.

The Last Judgment, when all those are Cast away who trouble Religion with Questions concerning Good & Evil or Eating of the Tree of those Knowledges or Reasonings which hinder the Vision of God, turning all into a Consuming fire. When Imaginative Art & Science & all Intellectual Gifts, all the Gifts of the Holy Ghost, are looked upon as of no use & only Contention remains to Man; then the Last Judgment begins & its Vision is seen by the Imaginative Eye of Everyone according to the situation he holds.

The Last Judgment is not Fable or Allegory, but Vision. Fable or Allegory are a totally distinct & inferior kind of Poetry. Vision or Imagination is a Representation of what Eternally Exists, Really & Unchangeably. Fable or Allegory is Formed by the daughters of Memory. Imagination is Surrounded by the daughters of Inspiration, who in the aggregate are called Jerusalem. Fable is Allegory, but what Critics call The Fable is Vision itself. The Hebrew Bible & the Gospel of Jesus are not Allegory, but Eternal Vision or Imagination of All that Exists. Note here that Fable or Allegory is Seldom without some Vision. Pilgrim's Progress is full of it, the Greek Poets the same; but Allegory & Vision ought to be known as Two Distinct Things & so called for the Sake of Eternal Life. Plato has made Socrates say that Poets & Prophets do not know or Understand what they write or Utter. This is a most Pernicious Falsehood. If they do not, pray, is an inferior Kind to be called Knowing? Plato confutes himself.

The Last Judgment is one of these Stupendous Visions. I have represented it as I saw it. To different People it appears differently, as every thing else does; for though on Earth things seem Permanent, they are less permanent than a Shadow, as we all know too well.

570

The Nature of Visionary Fancy or Imagination is very little Known, & the Eternal nature & permanence of its ever Existent Images is considered as less permanent than the things of Vegetative & Generative Nature; yet the Oak dies as well as the Lettuce, but Its Eternal nature & the Individuality never dies, but renews by its seed. Just so the Imaginative Image returns by the seed of Contemplative Thought. The Writings of the Prophets illustrate these conceptions of the Visionary Fancy by their various sublime & Divine Images as seen in the Worlds of Vision.

[a passage is here obliterated] when they Assert that Jupiter usurped the Throne of his Father Saturn & brought on an Iron Age & Begat on Mnemosyne or Memory The Greek Muses, which are not Inspiration, as the Bible is. Reality was Forgot & the Vanities of Time & Space only Remembered & called Reality. Such is the Mighty difference between Allegoric Fable & Spiritual Mystery. Let it here be Noted that the Greek Fables originated in Spiritual Mystery & Real Visions, Which are lost & clouded in Fable & Allegory, while the Hebrew Bible & the Greek Gospel are Genuine, Preserved by the Saviour's Mercy. The Nature of my Work is Visionary or Imaginative; it is an Endeavour to Restore what the Ancients called the Golden Age.

This world of Imagination is the World of Eternity; it is the Divine bosom into which we shall all go after the death of the Vegetated body. This World of Imagination is Infinite & Eternal, whereas the world of Generation or Vegetation is Finite & Temporal. There Exist in that Eternal World the Permanent Realities of Everything which we see reflected in this Vegetable Glass of Nature.

All Things are comprehended in their Eternal Forms in the Divine body of the Saviour, the True Vine of Eternity, The Human Imagination, who appeared to Me as Coming to Judgment among his Saints & throwing off the Temporal, that the Eternal might be Established. Around him were seen the Images of Existences according to a certain order suited to my Imaginative Eye as follows:

Jesus seated between the Two Pillars, Jachin & Boaz, with the Word of Divine Revelation on his knees, & on each side the four & twenty Elders sitting in judgment, the Heavens opening around him by unfolding the clouds around his throne. The Old Heaven & old Earth are passing away & the New Heaven & New Earth descending. The Just arise on his right & the wicked on his Left hand. A Sea of fire Issues from before the throne. Adam & Eve appear first before the Judgment Seat in humiliation. Abel, surrounded by Innocents & Cain with the flint in his hand with which he slew his brother, falling with the head downward. From the Cloud on which Eve stands Satan is seen falling headlong, wound round by the tail of the serpent, whose bulk, nailed to the Cross round which he wreathes, is falling into the Abyss. Sin is also represented as a female bound in one of the Serpent's folds, surrounded by her fiends. Death is Chained to the Cross, & Time falls together with death, dragged down by a Demon crowned with Laurel. Another demon with a Key has the charge of Sin & is dragging her down by the hair. Beside them a figure is seen scaled with iron scales from head to feet, precipitating himself into the Abyss with the Sword & Balances. He is Og, King of Bashan.

On the Right, Beneath the Cloud on which Abel kneels, is Abraham with Sarah & Isaac, also Hagar & Ishmael. Abel kneels on a bloody Cloud, descriptive of those Churches before the flood, that they were filled with blood & fire & vapour of smoke. Even till Abraham's time the vapour & heat was not Extinguished. These States Exist now. Man Passes on, but States remain forever. He passes through them like a traveller who may as well suppose that the places he has passed through exist no more, as a Man may suppose that the States he has passed through Exist no more. Everything is Eternal.

In Eternity one Thing never Changes into another Thing. Each Identity is Eternal. Consequently Apuleius's Golden Ass & Ovid's Metamorphosis & others of the like kind are Fable; yet they contain Vision in a Sublime degree, being derived from real Vision in More Ancient Writings. Lot's Wife being Changed into Pillar of Salt alludes to the Mortal Body being rendered a Permanent Statue, but not Changed or Transformed into Another Identity while it retains its own Individuality. A Man can never become Ass nor Horse. Some are born with shapes of Men who may be both, but Eternal Identity is one thing, & Corporeal Vegetation is another thing. Changing Water into Wine by Jesus & into Blood by Moses relates to Vegetable Nature also.

Beneath Ishmael is Mahomet, & on the left beneath the falling figure of Cain is Moses casting his tables of stone into the deeps. It ought to be understood that the Persons Moses & Abraham are not here meant but the States Signified by those Names, the Individuals being representatives or Visions of those States as they were revealed to Mortal Man in the Series of Divine Revelations as they are written in the Bible. These various States I have seen in my Imagination; when distant they appear as One Man, but as you approach they appear Multitudes of Nations. Abraham hovers above his posterity, which appear as Multitudes of Children ascending from the Earth, surrounded by Stars, as it was said, "As the Stars of Heaven for Multitude." Jacob & his Twelve Sons hover beneath the feet of Abraham & receive their children from the Earth. I have seen, when at a distance, Multitudes of Men in Harmony appear like a single Infant, sometimes in the Arms of a Female. This represented the Church.

But to proceed with the description of those on the Left hand: Beneath the Cloud on which Moses kneels is two figures, a Male & Female chained together by the feet. They represent those who perished by the flood. Beneath them a multitude of their associates are seen falling headlong. By the side of them is a Mighty fiend with a Book in his hand, which is Shut. He represents the person named in Isaiah XXII.c. & 20.v., Eliakim, the Son of Hilkiah. He drags Satan down headlong; he is crowned with oak. By the side of the Scaled figure representing Og, King of Bashan, is a Figure with a Basket emptying out the vanities of Riches & Worldly Honours. He is Araunah, the Jebusite, master of the threshing floor. Above him are two figures elevated on a Cloud, representing the Pharisees, who plead their own Righteousness before the throne; they are weighed down by two fiends. Beneath the Man with the Basket are three fiery fiends with grey beards & scourges of fire; they represent Cruel Laws: They scourge a group of figures down into the Deeps. Beneath them are various figures in attitudes of contention, representing various States of Misery, which, alas, everyone on Earth is liable to enter into, & against which we should all watch.

The Ladies will be pleased to see that I have represented the Furies by Three Men & not by three Women. It is not because I think the Ancients wrong, but they will be pleased to remember that mine is Vision & not Fable. The Spectator may suppose them Clergymen in the Pulpit, Scourging Sin instead of Forgiving it.

The Earth beneath these falling Groups of figures is rocky & burning and seems as if convulsed by Earthquakes. A Great City on fire is seen in the distance. The Armies are fleeing upon the Mountains. On the foreground, hell is opened, & many figures are descending into it down stone steps & beside a Gate beneath a rock where Sin & Death are to be closed Eternally by that Fiend who carries the Key in one hand & drags them down with the other. On the rock & above the Gate a fiend with wings urges the wicked onwards with fiery darts; he is Hazael, the Syrian, who drives abroad all those who rebel against their Saviour. Beneath the steps Babylon, represented by a King crowned, Grasping his Sword & his Scepter. He is just awakened out of his Grave; around him are other Kingdoms arising to Judgment, represented in this Picture as Single Personages according to the descriptions in the Prophets. The Figure dragging up a Woman by her hair represents the Inquisition, as do those contending on the sides of the Pit; & in Particular the Man Strangling two Women represents a Cruel Church.

Two persons, one in Purple, the other in Scarlet, are descending down the Steps into the Pit. These are Caiaphas & Pilate, Two States where all those reside who Calumniate & Murder under Pretense of Holiness & Justice. Caiaphas has a Blue Flame like a Miter on his head. Pilate has bloody hands that never can be cleansed. The Females behind them represent the Females belonging to such States, who are under perpetual terrors & vain dreams, plots & secret deceit. Those figures that descend into the Flames before Caiaphas & Pilate are Judas & those of his Class. Achitophel is also here with the cord in his hand.

Between the Figures of Adam & Eve appears a fiery Gulph descending from the sea of fire Before the throne; in this Cataract Four Angels descend headlong with four trumpets to awake the dead; beneath these is the Seat of the Harlot named Mystery in the Revelations. She is seized by Two Beings, each with three heads; they Represent Vegetative Existence. As it is written in Revelations, they strip her naked & burn her with fire; it repre-

sents the Eternal Consummation of Vegetable Life & Death with
its Lusts. The wreathed Torches in their hands represents Eternal Fire, which is the fire of Generation or Vegetation; it is an
Eternal Consummation. Those who are blessed with Imaginative Vision see This Eternal Female & tremble at what others
fear not, while they despise & laugh at what others fear. Her Kings
& Counsellors & Warriors descend in Flames, Lamenting & looking upon her in astonishment & Terror; & Hell is opened beneath
her Seat on the Left hand. Beneath her feet is a flaming Cavern
in which is seen the Great Red Dragon with Seven heads & ten
Horns. He has Satan's book of Accusations lying on the rock open
before him. He is bound in chains by Two strong demons. They
are Gog & Magog, who have been compelled to subdue their
Master (Ezekiel XXXVIII c. 8 v.) with their Hammer & Tongs,
about to new-Create the Seven-Headed Kingdoms. The Graves
beneath are opened, & the dead awake & obey the call of the
Trumpet. Those on the Right hand awake in joy, those on the
Left in Horror. Beneath the Dragon's Cavern a Skeleton begins
to Animate, starting into life at the Trumpet's sound, while the
Wicked contend with each other on the brink of perdition. On
the Right a Youthful couple are awaked by their Children; an
Aged patriarch is awaked by his aged wife. He is Albion, our An-
cestor, patriarch of the Atlantic Continent, whose History Pre-
ceded that of the Hebrews, & in whose Sleep or Chaos Creation
began; at their head the Aged Woman is Britannica, the Wife
of Albion. Jerusalem is their daughter. Little Infants creep out
of the flowery mould into the Green fields of the blessed, who
in various joyful companies embrace & ascend to meet Eternity.

The Persons who ascend to Meet the Lord, coming in the Clouds
with power & great Glory, are representations of those States
described in the Bible under the Names of the Fathers before
& after the Flood. Noah is seen in the Midst of these, Canopied
by a Rainbow, on his right hand Shem & on his Left Japhet. These
three Persons represent Poetry, Painting & Music, the three Powers in Man of conversing with Paradise, which the flood did not
Sweep away.

Above Noah is the Church Universal, represented by a Woman
Surrounded by Infants. There is such a State in Eternity; it is com-

posed of the Innocent, civilized Heathen & the Uncivilized Savage, who, having not the Law, do by Nature the things contained in the Law. This State appears like a Female crowned with Stars driven into the Wilderness. She has the Moon under her feet.

The Aged Figure with Wings, having a writing tablet & taking account of the numbers who arise, is That Angel of the Divine Presence mentioned in Exodus XIV c. 19 v. & in other Places. This Angel is frequently called by the Name of Jehovah Elohim, The "I Am" of the Oaks of Albion.

Around Noah & beneath him are various figures Risen into the Air; among these are Three Females, representing those who are not of the dead but of those found Alive at the Last Judgment; they appear to be innocently gay & thoughtless, not being among the Condemned because ignorant of crime in the midst of a corrupted Age. The Virgin Mary was of this Class. A Mother Meets her numerous Family in the Arms of their Father; these are representations of the Greek Learned & Wise as also of those of other Nations, such as Egypt & Babylon, in which were multitudes who shall meet the Lord coming in the Clouds.

The Children of Abraham, or Hebrew Church, are represented as a Stream of Figures on which are seen Stars somewhat like the Milky way. They ascend from the Earth, where Figures kneel Embracing above the Graves, & Represent Religion or Civilized Life, such as it is in the Christian Church, who are the Offspring of the Hebrew.

Just above the graves & above the spot where the Infants creep out of the Ground Stand two, a Man & Woman; these are the Primitive Christians. The two Figures in purifying flames by the side of the Dragon's cavern represents the Latter state of the Church when on the verge of Perdition, yet protected by a Flaming Sword. Multitudes are seen ascending from the Green fields of the blessed, in which a Gothic Church is representative of true Art, Called Gothic in All Ages by those who follow the Fashion, as that is called which is without Shape or Fashion. On the right hand of Noah a Woman with Children represents the State Called Laban, the Syrian; it is the Remains of Civilization in the State from whence Abraham was taken. Also On the right hand of Noah, A Female descends to meet her Lover or Husband, representative of that Love called Friendship, which Looks for no other heaven than their Beloved & in him sees all reflected as in a Glass of Eternal Diamond.

On the right hand of these rise the diffident & Humble, & on their left a solitary Woman with her infant: these are caught up by three aged Men, who appear as suddenly emerging from the blue sky for their help. These three Aged Men represent Divine Providence as opposed to & distinct from divine vengeance, represented by three Aged men on the side of the Picture among the Wicked, with scourges of fire.

If the Spectator could Enter into these Images in his Imagination, approaching them on the Fiery Chariot of his Contemplative Thought, if he could Enter into Noah's Rainbow or into his bosom or could make a Friend & Companion of one of these Images of wonder, which always entreats him to leave mortal things, as he must know, then would he arise from his Grave, then would he meet the Lord in the Air, & then he would be happy. General Knowledge is Remote Knowledge; it is in Particulars that Wisdom consists, & Happiness too. Both in Art & in Life General Masses are as Much Art as a Pasteboard Man is Human. Every Man has Eyes, Nose & Mouth; this Every Idiot knows, but he who enters into & discriminates most minutely the Manners & Intentions, the Characters in all their branches, is the alone Wise or Sensible Man; & on this discrimination All Art is founded. I entreat then that the Spectator will attend to the Hands & Feet, to the Lineaments of the Countenances; they are all descriptive of Character, & not a line is drawn without intention, & that most discriminate & particular. As Poetry admits not a Letter that is Insignificant, so Painting admits not a Grain of Sand or a Blade of Grass Insignificant, much less an Insignificant Blur or Mark.

Above the Head of Noah is Seth. This State called Seth is Male & Female in a higher state of Happiness & wisdom than Noah, being nearer the State of Innocence. Beneath the feet of Seth two figures represent the two Seasons of Spring & Autumn, while beneath the feet of Noah Four Seasons represent the Changed State made by the flood.

By the side of Seth is Elijah; he comprehends all the Prophetic Characters; he is seen on his fiery Chariot, bowing before the throne of the Saviour. In like manner The figures of Seth & his wife Comprehends the Fathers before the flood & their Generations; when seen remote they appear as One Man. A little below Seth on his right are Two Figures, a Male & Female with numerous Children; these represent those who were not in the Line of the Church & yet were Saved from among the Antediluvians, who Perished; between Seth & these a female figure represents the Solitary State of those who, previous to the Flood, walked with God.

All these arise toward the opening Cloud before the Throne, led onward by triumphant Groups of Infants, & the Morning Stars sang together. Between Seth & Elijah three Female Figures crowned with Garlands Represent Learning & Science, which accompanied Adam out of Eden.

The Cloud that opens, rolling apart before the throne & before the New Heaven & the New Earth, is Composed of Various Groups of Figures, particularly the Four Living Creatures mentioned in Revelations as Surrounding the Throne; these I suppose to have the chief agency in removing the old heavens & the old Earth to make way for the New Heaven & the New Earth to descend from the throne of God & of the Lamb. That Living Creature on the Left of the Throne Gives to the Seven Angels the Seven Vials of the wrath of God, with which they, hovering over the Deeps beneath, pour out upon the wicked their Plagues. The Other Living Creatures are descending with a Shout & with the Sound of the Trumpet, Directing the Combats in the upper Elements. In the two Corners of the Picture, on the Left hand Apollyon is foiled before the Sword of Michael, & on the Right the Two Witnesses are subduing their Enemies. On the Cloud are opened the Books of Remembrance of Life & of Death; before that of Life, on the Right, some figures bow in humiliation; before that of Death, on the left, the Pharisees are pleading their own Righteousness; the one Shines with beams of Light, the other utters Lightnings & tempests.

A Last Judgment is Necessary because Fools flourish. Nations Flourish under Wise Rulers & are depressed under foolish Rulers. It is the same with Individuals as Nations. Works of Art can only be produced in Perfection where Man is either in Affluence or is Above the Care of it. Poverty is the Fool's Rod, which at last is turned on his own back. This is A Last Judgment: when Men of Real Art Govern, & Pretenders Fall. Some People & not a few Artists have asserted that the Painter of this Picture would not have done so well if he had been properly Encouraged. Let those who think so reflect on the State of Nations under Poverty & their incapability of Art. Though Art is Above Either, the Argument is better for Affluence than Poverty, & though he would have been a greater Artist yet he would have produced Greater works of Art in proportion to his means. A Last Judgment is not for the purpose of making Bad Men better, but for the Purpose of hindering them from oppressing the Good with Poverty & Pain by means of Such Vile Arguments & Insinuations.

Around the Throne Heaven is opened & the Nature of Eternal Things Displayed, All Springing from the Divine Humanity. All beams from him. He is the Bread & the Wine; he is the Water of Life. Accordingly on Each Side of the opening Heaven appears an Apostle; that on the Right Represents Baptism, that on the Left Represents the Lord's Supper. All Life consists of these Two: Throwing off Error & Knaves from our company continually & receiving Truth or Wise Men into our Company Continually. He who is out of the Church & opposes it is no less an Agent of Religion than he who is in it. To be an Error & to be Cast out is a part of God's Design. No man can Embrace True Art till he has Explored & Cast out False Art—such is the Nature of Mortal Things—or he will be himself Cast out by those who have Already Embraced True Art. Thus My Picture is a History of Art & Science, the Foundation of Society, Which is Humanity itself. What are all the Gifts of the Spirit but Mental Gifts? Whenever any Individual Rejects Error & Embraces Truth, a Last Judgment passes upon that Individual.

Over the Head of the Saviour & Redeemer The Holy Spirit, like a Dove, is surrounded by a blue Heaven, in which are the two Cherubim that bowed over the Ark; for here the temple is opened in Heaven, & the Ark of the Covenant is as a Dove of Peace. The Curtains are drawn apart, Christ having rent the

Veil. The Candlestick & the Table of Shewbread appear on Each Side; a Glorification of Angels with Harps surround the Dove.

The Temple stands on the Mount of God; from it flows on each side the River of Life, on whose banks Grows the Tree of Life, among whose branches temples & Pinnacles, tents & pavilions, Gardens & Groves display Paradise with its Inhabitants walking up & down in Conversations concerning Mental Delights.

Here they are no longer talking of what is Good & Evil or of what is Right or Wrong & puzzling themselves in Satan's Labyrinth, But are Conversing with Eternal Realities as they Exist in the Human Imagination. We are in a World of Generation & death, & this world we must cast off if we would be Painters Such as Rafael, Mich. Angelo & the Ancient Sculptors. If we do not cast off this world we shall be only Venetian Painters, who will be cast off & Lost from Art.

Jesus is surrounded by Beams of Glory in which are seen all around him Infants emanating from him. These represent the Eternal Births of Intellect from the divine Humanity. A Rainbow surrounds the throne & the Glory in which youthful Nuptials receive the infants in their hands. In Eternity Woman is the Emanation of Man; she has No Will of her own. There is no such thing in Eternity as a Female Will.

On the Side next Baptism are seen those called in the Bible Nursing Fathers & Nursing Mothers. They represent Education. On the Side next the Lord's Supper, The Holy Family consisting of Mary, Joseph, John the Baptist, Zacharias & Elizabeth receiving the Bread & Wine among other Spirits of the Just made perfect. Beneath these, a Cloud of Women & Children are taken up, fleeing from the rolling Cloud which separates the Wicked from the Seats of Bliss. These represent those who, though willing, were too weak to Reject Error without the Assistance & Countenance of those Already in the Truth; for a Man Can only Reject Error by the Advice of a Friend or by the Immediate Inspiration of God. It is for this Reason among many others that I have put the Lord's Supper on the Left hand of the Throne, for it appears so at the Last Judgment for a Protection.

Many suppose that before the Creation All was Solitude & Chaos. This is the most pernicious Idea that can enter the Mind, as it takes away all sublimity from the Bible & Limits All Existence to Creation & to Chaos, To the Time & Space fixed by the Corporeal Vegetative Eye, & leaves the Man who entertains such an Idea the habitation of Unbelieving Demons. Eternity Exists, and All things in Eternity, Independent of Creation, which was an act of Mercy. I have represented those who are in Eternity by some in a Cloud within the Rainbow that surrounds the Throne; they merely appear as in a Cloud when anything of Creation, Redemption or Judgment are the Subjects of Contemplation, though their Whole Contemplation is Concerning these things. The Reason they so appear is the Humiliation of the Reasoning & doubting Selfhood & the Giving all up to Inspiration. By this it will be seen that I do not consider either the Just or the Wicked to be in a Supreme State, but to be every one of them States of the Sleep which the Soul may fall into in its deadly dreams of Good & Evil when it leaves Paradise following the Serpent.

The Greeks represent Chronos or Time as a very Aged Man; this is Fable, but the Real Vision of Time is in Eternal Youth. I have, however, somewhat accommodated my Figure of Time to the Common opinion, as I myself am also infected with it & my Visions also infected, & I see Time Aged, alas, too much so.

Allegories are things that Relate to Moral Virtues. Moral Virtues do not Exist; they are Allegories & dissimulations. But Time & Space are Real Beings, a Male & a Female. Time is a Man; Space is a Woman, & her Masculine Portion is Death.

The Combats of Good & Evil is Eating of the Tree of Knowledge. The Combats of Truth & Error is Eating of the Tree of Life. These are not only Universal but Particular. Each are Personified. There is not an Error but it has a Man for its Agent, that is, it is a Man. There is not a Truth but it has also a Man. Good & Evil are Qualities in Every Man, whether a Good or Evil Man. These are Enemies & destroy one another by every Means in their power, both of deceit & of open Violence. The Deist & the Christian are but the Results of these Opposing Natures. Many are Deists who would in certain Circumstances have been Christians in outward appearance. Voltaire was one of this number; he was as intolerant as an Inquisitor. Manners make the Man, not Habits. It is the same in Art: by their Works ye shall know them. The Knave who is Converted to Deism & the Knave who is Converted to Christianity is still a Knave, but he himself will not know it, though Everybody else does. Christ comes as he came at first, to deliver those who were bound under the Knave, not to deliver the Knave. He Comes to Deliver Man the Accused & not Satan the Accuser. We do not find anywhere that Satan is Accused of Sin; he is only accused of Unbelief & thereby drawing Man into Sin that he may accuse him. Such is the Last Judgment, a Deliverance from Satan's Accusation. Satan thinks that Sin is displeasing to God; he ought to know that Nothing is displeasing to God but Unbelief & eating of the Tree of Knowledge of Good & Evil.

Men are admitted into Heaven not because they have curbed & governed their Passions or have No Passions, but because they have Cultivated their Understandings. The Treasures of Heaven are not Negations of Passion but Realities of Intellect from which All the Passions Emanate Uncurbed in their Eternal Glory. The Fool shall not enter into Heaven, let him be ever so Holy. Holiness is not The Price of Entrance into Heaven. Those who are cast out Are All Those, who, having no Passions of their own because No Intellect, Have spent their lives in Curbing & Governing other People's by the Various arts of Poverty & Cruelty of all kinds. Woe, Woe, Woe to you Hypocrites. Even Murder the Courts of Justice, more merciful than the Church, are compelled to allow is not done in Passion, but in Cool-Blooded Design & Intention.

The Modern Church Crucifies Christ with the Head Downwards.

Many Persons such as Paine & Voltaire with some of the Ancient Greeks say we will not converse concerning Good & Evil, we will live in Paradise & Liberty. You may do so in Spirit, but not in the Mortal Body as you pretend, till after the Last Judgment; for in Paradise they have no Corporeal & Mortal Body that originated with the Fall & was called Death & cannot be removed but by a Last Judgment. While we are in the world of Mortality we Must Suffer. The Whole Creation Groans to be delivered. There will always be as many Hypocrites born as Honest Men, & they will always have superior Power in Mortal Things. You cannot have Liberty in this World without what you call Moral Virtue, & you cannot have Moral Virtue without the Slavery of that half of the Human Race who hate what you call Moral Virtue.

The Nature of Hatred & Envy & of All the Mischiefs in the World are here depicted. No one Envies or Hates one of his Own Party; even the devils love one another in their Way. They torment one another for other reasons than Hate or Envy; these are only employed against the Just. Neither can Seth Envy Noah, or Elijah Envy Abraham, but they may both of them Envy the Success of Satan or of Og or Molech. The Horse never Envies the Peacock, nor the Sheep the Goat, but they Envy a Rival in Life & Existence whose ways & means exceed their own, let him be of what Class of Animals he will. A Dog will envy a Cat who is pampered at the expense of his comfort, as I have often seen. The Bible never tells us that Devils torment one another through Envy; it is through this that they torment the Just. But for what do they torment one another? I answer: For the Coercive Laws of Hell, Moral Hypocrisy. They torment a Hypocrite when he is discovered; they Punish a Failure in the tormentor who has suffered the Subject of his torture to Escape. In Hell all is Self-Righteousness; there is no such thing there as Forgiveness of Sin. He who does Forgive Sin is Crucified as an Abettor of Criminals, & he who performs Works of Mercy in Any shape whatever is punished & if possible destroyed, not through Envy or Hatred or Malice, but through Self-Righteousness, that thinks it does God service, which God is Satan. They do not Envy one another. They contemn & despise one another. Forgiveness of Sin is only at the Judgment Seat of Jesus, the Saviour, where the Accuser is cast out, not because he Sins, but because he torments the Just & makes them do what he condemns as Sin & what he knows is opposite to their own Identity.

It is not because Angels are Holier than Men or Devils that makes them Angels, but because they do not Expect Holiness from one another, but from God only.

The Player is a liar when he says Angels are happier than Men because they are better. Angels are happier than Men & Devils because they are not always Prying after Good & Evil in one Another & eating the Tree of Knowledge for Satan's Gratification.

Thinking as I do that the Creator of this World is a very Cruel Being, & being a Worshipper of Christ, I cannot help saying, "The Son, O how unlike the Father!" First God Almighty comes with a Thump on the Head. Then Jesus Christ comes with a balm to heal it.

The Last Judgment is an Overwhelming of Bad Art & Science. Mental Things are alone Real. What is Called Corporeal, Nobody Knows of its dwelling Place. It is in Fallacy, & its Existence an Imposture. Where is the Existence Out of Mind or Thought? Where is it but in the Mind of a Fool? Some People flatter themselves that there will be No Last Judgment & that Bad Art will be adopted & mixed with Good Art, That Error or Experiment will make a Part of Truth; & they Boast that it is its Foundation. These People flatter themselves. I will not Flatter them. Error is Created; Truth is Eternal. Error or Creation will be Burned Up; & then, & not till then, Truth or Eternity will appear. It is Burnt up the Moment Men cease to behold it. I assert for Myself that I do not behold the Outward Creation & that to me it is hindrance & not Action. It is as the Dirt upon my feet, No part of Me. "What," it will be Questioned, "When the Sun rises do you not see a round Disk of fire somewhat like a Guinea?" "O no, no, I see an Innumerable company of the Heavenly host crying, 'Holy, Holy, Holy is the Lord God Almighty.'" I question not my Corporeal or Vegetative Eye any more than I would Question a Window concerning a Sight. I look through it & not with it.

Aphorisms from *The Laocoön* (circa 1820)

Jehovah & his two Sons, Satan & Adam, as they were copied from the Cherubim of Solomon's Temple by three Rhodians & applied to Natural Fact or History of Ilium.

He repented that he had made Adam (Of the Female, the Adamah), & it grieved him at his heart.

Satan's Wife, The Goddess Nature, is War & Misery, & Heroism a Miser.

Good & Evil are Riches & Poverty, a Tree of Misery, propagating Generation & Death.

What can be Created Can be Destroyed. Adam is only The Natural Man & not the Soul or Imagination.

The Eternal Body of Man is The Imagination, that is

God himself
The Divine Body } Jesus: we are his Members.

It manifests itself in his Works of Art (In Eternity All is Vision).

All that we See is Vision, from Generated Organs gone as soon as come, Permanent in The Imagination, considered as Nothing by the Natural Man.

Hebrew Art is called Sin by the Deist Science.

The whole Business of Man Is The Arts & All Things Common.

Christianity is Art & not Money. Money is its Curse.

The Old & New Testaments are the Great Code of Art.

Jesus & His Apostles & Disciples were all Artists. Their Works were destroyed by the Seven Angels of the Seven Churches in Asia, Antichrist Science.

Science is the Tree of Death.

Art is the Tree of Life; God is Jesus.

The Gods of Priam are the Cherubim of Moses & Solomon, The Hosts of Heaven.

The Gods of Greece & Egypt were Mathematical Diagrams. See Plato's Works.

There are States in which all Visionary Men are accounted Mad Men. Such are Greece & Rome. Such is Empire or Tax. See Luke, Ch. 2. v. 1.

Art Degraded, Imagination Denied, War Governed the Nations.

Divine Union Deriding, And Denying Immediate Communion with God, The Spoilers say, "Where are his Works That he did in the Wilderness? Lo, what are these? Whence came they? These are not the Works of Egypt nor Babylon, Whose Gods are the Powers of this World, Goddess Nature, Who first spoil & then destroy Imaginative Art; For their Glory is War and Dominion."

Empire against Art. See Virgil's Eneid. Lib. VI. v. 848.

Spiritual War: Israel delivered from Egypt is Art delivered from Nature & Imitation.

What we call Antique Gems are the Gems of Aaron's Breast Plate.

Prayer is the Study of Art. Praise is the Practice of Art. Fasting &c. all relate to Art. The outward Ceremony is Antichrist. Without Unceasing Practice, nothing can be done. Practice is Art. If you leave off you are Lost.

A Poet, a Painter, a Musician, an Architect: the Man Or Woman who is not one of these is not a Christian.

You must leave Fathers & Mothers & Houses & Lands if they stand in the way of Art.

The unproductive Man is not a Christian, much less the Destroyer.

The True Christian Charity not dependent on Money (the life's blood of Poor Families) that is on Caesar or Empire or Natural Religion.

For Every Pleasure Money Is Useless.

Money, which is The Great Satan or Reason, the Root of Good & Evil In the Accusation of Sin.

Where any view of Money exists Art cannot be carried on, but War only (Read Matthew C. X: 9 & 10 v.) by pretenses to the Two Impossibilities, Chastity & Abstinence, Gods of the Heathen.

Is not every Vice possible to Man described in the Bible openly?

All is not Sin that Satan calls so: all the Loves & Graces of Eternity.

If Morality was Christianity, Socrates was the Saviour.

Art can never exist without Naked Beauty displayed.

No Secrecy in Art.

On Homer's Poetry (circa 1820)

Every Poem must necessarily be a perfect Unity, but why Homer's is peculiarly so, I cannot tell; he has told the story of Bellerophon & omitted the Judgment of Paris, which is not only a part, but a principal part, of Homer's subject.

But when a Work has Unity it is as much in a Part as in the Whole. The Torso is as much a Unity as the Laocoön.

As Unity is the cloak of folly, so Goodness is the cloak of knavery. Those who will have Unity exclusively in Homer come out with a Moral like a sting in the tail. Aristotle says Characters are either Good or Bad; now Goodness or Badness has nothing to do with Character. An Apple tree, a Pear tree, a Horse, a Lion are Characters; but a Good Apple tree or a Bad, is an Apple tree still; a Horse is not more a Lion for being a Bad Horse. That is its Character; its Goodness or Badness is another consideration.

It is the same with the Moral of a whole Poem as with the Moral Goodness of its parts. Unity & Morality are secondary considerations & belong to Philosophy & not to Poetry, to Exception and not to Rule, to Accident & not to Substance. The Ancients called it eating of the tree of good & evil.

The Classics, it is the Classics, & not Goths nor Monks, that Desolate Europe with Wars.

On Virgil (circa 1820)

Sacred Truth has pronounced that Greece & Rome, as Babylon & Egypt, so far from being parents of Arts & Sciences as they pretend, were destroyers of all Art. Homer, Virgil & Ovid confirm this opinion & make us reverence The Word of God, the only light of antiquity that remains unperverted by War. Virgil in the Eneid, Book VI, Line 848, says, "Let others study Art; Rome has somewhat better to do, namely War & Dominion."

Rome & Greece swept Art into their maw & destroyed it. A Warlike State never can produce Art. It will Rob & Plunder & accumulate into one place, & Translate & Copy & Buy & Sell & Criticize, but not Make. Grecian is Mathematic Form. Gothic is Living Form. Mathematic Form is Eternal in the Reasoning Memory. Living Form is Eternal Existence.

Part Four
SELECTED MARGINALIA

Annotations to Lavater's
Aphorisms on Man (circa 1788)

224. Who writes what he should tell, and dares not tell what he writes, is either like a wolf in sheep's clothing or like a sheep in a wolf's skin.

Some cannot tell what they can write, though they dare.

309. He who, at a table of forty covers, thirty-nine of which are exquisite, and one indifferent, lays hold of that, and with a "damn your dinner" dashes it in the landlord's face, should be sent to Bethlem or to Bridewell—and whither he, who blasphemes a book, a work of art, or perhaps a man of nine-and-thirty good and but one bad quality, and calls those fools or flatterers who, engrossed by the superior number of good qualities, would fain forget the bad one.

To hell till he behaves better. Mark that I do not believe there is such a thing literally. But hell is the being shut up in the possession of corporeal desires, which shortly weary the man, for all life is holy.

342. Superstition always inspires littleness, religion grandeur of mind: the superstitious raises beings inferior to himself to deities.

No man was ever truly superstitious who was not truly religious as far as he knew.

True superstition is ignorant honesty, & this is beloved of god & man.

I do not allow that there is such a thing as Superstition taken in the strict sense of the word.

A man must first deceive himself before he is thus Superstitious, & so he is a hypocrite.

Hypocrisy is as distant from superstition as the wolf from the lamb.

407. Whatever is visible is the vessel or veil of the invisible past, present, future—as man penetrates to this more, or perceives it less, he raises or depresses his dignity of being.

A vision of the Eternal Now.

409. He alone is good, who, though possessed of energy, prefers virtue, with the appearance of weakness, to the invitation of acting brilliantly ill.

Noble. But Mark: Active Evil is better than Passive Good.

489. An entirely honest man, in the severe sense of the word, exists no more than an entirely dishonest knave: the best and the worst are only approximations of those qualities. Who are those that never contradict themselves? Yet honesty never contradicts itself: Who are those that always contradict themselves? Yet knavery is mere self-contradiction. Thus the knowledge of man determines not the things themselves, but their proportions, the quantum of congruities and incongruities.

Man is a twofold being, one part capable of evil & the other capable of good. That which is capable of good is not also capable of evil, but that which is capable of evil is also capable of good. This aphorism seems to consider man as simple & yet capable of evil. Now both evil & good cannot exist in a simple being, for thus two contraries would spring from one essence, which is impossible, but if man is considered as only evil & god only good, how then is regeneration effected, which turns the evil to good by casting out the evil by the good? See Matthew, XII Ch., 26, 27, 28, 29 v.

532. Take from Luther his roughness and fiery courage; from Calvin his hectic obstinacy; from Erasmus his timid prudence; hypocrisy and fanaticism from Cromwell; from Henry IV his sanguine character; mysticism from Fenelon; from Hume his all-unhinging wit; love of paradox and brooding suspicion from Rousseau; naiveté and elegance of knavery from Voltaire; from Milton the extravagance of his all-personifying fancy; from Raffaelle his dryness and nearly hard precision; and from Rubens his supernatural luxury of colours:—deduct this oppressive exuberance from each; rectify them according to your own taste—what will be the result? Your own correct, pretty, flat, useful—for me, to be sure, quite convenient vulgarity. And why this amongst maxims of humanity? That you may learn to know this exuberance, this leaven, of each great character, and its effects on contemporaries and posterity—that you may know where d, e, f, is, there must be a, b, c: he alone has knowledge of man, who knows the ferment that raises

each character, and makes it that which it shall be, and something more or less than it shall be.

Deduct from a rose its redness, from a lily its whiteness, from a diamond its hardness, from a sponge its softness, from an oak its height, from a daisy its lowness, & rectify everything in Nature as the Philosophers do, & then we shall return to Chaos, & God will be compelled to be Eccentric if he Creates, O happy Philosopher.

Variety does not necessarily suppose deformity, for a rose & a lily are various & both beautiful.

Beauty is exuberant, but not of ugliness, but of beauty; & if ugliness is adjoined to beauty, it is not the exuberance of beauty. So if Rafael is hard & dry, it is not his genius but an accident acquired; for how can Substance & Accident be predicated of the same Essence I cannot conceive.

But the substance gives tincture to the accident & makes it physiognomic.

Aphorism 47 speaks of the heterogeneous, which all extravagance is, but exuberance not.

539. A great woman not imperious, a fair woman not vain, a woman of common talents not jealous, an accomplished woman, who scorns to shine—are four wonders, just great enough to be divided among the four quarters of the globe.

Let the men do their duty & the women will be such wonders; the female life lives from the light of the male. See a man's female dependents, you know the man.

605. He who pursues the glimmering steps of hope, with steadfast, not presumptuous, eye, may pass the gloomy rock, on either side of which superstition and incredulity their dark abysses spread.

Superstition has been long a bugbear by reason of its being united with hypocrisy. But let them be fairly separated, & then superstition will be honest feeling, & God, who loves all honest men, will lead the poor enthusiast in the paths of holiness.

630. A god, an animal, a plant, are not companions of man; nor is the faultless—then judge with lenity of all; the coolest, wisest, best,

all without exception, have their points, their moments of enthusiasm, fanaticism, absence of mind, faintheartedness, stupidity—if you allow not for these, your criticisms on man will be a mass of accusations or caricatures.

It is the God in all that is our companion & friend, for our God himself says: "You are my brother, my sister & my mother," & St. John: "Whoso dwelleth in love dwelleth in God & God in him," & such an one cannot judge of any but in love, & his feelings will be attractions or repulses.

God is in the lowest effects as well as in the highest causes, for he is become a worm that he may nourish the weak.

For let it be remembered that creation is God descending according to the weakness of man, for our Lord is the word of God, & everything on earth is the word of God & in its essence is God.

640. Man is bad or good as he unites himself with bad or good spirits. Tell me with whom you go & I'll tell you what you do.

As we cannot experience pleasure but by means of others who experience either pleasure or pain through us, And as all of us on earth are united in thought, for it is impossible to think without images of somewhat on earth, So it is impossible to know God or heavenly things without conjunction with those who know God & heavenly things. Therefore, all who converse in the Spirit converse with Spirits.

For these reasons I say that this Book is written by consultation with Good Spirits, because it is Good, & that the name Lavater is the amulet of those who purify the heart of man.

There is a strong objection to Lavater's principles (as I understand them) & that is, He makes every thing originate in its accident; he makes the vicious propensity not only a leading feature of the man but the stamina on which all his virtues grow. But as I understand Vice it is a Negative. It does not signify what the laws of Kings & Priests have called Vice. We who are philosophers ought not to call the Staminal Virtues of Humanity by the same name that we call the omissions of intellect springing from poverty.

Every man's leading propensity ought to be called his leading Virtue & his good Angel. But the Philosophy of Causes & Consequences misled Lavater as it has all his Cotemporaries. Each thing is its own cause & its own effect. Accident is the omission of act in self & the hindering of act in another. This is Vice, but all Act is Virtue. To hinder another is not an act; it is the contrary; it is a restraint on action both in ourselves & in the person hindered, for he who hinders another omits his own duty at the same time.

Murder is Hindering Another.

Theft is Hindering Another.

Backbiting, Undermining, Circumventing & whatever is Negative is Vice. But the origin of this mistake in Lavater & his cotemporaries is, They suppose that Woman's Love is Sin; in consequence all the Loves & Graces with them are Sins.

Annotations to Swedenborg's
Wisdom of Angels Concerning Divine Love and Divine Wisdom (circa 1788)

Hence it may appear, that Man from a merely natural Idea cannot comprehend that the Divine is everywhere, and yet not in Space; and yet that Angels and Spirits clearly comprehend this; consequently that Man also may, if so be he will admit something of spiritual Light into his Thought;

Observe the distinction here between Natural & Spiritual as seen by Man.

The Reason why Man may comprehend it is, because his Body doth not think, but his Spirit, therefore not his natural but his spiritual Part.

Man may comprehend, but not the natural or external man.

It hath been said, that in the spiritual World Spaces appear equally as in the natural World. . . . Hence it is that the Lord, although he is in the Heavens with the Angels everywhere, nevertheless appears high above them as a Sun: And whereas the Reception of Love and Wisdom constitutes Affinity with him, therefore those Heavens appear nearer to him where the Angels are in a nearer Affinity from Reception, than where they are in a more remote Affinity.

He who Loves feels love descend into him & if he has wisdom may perceive it is from the Poetic Genius, which is the Lord.

In all the Heavens there is no other Idea of God than that of a Man.

Man can have no idea of anything greater than Man, as a cup cannot contain more than its capaciousness. But God is a man, not because he is so perceived by man, but because he is the creator of man.

The Gentiles, particularly the Africans. . . . entertain an Idea of God as of a Man, and say that no one can have any other Idea of God: When they hear that many form an Idea of God as existing in the Midst of a Cloud, they ask where such are.

Think of a white cloud as being holy, you cannot love it; but think of a holy man within the cloud, love springs up in your thought. For to think of holiness distinct from man is impossible to the affections. Thought alone can make monsters, but the affections cannot.

They who are wiser than the common People pronounce God to be invisible.

Worldly wisdom or demonstration by the senses is the cause of this.

What Person of Sound Reason doth not perceive, that the Divine is not divisible; . . . If another, who hath no Reason, should say that it is possible there may be several Infinities, Uncreates, Omnipotents and Gods, provided they have the same Essence, and that thereby there is one Infinite, Uncreate, Omnipotent and God—is not one and the same Essence but one and the same Identity?

Answer: Essence is not Identity, but from Essence proceeds Identity, & from one Essence may proceed many Identities, as from one Affection may proceed many thoughts. Surely this is an oversight.

That there is but one Omnipotent, Uncreate & God I agree, but that there is but one Infinite I do not; for if all but God is not Infinite, they shall come to an End, which God forbid.

If the Essence was the same as the Identity, there could be but one Identity, which is false.

Heaven would upon this plan be but a Clock; but one & the same Essence is therefore Essence & not Identity.

Man is only a Recipient of Life. From this Cause it is, that Man, from his own hereditary Evil, reacts against God; but so far as he believes that all his Life is from God, and every Good of Life from the Action of God, and every Evil of Life from the Reaction of Man, Reaction thus becomes correspondent with Action, and Man acts with God as from himself.

Good & Evil are here both Good, & the two contraries Married.

But he who knows how to elevate his Mind above the Ideas of Thought which are derived from Space and Time, such a Man passes from Darkness to Light, and becomes wise in Things spiritual and

Divine . . . and then by Virtue of that Light he shakes off the Darkness of natural Light, and removes its Fallacies from the Center to the Circumference.

When the fallacies of darkness are in the circumference, they cast a bound about the infinite.

That without two Suns, the one living and the other dead, there can be no Creation.

False philosophy according to the letter, but true according to the spirit.

That all Things were created from the Lord by the living Sun, and nothing by the dead Sun, may appear from this Consideration.

The dead Sun is only a phantasy of evil Man.

From these Considerations a Conclusion was drawn, that the Whole of Charity and Faith is in Works.

The Whole of the New Church is in the Active Life & not in Ceremonies at all.

These three Degrees of Altitude are named Natural, Spiritual and Celestial. . . . Man, at his Birth, first comes into the natural Degree, and this increases in him by Continuity according to the Sciences, and according to the Understanding acquired by them, to the Summit of Understanding which is called Rational.

> Study Sciences till you are blind.
> Study intellectuals till you are cold.
> Yet Science cannot teach intellect.
> Much less can intellect teach Affection.

How foolish then is it to assert that Man is born in only one degree, when that one degree is reception of the 3 degrees, two of which he must destroy or close up or they will descend; if he closes up the two superior, then he is not truly in the 3rd, but descends out of it into mere Nature or Hell. . . .

Is it not also evident that one degree will not open the other, & that science will not open intellect, but that they are discrete & not continuous so as to explain each other except by correspondence, which has nothing to do with demonstration; for you cannot demonstrate one degree by the other; for how can science be brought to demonstrate intellect without making them continuous & not discrete?

Figure 7. "Elohim Creating Adam." By permission of the Tate Gallery, London.

Annotations to Bishop Watson's
Apology for the Bible (1798)

To defend the Bible in this year 1798 would cost a man his life.
The Beast & the Whore rule without control.

It is an easy matter for a Bishop to triumph over Paine's attack,
but it is not so easy for one who loves the Bible.

The Perversions of Christ's words & acts are attacked by Paine
& also the perversions of the Bible; Who dare defend either the
Acts of Christ or the Bible Unperverted?

But to him who sees this mortal pilgrimage in the light that
I see it, Duty to his country is the first consideration & safety the
last.

Read patiently; take not up this Book in an idle hour. The consideration of these things is the whole duty of man & the affairs
of life & death trifles, sports of time. But these considerations
business of Eternity.

I have been commanded from Hell not to print this, as it is what
our Enemies wish.

> You hold it impossible that the Bible can be the Word of God, be-
> cause it is therein said, that the Israelites destroyed the Canaanites
> by the express command of God: and to believe the Bible to be true,
> we must, you affirm, unbelieve all our belief of the moral justice of
> God; . . . I am astonished that so acute a reasoner should attempt
> to disparage the Bible by bringing forward this exploded and frequent-
> ly refuted objection. . . . The word of God is in perfect harmony with
> his work; crying or smiling infants are subjected to death in both.

To me, who believe the Bible & profess myself a Christian,
a defense of the Wickedness of the Israelites in murdering so
many thousands under pretense of a command from God is altogether Abominable & Blasphemous. Wherefore did Christ
come? Was it not to abolish the Jewish Imposture? Was not Christ
murdered because he taught that God loved all Men & was their
father & forbade all contention for Worldly prosperity in opposi-

tion to the Jewish Scriptures, which are only an Example of the wickedness & deceit of the Jews & were written as an Example of the possibility of Human Beastliness in all its branches. Christ died as an Unbeliever, & if the Bishops had their will so would Paine. . . . But he who speaks a word against the Son of man shall be forgiven. Let the Bishop prove that he has not spoken against the Holy Ghost, who in Paine strives with Christendom, as in Christ he strove with the Jews.

> When I consider how nearly man, in a savage state, approaches to the brute creation, as to intellectual excellence; and when I contemplate his miserable attainments, as to the knowledge of God,.in a civilized State, when he has had no divine instruction on the subject, or when that instruction has been forgotten, . . . I cannot but admire the wisdom and goodness of the Supreme Being, in having let himself down to our apprehensions.

Read the Edda of Iceland, the Songs of Fingal, the accounts of North American Savages (as they are called); Likewise Read Homer's *Iliad*. He was certainly a Savage in the Bishop's sense. He knew nothing of God in the Bishop's sense of the word, & yet he was no fool.

The Bible or Peculiar Word of God, Exclusive of Conscience or the Word of God Universal, is that Abomination which, like the Jewish ceremonies is forever removed, & henceforth every man may converse with God & be a King & Priest in his own house.

> Had, indeed, Moses said that he wrote the five first books of the Bible . . . and had it been found, that Moses . . . did not write these books; then, I grant, the authority of the whole would have been gone at once.

If Paine means that a history, though true in itself, is false When it is attributed to a wrong author, he's a fool. But he says that Moses being proved not the author of that history which is written in his name & in which he says I did so & so Undermines the veracity entirely. The writer says he is Moses; if this is proved false, the history is false (Deut. xxxi, v. 24). But perhaps Moses is not the author & then the Bishop loses his Author.

> The evidence for the miracles recorded in the Bible is . . . so greatly superior to that for the prodigies mentioned by Livy, or the miracles

related by Tacitus, as to justify us in giving credit to the one as the work of God, and in withholding it from the other as the effect of superstition and imposture.

Jesus could not do miracles where unbelief hindered; hence we must conclude that the man who holds miracles to be ceased puts it out of his own power to ever witness one. The manner of a miracle being performed is in modern times considered as an arbitrary command of the agent upon the patient, but this is an impossibility, not a miracle. Neither did Jesus ever do such a miracle. Is it a greater miracle to feed five thousand men with five loaves than to overthrow all the armies of Europe with a small pamphlet? Look over the events of your own life, & if you do not find that you have both done such miracles & lived by such, you do not see as I do. True, I cannot do a miracle through experiment & to domineer over & prove to others my superior power, as neither could Christ. But I can & do work such as both astonish & comfort me & mine. How can Paine, the worker of miracles ever doubt Christ's in the above sense of the word "miracle"? But how can Watson ever believe the above sense of a miracle, who considers it as an arbitrary act of the agent upon an unbelieving patient, whereas the Gospel says that Christ could not do a miracle because of Unbelief?

If Christ could not do miracles because of Unbelief, the reason alleged by Priests for miracles is false; for those who believe want not to be confounded by miracles. Christ & his prophets & Apostles were not ambitious miracle mongers.

You esteem all prophets to be such lying rascals, that I dare not venture to predict the fate of your book.

Prophets in the modern sense of the word have never existed. Jonah was no prophet in the modern sense, for his prophecy of Nineveh failed. Every honest man is a Prophet; he utters his opinion both of private & public matters. Thus, If you go on So, the result is So. He never says such a thing Shall Happen, let you do what you will. A Prophet is a Seer, not an Arbitrary Dictator. It is man's fault if God is not able to do him good, for he gives to the just & to the unjust, but the unjust reject his gift.

What if I should admit, that Samuel, or Ezra, or some other learned Jew composed these books, from public records, many years after the death of Moses? Will it follow that there was no truth in them? According to my logic, it will only follow, that they are not genuine books; every fact recorded in them may be true.

Nothing can be more contemptible than to suppose Public Records to be true. Read them & Judge, if you are not a Fool.

Of what consequence is it whether Moses wrote the Pentateuch or no? If Paine trifles in some of his objections, it is folly to confute him so seriously in them & leave his more material ones unanswered. Public Records! As If Public Records were True! Impossible, for the facts are such as none but the actor could tell. If it is True, Moses & none but he could write it unless we allow it to be Poetry, & that Poetry inspired.

If historical facts can be written by inspiration, Milton's *Paradise Lost* is as true as *Genesis* or *Exodus*; but the Evidence is nothing, for how can he who writes what he has neither seen nor heard of be an Evidence of The Truth of his history?

> Having done with what you call the grammatical evidence that Moses was not the author of the books attributed to him, you come to your historical and chronological evidence; and you begin with *Genesis*.

I cannot conceive the Divinity of the books in the Bible to consist either in who they were written by or at what time or in the historical evidence, which may be all false in the eyes of one man & true in the eyes of another, but in the Sentiments & Examples which, whether true or Parabolic are Equally useful as Examples given to us of the perverseness of some & its consequent evil & the honesty of others & its consequent good. This sense of the Bible is equally true to all & equally plain to all. None can doubt the impression which he receives from a book of Examples. If he is good he will abhor wickedness in David or Abraham; if he is wicked he will make their wickedness an excuse for his, & so he would do by any other book.

> You may as reasonably attribute cruelty and murder to the judge of the land in condemning criminals to death, as butchery and massacre to Moses in executing the command of God.

All Penal Laws court Transgression & therefore are cruelty & Murder.

The laws of the Jews were (both ceremonial & real) the basest & most oppressive of human codes &, being like all other codes given under pretense of divine command, were what Christ pronounced them, The Abomination that maketh desolate; i.e. State Religion, which is the Source of all Cruelty.

It appears to me Now that Tom Paine is a better Christian than the Bishop. I have read this Book with attention & find that the Bishop has only hurt Paine's heel, while Paine has broken his head. The Bishop has not answered one of Paine's grand objections.

Annotations to Bacon's *Essays*
(*circa 1798*)

I am astonished how such Contemptible Knavery & Folly as this Book contains can ever have been called Wisdom by Men of Sense, but perhaps this never was the Case & all Men of Sense have despised the Book as much as I do.

Everybody Knows that this is Epicurus and Lucretius & Yet Everybody Says that it is Christian Philosophy. How is this Possible? Everybody must be a Liar & deceiver, but Everybody does not do this, But The Hirelings of Kings & Courts who make themselves Everybody & Knowingly propagate Falsehood.

It was a Common opinion in the Court of Queen Elizabeth that Knavery Is Wisdom. Cunning Plotters were considered as wise Machiavels.

Self-Evident Truth is one Thing, and Truth the result of Reasoning is another Thing. Rational Truth is not the Truth of Christ, but of Pilate. It is the Tree of the Knowledge of Good & Evil.

But it is not only the difficulty and labour which men take in finding out of truth; nor again, that, when it is found, it imposeth upon men's thoughts, that doth bring lies in favour; but a natural, though corrupt love of the lie itself. One of the later school of the Grecians examineth the matter, and is at a stand to think what should be in it, that men should love lies, where neither they make for pleasure, as with poets; nor for advantage, as with the merchant; but for the lie's sake. But I cannot tell: this same truth is a naked and open daylight, that doth not show the masques, and mummeries, and triumphs of the world half so stately and daintily as candlelights.

What Bacon calls Lies is Truth itself.

The reason was, because the religion of the heathen consisted rather in rites and ceremonies, than in any constant belief: for you may imagine what kind of faith theirs was, when the chief doctors and fathers of their church were the poets.

Prophets.

It was great blasphemy when the devil said, "I will ascend and be like the Highest"; but it is greater blasphemy to personate God, and bring him in saying, "I will descend, and be like the prince of darkness."

Did not Jesus descend & become a Servant? The Prince of darkness is a Gentleman & not a Man; he is a Lord Chancellor.

This public envy seemeth to beat chiefly upon principal officers or ministers, rather than upon kings and estates themselves.

A Lie! Everybody hates a King. Bacon was afraid to say that the Envy was upon a King, but is This Envy or Indignation?

But power to do good is the true and lawful end of aspiring; for good thoughts (though God accept them), yet towards men are little better than good dreams, except they be put in act.

Thought is Act. Christ's Acts were Nothing to Caesar's if this is not so.

Also, when discords, and quarrels, and factions are carried openly and audaciously it is a sign the reverence of government is lost.

When the Reverence of Government is Lost, it is better than when it is found. Reverence is all for Reverence.

The things to be seen and observed are the courts of princes, especially when they give audience to ambassadors; the courts of justice . . . the churches and monasteries . . . the walls and fortifications . . . and so the havens and harbours, antiquities and ruins, libraries, colleges, disputations, and lectures where any are; shipping and navies; houses and gardens of state and pleasure near great cities; armories, arsenals, magazines, exchanges, burses, warehouses, exercises of horsemanship, fencing, training of soldiers, and the like; comedies . . . treasures of jewels and robes; cabinets and rarities.

The Things worthy to be seen are all the Trumpery he could rake together.

Nothing of Arts or Artists or Learned Men or of Agriculture or any Useful Thing. His Business & Bosom was to be Lord Chancellor.

Certainly, if a man will keep but of even hand, his ordinary expenses ought to be but to the half of his receipts; and if he think to wax rich, but to the third part.

If this is advice to the Poor, it is mocking them. If to the Rich, it is worse still; it is The Miser. If to the Middle Class, it is the direct Contrary to Christ's advice.

It is certain, that sedentary and within-door arts, and delicate manufactures, (that require rather the finger than the arm,) have in their nature a contrariety to a military disposition . . . therefore it was great advantage in the ancient states of Sparta, Athens, Rome and others that they had the use of slaves, which commonly did rid those manufactures; but that is abolished, in greatest part, by the Christian law. That which cometh nearest to it is, to leave those arts chiefly to strangers . . . and to contain the principal bulk of the vulgar natives within those three kinds, tillers of the ground, free servants, and handicraftmen of strong and manly arts; as smiths, masons, carpenters, &c. not reckoning professed soldiers.

Bacon calls Intellectual Arts Unmanly. Poetry, Painting, Music are in his opinion Useless; & so they are for Kings & Wars & shall in the End annihilate them.

Annotations to Boyd's "Historical Notes" to *A Translation of the Inferno in English Verse (circa 1800)*

Antecedent to and independent of all laws, a man may learn to argue on the nature of moral obligation, and the duty of universal benevolence, from Cumberland, Wollaston, Shaftesbury, Hutcheson; but would he feel what vice is in itself . . . let him enter into the passions of Lear, when he feels the ingratitude of his children; of Hamlet, when he learns the story of his father's murder; . . . and he will know the difference of right and wrong much more clearly than from all the moralists that ever wrote.

The grandest Poetry is Immoral, the Grandest characters Wicked Very; Satan, Capanius, Othello a murderer, Prometheus, Jupiter, Jehovah, Jesus a wine bibber.

Cunning & Morality are not Poetry but Philosophy. The Poet is Independent & Wicked; the Philosopher is Dependent & Good.

Poetry is to excuse Vice & show its reason & necessary purgation.

Annotations to Reynolds'
Discourses *(circa 1808)*

This Man was Hired to Depress Art. This is the opinion of Will Blake; my Proofs of this Opinion are given in the Following Notes:

Advice of the Popes who succeeded the Age of Rafael:
Degrade first the Arts if you'd Mankind degrade;
Hire Idiots to Paint with cold light & hot shade;
Give high Price for the worst, leave the best in
    disgrace,
And with Labours of Ignorance fill every place.

Having spent the Vigour of my Youth & Genius under the Oppression of Sir Joshua & his Gang of Cunning Hired Knaves Without Employment & as much as could possibly be Without Bread, The Reader must Expect to Read in all my Remarks on these Books Nothing but Indignation & Resentment. While Sir Joshua was rolling in Riches, Barry was Poor & Unemployed except by his own Energy. Mortimer was called a Madman, & only Portrait Painting applauded & rewarded by the Rich & Great. Reynolds & Gainsborough Blotted & Blurred one against the other & Divided all the English World between them. Fuseli, Indignant, almost hid himself—I am hid.

The Arts & Sciences are the Destruction of Tyrannies or Bad Governments. Why should A Good Government endeavour to Depress What is its Chief & only Support?
The Foundation of Empire is Art & Science. Remove them or Degrade them & the Empire is No More. Empire follows Art & not Vice Versa as Englishmen suppose.

TO THE KING

The regular progress of cultivated life is from necessaries to accommodations, from accommodations to ornaments.

The Bible says That Cultivated Life Existed First. Uncultivated Life comes afterwards from Satan's Hirelings. Necessaries, Accommodations & Ornaments are the whole of Life. Satan took away Ornament First. Next he took away Accommodations, & Then he became Lord & Master of Necessaries.

To give advice to those who are contending for royal liberality, . . .

Liberality! We want not Liberality. We want a Fair Price & Proportionate Value & a General Demand for Art.

Let not that Nation where Less than Nobility is the Reward Pretend that Art is Encouraged by that Nation; Art is the First in Intellectuals & Ought to be First in Nations.

Invention depends Altogether upon Execution or Organization. As that is right or wrong so is the Invention perfect or imperfect. Whoever is set to Undermine the Execution of Art is set to Destroy Art. Michael Angelo's Art Depends on Michael Angelo's Execution Altogether.

How incapable of producing anything of their own, those are, who have spent most of their time in making finished copies, is an observation well known to all who are conversant with our art.

Finished! What does he Mean? Niggling Without the Correct & Definite Outline? If he means That Copying Correctly is a hindrance he is a Liar, for that is the only School to the Language of Art.

[The editor denies rumors that the Discourses were written by Johnson or Burke.]

The Contradictions in Reynolds' Discourses are Strong Presumptions that they are the Work of Several Hands, But this is no Proof that Reynolds did not Write them. The Man, Either Painter or Philosopher, who Learns or Acquires all he Knows from Others, Must be full of Contradictions.

> But this disposition to abstractions, to generalizing and classification, is the great glory of the human mind.

To Generalize is to be an Idiot. To Particularize is the Alone Distinction of Merit. General Knowledges are those Knowledges that Idiots possess.

DISCOURSE I

I consider Reynolds' Discourses to the Royal Academy as the Simulations of the Hypocrite who smiles particularly where he means to Betray. His Praise of Rafael is like the Hysteric Smile of Revenge. His Softness & Candour, the hidden trap & the poisoned feast. He praises Michael Angelo for Qualities which Michael Angelo Abhorred, & He blames Rafael for the only Qualities which Rafael Valued. Whether Reynolds knew what he was doing is nothing to me; the Mischief is just the same whether a Man does it Ignorantly or Knowingly. I always considered True Art & True Artists to be particularly Insulted & Degraded by the Reputation of these Discourses, As much as they were Degraded by the Reputation of Reynolds' Paintings, & that Such Artists as Reynolds are at all times Hired by the Satans for the Depression of Art—A Pretense of Art, to Destroy Art.

Reynolds' Opinion was that Genius May be Taught & that all Pretense to Inspiration is a Lie & a Deceit, to say the least of it. For if it is a Deceit, the Whole Bible is Madness. This Opinion originates in the Greeks Calling the Muses Daughters of Memory.

The Inquiry in England is not whether a Man has Talents & Genius, But whether he is Passive & Polite & a Virtuous Ass & obedient to Noblemen's Opinions in Art & Science. If he is, he is a Good Man. If Not, he must be Starved.

Raffaelle, it is true, had not the advantage of studying in an Academy; but all Rome, and the works of Michael Angelo in particular, were to him an Academy. On the site of the Capella Sistina, he immediately from a dry, Gothick, and even insipid manner, which attends to the minute accidental discriminations of particular and individual objects, assumed that grand style of painting which improves partial representation by the general and invariable ideas of nature.

I do not believe that Rafael taught Mich. Angelo, or that Mich. Angl. taught Rafael, any more than I believe that the Rose teaches the Lily how to grow or the Apple tree teaches the Pear tree how to bear Fruit. I do not believe the tales of Anecdote writers when they militate against Individual Character.

Minute Discrimination is Not Accidental. All Sublimity is founded on Minute Discrimination.

When we read the lives of the most eminent Painters, every page informs us, that no part of their time was spent in dissipation.

The Lives of Painters say that Rafael died of Dissipation. Idleness is one Thing & Dissipation Another. He who has Nothing to Dissipate Cannot Dissipate. The Weak Man may be Virtuous Enough, but will Never be an Artist. Painters are noted for being Dissipated & Wild.

DISCOURSE II

How incapable those are of producing anything of their own, who have spent much of their time in making finished copies.

This is most False, for no one can ever Design till he has learned the Language of Art by making many Finished Copies, both of Nature & Art & of whatever comes in his way from Earliest Childhood.

The difference between a bad Artist & a Good One Is: the Bad Artist Seems to Copy a Great Deal, The Good one Really Does Copy a Great Deal.

You cannot do better than have recourse to nature herself, who is always at hand, and in comparison of whose true splendour the best coloured pictures are but faint and feeble.

Nonsense! Every Eye Sees differently. As the Eye, Such the Object.

Labour to invent on their general principles. . . . how a Michael Angelo or a Raffaelle would have treated this subject: . . .

General Principles Again! Unless You Consult Particulars You Cannot even Know or See Mich. Ang. or Rafael or anything Else.

But as mere enthusiasm will carry you but a little way. . . .

Mere Enthusiasm is the All in All! Bacon's Philosophy has ruined England. Bacon is only Epicurus over again.

The well-grounded painter . . . is contented that all shall be as great as himself, who have undergone the same fatigue.

The Man who asserts that there is no Such Thing as Softness in Art & that everything in Art is Definite & Determinate has not been told this by Practice, but by Inspiration & Vision, because Vision is Determinate & Perfect, & he Copies That without Fatigue, Everything being Definite & determinate. Softness is Produced Alone by Comparative Strength & Weakness in the Marking out of the Forms.

I say These Principles could never be found out by the Study of Nature without Con-, or Innate, Science.

DISCOURSE III

A Work of Genius is a Work "Not to be obtained by the Invocation of Memory & her Siren Daughters, but by Devout prayer to that Eternal Spirit, who can enrich with all utterance & knowledge & sends out his Seraphim with the hallowed fire of his Altar to touch & purify the lips of whom he pleases." Milton.

The following Discourse is particularly Interesting to Block-heads, as it Endeavours to prove That there is No such thing as Inspiration & that any Man of a plain Understanding may by Thieving from Others become a Mich. Angelo.

> The wish of the genuine painter must be more extensive; instead of endeavouring to amuse mankind with the minute neatness of his imitations, he must endeavour to improve them by the grandeur of his ideas.

Without Minute Neatness of Execution, The Sublime cannot Exist! Grandeur of Ideas is founded on Precision of Ideas.

> He never travelled to heaven to gather new ideas; and he finds himself possessed of no other qualifications than what mere common observation and a plain understanding can confer.

The Man who never in his Mind & Thoughts travelled to Heaven Is No Artist.

Artists who are above a plain Understanding are Mocked & Destroyed by this President of Fools.

> The whole beauty of art consists . . . in being able to get above all singular forms, local customs, particularities, and details of every kind.

A Folly!

Singular & particular Detail is the Foundation of the Sublime.

> This idea of the perfect state of nature, which the Artist calls the Ideal Beauty, is the great leading principle by which works of genius are conducted.

Knowledge of Ideal Beauty is Not to be Acquired. It is Born with us. Innate Ideas are in Every Man Born with him; they are truly Himself. The Man who says that we have No Innate Ideas must be a Fool & Knave, Having No conscience or Innate Science.

> Thus it is from a reiterated experience and a close comparison of the objects in nature, that an artist becomes possessed of the idea of that central form . . . from which every deviation is deformity.

One Central Form Composed of all other Forms being Granted, it does not therefore follow that all other Forms are Deformity.

The ancient sculptors . . . being indefatigable in the school of nature, have left models of that perfect form. . . .

All Forms are Perfect in the Poet's Mind, but these are not Abstracted nor Compounded from Nature, but are from Imagination.

Even the great Bacon treats with ridicule the idea of confining proportion to rules, or of producing beauty by selection.

The Great Bacon he is Called (I call him the Little Bacon) says that Everything must be done by Experiment. His first principle is Unbelief, And Yet here he says that Art must be produced Without such Method. He is, Like Sir Joshua, full of Self-Contradiction & Knavery.

There is a rule, obtained out of general nature, to contradict which is to fall into deformity.

What is General Nature? Is there Such a Thing?
What is General Knowledge? Is there such a Thing? Strictly Speaking, All Knowledge is Particular.

Still none of them is the representation of an individual, but of a class.

Every Class is individual.

The painter must divest himself of all prejudices . . . disregard all local and temporary ornaments, and look only on those general habits, which are everywhere and always the same.

Generalizing in Everything, the Man would soon be a Fool, but a Cunning Fool.

Albert Dürer, as Vasari has justly remarked, would, probably, have been one of the first painters of his age, (and he lived in an era of great artists,) had he been initiated into those great principles. . . .

What does this mean "Would have been one of the first Painters of his Age"? Albert Dürer Is! Not would have been! Besides, let them look at Gothic Figures & Gothic Buildings & not talk of Dark Ages or of Any Age! Ages are All Equal. But Genius is Always Above The Age.

DISCOURSE IV

The errors of genius, however, are pardonable. . . .

Genius has no Error; it is Ignorance that is Error.

DISCOURSE V

Gainsborough told a Gentleman of Rank & Fortune that the Worst Painters always chose the Grandest Subjects. I desired the Gentleman to Set Gainsborough about one of Rafael's Grandest Subjects, Namely Christ delivering the Keys to St. Peter, & he would find that in Gainsborough's hands it would be a Vulgar Subject of Poor Fishermen & a Journeyman Carpenter.

The following Discourse is written with the same End in View that Gainsborough had in making the Above assertion, Namely To Represent Vulgar Artists as the Models of Executive Merit.

If you mean to preserve the most perfect beauty in its most perfect state, you cannot express the passions, all of which produce distortion and deformity, more or less, in the most beautiful faces.

What Nonsense!

Passion & Expression is Beauty Itself. The Face that is Incapable of Passion & Expression is Deformity Itself. Let it be Painted & Patched & Praised & Advertised forever, it will only be admired by Fools.

DISCOURSE VI

As . . . art shall advance, its powers will be still more and more fixed by rules.

If Art was Progressive We should have had Mich. Angelos &
Rafaels to Succeed & to Improve upon each other, But it is not
so. Genius dies with its Possessor & comes not again till Another is Born with It.

We should to the last moment of our lives continue a settled inter-
course with all the true examples of grandeur.

Reynolds Thinks that Man Learns all that he Knows. I say on
the Contrary That Man Brings All that he has or Can have Into
the World with him. Man is Born Like a Garden ready Planted
& Sown. This World is too poor to produce one Seed.

The mind is but a barren soil; a soil which is soon exhausted, and
will produce no crop.

The Mind that could have produced this Sentence must have
been a Pitiful, a Pitiable Imbecility. I always thought that the
Human Mind was the most Prolific of All Things & Inexhaust-
ible. I certainly do Thank God that I am not like Reynolds.

Men who although thus bound down by the almost invincible powers of early habits, have still exerted extraordinary abilities.

He who Can be bound down is No Genius. Genius cannot be
Bound; it may be Rendered Indignant & Outrageous.
"Oppression makes the Wise Man Mad"
                                        Solomon.

DISCOURSE VII

The Purpose of the following Discourse is to Prove That Taste
& Genius are not of Heavenly Origin & that all who have Sup-
posed that they Are so Are to be Considered as Weak-headed
Fanatics.

The obligations Reynolds has laid on Bad Artists of all Classes will at all times make them his Admirers, but most especially for this Discourse in which it is proved that the Stupid are born
with Faculties Equal to other Men, Only they have not Cultivated them because they thought it not worth the trouble.

To understand literally these metaphors or ideas expressed in poetical language seems . . . absurd.

The Ancients did not mean to Impose when they affirmed their belief in Vision & Revelation. Plato was in Earnest; Milton was in Earnest. They believed that God did Visit Man Really & Truly & not as Reynolds pretends.

That because painters sometimes represent poets writing from the dictates of a little winged boy or genius, that this same genius did really inform him in a whisper what he was to write; and that he himself is but a mere machine unconscious of the operations of his own mind.

How very Anxious Reynolds is to Disprove & Contemn Spiritual Perception.

We often appear to differ in sentiments from each other merely from the inaccuracy of terms. . . .

It is not in Terms that Reynolds & I disagree. Two Contrary Opinions can never by any Language be made alike. I say Taste & Genius are Not Teachable or Acquirable, but are born with us. Reynolds says the Contrary.

It is the very same taste which relishes a demonstration in geometry, that is pleased with the resemblance of a picture to an original, and touched with the harmony of music.

Demonstration, Similitude & Harmony are Objects of Reasoning. Invention, Identity & Melody are Objects of Intuition.

Colouring is true . . . from brightness, from softness, from harmony, from resemblance; because these agree with their object, nature, and therefore are true; as true as mathematical demonstration; . . .

God forbid that Truth should be Confined to Mathematical Demonstration.

DISCOURSE VIII

Burke's Treatise on the Sublime & Beautiful is founded on the Opinions of Newton & Locke. On this Treatise Reynolds has

grounded many of his assertions in all his Discourses. I read
Burke's Treatise when very Young; at the same time I read Locke
on Human Understanding & Bacon's *Advancement of Learning.*
On Every one of these Books I wrote my Opinions & on looking
them over find that my Notes on Reynolds in this Book are exactly Similar. I felt the Same Contempt & Abhorrence then that
I do now. They mock Inspiration & Vision. Inspiration & Vision
was then, & now is & I hope will always Remain, my Element,
my Eternal Dwelling place. How can I then hear it Contemned
without returning Scorn for Scorn?

The conduct of Titian in the picture of Bacchus and Ariadne, has
been much celebrated, and justly, for the harmony of colouring.

Such Harmony of Colouring is destructive of Art. One Species of General Hue over all is the Cursed Thing called Harmony;
it is like the Smile of a Fool.

Annotations to Spurzheim's *Observations on the Deranged Manifestations of the Mind, or Insanity*

(circa 1819)

Religion is another fertile cause of insanity. Mr. Haslam, though he declares it sinful to consider religion as a cause of insanity, adds, however, that he would be ungrateful, did he not avow his obligations to Methodism for its supply of numerous cases. Hence the primitive feelings of religion may be misled and produce insanity; that is what I would contend for, and in that sense religion often leads to insanity.

Cowper came to me & said: "O that I were insane always. I will never rest. Can you not make me truly insane? I will never rest till I am so. O that in the bosom of God I was hid. You retain health & yet are as mad as any of us all—over us all—mad as a refuge from unbelief—from Bacon, Newton & Locke."

Annotations to Berkeley's
Siris (circa 1820)

God knoweth all things, as pure mind or intellect, but nothing by sense, nor in nor through a sensory. Therefore to suppose a sensory of any kind, whether space or any other, in God would be very wrong, and lead us into false conceptions of his nature.

Imagination or the Human Eternal Body in Every Man.

But in respect of a perfect spirit, there is nothing hard or impenetrable: there is no resistance to the deity. Nor hath he any Body: Nor is the supreme being united to the world, as the soul of an animal is to its body, which necessarily implieth defect, both as an instrument and as a constant weight and impediment.

Imagination or the Divine Body in Every Man.

Natural phenomena are only natural appearances. . . . They and the phantoms that result from those appearances, the children of imagination grafted upon sense, such for example as pure space, are thought by many the very first in existence and stability, and to embrace and comprehend all beings.

The All in Man. The Divine Image or Imagination.
The Four Senses are the Four Faces of Man & the Four Rivers of the Water of Life.

Plato and Aristotle considered God as abstracted or distinct from the natural world. But the Egyptians considered God and nature as making one whole, or all things together as making one universe.

They also considered God as abstracted or distinct from the Imaginative World, but Jesus, as also Abraham & David, considered God as a Man in the Spiritual or Imaginative Vision.

Jesus considered Imagination to be the Real Man & says I will not leave you Orphaned and I will manifest myself to you; he says also the Spiritual Body or Angel as little Children always behold the Face of the Heavenly Father.

The perceptions of sense are gross: but even in the senses there is a difference. Though harmony and proportion are not objects of sense, yet the eye and the ear are organs, which offer to the mind such materials, by means whereof she may apprehend both the one and the other.

Harmony and Proportion are Qualities & Not Things. The Harmony & Proportion of a Horse are not the same with those of a Bull. Everything has its own Harmony & Proportion, Two Inferior Qualities in it. For its Reality is its Imaginative Form.

By experiments of sense we become acquainted with the lower faculties of the soul; and from them, whether by a gradual evolution or ascent, we arrive at the highest. These become subjects for fancy to work upon. Reason considers and judges of the imaginations. And these acts of reason become new objects to the understanding.

Knowledge is not by deduction, but Immediate by Perception or Sense at once. Christ addresses himself to the Man, not to his Reason. Plato did not bring Life & Immortality to Light. Jesus only did this.

There is according to Plato properly no knowledge, but only opinion concerning things sensible and perishing, not because they are naturally abstruse and involved in darkness: but because their nature and existence is uncertain, ever fleeting and changing.

Jesus supposes everything to be Evident to the Child & to the Poor & Unlearned. Such is the Gospel.

The Whole Bible is filled with Imagination & Visions from End to End, & not with Moral Virtues; that is the business of Plato & the Greeks & all Warriors. The Moral Virtues are continual Accusers of Sin & promote Eternal Wars & Dominancy over others.

Aristotle maketh a threefold distinction of objects according to the three speculative sciences. Physics he supposeth to be conversant about such things as have a principle of motion in themselves, mathematics about things permanent but not abstracted, and theology about being abstracted and immovable, which distinction may be seen in the ninth book of his metaphysics.

God is not a Mathematical Diagram.

It is a maxim of the Platonic philosophy, that the soul of man was originally furnished with native inbred notions, and stands in need of sensible occasions, not absolutely for producing them, but only for awakening, rousing or exciting into act what was already pre-existent, dormant, and latent in the soul.

The Natural Body is an Obstruction to the Soul or Spiritual Body.

It may be inferred that all beings are in the soul. For, saith [Themistius], the forms are the beings. By the form every thing is what it is. And, he adds, it is the soul that imparteth forms to matter.

This is my Opinion, but Forms must be apprehended by Sense or the Eye of Imagination. Man is all Imagination. God is man, & exists in us, & we in him.

What Jesus came to Remove was the Heathen or Platonic Philosophy, which blinds the Eye of Imagination, The Real Man.

Annotations to Wordsworth's *Poems*

(1826)

PREFACE

The powers requisite for the production of poetry are, first, those of observation and description, . . . whether the things depicted be actually present to the senses, or have a place only in the memory. . . . 2ndly, Sensibility, ...

One Power alone makes a Poet—Imagination, The Divine Vision.

Poems Referring to the Period of Childhood

I see in Wordsworth the Natural Man rising up against the Spiritual Man Continually, & then he is No Poet but a Heathen Philosopher at Enmity against all true Poetry or Inspiration.

> And I could wish my days to be
> Bound each to each by natural piety.

There is no such Thing as Natural Piety, Because The Natural Man is at Enmity with God.

To H.C. Six Years Old

This is all in the highest degree Imaginative & equal to any Poet, but not Superior. I cannot think that Real Poets have any competition. None are greatest in the Kingdom of Heaven; it is so in Poetry.

Influence of Natural Objects
In calling forth and strengthening the Imagination
in Boyhood and early Youth.

Natural Objects always did & now do Weaken, deaden & obliterate Imagination in Me. Wordsworth must know that what he Writes Valuable is Not to be found in Nature. Read Michael Angelo's Sonnet, vol. 2, p. 179.

Essay, Supplementary to the Preface.

I do not know who wrote these Prefaces. They are very mischievous & direct contrary to Wordsworth's own Practice.

> From what I saw with my own eyes, I knew that the Imagery was spurious. In nature everything is distinct, yet nothing defined into absolute independent singleness. In Macpherson's work, it is exactly the reverse; everything (that is not stolen) is in this manner defined, insulated, dislocated, deadened,—yet nothing distinct. It will always be so when words are substituted for things. . . . Yet, much as these pretended treasures of antiquity have been admired, they have been wholly uninfluential upon the literature of the country . . . no Author in the least distinguished, has ventured formally to imitate them—except the Boy, Chatterton, on their first appearance.

I Believe both Macpherson & Chatterton, that what they say is Ancient Is so. I own myself an admirer of Ossian equally with any other Poet, whatever; Rowley & Chatterton also.

> He . . . takes leave of his Readers by assuring them that if he were not persuaded that the Contents of these Volumes and the work to which they are subsidiary evinced something of the "Vision and the Faculty divine," . . . he would not, if a wish could do it, save them from immediate destruction.

It appears to me as if the last Paragraph beginning With "Is it the result" Was writ by another hand & mind from the rest of these Prefaces. Perhaps they are the opinions of a Portrait or Landscape Painter. Imagination is the Divine Vision, not of The World, nor of Man, nor from Man as he is a Natural Man, but only as he is a Spiritual Man. Imagination has nothing to do with Memory.

Annotations to Wordsworth's Preface to *The Excursion, Being a Portion of the Recluse, A Poem* (circa 1826)

All strength, all terror, single or in bands
That ever was put forth in personal Form
Jehovah—with his thunder & the choir
Of shouting Angels & the empyreal thrones—
I pass them unalarmed, . . .   5

    Solomon, when he Married Pharaoh's daughter & became a
Convert to the Heathen Mythology, Talked exactly in this way
of Jehovah as a Very inferior object of Man's Contemplations;
he also passed him by unalarmed & was permitted. Jehovah
dropped a tear & followed him by his Spirit into the Abstract
Void; it is called the Divine Mercy, Satan dwells in it, but Mercy
does not dwell in him; he knows not to Forgive.

How exquisitely the individual Mind
(And the progressive powers perhaps no less
(Of the whole species) to the external World
Is fitted.—& how exquisitely too,
Theme this but little heard of among Men   5
The external World is fitted to the Mind.

    You shall not bring me down to believe such fitting & fitted.
I know better, & Please your Lordship.

—Such grateful haunts forgoing, if I oft
Must turn elsewhere—to travel near the tribes
And fellowships of Men, & see ill sights
Of madding passions mutually inflamed
Must hear Humanity in fields & groves   5
Pipe solitary anguish; or must hang
Brooding above the fierce confederate storm
Of Sorrow barricaded evermore
Within the walls of cities; may these sounds

Have their authentic comment—that even these   10
Hearing I be not downcast nor forlorn.

Does not this Fit, & is it not Fitting most Exquisitely too, but
to what? Not to Mind, but to the Vile Body only, & to its Laws
of Good & Evil & its Enmities against Mind.

Annotations to Thornton's
The Lord's Prayer, Newly Translated (1827)

I look upon this as a Most Malignant & Artful attack upon the Kingdom of Jesus By the Classical Learned through the Instrumentality of Dr. Thornton. The Greek & Roman Classics is the Antichrist. I say Is & not Are as most expressive & correct too.

Doctor Johnson on the Bible:
The Bible is the most difficult book in the world to comprehend, nor can it be understood at all by the unlearned, except through the aid of critical and explanatory notes. . . ."

Christ & his Apostles were Illiterate Men. Caiaphas, Pilate & Herod were Learned.

Lord Byron on the Ethics of Christ:
What made Socrates the greatest of men? His moral truths—his ethics. What proved Jesus Christ to be the son of God, hardly less than his miracles did? His moral precepts. . . ."

If Morality was Christianity, Socrates was The Saviour.
The Beauty of the Bible is that the most Ignorant & Simple Minds Understand it Best. Was Johnson hired to Pretend to Religious Terrors while he was an Infidel, or how was it?

THE LORD'S PRAYER
Translated from the Greek, by Dr. Thornton

Come let us worship, and bow down, and kneel, before the Lord, our Maker. Psalm XCV.

O Father Of Mankind, Thou, who dwellest in the highest of the Heavens, Reverenced be Thy Name!

May Thy Reign be, everywhere, proclaimed so that Thy Will may be done upon the Earth, as it is in the mansions of Heaven:

Grant unto me, and the whole world, day by day, an abundant supply of spiritual and corporeal Food:

Forgive us our Transgressions against Thee, as we extend our Kindness, and Forgiveness, to all:
   O God! Abandon us not, when surrounded, by Trials;
   But Preserve Us from the Dominion of Satan: For Thine only, is
the Sovereignty, the power, and the glory, throughout Eternity!!!
                                              Amen.

This is Saying the Lord's Prayer Backwards, which they say
Raises the Devil.

Doctor Thornton's Tory Translation, Translated out of its disguise in the Classical & Scotch language into the vulgar English:

Our Father Augustus Caesar, who art in these thy Substantial
Astronomical Telescopic Heavens, Holiness to thy Name or Title,
& reverence to thy Shadow. Thy Kingship come upon Earth first
& thence in Heaven. Give us day by day our Real Taxed Substantial Money-bought Bread; deliver from the Holy Ghost whatever
cannot be Taxed, for all is debts & Taxes between Caesar & us
& one another; lead us not to read the Bible, but let our Bible
be Virgil & Shakespeare, & deliver us from Poverty in Jesus, that
Evil One. For thine is the Kingship, or Allegoric Godship, & the
Power, or War, & the Glory, or Law, Ages after Ages in thy De-
scendants; for God is only an Allegory of Kings & nothing Else.
Amen.

Thus we see that the Real God is the Goddess Nature, & that
God Creates nothing but what can be Touched & Weighed &
Taxed & Measured. All else is Heresy & Rebellion against Cae-
sar, Virgil's Only God. See Eclogue i. For all this we thank Dr.
Thornton.

Part Five
SELECTED LETTERS

To Dr. Trusler

Rev'd Sir,

I find more & more that my Style of Designing is a Species by itself, & in this which I send you have been compelled by my Genius or Angel to follow where he led; if I were to act otherwise it would not fulfill the purpose for which alone I live, which is, in conjunction with such men as my friend Cumberland, to renew the lost Art of the Greeks.

I attempted every morning for a fortnight together to follow your Dictate, but when I found my attempts were in vain, resolved to show an independence which I know will please an Author better than slavishly following the track of another, however admirable that track may be. At any rate, my Excuse must be: I could not do otherwise; it was out of my power!

I know I begged of you to give me your Ideas & promised to build on them; here I counted without my host. I now find my mistake.

The Design I have Sent Is:

A Father taking leave of his Wife & Child Is watched by Two Fiends incarnate, with intention that when his back is turned they will murder the mother & her infant. If this is not Malevolence with a vengeance, I have never seen it on Earth; & if you approve of this, I have no doubt of giving you Benevolence with Equal Vigor, as also Pride & Humility, but cannot previously describe in words what I mean to Design, for fear I should Evaporate the Spirit of my Invention. But I hope that none of my Designs will be destitute of Infinite Particulars which will present themselves to the Contemplator. And though I call them Mine, I know that they are not Mine, being of the same opinion with Milton when he says That the Muse visits his Slumbers & awakes & governs his Song when Morn purples the East, & being also in the predicament of that prophet who says: I cannot go beyond the command of the Lord, to speak good or bad.

If you approve of my Manner, & it is agreeable to you, I would rather Paint Pictures in oil of the same dimensions than make

Drawings, & on the same terms; by this means you will have a number of Cabinet pictures which I flatter myself will not be unworthy of a Scholar of Rembrandt & Teniers, whom I have Studied no less than Rafael & Michael Angelo. Please to send me your orders respecting this, & In my next Effort I promise more Expedition.

I am, Rev'd Sir,
Your very humble serv't
Will'm Blake

Hercules Build'gs
Lambeth
Aug'st 16, 1799

To Dr. Trusler

23 August 1799

Rev'd Sir,

I really am sorry that you are fallen out with the Spiritual World, Especially if I should have to answer for it. I feel very sorry that your Ideas & Mine on Moral Painting differ so much as to have made you angry with my method of Study. If I am wrong, I am wrong in good company. I had hoped your plan comprehended All Species of this Art, & Especially that you would not regret that Species which gives Existence to Every other, namely, Visions of Eternity. You say that I want somebody to Elucidate my Ideas. But you ought to know that What is Grand is necessarily obscure to Weak men. That which can be made Explicit to the Idiot is not worth my care. The wisest of the Ancients considered what is not too Explicit as the fittest for Instruction, because it rouses the faculties to act. I name Moses, Solomon, Aesop, Homer, Plato.

But as you have favored me with your remarks on my Design, permit me in return to defend it against a mistaken one, which is That I have supposed Malevolence without a Cause. Is not Merit in one a Cause of Envy in another, & Serenity & Happiness & Beauty a Cause of Malevolence? But Want of Money & the Distress of A Thief can never be alleged as the Cause of his Thieving, for many honest people endure greater hardships with Fortitude. We must therefore seek the Cause elsewhere than in want of Money, for that is the Miser's passion, not the Thief's.

I have therefore proved your Reasonings Ill-proportioned, which you can never prove my figures to be; they are those of Michael Angelo, Rafael & the Antique, & of the best living Models. I perceive that your Eye is perverted by Caricature Prints, which ought not to abound so much as they do. Fun I love, but too much Fun is of all things the most loathsome. Mirth is better than Fun, & Happiness is better than Mirth. I feel that a Man may be happy in This World. And I know that This World Is a World of Imagination & Vision. I see Everything I paint In This World, but Everybody does not see alike. To the Eyes of a Miser a Guinea is more beautiful than the Sun, & a bag worn with the use of Money has more beautiful proportions than a Vine filled with Grapes. The tree which moves some to tears of joy is in the Eyes of others only a Green thing that stands in the way. Some See Nature all Ridicule & Deformity, & by these I shall not regulate my proportions; & Some Scarce see Nature at all. But to the Eyes of the Man of Imagination, Nature is Imagination itself. As a man is, So he Sees. As the Eye is formed, such are its Powers. You certainly Mistake when you say that the Visions of Fancy are not to be found in This World. To Me This World is all One continued Vision of Fancy or Imagination, & I feel Flattered when I am told so. What is it sets Homer, Virgil & Milton in so high a rank of Art? Why is the Bible more Entertaining & Instructive than any other book? Is it not because they are addressed to the Imagination, which is Spiritual Sensation, & but mediately to the Understanding or Reason? Such is True Painting, and such was alone valued by the Greeks & the best modern Artists. Consider what Lord Bacon says: "Sense sends over to Imagination before Reason have judged, & Reason sends over to Imagination before the Decree can be acted." See *Advancem't of Learning,* Part 2, P. 47, of first Edition.

But I am happy to find a Great Majority of Fellow Mortals who can Elucidate My Visions, & Particularly they have been Elucidated by Children, who have taken a greater delight in contemplating my Pictures than I even hoped. Neither Youth nor Childhood is Folly or Incapacity. Some Children are Fools, & so are some Old Men. But There is a vast Majority on the side of Imagination or Spiritual Sensation.

To Engrave after another Painter is infinitely more laborious than to Engrave one's own Inventions. And of the size you require my price has been Thirty Guineas, & I cannot afford to do it for less. I had Twelve for the Head I sent you as a Specimen; but after my own designs I could do at least Six times the quantity of labour in the same time, which will account for the difference of price as also that Chalk Engraving is at least six times as laborious as Aqua tinta. I have no objection to Engraving after another Artist. Engraving is the profession I was apprenticed to, & should never have attempted to live by anything else, If orders had not come in for my Designs & Paintings, which I have the pleasure to tell you are Increasing Every Day. Thus If I am a Painter it is not to be attributed to Seeking after. But I am contented whether I live by Painting or Engraving.

I am, Rev'd Sir, your very obedient servant,

William Blake

13 Hercules Buildings
Lambeth
August 23, 1799

To George Cumberland

26 August 1799

Dear Cumberland:

I ought long ago to have written to you to thank you for your kind recommendation to Dr. Trusler, which, though it has failed of success, is not the less to be remembered by me with Gratitude.

I have made him a Drawing in my best manner; he has sent it back with a Letter full of Criticisms, in which he says It accords not with his Intentions, which are to Reject all Fancy from his Work. How far he Expects to please I cannot tell. But as I cannot paint Dirty rags & old shoes where I ought to place Naked Beauty or simple ornament, I despair of Ever pleasing one Class of Men. Unfortunately our authors of books are among this Class; how soon we Shall have a change for the better I cannot Prophesy. Dr. Trusler says: "Your Fancy, from what I have seen of it, & I have seen variety at Mr. Cumberland's, seems to be in the other world, or the World of Spirits, which accords not my Intentions, which, whilst living in This World, Wish to follow the Nature of it." I could not help Smiling at the difference between the doctrines of Dr. Trusler & those of Christ. But, however, for his own sake I am sorry that a Man should be so enamoured of Rowlandson's caricatures as to call them copies from life & manners or fit Things for a Clergyman to write upon.

Pray let me entreat you to persevere in your Designing; it is the only source of Pleasure. All your other pleasures depend upon it. It is the Tree; your Pleasures are the Fruit. Your Inventions of Intellectual Visions are the Stamina of everything you value. Go on, if not for your own sake, yet for ours, who love & admire your works, but, above all, For the Sake of the Arts. Do not throw aside for any long time the honour intended you by Nature to revive the Greek workmanship. I study your outlines as usual, just as if they were antiques.

As to Myself, about whom you are so kindly Interested, I live by Miracle. I am Painting small Pictures from the Bible. For as to Engraving, in which art I cannot reproach myself with any neglect, yet I am laid by in a corner as if I did not Exist; & Since my Young's *Night Thoughts* have been published, Even Johnson & Fuseli have discarded my Graver. But as I know that He who Works & has his health cannot starve, I laugh at Fortune & Go on & on. I think I foresee better Things than I have ever seen. My Work pleases my employer, & I have an order for Fifty small Pictures at One Guinea each, which is Something better than mere copying after another artist. But above all, I feel myself happy & contented, let what will come; having passed now near twenty years in ups & downs, I am used to them, & perhaps a little practice in them may turn out to benefit. It is now Exactly Twenty years since I was upon the ocean of business, & Though I laugh at Fortune, I am persuaded that She Alone is the Governor of Worldly Riches, & when it is Fit She will call on me; till then I wait with Patience, in hopes that She is busied among my Friends.

With Mine and My Wife's best compliments to Mrs. Cumberland, I remain,

Yours sincerely,
Will'm Blake

Hercules Buildings
Lambeth
Aug'st 26, 1799

To William Hayley

6 May 1800

Dear Sir,

I am very sorry for your immense loss, which is a repetition of what all feel in this valley of misery & happiness mixed. I send the Shadow of the departed Angel; hope the likeness is improved. The lip I have again lessened as you advised & done a good many other softenings to the whole. I know that our deceased friends are more really with us than when they were apparent to our mortal part. Thirteen years ago I lost a brother, & with his spirit I converse daily & hourly in the Spirit & See him in my remembrance in the regions of my Imagination. I hear his advice & even now write from his Dictate. Forgive me for Expressing to you my Enthusiasm, which I wish all to partake of, Since it is to me a Source of Immortal Joy; even in this world by it I am the companion of Angels. May you continue to be so more & more & to be more & more persuaded that every Mortal loss is an Immortal Gain. The Ruins of Time builds Mansions in Eternity. I have also sent A Proof of Pericles for your Remarks, thanking you for the Kindness with which you Express them & feeling heartily your Grief with a brother's Sympathy.

I remain, Dear Sir, Your humble Servant,

William Blake

Lambeth. May 6, 1800

To John Flaxman

21 September 1800

Dear Sculptor of Eternity,

We are safe arrived at our Cottage, which is more beautiful than I thought it, & more convenient. It is a perfect Model for Cottages &, I think, for Palaces of Magnificence, only Enlarging, not altering its proportions, & adding ornaments & not principals. Nothing can be more Grand than its Simplicity & Usefulness. Simple without Intricacy, it seems to be the Spontaneous Effusion of Humanity, congenial to the wants of Man. No other formed House can ever please me so well; nor shall I ever be persuaded, I believe, that it can be improved either in Beauty or Use.

Mr. Hayley received us with his usual brotherly affection. I have begun to work. Felpham is a sweet place for Study because it is more Spiritual than London. Heaven opens here on all sides her golden Gates; her windows are not obstructed by vapours; voices of Celestial inhabitants are more distinctly heard, & their forms more distinctly seen, & my Cottage is also a Shadow of their houses. My Wife & Sister are both well, courting Neptune for an Embrace.

Our Journey was very pleasant; & though we had a great deal of Luggage, No Grumbling, All was Cheerfulness & Good Humour on the Road, & yet we could not arrive at our Cottage before half past Eleven at night, owing to the necessary shifting of our Luggage from one Chaise to another; for we had Seven Different Chaises, & as many different drivers. We set out between Six & Seven in the Morning of Thursday with Sixteen heavy boxes & portfolios full of prints. And Now Begins a New life, because another covering of Earth is shaken off. I am more famed in Heaven for my works than I could well conceive. In my Brain are studies & Chambers filled with books & pictures of old, which I wrote & painted in ages of Eternity before my mortal life; & those works are the delight & Study of Archangels. Why, then, should I be anxious about the riches or fame of mortality? The Lord our father will do for us & with us according to his Divine will for our Good.

You, O Dear Flaxman, are a Sublime Archangel, My Friend & Companion from Eternity; in the Divine bosom is our Dwelling place. I look back into the regions of Reminiscence & behold our ancient days before this Earth appeared in its vegetated mortality to my mortal vegetated Eyes. I see our houses of Eternity, which can never be separated, though our Mortal vehicles should stand at the remotest corners of heaven from each other.

Farewell, My Best Friend. Remember Me & My Wife in Love & Friendship to our Dear Mrs. Flaxman, whom we ardently desire to Entertain beneath our thatched roof of rusted gold, & believe me forever to remain

Your Grateful & Affectionate,

William Blake

Felpham
Sept'r 21, 1800
Sunday Morning

To Thomas Butts

2 October 1800

Friend of Religion & Order,

I thank you for your very beautiful & encouraging Verses, which I account a Crown of Laurels, & I also thank you for your reprehension of follies by me fostered. Your prediction will, I hope, be fulfilled in me, & in future I am the determined advocate of Religion & Humility, the two bands of Society. Having been so full of the Business of Settling the sticks & feathers of my nest, I have not got any forwarder with "the three Marys" or with any other of your commissions; but hope, now I have commenced a new life of industry, to do credit to that new life by Improved Works. Receive from me a return of verses, such as Felpham produces by me, though not such as she produces by her Eldest Son; however, such as they are, I cannot resist the temptation to send them to you.

To my Friend Butts I write
My first Vision of Light,
On the yellow sands sitting.
The Sun was Emitting
His Glorious beams
From Heaven's high Streams.
Over Sea, over Land
My Eyes did Expand
Into regions of air
Away from all Care;
Into regions of fire
Remote from Desire;
The Light of the Morning
Heaven's Mountains adorning,
In particles bright
The jewels of Light
Distinct shone & clear.
Amazed & in fear
I each particle gazed,
Astonished, Amazed;
For each was a Man
Human-formed. Swift I ran,
For they beckoned to me,
Remote by the Sea,
Saying Each grain of Sand,
Every Stone on the Land,
Each rock & each hill,
Each fountain & rill,
Each herb & each tree;
Mountain, hill, earth & sea,
Cloud, Meteor & Star

Are Men Seen Afar.
I stood in the Streams
Of Heaven's bright beams
And Saw Felpham sweet
Beneath my bright feet
In soft Female charms;
And in her fair arms
My Shadow I knew
And my wife's shadow too,
And My Sister & Friend.
We like Infants descend
In our Shadows on Earth
Like a weak mortal birth.
My Eyes more & more
Like a Sea without shore
Continue Expanding,
The Heavens commanding,
Till the Jewels of Light,
Heavenly Men beaming bright,
Appeared as One Man,
Who Complacent began
My limbs to enfold
In his beams of bright gold;
Like dross purged away
All my mire & my clay.
Soft consumed in delight
In his bosom Sun bright
I remained. Soft he smiled,
And I heard his voice Mild
Saying: "This is My Fold,
O thou Ram horned with gold,
Who awakest from Sleep
On the Sides of the Deep.
On the Mountains around
The roarings resound
Of the lion & wolf,
The loud Sea & deep gulf.
These are guards of My Fold,

O thou Ram horned with gold!"
And the voice faded mild.
I remained as a Child;
All I ever had known
Before me bright Shone.
I saw you & your wife
By the fountains of Life.
Such the Vision to me
Appeared on the Sea.

   Mrs. Butts will, I hope, Excuse my not having finished the Portrait. I wait for less hurried moments. Our Cottage looks more & more beautiful. And though the weather is wet, the Air is very Mild, much Milder than it was in London when we came away. Chichester is a very handsome City, Seven miles from us; we can get most Conveniences there. The Country is not so destitute of accommodations to our wants as I expected it would be. We have had but little time for viewing the Country, but what we have seen is Most Beautiful, & the People are Genuine Saxons, handsomer than the people about London. Mrs. Butts will Excuse the following lines:

To Mrs. Butts

Wife of the Friend of those I most revere;
Receive this tribute from a Harp sincere;
Go on in Virtuous Seed sowing on Mold
Of Human Vegetation, & Behold
Your Harvest Springing to Eternal life,
Parent of Youthful Minds, & happy Wife!

W. B.

I am forever Yours,
William Blake

Felpham
Oct'r. 2nd, 1800

To Thomas Butts

Felpham Jan'y 10, 1802

Dear Sir,

Your very kind & affectionate Letter & the many kind things you have said in it called upon me for an immediate answer; but it found My Wife & Myself so Ill, & My wife so very ill, that till now I have not been able to do this duty. The Ague & Rheumatism have been almost her constant Enemies, which she has combated in vain ever since we have been here; & her sickness is always my sorrow, of course. But what you tell me about your sight afflicted me not a little, & that about your health, in another part of your letter, makes me entreat you to take due care of both; it is a part of our duty to God & man to take due care of his Gifts; & though we ought not to think more highly of ourselves, yet we ought to think As highly of ourselves as immortals ought to think.

When I came down here, I was more sanguine than I am at present; but it was because I was ignorant of many things which have since occurred, & chiefly the unhealthiness of the place. Yet I do not repent of coming on a thousand accounts; & Mr. H., I doubt not, will do ultimately all that both he & I wish—that is, to lift me out of difficulty; but this is no easy matter to a man who, having Spiritual Enemies of such formidable magnitude, cannot expect to want natural hidden ones.

Your approbation of my pictures is a Multitude to Me, & I doubt not that all your kind wishes in my behalf shall in due time be fulfilled. Your kind offer of pecuniary assistance I can only thank you for at present, because I have enough to serve my present purpose here; our expenses are small, & our income, from our incessant labour, fully adequate to them at present. I am now engaged in Engraving 6 small plates for a New Edition of Mr. Hayley's *Triumphs of Temper,* from drawings by Maria Flaxman, sister to my friend the Sculptor, and it seems that other things will follow in course, if I do but Copy these well; but Patience! if Great things do not turn out, it is because such things depend

on the Spiritual & not on the Natural World; & if it was fit for
me, I doubt not that I should be Employed in Greater things;
& when it is proper, my Talents shall be properly exercised in
Public, as I hope they are now in private; for, till then, I leave
no stone unturned & no path unexplored that tends to improvement in my beloved Arts. One thing of real consequence I have
accomplished by coming into the country, which is to me consola-
tion enough; namely, I have recollected all my scattered thoughts
on Art & resumed my primitive & original ways of Execution
in both painting & engraving, which in the confusion of London
I had very much lost & obliterated from my mind. But whatever
becomes of my labours, I would rather that they should be preserved in your Green House (not, as you mistakenly call it, dung
hill) than in the cold gallery of fashion. The Sun may yet shine,
& then they will be brought into open air.

But you have so generously & openly desired that I will divide
my griefs with you, that I cannot hide what it is now become my
duty to explain. My unhappiness has arisen from a source which,
if explored too narrowly, might hurt my pecuniary circumstances, As my dependence is on Engraving at present, & particularly on the Engravings I have in hand for Mr. H., & I find on all
hands great objections to my doing anything but the mere drudgery of business, & intimations that if I do not confine myself to
this, I shall not live; this has always pursued me. You will understand by this the source of all my uneasiness. This from Johnson
& Fuseli brought me down here, & this from Mr. H. will bring
me back again; for that I cannot live without doing my duty to
lay up treasures in heaven is Certain & Determined, & to this
I have long made up my mind, & why this should be made an objection to Me, while Drunkenness, Lewdness, Gluttony & even
Idleness itself does not hurt other men, let Satan himself Explain.
The Thing I have most at Heart—more than life, or all that seems
to make life comfortable without—Is the Interest of True Religion & Science, & whenever anything appears to affect that Interest (Especially if I myself omit any duty to my Station as a Soldier of Christ), It gives me the greatest of torments. I am not
ashamed, afraid, or averse to tell you what Ought to be Told: That
I am under the direction of Messengers from Heaven Daily &
Nightly; but the nature of such things is not, as some suppose,

without trouble or care. Temptations are on the right hand & left; behind, the sea of time & space roars & follows swiftly; he who keeps not right onward is lost, & if our footsteps slide in clay, how can we do otherwise than fear & tremble? But I should not have troubled You with this account of my spiritual state, unless it had been necessary in explaining the actual cause of my uneasiness, into which you are so kind as to Inquire; for I never obtrude such things on others unless questioned, & then I never disguise the truth. But if we fear to do the dictates of our Angels & tremble at the Tasks set before us; if we refuse to do Spiritual Acts because of Natural Fears of Natural Desires, Who can describe the dismal torments of such a state! I too well remember the Threats I heard! If you, who are organized by Divine Providence for Spiritual communion, Refuse & bury your Talent in the Earth, even though you should want Natural Bread, Sorrow & Desperation pursues you through life, & after death shame & confusion of face to eternity. Everyone in Eternity will leave you, aghast at the Man who was crowned with glory & honour by his brethren & betrayed their cause to their enemies. You will be called the base Judas who betrayed his Friend! Such words would make any stout man tremble, & how then could I be at ease? But I am now no longer in That State & now go on again with my Task, Fearless; and though my path is difficult, I have no fear of stumbling while I keep it.

My wife desires her kindest Love to Mrs. Butts, & I have permitted her to send it to you also; we often wish that we could unite again in Society & hope that the time is not distant when we shall do so, being determined not to remain another winter here, but to return to London.

> I hear a voice you cannot hear, that says I must
> not stay;
> I see a hand you cannot see, that beckons me away.

Naked we came here, naked of Natural things; & naked we shall return; but while clothed with the Divine Mercy, we are richly clothed in Spiritual & suffer all the rest gladly. Pray give my Love to Mrs. Butts & your family. I am, Yours Sincerely,

William Blake

P.S. Your Obliging proposal of Exhibiting my Two Pictures likewise calls for my thanks; I will finish the other, & then we shall judge of the matter with certainty.

To Thomas Butts

Felpham, Nov'r. 22, 1802

Dear Sir,

My Brother tells me that he fears you are offended with me. I fear so too, because there appears some reason why you might be so. But when you have heard me out, you will not be so.

I have now given two years to the intense study of those parts of the art which relate to light & shade & colour & am Convinced that either my understanding is incapable of comprehending the beauties of Colouring, or the Pictures which I painted for you Are Equal in Every part of the Art, & superior in One, to anything that has been done since the age of Rafael. All Sir J. Reynolds' discourses to the Royal Academy will show that the Venetian finesse in Art can never be united with the Majesty of Colouring necessary to Historical beauty; & in a letter to the Rev'd Mr. Gilpin, author of a work on Picturesque Scenery, he says Thus: "It may be worth consideration whether the epithet 'Picturesque' is not applicable to the excellencies of the Inferior Schools rather than to the higher. The works of Michael Angelo, Rafael, &c., appear to me to have nothing of it; whereas Rubens & the Venetian Painters may almost be said to have Nothing Else. Perhaps 'Picturesque' is somewhat synonymous to the word 'Taste,' which we should think improperly applied to Homer or Milton, but very well to Prior or Pope. I suspect that the application of these words are to Excellencies of an inferior order, & which are incompatible with the Grand Style. You are certainly right in saying that variety of Tints & Forms is Picturesque; but it must be remembered, on the other hand, that the reverse of this (uniformity of Colour & a long continuation of lines) produces Grandeur." So Says Sir Joshua, and So say I; for I have now proved that the parts of the art which I neglected to display in those little pictures & drawings which I had the pleasure & profit to do for you are incompatible with the designs. There is nothing in the Art which our Painters do that I can confess myself ignorant of. I also Know & Understand & can assuredly affirm that the works I have done for You are Equal to Carrache or Rafael (and I am now Seven years older than Rafael was when he died); I say they are Equal to Carrache or Rafael, or Else I am Blind, Stupid, Ignorant and Incapable in two years' Study to understand those things which a Boarding School Miss can comprehend in a fortnight. Be assured, My dear Friend, that there is not one touch in those Drawings & Pictures but what came from my Head & my Heart in Unison; That I am Proud of being their Author and Grateful to you my Employer; & that I look upon you as the Chief of my Friends, whom I would endeavour to please, because you, among all men, have enabled me to produce these things. I would not send you a Drawing or a Picture till I had again reconsidered my notions of Art & had put myself back as if I was a learner. I have proved that I am Right & shall now Go on with the Vigour I was in my Childhood famous for.

But I do not pretend to be Perfect: but, if my Works have faults, Carrache, Corregio, & Rafael's have faults also; let me observe that the yellow leather flesh of old men, the ill-drawn & ugly young women, &, above all, the daubed black & yellow shadows that are found in most fine, ay, & the finest pictures, I altogether reject as ruinous to Effect, though Connoisseurs may think otherwise.

Let me also notice that Carrache's Pictures are not like Correggio's, nor Correggio's like Rafael's; &, if neither of them was to be encouraged till he did like any of the others, he must die without Encouragement. My Pictures are unlike any of these Painters, & I would have them to be so. I think the manner I adopt

More Perfect than any other; no doubt They thought the same of theirs.

You will be tempted to think that, as I improve, The Pictures &c. that I did for you are not what I would now wish them to be. On this I beg to say That they are what I intended them & that I know I never shall do better; for, if I were to do them over again, they would lose as much as they gained, because they were done in the heat of My Spirits.

But You will justly inquire why I have not written all this time to you. I answer I have been very Unhappy & could not think of troubling you about it or any of my real Friends. (I have written many letters to you which I burned & did not send.) & why I have not before now finished the Miniature I promised to Mrs. Butts. I answer I have not, till now, in any degree pleased myself, & now I must entreat you to Excuse faults, for Portrait Painting is the direct contrary to Designing & Historical Painting in every respect. If you have not Nature before you for Every Touch, you cannot Paint Portrait; & if you have Nature before you at all, you cannot Paint History; it was Michael Angelo's opinion & is Mine. Pray Give My Wife's love with mine to Mrs. Butts; assure her that it cannot be long before I have the pleasure of Painting from you in Person, & then that She may Expect a likeness, but now I have done All I could & know she will forgive any failure in consideration of the Endeavour.

And now let me finish with assuring you that, Though I have been very unhappy, I am so no longer. I am again Emerged into the light of day; I still & shall to Eternity Embrace Christianity and Adore him who is the Express image of God; but I have travelled through Perils & Darkness not unlike a Champion. I have Conquered and shall still Go on Conquering. Nothing can withstand the fury of my Course among the Stars of God & in the Abysses of the Accuser. My Enthusiasm is still what it was, only Enlarged and confirmed.

I now Send Two Pictures & hope you will approve of them. I have enclosed the Account of Money received & Work done, which I ought long ago to have sent you; pray forgive Errors in omissions of this kind. I am incapable of many attentions which it is my Duty to observe towards you through multitude of employment & through hope of soon seeing you again. I often omit to Inquire of you. But pray let me now hear how you do & of the welfare of your family.

Accept my Sincere love & respect.

I remain Yours Sincerely,

Will'm Blake

A Piece of Seaweed serves for a Barometer; it gets wet & dry as the weather gets so.

To Thomas Butts

22 November 1802

Dear Sir,

After I had finished my Letter, I found that I had not said half what I intended to say, & in particular I wish to ask you what subject you choose to be painted on the remaining Canvas which I brought down with me (for there were three) and to tell you that several of the Drawings were in great forwardness; you will see by the Enclosed Account that the remaining Number of Drawings which you gave me orders for is Eighteen. I will finish these with all possible Expedition, if indeed I have not tired you, or as it is politely called, Bored you too much already; or, if you would rather cry out, "Enough, Off, Off!," tell me in a Letter of forgiveness if you were offended & of accustomed friendship if you were not. But I will bore you more with some Verses which My Wife desires me to Copy out & send you with her kind love & Respect; they were Composed above a twelve-month ago, while walking from Felpham to Lavant to meet my Sister:

With happiness stretched across the hills
In a cloud that dewy sweetness distills,
With a blue sky spread over with wings
And a mild sun that mounts & sings,
With trees & fields full of Fairy elves
And little devils who fight for themselves,
Rememb'ring the Verses that Hayley sung
When my heart knocked against the root of my tongue,
With Angels planted in Hawthorn bowers
And God himself in the passing hours,
With Silver Angels across my way
And Golden Demons that none can stay,
With my Father hovering upon the wind
And my Brother Robert just behind
And my Brother John, the evil one,
In a black cloud making his moan;
Though dead, they appear upon my path,
Notwithstanding my terrible wrath;
They beg, they entreat, they drop their tears,
Filled full of hopes, filled full of fears;
With a thousand Angels upon the Wind
Pouring disconsolate from behind
To drive them off, & before my way
A frowning Thistle implores my stay.
What to others a trifle appears
Fills me full of smiles or tears;
For double the vision my Eyes do see,
And a double vision is always with me.
With my inward Eye 'tis an old Man grey;
With my outward, a Thistle across my way.
"If thou goest back," the thistle said,
"Thou art to endless woe betrayed;
For here does Theotormon lower,
And here is Enitharmon's bower,
And Los the terrible thus hath sworn,
Because thou backward dost return,
Poverty, Envy, old age & fear
Shall bring thy Wife upon a bier;

And Butts shall give what Fuseli gave,
A dark black Rock & a gloomy Cave."

I struck the Thistle with my foot,
And broke him up from his delving root.
"Must the duties of life each other cross?
Must every joy be dung & dross?
Must my dear Butts feel cold neglect
Because I give Hayley his due respect?
Must Flaxman look upon me as wild,
And all my friends be with doubts beguiled?
Must my Wife live in my Sister's bane,
Or my Sister survive on my Love's pain?
The curses of Los, the terrible shade,
And his dismal terrors make me afraid."

So I spoke & struck in my wrath
The old man weltering upon my path.
Then Los appeared in all his power;
In the Sun he appeared, descending before
My face in fierce flames; in my double sight
'Twas outward a Sun, inward Los in his might.
"My hands are laboured day and night,
And Ease comes never in my sight.
My Wife has no indulgence given
Except what comes to her from Heaven.
We eat little, we drink less;
This Earth breeds not our happiness.
Another Sun feeds our life's streams,
We are not warmed with thy beams;
Thou measurest not the Time to me,
Nor yet the Space that I do see;
My Mind is not with thy light arrayed.
Thy terrors shall not make me afraid."

When I had my Defiance given,
The Sun stood trembling in heaven;
The Moon, that glowed remote below,
Became leprous & white as snow;

And every soul of men on the Earth
Felt affliction & sorrow & sickness & dearth.
Los flamed in my path, & the Sun was hot
With the bows of my Mind & the Arrows of Thought.
My bowstring fierce with Ardour breathes;
My arrows glow in their golden sheaves;
My brothers & father march before;
The heavens drop with human gore.

Now I a fourfold vision see,
And a fourfold vision is given to me;
'Tis fourfold in my supreme delight
And threefold in soft Beulah's night
And twofold Always. May God us keep
From Single vision & Newton's sleep!

I also enclose you some Ballads by Mr. Hayley, with prints to
them by Your H'ble Serv't. I should have sent them before now
but could not get anything done for You to please myself; for
I do assure you that I have truly studied the two little pictures
I now send, & do not repent of the time I have spent upon them.
God bless you.

Yours,
W. B.

P.S. I have taken the liberty to trouble you with a letter to my
Brother, which you will be so kind as to send or give him, & oblige
yours, W. B.

To Thomas Butts

25 April 1803

Dear Sir,

I write in haste, having received a pressing Letter from my Brother. I intended to have sent the Picture of the Riposo, which is nearly finished much to my satisfaction, but not quite; you shall have it soon. I now send the 4 Numbers for Mr. Birch, with best Respects to him. The Reason the Ballads have been suspended is the pressure of other business, but they will go on again soon.

Accept of my thanks for your kind & heartening Letter. You have Faith in the Endeavours of Me, your weak brother & fellow Disciple; how great must be your faith in our Divine Master! You are to me a Lesson of Humility, while you Exalt me by such distinguishing commendations. I know that you see certain merits in me, which, by God's Grace, shall be made fully apparent & perfect in Eternity; in the meantime I must not bury the Talents in the Earth, but do my endeavour to live to the Glory of our Lord & Saviour; & I am also grateful to the kind hand that endeavours to lift me out of despondency, even if it lifts me too high.

And now, My Dear Sir, Congratulate me on my return to London, with the full approbation of Mr. Hayley & with Promise—But, Alas!

Now I may say to you, what perhaps I should not dare to say to anyone else: That I can alone carry on my visionary studies in London unannoyed, & that I may converse with my friends in Eternity, See Visions, Dream Dreams & prophesy & speak Parables unobserved & at liberty from the Doubts of other Mortals, perhaps Doubts proceeding from Kindness; but Doubts are always pernicious, Especially when we Doubt our Friends. Christ is very decided on this Point: "He who is Not With Me is Against Me." There is no Medium or Middle state; & if a Man is the Enemy of my Spiritual Life while he pretends to be the Friend of my Corporeal, he is a Real Enemy; but the Man may be the friend of my Spiritual Life while he seems the Enemy of my Corporeal, but Not Vice Versa.

What is very pleasant, Everyone who hears of my going to London again Applauds it as the only course for the interest of all concerned in My Works, Observing that I ought not to be away from the opportunities London affords of seeing fine Pictures and the various improvements in Works of Art going on in London.

But none can know the Spiritual Acts of my three years' Slumber on the banks of the Ocean, unless he has seen them in the Spirit, or unless he should read My long Poem descriptive of those Acts; for I have in these three years composed an immense number of verses on One Grand Theme, Similar to Homer's *Iliad* or Milton's *Paradise Lost,* the Persons & Machinery entirely new to the Inhabitants of Earth (some of the Persons Excepted). I have written this Poem from immediate Dictation, twelve or sometimes twenty or thirty lines at a time, without Premeditation & even against my Will; the Time it has taken in writing was thus rendered Non-Existent, & an immense Poem Exists which seems to be the Labour of a long Life, all produced without Labour or Study. I mention this to show you what I think the Grand Reason of my being brought down here.

I have a thousand & ten thousand things to say to you. My heart is full of futurity. I perceive that the sore travel which has been given me these three years leads to Glory & Honour. I rejoice & I tremble: "I am fearfully & wonderfully made." I had been reading the 139th Psalm a little before your Letter arrived. I take your advice. I see the face of my Heavenly Father; he lays his Hand upon my Head & gives a blessing to all my works. Why should I be troubled? Why should my heart & flesh cry out? I will go on in the Strength of the Lord; through Hell will I sing forth his Praises, that the Dragons of the Deep may praise him, & that those who dwell in darkness & in the Seacoasts may be gathered into his Kingdom. Excuse my perhaps too great Enthusiasm. Please to accept of & give our Loves to Mrs. Butts & your amiable Family, and believe me to be,

Ever Yours Affectionately,
Will Blake

Felpham
April 25, 1803

To Thomas Butts

6 July 1803

Dear Sir,

I send you the Riposo, which I hope you will think my best Picture in many respects. It represents the Holy Family in Egypt, Guarded in their Repose from those Fiends, the Egyptian Gods, and though not directly taken from a Poem of Milton's (for till I had designed it Milton's Poem did not come into my Thoughts), Yet it is very similar to his Hymn on the Nativity, which you will find among his smaller Poems and will read with great delight. I have given in the background a building, which may be supposed the ruin of a Part of Nimrod's tower, which I conjecture to have spread over many Countries; for he ought to be reckoned of the Giant brood.

I have now on the Stocks the following drawings for you: 1. Jephthah sacrificing his Daughter; 2. Ruth & her mother-in-law & Sister; 3. The three Marys at the Sepulcher; 4. The Death of Joseph; 5. The Death of the Virgin Mary; 6. St. Paul Preaching; & 7. The Angel of the Divine Presence clothing Adam & Eve with Coats of Skins.

These are all in great forwardness, & I am satisfied that I improve very much & shall continue to do so while I live, which is a blessing I can never be too thankful for both to God & Man.

We look forward every day with pleasure toward our meeting again in London with those whom we have learned to value by absence no less perhaps than we did by presence; for recollection often surpasses everything; indeed, the prospect of returning to our friends is supremely delightful. Then I am determined that Mrs. Butts shall have a good likeness of You, if I have hands & eyes left; for I am become a likeness taker & succeed admirably well; but this is not to be achieved without the original sitting before you for Every touch, all likenesses from memory being necessarily very, very defective; but Nature & Fancy are Two Things & can Never be joined; neither ought anyone to attempt it, for it is Idolatry & destroys the Soul.

I ought to tell you that Mr. H. is quite agreeable to our return, & that there is all the appearance in the world of our being fully employed in Engraving for his projected Works, Particularly Cowper's *Milton,* a Work now on foot by Subscription, & I understand that the Subscription goes on briskly. This work is to be a very Elegant one & to consist of All Milton's Poems, with Cowper's Notes and translations by Cowper from Milton's Latin & Italian Poems. These works will be ornamented with Engravings from Designs from Romney, Flaxman & Y'r h'ble Serv't, & to be Engraved also by the last mentioned. The Profits of the work are intended to be appropriated to Erect a Monument to the Memory of Cowper in St. Paul's or Westminster Abbey. Such is the Project, & Mr. Addington & Mr. Pitt are both among the Subscribers, which are already numerous & of the first rank: the price of the Work is Six Guineas. Thus I hope that all our three years' trouble Ends in Good Luck at last & shall be forgot by my affections & only remembered by my Understanding; to be a Memento in time to come & to speak to future generations by a Sublime Allegory, which is now perfectly completed into a Grand Poem. I may praise it, since I dare not pretend to be any other than the Secretary; the Authors are in Eternity. I consider it as the Grandest Poem that this World Contains. Allegory addressed to the Intellectual powers, while it is altogether hidden from the Corporeal Understanding, is My Definition of the Most Sublime Poetry; it is also somewhat in the same manner defined by Plato. This Poem shall, by Divine Assistance, be progressively Printed & Ornamented with Prints & given to the Public. But of this work I take care to say little to Mr. H., since he is as much averse to my poetry as he is to a Chapter in the Bible. He knows that I have writ it, for I have shown it to him, & he has read Part by his own desire & has looked with sufficient contempt to enhance my opinion of it. But I do not wish to irritate by seeming too obstinate in Poetic pursuits. But if all the World should set their faces against This, I have Orders to set my face like a flint (*Ezekiel,* III, 9) against their faces, & my forehead against their foreheads.

As to Mr. H., I feel myself at liberty to say as follows upon this ticklish subject: I regard Fashion in Poetry as little as I do in Painting; so, if both Poets & Painters should alternately dislike (but I know the majority of them will not), I am not to regard it at all, but Mr. H. approves of My Designs as little as he does of my Poems, and I have been forced to insist on his leaving me in both to my own Self Will; for I am determined to be no longer Pestered with his Genteel Ignorance & Polite Disapprobation. I know myself both Poet & Painter, & it is not his affected Contempt that can move me to anything but a more assiduous pursuit of both Arts. Indeed, by my late Firmness I have brought down his affected Loftiness, & he begins to think I have some Genius; as if Genius & Assurance were the same thing! But his imbecile attempts to depress Me only deserve laughter. I say thus much to you, knowing that you will not make a bad use of it. But it is a Fact too true That, if I had only depended on Mortal Things, both myself & my Wife must have been Lost. I shall leave everyone in This Country astonished at my Patience & Forbearance of Injuries upon Injuries; & I do assure you that, if I could have returned to London a Month after my arrival here, I should have done so, but I was commanded by my Spiritual friends to bear all, to be silent, &, to go through all without murmuring, &, in fine, hope, till my three years should be almost accomplished, at which time I was set at liberty to remonstrate against former conduct & to demand Justice & Truth, which I have done in so effectual a manner that my antagonist is silenced completely, & I have compelled what should have been of freedom—My Just Right as an Artist & as a Man; & if any attempt should be made to refuse me this, I am inflexible & will relinquish any engagement of Designing at all, unless altogether left to my own Judgment, As you, My dear Friend, have always left me, for which I shall never cease to honour & respect you.

When we meet, I will perfectly describe to you my Conduct & the Conduct of others toward me, & you will see that I have laboured hard indeed & have been borne on angel's wings. Till we meet I beg of God our Saviour to be with you & me, & yours & mine. Pray give my & my wife's love to Mrs. Butts & Family, & believe me to remain,

Yours in truth & sincerity,
Will Blake

Felpham July 6, 1803

Scofield's Information and Complaint Against Blake

15 August 1803

The Information and Complaint of John Scofield, a Private Soldier in His Majesty's First Regiment of Dragoons, taken upon his Oath, this 15th Day of August, 1803, before me, One of His Majesty's Justices of the Peace, in and for the County aforesaid.

Who saith that on the twelfth Day of this Instant, August, at the Parish of Felpham, in the County aforesaid, one _____ Blake, a Miniature Painter, and now residing in the said Parish of Felpham, did utter the following seditious expressions, viz, that we (meaning the People of England) were like a Parcel of Children; that they would play with themselves till they got scalded and burnt; that the French knew our Strength very well, and if Bonaparte should come he would be master of Europe in an Hour's Time; that England might depend upon it; that when he set his Foot on English Ground that every Englishman would have his choice, whether to have his Throat cut, or to join the French, & that he was a strong Man, and would certainly begin to cut Throats, and the strongest Man must conquer; that he damned the King of England, his Country, & his Subjects; that his Soldiers were all bound for Slaves, and all the Poor People in general; that his Wife then came up and said to him, this is nothing to you at present, but that the King of England would run himself so far into the Fire, that he might get himself out again, & although she was but a Woman, she would fight as long as she had a drop of Blood in her, to which the said _____ Blake said, my Dear, you would not fight against France; she replied no, I would for Bonaparte as long as I am able; that the said _____ Blake, then addressing himself to this Informant, said, though you are one of the King's Subjects, I have told what I have said before greater People than you, and that this Informant was sent by his Captain to Esquire Hayley to hear what he had to say, & to go and tell them; that his Wife then told her said Husband to turn this Informant out of the Garden; that this Informant thereupon

turned round to go peaceably out, when the said _____ Blake
pushed this Deponent out of the Garden into the Road, down
which he followed this Informant, & twice took this Informant by
the Collar without this Informant's making any Resistance, & at
the same Time the said Blake damned the King, and said the Soldiers were all Slaves.

John Scofield

Blake's Memorandum Against Scofield

August 1803

Blake's Memorandum in Refutation of the Information and Complaint of John Scofield, a private Soldier, &c.

The Soldier has been heard to say repeatedly that he did not
know how the Quarrel began, which he would not say if such
seditious words were spoken.

Mrs. Haynes Evidences that she saw me turn him down the
Road, & all the while we were at the Stable Door, and that not
one word of charge against me was uttered, either relating to
Sedition or anything else; all he did was swearing and threatening.

Mr. Hosier heard him say that he would be revenged and would
have me hanged if he could. He spoke this the Day after my turning him out of the Garden. Hosier says he is ready to give Evidence
of this, if necessary.

The Soldier's Comrade swore before the Magistrates, while
I was present, that he heard me utter seditious words at the Stable Door and, in particular, said that he heard me D—n the

K — g. Now I have all the Persons who were present at the Stable Door to witness that no Word relating to Seditious Subjects was uttered, either by one party or the other; and they are ready, on their Oaths, to say that I did not utter such Words.

Mrs. Haynes says very sensibly that she never heard People quarrel but they always charged each other with the Offense and repeated it to those around; therefore as the Soldier charged not me with Seditious Words at that Time, neither did his Comrade, the whole Charge must have been fabricated in the Stable afterwards.

If we prove the Comrade perjured who swore that he heard me D — n the K — g. I believe the whole Charge falls to the Ground.

Mr. Cosens, owner of the Mill at Felpham, was passing by in the Road and saw me and the Soldier and William standing near each other; he heard nothing, but says we certainly were not quarreling.

The whole Distance that William could be at any Time of the Conversation between me and the Soldier (supposing such Conversation to have existed) is only 12 Yards, & W _____ says that he was backwards and forwards in the Garden. It was a still Day; there was no Wind stirring.

William says on his Oath that the first Words that he heard me speak to the Soldier were ordering him out of the Garden; the truth is, I did not speak to the Soldier till then, & my ordering him out of the Garden was occasioned by his saying something that I thought insulting.

The Time that I & the Soldier were together in the Garden was not sufficient for me to have uttered the Things that he alleged.

The Soldier said to Mrs. Grinder that it would be right to have my House searched, as I might have plans of the Country which I intended to send to the Enemy; he called me a Military Painter, I suppose mistaking the Words "Miniature Painter," which he might have heard me called. I think that this proves his having come into the Garden with some bad Intention, or at least with a prejudiced Mind.

It is necessary to learn the Names of all that were present at the Stable Door, that we may not have any Witnesses brought against us that were not there.

All the Persons present at the Stable Door were: Mrs. Grinder and her Daughter, all the Time; Mrs. Haynes & her Daughter, all the Time; Mr. Grinder, part of the Time; Mr. Hayley's Gardener, part of the Time. Mrs. Haynes was present from my turning him out at my Gate, all the rest of the Time. What passed in the Garden, there is no Person but William & the Soldier & myself can know.

There was not anybody in Grinder's Tap-room, but an Old Man, named Jones, who (Mrs. Grinder says) did not come out. He is the same Man who lately hurt his Hand & wears it in a sling.

The Soldier, after he and his Comrade came together into the Tap-room, threatened to knock William's Eyes out (this was his often repeated Threat to me and to my Wife) because W_____ refused to go with him to Chichester and swear against me. William said that he would not take a false Oath, for that he heard me say nothing of the Kind (i.e. Sedition). Mr. Grinder then reproved the Soldier for threatening William, and Mr. Grinder said that W_____ should not go, because of those Threats, especially as he was sure that no seditious Words were spoken.

William's timidity in giving his Evidence before the Magistrates and his fear of uttering a Falsehood upon Oath proves him to be an honest Man & is to me an host of strength. I am certain that if I had not turned the Soldier out of my Garden I never should have been free from his Impertinence & Intrusion.

Mr. Hayley's Gardener came past at the Time of the Contention at the Stable Door & going to the Comrade, said to him, "Is your Comrade drunk?" — a Proof that he thought the Soldier abusive & in an Intoxication of Mind.

If such a Perjury as this can take effect, any Villain in future may come & drag me and my Wife out of our House & beat us in the Garden or use us as he please or is able & afterwards go and swear our Lives away.

Is it not in the Power of any Thief who enters a Man's Dwelling & robs him or misuses his Wife or Children to go & swear as this Man has sworn?

To Thomas Butts

Felpham, August 16, 1803

Dear Sir,

I send 7 Drawings, which I hope will please you; this, I believe, about balances our account. Our return to London draws on apace; our Expectation of meeting again with you is one of our greatest pleasures. Pray tell me how your Eyes do. I never sit down to work but I think of you & feel anxious for the sight of that friend whose Eyes have done me so much good. I omitted (very unaccountably) to copy out in my last Letter that passage in my rough sketch which related to your kindness in offering to Exhibit my 2 last Pictures in the Gallery in Berners Street; it was in these Words: "I sincerely thank you for your kind offer of Exhibiting my 2 Pictures; the trouble you take on my account I trust will be recompensed to you by him who seeth in secret; if you should find it convenient to do so, it will be gratefully remembered by me among the other numerous kindnesses I have received from you."

I go on with the remaining Subjects which you gave me commission to Execute for you, but shall not be able to send any more before my return, though perhaps I may bring some with me finished. I am at Present in a Bustle to defend myself against a very unwarrantable warrant from a Justice of Peace in Chichester, which was taken out against me by a Private in Capt'n Leathes's troop of 1st or Royal Dragoons, for an assault & Seditious words. The wretched Man has terribly Perjured himself, as has his Comrade; for, as to Sedition, not one Word relating to the King or Government was spoken by either him or me. His Enmity arises from my having turned him out of my Garden, into which he was invited as an assistant by a Gardener at work therein, without my knowledge that he was so invited. I desired him, as politely as was possible, to go out of the Garden; he made me an impertinent answer. I insisted on his leaving the Garden; he refused. I still persisted in desiring his departure; he then threatened to knock out my Eyes, with many abominable imprecations & with some contempt for my Person; it affronted my foolish Pride. I therefore took him by the Elbows & pushed him before me till I had got him out; there I intended to have left him, but he, turning about, put himself into a Posture of Defiance, threatening & swearing at me. I, perhaps foolishly & perhaps not, stepped out at the Gate, &, putting aside his blows, took him again by the Elbows, &, keeping his back to me, pushed him forwards down the road about fifty yards, he all the while endeavouring to turn round & strike me, & raging & cursing, which drew out several neighbours; at length, when I had got him to where he was Quartered, which was very quickly done, we were met at the Gate by the Master of the house, The Fox Inn (who is the proprietor of my Cottage), & his wife & Daughter & the Man's Comrade & several other people. My Landlord compelled the Soldiers to go indoors, after many abusive threats against me & my wife from the two Soldiers; but not one word of threat on account of Sedition was uttered at that time. This method of Revenge was Planned between them after they had got together into the Stable. This is the whole outline. I have for witnesses: The Gardener, who is Hostler at the Fox & who Evidences that, to his knowledge, no word of the remotest tendency to Government or Sedition was uttered; Our next door Neighbour, a Miller's wife, who saw me turn him before me down the road & saw & heard all that happened at the Gate of the Inn, who Evidences that no Expression of threatening on account of Sedition was uttered in the heat of their fury by either the Dragoons; this was the woman's own remark & does high honour to her good sense, as she observes that, whenever a quarrel happens, the offense is always repeated. The Landlord of the Inn & His Wife & daughter will Evidence the Same & will evidently prove the Comrade perjured, who swore that he heard me, while at the Gate, utter Seditious words & D——— the K———, without which perjury I could not have been committed; & I had no witness with me before the Justices who could combat his assertion, as the Gardener remained in my Garden all the while, & he was the only person I thought necessary to take with me. I have been before a Bench of Justices at Chichester this morning; but they, as the Lawyer who wrote down the Accusation told me in private, are compelled by the Military to suffer a prosecution to be entered into; although they must know, & it is manifest, that the whole is a Fabricated Perjury. I have been forced to find Bail. Mr. Hayley was kind enough to come forwards, & Mr. Seagrave, Printer at Chichester; Mr. H. in 100£, & Mr. S. in 50£; & myself am bound in 100 £ for my appearance at the Quarter Sessions, which is after Michaelmas. So I shall have the satisfaction to see my friends in Town before this Contemptible business comes on. I say Contemptible, for it must be manifest to everyone that the whole accusation is a wilful perjury. Thus, you see, my dear Friend, that I cannot leave this place without some adventure; it has struck a consternation through all the Villages round. Every Man is now afraid of speaking to, or looking at, a Soldier; for the peaceable Villagers have always been forward in expressing their kindness for us, & they express their sorrow at our departure as soon as they hear of it. Everyone here is my Evidence for peace & Good Neighbourhood; & yet, such is the present state of things, this foolish accusation must be tried in public. Well, I am content; I murmur not & doubt not that I shall receive Justice & am only sorry for the trouble & expense. I have heard that my Accuser is a disgraced Sergeant; his name is John Scofield; perhaps it will be in your power to learn somewhat about the Man. I am very ignorant of what I am requesting of you; I only suggest what I know you will be kind enough to Excuse if you can learn nothing about him, & what, I as well know, if it is possible, you will be kind enough to do in this matter.

Dear Sir, This perhaps was suffered to Clear up some doubts & to give opportunity to those whom I doubted to clear themselves of all imputation. If a Man offends me ignorantly & not designedly, surely I ought to consider him with favour & affection. Perhaps the simplicity of myself is the origin of all offenses committed against me. If I have found this, I shall have learned a most valuable thing, well worth three years' perseverance. I have found it. It is certain that a too passive manner, inconsistent with my active physiognomy, had done me much mischief. I must now express to you my conviction that all is come from the spiritual World for Good, & not for Evil.

Give me your advice in my perilous adventure; burn what I have peevishly written about any friend. I have been very much degraded & injuriously treated; but if it all arise from my own fault, I ought to blame myself.

O why was I born with a different face?
Why was I not born like the rest of my race?
When I look, each one starts! When I speak, I offend;
Then I'm silent & passive & lose every Friend.

Then my verse I dishonour, My pictures despise,
My person degrade & my temper chastise;
And the pen is my terror, the pencil my shame;
All my Talents I bury, and dead is my Fame.

I am either too low or too highly prized;
When Elate I am Envied, When Meek I'm despised.

This is but too just a Picture of my Present state. I pray God to keep you & all men from it & to deliver me in his own good time. Pray write to me & tell me how you & your family enjoy health. My much terrified Wife joins me in love to you & Mrs. Butts & all your family. I again take the liberty to beg of you to cause the Enclosed Letter to be delivered to my Brother, & remain Sincerely & Affectionately Yours,

William Blake

To William Hayley

London, October 7, 1803

Dear Sir,

Your generous & tender solicitude about your devoted rebel makes it absolutely necessary that he should trouble you with an account of his safe arrival, which will excuse his begging the favor of a few lines to inform him how you escaped the contagion of the Court of Justice. I fear that you have & must suffer more on my account than I shall ever be worth. Arrived safe in London, my wife in very poor health; still I resolve not to lose hope of seeing better days.

Art in London flourishes. Engravers in particular are wanted. Every Engraver turns away work that he cannot execute from his superabundant Employment. Yet no one brings work to me. I am content that it shall be so as long as God pleases. I know that many works of a lucrative nature are in want of hands; other Engravers are courted. I suppose that I must go a-Courting, which I shall do awkwardly; in the meantime I lose no moment to complete Romney to satisfaction.

How is it possible that a Man almost 50 Years of Age, who has not lost any of his life since he was five years old without incessant labour & study, how is it possible that such a one with ordinary common sense can be inferior to a boy of twenty, who scarcely has taken or deigns to take a pencil in hand, but who rides about the Parks or Saunters about the Playhouses, who Eats & drinks for business, not for need, how is it possible that such a fop can be superior to the studious lover of Art can scarcely be imagined. Yet such is somewhat like my fate & such it is likely to remain. Yet I laugh & sing, for, if on Earth neglected, I am in heaven a Prince among Princes, & even on Earth beloved by the Good as a Good Man; this I should be perfectly contented with, but at certain periods a blaze of reputation arises round me in which I am considered as one distinguished by some mental perfection, but the flame soon dies again, & I am left stupefied

and astonished. O that I could live as others do in a regular succession of Employment; this wish I fear is not to be accomplished to me. Forgive this Dirge-like lamentation over a dead
horse; & now I have lamented over the dead horse let me laugh &
be merry with my friends till Christmas, for as Man liveth not by
bread alone, I shall live, although I should want bread; nothing
is necessary to me but to do my Duty & to rejoice in the exceeding joy that is always poured out on my Spirit, to pray that my
friends & you above the rest may be made partakers of the joy
that the world cannot conceive, that you may still be replen-
ished with the same & be as you always have been, a glorious &
triumphant Dweller in immortality. Please to pay for me my best
thanks to Miss Poole; tell her that I wish her a continued Excess
of Happiness. Some say that Happiness is not Good for Mortals,
& they ought to be answered that Sorrow is not fit the Immortals
& is utterly useless to anyone; a blight never does good to a tree,
& if a blight kill not a tree but it still bear fruit, let none say that
the fruit was in consequence of the blight. When this Soldier-like
danger is over I will do double the work I do now, for it will hang
heavy on my Devil, who terribly resents it; but I soothe him to
peace, & indeed he is a good-natured Devil after all & certainly
does not lead me into scrapes. He is not in the least to be blamed
for the present scrape, as he was out of the way all the time on
other employment, seeking amusement in making Verses, to which
he constantly leads me, very much to my hurt & sometimes to
the annoyance of my friends; as I perceive he is now doing the
same work by my letter, I will finish it, wishing you health & joy
in God our Saviour.

To Eternity yours,
Will'm Blake

To William Hayley

London Jan'y 14, 1804

Dear Sir,

I write immediately on my arrival. Not merely to inform you that I am safe arrived, but also to inform you that in a conversation with an old Soldier who came in the Coach with me I learned that no one, not even the most expert horseman, ought ever to mount a Trooper's Horse; they are taught so many tricks, such as stopping short, falling down on their knees, running sideways, & in various & innumerable ways endeavouring to throw the rider, that it is a miracle if a stranger escapes with Life. All this I learned with some alarm & heard also what the soldier said confirmed by another person in the coach. I therefore, as it is my duty, beg & entreat you never to mount that wicked horse again, nor again trust to one who has been so Educated. God our Saviour watch over you & preserve you.

I have seen Flaxman already, as I took to him early this morning your present to his Scholar; he & his are all well & in high spirits & welcomed Me with kind affection & generous exultation in my escape from the arrows of darkness. I intend to see Mrs. Lambert & Mr. Johnson, bookseller, this afternoon. My poor wife has been near the Gate of Death, as was supposed by our kind & attentive fellow inhabitant, the young & very amiable Mrs. Enoch, who gave my wife all the attention that a daughter could pay to a mother, but my arrival has dispelled the formidable malady & my dear & good woman again begins to resume her health & strength. Pray, my dear Sir, favour me with a line concerning your health & how you have escaped the double blow both from the wicked horse & from your innocent humble servant, whose heart & soul are more & more drawn out towards you & Felpham & its kind inhabitants. I feel anxious, & therefore pray to my God & father for the health of Miss Poole, hope that the pang of affection & gratitude is the Gift of God for good. I am thankful that I feel it; it draws the soul towards Eternal life

& conjunction with Spirits of just men made perfect by love & gratitude—the two angels who stand at heaven's gate ever open, ever inviting guests to the marriage. O foolish Philosophy! Gratitude is Heaven itself; there could be no heaven without Gratitude. I feel it & I know it. I thank God & Man for it & above all You, My dear friend & benefactor in the Lord. Pray give my & my wife's duties to Miss Poole; accept them yourself & believe me to be,

Yours in sincerity,
Will'm Blake

To William Hayley

28 May, 1804

Dear Sir,

I thank you heartily for your kind offer of reading, &c. I have read the book through attentively and was much entertained and instructed, but have not yet come to the *Life of Washington.* I suppose an American would tell me that Washington did all that was done before he was born, as the French now adore Bonaparte and the English our poor George; so the Americans will consider Washington as their god. This is only Grecian, or rather Trojan, worship, and perhaps will be revised in an age or two. In the meantime I have the happiness of seeing the Divine countenance in such men as Cowper and Milton more distinctly than in any prince or hero. Mr. Phillips has sent a small poem; he would not tell the author's name, but desired me to enclose it for you with Washington's *Life.*

. . . .

23 October 1804

Dear Sir,

I received your kind letter with the note to Mr. Payne and have
had the cash from him. I should have returned my thanks immediately on receipt of it, but hoped to be able to send, before now,
proofs of the two plates, the *Head of R*[omney] and the *Shipwreck,*
which you shall soon see in a much more perfect state. I write
immediately because you wish I should do so, to satisfy you that
I have received your kind favour.

I take the extreme pleasure of expressing my joy at our good
Lady of Lavant's continued recovery, but with a mixture of sincere sorrow on account of the beloved Councillor. My wife returns her heartfelt thanks for your kind inquiry concerning her
health. She is surprisingly recovered. Electricity is the wonderful cause; the swelling of her legs and knees is entirely reduced.
She is very near as free from rheumatism as she was five years
ago, and we have the greatest confidence in her perfect recovery.

The pleasure of seeing another poem from your hands has truly
set me longing (my wife says I ought to have said "us") with desire
and curiosity; but, however, "Christmas is a-coming."

Our good and kind friend Hawkins is not yet in town—hope
soon to have the pleasure of seeing him, with the courage of conscious industry, worthy of his former kindness to me. For now! O
Glory! and O Delight! I have entirely reduced that spectrous Fiend
to his station, whose annoyance has been the ruin of my labours
for the last passed twenty years of my life. He is the enemy of
conjugal love and is the Jupiter of the Greeks, an ironhearted
tyrant, the ruiner of ancient Greece. I speak with perfect confidence and certainty of the fact which has passed upon me. Neb-
uchadnezzar had seven times passed over him; I have had twenty;
thank God I was not altogether a beast as he was; but I was a slave
bound in a mill among beasts and devils; these beasts and these
devils are now, together with myself, become children of light
and liberty, and my feet and my wife's feet are free from fetters.

O lovely Felpham, parent of Immortal Friendship, to thee I am eternally indebted for my three years' rest from perturbation and the strength I now enjoy. Suddenly, on the day after visiting the Truchsessian Gallery of pictures, I was again enlightened with the light I enjoyed in my youth, and which has for exactly twenty years been closed from me as by a door and by window-shutters. Consequently I can, with confidence, promise you ocular demonstration of my altered state on the plates I am now engraving after Romney, whose spiritual aid has not a little conduced to my restoration to the light of Art. O, the distress I have undergone, and my poor wife with me, incessantly labouring and incessantly spoiling what I had done well. Every one of my friends was astonished at my faults, and could not assign a reason; they knew my industry and abstinence from every pleasure for the sake of study, and yet—and yet—and yet there wanted the proofs of industry in my works. I thank God with entire confidence that it shall be so no longer; he is become my servant who domineered over me, he is even as a brother who was my enemy. Dear Sir, excuse my enthusiasm or rather madness, for I am really drunk with intellectual vision whenever I take a pencil or graver into my hand, even as I used to be in my youth, and as I have not been for twenty dark, but very profitable years. I thank God that I courageously pursued my course through darkness. In a short time I shall make my assertion good that I am become suddenly as I was at first, by producing the *Head of Romney* and the *Shipwreck,* quite another thing from what you or I ever expected them to be. In short, I am now satisfied and proud of my work, which I have not been for the above long period.

If our excellent and manly friend Meyer is yet with you, please to make my wife's and my own most respectful and affectionate compliments to him, also to our kind friend at Lavant.

I remain, with my wife's joint affection,

Your sincere and obliged servant,
Will Blake

23 October 1804

To William Hayley

11 December 1805

Dear Sir,

I cannot omit to Return you my sincere & Grateful Acknowledgments for the kind Reception you have given my New Projected Work. It bids fair to set me above the difficulties I have hitherto encountered. But my Fate has been so uncommon that I expect Nothing. I was alive & in health & with the same Talents I now have all the time of Boydell's, Machlin's, Bowyer's, & other Great Works. I was known by them and was looked upon by them as Incapable of Employment in those Works; it may turn out so again, notwithstanding appearances. I am prepared for it, but at the same time sincerely Grateful to Those whose Kindness & Good opinion has supported me through all hitherto. You, Dear Sir, are one who has my Particular Gratitude, having conducted me through Three that would have been the Darkest Years that ever Mortal Suffered, which were rendered through your means a Mild & Pleasant Slumber. I speak of Spiritual Things, Not of Natural; Of Things known only to Myself & to Spirits Good & Evil, but Not known to Men on Earth. It is the passage through these Three Years that has brought me into my Present State, & I know that if I had not been with You I must have Perished. Those Dangers are now Passed, & I can see them beneath my feet. It will not be long before I shall be able to present the full history of my Spiritual Sufferings to the Dwellers upon Earth & of the Spiritual Victories obtained for me by my Friends. Excuse this Effusion of the Spirit from One who cares little for this World, which passes away, whose Happiness is Secure in Jesus our Lord & who looks for Suffering till the time of complete deliverance. In the meanwhile I am kept Happy, as I used to be, because I throw Myself & all that I have on our Saviour's Divine Providence. O What Wonders are the Children of Men! Would to God that they would consider it, That they would consider their Spiritual Life, Regardless of that faint Shadow called Natural Life, & that they would Promote Each other's Spiritual Labours, Each according to its Rank, & that they would know that Receiving a Prophet As a Prophet is a Duty which If omitted is more Severely Avenged than Every Sin & Wickedness beside. It is the Greatest of Crimes to Depress True Art & Science. I know that those who are dead from the Earth & who mocked and Despised the Meekness of True Art (and such, I find, have been the situations of our Beautiful, Affectionate Ballads), I know that such Mockers are Most Severely Punished in Eternity. I know it, for I see it & dare not help. The Mocker of Art is the Mocker of Jesus. Let us go on, Dear Sir, following his Cross; let us take it up daily, Persisting in Spiritual Labours & the Use of that Talent which it is Death to Bury, & of that Spirit to which we are called.

Pray Present My Sincerest Thanks to our Good Paulina, whose kindness to Me shall receive recompense in the Presence of Jesus. Present also my Thanks to the Generous Seagrave, In whose debt I have been too long, but perceive that I shall be able to settle with him soon what is between us. I have delivered to Mr. Sanders the 3 Works of Romney, as Mrs. Lambert told me you wished to have them; a very few touches will finish the Shipwreck; those few I have added upon a Proof before I parted with the Picture. It is a Print that I feel proud of, on a New inspection. Wishing you & All Friends in Sussex a Merry & a Happy Christmas,

I remain, Ever Your Affectionate,

Will Blake & his Wife Catherine Blake

S'th Molton Street
Decemb'r 11, 1805

To Richard Phillips

Sir,

My indignation was exceedingly moved at reading a criticism in *Bell's Weekly Messenger* (25th May) on the picture of Count Ugolino, by Mr. Fuseli, in the Royal Academy Exhibition; and your Magazine being as extensive in its circulation as that Paper, and as it also must from its nature be more permanent, I take the advantageous opportunity to counteract the widely diffused malice which has for many years, under the pretense of admiration of the arts, been assiduously sown and planted among the English public against true art, such as it existed in the days of Michael Angelo and Raphael. Under pretense of fair criticism and candour, the most wretched taste ever produced has been upheld for many, very many years; but now, I say, now its end is come. Such an artist as Fuseli is invulnerable, he needs not my defense; but I should be ashamed not to set my hand and shoulder, and whole strength, against those wretches who, under pretense of criticism, use the dagger and the poison.

My criticism on this picture is as follows: Mr. Fuseli's Count Ugolino is the father of sons of feeling and dignity, who would not sit looking in their parent's face in the moment of his agony, but would rather retire and die in secret, while they suffer him to indulge his passionate and innocent grief, his innocent and venerable madness and insanity and fury, and whatever paltry, coldhearted critics cannot, because they dare not, look upon. Fuseli's Count Ugolino is a man of wonder and admiration, of resentment against man and devil, and of humiliation before God; prayer and parental affection fill the figure from head to foot. The child in his arms, whether boy or girl, signifies not (but the critic must be a fool who has not read Dante, and who does not know a boy from a girl); I say the child is as beautifully drawn as it is coloured—in both, inimitable! And the effect of the whole is truly sublime, on account of that very colouring which our critic calls black and heavy. The German flute colour, which was used by the Flemings (they call it burnt bone), has possessed the eye of certain connoisseurs, that they cannot see appropriate colouring, and are blind to the gloom of a real terror.

The taste of English amateurs has been too much formed upon pictures imported from Flanders and Holland; consequently our countrymen are easily browbeat on the subject of painting; and hence it is so common to hear a man say: "I am no judge of pictures." But O Englishmen! Know that every man ought to be a judge of pictures, and every man is so who has not been connoisseured out of his senses.

A gentleman who visited me the other day said, "I am very much surprised at the dislike that some connoisseurs show on viewing the pictures of Mr. Fuseli; but the truth is, he is a hundred years beyond the present generation." Though I am startled at such an assertion, I hope the contemporary taste will shorten the hundred years into as many hours; for I am sure that any person consulting his own eyes must prefer what is so supereminent; and I am as sure that any person consulting his own reputation, or the reputation of his country, will refrain from disgracing either by such ill-judged criticisms in future.

Yours,
Wm. Blake

To John Linnell

1 February 1826

Dear Sir,

I am forced to write, because I cannot come to you, & this on two accounts. First, I omitted to desire you would come & take a Mutton chop with us the day you go to Cheltenham, & I will go with you to the Coach; also, I will go to Hampstead to see Mrs.

Linnell on Sunday, but will return before dinner (I mean if you set off before that), & Second, I wish to have a copy of *Job* to show to Mr. Chantry.

For I am again laid up by a cold in my stomach; the Hampstead Air, as it always did, so I fear it always will do this, Except it be the Morning air; & That, in my Cousin's time, I found I could bear with safety & perhaps benefit. I believe my Constitution to be a good one, but it has many peculiarities that no one but myself can know. When I was young, Hampstead, Highgate, Hornsea, Muswell Hill, & even Islington & all places North of London always laid me up the day after, & sometimes two or three days, with precisely the same Complaint & the same torment of the Stomach, Easily removed, but excruciating while it lasts & enfeebling for some time after. Sir Francis Bacon would say it is want of discipline in Mountainous Places. Sir Francis Bacon is a Liar. No discipline will turn one Man into another, even in the least particle; & such discipline I call Presumption & Folly. I have tried it too much not to know this & am very sorry for all such who may be led to such ostentatious Exertion against their Eternal Existence itself, because it is Mental Rebellion against the Holy Spirit, & fit only for a Soldier of Satan to perform.

Though I hope in a morning or two to call on you in Cirencester Place, I feared you might be gone, or I might be too ill to let you know how I am & what I wish.

I am, dear sir,
Yours Sincerely,
William Blake

Feb'y 1, 1826

To John Linnell

Dear Sir,

I thank you for the Five Pounds received today; am getting better every Morning, but slowly, as I am still feeble & tottering, though all the Symptoms of my complaint seem almost gone as the fine weather is very beneficial & comfortable to me. I go on, as I think improving my Engravings of Dante more & more, & shall soon get Proofs of these Four which I have, & beg the favour of you to send me the two Plates of Dante which you have, that I may finish them sufficiently to make some show of Colour & Strength.

I have thought & thought of the Removal & cannot get my Mind out of a state of terrible fear at such a step; the more I think the more I feel terror at what I wished at first & thought it a thing of benefit & Good hope; you will attribute it to its right Cause— Intellectual Peculiarity, that must be Myself alone shut up in Myself, or Reduced to Nothing. I could tell you of Visions & dreams upon the Subject. I have asked & entreated Divine help, but fear continues upon me, & I must relinquish the step that I had wished to take, & still wish, but in vain.

Your Success in your Profession is above all things to me most gratifying; may it go on to the Perfection you wish & more. So wishes also

Yours Sincerely,
William Blake

To George Cumberland

12 April 1827

Dear Cumberland,

I have been very near the Gates of Death & have returned very weak & an Old Man, feeble & tottering, but not in Spirit & Life, not in The Real Man, The Imagination, which Liveth forever. In that I am stronger & stronger as this Foolish Body decays. I thank you for the Pains you have taken with Poor *Job.* I know too well that a great majority of Englishmen are fond of The Indefinite, which they Measure by Newton's Doctrine of the Fluxions of an Atom, A Thing that does not Exist. These are Politicians & think that Republican Art is Inimical to their Atom. For a Line or Lineament is not formed by Chance; a Line is a Line in its Minutest Subdivisions; Straight or Crooked, It is Itself & Not Intermeasurable with or by anything Else. Such is *Job,* but since the French Revolution Englishmen are all Intermeasurable One by Another, Certainly a happy state of Agreement to which I for One do not Agree. God keep me from the Divinity of Yes & No too, The Yea Nay Creeping Jesus, from supposing Up & Down to be the same Thing, as all Experimentalists must suppose.

You are desirous I know to dispose of some of my Works & to make them Pleasing. I am obliged to you & to all who do so. But having none remaining of all that I had Printed, I cannot Print more Except at a great loss, for at the time I printed those things I had a whole House to range in; now I am shut up in a Corner, therefore am forced to ask a Price for them that I scarce expect to get from a Stranger. I am now Printing a Set of the *Songs of Innocence & Experience* for a Friend at Ten Guineas, which I cannot do under Six Months consistent with my other Work, so that I have little hope of doing any more of such things. The Last Work I produced is a Poem Entitled *Jerusalem, the Emanation of the*

Giant Albion, but find that to Print it will Cost my Time the amount of Twenty Guineas. One I have Finished. It contains 100 Plates, but it is not likely that I shall get a Customer for it.

As you wish me to send you a list with the Prices of these things they are as follows:

	£	s	d
America	6.	6.	0
Europe	6.	6.	0
Visions &c.	5.	5.	0
Thel	3.	3.	0
Songs of Inn. & Exp.	10.	10.	0
Urizen	6.	6.	0

The Little Card I will do as soon as Possible, but when you Consider that I have been reduced to a Skeleton from which I am slowly recovering, you will, I hope, have Patience with me.

Flaxman is Gone, & we must All soon follow, everyone to his Own Eternal House, Leaving the Delusive Goddess Nature & her Laws to get into Freedom from all Law of the Members into The Mind, in which everyone is King & Priest in his own House. God send it so on Earth as it is in Heaven.

I am, Dear Sir, Yours Affectionately,

William Blake

12 April 1827
N. 3 Fountain Court Strand

NOTES AND COMMENTARIES

PART ONE: SHORTER POEMS

There is no attempt here to offer detailed commentaries on the shorter poems. Remarks are limited to those useful to a beginning reader. References are often supplied to extended readings elsewhere.

POETICAL SKETCHES

Poetical Sketches was printed for Blake in 1783. At the time, Blake had become attached to a group of bluestockings that included Anna Barbauld, a writer of children's songs. The "Rev. Henry Mathew," actually the Rev. Anthony Stephen Matthews, apparently the group's leader, wrote the preface to the volume:

> The following Sketches were the production of untutored youth, commenced in his twelfth, and occasionally resumed by the author till his twentieth year; since which time, his talents have been wholly directed to the attainment of excellence in his profession, he has been deprived of the leisure requisite to such a revisal of these sheets, as might have rendered them less unfit to meet the public eye.
>
> Conscious of the irregularities and defects to be found in almost every page, his friends have still believed that they possessed a poetic originality which merited some respite from oblivion. These their opinions remain, however, to be now reproved or confirmed by a less partial public.

Perhaps the condescension of the preface with its reference to Blake's lack of formal education annoyed Blake, for no copies were ever put up for sale. Among the most interesting of these poems are "Mad Song," which is a considerable technical achievement and an anticipation of the "Spectre" of the Prophecies, "Love and harmony combine. . . ." which offers Blake's first use of the tree of life, later associated with the unfallen Albion, and "How

sweet I roamed. . . ." (said to have been composed at age fourteen), which anticipates *Songs of Experience* and *Vala* in its pre-
sentation of a caged bird and a repressive "prince of love."

The poems display a variety of influences, including *Ossian,*
Chatterton, Renaissance lyrics, and Percy's *Reliques.* These influences, if nothing else, identify Blake as more closely related
to the poetry of his time than has often been supposed.

For commentary see Margaret Ruth Lowery, *Windows of the
Morning* (1940), Northrop Frye, *Fearful Symmetry* (1947), pp.
172 - 182; and Harold Bloom, *Blake's Apocalypse* (1963), pp. 13 -
22. For a discussion of the four poems to the seasons, see Robert
F. Gleckner, "Blake's Seasons," *Studies in English Literature,
1500 - 1900* V (3), 1965, pp. 533 - 551.

SONGS OF INNOCENCE

The earliest copies are dated 1789. Early drafts of three songs
appear in the manuscript of *An Island in the Moon.* Commentary is plentiful but of uneven quality. As a beginning there is
Joseph Wicksteed's *Blake's Innocence and Experience* (1928),
more useful as a discussion of the designs than of the text; later
studies are Robert F. Gleckner's *The Piper and the Bard* (1959);
Hazard Adams's *William Blake: A Reading of the Shorter Poems*
(1963), which includes an index of criticism to 1960; and E. D.
Hirsch, Jr.'s *Innocence and Experience* (1964). An excellent facsimile of *Songs of Innocence and Experience,* with introduction
and commentary by Sir Geoffrey Keynes, was published by Ru-
pert Hart-Davis in 1967. The poems are best read, of course, in
the form in which Blake engraved them.

INTRODUCTION   The poem has occasioned some debate but
it is relatively direct and simple. The poet asserts that the child
on the cloud, a sort of spirit of innocence, has called upon him to
pipe, then sing, then write out his songs.

THE SHEPHERD   We begin to be introduced to the anatomy
of innocence. Major archetypes, renewed in Blake's treatment
of Tharmas at the end of *The Four Zoas,* are the shepherd and

flocks of *Psalms,* XXIII. Innocence, later Beulah, is a protective, loving, idyllic, surrounding world associated with a benevolent mother and protective shepherd-father-god.

THE ECHOING GREEN   Though some have seen intimations of experience in ll. 11-13 and 29-30, the poem presents a world of animation different from the fallen world of living subject and dead object. Though darkness comes, it will recede before the sun's rebirth, and in the intervening darkness there is the protection of the society of the family. Later the white-haired old man and the oak tree will be used as ominous symbols of experience, related to Druidism and human sacrifice.

THE LAMB   Paired with "The Tiger" of *Songs of Experience,* the poem works towards the identity of child and lamb, which becomes a figure, as in the Bible, of the infant Jesus. The contrast is to the alien majesty of the tiger, as it is represented by the speaker of that poem.

THE LITTLE BLACK BOY   The poem has been frequently discussed. It is an example of an irony present even in *Songs of Innocence,* since there is a good deal of pathos in the black boy's statement. We can well imagine his emergence from innocence. Both black and white bodies are seen as clouds, but the white child has obviously made too much of the difference. Longing to be loved, the black boy anticipates that he may be able to shade the white boy, unprepared for the light of God, until he is ready for it. The poem perhaps supports the activities of the Society for Effecting the Abolition of the Slave Trade, formed in 1787. In 1792-1793 Blake did a number of etchings for J. G. Stedman's *A Narrative, of a Five Years' expedition, against the revolted Negroes of Surinam* (1796), which describes a number of atrocities against black people.

THE BLOSSOM   The blossom is speaking; it is a flower on the tree of life. The relation of bird to blossom suggests gratified sexual desire and, at the same time, loving protection. In the illustration, the plant suggests a phallic flame from which tiny angels emerge.

THE CHIMNEY SWEEPER   Paired with "The Chimney Sweeper" in *Songs of Experience.* The poem's irony arises from the pathos of Tom Dacre's dream and the "moral" of the concluding line. David V. Erdman (*Blake: Prophet Against Empire,* p. 120) reports that in 1788 a law was passed that prevented a boy from being apprenticed as a sweep before age eight, required his being washed once a week, and forbade his being sent up an ignited chimney. Erdman suggests that the "bright key" may be passage of the bill containing these provisions. Perhaps so, but is is clearly more than that; it is the hope for freedom. "'Weep" may be the young boy's effort to pronounce "sweep" as he walks through the streets soliciting trade. The black coffins are, of course, chimneys. At the end, the poem teeters on the edge of bitter parody of the tone of pious songs for children such as those of Mrs. Barbauld. See also Martin K. Nurmi, "Fact and Symbol in 'The Chimney Sweeper' of Blake's *Songs of Experience,"* *Bulletin of the New York Public Library* LXVIII (4), 1964, pp. 249 - 256.

THE LITTLE BOY LOST and THE LITTLE BOY FOUND   These poems express the child's fear of the unknown terrors of the darkness, as do the poems "Night" and "A Dream." At this stage the child is aware of danger on the edges of his consciousness. In innocence, there is protection in the child's capacity to believe in the benevolence of a father-god.

LAUGHING SONG   The poem is notable for the subtle progressive heightening of the sense of human life in all things through the attribution of, first, a metaphorical laughter to objects and, ultimately, literal laughter to everything.

CRADLE SONG   The poem ends by dissolving the historical Jesus into present identity with the child, thus lifting Jesus out of linear time.

THE DIVINE IMAGE   Paired with the bitter "A Divine Image," which was probably designed as an addition to *Songs of Experience.* Terms like mercy, pity, peace, and love are mere abstractions until given human form. The poem affirms that such abstractions have their reality only in concrete acts.

HOLY THURSDAY   Paired with "Holy Thursday" of *Songs of Experience,* the poem refers to Ascension Day. Annually on that day in London, over six thousand children from charity schools marched in uniform to St. Paul's Cathedral, where they attended service and sang. The "grey-headed beadles" will later appear from the perspective of innocence to be Urizenic "angels." The "mighty wind" and "harmonious thunderings" reveal a potential for Orcan revolt among the children and intimations of apocalypse. The moral last line is ironic from the perspective of experience, angels in experience and in Blake's *Marriage of Heaven and Hell* being representative of the *status quo.* Compare "The Human Abstract" in *Songs of Experience:* "Pity would be no more/If we did not make somebody Poor."

NIGHT   There is a cruel world beyond the sheepfold, but lullaby visions of peace and protection are available. Frye points out that the vision of the lion and lamb lying down together is clearly from the lamb's point of view. In experience the lamb is the prolific, the lion the devourer. These terms, amplified in *The Marriage of Heaven and Hell* and elsewhere, suggest that the lamb and the tiger are contraries, each of which acts according to its own nature. For the lion to devour is not sinful. That is its nature.

SPRING   The poem is spoken by a voice that gradually becomes, in innocent love, all that it beholds. To become what one beholds in experience is something else.

NURSE'S SONG   Paired with "Nurse's Song" in *Songs of Experience.* The speaker of this poem clearly presents an attitude at peace with experience, while the nurse of experience is bitter and does not hide it from the children. Here the imagery of sleep and darkness is not dwelt on ominously by the speaker.

INFANT JOY   Paired with "Infant Sorrow" in *Songs of Experience,* the poem is a dialogue imagined by the mother, who sees what is usually an abstraction, "joy," living before her *as* her child. The illustration shows mother, child, and winged angel inside the bud of a flower. Innocence absorbs abstractions in particulars.

A DREAM   The range of protection in innocence runs to the lowest of creatures. It is not so much a chain of being as a humanization of all things.

ON ANOTHER'S SORROW   The sense of cooperation and identification of all things is completed in this song by its incarnation in the image and loving acts of Jesus.

SONGS OF EXPERIENCE

Once one reads *Songs of Experience,* the *Songs of Innocence* take on new implications simply by juxtaposition with the later poems. Never published separately from *Songs of Innocence,* these poems are dated 1794. Four of them were originally published among *Songs of Innocence* but subsequently transferred. Early drafts of some of the poems appear in the Rossetti manuscript. For a list of extended commentary see the note to *Songs of Innocence.*

INTRODUCTION and EARTH'S ANSWER   Much discussed because of their cryptic compressed symbolism, these poems are best interpreted by Northrop Frye in *Huntington Library Quarterly* XXI (1), pp. 57-68. See also Gleckner, pp. 77-78, pp. 231-239; Adams, pp. 21-27. The reference in ll. 4-5 is to *Genesis* 3:8. The "lapsed Soul" of l. 6 is, later in Blake's story, Albion, the archetypal man, who lapses into the fall and the sleep of history. Here it is "Earth" or nature, who is later Vala, man's emanation separated and alienated from him. The "slumberous mass" (l. 15) is the sleeping, chaotic, fallen world, bereft of imaginative shaping. The "starry floor" (l. 18) forms the base of the fall into the sky, just as the "wat'ry shore" (l. 19) is a wall against chaos. In a world turned upside down, the stars are on the floor. They are the lowest limit of the fall, set by God's mercy. Later Blake calls this limit the twofold limit of contraction (Adam) and opacity (Satan). "Break of day" (l. 20) is, of course, the apocalypse. The poem prepares us to read the poems of *Experience* symbolically, it being much more indirect and cryptic than the direct approach of "Introduction" to *Songs of Experience.* In "Earth's Answer," Earth, like Albion in the prophecies, is imprisoned by a "starry" old man or god of the sky, the oppressive giver of abstract external law. In later works this oppressor is Urizen.

THE CLOD AND THE PEBBLE   This song forces innocence and experience into contrariety. One can imagine weaknesses in either position. One wishes to struggle like Orc out of the position of the clod but to reject the selfish hedonism of the pebble. *Songs of Experience* will not simply imply the existence of the contrary state, as does *Songs of Innocence;* it will insist on the opposition and seek to build something from it.

HOLY THURSDAY   Paired with "Holy Thursday" of *Songs of Innocence;* the poem makes us rethink the earlier song. The speaker presents another interpretation of the treatment of poverty by society.

THE LITTLE GIRL LOST and LITTLE GIRL FOUND   These poems were first located in *Songs of Innocence.* The whole movement of history toward apocalypse and the awakening of earth is here figured forth in microcosm in the efforts of Lyca to be lost and found again. The hysterical parents, who become more childish as the story proceeds, must adjust themselves to the child's new condition. They are no longer the protective figures of innocence but the "starry" external oppressors from whom Lyca must be emancipated. Lengthy interpretations of these poems occur in Kathleen Raine, "The Little Girl Lost and Found," *The Divine Vision* (V. de S. Pinto, ed.), London, 1957, pp. 19-49; Gleckner, pp. 219-228; Adams, pp. 210-218.

THE CHIMNEYSWEEPER   Paired with "The Chimney Sweeper" from *Songs of Innocence,* the poem presents a somewhat accusing questioner and a small child who answers with a devastating attack on church and state. That the speaker is a child emphasizes the directness and the clarity of his vision. A dream like that of the child's counterpart in innocence is not sufficient to cloud this child's direct understanding of the situation.

NURSE'S SONG   Paired with "Nurse's Song" in *Songs of Innocence,* this poem presents a hysterical reaction to the children's emergence from innocence. In a self-pitying way this nurse would drag the children into experience, insisting on the allegorical foreboding of the sunset.

THE SICK ROSE   This poem packs a great deal into its eight lines. In the illustrations to *Songs of Innocence* flowers contain babes or birds or angels. They are the wombs from which innocent life springs. Experience presents another picture. The phallic worm within the rose has raped it and now destroyed its life. The poem can be read on many levels from literal to macrocosmic, where the rose becomes the world itself.

THE FLY   This apparently simple poem has become the subject of recent comment. See John E. Grant, "Misreadings of 'The Fly'," *Essays in Criticism* XI (4), 1961, pp. 481-487; Adams, pp. 287-288; Warren Stevenson, "Artful Irony in Blake's 'The Fly'," *Texas Studies in Literature and Language* X (1), 1968, pp. 77-82.

THE ANGEL   Having joyed in her angel's loss of ease, the speaker discovers that the angel has departed. On his return she is now committed to her own defenses against the world. She has failed to catch the joy as it flies.

THE TIGER   The poem is paired with "The Lamb" of *Songs of Innocence*. Here the speaker faces an alien and frightening beast. He must, however, come to terms with its "fearful symmetry" as Job (XL, XLI, XLII) came to understand the leviathan and behemoth as part of creation, for the tiger is beautiful as well as frightening. For extended discussion see Martin K. Nurmi, "Blake's Revisions of 'The Tyger'," *PMLA* LXXI (4), 1956, pp. 669-685; Adams, pp. 52-74; John E. Grant, "The Art and Argument of 'The Tyger'," *Texas Studies in Literature and Language* II, 1960, pp. 38-60.

MY PRETTY ROSE TREE, AH! SUNFLOWER, and THE LILY   These poems appear together on a single plate. In the first we have a little allegory of misunderstanding and jealousy. The rose tree is jealous even though the speaker has adhered to the moral law; to be honestly admiring of the flower was too much. The sunflower is a figure for the pining natural man of experience, who seeks consummation of desire beyond nature. The rose and sheep of

"The Lily" symbolize the protection of selfhood already described tragically in "The Angel." The lily itself, by contrast, offers no such defenses and thus is capable of delighting in love.

THE GARDEN OF LOVE   The title is ironic, for the garden of innocence is now a graveyard, the burial place of desire in the prohibitions of organized religion. It is worth comparing this song with "I saw a chapel all of gold" from the Rossetti manuscript.

THE LITTLE VAGABOND   This poem was thought to be too inflammatory and was suppressed from the first printed edition of *Songs* in 1839. We have here again the incisive social criticism of the innocent child.

LONDON   One of Blake's most accomplished poems, "London" offers many of the symbols of the fallen world—the child of "Infant Sorrow," the church of "The Garden of Love," the soldier and palace of the minor prophecies, the harlot of the later works, and the chimney sweeper. Note the complex figures of stanzas three and four. See Adams, pp. 275-286, for the poem's relation to the later prophecies.

THE HUMAN ABSTRACT   A poem from the Rossetti manuscript, "I heard an angel singing," anticipates the first stanza. The poem then describes the growth of the Tree of Mystery or the Tree of the Knowledge of Good and Evil. Compare "Love and harmony combine. . . ." from *Poetical Sketches,* which could well have been paired with this poem in *Songs of Innocence.* For Blake, humility (l. 11) is always hypocritical. The fruit of deceit appears in "A Poison Tree." W. B. Yeats appropriated Blake's raven for his lyric "The Two Trees."

INFANT SORROW   This is the situation of "Infant Joy" seen from the perspective of the child, now grown into the state of Orcan revolt and looking backward on his infanthood, believing that from the beginning he had been imprisoned in his "swaddling bands."

A POISON TREE   The poem describes how the fruit of resentment is properly grown, by repression of feeling, which blooms as desire for revenge.

A LITTLE BOY LOST   Like the little vagabond this child in his innocence sees things too clearly and seems, to the priest, to have affronted "holy mystery." Paired with "The Little Boy Lost" and "The Little Boy Found," the poem ironically twists the idea of being "lost."

A LITTLE GIRL LOST   As in the poems "The Little Girl Lost" and "The Little Girl Found," it is the parent who is lost or trapped in the moral law and his own fears. The "father white" is clearly Urizen.

TO TIRZAH   This poem is a late addition to the *Songs* and the only one of them that introduces a character from the prophetic books by name. She is the fifth daughter of Zelophehad, who had no sons, and thus she sought a female inheritance. She is a symbol, then, of the separate "female will," which always seeks domination. (*Numbers* 27: 1-8; *Joshua* 17: 3-4.) Tirzah is also mentioned in *The Song of Solomon* (6:4). In *Vala* and *Milton* she appears as a younger, chaste form of Rahab. She is also the mother of mortality, in that, asserting her separateness from man, she creates the physical body and limits the senses. Lines 4 and 15 repeat the words of Jesus to Mary (*John* 2:4), emphasizing the necessity of emancipation from innocence and mother-protection. The poem indicates that man must be planted and generated. A merciful god created the fallen world, the sleep of fallen history, and sexuality, in order to prevent total chaos.

THE SCHOOL BOY   Once in *Songs of Innocence,* this poem of complaint belongs more properly where it now is. The cycles of growth and of the seasons and the imagery of the caged bird were all introduced in *Poetical Sketches.*

THE VOICE OF THE ANCIENT BARD   This poem originally appeared in *Songs of Innocence,* but clearly it discusses the state of experience and calls on youth not merely to criticize experience but also to see beyond it to a reordered society.

A DIVINE IMAGE   Not actually included in the *Songs,* the poem is a savage contrary to "The Divine Image" of *Songs of Innocence.* The illustration shows Blake's prophet-hero Los hammering at his forge, shaping the body of the sun, Urizen. When cruelty, jealousy, terror, and secrecy are given human form, then they will be incapable of shrouding themselves in mystery, which is their only power.

POEMS, EPIGRAMS AND FRAGMENTS
FROM THE ROSSETTI MANUSCRIPT.

This notebook, belonging originally to Blake's brother Robert, came into the possession of the poet Dante Gabriel Rossetti. Reproduced in facsimile by Sir Geoffrey Keynes (1935), it is composed of fifty-eight leaves and contains poems, prose essays, epigrams, designs, and drawings.

NEVER PAIN TO TELL THY LOVE   l. 1. Originally Blake wrote "seek" for "pain." ll. 1-4. Then Blake deleted the whole first stanza. l. 12. Originally Blake wrote: "He took her with a sigh."

I SAW A CHAPEL ALL OF GOLD   This poem takes the irony of "The Garden of Love" one step further. The poet here observes the rebellion that is only about to brew in the mind of the speaker of "The Garden of Love." The phallic serpent, like the revolutionary oedipal boy Orc, who is thwarted desire, tears down the doors of the chapel, which is also a symbol of female chastity, defiling the sacraments. But the sacraments, or joyful love, have been hidden away from man. Seeing that outrageous repression has brought about outrageous revolt, the speaker turns with bitterness to the sty and the swine, as if to seek a way back into a simple life. Jesus was, after all, born in a manger.

I ASKED A THIEF TO STEAL ME A PEACH   Blake changed l. 11 to "And still as a maid," retaining the new line in a fair copy dated 1796. I think the change was a mistake and therefore presumptuously print the poem with its original line. Angels are clearly of Urizen's party once we leave *Songs of Innocence.*

I HEARD AN ANGEL SINGING   This poem was plundered for "The Human Abstract" of *Songs of Experience.*

A CRADLE SONG This poem is different enough from "A Cradle Song" in *Songs of Innocence* to be considered in its own right.

THOU HAST A LAP FULL OF SEED   The poem is interpreted by Damon (p. 288) as a sexual allegory, the sand being marriage with a chaste woman, as opposed to the unchaste ground where weeds already grow.

TO NOBODADDY   The name, coined as far as I know by Blake, is really a nickname for Urizen; the poem discusses some of the results of Urizen's dark activity. His laws are responsible for jealousy.

ETERNITY   Blake's idea of eternity is neither endless time nor some place out of time. Eternity is the now in which work is done and in which time is made significant.

MOTTO TO THE SONGS OF INNOCENCE AND EXPERIENCE   This poem was never included among the *Songs*. The fairies and elves are emblematic of freedom and joy, which are lost in experience. Grounds then develop for knowing the difference between the creatures of day and night, eagle and owl, and their symbolic values.

LET THE BROTHELS OF PARIS BE OPENED   This much revised poem is sometimes called "Fayette." Lafayette perceives that the king and queen are wrong, having sided with Nobodaddy, but he protects them out of loyalty. The questions of the last stanza treat Lafayette's dilemma as tragic.

WHEN KLOPSTOCK ENGLAND DEFIED   The German poet Klopstock, who wrote a long poem *The Messiah,* criticized English diction as too coarse for epic verse, blaming the influence of Swift. Blake considered Klopstock's poem a defiance of English poets, who had not followed adequately in Milton's tradition. Blake would take up the challenge with his own *Milton.* The poem may or may not have been written before the Blakes moved to Felpham. Lines 29-32 were considered illegible by Keynes. I have adopted Erdman's new transcription of them.

A FAIRY SKIPPED UPON MY KNEE   l. 1. Keynes reads "leapt" for "skipped."

MY SPECTRE AROUND ME NIGHT & DAY   There is an extended discussion of the poem in Adams, pp. 101-120. See also Bloom, pp. 285-288. The poem is revised but unfinished. The additional stanzas were never worked into the poem. Fallen man divides into a wolflike, devouring, reasoning selfhood and a separate, chaste, tormenting, female emanation. The speaker is aware of the tragic split in himself that results in the chase and struggle of the poem.

ON THE VIRGINITY OF THE VIRGIN MARY AND JOHANNA SOUTHCOTT Joanna Southcott (1750-1814) was a religious fanatic who at age sixty-four proclaimed that she was pregnant by the Holy Ghost. But her pregnancy was only dropsy.

MOCK ON, MOCK ON, VOLTAIRE, ROUSSEAU   Blake considered Voltaire and Rousseau mockers against spiritual vision. The sand is perhaps a figure for materialism, which in turn blinds them, metamorphosing in the eyes of a visionary into gems.

TO H   Robert Hunt, who viciously attacked Blake's exhibition in the *Examiner* and who may have attacked Fuseli two years earlier, was the brother of Leigh Hunt.

TO F   John Flaxman, the artist. But Blake and Flaxman were usually on friendly terms except when Blake became suspicious that Flaxman was jealous of his talent.

ON H_____Y'S FRIENDSHIP and TO H   Reference is to William Hayley.

ON H_____THE PICK THANK   William Hayley again.

TO GOD   The circle is the compass-work of Blake's "Ancient of Days," depicted in a famous painting. The circle is also the enclosure of material space and measured time, called the Circle of Destiny and the Mundane Shell in the Prophecies.

NOW ART HAS LOST ITS MENTAL CHARMS   Blake once wrote: "Let us teach Bonaparte and whomsoever else it may concern that it is not Arts that follow and attend upon Empire, but Empire that attends upon and follows the Arts." The poem describes a charge to Blake to renew English art and thereby win a spiritual victory over France.

THE CAVERNS OF THE GRAVE I'VE SEEN   Blake has dedicated the illustrations to Blair's *Grave* to the queen. The poem wonders to whom he can dedicate his visions of "the Caves of Hell." It has been thought that he refers to his "Last Judgment," to be dedicated to the Countess of Egremont.

POEMS FROM THE PICKERING MANUSCRIPT

The manuscript, about which very little is known, is composed of ten poems in fair copy. It is named after a nineteenth-century owner, B. M. Pickering. The most complete discussions of these poems occur in Adams, pp. 77-169. 205-208. See also the more general discussions of Damon, Frye, Bloom and Hirsch.

THE SMILE   See Adams, pp. 152-154.

THE GOLDEN NET   The three virgins are the "triple female" of the prophetic books that Blake associates with Rahab-Tirzah-Vala. The young man is captured by these "virgin harlots" in their net of nature and religion. See Damon, p. 297; Frye, p. 266; Adams, pp. 129-131.

THE MENTAL TRAVELLER   This poem has been variously interpreted. The cyclic process includes a male figure who ages as his female opposite becomes younger. In this way all the relationships between male and female are explored. The male has been identified by some as Orc-Urizen and the female as Tirzah-Rahab. The cycle has been named the Orc cycle by Frye, that is, the endless principle of tyranny and revolt. For extensive discussion see Frye, pp. 227-229; John H. Sutherland, "Blake's 'Mental Traveller'," *English Literary History* XXII (2), 1955, pp. 136-147; Adams, pp. 77-100; Bloom, pp. 289-297; and Martin K. Nurmi, "Joy, Love, and Innocence in Blake's 'The Mental Traveller'," *Studies in Romanticism* III (2), 1964, pp. 109-117.

THE LAND OF DREAMS   See Adams, pp. 205-208.

MARY   Lines 21-22 are revised from a poem in a letter to Thomas Butts, 16 August, 1803. See Adams, pp. 137-141.

THE CRYSTAL CABINET   See Frye, pp. 234; Adams, pp. 121-128; Bloom, pp. 297-301. This poem is spoken by someone who recalls a state of unrestrained innocence where he meets a maiden and subsequently falls from innocent love into sexuality and then into experience. The poem is closely connected to the symbolism of "The Mental Traveller."

THE GREY MONK   The poem is condensed from a longer unfinished poem in the Rossetti manuscript, which also apparently forms the basis for the introductory poem to *Jerusalem,* Chapter 3. See Erdman, pp. 385-386, for biographical comment; Adams, pp. 149-152.

AUGURIES OF INNOCENCE   Almost all treatments of Blake get around to discussing auguries from this poem. Extended discussions are found in Bloom, pp. 301-303; Adams, pp. 155-169. The mixture of auguries suggests that Blake is telling us that all of the themes suggested are connected to each other, are indeed one theme: Man must look through the eye rather than with it, that is, among other things, look with the spirit, not divide himself as subject off from other things as objects.

LONG JOHN BROWN & LITTLE MARY BELL   See Adams, pp. 134-137.

WILLIAM BOND   See Adams, pp. 142-148.

THE EVERLASTING GOSPEL   The text of this poem is confused, for passages are scattered here and there through the Rossetti manuscript. There is an extensive discussion of the text by David V. Erdman, "'Terrible Blake in His Pride,' An Essay on *The Everlasting Gospel," From Sensibility to Romanticism: Essays Presented to Frederick A. Pottle,* New York, 1965, pp. 331-356. For interpretive commentary see J. G. Davies, *The Theology of William Blake,* Oxford, 1948, pp. 110-121; Arthur L. Morton, *The Everlasting Gospel: A Study in the Sources of William Blake,* London, 1958; also Damon, pp. 292-297; Frye, pp. 78-84; Adams, pp. 180-200. Blake's interpretation of Jesus makes him a rebel against external codes or laws. Thus, Blake has him flout the ten commandments and substitute the principle of the forgiveness of sins for the moral law.

TO THE ACCUSER WHO IS THE GOD OF THIS WORLD   This is the epilogue to *For The Sexes: The Gates of Paradise,* added to the work perhaps as late as 1818. See Bloom, pp. 435-436.

PART TWO: PROPHECIES

These commentaries do not attempt to identify or explain all of the many references, mainly to the Bible, in Blake. Students will find excellent notes of this sort and extended commentary by Harold Bloom in *The Poetry and Prose of William Blake* and much information in S. Foster Damon's *A Blake Dictionary*.

The aim here is to offer a helpful brief running commentary that will guide the reader through the major events of these difficult poems. Blake's poems work by accumulation of overtones; as a poem proceeds, these overtones throng together even in single words. Unless the commentaries are to become prohibitively long, they must remain superficial.

THERE IS NO NATURAL RELIGION (a)

Blake rejects the assumption that man is born into the world a *tabula rasa* (blank tablet). If one reasons from his perceptions of a fallen natural world, he can never pass into full imaginative life. But man can so pass; therefore, there is escape from the "same dull round" of generalization from sense data.

THERE IS NO NATURAL RELIGION (b)

The "mill" and "complicated wheels" will reappear in Blake, always associated with the reasoning power once it attempts to capture all of the human spirit. In order to see God one must see Him from His own point of view, that is, become God himself. To do otherwise is to divide God analytically, to be bounded by organs of perception, from which one reasons in a circle and makes an abstract idea of God. This is the reason that Jesus in

Jerusalem 1:18-19 insists that he is inside Albion and that Albion is also inside him.

ALL RELIGIONS ARE ONE

The "voice" mentioned here is developed in *The Marriage of Heaven & Hell* into Rintrah, righteous wrath, and is a prophetic John the Baptist figure in Blake. In the later works he is a Son of Los, an aspect of the imagination. The idea of the "poetic genius" suggests a connection among men, who harbor the genius, and suggests, as Frye has pointed out, that there is a universal poetic language of which all religions are efforts at grammars.

THE BOOK OF THEL

The motto borrowed in part from *Ecclesiastes* 12:6, suggests that, to know experience, one must descend into it, that is, converse with the mole. The rod and bowl are sexual symbols of generation, into which every human will must descend. Thel, whose name in Greek is "will," refuses the descent, however, and remains ungenerated. The result, only hinted at as the poem ends, is monstrous.

"Mne" (1:1) has been variously but never convincingly interpreted. Some think it a misprint. Thel, a daughter of the Seraphim, exists in a pregenerative world, a sort of biblical Eden, to which there is a reference in 1:14. In Thel's opening lament (1:6-1:14) she fears that she will pass away in the cycle of nature that surrounds her. Indeed, she must pass out of it if she is not to become monstrously childish and without identity, since she must pass into experience, and in experience there must be contrariety. Fearing this absence of identity, she wishes to be of use, and she asks the lily and the cloud how they can live without her fears.

The lily makes an apology for the natural cycle and rejoices in the love of the sun. The cloud, who mentions, incidentally, the first of Blake's "giant forms" or Zoas, Luvah, insists that its own form may pass away, but not its substance, which is food for flowers.

That Thel might be food for worms (3:25) and thus useful only frightens her. The worm symbolizes sexuality and death. It is helpless like a child, but it is phallic, and it devours the body. Its appearance in the poem sets the stage for clay's invitation to Thel to descend into generation, which will include sexuality and death, where indeed she may, in her progress back to a higher innocence, be of service to worms. Thel refuses experience after hearing the lamentations of her own future, experienced self.

The eternal gates (6:1) are a remembrance from *Odyssey XIII* as interpreted by Porphyry; through them, souls descend to generation. Har (6:22) appears earlier in Blake's *Tiriel,* where with Heva he inhabits a world of monstrous extended childhood.

THE MARRIAGE OF HEAVEN AND HELL

Martin K. Nurmi's *Blake's Marriage of Heaven and Hell: A Critical Study,* Kent, Ohio, 1957, is a useful extended commentary, though it gives an excess of space to emphasis on the influence of Swedenborg and Boehme. Helpful discussions occur in Harold Bloom, *Blake's Apocalypse,* pp. 69-98, and Northrop Frye, *Fearful Symmetry,* pp. 194-201.

The *Marriage* is perhaps best described by Northrop Frye's use of the word "anatomy" in his *Anatomy of Criticism.* As such it is comparable to W. B. Yeats's *A Vision.* In some respects it is an answer to the writings of Emanuel Swedenborg, the mystical theologian. Swedenborg's work interested Blake at one time, but he soon became critical of Swedenborg's materialism. Blake's "Memorable Fancies" parody Swedenborg's "Memorable Relations," which describe the spiritual order.

The "Argument" introduces Rintrah, who appears in the later works as righteous wrath, a Son of Los. Here Rintrah is also the revolutionary turmoil of Blake's time. The remainder of the poem presents human history in greatly compressed form. Originally man walked on the perilous path through the contraries of life, but gradually civilization planted the path and brought forth a new man, or Adam, from the red clay. In this new order the villain (Satan), or the villainous aspects of culture, drove the just man into the wilderness, a wandering John the Baptist. As a result, the villain runs society and is "angelic" while the just man rages as a "devil" in the wilds. The inversion of the terms "angel" and "devil" is exploited throughout the *Marriage.* Repetition of the argument's opening lines suggests some impending great event.

Plate 3 takes up this matter: Swedenborg had announced that the beginning of the Last Judgment would take place in 1757. This was the year of Blake's birth. In 1790, the year of publication of the *Marriage,* Blake was thirty-three, the age of Christ at his death. Swedenborg is called the angel sitting at the tomb of Jesus after the resurrection. The linen clothes, Swedenborg's writings, are cast aside as useless to this new condition of true life. The biblical passage *Isaiah* 34 describes the terrible judgment of God upon the earth: "Behold, the Lord maketh the earth empty, and maketh it waste, and turneth it upside down, and scattereth abroad the inhabitants thereof." In 35, the prophet praises God, who will destroy "the face of the covering cast over all people, and the veil that is spread over all nations." In Chapter 63 Isaiah prophesies the coming of the outcast red man of Edom, Esau, who, it had been prophesied, would finally gain dominion over Jacob. This red man is the outcast representative of energy, and becomes the revolutionary Orc in the later poems.

The principle of contrariety is next presented. Blake notes that the religious call passivity good and active energy evil. For this reason the *Marriage,* taking the side of energy, will reject the terms good and evil and insist that reason and energy are necessary "contraries," while good and evil are "negations" of each other.

The Devil of Plate 4 is a representative of energy. Hell is the place of energy, Heaven the place of passivity. The devil argues that the distinction between body and soul arises falsely from the reduction of reason and energy to good and evil, with good assigned to soul and evil to body. The body is what the five senses, left to man after the fall, can see of the soul, but body and soul are not distinct from each other.

Plates 5-6 have been much misunderstood by casual readers. What Blake does here is to make a criticism of the poet he admired above all others, Milton. He sees the writing and the movement of *Paradise Lost* as a gradual ebbing out of desire or energy in the face of an increasingly remote principle of restraint and reason. Milton's own desire having weakened, he restrained the principle of desire in his poem. As a result, Milton's "devils," which in Blake are principles of active energy, appear to be submerged in Satan, who unfortunately represents sin and death. The accuser, or restraining force in the *Book of Job* was Satan, but in *Paradise Lost* it is the Messiah who created a hell of punishment. Thus Milton's poem separates creative energy from the good; there is no place for energy to go unless it goes to Satan, and Satan must be evil. As *Paradise Lost* proceeds, the energetic Satan ebbs into the shape he has in *Job,* and there is no principle of energy left in the poem. Milton's early treatment of Satan is the truly poetic or energetic part of his poem.

When Blake says Milton was of the devil's party, he does not mean that he satanically inverted good and evil but only that as a poet he could not fully suppress the poetic energy that forced him to make something in his poem representative of energy, if only for a while, even against the force in him that turned reason and energy into good and evil.

From this point on in the *Marriage,* hell is the area that the good have assigned to energy. This predicts the symbolism of the later poems, where the heroic blacksmith-artist Los, the imagination, works properly in the caves of the earth, an unfallen "hell."

In the first "Memorable Fancy" Blake walks in the fires of creativity and observes a devil (an artist like Blake himself) engraving with corrosives. The "Proverbs of Hell" which follow are meant as a contrary to the "Book of Proverbs" in the Old Testament, which are the proverbs of orthodox, prudent action.

Plate 11 describes the decline of true vision into priesthood and law, poetry into abstract thought. The early poets acknowledged the living quality of everything; the later priests separated the deity from what could be immediately imagined.

The Memorable Fancy of Plates 12-13 endorses the way of the ancient poets. Isaiah asserts that his "senses discovered the infinite in everything." Both Ezekiel and Isaiah express the idea that the prophet must in some way shock his listeners into higher perception.

On Plate 14, Blake sees his special method of printing by corrosives as symbolic of the clearing away of veils that man has put upon the infinite. The result will be that, indeed, man will see every bird as a universe. The cavern in which man is closed up is his idea of his own body. Blake does not deny the body; he denies a philosophy which rejects the body as a means of fulfillment.

The "Memorable Fancy" of Plate 15 is an allegory of creativity. A phallic dragon clears away rubbish in order to improve sexual enjoyment. The viper is the contrary to the dragon's activity, the outward bound or circumference, restraint, which must be present, else expansion would explode into chaos. It is within the cave, therefore, that infinity must be found, for the cave is the body.

The metals melted by the lions are the raw materials of imagination mined deep within the earth. In the process, the culture is created and made into books. This is the making of history and art out of the flux that would otherwise be lost. Culture is an imaginative achievement.

The Giants of Plates 16-17 are the great energies of man. Blake calls them the prolific and warns that the devourers are necessary to receive the creations of the prolific, to drown its excesses. Energy and reason are prolific and devourer respectively. They depend upon each other, but they cannot be reconciled. Religion attempts reconciliation by chaining energy to religious law. Jesus recognized this and came to attack religious law.

The "Memorable Fancy" of Plates 17ff. is a satire on the view of hell offered by organized religion. The angel's state of mind and his metaphysics creates what he sees. The angel is frightened by his vision, but Blake is not. The angel's true lot is to exist in the void of space, which is the world of materialist science. Note that Swedenborg's volumes are used for ballast, being materialistic. The monkey house is perhaps an allegory of theological controversy, as Bloom suggests.

On Plates 21-22 Blake attacks Swedenborg as simply a rearranger of old truths. Since much has been made of Blake's debts to

Swedenborg, Boehme, and other mystical theologians, it is well to note here that Blake is very critical of their procedures, which he indicates are not his own.

The last "Memorable Fancy" gives the devil the last word in his argument with an angel who has great difficulty practicing restraint. The Devil's speech may be compared to "The Ever-lasting Gospel." The angel here is clearly a forerunner of Blake's Zoa, Urizen.

"A Song of Liberty" was composed somewhat later than the rest of the work. The "Eternal Female" (later Enitharmon) is in labor with a rebel child (later Orc). He is born, jealousy hurls him through the night, and he falls into the western sea. Awakened by this, the "hoary element" (later Urizen) also falls. Then he tries to rally his legions, as did Satan in *Paradise Lost.* But the "son of fire" is reborn in the East. This poem tells briefly a story, elaborated later, of the birth of Orc, son of Enitharmon and Los and the subsequent oedipal struggle of Orc (desire) with Urizen (restraint).

VISIONS OF THE DAUGHTERS OF ALBION

The "argument" offers a preview of the poem up to 1:16. At the outset of the poem proper Oothoon plucks a flower in the vale of Leutha, a state of sexual innocence and timidity. She intends to bring the flower to Theotormon as an emblem of innocent love, but she is raped by Bromion. The rest of the poem delineates the attitudes of the three characters involved.

Bromion is a puritanical hypocrite, but a complex one. After he rapes Oothoon he accuses her of harlotry (1:18-2:2). His later speech (4:13-24) is perhaps more insidious than his first, violent one, for there he acknowledges the possible existence of other fruits and other wars (the intellectual wars of Eden that Blake later praises) and other woes and joys than those realizable within the terms of his philosophy. But he clings to that philosophy and shuts out much of reality. He ends by reducing all life to one law, contradicting the proverbs of Hell in *The Marriage of Heaven and Hell.* This conclusion condemns Oothoon to punishment.

Theotormon, whose name suggests that he is tormented by his religion, is a victim of jealousy. He ties Oothoon and Bromion together back to back in the cavern of his mind. A victim of his own lust as well as his own jealousy, he torments both Oothoon and himself.

Oothoon cannot cry and calls upon "Theotormon's Eagles to prey upon her flesh." (2:13-15). At first this suggests that she believes she should be punished, but a closer look suggests masochism as a substitute gratification for those desires now released in her by Bromion's rape and, at the same time, a Promethean defiance of the moral code. Her calling for punishment is parallel to Prometheus' defiance of Zeus. Her speech ends with an argument in behalf of her own purity (3:16-20).

The Zoa Urizen appears for the first time in this poem (5:3). He is the reasoning power, restraint, and, in the fall, creator of the one law, of abstract ideas and Spectres. The whole of Oothoon's speech (5:3-8:10) develops the idea of the *Marriage* that "One Law for the Lion & Ox is Oppression."

EUROPE: A PROPHECY

The most useful commentaries are David V. Erdman, *Blake: Prophet Against Empire,* pp. 193-207, for the political allegory, and Harold Bloom, *Blake's Apocalypse,* pp. 146-161.

In the introductory passage of Plate iii an impudent fairy describes the five senses and remarks that through the sexual window man can actually move beyond himself, but he does not, for he enjoys stealth and secrecy.

The "nameless shadowy female (1:1) " who first appeared in *America* as Orc's lover, laments the cyclical pattern of nature, which makes Orc always a dying god. She describes herself as an upside down tree (1:8-10). As the fallen world she is a reversed analogy of the unfallen. She describes all that she gives birth to as falling into the natural cycle of birth and death, tyranny and revolt.

The "Prophecy" begins with a suggestion of Milton's "On the Morning of Christ's Nativity" (3:1-3). The secret child, however, brings only the illusion of peace, for he is an Orc, the son of Enitharmon and Los, and represents energetic revolt. Los does not quite understand his son; Orc is bound down by his parents, and Los thinks sentimentally of Orc as a prolongation of their peaceful moony night.

Enitharmon is the female will (6:1ff.), which surrounds and represses energy in the form of Deistic science and morality. The mythological figures she addresses are separated from their emanations under the domination of sexual jealousy and the moral code. Plate 9 describes the sleep of Enitharmon, her world of female domination intact through the eighteen centuries of modern history. Then recent history is described (9:8ff), in which Albion's Angel (George III) is smitten by revolution in America and subsequent unrest.

The Angel, or King, retires to his Druidic temple (10:1-15). For Blake, Druidism was the most obvious form of nature worship, of which Deism is a modern version (see P. F. Fisher, *The Valley of Vision,* Toronto, 1961, 32-53, 63-66, and throughout.) Nature being the female emanation in Blake, nature worship is worship of the female will. It is also, as in Druidism, worship of trees, the "shadowy female" being an upside down tree. Bloom suggests that the serpent probably refers to the serpentine temple at Avebury. The Angel goes to Verulam (10:6) because Verulam was the home of Sir Francis Bacon, who championed a philosophy of nature and empiricism and is one of Blake's villainous triad "Bacon, Newton, Locke." The temple is built in Zodiacal form to represent the Urizenic world of abstract ideas (10:6-10). Deism, which Blake considered a Druidical religion, is the cause of the shrinking of man's perceptions (10:10-15). The passage recalls the opening lines of the poem.

10:16-23 collects numerous images of fallen nature: the serpent, the devouring flame, the forests of the night, the ocean of indefiniteness, the wheel of religion, the world ordered by Urizen as a great cyclical movement. All suggest the triumph of Deism.

10:24-31 describes Albion's Angel, or the King, arriving at the southern, or Urizenic, quarter of his temple, that of the reason. It is planted with trees, a forest of the night. Once the head, this southern quarter is now "sunk beneath th'attractive North," the area of Los, the imagination. This is a figure for the upside down man or, in the later poems, Albion himself.

The king reaches the high stone, or altar, and views the Bible of conventional religion (11:1-3). The youth of England speak here (12:5) as they do in some of the Songs of Experience. In 12:25ff. Enitharmon continues her domination in spite of the previous revolts. We are reminded of the lyrics, "The Garden of Love" and "London." Newton blows the last trumpet (13:5) because his system is the complete delineation of the error known as Deistic materialism. The three efforts that failed to blow the trumpet (13:3) are, in the historical allegory (see Erdman, pp. 195-196), William Pitt's three efforts to bring about war with France.

Enitharmon, now awake, calls upon several of her children formerly under her sway, but they disregard her (14:32-36), and Orc appears as revolution in France, a portent of apocalypse. Note that, although Los is a prophetic spirit, he arises through the snaky thunders of the Deistic order (5:9).

THE [FIRST] BOOK OF URIZEN

The "First" of the title is deleted in some copies. Apparently the *Book of Ahania* would have been book two and the *Book of Los,* perhaps, book three, but Blake changed his plan.

The poem tells of the fall and creation of the world of materialism, the moral law, and priesthood, as a result of Urizen's mental errors. Urizen unfallen is a true prince of light, the Zoa representing the highest powers of the intellect, the reason.

The "primeval Priest" of 2:1 is Urizen. The north (2:3) is not Urizen's proper quarter. He properly belongs in the south with the sun. Chapter I shows Urizen thinking darkly, his mind in conflict with its own creations; yet the world (Chapter III) is not yet fallen. "Globes of attraction" (3:36), isolated selfhoods in a Newtonian cosmos, do not exist. But Urizen insists on his own holiness (4:7) and his own ordering of things according to one law which he has heroically fought to create. Urizen's books suggest the moral law given by Jehovah to Moses on Mt. Sinai (4:24-40). In creating the one law, Urizen has created opposition and sin (4:45-5:2). This enrages the other eternals, and the fall occurs (5:3ff).

Los, the poetic spirit or imagination, is badly hurt by Urizen's act, finding it difficult to work separated from the intellect (6:2-3). Urizen is separated from Los as Eve is from Adam (6:4); the fall of Urizen later brings about the separation of each Zoa from his female emanation.

Urizen's changes (11:1ff.) are the result of his mind's creating the idea of matter. The seven ages are a parody of the seven days of *Genesis.* Los meanwhile is desperately trying to give shape to these changes, but he is frightened and disillusioned by the results. Note that in this process Los has created measurable time (10:17-10:18). Los's failure is not that he has shaped Urizen's body but that he has been unable to delineate it fully. He has not been able to wake him up. So Los himself is weakened into sentimental pity for the sleeping monster (13:51) and is divided from his emanation, Enitharmon (18:10). The "Tent" of 19:2 is the completion of the material world of Newtonian science, an enclosure which will be called later in Blake the "mundane shell" and the "circle of destiny."

The relation of Los and Enitharmon reveals the nature of fallen sexual life (19:10-13). It results in the birth of the oedipal child Orc, who is bound down like Prometheus to a mountaintop (20:21-23).

Urizen's explorations (20:46ff) are his attempt to control the alien world his mind insists upon. Here Blake again borrows from Satan's journey in *Paradise Lost.* The web (25:10) is not only religion but also the phenomenal world itself as a devouring prison. All the inhabitants of this world experience a shrinking of the senses which is a parody of creation (25:23-42). This state is allied with the biblical Egypt (28:10), and Fuzon, a fiery child of Urizen, seeks to lead the remaining children out of it (28:19-22). The last line of the poem, with overtones of the flood of *Genesis,* the waters unparted, and Atlantis, pictures a world that is now a globe containing chaos.

THE BOOK OF AHANIA

This book takes up where *Urizen* leaves off. Fuzon is clearly a revolutionary leader, associated with Moses, and this relates Urizen to Pharaoh. Fuzon is correct to call his father an "abstract non-Entity" (2:11), for Urizen fallen is abstract thought. But Fuzon has only his father's world to hurl back at him, a globe, which lengthens into a beam and wounds Urizen in the genitals (2:29). Fuzon's revolt, then, seems only to enforce Urizen's anticreative tendencies and is followed by Urizen's attempt to hide his emanation Ahania from sight (2:31-37). This makes her a part of a remote nature (2:38-43), a cyclical world.

Fuzon's beam is the biblical pillar of fire (2:45) until Los can restore it to the sun. The rock with which Urizen fells Fuzon becomes the Mount of the tables of the law (3:46). The Tree of Mystery (3:63) is the "human abstract" of *Songs of Experience.* It multiplies into the labyrinth which is the "forests of the night" of "The Tiger." Fuzon is crucified on it as a challenge, like Jesus, to its mysterious law. But Fuzon's revolutionary powers, described by Blake as his children, "harden" (4:41) and "reptilize" (4:43), his cycle of energy having waned.

The remainder of the poem is devoted to the lament of Ahania, Urizen's emanation.

5:29 recalls "Thou hast a lap full of seed" (p. 56), and the whole lament echoes the situation of Earth in "Earth's Answer," particularly 5:40ff.

SELECTIONS FROM "VALA; OR THE FOUR ZOAS"

The most useful commentaries are Northrop Frye, *Fearful Symmetry,* pp. 269-309; Harold Bloom, *Blake's Apocalypse,* pp. 189-284. A conjectural early vision of *Vala* is offered by H. M. Margoliouth, *Vala, Blake's Numbered Text* (1956). A large photographic facsimile with a study of the text is provided by G. E. Bentley, Jr. (1963).

Blake never finished the poem, and there remains only a much worked over manuscript. The poem is written partly on proof sheets for Blake's illustrations to Edward Young's *Night Thoughts.* Thus the illustrations in much of the manuscript have nothing to do with the poem. Other sheets, however, have preliminary drawings for the poem.

Blake's first title was *Vala.* Later he named the poem *The Four Zoas* and subtitled it *The Torments of Love and Jealousy in the*

Death and Judgment of Albion the Ancient Man. The term "Zoa" has its source in the four creatures of Ezekiel's vision and in the Greek term that denotes them in *Revelation.* The four Zoas—Urizen, Tharmas, Luvah, and Urthona—compose Albion, the eternal man. The poem tells the story of Albion's fall into the sleep or "death" of history as this is figured forth by the disruption of the proper relationship among the Zoas and between the Zoas and their emanations. The Poem ends with the apocalypse, in which the Zoas are again properly ordered within Albion. Urthona, of whom Los is the fallen form, possessed the earth (3:11-12) before the fall. Eden (4:1) is the state of the unfallen eternal man Albion, who with his emanations, in the aggregate called Jerusalem, "propagated fairies of Albion" (4:2-3). These fairies, true deities of the imagination, became in the course of the development of religion, "gods of the Heathen (4:3)." They became more and more abstracted from human experience. For a discussion of this point see *The Marriage of Heaven and Hell,* plate 11.

The poem begins with the fall of Tharmas, the Zoa who represents instinct, the unifying power in Albion. When Tharmas falls, the chaos of a huge flood covers the earth. He separates from his emanation Enion, who, unfallen, is a benevolent mother, but becomes a separate "other" or distant nature in the fall. The first excerpt (3:1-6:8) introduces the poem and proceeds to a dialogue between fallen Tharmas and Enion. Enion has become jealous because the other emanations have come to Tharmas for protection in the fall (4:16-17). In her jealousy Enion accuses Tharmas of sin. Tharmas accuses her of turning their relationship into one of rational analysis (4:30-36), but he accepts the idea of sin nevertheless and sinks into despair (4:36-46).

A description of the unfallen state of the Zoas and emanations interrupts briefly (5:1-4) before Tharmas and Enion are completely separated. Tharmas embraces the fallen Circle of Destiny, the endless cycle of growth and decay, and becomes a Spectre (5:14-15) Another way of seeing this is to observe Enion working on her loom and weaving the disorganized chaos which is the mortal Tharmas into the fallen cyclical order of time (5:16-28). It is characteristic of Blake to offer a number of views of the same events.

The Daughters of Beulah, which is the state of "Marriage," of repose and restoration of strength, observe the chaos of Tharmas and create Ulro in order to confine chaos and to prevent further fall (5:29-42). But, frightened of the Spectre, they "close the Gate of the Tongue" (5:43) and separate Tharmas from feeling. The completion of the spectral Tharmas is described in 6:1-7, a Satanic figure.

Night II describes the fall of Luvah, the passions, into torment. The first excerpt from this Night (23:9-25:20) forms part of the description of the building of the mundane shell, the symbolic form of materialism, by Urizen. The second excerpt (34:55-36:13) comprises the laments of Enitharmon and Enion as a result of the fall. Night III describes the fall of Urizen, the intellect. Night IV introduces Los laboring to limit Urizen's fall. In Night V the birth of Orc is described much as we have it in the *Book of Urizen*. The excerpt from Night V shows Enitharmon nursing Orc and Los building Golgonooza (60:3), which is the city of art or vision. Luban (60:4) is Golgonooza's gate. But Orc frightens Los, who chains him to a mountaintop (60:6-30). Then the parents repent, only to discover that they cannot themselves free Orc (62:9-63:6).

Night VI presents Urizen exploring his dens, the world that his mind has created in the fall. First, he meets the "three terrific women," (67:5) whom we remember from "The Golden Net"; they are his daughters, but they are alienated from him. 70 and 71 describe not only Urizen exploring his dens but also Urizen's mental state. One is reminded of Satan's journey in *Paradise Lost, 2.* Urizen's world is a dead world, "dishumanized" and without an answering voice. It is a world of "cumbrous wheels," like the Circle of Destiny or the wheel of religion that is mentioned in *Jerusalem.* The Vortex (72:13, 16, 30) is discussed in the commentary on *Milton.* Here it is a place, stance, or attitude from which things may be seen and ordered. Urizen cannot order his world, cannot maintain a vortex, even though he is supposed to be the "outward bound and circumference of energy." There is no up or down. He cannot, in other words, find any place to stand from which to move the earth. So ultimately he makes an arbitrary choice of where to seek to rebuild the world (73:14). He will rebuild on abstract thought (73:16-23).

There are two versions of Night VII. Version A is undoubtedly the later and is more interesting, in that it includes the meeting between Urizen and Orc. The caves of Orc contain the energies closed up by Urizenic repression. The horses and tigers are all frustrated, for they are kept from their properly contrary tasks (77:6-10). Orc is an aspect of Albion that is suppressed in the fallen world. Urizen envies Orc, for Urizen is old law and Orc young energy. Urizen's books (77:19), the root of Mystery (78:5), and the labyrinths (78:8) are familiar from the *Book of Urizen* and *Ahania*. They are aspects of the web or cavern that represents Urizen's solipsism, his alienation from nature, and religious repression.

In 78:15 Urizen views Orc from a position similar to that of the angel viewing hell in the *Marriage* (Plates 17-20). To Urizen Orc is a devil, but he is clearly meant to be a Promethean figure to the reader; and Urizen, like Jupiter, fears him and the future he represents (78:41). The daughters of Urizen feed Orc, that is, intensify his frustrations (79:25-37). Urizen's speech (80:2-26) expresses the savage ironies that Blake sees implicit in natural religion. Orc's reply (80:27-42) establishes clearly that he is the fallen Luvah, the repressed passions. Orc and Urizen become locked in a cycle of revolt and tyranny that neither can break, since a successful Orc becomes Urizen in turn. An example of this is Jesus, who comes as an Orc but whose body, crucified on a Tree of Mystery, becomes serpentine, the Urizenic Christian church. In modern times the waning of the French Revolution into despotism marks a similar cycle. From this point in the poem it is clear that Orc offers only Urizen again and that another hero must work toward true vision. At this point Los begins to emerge clearly as that hero.

The first excerpt from Night VIII shows Urizen terrified at Orc's appearance as Jesus (101:1-16). Polarized against Orc, who epitomizes human desire, Urizen comes into the presence of his own ultimate fallen form. It is Satan, a hermaphrodite (101:43) because the ultimate fallen condition is that of a subject surrounded by an object. Meanwhile Los builds Golgonooza and seeks to humanize life against the dehumanizing powers of Satan. Los's creations are dehumanized without Los's perpetual work, for Urizen seeks to "pervert all the faculties of sense" (102:20). Note that Urizen is never happy with his own creations and works desperately to avert his own despair (102:21-22).

In the second excerpt, Jesus is described by Los as coming to "put off Mystery" (104:33). The mystery Blake complains about is religion abstracted and divorced from direct individual experience and put in the hands of priesthood. Rahab appears among the jury judging Jesus. She epitomizes all that we have seen as abhorrent in church religion (105:15). 105:28-29 associate her with human sacrifices as in the archetype of natural religion, Druidism.

Jerusalem's reaction to the crucifixion in the third excerpt (106: 7-13) is frantic and misguided, for Jesus dead is Urizen again, the church that corrupted Jesus' revolt against moral law. In this confusion, it is no surprise that Rahab "triumphs over all." She is the great whore of *Revelation*. She captures the revolutionary impulses in Orc (111:11) and orders them in the Urizenic form (111:11-12) of a religion that seems revolutionary but is really only "Babylon again in Infancy" (111:24). This appearance of the stupendous form of error prepares for the apocalypse of Night IX. Meanwhile we are presented with a description of the reptilization of Urizen (in the fourth excerpt), which associates him with Leviathan and Ultimately with the serpent boy Orc, in so far as Urizen is an aged Orc, Orc a youthful Urizen.

As Night IX begins Los and Enitharmon labor in error though with the best of intentions. They weep over Jesus' death, for they deem the death of the body non-existent (117:1-6). Terrified and frustrated in his efforts, Los begins the stirring toward apocalypse by smashing the orderly clock-world of the fall (117:6-9). Revolution is the result. The spectral forms of Los and Enitharmon are cast away (117:24-118:5). Since Los and Enitharmon are time and space respectively, their Spectres are measured time and measured space. The greatest commotion is in the south, which is the proper quarter of Urizen; the turmoil is sensed by animals, which are suddenly humanized (118:30-38).

On a rock the eternal man Albion hears the commotion but misinterprets its meaning, lamenting his state (119:32-120:12). All that occurs is actually within him. His state of mind is changing; awake now, he calls on Urizen to arise from "cold abstraction" (120:19). Albion judges the relative danger of Urizen and Luvah fairly accurately in 120:32-33 and 42-45. Luvah's rage will subside somewhat if Urizen does not send his daughters to feed his frustrations. Urizen weeps and repents (121:1-26), and ascends (121:27-32). Ahania comes to meet him but dies (121:32-39), to be reborn later. Apparently Urizen cannot be united with his emanation until he reachieves his proper relation to the other Zoas. In 122:27 there are further apocalyptic strokes. All things fly from their centers, that is, become circumferences which contain the "other" within them. (See *Jerusalem* 1:19.) This occurrence is a result of Urizen's speech (122:21-25). Many lines on pp. 122-123 recall *Revelation*. The events preceding apocalypse appear disordered, and the struggle is not always enlightened, as in the revengeful act of 123:32.

The sons of Urizen set about the reordering by preparing the Plow of 124:6. The hell of Albion's mental state must be plowed up and the ground newly planted and harrowed. Urthona's Sons provide some of the necessary agricultural tools (124:20-22) in the "dens of death," which are properly the caves of an unfallen Ulro, where the sources of creative thought lie. With Urizen now contributing to creative work, Ahania is reborn in the great harvest (125:26). Albion, still partially in error but awake, wishes to put off his "new risen body" (125:37) and thus the apocalypse is not yet quite achieved, but mercy redeems his body. Orc as a fallen form is consumed and restored as Luvah and Vala (126:1-17), and they return to the genitals. The sexual life is thus restored to man in the form of the unfallen realm of generation. The long pastoral interlude (126:18-129:16) reflects the adjustment of Vala to her new state.

Tharmas and Enion are the next to be reintegrated with the whole. The new Beulah will be the result of their renewal out of the watery chaos that had been Tharmas' domain during fallen time (129:17-131:21). Their remarriage must be prepared for by a new childhood, which is a restored but higher innocence.

Urizen, returned to the head of eternal man, announces the end of time (131:31). This is followed by a harvesting. Albion arises at a feast where past errors are reviewed, particularly the separation of the emanations (133:5-9). The Eternal's speech that follows recapitulates from the perspective of eternity what ought to have been learned about human life (133:11-26).

There follows the winnowing and the tossing out of the chaff—nations and all the mystery of organized religion. In the passage involving the winepress of Luvah the crown of thorns falls from Luvah's head (135:23), and he is reborn, not as another dying Jesus, but as an eternal. The association is with Dionysus. Luvah's winepresses are taking the blood of the temporal wars that have been precursors of apocalypse and turning it into the wine of eternity. Luvah is undergoing a change. He is no longer the sexual frustration that leads to masochistic and sadistic violence (135:21 - 137:4) and results in cyclical revolt. He is instead an image of achievable desire.

Urthona appears limping in 137:8 and is thus associated with the lame artist-blacksmith god Hephaestos.

The emotional being is the most difficult to restore to order. Tharmas and Urthona descend to the winepresses to separate the wine from the lees and to break through the dying-god cycle once and for all. A final winter then descends, during which Urthona prepares with Tharmas the "Bread of Ages" (138:17). Fallen time is dead, and now, with the bread and wine or body of Albion remade, the apocalypse occurs. The Zoas are restored to their proper places (138:33 - 35). Yet this is no timeless world of stasis (that is the world of Ulro); this is a world of real time converted into work, intellectual war instead of the war of swords (139:9).

SELECTIONS FROM 'MILTON'

The most useful commentaries are: Northrop Frye, *Fearful Symmetry,* pp. 313 - 355, and "Notes for a Commentary on *Milton,"* *The Divine Vision* (V. de Sola Pinto, ed.), London, 1957, pp. 99 - 137; Harold Bloom, *Blake's Apocalypse,* pp. 304 - 364.

Milton was doubtless begun during Blake's three years at Felpham; the last plates were probably completed by 1810. Blake remarked in 1803 that he had composed "an immense number of verses" describing the "spiritual acts" of the years at Felpham. He may have been referring to an earlier version of *Milton* or materials eventually used in the poem we now have. There are four copies of the poem extant, and none is complete. Of the four, copy D of Keynes's census is the fullest, but it lacks the preface with its famous lyric.

The plot of *Milton,* like that of *The Four Zoas,* is not easy to follow, for it is absorbed by a poetic structure that seldom lays out time in linear fashion. The poem's structure reflects Blake's remark that his hero can walk back and forth in time and that all time can be reduced to a "pulsation of the artery."

The Preface asserts obliquely Blake's affinity with Milton and directly that the poem, like *Paradise Lost,* will "justify the ways of God to man." However, *Milton* is nearer in spirit to *Paradise Regained* than to *Paradise Lost.* The poem leads up to the vision of a renewed Jerusalem "in England's green and pleasant land" (ll. 15-16). Blake's call for a "Chariot of fire" (l. 12) is reminiscent of the vision of Ezekiel and of Milton's chariot in Gray's *Progress of Poesy.* The "dark Satanic Mills" (l. 8), erroneously associated by some with industrialization, appear elsewhere in Blake and represent the unprolific, dark, revolving, solipsistic activity of Urizen.

BOOK THE FIRST   The poem begins in a traditional manner with an invocation (2:1-20). Blake asks his muses, the Daughters of Beulah, to tell the story of the return of Milton to earth over a century after his death, also the story of the "false tongue," who is the fallen Tharmas and the human condition in history. (*The Four Zoas* began with the fall of Tharmas.) Milton's activity in the poem is thus immediately opposed to fallen history. Milton's resolve to return from Eternity after "pondering the intricate mazes of Providence" (2:17) is occasioned by a sense that he had failed as a prophetic reformer, yet also by a knowledge that his aims were correct and ought to be achieved. He must return to redeem his "Sixfold Emanation" (2:19), the totality of all that he loves, and at the same time to annihilate the selfhood in himself. The emanation is sixfold presumably because Milton had three wives and three daughters and also because six is a multiple of three, in Blake the alienated female figure is usually threefold (as in "The Golden Net"), a parody of the threefold vision that is the state of Beulah. The selfhood, or Spectre, includes for Milton the dualistic attitude expressed in *Paradise Lost* that resulted ultimately in the assignment of energy to Satan and reason to God.

(See *The Marriage of Heaven and Hell,* plates 5-6.) In other words, Milton's selfhood is his Puritanism, though the real Milton was of the class of the energetic. Should Milton not cast out his selfhood, his search for the emanation would result in the same dreadful relation of spectral wolf to domineering emanation described in "My Spectre around me. . . ." The return of Milton involves his inhabiting and becoming identical with Blake, whom he redeems for prophecy, and who as a result composes the poem we have before us.

Following the invocation there is a long "Bard's song" (12:25-13:44), none of which is excerpted here. The story it presents, if story is quite the word, carries inside itself a personal allegory. The great archetypal events of the poem are referred microcosmically, so to speak, to events in Blake's life. The song begins with the building of Urizen's body by Los, as it was first described in *The Book of Urizen.* There follows the birth of Orc from Enitharmon and the building of Golgonooza. Then there is the report of Los rejecting Satan, followed by Los's creation of the three classes of men—the reprobate, the redeemed, and the elect. The terms are taken ironically from Calvin. Blake calls the reprobate and redeemed the two contraries (they are similar to the prolific and the devourer of the *Marriage*); the elect is the "reasoning negative." This fixing of the classes of men, like the limits of opacity and contraction (Satan and Adam) and the "starry floor," limits the extent of the fall.

In an ensuing allegory of Blake's relations with Hayley at Felpham, Satan (Hayley, the elect) and Palamabron (Blake, the redeemed) enter into a prolonged struggle in which Satan (a miller) seeks to turn Palamabron (a harrower) from his fundamental task. Involved in the dispute is Rintrah, the reprobate, a figure who broods over the prelude to the *Marriage* as the spirit of prophecy. At Felpham Satan in the form of Hayley sought to turn Blake away from his vocation of prophet to become a painter of miniatures. The author of *The Triumphs of Temper* would then assume the harrow of Palamabron that is, replace Blake as the true artist. The question of whether Satan's intentions are good or not becomes secondary, that is, it is finally of not much account whether jealousy or lack of confidence in Blake motivated

Hayley. In any case, "Satan's self believed/That he had not oppressed the horses of the harrow." As the dispute continues, Satan reveals himself as Urizen, and the struggle between Satan and Palamabron reveals itself in its more universal form as the struggle of Urizen and Los. When this struggle takes place the respective emanations play their customary parts. Leutha, Satan's emanation, or muse, clearly prefers Palamabron, but she is repulsed by Elynittria, Palamabron's emanation. The problem of love and jealousy is a complicated one, for Blake recognized that his relation to Hayley was complex.

After the Bard's song, the second excerpt (14:10 - 17:30) shows Milton making his descent from Eternity. His own work had been meant to destroy the "detestable Gods of Priam," the Blakean deities of war, but had failed. Thus his own purification, the annihilation of his own selfhood, has not been completed. He had created in *Paradise Regained* a Christ who had rejected classical wisdom because it was "natural religion," but Milton has not quite subdued natural religion in himself.

The descent is a complex one. First Milton must enter into his own shadow, the hermaphrodite, which represents in Blake not a unification of the sexes but the split and warfare between them. But Milton is not merely sent down into Generation; the "seven angels" or "seven eyes of God" or seven cycles of history provide him with a visionary perspective at the same time that he seems to himself "a wanderer lost in dreary night."

Harold Bloom describes a vortex as "a whirlpool drawing existence in." We can imagine it here as a cone with the perceived object as its apex. In order to descend into the lower world, Milton must pass through the vortex of Albion, whom he sees from Eternity as stretched "deadly pale" upon a rock. Once he passes through Albion's bosom, or the vortex of his vision of him, and proceeds into the fallen world, the view he has of Albion changes, rolling back behind Milton, "a cloudy heaven mingled with stormy seas in loudest ruin." It is the fallen world of Urizen and Tharmas. No longer surrounding his vision, Milton is now enclosed by it. To put it another way, no longer looking down at Albion, he seems to be looking up. Albion is, of course, an upside-down man.

The passage 15:36-43 helps us to understand the preceding one (15:21-35). When Milton passed into the fallen world through the vortex of his vision of Albion, Albion became "dishumanized." But though the traveller will see the object roll behind him as a globe, he ought also to behold still the object in its human form. He does this by "encompassing its vortex." Thus, although the eye seems to be at the center and to be looking in all directions, actually it *is* the circumference, enclosing all it sees in the human form of the viewer. The reader might well compare the gyres of Yeats and his own paradoxes expressing a similar situation. (See Hazard Adams, *Blake and Yeats: The Contrary Vision,* throughout).

Milton descends much as Satan does in *Puradise Lost*. This accounts for the fear of him expressed by some of the characters. Blake sees him, and Milton enters Blake via Blake's left foot (15:49). It is the foot because that is the area of the unfallen Urthona; it is left because left is traditionally the fallen side. Note that Milton manages to maintain his view from the circumference even in his descent. He sees his wives and daughters. Their names, except for Rahab, are from *Numbers 26:33.* They are the five daughters of Zelophehad, who sought and obtained a female inheritance and therefore for Blake represent triumphant female will, which is what the emanation is when separated from man. In 17:9-17 Milton sees himself as he was in time, a Urizen in bondage to his own idea of a separate female will, trying to legislate the relation of man to emanation and finally creating Spectres.

The Mundane Shell (17:21-28) is the spatial vision of the fallen world. From within this world is a cave, from without it appears to be an egg.

Milton's travel has been outward to the limit of opacity, but the aim is to convert all that is contained by the journey into a prophetic vision, which will be inward (17:29-30), that is, containing what it observes.

The third excerpt describes the world after Albion is "slain." Previous to this passage, Los and Enitharmon see Milton's descent, both misinterpreting his purpose. For a moment Los thinks Milton is Satan. Milton joins in a struggle with Urizen (19:8-9) in which Urizen tries to baptize him with the icy water of reason and Milton tries to remold Urizen's body with red clay. "Red clay" is the meaning of the word "Adam." The seven angels help Milton to maintain his visionary perspective.

A few lines later Albion shows some signs of life (20:25-42), and Blake insists on the humanization of all things in his description of the fly, turning the reader away from a search for a sky god, which will lead only to chaos and "ancient Night" (20:33).

As already mentioned, the feet are properly the area of Los (21:4). The spirit of Milton as poet enters Blake's poetic part, and Blake's vision is renewed. All nature is seen in a new and glittering light (21:12-14). Blake is thus redeemed by the reprobate Milton. In the next excerpt (22:4ff) Blake is one with Los, who walks up and down in time, making permanent those acts which would otherwise be lost in the flux.

In the passage before the description of Los as time (24:68-76), Blake accompanies Los to the gate of Golgonooza, where they meet Rintrah and Palamabron, who express their fear of Milton, thinking him an Orc. They are frightened by Milton's religion, not realizing that Milton is descending specifically to cast off Puritanism and selfhood. But Los tries to calm their fears by assuring them that Milton's descent is a signal of apocalypse. They are unconvinced, however, and descend into Bowlahoola (law), where they view workers at the vintage.

Blake elsewhere insists that time should not be depicted as an old man with a scythe. That is destructive time, the time of measurement. Creative time is ever young, the spirit of the future (24:68-76).

Los's speech to the laborers of the vintage (25:16-39) directs them to separate the sheaves into the three classes of reprobate, redeemed, and elect. In long subsequent passages not excerpted here, the activities of Los and his sons are described. Also the world of generation is seen as redeemable through the power of prophecy. The winepress of war refers to the wars of Blake's own time as disturbances prophetic of the last judgment.

The work of Los and his Sons is no less than the building of culture and is redemptive of time from the devouring flux on the one hand and from linear distancing on the other (28:44-29:3). Space (29:4-22) also must be redeemed from measurement so that it can be drawn into the human imagination. What our mind sees is a flat world. When we move, that world accompanies us. Space is symbolic. The biblical lands and England are one. The "Globe rolling through Voidness" (29:16) is a creation of abstract reason.

In spite of Los's work, Book I ends ominously with the report, not excerpted here, that Rahab and Tirzah are busy weaving the woof of death, "the veil of human miseries" (29:53 - 63). However, it has been shown that the generative world into which Milton has descended and in which work must go on, is capable of redemption through that work.

BOOK THE SECOND   Book II begins with a description of Beulah (30:1 - 31:11) which is well analyzed by Frye, *Fearful Symmetry,* pp. 227 - 235. One of the four Blakean states, Beulah is the biblical Garden of Eden, the state of innocence, protection, repose, rest, of lover and beloved. Below the Blakean highest state (Eden), it can turn into Ulro if one tarries in it too long. (This is the fate of Thel.) Beulah is the innocent state in which nature is seen as a benevolent and loving mother; it is also the "married land" of *Isaiah.*

Ololon, Milton's emanation, descends to seek him. There follows (31:28 - 63) "a Vision of the lamentation of Beulah over Ololon." From the perspective of Beulah, Ololon's descent is to be lamented; from Generation, below Beulah, the lament is a morning song of spring and new birth.

The giants Og and Anak (31:49) are biblical figures. Blake apparently allies them with Satan, but they are, like the Spectre of Los, capable of imaginative use. They here mark the limits of materialism. A center (31:46) in imaginative life is any point from which the mind imagines the world. Thus it is really an opening to a circumference that contains the world. It becomes, then, the human form itself. Blake describes this center as so expanding. When centers "close" there is trouble.

Milton is next seen (32:1 - 7) rejecting the condition in which he plays Spectre to Ololon's female will. This passage is clearly related to the poem "My Spectre around me . . . " and describes, as do later passages, a diabolical negation of true marriage. Meanwhile Ololon continues her descent in search of Milton's couch.

The moment in which she comes into the mundane world is described in 35:42-37:3. It is an expanded center of time, "a wide road . . . open to Eternity" (35:35). It is a moment of creativity. The lark and wild thyme, already introduced into the poem, are its harbingers. The fountain mentioned provides two rivers of life, one representing the artist's creative vision, for it flows through Golgonooza; and the other representing the sum of all time laid out in linear terms, flowing through the "aerial void" and all the "churches" of history. So it seems that linear time, too, would be prophetic if we could grasp it all at once as ideally it should be grasped by the historian.

The seven eyes of God and the twenty-seven churches are symbolic of phases of history, the present one being "Luther," the twenty-eighth yet to come. The lark, Los's messenger, travels back through time, continually awakening all the churches, that is, insisting on their presence in the present moment. The twenty-eighth or apocalyptic lark meets Ololon as she descends into Blake's garden at Felpham. She is the "they" of 36:14, the sixfold emanation of Milton now seen as one. Blake invites her into his cottage to comfort his wife, who is ill and probably despondent over Blake's problems with Hayley and, perhaps, with his poem (36:32).

Ololon (37:1-3) feels that she has been responsible for Milton's descent, and now she seeks to be reunited with him. With Ololon ready to reject "female love" or domination, Milton too descends into Blake's garden (38:5-8). He appears to be the "severe and silent" Puritan. Out on the sea stands Satan, whom Blake sees from within, for Satan is the fallen world (38:15-27). In this confrontation Milton casts off error and prepares the way for the greater apocalypse called for in 39:10-13.

Albion tries to rise up, makes a great effort, but fails, Nevertheless, this is a good sign. In the final passages Rahab-Babylon appears and ceases to delude. She has been imaginatively delineated. Milton describes the important differences between contrariety and negation. The garments of false religion and chastity must be cast off. Milton and Ololon are united, and Blake, falling upon his garden path, remains to imagine the preparation for a great apocalypse.

JERUSALEM

Useful introductory commentaries are Northrop Frye, *Fearful Symmetry,* pp. 356-403, and Harold Bloom, *Blake's Apocalypse,* pp. 365-433. Interesting speculations occur in Karl Kiralis, "The Theme and Structure of William Blake's *Jerusalem,*" *The Divine Vision* (V. de Sola Pinto, ed.), pp. 141-162, and "A Guide to the Intellectual Symbolism of William Blake's Later Prophetic Writings," *Criticism* I, 3 (Summer 1959), pp. 190-210.

Jerusalem as published by Blake is an illuminated book of one hundred plates. Six copies done by him are extant, as well as three more posthumously printed. There is a variation in the arrangement of plates in Chapter 2. I have followed the arrangement of copies A, C. and F of Keynes's census, which is the same as that adopted by Erdman. Numbers in brackets indicate the order of copies D and E, adopted by Keynes.

The poem bears the date 1804 on its title page, but parts of it may not have been completed until as late as 1820.

Jerusalem is Blake's most ambitious poem and his most difficult. Recently its complexities have become better understood. Perhaps the best introductory statement about its structure is Harold Bloom's. He notes similarities to the *Book of Ezekiel* and then suggests that each chapter of *Jerusalem* presents two opposing forces. In Chapter 1, Los, creativity among the English people and the imagination, is set against Albion, who, fallen, is mental chaos. In Chapter 2, Los "seeks to form an image of salvation from the repetitive cycle of nature and history that Albion has become." In Chapter 3, this opposition becomes that between Jesus and Deism. In Chapter 4, there is the confrontation between truth and error and finally, the last judgment. The process through the whole work is a progressive one, for the antithesis sharpens even as it broadens to include more of the cultural situation.

This may be a little neat, but clearly there is a growing delineation of the opposition as Los proceeds to clarify what it is that he is trying to do. Albion holds the center of the stage with Los in Chapter 1. In Chapters 3 and 4 there is a gradual deepening of the trouble of history into the cycle of nature, of revenge and tyranny. The increasing horror of the poem is partly the work of Los, who is trying to reveal that horror, from his journey through Albion's bosom in Chapter 2 to his revelation of Hand and the triple female will in Chapter 3.

CHAPTER 1   *Jerusalem* begins in *medias res* after a very brief introduction (4:1-5). The fall has occurred, though there is also a sense in which the fall is *always* occurring in history. The Saviour's initial speech (4:6-21), with its emphasis on expansion of the selfish center of Albion and insistence on the Saviour's own presence within the Eternal Man (and thus His denial of material space), is rejected by Albion (4:23-31), whose imagination has hardened and whose center is closed. He misinterprets the place of God and is alienated from his own emanations. He will hide in the barren, rugged mountains of his selfhood.

The situation is then seen from the poet's point of view (5:1-15). The mind of Albion is corrupted by the vision of the starry wheels of Newtonian space. There is revolutionary turmoil; human centers are closed and withered; Jerusalem is scattered (like the atoms of which the world is supposedly composed) abroad through the void; religion is the religion of revenge and sacrifice. The passage offers a collection of the characteristics of the fallen world, which will be developed as the poem proceeds. In brief, analytical modes of thought have appeared to order a clock-like universe but have actually divided and scattered the world into its parts.

The poet's remarks about his own task (5:16-26) suggest that reality is "inward" while error is "outward" toward the vision of the starry wheels of infinite space.

The Sons and Daughters of Albion are aspects of Albion's attitudes, as is everything he sees or "creates." Particularly they suggest his tendency, under the domination of Urizen, to reduce reality by analysis to ever and ever smaller particles. Hand, Hyle and Coban (15:25) are invented names. Bloom and Erdman suggest that Hand is meant to recall Robert Hunt, who attacked Blake's exhibition in a review, and that Hyle has overtones of William Hayley. Coban seems to be an anagram for Francis Bacon, who appears later in the poem as part of the villainous empiricist triumvirate of "Bacon, Newton, Locke." Hand and Hyle are paired as the dominant oldest Sons of Albion. Later in the poem Hand acts for all of them. Scofield and Kox (Cock) were the soldiers who accused Blake of treason; Guantok, Peachey, and Brereton were judges at the trial. Of Slade, Hutton, Kotope, and Bowen nothing is known. They may have been involved in the trial in some way. These Sons revolve (15:27) like the starry wheels and are clearly stars in the firmament of Albion's mind.

The Daughters of Albion have names adopted from Geoffrey of Monmouth's history of Britain. Tirzah and Rahab together (sometimes with Vala) form the female will or alienated emanation or "nature" in the fallen world.

6:1-14:34 describes Los's titanic struggle with his Spectre, the building of Golgonooza, and the city itself. The Spectre of Los plays the part of the recalcitrant egoistic part of Los's being. He is like a machine "driven by the Starry Wheels of Albion's sons" (6:1). He hates Los for his love of Albion and would divide Los from his task by insidious analysis of Albion's attitudes (7:1-50). He offers some impressive arguments, culminating in his re-porting that Luvah has been thrown into Albion's furnaces and tormented by Vala. But Los is no longer the occasionally error-prone giant of *The Four Zoas.* He will seldom succumb to uncontrolled wrath or despair, and then only for moments; he will remain steadfast in his work of building Golgonooza (7:51-64). He will pity Albion, but without sentimentality. He fearlessly threatens his Spectre (8:9-12): It is possible to exercise patience if one knows one's proper task (8:15-18). The Spectre is particularly obnoxious because of his pretenses to chastity, his hypocritical innocence. "Holy" in Blake (8:33) usually means "hypocritically self-righteous."

The "condensation" of 8:43 signifies the hardening of the em-anations into separate material female wills, which, like material particles or counters of the understanding, can be generalized into Rahab and Tirzah. While Los works at his forge in one way, Hand, representing the Sons of Albion, works as a demonic blacksmith against him (8:43-9:6). The results Los describes in 9:16ff. He describes his own answering acts in 9:17-25. Often

Los's acts seem to turn against him, as they did in earlier books, but now he knows that error must be given a body, "That he who will not defend Truth may be compelled to defend / A Lie" (9:29 - 30).

The Spaces of Erin (9:34), Ireland in the West, are a wall against the flood that destroyed Atlantis, which is associated with the unfallen world. The Sons and Daughters of Jerusalem are her lost hopes. Los seeks to adopt them (10:3 - 5).

In the important passage 10:7 - 16, Blake attacks the Lockean distinction between primary and secondary qualities, objectivity and subjectivity, outer and inner. The Sons of Albion equate outer with good, inner with evil, negating the mind and the unity of man. Thus Los must create a way of vision contrary to the analytic, divisive powers of the Sons (10:20 - 21), a system or, more accurately, a non-system designed to oppose the dominant system. The Spectre tries to undermine Los's activities by appealing to a latent sense of sinfulness in Los (10:37 - 59) and to the idea of an alien, revengeful god. In the process the Spectre reveals his misunderstanding of what a true contrary is (10:56). After a great show of will, described in a moving passage (10:65 - 11:7), Los succeeds in drawing imaginative power out of the furnaces (11:8 - 15). But this is only the beginning of his work, for Jerusalem is in great danger of being metamorphosed into Vala, the surrounding alien material nature.

The building of Golgonooza and the plan of the completed city is now presented (12:24ff). Golgonooza is perhaps the new Golgotha, place of the skull in the Bible and of the crucifixion; as such it is the lowest limit of the fall, from which rebuilding can begin. It is also a center for expansion. Tyburn is London's equivalent to Golgotha, being the site of a famous gallows. Paddington was a London slum. Golgonooza is a city of mental states (12:29 - 37). Lambeth (12:41) is given special prominence probably because it was Blake's home when he composed the earlier prophecies.

12:45 - 13:29 describes Golgonooza. The directional descriptions and the fourfold nature of each gate defy adequate diagram. The city is, after all, a mental city, not subject to materialist space. The four faces are clearly related to Ezekiel's vision, and the whole description owes much in spirit to *Revelation*. Golgonooza is surrounded by the fallen world; thus its gates are closed until the last day, and it is a fortress. It is material substance being made into visionary or mental forms by the work of Los. After the visionary city there comes a description of the fallen Ulro (13:30-55). The passage is a catalogue of fallen imagery; but note that even here there is mercy, because the fall could have plunged man into even greater chaos (13:44-45). The twenty-seven heavens are the phases of Ulro history. "Heaven" is always used ironically by Blake (13:51) to describe the creative efforts and accomplishments of the Urizens of this world. Los must build with the fallen materials at hand (13:56-14:15). Los's Sons and Daughters (14:16-30) are his creations, visionary works. Note that their western gates are closed, signifying both their own imperfections and their function as a bulwark against chaos.

After laying out the mental topography of Golgonooza and Ulro, the poem turns to Blake himself and a vision of England. Reuben (15:25), who appears here and there in the poem, is the natural man to be redeemed. The Valley of the Son of Hinnom (15:34) was a place of human sacrifice in the Bible. 16:1-15 presents a chaos of sounds in England. Opposing Bromion and Theotormon, remembered from *Visions of the Daughters of Albion,* are Palamabron and Rintrah. All are Sons of Los working as contraries. The effort of Los and his Sons is to unify England and the Holy Land in the imagination (16:28-60), that is, to unify mental space and time and to oppose measurable space and time, which insists on separate entities. This unification is seen in a vision in 16:61-69.

While all of this goes on we are required to remember that Los's struggle with his Spectre is constant and that his own work must often proceed by indirection (17:1-9). This passage and Los's speech following it offer a poignant example of the state of isolation felt by the creative man in his work. This is reflected also in Los's relations with Enitharmon, which are tormented by his fears of turning her into a negation.

There is a historical allegory behind 17:59-63, discussed by Erdman (p. 383), but it is basically a direct assertion by Los of his intentions to proceed, turning even hatred to creative ends.

The poem now turns to the relationship between Albion and Jerusalem. The speech of Hand and Hyle inveighs against sin and accuses Jerusalem (18:11-35). It is an example of the creeping hypocrisy of the religious "elect." Out of such hypocrisy the "Polypus" (18:40) grows. All of Albion's children are now externalized (19:1-27) and thus made analytical and material. This material Los must transform back into true affections. As more of Albion is externalized, Albion flees inward (19:39) to be surrounded by himself and his ideas. Plate 20 explores the problem of love and jealousy and the resultant failure of the participants to forgive, the accusation of sin. It is well to remember that Vala here is really an aspect of Jerusalem, Jerusalem as an object of Albion's understanding, or nature; she could be a garden to be planted and nurtured, but when jealousy intervenes nature becomes foreign, as in Albion's speech (21:1ff.), where he falls victim to his own sense of sin and insists on weaving "a chaste/ Body over an unchaste Mind" (21:11-12), thereby ultimately killing Luvah, the passions. Soon everything appears sinful to Albion, and his fears lead to cruelty and war. Albion cannot understand Jerusalem's appeal of 22:19-24. He realizes something has gone wrong but is so locked in the idea of good and evil, revenge and punishment, that he can only castigate himself (22:26-32). He sees Jerusalem's protestations as further examples of her sinfulness (22:34-23:19) and desperately tries to order life by imposing the veil of moral virtue upon it (23:22-23). Like Job, Albion cannot quite understand his torment, for he has been righteous. He thinks back into history to explain his case; he recites his sins in a mixture of self-castigation and self-pity, but he is incapable of discovering a cure for his mental condition. He refuses belief in a merciful and forgiving God (24:53). The chaotic ocean rolls, and the eternals lament.

CHAPTER 2   In Chapter 2 the chaos of the fall becomes more frightful and the struggle between Los and Albion deepens. Albion's own state spreads everywhere. After various efforts by the cities of England to save Albion, Los sets out to journey through Albion himself to "search the tempters out."

The prefatory material, addressed to the Jews, asks them to consider the true prophetic meaning of their history. In Chapter 1 the identity of Britain and the Holy Land was imaginatively established. Blake next follows up the implications of that imaginative unity. The unity is not to be taken in a literal or historical sense such as that insisted on by the British Israelites and others but as a vision like that of Blake's *All Religions Are One,* though some religions are "Druidical" or debased. They are debased because internal reality has been negated, all reality externalized: the "starry heavens are fled from the mightly limbs of Albion."

The prefatory lyric treats the whole story of *Jerusalem* in the microcosm of Blake's life, which in the imagination can contain all of time. The places mentioned are recalled from Blake's youth and inhabit a world of primal innocence. Satan won a victory in the slum of Paddington, where Los now tries to rebuild. Tyburn, the gallows site, becomes associated with Druidical sacrifice. Satan was victorious, but the mortal worm, to which the human form was reduced by analysis, still had a lovely interior. There is hope for redemption through struggle with the Spectre.

As Chapter 2 begins, Albion is not only suffering from guilt but also has become a Urizenic judge of all his creations (28:4). Around him grows the Tree of Mystery, familiar from earlier works. It multiplies characteristically into a labyrinth or forest of the night (28:14-19). Albion's Spectre appears before him and expresses the philosophy of man that his state of mind requires (29:5-16). The Spectre, who is Satan, is a wheel and at the same time a many-headed, many-armed monster (29:18-24). Under these conditions Vala, rather than Jerusalem, appears as Albion's emanation. In her lament (29:36-30:1) Vala is either attempting to delude or is herself deluded, for she finally comes around to asserting the female will. Albion's lament in reply is answered by Los's defiant attack upon the separate, secret female and his assertion that Albion is engaging in nature worship. Bashan (*Numbers* 32:33) is the environment of fallen natural man, Reuben. Merlin is his latent imaginative powers.

Los sends Reuben over Jordan several times in order to establish the senses of man as a base from which to rebuild the imaginative powers. The order of these efforts is: scent (30:47-48), sight (30:53-54), touch or taste (32:5-6), hearing (32:13). In each case there is terror at the appearance of the natural man. It is explained that perceivers tend to become what they behold and that what they see varies as their mental powers vary.

A limit is put upon the contracting of the sense perceptions (31:1). Fallen natural man's emanation is Tirzah, who closed man's senses in *Songs of Experience.*

After a recapitulation of some of the familiar results of these events, the Eternals summarize with awful sarcasm (32:43-48).

There follows the flight of Albion (33:10ff.) with the Saviour in pursuit seeking to explain the nature of true intellectual warfare and wrath and the idea of unity in man (34:14-26). Blake himself sees London lamenting (34:29-39). Blake's home at this time was in South Molton Street (34:42). A call now goes out to the cities of England to save Albion. In London is the gate of Los, which takes one *in* to Golgonooza but *out* to the "Mill" of Satan 35:3-5). Albion in despair seeks to flee out of the gate, and the Zoas try to save him, calling on the twenty-four cities for aid (36:3-21). There is a narrow escape here from the situation of Satan in *Paradise Lost* (36:31-42). But the fall of Albion's Spectre into hell is averted because of the mercy of the Divine Family. Various cities attempt to help Albion. The reference to Selsey and Chichester recalls the removal of the seat of the Church from one to the other because of the erosion of the seacoast at Selsey (36:48-50).

In the midst of these efforts Los, the artist, builds the language in order to keep the power of expression open for Albion (36:58-60). Meanwhile Jerusalem, too, flees and is hidden, protected by the Daughters of Beulah (37:11-14). Oothoon's palace would seem to be Blake's own imagination or art, since it is located in Lambeth, where Blake long resided.

In the passage of history through the twenty-eight churches the Zoas all fall, and the world, or Albion, takes the form of a cyclical order. The speech of Los in response to the despair of the Zoas (38:12-79) sets forth the differences between the fallen and unfallen worlds, but the speech ends in desperation, for Los feels alone in his work. However, the Zoas make an effort to bring Albion back through Los's Gate (39:1-5), only to be frustrated by Albion's own "Starry Wheels." The two sets of wheels, the visionary wheels of Ezekiel's vision and the Satanic Mills, are pitted against each other. The effort fails, and Erin, the land between fallen man and chaos, is invaded by the religion of jealousy.

Bath and Oxford both make efforts to awaken Albion to his errors (40:1-32 and 41:7-15), but the efforts, though sincere enough, are sentimentally ineffectual and more like funeral eulogies than convincing calls to action. These cities seem affected by the Deistic disease (41:17-28).

Los is even more isolated after these failures, but he answers Albion's attacks vigorously (42:19-45) with a defense of his art. It is as if Los is trying to bring Albion's indefiniteness out into the open so that he can grasp and shape it.

Albion calls for justice (that is, vengeance) against Los (42:47-54), but while the cities of Albion lament, Los continues to build the Mundane Shell as insurance against chaos (42:77-79). The times are bad. The Divine Vision appears as a setting sun, but he speaks words that are both wearying and prophetic of eventual redemption. Albion's Reactor, his Spectre, Satan, lurks in the forests like the tiger and will do so until his place is prepared. Los must continue to build visions of clarity (43:6-26). Then Albion will arise.

From the calamity of these events and the experience of seeing Albion slay his own humanity and bring about the fall of Luvah and Vala, Enitharmon and the Spectre of Urthona have escaped (43:28-44:1), the latter having "kept the Divine Vision in time of trouble" (44:15).

In Los's comment on the suppression of the passions it is important to notice that "sex" or "sexual" always means a separation of the sexes, chastity, and the mystery with which religion surrounds sexuality. Blake is not defending asceticism when he says, "Humanity knows not of sex." He is equating the word with repression and the situation of Spectre and Emanation.

Plate 45 begins Los's heroic journey into Albion's bosom to search out "Albion's tempters" (45:6). He discovers that Albion's being has been given over to abstract reasoning. Minute particulars, or the real texture of life, have been murdered. There follows a spectacular metaphor, in which (45:9-12) the "articulalations" of men's souls are framed, baked in ovens, and used to build pyramids, symbols of tyranny.

Having viewed Jerusalem and Vala, and having heard their laments, Los reaches London Stone, Albion's center, and sees everything reversed, as presumably everything appears to Albion (46:7). He confronts the Sons of Albion and Albion himself, borne on a golden couch. At this, Luvah appears in revolt, but cruelly suppressed. The cyclical fallen world of revenge and tyranny is now revealed (47:1-15). Man is *inside* history; Albion dies without hope, but in the Saviour's arms. Jerusalem, protected to this moment in Beulah, descends into separation from Albion (48:13-52). Erin now laments over Albion's death, collecting in her speech many of the symbols central to the poem. Albion's god now surrounds him rather than being within him, and the senses of man have shrunk. The fallen cyclical world of distant stars and covering ocean prevails (50:18-21).

CHAPTER 3   In Chapter 3 the opposition of Los to Albion and his cyclical world hardens further into the modern one of visionary experience, represented by Jesus, and Deism. The prefatory lyric, similar in parts to "The Grey Monk" (Pickering manuscript), defends those who argue for the vision of Jesus' life as against the Satanic law abstracted from his life. Chapter 2 moved toward Los's search through Albion's bosom. Chapter 3 moves toward the display of the triple female will through Los's efforts. Chapter 2 had shown the opposition of Los to Albion as natural man in the cyclic word of generation and decay. Albion is now clearly the archetype of that world and falls into the oedipal cycle in jealous opposition to his sons, who "assimilate" with Luvah.

The chapter begins with Los, the "vehicular form" of Urthona, his shape in history, continually building Golgonooza. Los, a timespirit, is creative change. He must constantly renew his efforts.

In 55:30-32, the Eternals, who wish to protect Albion from chaos, try to order history into seven major historical cycles. They name the eighth, apocalyptic movement, yet to be revealed. The fall does not prevent a return to vision, as 55:36-46 explains. The whole effort of creative work will be to bring about a cleansing of the perceptions along the lines suggested in 55:57-66.

On plate 56, Los speaks first (3-25), and the Daughters answer (26-28). At the end of their exchange, and in response to their timid chastity, Los invites them to look back into the seventy-fourth historical "church," that named Paul, which followed the crucifixion, and see the three women around the cross. They represent the triumph of the triple female will in corrupting the vision of Jesus into the religion of chastity (56:41-43).

There is chaos in England (57:1-4), and the voice of the Atlantic is not heard by Albion because he flees further into cyclic death (57:12-16). The triumph of Deism is expressed by the orgiastic dance of the Daughters and by their bloody sacrifices, which are representative of war and of analytic modes of thought run rampant (58:1-20). Urizen builds his domain from these divisions and units, making the Mundane Shell and the Circle of Destiny (58:21-30). But Los also works to build these objects in order to preserve life against further fall, and eventually to redeem life. The areas around Los's creation remain chaotic (59:10-21). The looms of Cathedron in Golgonooza are the places in which the Daughters of Los combat the divisive spinnings of the Daughters of Albion. (59:22-55).

Plate 60 begins by identifying Albion's spectre with Luvah, which is to say that Albion as Urizen is locked in an endless cycle with Luvah. This is followed by an effort of the Divine Vision to redeem Jerusalem (60:10-37), but she is a victim of insidious reason (60:39-49) and of the female will within her. The Divine Vision offers the Blakean interpretation of how Jesus was conceived, in order to emphasize the fundamental idea of forgiveness (61:1-52). But Jerusalem is the victim of Albion's attitudes (62:2-7). Jesus offers comfort (62:18-29); he will bring Luvah to rebirth in another cycle (62:20, 62:30-34).

We are now in modern history, perhaps the events in France from revolution through Napoleon (63:5-6). It is an era of violence, which startles even Los (63:36-40), yet he continues to speak out. As things grow worse, and Los persists in trying to complete his vision, Vala begins to reveal her nature fully (64:6ff.). The crucifixion of Luvah is an inevitable turn of the cyclic wheel, as is the retreat of the Sons of Urizen from their proper work (65:12-28). In the chaos of war and sacrifice, under the smiling domination of Vala and Rahab-Tirzah, we see the cyclic world and its horrors epitomized (65 through 68). This includes the association of sexual frustration with war.

The Sons of Albion also combine into a giant spectral form or Polypus (69:1-7) opposed by Los. The Beulah state of love is opposed by the female tabernacle of sexual mystery (69:9-37). Jesus' rending of the veil (69:38-44) has a sexual meaning for Blake. Mystery is the creation of a vague surrounding and yet alien nature, but it also is the result of sexual conventions glorifying chastity.

Hand (70:1-16) is the sum of Albion's Sons. He is identified with Bacon, Newton, Locke, the empirical tradition that culminates in Deism. Inside Hand is Rahab, now fully revealed (70:17-31) as fallen Vala.

The world of Albion's Sons is spread before us (71:1-49), but always opposed to this is the possibility of inward vision (71:6-8). Los apparently feels that he must now work by stealth (71:58-60). In the catalogue of English, Scottish, and Welsh counties, the counties are presided over by the Sons of Albion; thus they are not part of imaginative space. If they were, they would be associated with the Holy Land, as they should be in the imagination. This is not true of the western isle, Ireland (72:1-37), which is the land of hope. There the counties are associated with names from the Holy Land.

It is not just the ancient lands that must be united with Albion, but all nations (72:28-44).

Los and his work, which involves propping up the fallen world (73:25-27), is now ranged against the Deism of Voltaire (73:29-31). This opposition results in two different lines, kings and tyrants (73:35-37), and prophets (73:39-40). The chapter ends with Blake's own visionary recapitulation of events (74:1-51), which culminates in the opposed figures of Dinah (74:52-54) and Rahab (75:1-6). Dinah, in revenge of whom Simeon and Levi murdered the Shechemites, is Erin (74:54) and a precursor of apocalypse, which will apparently be violent. By now, Rahab is being shaped by Los (75:6-9) into a dragon harlot. The Mundane Shell is complete (75:23-25), and Jesus has broken into it to arrest its endless turning (75:21).

CHAPTER 4   The line "Saul, Saul . . ." refers to the "Church Paul" or the phase of spiritual history following Jesus. The Wheel of fire of the prefatory lyric recalls the wheel to which Lear said he was bound. It is the familiar starry wheel of Urizen, now associated with natural religion and the resultant cyclical world.

The first clear manifestation of Rahab toward the end of Chapter 3 has not brought immediate apocalypse, but Los seems stronger as Chapter 4 begins. Yet the events of Chapter 3 seem, if anything, to intensify the disorder and violence. Surely some revelation is at hand. Jerusalem's lament (78:31-80:21) is the most disturbed and frantic of the poem. England no longer encompasses the nations (79:22), and Druid temples have spread over the earth (79:66-67). She implores Vala for an explanation (79:68); at the same time she tries to correct Vala's errors (79:74-80). In these depths of fallen time Vala suffers terrible torments, for error is beginning to complete its shape. She blames Albion's death on Luvah, and she seems resentful of the cyclical world of nature that requires Luvah's periodic death. As a result she has tried to keep Albion "embalmed in moral laws" lest he continue to kill Luvah (80:27-29). This is a bit of confused self-justification, but it is a confusing and desperate time.

Rahab has managed to hide herself in indefiniteness again in this new cycle, but her previous more definite appearance was a sign of her loss of power. Here she is a "dismal and indefinite hovering Cloud" (80:51).

We now turn to Hand and Hyle and their emanations Cambel and Gwendolen. Their divisions are intensified by Rahab's ubiquity. These two fierce emanations seek to dominate Hand and Hyle by delusive arts, including reducing them to infants. Gwendolen falsely reports a conversation of Enitharmon and Los (82:22-44). Having observed this deceit, Los draws Cambel into his furnaces, insisting upon her bringing forth not an infant worm, as she would want Hand to be under her domination, but a "mighty form" (82:63). Cambel submits to an act of love. Moved to repentence, Gwendolen does likewise (82:72-76).

Much cheered by this success, Los announces his identity with Urthona (82:81). His long speech (82:81-83:65) recognizes the fallen situation, vows continued work, and prophesies redemption. Los's own actions seem now more self-assured (83:66-81). The Daughters of Albion follow with a lament that calls on Los for aid against the appearance of Hand (83:85-84:25). Their speech suggests a change of heart, but it is not complete, since they do welcome Hand. The description of London (84:11-12) is coupled with a plate like that for "London" in *Songs of Experience*. The confusion of the Daughters unites them again with Rahab (84:27). In spite of themselves the spaces they weave are material for Los, who peoples the spaces with Reuben (84:28-85:9), and converts them to use.

Los has been imaginatively creating Jerusalem again (85:22-86:32). He describes her visionary form. He must still, however, reunite with Enitharmon. In this story of their separation (86:50-87:24) Enitharmon is jealous of Jerusalem. However, Los is ever more steadfast and keeps resolutely at work, meeting Enitharmon's arguments (88:1-15). Los's Spectre smiles at the division (88:34-48), but Los continues to work even as Enitharmon "scattered his love on the wind" (88:51) and Jerusalem accepts Vala's bloody cup.

These events and Los's continued efforts bring about the appearance of the great Satanic hermaphrodite (89:52-62). The dreadful creatures that compose the hermaphrodite presage apocalypse, and their appearance is Los's work. He wishes to destroy the error they represent by delineating their form. Some of the implications of the dominion of these creatures are explored in 90:1-13, particularly the split between the sublime and pathos.

From 90:28 Los is in greater and greater control, fixing imaginative attitudes against divisive ones. No individual can attempt to assume universality, Los tells us, without falling into division, for to seek universality is to seek domination of the other. 91:1-30 displays Los reordering the imagination in a speech that collects most of the themes of the poem.

The Spectre is now working desperately to draw Los back into abstract reasoning, including occultism (91:32-35), but Los' inspiration is now far too great and is able finally even to "alter" his Spectre (91:50-52) and to escape the dualism of body and soul. The effort leaves Los shaken and weeping but still in control (91:53-92:6). He must still deal with Enitharmon, confused by her own separation though sensing impending apocalypse (92:7-12). Meanwhile Los sees the nations once again returning to Albion (92:1-6).

The naming of mystery (93:18-26) by Los brings about Albion's awakening (95:1) and the restoration of England (94:20). The poem moves to its climax in the apocalypse, which includes Albion's repentance, the awakening of Jerusalem, the annihilation of the Spectre, and the restoration of fourfold man. The world of 99:1-5 is no longer the fallen material cycle but the world of work and creativity.

PART THREE: MISCELLANEOUS PROSE

AN ISLAND IN THE MOON   This burlesque work was left unfinished in manuscript. The title, not supplied by Blake, has been used since its first printing by Edwin J. Ellis in 1907. A number of people may be satirized in the work: Thomas Taylor (Sipsop the Pythagorean), Joseph Priestley (Inflammable Gas). Quid is perhaps Blake himself. Probably the most useful discussion of the work is Erdman, *Blake: Prophet Against Empire,* principally pp. 86-116.

A DESCRIPTIVE CATALOGUE   This catalogue of twenty-eight pages was printed for Blake's exhibition at his brother's house, 28 Broad Street, in 1809. Of the paintings described, numbers V, VI, VII, VIII, X are lost. Of the others I, II, IV, XV, XVI are in the Tate Gallery, London.

The rival to whom Blake refers is Thomas Stothard, who painted a competing picture of the Canterbury pilgrims.

SELECTIONS FROM "A PUBLIC ADDRESS"   This essay, never published, is written here and there throughout the Rossetti Manuscript.

The poem Blake refers to in the first extract is probably *Milton.* Thomas Macklin employed Blake to color some prints.

A VISION OF THE LAST JUDGMENT   This description, scattered in parts through the Rossetti Manuscript, was probably written in anticipation of another exhibition. The picture, 7' x 5', is lost. The smaller "Last Judgment," not like it, and several preliminary sketches to the later work, are extant.

The ordering of the text here is that of Keynes.

APHORISMS FROM "THE LAOCOÖN"   These aphorisms appear on an engraving of the Laocoön group executed by Blake in about 1820.

ON HOMER'S POETRY and ON VIRGIL   These two works compose a single plate executed in about 1820.

PART FOUR: SELECTED MARGINALIA

The books annotated are:

Aphorisms on Man, translated from the Original Manuscript of of the Rev. John Casper Lavater, Citizen of Zuric. London, 1788.

The Wisdom of Angels, concerning Divine Love and Divine Wisdom, by Emanuel Swedenborg. Translated from the Original Latin, London, 1788.

An Apology for the Bible, in a Series of Letters, addressed to Thomas Paine, by R. Watson, Lord Bishop of Landaff, and Regius Professor of Divinity in the University of Cambridge, eighth edition, London, 1797.

Essays Moral, Economical and Political, by Francis Bacon, London, 1798.

A Translation of the Inferno in English Verse, with Historical Notes, and a Life of Dante, by Henry Boyd, Dublin, 1785.

The Works of Sir Joshua Reynolds, Knight; Later President of the Royal Academy. . . , and An Account of the Life and Writings of the Author, By Edmond Malone, Vol. I, London, 1798.

Observations on the Deranged Manifestations of the Mind, or Insanity, by J. G. Spurzheim, London, 1817.

Siris: A Chain of Philosophical Reflexions and Inquiries Concerning the Virtues of Tar Water, And divers other Subjects connected together and arising from one another, by George Berkeley, Lord Bishop of Cloyne, Dublin, 1744.

Poems: including Lyrical Ballads. . . , by William Wordsworth, Vol. I, London, 1815.

Preface to *The Excursion, being a portion of* The Recluse, *A Poem,* by William Wordsworth, London, 1814.

The Lord's Prayer, Newly Translated. . . , by Robert John Thornton, M.D. of Trinity College, Cambridge, and Member of the Royal London College of Physicians, London, 1827.

All of the annotations are provided here only for the books of Berkeley and Wordsworth. Selections have been made from annotations to all of the other books.

PART FIVE: SELECTED LETTERS

The standard edition is *The Letters of William Blake* (Geoffrey Keynes, ed.), rev. ed., Cambridge, U.S.A., 1969.

RECIPIENTS OF THE LETTERS:

DR. TRUSLER (1735-1820), a rather eccentric clergyman, was the author of *The Way to be Rich and Respectable. Hogarth Moralized,* and other works. He had given Blake a commission but was not pleased with the results. On his second letter from Blake, he wrote "Blake, dimmed by superstition."

GEORGE CUMBERLAND (b. 1754), a business man interested in the arts, was Blake's friend for many years and bought a number of his works.

WILLIAM HAYLEY (1745-1820), who had some repute as a poet, was the patron who brought Blake to Felpham, gave him commissions, and came to his aid at the time of his trial for treason. However, Hayley had no comprehension of Blake's genius and attempted to dissuade him from pursuing his visionary work. See Morchard Bishop, *Blake's Hayley,* London, 1951.

JOHN FLAXMAN Flaxman (1755-1826) was a prominent artist and sculptor. He introduced Blake to Hayley. Though for a time Blake suspected him of professional envy, they were friends.

THOMAS BUTTS (d. 1845) was a friend of Blake. Chief clerk in the Muster-master General's office and apparently possessed of a private income, he made a large collection of Blake's works. See G. E. Bentley, Jr., "Thomas Butts, White Collar Maecenas," *PMLA* LXXI (1956), 5, pp. 1052-1066.

RICHARD PHILLIPS (1767-1840) was publisher and editor of *The Monthly Magazine.*

JOHN LINNELL (1792-1882), the painter, was, as a young man, a friend of Blake.

NOTES

TO CUMBERLAND, 26 AUGUST 1799   Johnson was a bookseller who gave Blake commissions for engravings. Fuseli was a well-known artist, whose work Blake admired and who admired Blake's.

TO HAYLEY, 6 MAY 1800   Hayley's loss was the death of his illegitimate son, on May 2. The shadow is Blake's engraving of Hayley's son. Blake's brother Robert died in 1787.

TO BUTTS, OCTOBER 1800   Felpham's "eldest son" is Hayley.

TO BUTTS, 10 JANUARY 1802   The edition of Hayley's poem was *The Triumphs of Temper, A Poem: In Six Cantos,* Twelfth edition, 1803, with six plates by Blake.

The lines quoted are not Blake's but from Percy's *Reliques of Ancient English Poetry.*

TO BUTTS, 22 NOVEMBER 1802 (a)   The quotation is from Gilpin's *Three Essays on Picturesque Beauty* (1792).

TO BUTTS, 22 NOVEMBER 1802 (b)   Of Blake's brother John little is known. Apparently he served in the army, later begged from William, died young.

TO HAYLEY, 7 OCTOBER 1803   Blake refers to an engraving of Romney for Hayley's *Life of Romney.* It was not used in the book.

TO HAYLEY, 23 OCTOBER 1804   "The beloved Councillor" was Samuel Rose, who defended Blake at his trial. He died shortly afterwards.

The Truchsessian Gallery was a collection brought to London by Joseph, Count Truchsess. It is said that it was not a very distinguished collection.

TO RICHARD PHILLIPS, JUNE 1806   The letter was published in *The Monthly Magazine* 1 July 1806.

Rinehart Editions